6. Can a local account be used in a trust relationship? Explain.

7. In a complete trust domain model that uses 4 different domains, what is the total number of trust relationships required to use a complete trust domain model?

A. Single-domain model

B. Single-master domain model

C. Multiple-master domain model

D. Complete-trust domain model

5. What must be created to allow a user account from one domain to access resources in a different domain?

A. Complete Trust Domain Model

B. One Way Trust Relationship

C. Two Way Trust Relationship

D. Master-Domain Model

Exam Questions

The following questions are similar to those you will face on the Microsoft exam. Answers to these questions can be found in section Answers and Explanations, later in the chapter. At the end of each of those answers, you will be informed of where (that is, in what section of the chapter) to find more information..

1. ABC Corporation has locations in Toronto, New York, and San Francisco. It wants to install Windows NT Server 4 to encompass all its locations in a single WAN environment. The head office is located in New York. What is the best domain model for ABCís directory services implementation?

A. Single-domain model

B. Single-master domain model

C. Multiple-master domain model

D. Complete-trust domain model

2. JPS Printing has a single location with 1,000 users spread across the LAN. It has special printers and applications installed on the servers in its environment. It needs to be able to centrally manage the user accounts and the resources. Which domain model would best fit its needs?

Answers to Review Questions

1. Single domain, master domain, multiple-master domain, complete-trust domain. See section, Windows NT Server 4 Domain Models, in this chapter for more information. (This question deals with objective Planning 1.)

2. One user, one account, centralized administration, universal resource access, synchronization. See section, Windows NT Server 4 Directory Services, in this chapter for more information. (This question deals with objective Planning 1.)

6. Local accounts cannot be given permissions across trusts. See section, Accounts in Trust Relationships, in this chapter for more information. (This question deals with Planning 1.)

Answers and Explanations: For each of the Review and Exam questions, you will find thorough explanations located at the end of the section. They are easily identifiable because they are in blue type.

Exam Questions: These questions reflect the kinds of multiple-choice questions that appear on the Microsoft exams. Use them to become familiar with the exam question formats and to help you determine what you know and what you need to review or study more.

TROUBLESHOOTING (CHAPTERS 11, 12, 13, 14, AND 15)

THIS OBJECTIVE	IS COVERED HERE:
Choose the appropriate course of action to take to resolve installation failures.	1)Body-of-text coverage—Section "Installation Errors" 2)Step-by-step examples (these are placed in different spots within the body of the chapter)—None 3)Review Questions—1 4)Exercises—None 5)Exam Questions—6, 10, 12
Choose the appropriate course of action to take to resolve boot failures.	1)Body-of-text coverage—Section "Startup Errors" 2)Step-by-step examples (these are placed in different spots within the body of the chapter)—12.1 3)Review Questions—2, 3, 6, 7 4)Exercises—12.1 5)Exam Questions—5, 7, 8
Choose the appropriate course of action to take to resolve configuration errors. Tasks include: · Backing up and restoring the Registry · Editing the Registry	1)Body-of-text coverage—Section "Configuration Problems" 2)Step-by-step examples (these are placed in different spots within the body of the chapter)—None 3)Review Questions—4 4)Exercises—12.2 5)Exam Questions—1, 2, 4, 11, 13
Choose the appropriate course of action to take to resolve printer problems.	1)Body-of-text coverage—Section "Troubleshooting Printer Problems" 2)Step-by-step examples (these are placed in different spots within the body of the chapter)—12.2 3)Review Questions—5 4)Exercises—12.3 5)Exam Questions—3, 9, 14
Choose the appropriate course of action to take to resolve RAS problems.	1)Body-of-text coverage—Section "Remote Access Service" 2)Step-by-step examples—13.1–13.5 3)Review Questions—1, 3–6 4)Exercises—13.1 5)Exam Questions—1–7
Choose the appropriate course of action to take to resolve connectivity problems.	1)Body-of-text coverage—Section "Connectivity Issues" 2)Step-by-step examples—13.6 3)Review Questions—2, 7–8 4)Exercises—None 5)Exam Questions—8
Choose the appropriate course of action to take to resolve resource access and permission problems.	1)Body-of-text coverage—Section "Sharing Problems" 2)Step-by-step examples—None 3)Review Questions—3 4)Exercises—None 5)Exam Questions—1
Choose the appropriate course of action to take to resolve fault-tolerance failures. Fault-tolerance methods include: · Tape backup · Mirroring · Stripe set with parity	1)Body-of-text coverage—Section "Fault Tolerance Problems" 2)Step-by-step examples—14.1–14.4 3)Review Questions—1, 2, 4–6 4)Exercises—14.1 5)Exam Questions—2–5
Perform advanced problem resolution. Tasks include: · Diagnosing and interpreting a blue screen · Configuring a memory dump · Using the event log service	1)Body-of-text coverage–15 2)Step-by-step examples—15.1–15.3 3)Review Questions—1–4

MCSE Training Guide: Windows NT Server 4 Enterprise, Second Edition

PLANNING (Chapter 1 and 2)

THIS OBJECTIVE	IS COVERED HERE:
Plan the implementation of a directory services architecture. Considerations include: • Selecting the appropriate domain model • Supporting a single logon account • Allowing users to access resources in different domains	1)(b)Planning, Ch 1, p. 1 2)Step-by-step examples (these are placed in different spots within the body of the chapter)—Step-by-step example 1.1 3)Review Questions—1–6 4)Exercises—1.1 – 1.3 5)Exam Questions—1–5
Plan the disk drive configuration for various requirements. Requirements include choosing a fault-tolerance method.	1)Body-of-text coverage—Section "Planning the Fault Tolerance Configurations for Windows NT Server 4" 2)Step-by-step examples (these are placed in different spots within the body of the chapter)—None 3)Review Questions—1–2 4)Exercises—None 5)Exam Questions—1–3
Choose a protocol for various situations. Protocols include: • TCP/IP • TCP/IP with DHCP and WINS • NWLink IPX/SPX-Compatible Transport • Data Link Control (DLC) • AppleTalk	1)Body-of-text coverage—Section "Selecting the Proper Protocol" 2)Step-by-step examples (these are placed in different spots within the body of the chapter)—None 3)Review Questions—3–6 4)Exercises—2.1 5)Exam Questions—4–5

INSTALLATION AND CONFIGURATION (Chapter 3)

THIS OBJECTIVE	IS COVERED HERE:
Install Windows NT Server to perform various server roles. Server roles include: • Primary Domain Controller • Backup Domain Controller • Member server	1)Body-of-text coverage—Section "Installing Windows NTServer 4 in Various Server Roles" 2)Step-by-step examples (these are placed in different spots within the body of the chapter)—None 3)Review Questions—1–5 4)Exercises—3.1 5)Exam Questions—1, 7–8
Configure protocols and protocol bindings. Protocols include: • TCP/IP • TCP/IP with DHCP and WINS • NWLink IPX/SPX-Compatible Transport Protocol • DLC • AppleTalk	1)Body-of-text coverage—Section "Configuring Networking Protocols and Protocol Bindings" 2)Step-by-step examples (these are placed in different spots within the body of the chapter)—3.1 3)Review Questions—6–10 4)Exercises—3.2 5)Exam Questions—2, 11
Configure Windows NT Server core services. Services include: • Directory Replicator • Computer Browser	1)Body-of-text coverage—Section "Configuring Windows NT Server Core Services" 2)Step-by-step examples (these are placed in different spots within the body of the chapter)—3.2 3)Review Questions—12–13 4)Exercises—3.3 5)Exam Questions—12
Configure hard disks to meet various requirements. Requirements include: • Providing redundancy • Improving performance	1)Body-of-text coverage—Section "Configuring Hard Disks to Improve Performance and to Provide Redundancy" 2)Step-by-step examples (these are placed in different spots within the body of the chapter)—3.3–3.4 3)Review Questions—15 4)Exercises—None 5)Exam Questions—3–6
Configure printers. Tasks include: • Adding and configuring a printer • Implementing a printer pool • Setting print priorities	1)Body-of-text coverage—Section "Configuring Printers" 2)Step-by-step examples (these are placed in different spots within the body of the chapter)—3.5–3.7 3)Review Questions—14 4)Exercises—3.4–3.5 5)Exam Questions—9–10

Install and configure Internet Information Server	1)Body-of-text coverage—Section "Install and Configure Internet Information Server" 2)Step-by-step examples (these are placed in different spots within the body of the chapter)—7.4 3)Review Questions—4 4)Exercises—7.3 5)Exam Questions—2–4

Install and configure Internet services.
 Services include:
   • World Wide Web
   • DNS
   • Intranet
	1)Body-of-text coverage—Section "Install and Configure Internet Information Server"
	 2)Step-by-step examples (these are placed in different spots within the body of the chapter)—None
	 3)Review Questions—5
	 4)Exercises—7.3
	 5)Exam Questions—None

Install and configure Remote Access Services
 Configuration options include:
   • Configuring RAS communications
   • Configuring RAS protocols
   • Configuring RAS security
	1)Body-of-text coverage—Section "Remote Access Service (RAS)"
	 2)Step-by-step examples (these are placed in different spots within the body of the chapter)— 7.5–7.8
	 3)Review Questions—6–8
	 4)Exercises—7.4–7.5
	 5)Exam Questions—5–10

MONITORING AND OPTIMIZATION (CHAPTERS 8, 9, AND 10)

THIS OBJECTIVE	IS COVERED HERE:
Establish a baseline for measuring system performance. Tasks include creating a database of measurement data.	1)Body-of-text coverage—Section "Establishing a Baseline" and section "Establishing a Database" 2)Step-by-step examples (these are placed in different spots within the body of the chapter)—None 3)Review Questions—2 4)Exercises—None 5)Exam Questions—None

Monitor performance of various functions by using Performance Monitor. Functions include:
   • Processor
   • Memory
   • Disk
   • Network
	1)Body-of-text coverage—Section(s) "Performance Analysis"
	 2)Step-by-step examples—None
	 3)Review Questions—3–6
	 4)Exercises—9.1–9.4
	 5)Exam Questions—1

Monitor network traffic by using Network Monitor. Tasks include:
   • Collecting data
   • Presenting data
   • Filtering data
	1)Body-of-text coverage—Section "Using Network Monitor"
	 2)Step-by-step examples—None
	 3)Review Questions—2, 4–9
	 4)Exercises—10.1
	 5)Exam Questions—1, 3, 7–8

Identify performance bottlenecks.	1)Body-of-text coverage—Ch 9, Section(s) "Analysis of a File and and Print Server" and "Analysis of an Application Server"; Ch 10, Section "Analyzing Data" 2)Step-by-step examples—None 3)Review Questions—(Ch 9)1, 2, 7, 8; (Ch 10)3 4)Exercises—9.1–9.4, 10.1 5)Exam Questions—(Ch 9)2, 5; (Ch10)5
Optimize performance for various results. Results include: • Controlling network traffic • Controlling server load	1)Body-of-text coverage—(Ch 9)Section(s) "Finding Memory Bottlenecks," "Finding Processor Bottlenecks," "Finding Disk Bottlenecks," and "Finding Network Bottlenecks"; (Ch 10) Section "Client Traffic and Optimization" and "Client-to-Server Traffic and Optimization" 2)Step-by-step examples—None 3)Review Questions—(Ch 9)1–2; (Ch10)1–3 4)Exercises—None 5)Exam Questions—(Ch 9)3–4; (Ch 10)2, 4, 6, 9

Configure a Windows NT Server computer for various types of client computers. Client computer types include: • Windows NT Workstation • Windows 95 • Macintosh	1)Body-of-text coverage—Section "Configuring Windows NT Server for Various Types of Clients" 2)Step-by-step examples (these are placed in different spots within the body of the chapter)—3.8 3)Review Questions—11 4)Exercises—None 5)Exam Questions—None

MANAGING RESOURCES (CHAPTERS 4 AND 5)

THIS OBJECTIVE	IS COVERED HERE:
Manage user and group accounts. Considerations include: • Managing Windows NT user accounts • Managing Windows NT user rights • Managing Windows NT groups • Administering account policies • Auditing changes to the user account database	1)Body-of-text coverage—Section "Managing User and Group Accounts" 2)Step-by-step examples (these are placed in different spots within the body of the chapter)—4.1–4.3 3)Review Questions—1–3 4)Exercises—4.1–4.3, 4.5–4.7 5)Exam Questions—1, 2, 3, 8
Create and manage policies and profiles for various situations. Policies and profiles include: • Local user profiles • Roaming user profiles • System policies	1)Body-of-text coverage—Section "Creating and Managing System Policies and User Profiles" 2)Step-by-step examples (these are placed in different spots within the body of the chapter)—4.4–4.7 3)Review Questions—4, 5 4)Exercises—4.4 5)Exam Questions—4–7
Administer remote servers from various types of client computers. Client computer types include: • Windows 95 • Windows NT Workstation	1)Body-of-text coverage—Section "Remote Administration of Windows NT" 2)Step-by-step examples (these are placed in different spots within the body of the chapter)—5.1–5.4 3)Review Questions—1, 3 4)Exercises—5.1 5)Exam Questions—2, 4
Manage disk resources. Tasks include: • Creating and sharing resources • Implementing permissions and security • Establishing file auditing	1)Body-of-text coverage—Sections "Managing Disk Resources" and "Implementing Auditing in Windows NT" 2)Step-by-step examples (these are placed in different spots within the body of the chapter)—5.5–5.6 3)Review Questions—2, 4, 5 4)Exercises—5.2–5.3 5)Exam Questions—1, 3, 5, 6

CONNECTIVITY (CHAPTERS 6 AND 7)

THIS OBJECTIVE	IS COVERED HERE:
Configure Windows NT Server for interoperability with NetWare servers by using various tools. Tools include: • Gateway Service for NetWare • Migration Tool for NetWare	1)Body-of-text coverage—Section "Interoperability with NetWare" 2)Step-by-step examples (these are placed in different spots within the body of the chapter)—7.1–7.3 3)Review Questions—1–3 4)Exercises—7.1–7.2 5)Exam Questions—1, 11–13
Install and configure multiprotocol routing to serve various functions. Functions include: • Internet router • BOOTP/DHCP Relay Agent • IPX Router	1)Body-of-text coverage—Section "Installing and Configuring Multiprotocol Routing" 2)Step-by-step examples (these are placed in different spots within the body of the chapter)—None 3)Review Questions—1–2 4)Exercises—None 5)Exam Questions—None

TRAINING GUIDE

MCSE

Second Edition

Windows NT®
Server 4 Enterprise

New Riders

Exam: 70-068

JASON SIROCKMAN

MCSE Training Guide: Windows NT® Server 4 Enterprise, Second Edition

International Standard Book Number: 1-56205-917-3

Library of Congress Catalog Card Number: 98-85731

Printed in the United States of America

First Printing: September, 1998

00   99   98   4   3

Trademarks

Warning and Disclaimer

EXECUTIVE EDITOR
Mary Foote

ACQUISITIONS EDITOR
Sean Angus

DEVELOPMENT EDITOR
Stacia Mellinger

MANAGING EDITOR
Sarah Kearns

PROJECT EDITOR
Christopher Morris

COPY EDITORS
Andrew Saff
Kris Simmons

INDEXER
Tim Wright

TECHNICAL EDITOR
Lyle Bryant

SOFTWARE DEVELOPMENT SPECIALIST
Jack Belbot

PRODUCTION
Jeanne Clark
Kim Cofer
Maribeth Echard
Mary Hunt
Nicole Ritch

Contents at a Glance

PART VII Final Review

PART VIII Appendixes

Table of Contents

PART I: Planning

PART II: Installation and Configuration

PART III: Managing Resources

PART IV: Connectivity

PART V: Monitoring and Optimization

PART VI: Troubleshooting

PART VII: Final Review

PART VIII: Appendixes

About the Author

Jason Sirockman has been involved in the information technology industry for the past eight years, and during the final stages of this book project he accepted an opportunity with Microsoft as a systems engineer in their Edmonton, Alberta offices. Prior to this recent change to his career he was employed with PBSC Computer Training Centres in Winnipeg, Manitoba, Canada as national technical marketing manager. He has played numerous roles within the IT field acting as a network analyst, technical trainer, and marketing manager and will continue to expand his experience within the industry. In addition to his fulltime career, he has authored several books with New Riders; some of these books include: *MCSE Training Guide: Systems Management Server, MCSE Training Guide: Windows NT Server 4 Enterprise*, and *MCSE Complete Version 1.1*. Jason lives in Edmonton, Alberta, Canada with his wife Christine and two children Megan and Eric. Jason can be reached via email at: jasonsi@microsoft.com.

Dedication

In preparing a dedication to this book, numerous individuals come to mind. Over my years, a number of people have influenced me and given me opportunities to grow as a person. Sean Angus, Nancy Maragioglio, and Dustin Sullivan from New Riders have allowed me to work on some great projects, and in the process have made it a very enjoyable experience. My parents, Roy and Denise Sirockman, who have supported me throughout my life and given me every opportunity to be successful. My friends at PBSC who made each day a rewarding adventure: Ramon, Gilbert, Bob, Al, Dennis, Glenn, Mike, Lyle, Lynne, Josy, Dave, Alain, etc...

And finally, to my beautiful wife Christine and our children Megan and Eric for their support and love throughout this project and many more to come...I dedicate this book to all of you.

Acknowledgments

As with any project, there are numerous individuals that rise to the challenge of completing and making the project successful. With the creation of the second edition of the Enterprise book, a great deal of feedback from the readers was used in order to offer you the best possible learning experience. I would like to thank Sean Angus, Stacia Mellinger, and the entire staff at New Riders for pulling together to develop this book. It was the experience and skill of each of you that made this possible. I would also like to acknowledge all of my peers and friends at PBSC Computer Training Centres for challenging me over the years and helping me expand my horizons within this industry.

Tell Us What You Think!

As the reader of this book, *you* are our most important critic and commentator. We value your opinion and want to know what we're doing right, what we could do better, what areas you'd like to see us publish in, and any other words of wisdom you're willing to pass our way.

As the Executive Editor for the Certification team at Macmillan Computer Publishing, I welcome your comments. You can fax, email, or write me directly to let me know what you did or didn't like about this book—as well as what we can do to make our books stronger.

Please note that I cannot help you with technical problems related to the topic of this book, and that due to the high volume of mail I receive, I might not be able to reply to every message.

When you write, please be sure to include this book's title and author, as well as your name and phone or fax number. I will carefully review your comments and share them with the author and editors who worked on the book.

Fax: 317-581-4663

Email: certification@mcp.com

Mail: Executive Editor
            Certification
            Macmillan Computer Publishing
            201 West 103rd Street
            Indianapolis, IN 46290 USA

How to Use This Book

New Riders Publishing has made an effort in the second editions of its Training Guide series to make the information as accessible as possible for the purposes of learning the certification material. Here, you have an opportunity to view the many instructional features that have been incorporated into the books to achieve that goal.

CHAPTER OPENER

Each chapter begins with a set of features designed to allow you to maximize study time for that material.

List of Objectives: Each chapter begins with a list of the objectives as stated by Microsoft.

Objective Explanations: Immediately following each objective is an explanation of it, providing context that defines it more meaningfully in relation to the exam. Because Microsoft can sometimes be vague in its objectives list, the objective explanations are designed to clarify any vagueness by relying on the authors' test-taking experience.

OBJECTIVES

Microsoft provides the following objectives for "Connectivity":

Add and configure the network components of Windows NT Workstation.

▶ This objective is necessary because someone certified in the use of Windows NT Workstation technology must understand how it fits into a networked environment and how to configure the components that enable it to do so.

Use various methods to access network resources.

▶ This objective is necessary because someone certified in the use of Windows NT Workstation technology must understand how resources available on a network can be accessed from NT Workstation.

Implement Windows NT Workstation as a client in a NetWare environment.

▶ This objective is necessary because someone certified in the use of Windows NT Workstation technology must understand how NT Workstation can be used as a client in a NetWare environment and how to configure the services and protocols that make this possible.

Use various configurations to install Windows NT Workstation as a TCP/IP client.

▶ This objective is necessary because someone certified in the use of Windows NT Workstation technology must understand how TCP/IP is important in a network environment and how Workstation can be configured to use it.

C H A P T E R 4

Connectivity

OUTLINE

Chapter Outline: Learning always gets a boost when you can see both the forest and the trees. To give you a visual image of how the topics in a chapter fit together, you will find a chapter outline at the beginning of each chapter. You will also be able to use this for easy reference when looking for a particular topic.

STUDY STRATEGIES

▶ Disk configurations are a part of both the planning and the configuration of NT Server computers. To study for Planning Objective 1, you will need to look at both the following section and the material in Chapter 2, "Installation Part 1." As with many concepts, you should have a good handle on the terminology and know the best applications for different disk configurations. For the objectives of the NT Server exam, you will need to know only general disk configuration concepts—at a high level, not the nitty gritty. Make sure you memorize the concepts relating to partitioning and know the difference between the system and the boot partitions in an NT system (and the fact that the definitions of these are counter-intuitive). You should know that NT supports both FAT and NTFS partitions, as well as some of the advantages and disadvantages of each. You will also need to know about the fault-tolerance methods available in NT—stripe sets with parity and disk mirroring—including their definitions, hardware requirements, and advantages and disadvantages.

Of course, nothing substitutes for working with the concepts explained in this objective. If possible, get an NT system with some free disk space and play around with the Disk Administrator just to see how partitions are created and what they look like.

You might also want to look at some of the supplementary readings and scan TechNet for white papers on disk configuration.

▶ The best way to study for Planning Objective 2 is to read, memorize, and understand the use of each protocol. You should know what the protocols are, what they are used for, and what systems they are compatible with.

As with disk configuration, installing protocols on your NT Server is something that you plan for, not something you do just because it feels good to you at the time. Although it is much easier to add or remove a protocol than it is to reconfigure your hard drives, choosing a protocol is still an essential part of the planning process because specific protocols, like spoken languages, are designed to be used in certain circumstances. There is no point in learning to speak Mandarin Chinese if you are never around anyone who can understand you. Similarly, the NWLink protocol is used to interact with NetWare systems; therefore, if you do not have Novell servers on your network, you might want to rethink your plan to install it on your servers. We will discuss the uses of the major protocols in Chapter 7, "Connectivity." However, it is important that you have a good understanding of their uses here in the planning stage.

Study Strategies: Each topic presents its own learning challenge. To support you through this, New Riders has included strategies for how to best approach studying in order to retain the material in the chapter, particularly as it is addressed on the exam.

INSTRUCTIONAL FEATURES WITHIN THE CHAPTER

These books include a large amount and different kinds of information. The many different elements are designed to help you identify information by its purpose and importance to the exam and also to provide you with varied ways to learn the material. You will be able to determine how much attention to devote to certain elements, depending on what your goals are. By becoming familiar with the different presentations of information, you will know what information will be important to you as a test-taker and which information will be important to you as a practitioner.

Objective Coverage Text: In the text before an exam objective is specifically addressed, you will notice the objective is listed and printed in color to help call your attention to that particular material.

Warning: In using sophisticated information technology, there is always potential for mistakes or even catastrophes that can occur through improper application of the technology. Warnings appear in the margins to alert you to such potential problems.

EXAM TIP

Only One NTVDM Supports Multiple 16-bit Applications Expect at least one question about running Win16 applications in separate memory spaces. The key concept is that you can load multiple Win16 applications into the same memory space only if it is the initial Win16 NTVDM. It is not possible, for example, to run Word for Windows 6.0 and Excel for Windows 5.0 in one shared memory space and also run PowerPoint 4.0 and Access 2.0 in another shared memory space.

Exam Tip: Exam Tips appear in the margins to provide specific exam-related advice. Such tips may address what material is covered (or not covered) on the exam, how it is covered, mnemonic devices, or particular quirks of that exam.

Note: Notes appear in the margins and contain various kinds of useful information, such as tips on the technology or administrative practices, historical background on terms and technologies, or side commentary on industry issues.

---

8   Chapter 1   PLANNING

INTRODUCTION

Microsoft grew up around the personal computer industry and established itself as the preeminent maker of software products for personal computers. Microsoft has a vast portfolio of software products, but it is best known for its operating systems.

Microsoft's current operating system products, listed here, are undoubtedly well-known to anyone studying for the MCSE exams:

◆ Windows 95

◆ Windows NT Workstation

◆ Windows NT Server

NOTE

Strange But True Although it sounds backward, it is true: Windows NT boots from the system partition and then loads the system from the boot partition.

Some older operating system products—namely MS-DOS, Windows 3.1, and Windows for Workgroups—are still important to the operability of Windows NT Server, so don't be surprised if you hear them mentioned from time to time in this book.

Windows NT is the most powerful, the most secure, and perhaps the most elegant operating system Microsoft has yet produced. It languished for a while after it first appeared (in part because no one was sure why they needed it or what to do with it), but Microsoft has persisted with improving interoperability and performance. With the release of Windows NT 4 which offers a new Windows 95-like user interface, Windows NT has assumed a prominent place in today's world of network-based computing.

WINDOWS NT SERVER AMONG MICROSOFT OPERATING SYSTEMS

WARNING

Don't Overextend Your Partitions and Wraps It is not necessary to create an extended partition on a disk; primary partitions might be all that you need. However, if you do create one, remember that you can never have more than one extended partition on a physical disk.

As we already mentioned, Microsoft has three operating system products now competing in the marketplace: Windows 95, Windows NT Workstation, and Windows NT Server. Each of these operating systems has its advantages and disadvantages.

Looking at the presentation of the desktop, the three look very much alike—so much so that you might have to click the Start button and read the banner on the left side of the menu to determine which operating system you are looking at. Each offers the familiar Windows 95 user interface featuring the Start button, the Recycling

STEP BY STEP

5.1 Configuring an Extension to Trigger an Application to Always Run in a Separate Memory Space

1. Start the Windows NT Explorer.

2. From the View menu, choose Options.

3. Click the File Types tab.

4. In the Registered File Types list box, select the desired file type.

5. Click the Edit button to display the Edit File Type dialog box. Then select Open from the Actions list and click the Edit button below it.

6. In the Editing Action for Type dialog box, adjust the application name by typing **cmd.exe /c start /separate** in front of the existing contents of the field (see Figure 5.15).

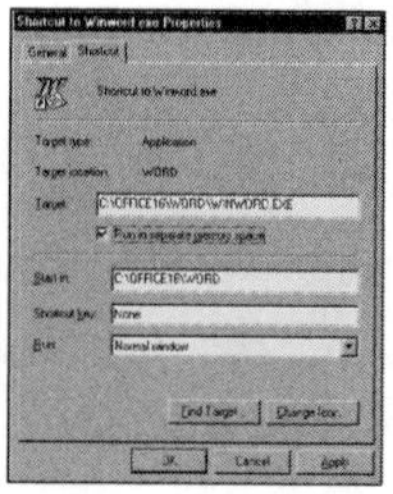

FIGURE 5.15
Configuring a shortcut to run a Win16 application in a separate memory space.

Step by Step: Step by Steps are hands-on tutorial instructions that walk you through a particular task or function relevant to the exam objectives.

Figure: To improve readability, the figures have been placed in the margins so they do not interrupt the main flow of text.

---

14   Chapter 1   PLANNING

You must use NTFS if you want to preserve existing permissions when you migrate files and directories from a NetWare server to a Windows NT Server system.

Windows 95 is Microsoft's everyday workhorse operating system. It provides a 32-bit platform and is designed to operate with a variety of peripherals. See Table 1.1 for the minimum hardware requirements for the installation and operation of Windows 95. Also, if you want to allow Macintosh computers to access files on the partition through Windows NT's Services for Macintosh, you must format the partition for NTFS.

MAKING REGISTRY CHANGES

To make Registry changes, run the REGEDT32.EXE program. The Registry in Windows NT is a complex database of configuration settings for your computer. If you want to configure the Workstation service, open the HKEY_LOCAL_MACHINE hive, as shown in Figure 3.22.

The exact location for configuring your Workstation service is

    HKEY_LOCAL_MACHINE\System\CurrentControlSet\Services\
    LanmanWorkstation\Parameters

To find additional information regarding this Registry item and others, refer to the Windows NT Server resource kit.

This summary table offers an overview of the differences between the FAT and NTFS file systems.

REVIEW   BREAK

Choosing a File System

But if the system is designed to store data, mirroring might produce disk bottlenecks. You might only know whether these changes are significant by setting up two identical computers, implementing mirroring on one but not on the other, and then running Performance Monitor on both under a simulated load to see the performance differences.

This summary table offers an overview of the differences between the FAT and NTFS file systems.

In-Depth Sidebar: These more extensive discussions cover material that perhaps is not as directly relevant to the exam, but which is useful as reference material or in everyday practice. In-Depths may also provide useful background or contextual information necessary for understanding the larger topic under consideration.

Review Break: Crucial information is summarized at various points in the book in lists or tables. At the end of a particularly long section, you might come across a Review Break that is there just to wrap up one long objective and reinforce the key points before you shift your focus to the next section.

CASE STUDIES

Case Studies are presented throughout the book to provide you with another, more conceptual opportunity to apply the knowledge you are developing. They also reflect the "real-world" experiences of the authors in ways that prepare you not only for the exam but for actual network administration as well. In each Case Study, you will find similar elements: a description of a Scenario, the Essence of the Case, and an extended Analysis section.

CASE STUDY: REALLY GOOD GUITARS

ESSENCE OF THE CASE

Here are the essential elements in this case:

- need for centralized administration
- the need for WAN connectivity nation-wide
- a requirement for Internet access and e-mail
- the need for Security on network shares and local files
- an implementation of Fault-tolerant systems

SCENARIO

Really Good Guitars is a national company specializing in the design and manufacture of custom acoustic guitars. Having grown up out of an informal network of artisans across Canada, the company has many locations but very few employees (300 at this time) and a Head Office in Churchill, Manitoba. Although they follow the best traditions of hand-making guitars, they are not without technological savvy and all the 25 locations have computers on-site which are used to do accounting, run MS Office applications, and run their custom made guitar design software. The leadership team has recently begun to realize that a networked solution is essential to maintain consistency and to provide security on what are becoming some very innovative designs and to provide their employees with e-mail and Internet access.

RGG desires a centralized administration of its

continues

Essence of the Case: A bulleted list of the key problems or issues that need to be addressed in the Scenario.

Scenario: A few paragraphs describing a situation that professional practitioners in the field might face. A Scenario will deal with an issue relating to the objectives covered in the chapter, and it includes the kinds of details that make a difference.

Analysis: This is a lengthy description of the best way to handle the problems listed in the Essence of the Case. In this section, you might find a table summarizing the solutions, a worded example, or both.

CASE STUDY: PRINT IT DRAFTING INC.

continued

too, which is unacceptable. You are to find a solution to this problem if one exists.

ANALYSIS

The fixes for both of these problems are relatively straightforward. In the first case, it is likely that all the programs on the draftspeople's workstations are being started at normal priority. This means that they have a priority of 8. But the default says that anything running in the foreground is getting a 2-point boost from the base priority, bringing it to 10. As a result, when sent to the background, AutoCAD is not getting as much attention from the processor as it did when it was the foreground application. Because multiple applications need to be run at once without significant degradation of the performance of AutoCAD, you implement the following solution:

1. On the Performance tab of the System Properties dialog box for each workstation, set the Application Performance slider to None to prevent a boost for foreground applications.

2. Recommend that users keep the additional programs running alongside AutoCAD at a minimum (because all programs will now get equal processor time).

The fix to the second problem is to run each 16-bit application in its own NTVDM. This ensures that the crashing of one application will not adversely affect the others, but it still enables interoperability between the applications because they use OLE (and not shared memory) to transfer data. To make the fix as transparent as possible to the users, you suggested that two things be done:

1. Make sure that for each shortcut a user has created to the office applications, the Run in Separate Memory Space option is selected on the Shortcut tab.

2. Change the properties for the extensions associated with the applications (for example, .XLS and .DOC) so that they start using the /separate switch. Then any file that is double-clicked invokes the associated program to run in its own NTVDM.

CHAPTER SUMMARY

KEY TERMS

Before you take the exam, make sure you are comfortable with the definitions and concepts for each of the following key terms:

- FAT
- NTFS
- workgroup
- domain

This chapter discussed the main planning topics you will encounter on the Windows NT Server exam. Distilled down, these topics revolve around two main goals: understanding the planning of disk configuration and understanding the planning of network protocols.

- ◆ Windows NT Server supports an unlimited number of inbound sessions; Windows NT Workstation supports no more than 10 active sessions at the same time.

- ◆ Windows NT Server accommodates an unlimited number of remote access connections (although Microsoft only supports up to 256); Windows NT Workstation supports only a single remote access connection.

Key Terms: A list of key terms appears at the end of each chapter. These are terms that you should be sure you know and are comfortable defining and understanding when you go in to take the exam.

Chapter Summary: Before the Apply Your Learning section, you will find a chapter summary that wraps up the chapter and reviews what you should have learned.

EXTENSIVE REVIEW AND SELF-TEST OPTIONS

At the end of each chapter, along with some summary elements, you will find a section called "Apply Your Learning" that gives you several different methods with which to test your understanding of the material and review what you have learned.

Chapter 1   PLANNING   23

APPLY YOUR LEARNING

This section allows you to assess how well you understood the material in the chapter. Review and Exam questions test your knowledge of the tasks and concepts specified in the objectives. The Exercises provide you with opportunities to engage in the sorts of tasks that comprise the skill sets the objectives reflect.

Exercises

1.1   Synchronizing the Domain Controllers

The following steps show you how to manually synchronize a backup domain controller within your domain. (This objective deals with Objective Planning 1.)

Time Estimate: Less than 10 minutes.

1. Click Start, Programs, Administrative Tools, and select the Server Manager icon.

2. Highlight the BDC (Backup Domain Controller) in your computer list.

3. Select the Computer menu, then select Synchronize with Primary Domain Controller.

12.2   Establishing a Trust Relationship between Domains

The following steps show you how to establish a trust relationship between multiple domains. To complete this exercise, you must have two Windows NT Server computers, each installed in their own domain. (This objective deals with objective Planning 1.)

Time Estimate: 10 minutes

1. From the trusted domain select Start, Programs, Administrative Tools, and click User Manager for Domains. The User Manager.

FIGURE 1.2
The login process on a local machine.

2. Select the Policies menu and click Trust Relationships. The Trust Relationships dialog box appears.

4. When the trusting domain information has been entered, click OK and close the Trust Relationships dialog box.

Review Questions

1. List the four domain models that can be used for directory services in Windows NT Server 4.

2. List the goals of a directory services architecture.

3. What is the maximum size of the SAM database in Windows NT Server 4.0?

4. What are the two different types of domains in a trust relationship?

5. In a trust relationship which domain would contain the user accounts?

Exercises: These activities provide an opportunity for you to master specific hands-on tasks. Our goal is to increase your proficiency with the product or technology. You must be able to conduct these tasks in order to pass the exam.

Review Questions: These open-ended, short-answer questions allow you to quickly assess your comprehension of what you just read in the chapter. Instead of asking you to choose from a list of options, these questions require you to state the correct answers in your own words. Although you will not experience these kinds of questions on the exam, these questions will indeed test your level of comprehension of key concepts.

6. Can a local account be used in a trust relationship? Explain.

7. In a complete trust domain model that uses 4 different domains, what is the total number of trust relationships required to use a complete trust domain model?

Exam Questions

The following questions are similar to those you will face on the Microsoft exam. Answers to these questions can be found in section Answers and Explanations, later in the chapter. At the end of each of those answers, you will be informed of where (that is, in what section of the chapter) to find more information..

1. ABC Corporation has locations in Toronto, New York, and San Francisco. It wants to install Windows NT Server 4 to encompass all its locations in a single WAN environment. The head office is located in New York. What is the best domain model for ABCís directory services implementation?

   A. Single-domain model

   B. Single-master domain model

   C. Multiple-master domain model

   D. Complete-trust domain model

2. JPS Printing has a single location with 1,000 users spread across the LAN. It has special printers and applications installed on the servers in its environment. It needs to be able to centrally manage the user accounts and the resources. Which domain model would best fit its needs?

   A. Single-domain model

   B. Single-master domain model

   C. Multiple-master domain model

   D. Complete-trust domain model

5. What must be created to allow a user account from one domain to access resources in a different domain?

   A. Complete Trust Domain Model

   B. One Way Trust Relationship

   C. Two Way Trust Relationship

   D. Master-Domain Model

Answers to Review Questions

1. Single domain, master domain, multiple-master domain, complete-trust domain. See section, Windows NT Server 4 Domain Models, in this chapter for more information. (This question deals with objective Planning 1.)

2. One user, one account, centralized administration, universal resource access, synchronization. See section, Windows NT Server 4 Directory Services, in this chapter for more information. (This question deals with objective Planning 1.)

6. Local accounts cannot be given permissions across trusts. See section, Accounts in Trust Relationships, in this chapter for more information. (This question deals with Planning 1.)

Exam Questions: These questions reflect the kinds of multiple-choice questions that appear on the Microsoft exams. Use them to become familiar with the exam question formats and to help you determine what you know and what you need to review or study more.

Answers and Explanations: For each of the Review and Exam questions, you will find thorough explanations located at the end of the section. They are easily identifiable because they are in blue type.

Introduction

MCSE Training Guide: Windows NT Server 4 Enterprise, Second Edition is designed for advanced end users, service technicians, and network administrators with the goal of certification as a Microsoft Certified Systems Engineer (MCSE). The "NT Server 4 Enterprise" exam (#70-068) measures your ability to implement, administer, and troubleshoot information systems that include Windows NT Server 4 Enterprise alone and with NetWare.

WHO SHOULD READ THIS BOOK

This book is designed to help you meet the goal of certification by preparing you for the "NT Server 4 Enterprise" exam.

This book is your one-stop shop. Everything you need to know to pass the exam is in here, and Microsoft has approved it as study material. You do not *need* to take a class in addition to buying this book to pass the exam. However, depending on your personal study habits or learning style, you may benefit from taking a class in addition to the book.

This book also can help advanced users and administrators who are not studying for the exam but are looking for a single-volume reference on networking.

HOW THIS BOOK HELPS YOU

This book leads you on a self-guided tour of all the areas covered by the "NT Server 4 Enterprise" exam and teaches you the specific skills you need to achieve your MCSE certification. You'll also find helpful hints, tips, real-world examples, exercises, and references to additional study materials. Specifically, this book is designed around four general concepts to help you learn.

◆ **Organization.** This book is organized first by major exam topics and then by individual exam objectives. Every objective you need to know for the "NT Server 4 Enterprise" exam is covered in this book. We attempted to make the information accessible in several different ways:

  • The full list of exam topics and objectives is included in this introduction.

  • Each chapter begins with a list of the objectives covered in that particular chapter, as well as the author's personal explanation of that objective.

  • Each chapter opener includes a Study Strategy, provided by the author, to guide you in the best ways to prepare for that particular section of the exam, whether it be memorization, hands-on practice, or conceptual understanding.

  • Each chapter also begins with an outline that provides an overview of the material in the chapter and the page numbers where particular topics can be found.

Individual objectives appear in color like this, immediately preceding the text that covers that particular objective.

  • To help you quickly locate where the objectives are addressed in the chapter, you will notice the objective listed and printed in color to help direct your attention to that particular material.

- The information on where the objectives are covered is also conveniently condensed on the tear card at the front of this book.

◆ **Instructional Features.** This book has been designed to provide you with multiple ways to access and reinforce the exam material. The book's instructional features include the following:

- *Objective Explanations.* As mentioned earlier, each chapter begins with a list of the objectives covered in the chapter. In addition, immediately following each objective is an explanation of it, in context that defines it more meaningfully.

- *Study Strategies.* The beginning of the chapter also includes strategies for how to approach studying and retaining the material in the chapter, particularly as it is addressed on the exam.

- *Exam Tips.* Exam tips appear in the margin to provide specific exam-related advice. Such tips may address what material is covered (or not covered) on the exam, how it is covered, mnemonic devices, or particular quirks of that exam.

- *Reviews and Summaries.* Crucial information is summarized at various points in the book in lists or tables. Each chapter ends with a summary as well.

- *Key Terms.* A list of key terms appears at the end of each chapter.

- *Notes and Tips.* These appear in the margin and contain various kinds of useful information, such as tips on the technology or administrative practices, historical background on terms and technologies, or side commentary on industry issues.

- *Warnings.* When you use sophisticated information technology, there is always potential for mistake or even catastrophe that can occur through improper application of the technology. Warnings appear in the margin to alert you to such potential problems.

- *In-Depth Sidebars.* These more extensive discussions cover material that is, perhaps, not directly relevant to the exam, but which is useful as reference material or in everyday practice. In-depth sidebars might also provide useful background or contextual information necessary for understanding the larger topic under consideration.

- *Step by Steps.* These are hands-on tutorial instructions that walk you through particular tasks or functions relevant to the exam objectives.

- *Exercises.* Found at the end of the chapters in the "Apply Your Learning" section, Exercises may include additional tutorial material as well as other types of problems and questions.

- *Case Studies.* Case studies are presented throughout the book. They provide you with another, more conceptual opportunity to apply the knowledge you are gaining. They include a description of a scenario, the essence of the case, and an extended analysis section. They also reflect the "real-world" experiences of the authors in ways that prepare you not only for the exam but for actual network administration as well.

◆ **Extensive Practice Test Options.** The book provides numerous opportunities for you to assess your knowledge and practice for the exam. The practice options include:

- *Review Questions.* These open-ended questions appear in the "Apply Your Learning" section at the end of each chapter. They allow you to quickly assess your comprehension of what you just read in the chapter. Answers to the questions are provided later in the chapter.

- *Exam Questions.* These questions also appear in the "Apply Your Learning" section. They reflect the kind of multiple-choice questions that appear on the Microsoft exams. Use them to practice for the exam and to help you determine what you know and what you need to review or study further. Answers and explanations for them are provided.

- *Practice Exam.* A Practice Exam is included in the "Final Review" section. The Final Review section and the Practice Exam are discussed below.

- *Top Score.* The Top Score software included on the CD-ROM provides further practice questions.

> **NOTE**   **Top Score**   For a complete description of New Riders' Top Score test engine, see Appendix D, "Using the Top Score Software."

❖ **Final Review.** This part of the book provides you with three valuable tools for preparing for the exam.

- *Fast Facts.* This condensed version of the information contained in the book will prove extremely useful for last-minute review.

- *Study and Exam Preparation Tips.* Read this section early on to help you develop study strategies. It also provides you with valuable exam-day tips and information on new exam

question formats, such as adaptive tests and simulation-based questions.

- *Practice Exam.* A full practice exam is included. Questions are written in the styles used on the actual exam. Use it to assess your readiness for the real thing.

The book includes other features, such as a glossary (Appendix A), an overview of the Microsoft certification program (Appendix B), and a description of what is on the CD-ROM (Appendix C). These and all the other book features mentioned above provide you with thorough preparation for the exam.

For more information about the exam or the certification process, contact Microsoft:

Microsoft Education: (800) 636-7544

Internet:
`ftp://ftp.microsoft.com/Services/MSEdCert`

World Wide Web:
`http://www.microsoft.com/train_cert`

CompuServe Forum: GO MSEDCERT

What the NT Server 4 Enterprise Exam (#70-068) Covers

The "NT Server 4 Enterprise" exam (#70-068) covers the four main topic areas represented by the conceptual groupings of the test objectives. Each chapter represents one or more of these main topic areas. The exam objectives are listed by topic area in the following sections.

Planning

Plan the implementation of a directory services architecture. Considerations include:

- Selecting the appropriate domain model

- Supporting a single logon account

- Allowing users to access resources in different domains

Plan the disk drive configuration for various requirements. Requirements include choosing a fault-tolerance method.

Choose a protocol for various situations. Protocols include:

- TCP/IP

- TCP/IP with DHCP and WINS

- NWLink IPX/SPX-Compatible Transport

- Data Link Control (DLC)

- AppleTalk

Installation and Configuration

Install Windows NT Server to perform various server roles. Server roles include:

- Primary Domain Controller

- Backup Domain Controller

- Member server

Configure protocols and protocol bindings. Protocols include:

- TCP/IP

- TCP/IP with DHCP and WINS

- NWLink IPX/SPX-Compatible Transport Protocol

- DLC

- AppleTalk

Configure Windows NT Server core services. Services include:

- Directory Replicator

- Computer Browser

Configure hard disks to meet various requirements. Requirements include:

- Providing redundancy

- Improving performance

Configure printers. Tasks include:

- Adding and configuring a printer

- Implementing a printer pool

- Setting print priorities

Configure a Windows NT Server computer for various types of client computers. Client computer types include:

- Windows NT Workstation

- Windows 95

- Macintosh

Managing Resources

Manage user and group accounts. Considerations include:

- Managing Windows NT user accounts

- Managing Windows NT user rights

- Managing Windows NT groups
- Administering account policies
- Auditing changes to the user account database

Create and manage policies and profiles for various situations. Policies and profiles include:

- Local user profiles
- Roaming user profiles
- System policies

Administer remote servers from various types of client computers. Client computer types include:

- Windows 95
- Windows NT Workstation

Manage disk resources. Tasks include:

- Creating and sharing resources
- Implementing permissions and security
- Establishing file auditing

Connectivity

Configure Windows NT Server for interoperability with NetWare servers by using various tools. Tools include:

- Gateway Service for NetWare
- Migration Tool for NetWare

Install and configure multiprotocol routing to serve various functions. Functions include:

- Internet router
- BOOTP/DHCP Relay Agent
- IPX Router

Install and configure Internet Information Server

Install and configure Internet services. Services include:

- World Wide Web
- DNS
- Intranet

Install and configure Remote Access Services (RAS). Configuration options include:

- Configuring RAS communications
- Configuring RAS protocols
- Configuring RAS security

Monitoring and Optimization

Establish a baseline for measuring system performance. Tasks include creating a database of measurement data.

Monitor performance of various functions by using Performance Monitor. Functions include:

- Processor
- Memory
- Disk
- Network

Monitor network traffic by using Network Monitor. Tasks include:

- Collecting data
- Presenting data
- Filtering data

Identify performance bottlenecks.

Optimize performance for various results. Results include:

- Controlling network traffic
- Controlling server load

Troubleshooting

Choose the appropriate course of action to take to resolve installation failures.

Choose the appropriate course of action to take to resolve boot failures.

Choose the appropriate course of action to take to resolve configuration errors. Tasks include:

- Backing up and restoring the Registry
- Editing the Registry

Choose the appropriate course of action to take to resolve printer problems.

Choose the appropriate course of action to take to resolve RAS problems.

Choose the appropriate course of action to take to resolve connectivity problems.

Choose the appropriate course of action to take to resolve resource access and permission problems.

Choose the appropriate course of action to take to resolve fault-tolerance failures. Fault-tolerance methods include:

- Tape backup
- Mirroring
- Stripe set with parity

Perform advanced problem resolution. Tasks include:

- Diagnosing and interpreting a blue screen
- Configuring a memory dump
- Using the event log service

ADVICE ON TAKING THE EXAM

More extensive tips are found in the Final Review section in the chapter titled "Study and Exam Preparation Tips." But keep the following suggestions in mind as you study:

- ◆ **Read all the material.** Microsoft has been known to include material on its exams that's not expressly specified in the objectives. This book has included additional information not reflected in the objectives in an effort to give you the best possible preparation for the examination and for the real-world network experiences to come.

- ◆ **Do the Step by Steps and complete the Exercises in each chapter.** They will help you gain experience using the Microsoft product. All Microsoft exams are task- and experienced-based and require you to have used the Microsoft product in a real networking environment.

- ◆ **Use the questions to assess your knowledge.** Don't just read the chapter content; use the questions to find out what you know and what you don't. Then study some more, review, and assess your knowledge again.

- ◆ **Review the exam objectives.** Develop your own questions and examples for each topic listed. If you can make and answer several questions for each topic, you should not find it difficult to pass the exam.

> **NOTE**
>
> **Preparation Includes Practice**
> Although this book is designed to prepare you to take and pass the NT Server 4 Enterprise certification exam, there are no guarantees. Read this book and work through the questions and exercises, and when you feel confident, take the Practice Exam and additional exams using the Top Score test engine. This should tell you whether or not you are ready for the real thing.
>
> When taking the actual certification exam, make sure you answer all the questions before your time limit expires. Do not spend too much time on any one question. If you are unsure about an answer, answer the question as best you can and mark it for later review; you can go back to it when you have finished the rest of the questions.

Remember, the primary object is not to pass the exam—it is to understand the material. If you understand the material, passing the exam should be simple. Knowledge is a pyramid: To build upward, you need a solid foundation. This book and the Microsoft Certified Professional programs are designed to ensure that you have that solid foundation.

Good luck!

NEW RIDERS PUBLISHING

The staff of New Riders Publishing is committed to bringing you the very best in computer reference material. Each New Riders book is the result of months of work by authors and staff who research and refine the information contained within its covers.

As part of this commitment to you, the NRP reader, New Riders invites your input. Please let us know if you enjoy this book, if you have trouble with the information or examples presented, or if you have a suggestion for the next edition.

Please note, however, that New Riders staff cannot serve as a technical resource during your preparation for the Microsoft certification exams or for questions about software- or hardware-related problems. Please refer instead to the documentation that accompanies the Microsoft products or to the applications' Help systems.

If you have a question or comment about any New Riders book, you can contact New Riders Publishing in several ways. We will respond to as many readers as we can. Your name, address, or phone number will never become part of a mailing list or be used for any purpose other than to help us continue to bring you the best books possible. You can write to us at the following address:

New Riders Publishing
Attn: Publisher
201 W. 103rd Street
Indianapolis, IN 46290

If you prefer, you can fax New Riders Publishing at:

(317) 581-4663

You also can send email to New Riders at the following Internet address:

certification@mcp.com

Thank you for selecting *MCSE Training Guide: Windows NT Server 4 Enterprise, Second Edition!*

PART

I

PLANNING

This chapter helps you to prepare for the Microsoft exam by covering the following objective under the Planning category:

Plan the implementation of a directory services architecture. Considerations include:

Selecting the appropriate domain model

Supporting a single logon account

Allowing users to access resources in different domains

▶ This objective introduces you to all of the components required while planning the implementation of your Enterprise system. A large component of it relates to the use of domain models and the trust relationships that are used to combine the domains into the appropriate domain model.

CHAPTER 1

Planning Directory Services for Windows NT 4.0

▶ In gaining the knowledge required to be successful in the planning section of the Enterprise exam, be sure that you fully understand the domain models and the requirements for each. As an additional preparation assignment, review case studies on network implementations and try to sketch out how the network could be installed using one of the domain models listed in this chapter. Make sure that you are analyzing the network design using the goals of directory services as your foundation for each design.

Much of the *Implementing and Supporting Microsoft Windows NT Server 4.0 in the Enterprise* exam is focused on planning an enterprise system. To understand the planning process, you need a solid understanding of the software and of the implementation goals you need to achieve. In this chapter, you look into the first planning objective Microsoft has laid out in the planning section of the exam. The main area of study in this chapter is understanding the Windows NT 4 directory services.

This chapter is based on the Microsoft implementation of the technology. It is designed to prepare you to correctly answer exam questions relating to planning an enterprise system with Windows NT Server 4.

The first objective covered in this book deals with the selection of the appropriate directory services architecture. Exam questions relating to this topic are scenario-based questions to which you apply directory services information. A large part of the exam is based on domain models, trust relationships, and the goals of implementing directory services. As you go through the various sections about directory services, think of different network scenarios to which you could apply this information.

Directory services can be implemented in small, medium, or very large organizations, although the actual setup and configuration for each would be dramatically different. One thing, however, remains the same throughout all implementations—the final goal of directory services. Before going into detail about actual implementation, this chapter first defines directory services in Windows NT Server 4 to ensure that you have a complete understanding of the objective.

The main sections in this chapter feature the topics of the Windows NT Server 4 directory services:

◆ Windows NT Server 4 directory services

◆ Trust relationships

◆ Windows NT Server 4 domain models

WINDOWS NT SERVER 4 DIRECTORY SERVICES

Whenever you install Windows NT Server, you must first decide how you want your network to function. If you're going to install multiple servers spread out across physical locations, you must first make a network design. The network design should start at a very high level of planning. Develop the domains you're going to set up and start thinking about how the domains will communicate with each other. These issues probably need to be answered with a directory services implementation.

The term *directory services* is used to define the network and, specifically, the account and security database used to combine your network into an organized structure. There are numerous implementations of directory services, and in previous versions of Windows NT, Microsoft referred to them as the domain models. In the following paragraphs, we will examine the various components of directory services in Windows NT 4.0 and the main function or goal of your directory services implementation.

Directory services enable you to extend your network, or domain, beyond its physical, and in some cases logical, size limitations. A single domain maintains all its directory database information in the Security Account Manager (SAM). The SAM contains all user accounts, Windows NT computer accounts, group accounts, and any account settings assigned in the domain. This database defines the actions that a user can carry out over the network. If not for this database, the network would be in a state of complete chaos. The previously mentioned physical limitation to a domain is based on the size of the SAM database. The SAM should not exceed 40MB in size because it could take several minutes to load into memory. Although it seems like 40MB is a large number, it can be reached easily in many large organizations. Table 1.1 breaks down how the contents of the SAM database fill the 40MB limit.

TABLE 1.1

SAM DATABASE LIMITATIONS

SAM Database Item	*Size per Item*
User Accounts	1KB
Local Groups	512 bytes per group plus 36 bytes per user
Global Groups	512 bytes per group plus 12 bytes per user
Computer Accounts	0.5KB

Table 1.1 shows the physical limitations of the domain, but there also can be a logical or departmental limitation. In every organization, the political side of the planning must be addressed in the design. In many organizations, each department requires control of its own resources. You should remember that most companies are likely to have a distributed domain environment.

So the big question is what can directory services do to help you control your network? Before you can answer that, you need to understand the goals of directory services. Then you can look at how to implement Windows NT Server 4 into directory services architecture.

Directory services are implemented to help you administer and maintain a consistent network environment throughout a LAN or WAN. The main goals of directory services are

◆ One user, one account

◆ Universal resource access

◆ Centralized administration

◆ Directory synchronization

To ensure that you have a thorough understanding of each goal, the following sections define them in more detail. Understanding the goals of directory services is crucial in ensuring that your implementation is complete.

One User, One Account

The purpose of "one user, one account" is to ensure that each user in your network has only one account name and one password. Assigning only one account per user simplifies administration of the system. If each user has a single account, you can assign permissions for resources to an individual, you can audit your system, and you can easily modify the user's permissions. But now look at it from a user perspective.

You have probably run into situations in which users have multiple accounts and passwords for accessing specific resources in the network environment. Did you ever have to reset a user's password because he forgot the password for the mail server? Or did you have to help a user connect to the laser printer because he used an improper user account for that resource? Anytime multiple user accounts are assigned, it causes you, the administrator, more work. You have to maintain more accounts than users, and you have to provide additional support for the users. The simple solution is to have each user have only one account. Some people would probably argue that it's not always an option to have one account per user. Your WAN, for example, might stretch across the country. But by implementing the proper directory service, you can achieve the goal of one user, one account.

> **NOTE**
>
> **BackOffice and One User, One Account** Microsoft BackOffice products work well with the "one user, one account" model. Programs such as SQL Server, Exchange, and SMS can take advantage of Windows NT user accounts as well as automate the login feature using service accounts instead of a regular user account. Users can access these programs with the same user name and password.

Universal Resource Access

Plan the implementation of a directory services architecture, allowing users to access resources in different domains.

Universal resource access enables users to access all resources from one account, regardless of physical location (see Figure 1.1). This makes it simple for an administrator to grant access to resources and to maintain consistency across the LAN/WAN.

Figure 1.1 shows that, by having universal resource access, User 1 from Domain A can access resources in the other domains (Domain B and Domain C). From a user's perspective, any individual user does not know that his connections have been extended beyond his own domain.

FIGURE 1.1
Universal resource access enables users from different domains to share resources.

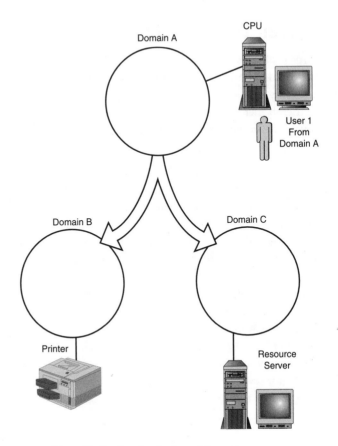

Centralized Administration

Centralized administration is probably the most important goal to you, the administrator, because you want to simplify the administration of your network as much as possible. Having full control of all user accounts and all resources from a central location is a timesaver for any administrator.

In any and probably all networks, obtaining centralized administration equals a great savings in both time and money in the total cost of ownership of your network environment. All user accounts, groups, and resources can be managed through a single user account or through a group of administrators.

Directory Synchronization

The most crucial part of the directory services architecture is ensuring that all your directory services information is available to all the computers in your environment. In a Windows NT environment the primary domain controller, or PDC, would hold the original account database. Additional copies of this database are then copied across to all of the backup domain controllers. The database, or directory, is used for all security and account verification in your network. If each directory, or database, isn't synchronized at regular intervals, your environment cannot be properly maintained. This makes it difficult to attain the directory services goals. Directory synchronization, however, is automatic within domains in Windows NT Server 4. By using trust relationships (discussed in the next section), you can enable domains to communicate with each other to share the database information.

A trust relationship doesn't really synchronize the information; it enables the databases to be accessed from another domain. The domains always cross-reference the domain databases through the trust. All database, or directory, synchronization is automated only within a domain structure. Each BDC and the PDC synchronize the database information at scheduled intervals to ensure that the directory is current.

Main Goals of Directory Services

REVIEW BREAK

Once again, the main goals of directory services are the following:

- One user, one account
- Universal resource access
- Centralized administration
- Directory synchronization

To ensure that you're selecting the best plan for your network, always address each of the goals of directory services.

TRUST RELATIONSHIPS

A *trust relationship* is a secured communication link between two domains. One domain acts as the trusted domain; the other is the trusting domain. The trusting domain permits users from the trusted domain to access its resources. It is this connection that gives a user account access across domains.

The trust is comprised of a remote procedure call (RPC) connection between the domain controllers of the two domains. The trusted and trusting domains use this RPC connection as a secured channel between the two domains. Using this RPC connection to look into the SAM of the trusted domain enables you to achieve the goal of one user, one account. By assigning resource permissions to this trusted account, you can have universal resource access. The use of trust relationships is critical to meeting the goals of directory services. The following sections discuss the different roles that the domains play in a trust.

Trusted Versus Trusting

Every trust relationship has a trusted domain and a trusting domain.

The *trusted domain* contains the user accounts; therefore, it also can be referred to as the *account domain*. Remembering this term for trusted domains makes it easier to determine which role your domain should play in the trust.

The *trusting domain* uses the accounts from the trusted domain. Located in the trusting domain are the resources you need to share. The trusting domain assigns security permissions to any user in its SAM, as well as to any user in a trusted domain's SAM. This makes it easy for departments to maintain control of their resources, and it still enables users to be administered centrally. An easy way to distinguish the trusting domain is to think of it as a *resource domain*.

Graphically Representing a Trust Relationship

To simplify a trust relationship as well as gain a better understanding of one, graphically representing the trust relationship is recommended. In a graphical representation of a trust relationship, you must define the domains and the direction of the trust relationship. In the diagrams on the Enterprise exam, the domains are shown as circles and the trust is an arrow (as shown in Figure 1.2). The direction of the arrow depends on the location of the trusted domain. Microsoft recommends that the arrow should always point toward the trusted domain. The arrowhead should point to the trusted domain (or account domain) that contains the users who can cross over the trust relationship.

In Figure 1.2 you can see two separate domains. Domain B has the printer, the resource you want to assign permissions to. Domain A contains the user accounts and, therefore, is the trusted domain.

Upcoming sections look at some examples of trust relationships. For now, take a look at the planning requirements for setting up a trust relationship.

Planning Trust Relationships

Setting up a trust relationship requires coordination between the trusted and trusting domains. A trust relationship cannot be established from one domain. Both domains must configure the trust. The requirements for setting up a trust are as follows:

◆ The trust relationship can only be established between Windows NT Server domains.

◆ The domains must be able to make an RPC connection. To establish an RPC connection, a network connection must exist between the domain controllers of all participating domains.

◆ The trust relationship must be set up by a user with administrator access.

◆ The number and type of trusts should be determined prior to the implementation.

◆ It must be decided where the user accounts reside, as that is the trusted domain.

Always define the role of your domain before the implementation. After the trusted domain and the trusting domain have been selected, you're ready to establish the trust relationship.

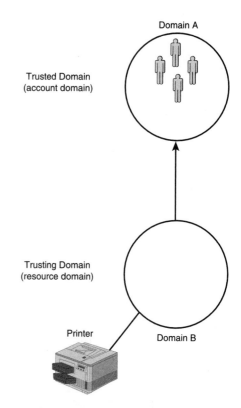

FIGURE 1.2
Graphically representing the trust relationship. In this figure, Domain A is the trusted domain and Domain B is the trusting domain. Take note as to the direction of the arrow—always point to the trusted domain that contains the user accounts.

EXAM TIP

Draw a Picture   Always draw the scenario shown in the exam questions. If you have the diagram in front of you, it's much easier to follow the trust relationship and to understand the question.

FIGURE 1.3

The Trust Relationships dialog box is used to define the role that your domain will play in the trust relationship.

FIGURE 1.4

A message stating that the trust was successfully established is displayed following the completion of both sides of the trust relationship.

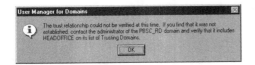

FIGURE 1.5

If the trust relationship has been set up incorrectly or in the opposite order, then you might encounter this message stating that the trust could not be verified.

FIGURE 1.6

The starting point for establishing a trust relationship is to open the User Manager and then select the Trust Relationships option from the Policies menu.

Establishing Trust Relationships

This section steps you through the tasks used in establishing a trust relationship. Prior to starting the trust relationship, verify that you have selected the trusted and the trusting domains.

An administrator from each domain must establish a trust relationship using the Trust Relationships dialog box (see Figure 1.3).

This dialog box contains two different sections:

❖ The Trusted Domains section is filled in by the administrator of the trusting domain.

❖ The Trusting Domains section is filled in by the administrator of the trusted domain.

The order in which you configure the trust relationship is not as important as ensuring that both sides complete the setup. If the trusted domain sets up the trust relationship first, when the trusting domain completes setup, it is presented with the message shown in Figure 1.4.

If the trust relationship is established in the opposite order, it can still be completed. You get a warning, however, that the trust cannot be verified (see Figure 1.5). If you see this message, you should verify the settings for your trust relationship.

To view all of the required steps involved in establishing a trust relationship, perform the tasks outlined in Step by Step 1.1.

STEP BY STEP

1.1 Creating a Trust Relationship

1. Start User Manager for Domains, then select Trust Relationships from the Policies menu (see Figure 1.6).

2. From the trusted domain, enter the name of the trusting domain in the Add Trusting Domain dialog box (see Figure 1.7). A password for the trust can be entered, but this is optional, depending on the security required at your site. If a password isn't used, then any user can establish the trust from the specified domain, and you cannot maintain a controlled environment.

3. Click OK. The trusting domain is added to the Trust Relationships dialog box (see Figure 1.8). Click Close.

4. From the trusting domain, open the Trust Relationships dialog box and add the name of the trusted domain (see Figure 1.9). Ensure that the password is correct for the trust relationship.

5. After the trusted domain is added, you should see the message telling you that the trust was successfully established.

When each of these steps has been completed, you have successfully created a trust relationship. This can be extended to include numerous domains, and each domain may be both a trusted domain and a trusting domain in your environment. These various methods are explained in the domain models in the upcoming sections of this chapter.

ADDED SECURITY

When a trust is established, NT creates a new password or changes the password used to establish the trust. The domain controllers in both domains know the new password; however, it isn't visible to users. Windows NT changes this password for added security. If one of the domains in the trust relationship breaks the trust, the trust cannot be reestablished without breaking both sides and starting the trust relationship over again. This is because the password is no longer the current correct password.

One-Way Trusts

The term *one-way trust* refers to a trust relationship with a single trusted domain and a single trusting domain. In a one-way trust, it's especially important to define the roles and then establish the trust in the proper direction (see Figure 1.10). The accounts are in the trusted domain, and the trusting domain is able to assign permissions to users in the trusted domain.

Two-Way Trusts

A *two-way trust* is basically two mutual one-way trusts—see Figure 1.11. In a two-way trust, both systems are trusted domains, and both are trusting domains. In this type of trust relationship, permissions can be assigned to any user in any of the domains.

FIGURE 1.7
Fill in the appropriate information in the dialog box to add a trusting domain with the password option filled in.

FIGURE 1.8
Once the trusting domain has been completed, you see a confirmation that the domain was entered.

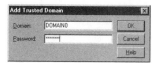

FIGURE 1.9
Fill in the appropriate information to configure the trusted domain.

EXAM TIP

Two-Way Trust Definition The definition of a two-way trust is two one-way trusts. This question has been on the past several versions of the Windows NT Server 4.0 exam, and it is here again in the Enterprise exam.

FIGURE 1.10
A one-way trust diagram showing the trusted domain with the user accounts and the trusting domain with the resources to be shared across domains.

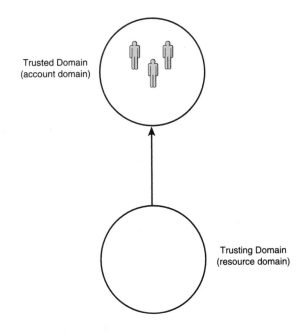

Trusted Domain
(account domain)

Trusting Domain
(resource domain)

Domain A

Trusted Domain   Trusting Domain

Trust relationship 1   Trust relationship 2

Trusting Domain   Trusted Domain

Domain B

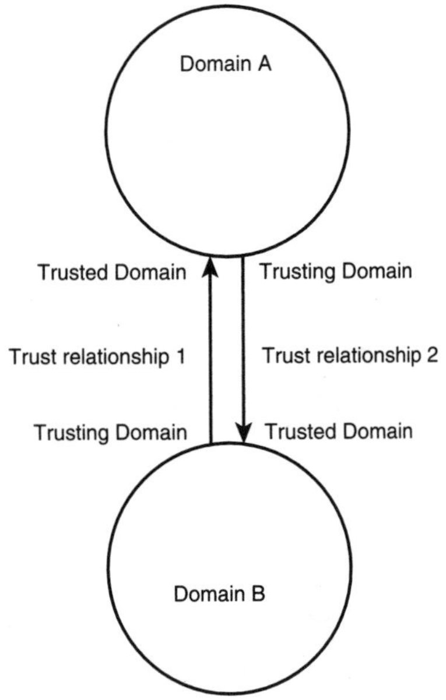

FIGURE 1.11
In a two-way trust diagram, both domains act as a trusted domain and a trusting domain with user accounts and resources located in both domains.

Trusts Are Non-Transitive

Trust relationships are non-transitive; in other words, you cannot pass through one trust into another. Every trust relationship must be explicitly established between each and every domain that's required.

In Figure 1.12, a user from Domain C can access resources in Domain B but cannot access resources in Domain A, even though Domain A and Domain B also have a trust relationship.

Removing Trusts

Removing a trust relationship is as simple as removing either side of the trust. If either domain—trusted or trusting—removes the opposite domain, the trust is broken. If the broken half of the trust tries to reestablish, the trust is not valid because the password is not valid. The trust cannot be reestablished without breaking both sides and starting the trust relationship over again.

Another way a trust can be removed, or broken, is if the domain name of a member of the trust relationship changes. The trust relationship is not reestablished, even if the name of the domain is changed back.

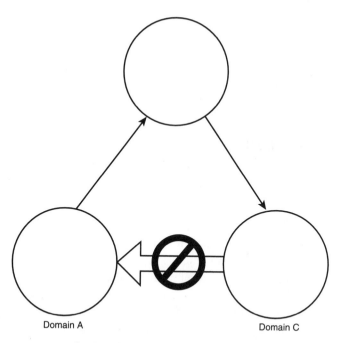

Can Domain C access resources on Domain A?

FIGURE 1.12
A non-transitive trust diagram. The user from Domain C cannot access resources on Domain A.

To remove a trust, you must open the User Manager for Domains, select the Trust Relationships option from the Policies menu, highlight the domain to remove, and click Remove.

Accounts in Trust Relationships

In an enterprise system that consists of trust relationships between domains, you have to ensure that you are using global accounts and not local accounts. Each of these account types are explained in the following section. In addition, the use of groups in the domains is essential to maintaining and administrating the enterprise system. You should be familiar with creating a global user account, and you should know that the user account can be used throughout the domain. But in a trust relationship you can use the accounts in the trusted domains as easily as you use your own domain accounts.

Before you look at using the accounts from trusted domains, you should examine the different types of accounts available and understand which accounts can be used across a trust and which ones are exclusive to your local domains.

> **NOTE**
>
> **Temporary Broken Trust** When the domain controllers in a domain are stopped, the trust is temporarily broken. If any domain controller for the domain comes back up, the trust is reestablished.

Global Accounts

A *global account* is the default user-account type. Every user has a global account unless you specifically change the type of user account. Global accounts are designed for use across trusts; they can be assigned access in your domain and all of the trusting domains.

Local Accounts

A *local account* is a special account type with some limitations:

◆ Local accounts cannot be given permissions across trusts.

◆ Local accounts do not support interactive logon processes.

◆ Local accounts require their own password. They are commonly used for accounts in non-trusted domains. Users are not able to automatically synchronize passwords.

The local account cannot be used across trusts; it is used only locally in your own domain. This type of account can be used to assign permissions to a user that needs access to only one domain in your enterprise. You can use local accounts for temporary employees, for example, who need to access only specific applications or resources.

To create a local user account, follow the normal setup procedures, making one small change in the user properties. In the Account Information dialog box, select the Local Account option (see Figure 1.13).

Global Groups and Local Groups

Microsoft recommends using groups for assigning all permissions. This statement is very important when taking the Enterprise exam. Users always belong to a group, and the group has the security permissions.

In Windows NT Server, there are two types of groups—local and global. Local groups are restricted to being used within their domains. Global groups are designed to contain users implemented across trusts.

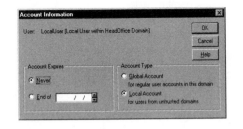

FIGURE 1.13
Setting up a local account in the Account Information dialog box can be accomplished by selecting the Local Account radio button.

Microsoft uses the acronym AGLP (Accounts, Global, Local, Permissions) for applying its group strategies. This acronym means user accounts get placed into global groups, global groups belong in local groups, and local groups are assigned all the permissions. The local group is restricted to the domain it's created in, whereas the global group can float across trusts. Following the acronym, place your user accounts into global groups and assign global groups into local groups of either your local domain or any trusting domain.

In preparation for the Enterprise exam, you should know all the built-in groups on Windows NT Server. Tables 1.2 and 1.3 show the different groups available. Table 1.2 shows the local groups, and Table 1.3 shows the global groups.

TABLE 1.2

BUILT-IN LOCAL GROUPS

Local Group	Initially Contains	Rights
Administrators	Domain Admins, Administrator	Administrate account; manage and maintain entire system.
Users	Domain Users	Access resources; perform day-to-day operation of computer system.
Guests	Domain Guests	Disabled by default.
Server Operators	None	Share and stop sharing resources; shutdown/lock servers; stop and start services; perform server maintenance; back up and restore server.
Print Operators	None	Share and stop sharing printers; manage printers.
Backup Operators	None	Back up and restore server.
Account Operators	None	Create and manage user and group accounts.
Replicators	None	Use for the Directory Replication service.

EXAM TIP

Exam Alert This section points out a few items that are very likely to be on the exam:

- Microsoft recommends using groups for assigning all permissions. Users always belong to a group, and the group has the security permissions.

- Be very familiar with all the built-in groups on Windows NT Server.

- The accounts that can be utilized across trust relationships are global groups and global accounts. Remember these account types.

TABLE 1.3		
BUILT-IN GLOBAL GROUPS		
Global Group	*Initial Accounts*	*Member of...*
Domain Admins	Administrator	Administrators
Domain Users	Administrator, all accounts created in domain	Users
Domain Guests	Guest	Guests

The accounts that can be utilized across trust relationships are global groups and global accounts. Remember these account types throughout your preparation for the Enterprise exam.

Assigning Permissions Across a Trust

To assign permissions across a trust relationship, you must place the global group or global account into a local group from the trusting domain. To select the trusted domain accounts, select the List Names From drop-down list in the Add Users and Groups dialog box (see Figure 1.14).

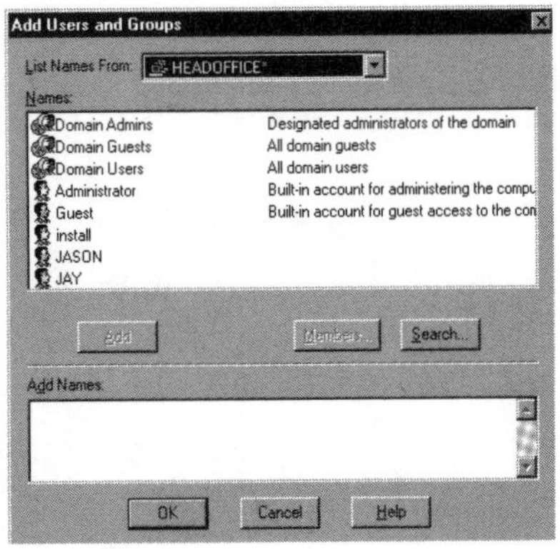

Notice in Figure 1.14 that local groups and local accounts cannot be seen in this view. Local accounts and local groups cannot be used across trusts. Assigning permissions across a trust is covered in Chapter 5, "Managing Resources."

FIGURE 1.14
Assigning permissions across a trust ensures that you select the appropriate domain from the List Names From drop-down box.

The NetLogon Service in a Trust

Plan the implementation of a directory services architecture, supporting a single logon account.

As a trust relationship is set up, users from trusted domains must be authenticated in order to gain access to the resources in a trusting domain. Similar to logging on to a domain, the user account must be verified, and the security permissions must be assigned to the user account. The NetLogon service is responsible for handling logon requests. When requests are made across a trust, the action is termed pass-through authentication.

Pass-Through Authentication

Pass-through authentication allows the trusting domain to handle the logon request, but it looks into the SAM of the trusted domain to verify that the account is valid.

In Figure 1.15 you can see that the User 1 account exists in Domain A; however, it is being validated by Domain B, a trusting domain. The communication between the two domains is pass-through authentication.

WINDOWS NT SERVER 4 DOMAIN MODELS

Trust relationships enable communication between domains. The trusts must be organized, however, to achieve the original goal of directory services.

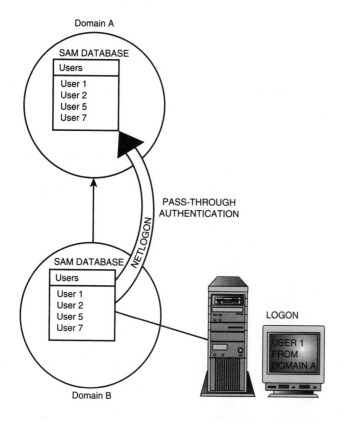

FIGURE 1.15
This illustration shows the process of pass-through authentication using a trust relationship.

EXAM TIP

Know Domain Models   Domain models are tested throughout the exam. If you have strong knowledge of the domain models and when to use each one, you should have no problems with the directory services planning on the Enterprise exam. The domain models incorporate all the information covered so far in this chapter and are tested extensively on the exam.

Windows NT domains can be organized into one of four different domain models:

◆ Single-domain model

◆ Single-master domain model

◆ Multiple-master domain model

◆ Complete-trust model

The upcoming sections analyze each domain model. Look at the accounts and trusts involved in the domain models and try to find reasons for selecting one domain model over another.

Selecting Your Domain Model

Plan the implementation of a directory services architecture, selecting the appropriate domain model.

When you're selecting a domain model, consider the following:

◆ How many user accounts are there?

◆ How many organizational (or departmental) domains are required?

◆ Is centralized account administration required?

◆ Is centralized or distributed resource administration required?

The responses to these questions are necessary to select the proper domain model for your network. In comparing the domain models, you must look at the trust relationships required to implement the domain model, and you must look at the account management within each domain model. The goal is always to select the proper domain model for your specific needs. By using the information gathered from the preceding questions, you should be able to select the domain model that meets your organizational needs.

Single-Domain Model

The single-domain model is the easiest to implement (see Figure 1.16). It places all users, groups, and resources into a single domain. The single domain is the starting point of all the domain models. In any implementation, you must ensure that each domain can function as a single domain before you consider any of the other models.

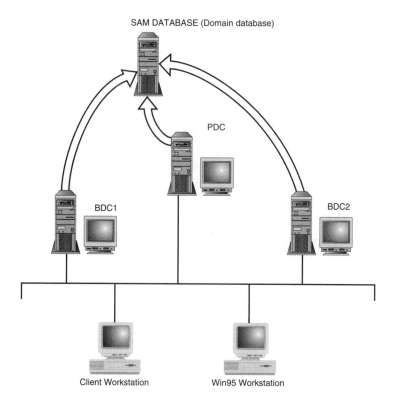

SAM DATABASE (Domain database)

PDC

BDC1

BDC2

Client Workstation

Win95 Workstation

FIGURE 1.16
A graphical representation of a single-domain model.

Examine the benefits and the limitations of the single-domain model to understand when a single-domain model is recommended. The benefits of a single-domain model are as follows:

◆ Easy installation—just install the first server as a primary domain controller and you have a single-domain model.

◆ Centralized administration of accounts, because there is only one domain database.

◆ Resources can be managed from one location.

◆ No trust relationships to establish.

The limitations of the single-domain model affect larger organizations with a distributed WAN environment. The limitations of the single-domain model are as follows:

◆ It can handle a recommended maximum of 40,000 accounts. This is due to the recommendation that the SAM database be limited to 40MB. The recommended number of users in a single domain is 20,000 users.

◆ No departmental administrative controls can be assigned as a result of the single-domain database for assigning security permissions.

◆ Browsing is slow if the domain contains a large number of servers and resources.

A single-domain model is best suited to organizations that have a single location with less than 20,000 users. When selecting the single-domain model, however, you need to ensure that the organization does not require departmental administration of resources.

Single-Master Domain Model

In a single-master domain, Windows NT Server uses trust relationships to extend the boundaries of the domain. This model maintains centralized administration by keeping all user accounts in the master domain. A big advantage of the single-master domain model, however, is that it allows other domains—resource domains—to exist (see Figure 1.17).

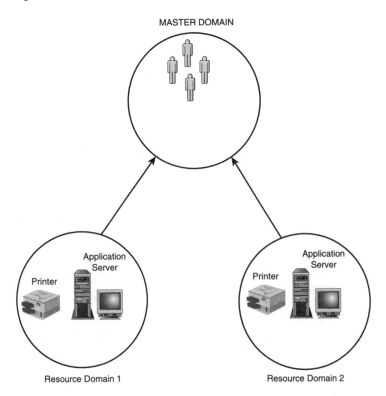

FIGURE 1.17
A graphical representation of a single-master domain model; notice that all resource domains trust the master domain.

These resource domains are able to maintain their own resources and permissions, with all user accounts living in the master domain. From a user's perspective, the domain appears to be one large system. Every user logs on to the master. Users connect to other domains in the environment without requiring additional user accounts or passwords.

Examine the main advantages and limitations of this model. The benefits of a single-master domain model are as follows:

◆ It has centralized administration of users accounts.

◆ Resources can be distributed and administered throughout resource domains.

◆ Each resource domain can have a domain administrator to maintain its resources, without giving access to the master domain.

◆ The trust relationships are fairly easy to implement.

◆ It maintains the "one user, one account" goal of directory services.

◆ Global groups can be maintained from the master domain.

The limitations of the single-master domain model are similar to those of the single-domain model. The single-master domain model also uses one domain database for all users. This model is recommended for domains having fewer than 20,000 user accounts and 40,000 overall accounts. Other limitations include the following:

◆ Local groups must be defined in each domain—master and resource domains.

◆ There is a limited number of users because of the 40MB limit for the SAM database.

◆ Resource domains have no control over user accounts assigned to the global groups from the master domain.

◆ Trust relationships have to be established in the proper direction in order to maintain the directory services structure.

The single-master domain model is best suited to organizations with less than 20,000 users that require some departmental resource administration. This model is excellent for companies with locations spread across a WAN, and the trust relationships allow for the centralized administration.

In the following sections, the use of trust relationships in a single-domain model will be discussed, along with a recommendation concerning using accounts in a single-master domain model.

Trusts in a Single-Master Domain Model

The trust relationships in a single-master domain model are relatively easy to implement (see Figure 1.18). The first step in setting up a single-master domain model is to select the master domain. The master domain holds all the user accounts and global groups, and it might have resources. After the master domain has been selected, all the other domains become resource domains. The trusted domain is the master domain, and the resource domains are the trusting domains. All resource domains trust the master domain.

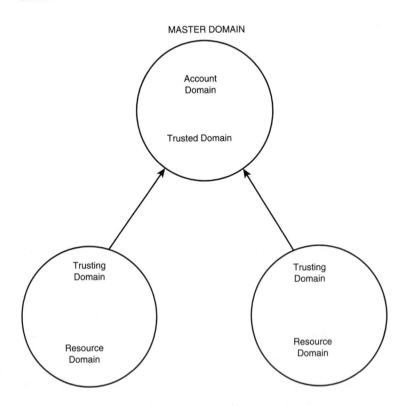

FIGURE 1.18
The use of trusts in a single-master domain model. Each resource domain trusts the master or account domain.

Accounts in a Single-Master Domain Model

By defining the master domain, you have already selected the domain that administers and maintains all the user accounts. If the user accounts live in the master domain, then all the global groups also are defined in the master domain. By establishing trust relationships with all resource domains trusting the master, you enable the resource domains to look into the SAM database of the master domain. If the resource domains trust the master, then they can assign permissions to any user or global group from the master domain.

At the resource domains, local groups must be created, and the permissions should be applied to the local groups. The members of the resource domain's local groups are the users and global groups from the master domain. As mentioned earlier, concentrate on using groups as opposed to users.

To assign administrator access for the resource domains, the selected users from the master domain should become members of the resource's local Administrators group. A normal scenario is to add the trusted domain's global domain Admins group to the trusting domain's local Administrators group.

Multiple-Master Domain Model

The multiple-master domain model is designed for very large organizations that have users distributed across multiple domains (see Figure 1.19). In this model, there can be multiple master, or account, domains. Each master domain contains user and global group accounts to be used by all other domains in the environment. The administration can still be centralized; however, you have to add the domain Admins global group from each master domain into the local Administrators group of all domains in the environment.

The multiple-master domain model is the most scaleable of the domain models. Each master domain can contain the recommended maximum number of user accounts and the full 40MB SAM. Multiple-master domains can be used in this model to expand the network to include an unlimited number of users. There is no limit to the number of master domains available in this model.

FIGURE 1.19

A graphical representation of a multiple-master domain model; take notice of the use of trust relationships in a multiple-master domain model.

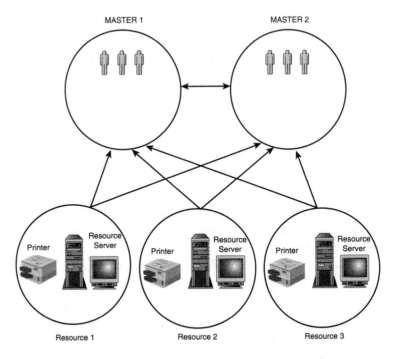

The advantages of the multiple-master domain are as follows:

◆ It is scaleable for networks with a large number of users.

◆ Resources are grouped into resource domains to allow distributed resource management.

◆ Each master domain can have a domain administrator, or they can be grouped to achieve centralized administration.

◆ User accounts and global groups are all maintained in the master domains.

The limitations or disadvantages of using this domain model are as follows:

◆ Complex trust relationships have to be configured to maintain this domain model.

◆ User accounts are distributed across multiple-master domains.

◆ Global groups might have to be defined multiple times, once in each master domain.

The multiple-master domain model requires more planning than the previous models presented. Each master domain must be identified, and the administration method for the master domains must be selected. Centralized administration can be achieved in this model by assigning the global domain Admins group from the master domains into the local Administrators group in all other domains, resources, and other master domains. The trust relationships are more complex in this model, and they require that all trusts be set in the proper direction.

The multiple-master domain model is best suited to large organizations—with more than 20,000 users—that want to maintain centralized control of user accounts while allowing resources to be administered departmentally.

The following sections put the entire picture together by looking at the trust relationships in a multiple-master domain model and the use of user accounts and groups in a multiple-master domain model.

Trusts in a Multiple-Master Domain Model

The trust relationships in a multiple-master domain model are configured similarly to the single-master domain. All resource domains trust the master domain. The only difference is that the multiple-master domain model contains numerous master domains. The resource domains trust *all* master domains. This increases the number of trusts, but there must also be a trust relationship between each of the master domains. In this model, each master sets up a two-way trust between all other masters (see Figure 1.20).

Each master domain has a two-way trust to all other master domains; every resource domain trusts every master. There are no trusts set up between resource domains.

The following is the formula to find the number of trusts required for this model:

```
M*(M-1)+(R*M)
```

M is the number of master domains, and R is the number of resource domains.

FIGURE 1.20
Trusts in a multiple-master domain model;
notice how all resource domains trust all master or account domains.

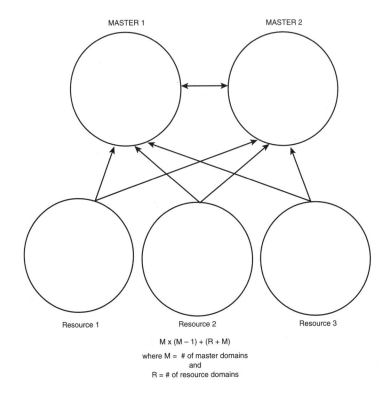

$$M \times (M - 1) + (R + M)$$

where M = # of master domains
and
R = # of resource domains

> **NOTE**
>
> **Two-Way Trust**   Remember that a
> two-way trust is actually two one-way
> trusts.

Using Figure 1.20 as an example, apply the formula to verify the
number of trust relationships required for a model that has two master domains and three resource domains:

$$2*(2-1)+(3*2) = 8$$

Can you visualize the eight trust relationships in Figure 1.20?

Accounts in a Multiple-Master Domain Model

The accounts in the multiple masters are distributed across multiple-
master domains. Each user still has only one account; global groups,
however, might have to be duplicated in all the master domains (see
Figure 1.21). If an organization has members of the marketing
department spread across both master domains, for example, and it
requires that all members of marketing access a database in one of
the resource domains, how can the users be assigned access?

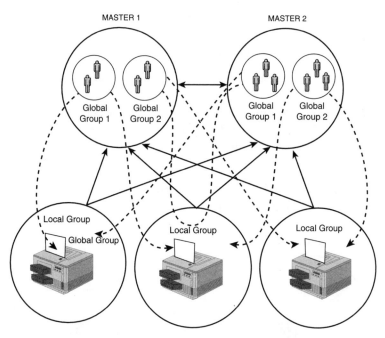

MASTER 1

MASTER 2

Global Group 1

Global Group 2

Global Group 1

Global Group 2

Local Group

Global Group

Local Group

Local Group

FIGURE 1.21
The use of user accounts and groups in a multiple-master domain model.

Each master domain is responsible for grouping its local users into a global marketing group. If this is done on both master domains, then you have two marketing global groups. When you assign access at the resource domain, the master domain places both marketing global groups into its local group that has permissions to the database.

The key points to remember regarding accounts in a multiple-master domain are as follows:

◆ User accounts are located in one of the master domains.

◆ Global groups are defined in all the master domains.

◆ Local groups are defined in resource domains and contain global groups from all the master domains.

Complete-Trust Model

The complete-trust model enables each domain to maintain control of its users and resources, and provides the opportunity to assign permissions to users of any other domain in the model (see

Figure 1.22). The complete-trust model implements two-way trust relationships between all domains in the environment. Each and every domain is an account domain and a resource domain.

This model is scaleable and very flexible, but it doesn't allow for the centralized administration of user accounts or resources. It enables each domain to control its users and resources. Each domain is able to access resources on other domains and is able to assign permissions to users from other domains.

The following sections introduce the trust relationships required for a complete trust, and the use of user accounts and global groups in a complete-trust domain model.

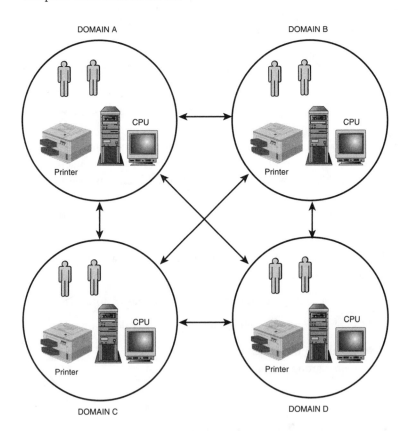

FIGURE 1.22
A graphical representation of the complete-trust model.

Trusts in a Complete-Trust Model

The trust relationships in a complete-trust model are numerous. Every domain has a two-way trust with every other domain (see Figure 1.23).

A formula can be used to find the number of trust relationships required. The formula is $N*(N-1)$. N is the total number of domains in the environment. If you have an environment with five domains, for example, how many trust relationships have to be established?

```
5*(5-1) = 20
```

Twenty trust relationships have to be established.

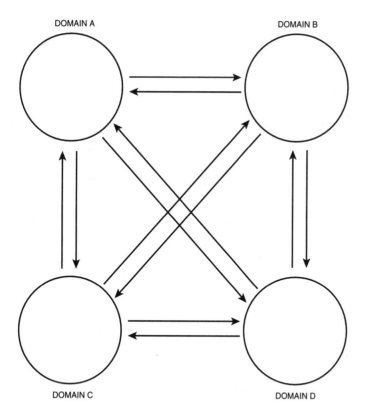

DOMAIN A

DOMAIN B

DOMAIN C

DOMAIN D

FIGURE 1.23

The trust in a complete-trust model: Every domain has a two-way trust with every other domain in the environment.

Accounts in a Complete-Trust Model

Every domain is responsible for administering the user accounts and global groups within its own domains. Global groups then are assigned to the local groups on each domain. This domain model makes it very difficult to centrally manage the user accounts. It is designed for environments that do not require centralized administration.

Weighing the Pros and Cons of Each Domain Model

Summary Table 1.1 recaps the advantages and disadvantages of each of the domain models.

SUMMARY TABLE 1.1
PROFILING THE DOMAIN MODELS

Domain Model	Advantages	Disadvantages
Single-domain model	Centralized administration	Limited to 40,000 user accounts No trust relationships No distribution of resources
Single-master domain model	Centralized Administration Distributed resources	Limited to 40,000 user accounts
Multiple-master domain model	Unlimited number of user accounts, each master domain can host 40,000 user accounts Distributed resources Complex trust relationships	No centralized administration of user accounts
Complete-trust model	Unlimited number of user accounts, each domain can host 40,000 user accounts Complex trust relationships	No centralized administration of user accounts

CASE STUDY: DEVELOPING A DESIRED WINDOWS NT MODEL

ESSENCE OF THE CASE

Here are the essential elements in this case:

- Each location needs to manage local resources.

- Winnipeg will manage all user accounts.

- All locations must be able to use the user accounts on Winnipeg server.

- 1,000 total users in the environment.

SCENARIO

A large organization with locations in Toronto, Ottawa, Winnipeg, Edmonton, and Vancouver requires a Windows NT model that allows each of the location to use a common user account database; however, each location must be able to add resources and administer them locally. The Winnipeg location is the corporate office and will handle all user account administration and central resources. All other locations will be responsible only for resources on their local servers. The organization has a total of 1,000 employees spread across all locations.

ANALYSIS

Each location will be installed as a separate domain. This allows them to manage and install resources locally. The Winnipeg domain will be set up as the master domain to all other locations. One-way trust relationships will be set up with all domains trusting Winnipeg domain—enabling the user accounts to be used in all locations. An administrator will be assigned in each location to allow them to manage the trusting sites and add resources. One master domain will be able to handle this organization because the total employee count is 1,000, well below the 20,000 recommended maximum limit for a domain.

CHAPTER SUMMARY

In any network design, the planning phase is one of the most important aspects of setting up the network. Ensure that you have a strong knowledge of the domain models and how to establish the trust relationships for each of the models to achieve the goals of the directory services.

To help you apply the information for the Enterprise exam, you should get into the habit of drawing the domain models, or more importantly, the trust relationships in the scenario-based questions. You will find them easier to understand. Watch for key phrases in the questions. They generally lead you to select the appropriate domain model. Some key phrases to watch for are as follows:

◆ **Centralized user accounts.** When centralized user accounts are required, it narrows your selection down to single domain, single master, or multiple master.

◆ **Distributed resource management.** This distribution of resources is available in single-master domain models, multiple-master domain models, and complete-trust domain models.

◆ **Distributed users and resources.** The only model that offers both of these is the complete-trust domain model.

◆ **Select domains to maintain user accounts with distributed resources.** The multiple master allows for numerous account (master) domains and distributed resource domains.

◆ **Very large organization with 20,000 or more users.** This is restricted to multiple-master and complete-trust domain models.

◆ **Small organizations with less than 20,000 users.** The best model is a single domain or single-master domain.

By combining all these items, you should be able to select the appropriate domain model in any situation on the Enterprise exam.

KEY TERMS

- directory services
- Security Account Manager (SAM) database
- directory synchronization
- trust relationships
- RPC—Remote Procedure Call
- AGLP
- domain
- primary domain controller (PDC)

APPLY YOUR LEARNING

This section enables you to assess how well you understood the material in the chapter. Review and exam questions test your knowledge of the tasks and concepts specified in the objectives. The exercises provide you with opportunities to practice the sorts of tasks that comprise the skill sets the objectives reflect.

For more review and exam type questions, see the Top Score test engine on the CD-ROM that came with this book.

Exercises

The following exercises provide you with an opportunity to apply what you've learned in this chapter. Each of these exercises deal in some part with the Planning 1 objective.

1.1   Synchronizing the Domain Controllers

The following steps show you how to manually synchronize a backup domain controller within your domain.

Time Estimate: Less than 10 minutes.

1. Click Start, Programs, Administrative Tools, and select the Server Manager icon.

2. Highlight the BDC (backup domain controller) in your computer list.

3. Select the Computer menu, then select Synchronize with Primary Domain Controller.

1.2   Establishing a Trust Relationship Between Domains

The following steps show you how to establish a trust relationship between multiple domains. To complete this exercise you must have two Windows NT Server computers, each installed in its own domain.

Time Estimate: 10 minutes

1. From the trusted domain, select Start, Programs, Administrative Tools, and click User Manager for Domains. The User Manager for Domains application starts.

2. Select the Policies menu and click Trust Relationships. The Trust Relationships dialog box appears.

3. In the Trusting Domain section, click Add and enter the name of your trusting domain. You can leave the password blank.

4. When the trusting domain information has been entered, click OK to close the Trust Relationships dialog box.

5. From the trusting domain, start the User Manager for Domains.

6. Select the Policies menu and click Trust Relationships.

7. Add the name of the trusted domain, then click OK.

8. You should then be presented with a message stating that the trust relationship was successfully established.

9. To test the trust relationship, log off from the trusting domain. When logging back on, select the drop-down list from the Domain section of the logon screen. You should see the name of the trusted domain and your current domain.

APPLY YOUR LEARNING

1.3   Designing a Network Domain Model

This exercise steps you through the planning phases of your Windows NT domain model. Look at the following situation, then work through the planning of a domain model.

Time Estimate: 15 minutes

Situation: The ABC Corporation has a building in Los Angeles, a production department in San Francisco, and a satellite location in San Diego. The Los Angeles location has 1,500 users and holds the central IT department that's responsible for all network administration. The other two locations, San Francisco and San Diego, each have a local administrator who is responsible for network servers and resources but does not need administrator access in Los Angeles.

Answer the following questions to help step you through the planning phases of your network.

1. How many domains would you require for this situation?

2. Which domain would hold all the user accounts?

3. Sketch the domain diagram for the scenario; make sure you include all trust relationships in the diagram.

4. What groups would the local administrator for the resource domains need to be placed in?

Solutions:

1. Three domains would be required for this situation.

2. The Los Angeles domain would contain all the user accounts.

3. See Figure 1.27.

4. The resource administrator would be placed into a global group on the Los Angeles domain. That global group would then be placed into the Administrators group on each of the resource domains.

Review Questions

1. List the four domain models that can be used for directory services in Windows NT Server 4.

2. List the goals of a directory services architecture.

3. What is the maximum size of the SAM database in Windows NT Server 4.0?

4. What are the two different types of domains in a trust relationship?

5. In a trust relationship, which domain would contain the user accounts?

6. Can a local account be used in a trust relationship? Explain.

7. In a complete-trust domain model that uses four different domains, what is the total number of trust relationships required to use a complete-trust domain model?

8. What are the disadvantages of a single-master domain model?

APPLY YOUR LEARNING

Exam Questions

1. ABC Corporation has locations in Toronto, New York, and San Francisco. It wants to install Windows NT Server 4 to encompass all its locations in a single WAN environment. The head office is located in New York, and all user accounts will be created at that location. In Toronto and San Francisco, ABC has numerous applications and resources that users from all three locations might need to access. What is the best domain model for ABC's directory services implementation?

   A. Single-domain model

   B. Single-master domain model

   C. Multiple-master domain model

   D. Complete-trust domain model

2. JPS Printing has a single location with 1,000 users spread across the LAN. It has special printers and applications installed on the servers in its environment. It needs to be able to centrally manage the user accounts and the resources. Which domain model would best fit its needs?

   A. Single-domain model

   B. Single-master domain model

   C. Multiple-master domain model

   D. Complete-trust domain model

3. Worldwide Training has locations around the world. The North American headquarters are located in Seattle; the European headquarters are in London, England. Smaller locations are distributed throughout the world. All the user accounts will be maintained from the two corporate headquarters, but each location needs to manage its own resources. Which domain model best fits this scenario?

   A. Single-domain model

   B. Single-master domain model

   C. Multiple-master domain model

   D. Complete-trust domain model

4. ABC Corporation has a single-domain model to maintain the directory services in its Toronto location. It manages all users and resources for its current network. ABC Corporation is merging with DEF Corporation. The two companies will still run as separate companies, but they would like to share network resources. Each domain will be completely responsible for its own user accounts and resources. What domain model would enable the two domains to maintain account and resource control, but would still allow access between the two domains?

   A. Single-domain model

   B. Single-master domain model

   C. Multiple-master domain model

   D. Complete-trust domain model

APPLY YOUR LEARNING

5. What must be created to allow a user account from one domain to access resources in a different domain?

   A. Complete trust domain model

   B. One-way trust relationship

   C. Two-way trust relationship

   D. Master-domain model

Answers to Review Questions

Each of the following answers (and their corresponding questions) deal in some part with the Planning 1 objective.

1. Single-domain, master-domain, multiple-master domain, complete-trust domain. See the section, "Windows NT Server 4 Domain Models" in this chapter for more information.

2. "One user, one account," centralized administration, universal resource access, directory synchronization. See the section "Windows NT Server 4 Directory Services" in this chapter for more information.

3. The SAM database has a maximum size of 40MB. See the section "Windows NT Server 4 Directory Services" in this chapter for more information.

4. A trust relationship is made up of a trusted domain and a trusting domain. See the section "Trust Relationships" in this chapter for more information.

5. The trusted domain, commonly referred to as the accounts domain, would hold the user accounts in a trust relationship. See the section "Trust Relationships" in this chapter for more information.

6. Local accounts cannot be given permissions across trusts. See the section "Accounts in Trust Relationships" in this chapter for more information.

7. The number of trust relationships can be figured out by using the formula $N * (N - 1)$, where N is the number of domains. Therefore, the answer is 12 trust relationships. See the section "Complete-Trust Model" in this chapter for more information.

8. The major disadvantage to the single-master domain model is the 40,000 limit on the number of user accounts. See the section "Single-Master Domain Model" in this chapter for more information.

Answers to Exam Questions

Each of the following answers (and their corresponding questions) deal in some part with the Planning 1 objective.

1. **B.** A single-master domain model would be the ideal solution in this scenario, with New York being the master domain, and Toronto and San Francisco acting as resource domains. See the section "Single-Master Domain Model."

APPLY YOUR LEARNING

2. **A**. A single-domain model would meet all of the needs of JPS Printing and its 1,000 user accounts and resources. See the section "Single-Domain Model."

3. **C**. A Multiple master domain model would meet the needs of the Worldwide Training organization. Both Seattle and the London domain would be a master domain, and all other remote sites would act as resource domains. See the section "Multiple-Master Domain Model."

4. **D**. A complete trust should be established between the two organizations to allow complete crossover of the domains, without giving up user account and resource management. See the section "Complete-Trust Model."

5. **B**. For two domains to be able to share user accounts and resources, a one-way trust relationship must be established between the two domains. See the section "Trust Relationships."

This chapter helps you to prepare for the Microsoft exam by covering the following remaining objectives within the "Planning" category:

Plan the disk drive configuration for various requirements. Requirements include choosing a fault tolerance method.

▶ This objective requires you to fully understand the fault tolerance options available in Windows NT Server and when they should be used in your enterprise environment.

Choose a protocol for various situations. Protocols include

- ❖ **TCP/IP**
- ❖ **TCP/IP with DHCP and WINS**
- ❖ **NWLink IPX/SPX-Compatible Transport**
- ❖ **Data Link Control (DLC)**
- ❖ **AppleTalk**

▶ To meet the requirements of this objective, you must understand all the protocols available in Windows NT Server 4.0 and where they apply in your enterprise environment.

CHAPTER 2

Planning Your Enterprise System: Fault Tolerance and Protocols

STUDY STRATEGIES

▶ In any planning section, you are introduced to procedures and detailed information on each of the components. To gain a strong understanding of each of these sections, you should read each of the sections and then cross-reference with the "Installation and Configuration" sections in this book to understand how each of these items is installed in a Windows NT system. Knowing the specific steps required in an installation gives the planning procedures more meaning.

This chapter covers the remaining objectives grouped in the planning section as defined by Microsoft. The main sections in this chapter—directly addressing these objectives—are as follows:

◆ Planning the fault tolerance configurations for Windows NT Server 4

◆ Selecting the proper protocol

The Enterprise exam focuses a great deal of its questions on the planning aspects of your enterprise system. If you have a strong understanding of the theory and the options available from your Windows NT Server system, you will have an easy time with the exam. This chapter will ensure that you can relate the various fault tolerance options available and the protocols for a heterogeneous enterprise environment.

PLANNING THE FAULT TOLERANCE CONFIGURATIONS FOR WINDOWS NT SERVER 4

Plan the disk drive configuration for various requirements. Requirements include choosing a fault tolerance method.

One of the major items tested in the planning section of the Enterprise exam is Microsoft's use of fault tolerance in Windows NT Server 4. This section reviews the different levels of RAID (Redundant Array of Inexpensive Disks) available for Windows NT Server 4. It looks into the requirements for each of the fault tolerance options as well as the limitations and disk restrictions. Many fault tolerance solutions today incorporate a hardware RAID, rather than software versions of the fault tolerance. In this chapter, we will look at the software fault tolerance as supported by Windows NT Server 4.0.

RAID Systems in Windows NT Server 4

In any enterprise system, you have to be prepared for system failure. Windows NT Server has some built-in hard disk fault tolerance capabilities. Later in this book, you will look at the steps required to implement the fault tolerance and how to recover from hardware failure. In this chapter about planning, however, you will look at the reasoning behind selecting a fault tolerance solution, and you will examine the benefits and limitations with each one. Windows NT Server 4 supports the following:

◆ RAID Level 0 (disk striping)

◆ RAID Level 1 (disk mirroring)

◆ RAID Level 5 (disk striping with parity)

The next few sections define each of these fault tolerance methods; they also give the reasoning for selecting these options.

RAID Level 0: Stripe Sets

Disk striping doesn't really belong in a section about fault tolerance because it offers no data redundancy. It is included, however, to help define the options and to serve as a reference against other fault tolerance options. The exam almost always uses disk striping as one of the options for fault tolerance under Windows NT, but keep in mind that it does not offer any disaster recovery of information.

Disk striping divides the data into 64KB blocks and writes the data across multiple physical disk drives (see Figure 2.1). Although this process improves the performance of your hard drives, it provides no method to recover lost data. A disk stripe set consists of multiple physical disks. A minimum of 2 disks is required with the stripe set, which can reach a maximum of 32 physical disks.

The benefits of a disk stripe set are

◆ Improved disk read performance

◆ Improved disk write performance

The limitations of a disk stripe set are

◆ No data redundancy or fault tolerance

◆ Inability to contain the system or boot partition in a stripe set

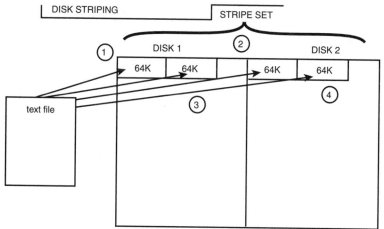

FIGURE 2.1

Disk striping writes the data across multiple physical disks in 64KB blocks of data.

(1) Writes data in 64KB block and disk 1 of stripe set

(2) Writes next 64KB block onto disk 2

(3) Back to disk 1 for next 64KB write

(4) Back to disk 2

RAID Level 1: Disk Mirroring

Disk mirroring is the process of duplicating the hard drive writes onto two physical disks. When a disk mirror is created, the information is written to both drives at the same time (see Figure 2.2). If each disk is controlled by its own hard drive controller, it is called *disk duplexing*.

This method of fault tolerance is more expensive per megabyte of data, due to the complete duplication of data. Every disk mirror requires two physical disks.

The benefits of disk mirroring are

◆ All drives and partitions can be mirrored, including boot and system partitions.

◆ Complete data duplication is done, enabling a complete recovery of data.

The drawbacks of disk mirroring are

◆ Higher cost per megabyte (50 percent of total available disk space is utilized)

◆ Moderate read and write performance

FIGURE 2.2
Disk mirroring duplicates the data across two
physical disks, ensuring that a complete copy
of the data exists on both disks.

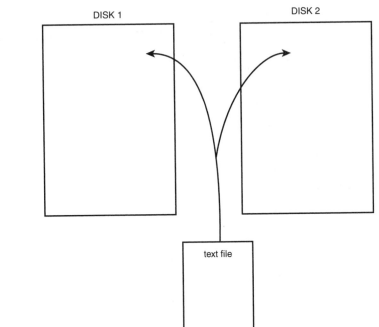

Duplicates all writes to both disks
within the mirror set

RAID Level 5: Stripe Sets with Parity

Disk striping with parity is the most common fault tolerance
method available through Windows NT Server 4. Disk striping with
parity uses the same basic process of disk striping. It writes the data
in 64KB blocks across multiple physical disks (see Figure 2.3). It also
calculates and writes parity information on one of the disks to ensure
that the data can be re-created in case of a disk failure.

The difference is that disk striping with parity uses a minimum of
three disks to spread parity information. With the parity information
available, the data can be regenerated on a stripe set. To implement
disk striping with parity, a minimum of 3 physical disks is required
and a maximum of 32 disks can be used. If any one of the disks in
the stripe set with parity fails, then the data can be regenerated from
the remaining disks.

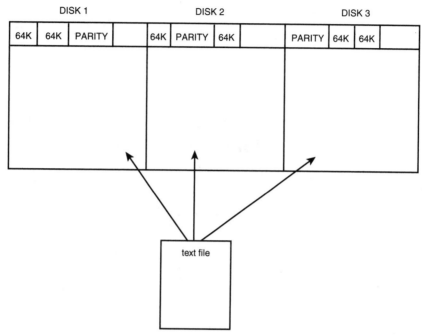

DISK STRIPING WITH PARITY

Data and Parity information distributed across all
disks in the stripe set with parity.

FIGURE 2.3
Disk striping with parity writes the data across
physical disks in 64KB blocks.

The benefits of a stripe set with parity are

- ◆ Data can be regenerated from parity information.
- ◆ Excellent read performance.
- ◆ Lower cost per megabyte than disk mirroring.

The limitations and drawbacks of a stripe set with parity are

- ◆ Requires a minimum of 3 disks and maximum of 32 disks.
- ◆ Provides only moderate write performance.
- ◆ Requires more system memory to implement due to calculation of parity.
- ◆ Cannot include system or boot partition.

Hardware RAID

Hardware solutions for fault tolerance are by far the best solutions available. For the Enterprise exam, however, you do not need to know any hardware solutions. Just know that they are available and are supported on the Windows NT Server 4 Hardware Compatibility List.

Implementing RAID in Windows NT Server 4

The steps required to implement fault tolerance in Windows NT Server 4 are covered in detail in Chapter 3, "Installing and Configuring Windows NT in the Enterprise."

Sector Sparing

Sector sparing is not a fault tolerance method; it is more of a self-recovery capability that is built into Windows NT Server 4. Sector sparing verifies each write of data onto the disk, and if it does not reread the data successfully, it moves the data to a different sector of the drive. After a sector of the disk has been marked as bad, the system does not use the bad sector until a disk defragmentation utility or a disk tool utility is executed. Sector sparing is supported on SCSI drives but does not offer any support for IDE or EIDE drives.

R E V I E W   B R E A K

Summary of Fault Tolerance in Windows NT Server 4

A comparison of the three fault tolerance options might help to summarize the information and ensure that you understand the options available in Windows NT Server 4 (see Table 2.1).

TABLE 2.1
FAULT TOLERANCE OPTIONS IN WINDOWS NT SERVER 4

Disk Striping	*Disk Mirroring/ Disk Duplexing*	*Disk Striping with Parity*
No fault tolerance.	Complete disk duplication.	Data regeneration from stored parity information.
Minimum of 2 physical disks; maximum of 32 disks.	Two physical disks.	Minimum of 3 physical disks; maximum of 32 disks.
100 percent available disk utilization.	50 percent available disk utilization.	Dedicates the equivalent of one disk's space in the set for parity information. The more disks, the higher the utilization.
Cannot include system/boot partition.	Includes all partition types.	Cannot include system/boot partition.
Excellent read/write performance.	Moderate read/write performance.	Excellent read, moderate write performance.

SELECTING THE PROPER PROTOCOL

Choose a protocol for various situations.

The interconnectivity of Windows NT with other operating systems and other NT systems is critical to the proper functionality of your enterprise system. The Enterprise exam focuses a great deal on the connectivity of Windows NT Server 4.

This section covers the planning of your protocols and the reasoning behind selecting certain protocols for interconnectivity with other systems. The installation and configuration of your protocols is covered in later chapters. Additional information about connection services within Windows NT Server 4 is covered in Part IV, "Connectivity." The main objective of this section is to give you the preliminary information required to select the proper protocol for various situations.

Windows NT Server 4 comes bundled with a number of protocols that you can use for interconnectivity with other systems and within a Windows NT environment. You will examine the various protocols and then define when each protocol would best fit your network needs. The protocols you need to know for the Enterprise exam include the following:

◆ NetBEUI

◆ TCP/IP

◆ NWLink IPX/SPX-Compatible Transport

◆ Data Link Control

◆ AppleTalk

NetBEUI

The NetBEUI protocol is the easiest to implement and has wide support across platforms. The NetBEUI protocol uses NetBIOS broadcasts to locate other computers on the network. This process of locating other computers requires additional network traffic and can slow down your entire network. Because NetBEUI uses broadcasts to locate computers, it is not routable; in other words, you cannot access computers that are not on your physical network. Most Microsoft and IBM OS/2 clients support this protocol. NetBEUI is best suited to small networks with no requirements for routing the information to remote networks or to the Internet.

TCP/IP

Transmission Control Protocol/Internet Protocol, or TCP/IP, is the most common protocol—more specifically, the most common suite of protocols. TCP/IP is an industry-standard protocol supported by most network operating systems. Because of this acceptance throughout the industry, TCP/IP enables your Windows NT system to connect to other systems with a common communication protocol.

TCP/IP is a routable protocol that lends itself directly to enterprise or WAN communication. Each computer is assigned a unique address, the IP address. The advantages of using TCP/IP in a Windows NT environment are

◆ The capability to connect dissimilar systems.

◆ The capability to use numerous standard connectivity utilities, including File Transfer Protocol, Telnet, and Ping.

◆ Internet access

The configuration of TCP/IP in your Windows NT system requires more work than that of the other supported protocols. Windows NT, however, has numerous services to simplify the administration and the configuration of your TCP/IP network. First, take a look at the interconnectivity, or heterogeneous connectivity, of TCP/IP within Windows NT. You will learn about some of the services available to simplify the administration and the configuration of your TCP/IP system.

The TCP/IP protocol is best suited to environments that require Internet access or access to dissimilar networks that are also running the TCP/IP protocol. The following sections will introduce the use of TCP/IP in a mixed or heterogeneous environment and some of the utilities that you can use to simplify this protocol and the configuration of it.

Heterogeneous Connectivity with TCP/IP

If your Windows NT system is using TCP/IP as a connection protocol, it can communicate with many non-Microsoft systems. Some of the systems it can communicate with are

◆ Any Internet-connected system

◆ UNIX systems

◆ IBM mainframe systems

◆ DEC Pathworks

◆ TCP/IP-supported printers directly connected to the network

Using a communication method that is supported throughout the industry is definitely a benefit to extending your Windows NT system into an enterprise system. TCP/IP has increased in popularity and is now supported by virtually all new operating systems. This acceptance of the TCP/IP protocol helps your Windows NT system maintain interconnectivity with the rest of the systems.

WINS and DHCP

TCP/IP can use the Windows Internet Naming Service (WINS) and the Dynamic Host Configuration Protocol (DHCP) to simplify administration of the system.

DHCP is a service that allocates TCP/IP addresses automatically to all the clients configured for DHCP. You do not have to configure every workstation in your environment to use this service. All you have to do is set up each client as a DHCP client. The DHCP client makes a request to the DHCP server for an IP address. The DHCP server holds a scope or range of IP addresses that are assigned to each of the client computers. You can manage this scope from the Windows NT Server that holds the DHCP server. DHCP is a great benefit to assigning IP addresses for your client computers.

Another utility that can help you in day-to-day TCP/IP use is WINS. A WINS server is a dynamic database that contains the names and IP addresses of all the computers on your network. This database is used to find computers on the network and to reduce the number of broadcast messages sent across the network. In a WINS environment, a WINS server is configured on a Windows NT Server system, and WINS clients are configured with the IP address of the WINS server. In WINS client configuration, you can set up a primary and a secondary WINS server. This system can be useful when your organization has remote locations you might need to access. If the computer does not find the computer name in the primary WINS server, it proceeds to the secondary WINS server to resolve the name to an IP address.

Both of these utilities are discussed in detail in later chapters. For the planning section of the exam, you need to know how you can use WINS and DHCP to simplify the administration and maintenance of TCP/IP addresses.

NWLink IPX/SPX-Compatible Transport

The IPX protocol has been used within the NetWare environment for years. By developing an IPX-compatible protocol, Microsoft enables Windows NT systems to communicate with NetWare systems.

NWLink is best suited to networks requiring communication with existing NetWare servers and for existing NetWare clients.

This protocol is discussed in detail throughout this book.

NetWare Connectivity

The main advantage of NWLink is the connectivity with NetWare systems. The NWLink IPX/SPX-Compatible Transport protocol enables the Windows NT system to run a compatible protocol for NetWare connections. You must install other utilities, however, to enable the Windows NT Server system to gain access to the NetWare security. Gateway Services for NetWare/Client Services for NetWare (GSNW/CSNW) must be installed on the Windows NT server to enable the computer to log on to a NetWare system. GSNW functions as a NetWare client, but it also has the capability to share the connection to the Novell box with users from the Windows NT system. This enables a controlled NetWare connection for file and print sharing on the NetWare box, without having to configure each NT client with a duplicate network redirector or client.

If your NetWare clients need to access your Windows NT system, you must configure another utility. The File and Print Services for NetWare (FPNW) is an add-on utility that you can use to enable your Windows NT system to emulate the functionality of a NetWare box for NetWare clients.

Data Link Control

The DLC protocol was originally used for connectivity in an IBM mainframe environment, and it maintains support for existing legacy systems and mainframes. The DLC protocol is also used for connections to some network printers.

AppleTalk

Windows NT Server can configure the AppleTalk protocol to provide connectivity with Apple Macintosh systems. This protocol is installed with the Services for Macintosh included with your Windows NT Server CD-ROM. The AppleTalk protocol enables Macintosh computers on your network to access files and printers set up on the Windows NT server. It also enables your Windows NT clients to print to Apple Macintosh printers. The AppleTalk protocol is best suited to connectivity with the Apple Macintosh.

Macintosh Connectivity

The AppleTalk protocol is installed with Services for Macintosh. This service was designed to enable connections from Macintosh computers to Windows NT systems. The Services for Macintosh and the AppleTalk protocol are covered in more detail later in this book.

The Protocols

The protocols available with Windows NT—to help provide connectivity within your enterprise system—include the following (know these for the exam):

- NetBEUI
- TCP/IP
- NWLink IPX/SPX-Compatible Transport
- Data Link Control
- AppleTalk

CASE STUDY: PROVIDING CONNECTIVITY

ESSENCE OF THE CASE

Here are the essential elements of this case:

- Windows 95 and Macintosh clients connectivity and support are required.
- Internet access via TCP/IP protocol.
- Novell NetWare 3.12 access, IPX protocol.

SCENARIO

ABC Corporation wants to use Windows NT Server as the network operating system for its user validation and home directories. A number of NetWare 3.12 servers in the environment are also used for specific network applications that users need to connect with. The client platforms used are mainly Windows 95, but some Macintosh clients are scattered throughout the environment. The company currently uses IPX/SPX protocol for connection to the NetWare servers. It would like to let all clients talk to the Windows NT Server systems, including the Macintosh clients; the individuals who require access to the NetWare applications will need to be able to access the Novell NetWare 3.12 servers. The company would also like to let all users access the Internet.

CASE STUDY: PROVIDING CONNECTIVITY

ANALYSIS

On the Windows NT Server system, install and use the TCP/IP protocol; also install the Services for Macintosh on this system to allow Macintosh connections. The Novell NetWare systems can remain as they are currently configured using the IPX protocol. The Windows 95 clients should all install and configure the TCP/IP protocol to have access to the Windows NT Server and the Internet. Any users requiring NetWare access should install NWLink IPX/SPX-Compatible Transport protocol. Macintosh clients should use the AppleTalk protocol to connect to the Windows NT Server system. This should meet all the requirements of ABC Corporation.

CHAPTER SUMMARY

A strong understanding of the supported fault tolerance methods available in Windows NT Server is important for the Enterprise exam. The disk configurations available for Windows NT Server 4.0 are

◆ RAID 0: Disk striping

◆ RAID 5: Disk striping with parity

◆ RAID 1: Disk mirroring

◆ RAID 1: Disk duplexing

The strength of Windows NT Server 4.0 in the enterprise is its use of common protocols and its flexibility to connect in a heterogeneous environment. The protocols included with Windows NT Server 4.0 are

◆ NetBEUI

◆ TCP/IP

◆ NWLink IPX/SPX-Compatible Transport

◆ Data Link Control

◆ AppleTalk

Make sure that you fully understand the strengths and compatibility of each of these protocols.

KEY TERMS

• RAID (Redundant Array of Inexpensive Disks)

• disk duplexing

• disk mirroring

• NetBIOS

• WINS

• DHCP

• IPX

APPLY YOUR LEARNING

This section allows you to assess how well you understood the material in the chapter. Review and exam questions test your knowledge of the tasks and concepts specified in the objectives. The exercises provide you with opportunities to engage in the sorts of tasks that compose the skill sets the objectives reflect.

For more review and exam questions, see the Top Score test engine on the CD-ROM that came with this book.

Exercise

The following exercise provides you with an opportunity to apply what you've learned in this chapter.

2.1 Selecting the Appropriate Protocol for Connectivity

This exercise has you select the appropriate protocols to use for a specific scenario. Select the best protocols for each scenario.

Time Estimate: Less than 10 minutes

1. Users need to access the Internet and to communicate with each other locally.

2. Users need to access a Novell server both running IPX and communicating with the Windows NT Server.

3. Users need to access resources on Novell servers, Windows NT systems, and UNIX systems.

4. A small number of users want to be able to share resources with no network configuration requirements. They do not need to access any computers outside the network.

2.1 Solutions:

1. TCP/IP.

2. NWLink IPX/SPX-Compatible Transport.

3. TCP/IP, NWLink IPX/SPX-Compatible Transport.

4. NetBEUI. All protocols would work; NetBEUI, however, is the easiest to configure and set up.

Review Questions

1. List the disk fault tolerance methods supported by Windows NT Server.

2. Which fault tolerance method enables recovery of the boot and system partitions?

3. List the network protocols supported by Windows NT Server.

4. Which protocol enables connectivity with UNIX systems and the Internet?

5. Which protocol is used for NetWare connectivity?

6. What other services in Windows NT Server are needed to enable connectivity with a NetWare system?

Exam Questions

1. Select all the disk fault tolerance functions that are supported by Windows NT Server 4.

    A. Disk mirroring

    B. Disk striping

APPLY YOUR LEARNING

C. Disk striping with parity

D. Sector sparing

2. Which of the following RAID classifications do not supply any recovery options?

A. RAID 0: Disk striping

B. RAID 1: Disk mirroring

C. RAID 5: Disk striping with parity

D. RAID 6: Hardware

3. Select the maximum number of disks that can be used in a stripe set with parity.

A. 3

B. 2

C. 24

D. 32

4. The production department needs to access a software product that can be installed only on a NetWare box. The department currently connects to the Windows NT system and would like to connect to both systems with one common protocol. What protocol allows access to both a NetWare system and a Windows NT System?

A. NetWare Connect Protocol

B. NetBEUI

C. NWLink IPX/SPX-Compatible Transport

D. GSNW

5. Users from your Windows NT system want to access your NetWare box, but you do not want to set up each one with the NetWare client. What is required to enable your NT system to share a NetWare connection for the NT users? Select all correct answers.

A. NWLink IPX/SPX-Compatible Transport

B. NetBEUI

C. GSNW

D. Services for Macintosh

Answers to Review Questions

1. Disk mirroring, stripe set with parity. See the section "Planning the Fault Tolerance for Windows NT Server 4" for more information.

2. Disk mirroring. See the section "Planning the Fault Tolerance for Windows NT Server 4" for more information.

3. TCP/IP, NetBEUI, NWLink IPX/SPX-Compatible Transport, DLC, AppleTalk. See the section "Selecting the Proper Protocol" for more information.

4. TCP/IP. See the section "Selecting the Proper Protocol" in this chapter for more information.

5. NWLink. See the section "Selecting the Proper Protocol" for more information.

6. Gateway Services for NetWare. See the section "Selecting the Proper Protocol" for more information.

APPLY YOUR LEARNING

Answers to Exam Questions

1. **A. C.** The software fault tolerance supported by Windows NT Server are disk mirroring and disk striping with parity. See the section "RAID Systems in Windows NT Server 4" for more information.

2. **A.** RAID 0, disk striping, can be used to increase performance of your hard disks; however, no recovery is available using a stripe set. See the section "RAID Systems in Windows NT Server 4" for more information.

3. **D.** The maximum number of disks that can be used in a stripe set with parity is 32 physical disks. See the section "RAID Level 5: Stripe Sets with Parity" for more information.

4. **C.** NWLink IPX/SPX-Compatible Transport protocol can be used to access both a Windows NT Server and Novell NetWare Server. See the section "NWLink IPX/SPX-Compatible Transport" for more information.

5. **A. C.** Sharing a connection to a NetWare box from an NT Server would require the NWLink IPX/SPX-Compatible Transport protocol and the Gateway Services for NetWare (GSNW). See the section "NWLink IPX/SPX-Compatible Transport" for more information.

INSTALLATION AND CONFIGURATION

This chapter helps you to prepare for the Microsoft exam by covering the following objectives within the "Installation and Configuration" category:

Install Windows NT Server to perform various server roles. Server roles include

- ◆ **Primary Domain Controller**

- ◆ **Backup Domain Controller**

- ◆ **Member server**

▶ This objective focuses on installing Windows NT Server by ensuring that the proper server role is selected. The server roles that you can use are Primary Domain Controller, Backup Domain Controller, and member server. Each of these roles allows the system to be optimized to its specific application in your enterprise environment.

Configure protocols and protocol bindings. Protocols include

- ◆ **TCP/IP**

- ◆ **TCP/IP with DHCP and WINS**

- ◆ **NWLink IPX/SPX-compatible Transport Protocol**

- ◆ **DLC**

- ◆ **AppleTalk**

▶ This objective has you focusing on the installation and configuration of networking protocols within Windows NT. The exam will focus on the TCP/IP configuration; however, you might see a question or two on the other listed protocols.

CHAPTER 3

Installing and Configuring Windows NT in the Enterprise

Configure Windows NT Server core services. Services include

◆ **Directory Replicator**

◆ **Computer Browser**

▶ This objective is listed to ensure that you have a firm understanding of the core services within Windows NT. You can configure these services to optimize your environment, and the enterprise exam will test you on these options.

Configure hard disks to meet various requirements. Requirements include

◆ **Providing redundancy**

◆ **Improving performance**

▶ Previous chapters have discussed the importance of the fault tolerance in your system; this objective ensures that you have all the skills required to implement the fault tolerance options and that you can select the best option to optimize your hard disk settings.

Configure printers. Tasks include

◆ **Adding and configuring a printer**

◆ **Implementing a printer pool**

◆ **Setting print priorities**

▶ Installing printers can be easy by using the Install Printer Wizard; however, you must be aware of the numerous available options to implement a printer in an enterprise environment. The printer pool can be an excellent network resource for your users, and the exam spends a bit of time with the procedure to implement one.

Configure a Windows NT Server computer for various types of client computers. Client computer types include

◆ **Windows NT Workstation**

◆ **Windows 95**

◆ **Macintosh**

▶ This entire book focuses on the Windows NT Server in an enterprise environment. However, the enterprise environment does not exist without client workstations. Understanding some basic configuration requirements to allow each of the listed client operating systems to connect to your Windows NT environment is crucial.

To have a strong foundation on the installation and configuration objectives, you must have experience with these items. Focus on the components that are listed in the preceding objectives, review each of the options available, and ensure that you understand how each option affects the system.

This chapter focuses on the installation and configuration of your Windows NT Server computer in an enterprise environment. It also covers the additional components and services that you can use in an enterprise environment.

The enterprise exam does not place a great deal of emphasis on the installation process; however, it is important to be aware of the various server roles for which your Windows NT Server can function. You also need strong knowledge of the configuration options and the reasons for selecting a specific configuration. The structure and content of this chapter is set up accordingly. As you read the sections in this chapter, you are introduced to the configuration options and the steps required to install and configure each component.

To prepare you for the exam, this chapter covers the following topics:

- ◆ Installing Windows NT Server in various server roles
- ◆ Configuring networking protocols and protocol bindings
- ◆ Configuring Windows NT Server core services
- ◆ Configuring hard disks to improve performance and to provide redundancy
- ◆ Configuring printers
- ◆ Configuring Windows NT Server for various types of clients

INSTALLING WINDOWS NT SERVER 4 IN VARIOUS SERVER ROLES

Install Windows NT Server to perform various server roles. Roles include Primary Domain Controller, Backup Domain Controller, and member server.

The installation of Windows NT Server is the starting point of any enterprise system. In this section, you learn the server roles available to your Windows NT Server installation, and you examine the reasons for installing NT Server in the different roles. The server roles available are tested in numerous scenarios in the exam, so make sure that you have a strong understanding of the different roles available in a Windows NT installation.

Defining Server Roles in Windows NT Server

The different server roles for which Windows NT Server can be installed are

◆ Primary Domain Controller

◆ Backup Domain Controller

◆ Member server

The server role defines how the system configures itself. Assigning the proper server role gives you dramatically better performance than not assigning the proper role.

Each role provides a specific function in your Windows NT system. The next three sections address each of the roles. You will gain an understanding of both the function each role performs and the reasons for selecting a particular server role for your Windows NT Server system.

Primary Domain Controllers

The Primary Domain Controller (PDC) is the first domain controller installed into a domain. As the first computer in the domain, the PDC creates the domain. This concept is important to understand because it establishes the rationale for needing a PDC in the environment. Each domain can contain only one PDC. All other domain controllers in the domain are installed as Backup Domain Controllers. The PDC handles user requests and logon validation, and it offers all the standard Windows NT Server functionality. The PDC contains the original copy of the Security Accounts Manager (SAM), which contains all user accounts and security permissions for your domain. The PDC runs the Netlogon service. The main function of the Netlogon service is to handle logon requests by users in your network. You also use the Netlogon service for synchronizing the SAM from the PDC with all Backup Domain Controllers (BDCs) in the domain. This synchronization process enables the SAM database to be passed across multiple domain controllers, all of which can handle logon requests.

NETLOGON SERVICE FUNCTIONS

The three main functions of the Netlogon service are covered in different sections of this chapter. Be sure you know the three functions of the Netlogon service, which are

- To handle logon requests from users

- To control database synchronization between PDCs and all BDCs

- To enable pass-through authentication of users across trust relationships

---

Backup Domain Controllers

The Backup Domain Controller (BDC) is an additional domain controller used to handle logon requests by users in the network. To handle the logon requests, the BDC must have a complete copy of the domain database, or SAM. The BDC also runs the Netlogon service; however, the Netlogon service in a BDC functions a little differently than that of a PDC. In the PDC, the Netlogon service handles synchronization of the SAM database to all the BDCs. The BDCs' role in synchronization is to receive any changes or updates to the SAM database from the PDC. The PDC maintains a change log of all the changes and updates and sends an up-to-date copy of the SAM back to each BDC. The PDC re-sends only the changes to the database, not the entire database, which results in less network traffic. The BDC helps the PDC to handle user requests and logon validation and also acts as a Windows NT Server, offering all the available options and functionality.

Member Server

In both of the domain controllers, PDC or BDC, the computer has an additional function. The domain controllers handle logon requests and ensure that the SAM is synchronized throughout the domain. These functions add overhead to the system. A computer that handles the server functionality you require without the overhead of handling logon validation is called a *member server*. A member server is a part of the domain, but it does not need a copy of the SAM database and does not handle logon requests. The main function of a member server is to share resources. The breakdown of typical roles is discussed later in the chapter.

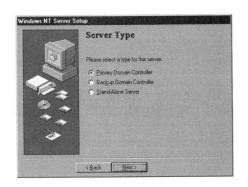

FIGURE 3.1
When selecting a server role, keep in mind that your Windows NT server system can be a PDC, BDC, or standalone server.

Installing Windows NT Server

During the installation of Windows NT Server, you are prompted for the server role (see Figure 3.1).

After selecting the appropriate server role, you are presented with different options during the installation process. If you install as a domain controller, either PDC or BDC, you are prompted for the name of your domain. If you're installing a BDC, you have to create a computer account for your domain on the PDC or have the administrator of the PDC create it for you. When installing your BDC, you must ensure that the PDC is available and turned on so the computer account can be created or verified. Each domain controller must have a corresponding computer account. By using this method, you ensure that an unauthorized user cannot join a domain without proper authorization.

NOTE

Two PDCs If you promote a BDC while the PDC is not stopped, you end up with two PDCs. The two PDCs are the promoted BDC and the existing PDC. The first server started starts the Netlogon service as the PDC, and the second server is not able to start the Netlogon service. To resolve this, when you start the Server Manager, highlight the grayed-out PDC and then select Computer | Demote Primary Domain Controller.

Changing Server Roles

After you install your computer into a specific server role, you might decide to change the role of the server. This can be a relatively easy task if you are changing a PDC to a BDC or vice versa. If you want to change a domain controller to a member server or member server to a domain controller, however, you must reinstall into the required server role. A member server has a local database that does not participate in domain synchronization. In changing roles, you must reinstall a member server to ensure that the account database and the appropriate services are installed.

BDC to PDC

To change the server role of a domain controller, use the Promote to Primary Domain Controller option in the Computer menu of the Server Manager (see Figure 3.2). You can access this option only by highlighting the appropriate BDC from the Server Manager list.

Selecting this option stops the Netlogon service of both the existing PDC and the BDC to be promoted. The Netlogon is then restarted with the role change in effect. The BDC starts as the PDC, and the old PDC restarts as a BDC. This is a relatively easy change and does not affect any of the other BDCs in the enterprise.

FIGURE 3.2
To change the server role of a domain controller, use the Promote to Primary Domain Controller option in the Computer menu of the Server Manager.

Member Server to Domain Controller

The only way to change the server role from a member server to a domain controller (or vice versa) is to do a reinstall. Be sure you do not upgrade your system; a reinstall is required. Remember that during an upgrade, the Windows NT software reinstalls into the same role for which it is currently set up.

Selecting a Server Role

When installing your Windows NT server, you must select the server role that it will play. Once again, the three server roles are as follows:

- *Primary Domain Controller.* The first domain controller installed within a Windows NT domain. The PDC maintains the working set of account and security databases for the domain.

- *Backup Domain Controller.* Backup copies of the account and security databases are maintained on the BDCs to assist in user account authentication (logons) and other related security tasks that require a verification from a secured database. The BDC receives copies of the SAM database from the PDC.

- *Member server.* Commonly referred to as a standalone server, this role does not maintain a copy of the domain database. A member server has its own local database that is only used by itself. Commonly used for application or file servers.

CONFIGURING NETWORKING PROTOCOLS AND PROTOCOL BINDINGS

Configure protocols and protocol bindings. Protocols include TCP/IP, TCP/IP with DHCP and WINS, NWLink IPX/SPX-Compatible Transport Protocol, DLC, and AppleTalk.

The network protocols that your system uses are its connection to the rest of your enterprise system. In Chapter 2, " Planning Your Enterprise System: Fault Tolerance and Protocols," you looked at reasons for selecting each of the protocols. In this chapter, you examine the configuration process for each protocol. You also learn the installation steps required to add any protocols you might need for communication with foreign systems.

Installing and configuring network protocols is controlled in the network properties of your Windows NT system. The first step toward installing a protocol in your NT Server system is to select the proper protocol. Remember that you can use each protocol in different scenarios. The following section covers the steps required to install a new protocol in your Windows NT Server system. Then, you will look at the configuration of each available protocol. The installation of each protocol is identical. The configuration of each protocol is different, however, so you have to understand the process required for configuring each of the supported protocols. Once you configure your protocols, you also can modify the order in which your system will use the protocols. This order is known as the binding order. Later in this section, you will review the procedure for modifying the binding order.

Installing Protocols

You install a new protocol in Windows NT Server through the Network dialog box. Perform the tasks outlined in Step by Step 3.1.

STEP BY STEP

3.1 Installing a Network Protocol

    1. Open the Network dialog box by double-clicking the Network icon in the control panel. The various tabs of the Network dialog box present all the options available for the networking components (see Figure 3.3).

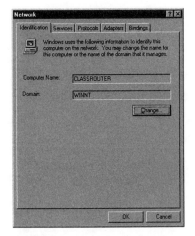

FIGURE 3.3
The Network dialog box presents all the options available for the networking components.

2. Select the Protocols tab (see Figure 3.4).

3. To see a list of the protocols available for you to install, click Add.

4. Highlight the protocol you are installing and then click OK (see Figure 3.5).

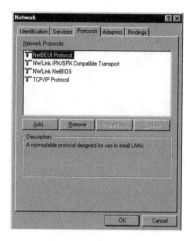

FIGURE 3.4
Select the Protocols tab.

The system then tries to locate the Windows NT installation files. If it cannot locate them, you are prompted to enter the directory location of the Windows NT Server 4 source files.

After the protocol is installed, you cannot configure it until it is bound to your network adapter. The binding process is completed when you click Close at the bottom of the Network dialog box. The system then may request that you reboot so the new protocol can be set up; if this protocol was previously installed, you might not be prompted to restart.

Configuring Protocols

You configure each protocol by changing its properties. You can access the properties of each protocol in the Protocols tab of the Network dialog box (refer to Figure 3.4).

On the Protocols tab, you should see a listing of all installed protocols. Highlight the protocol you want to configure and then select the Properties button.

The upcoming sections cover the following protocols and the configuration options available with each:

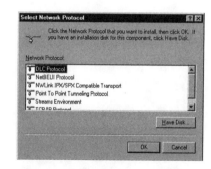

FIGURE 3.5
Select a network protocol from the list.

- ◆ TCP/IP
- ◆ NWLink IPX/SPX compatible
- ◆ DLC
- ◆ AppleTalk

The NetBEUI protocol is not covered because there are no configuration options available for this protocol.

> **EXAM TIP**
>
> **Know TCP/IP** Many of the questions on the Enterprise exam relate to the use of the TCP/IP protocol. Be sure you understand all the options available with the TCP/IP protocol.

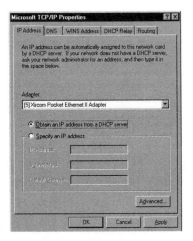

FIGURE 3.6
The Microsoft TCP/IP Properties dialog box contains multiple options for you to configure.

TCP/IP

TCP/IP is the most common protocol because it is accepted across virtually all platforms. It is the protocol that enables your system to access the Internet. The TCP/IP protocol also enables communication between various platforms, including UNIX systems and other systems that utilize the TCP/IP protocol.

To access the properties of the TCP/IP protocol, highlight TCP/IP Protocol in the Network dialog box and click Properties. The Microsoft TCP/IP Properties dialog box contains multiple options for you to configure (see Figure 3.6).

The tabs available for configuration in the Microsoft TCP/IP Properties dialog box are

◆ IP Address

◆ DNS

◆ WINS Address

◆ DHCP Relay

◆ Routing

You have to configure each tab in the Microsoft TCP/IP Properties dialog box to complete the configuration of your TCP/IP settings. Note that on the IP Address tab you have the option of selecting the network adapter you want to configure. Each network adapter card in your system can and should have different TCP/IP settings.

Configuring the IP Address

The IP Address tab enables you to configure the IP address, the subnet mask, and the default gateway. You also can enable the system to automatically allocate IP address information through the use of the DHCP server (see Figure 3.7).

An IP address is a 32-bit address broken into four octets that is used to identify your network adapter card as a TCP/IP host. Each IP

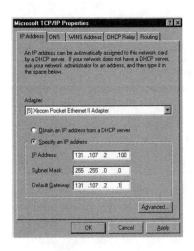

FIGURE 3.7
The IP Address tab of the Microsoft TCP/IP Properties dialog box enables you to configure the IP address, the subnet mask, and the default gateway.

address must be a unique address. If you have any IP address conflicts on your computer, you cannot use the TCP/IP protocol.

Your IP address is grouped into a subnet. The process you use to subnet your network is assigning a subnet mask. A *subnet mask* is used to identify the computers local to your network. Any address outside your subnet is accessed through the default gateway, also called the router. The default gateway is the address of the router that handles all routing of your TCP/IP information to computers, or hosts, outside your subnet.

In Figure 3.7, notice the IP address 131.107.2.100. This IP address must be a unique address. The subnet assigned is 255.255.0.0. By using this subnet, you are able to directly access any other computer that starts with 131.107. You should notice in the subnet that it blocks the first two sections of the IP address but allows the last two sections to be passed through. This type of subnet is a class B subnet. The IP address of the router in the figure is 131.107.2.1, which is also the default gateway.

If you want the computer to use the DHCP server, configure the settings as shown in Figure 3.8.

Note that the Obtain an IP address from a DHCP server option is selected. In upcoming sections, you will look more closely at installing and configuring a DHCP server.

Configuring DNS for Your TCP/IP Protocol

The Domain Name System (DNS) server translates TCP/IP host names of remote computers into IP addresses. Remember that an IP address is a unique address used for each computer. The DNS server contains a database of all the computers you can access by host name. This database is used when you access a Web page on the Internet. The naming scheme is easier than using the IP address of the computer.

The DNS tab shows you the options available for configuring your TCP/IP protocol to use a DNS server (see Figure 3.9).

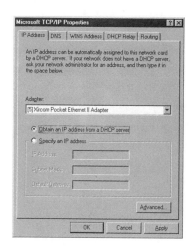

FIGURE 3.8
The DHCP server is used here to obtain an IP address.

FIGURE 3.9
The DNS tab shows you the options available for configuring your TCP/IP protocol to use a DNS server.

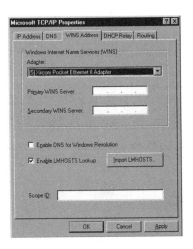

FIGURE 3.10
The WINS Address tab enables you to configure your primary and secondary Windows Internet Names Services (WINS) server addresses.

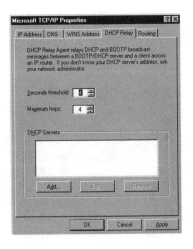

FIGURE 3.11
The DHCP Relay tab offers options in using the relay agent to find DHCP servers across the routers.

In configuring your DNS settings for the TCP/IP protocol, you must start by assigning a host name to your computer. This host name is part of the name other computers use to make TCP/IP connections to your computer system. The host name is then combined with the TCP/IP domain name. The TCP/IP domain name is a registered name that has been assigned to your organization. Any TCP/IP connection into a computer at Microsoft belongs to the microsoft.com domain. This domain name can be different from the one assigned to your Windows NT Server domain.

After you enter your computer host names, enter the IP address of the DNS server containing your name database. You can enter multiple DNS servers if you require names resolved by multiple databases. The top DNS server is the first DNS searched by your system, so place the servers in order of importance to your system. You can use the Up and Down buttons directly beside your DNS servers to modify your search order.

Assigning a WINS Address for Your TCP/IP Protocol

The WINS Address tab enables you to configure your primary and secondary Windows Internet Names Services (WINS) server addresses, as shown in Figure 3.10. WINS is used to reduce the number of NetBIOS broadcast messages sent across the network to locate a computer. Using a WINS server, the names of computers on your network are kept in a WINS database. The WINS database is dynamic. In other words, each of the computers is automatically entered into the database, enabling immediate lookup of computer names.

In configuring your WINS servers, you can enter your primary WINS server and a secondary WINS server. Your system first searches the primary WINS server database and then searches the secondary database if no match is found in the primary.

Two other options are available on this tab. The first enables your system to search the DNS for name searches in combination with the WINS server. The second option enables a local file, LMHOSTS, to be used as a local database of computer names. You can then configure the LMHOSTS file to enable named connections to your most common systems without using a DNS or WINS lookup.

Using a DHCP Relay Agent with Your TCP/IP Protocol

Figure 3.11 shows the DHCP relay agent options. The DHCP relay agent is used to find your DHCP servers across routers. DHCP addresses are handed out by the DHCP servers. The client request, however, is made with a broadcast message. Broadcast messages do not cross routers, which might place some restrictions on your systems. The solution is to use a DHCP relay agent to assist the clients in finding the DHCP server across a router. This can be a valuable tool for configuring your WAN environment.

In configuring your DHCP relay agent, you can specify the seconds threshold and the maximum number of hops to use in searching for the DHCP servers. At the bottom of the tab, you can enter the IP addresses of the DHCP servers you want to use.

Routing

In an environment in which multiple subnets are used, you can configure your Windows NT Server as a multihomed system. In other words, you can install multiple network adapters, each connecting to a different subnet. If you enable the Enable IP Forwarding option (see Figure 3.12), your computer acts as a router, forwarding the packets through the network cards in the multihomed system to the other subnet.

NWLink IPX/SPX Compatible

The NWLink IPX/SPX-compatible protocol was designed for NetWare connectivity, but it also can be used for network connectivity between any systems running an IPX-compatible protocol. The configuration of the NWLink protocol is simple in comparison to the TCP/IP protocol. This simplicity makes it a popular protocol to use.

To configure your NWLink protocol, highlight NWLink IPX/SPX-compatible Transport in the Network dialog box and then click Properties. Figure 3.13 shows the resulting NWLink IPX/SPX Properties dialog box.

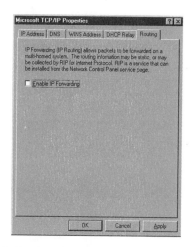

FIGURE 3.12
The Routing tab is where you configure your computer to act as a router.

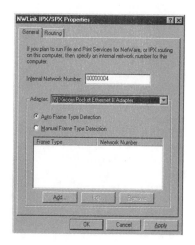

FIGURE 3.13
You use the NWLink IPX/SPX Properties dialog box to configure the NWLink protocol.

The NWLink IPX/SPX Properties dialog box has two tabs:

◆ General

◆ Routing

On the General tab, you have the option to assign an internal network number. This eight-digit hexadecimal number format is used by some programs with services that can be accessed by NetWare clients.

You also have the option to select a frame type for your NWLink protocol. The frame type you select must match the frame type of the remote computer you need communication with. By default, Windows NT Server uses the Auto Frame Type Detection setting, which scans the network and loads the first frame type it encounters. This feature can be handy when configuring the NWLink protocol between multiple Windows NT Servers because they all default to the same frame type. The frame types supported are based on the topology of your network adapters. Table 3.1 lists the topologies and frame types.

TABLE 3.1

SUPPORTED FRAME TYPES

Topology	Supported Frame Types
Ethernet	802.3, 802.2, Ethernet II, SNAP
Token ring	802.5, SNAP
FDDI	802.2, SNAP

To simplify the selection of your frame types, the default frame type is 802.2 in NetWare 3.12 and later. Earlier versions of NetWare use 802.3 as a default frame type.

The Routing tab of the NWLink IPX/SPX Properties dialog box is where you enable or disable the Routing Information Protocol (RIP). If you enable RIP routing over IPX, your Windows NT Server can act as an IPX router.

DLC

The Data Link Control (DLC) protocol is not like the other Windows NT–supported protocols. DLC does not support the TDI interface; in other words, the network services that Windows NT uses DLC does not support. This protocol is used to connect to other systems running the DLC protocol, such as IBM mainframes or HP printers running DLC.

You can install the DLC protocol by following the same process as you use for all other protocols; refer to the steps in the section "Installing Protocols," earlier in this chapter. However, you perform the configuration of DLC through Registry parameters. The DLC protocol is configured based on three timers:

◆ **T1.** The response timer

◆ **T2.** The acknowledgment delay timer

◆ **Ti.** The inactivity timer

The Registry contains the entries that can be modified to configure DLC. You find the entries at `HKEY_LOCAL_MACHINE\SYSTEM\CurrentControlSet\Services\DLC\Parameters\ELNKIII <adapter name>`.

Not on the Exam The configuration of the DLC protocol is not tested on the exam due to the rare use of it and the Registry requirements.

EXAM TIP

AppleTalk

To install the AppleTalk protocol, you install Services for Macintosh. You examine the requirements for that later in this chapter, but at this point, it is useful to look at the configuration options for the AppleTalk protocol. Select the AppleTalk protocol and then click Properties. You see the Microsoft AppleTalk Protocol Properties dialog box shown in Figure 3.14.

Reviewing the Protocols

Table 3.2 reviews the protocols that can be configured for your NT enterprise (including the subcomponents—tabs—of each protocol).

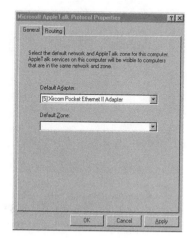

FIGURE 3.14
The Microsoft AppleTalk Protocol Properties dialog box displays the options available for AppleTalk.

<table>
<tr><td colspan="2">TABLE 3.2</td></tr>
</table>

TABLE 3.2

PROTOCOLS TO BE CONFIGURED

Protocol	Subcomponent (Tab)
TCP/IP	IP Address
	DNS
	WINS Address
	DHCP Relay
	Routing
NWLink IPX/SPX compatible	General Routing
AppleTalk	General Routing

The configuration and installation of network protocols is vital to your enterprise environment. Always ensure that you configure the protocols correctly and that you use only the required protocols so that you do not waste network bandwidth.

FIGURE 3.15
The Bindings tab in the Network dialog box enables you to configure the binding order.

Configuring the Binding Order

The binding order is the sequence your computer uses to select which protocol to use for network communication. Each protocol is listed for each network-based service, protocol, and adapter available.

Setting the binding order of your network services and protocols can be important in optimizing your network configuration. To modify the binding order, go to the Bindings tab in the Network dialog box (see Figure 3.15).

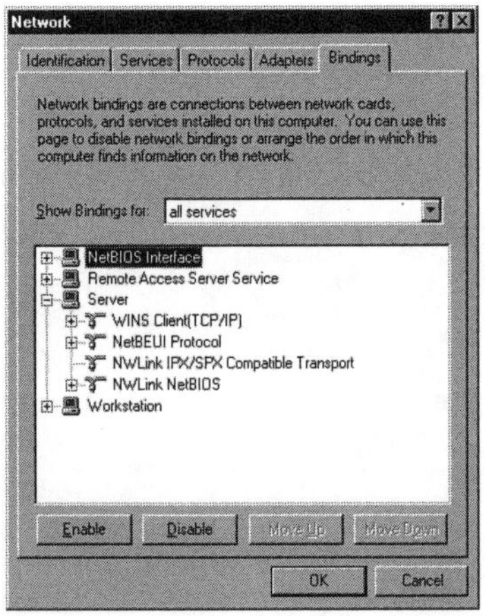

The Bindings tab contains an option, Show Bindings for, that you can use to select the service, adapter, or protocol you want to modify in the binding order. By clicking the appropriate button, you can enable or disable each binding or move it up or down in the binding order.

CONFIGURING WINDOWS NT SERVER CORE SERVICES

Configure Windows NT Server core services. Services include Directory Replicator and Computer Browser.

Windows NT takes full advantage of its multithreaded, multitasking capabilities by running services in the background. These services play a number of different roles. In this section, you will look at configuring some of the core services in Windows NT Server. These services are

◆ Server

◆ Workstation

◆ Computer Browser

◆ Directory Replicator

Server Service

The Server service answers network requests. By configuring Server service, you can change the way your server responds and, in a sense, the role it plays in your network environment. Servers in a network environment can be grouped into three different classes or roles:

◆ Logon server (domain controller)

◆ Application server

◆ File/print server

When configuring Server service, the first step is to select the role that your computer plays in your network environment. Some configuration settings also are available if your Windows NT Server computer is a desktop computer and not a server in the networking sense of the word.

To configure Server service, you must open the Network dialog box. To do this, double-click the Network icon in Control Panel. Select the Services tab, as shown in Figure 3.16.

To configure Server service, highlight Server and click Properties. You are then able to view the properties of your Server service, as shown in Figure 3.17.

The Server dialog box has four optimization settings. Each of these settings modifies memory management based on the role the server is playing. These options are described in the following sections.

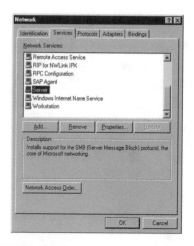

FIGURE 3.16
The Services tab in the Network dialog box enables you to configure the Server service.

<table>
<tr><td>EXAM TIP</td><td>**Know When to Use Each Optimization Setting** For the Enterprise exam, you need to know when you should use each optimization setting and the differences between the four settings.</td></tr>
</table>

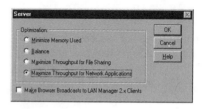

FIGURE 3.17
The Server dialog box displays the properties of your Server service.

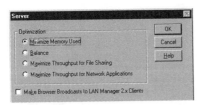

FIGURE 3.18
You use the Minimize Memory Used setting when your Windows NT Server system is accessed by few users.

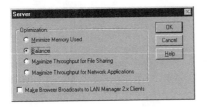

FIGURE 3.19
You use the Balance setting in the Server dialog box for a maximum of 64 network connections.

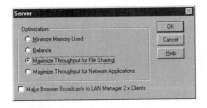

FIGURE 3.20
The Maximize Throughput for File Sharing option allocates the maximum amount of memory available for network connections.

Minimize Memory Used

You use the Minimize Memory Used setting, shown in Figure 3.18, when your Windows NT Server system is accessed by few users (fewer than 10).

You use this setting when the Windows NT Server computer is used as a user's desktop computer, not as a true server. This setting allocates memory so that a maximum of 10 network connections can be properly maintained. When you restrict the memory for network connections, more memory is available at the local or desktop level.

Balance

You can use the Balance setting, shown in Figure 3.19, for a maximum of 64 network connections.

This setting is the default when using NetBEUI software. Like the Minimize setting, Balance is best used for a relatively low number of users connecting to a server that also can be used as a desktop computer.

Maximize Throughput for File Sharing

The Maximize Throughput for File Sharing setting allocates the maximum amount of memory available for network connections (see Figure 3.20). It is the default on any Windows NT Server computer.

This setting is excellent for large networks in which the server is accessed for file and print sharing.

Maximize Throughput for Network Applications

If you are running distributed applications, such as SQL Server or Exchange Server, the network applications do their own memory caching. Therefore, you want your system to enable the applications to manage the memory. This is accomplished using the Maximize Throughput for Network Applications setting, shown in Figure 3.21. This setting also is used for very large networks.

Workstation Service

The Workstation service is your redirector in Windows NT Server. The Workstation service handles all outgoing network communication from your NT Server system. Workstation service has no configuration options through Control Panel, unlike the other services discussed. You can make some Registry changes that can optimize your Workstation service. Registry modification is not recommended unless you have a strong understanding of the Registry and its entries.

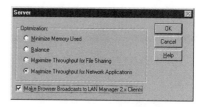

FIGURE 3.21
The Maximize Throughput for Network Applications option lets you configure your system to enable applications to manage their own memory.

MAKING REGISTRY CHANGES

To make Registry changes, run the REGEDT32.EXE program. The Registry in Windows NT is a complex database of configuration settings for your computer. If you want to configure the Workstation service, open the HKEY_LOCAL_MACHINE hive, as shown in Figure 3.22.

The exact location for configuring your Workstation service is

> HKEY_LOCAL_MACHINE\System\CurrentControlSet\Services\
> LanmanWorkstation\Parameters

To find additional information regarding this Registry item and others, refer to the Windows NT Server resource kit.

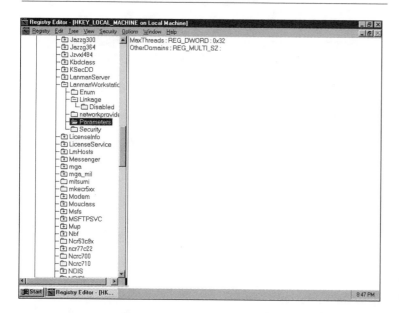

FIGURE 3.22
The Workstation service can be configured in the Registry.

Computer Browser

The Computer Browser service is responsible for maintaining the list of computers on the network. The browse list contains all the computers located on the physical network. As a Windows NT Server, your system plays a big role in the browsing of a network. The Windows NT Server acts as a master browser or backup browser.

The functions of a master or backup browser are to hold the list of computers in the domain and to share that list with other computers. In the Microsoft networking environment, all computers send broadcast messages across the network containing the domain/workgroup that they belong to as well as their computer names. The master browser in the domain gathers all these broadcast messages and stores them in the browse list for others to use. If your Windows NT environment gets too large for the master browser to handle all the computers, it elects a backup browser to hold copies of the browse list for computers to access.

The browsing happens automatically, so no configuration is required. You can, however, configure whether you want your server to be a master or backup browser. You do the configuration in the Registry, so you use REGEDT32.EXE (see Figure 3.23). The settings are found in

```
HKEY_LOCAL_MACHINE\System\CurrentControlSet\Services\
Browser\Parameters
```

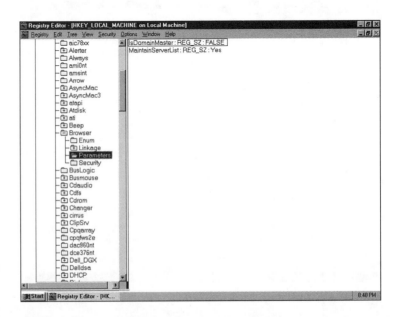

FIGURE 3.23

You can configure (in the Registry) whether you want your server to be a master or backup browser.

You can modify two entries to select whether you are a preferred master browser (in other words, that your computer is the master browser). The first entry is `IsDomainMaster` = `True/False`. You select `True` if you want your computer to be the master browser or select `False` if you do not want it to be the master browser.

The other entry is `MaintainServerList` = `Yes/No`. If this entry is set to `Yes`, you are able to play the role of the backup browser; if it is `No`, then you cannot be a backup browser.

Even with these Registry settings disabled, your system can still become a master browser or a backup browser. The selection of browsers is through an election. The election is called by any client computer or the startup of a preferred master browser computer. The election is based on broadcast messages. Every computer has the opportunity to nominate itself, and the computer with the highest settings wins the election.

The election criteria are based on three things:

◆ The operating system (Windows NT Server, Windows NT Workstation, Windows 95, Windows for Workgroups)

◆ The version of the operating system (NT 4.0, NT 3.51, NT 3.5)

◆ The current role of the computer (master browser, backup browser, potential browser)

This is a simplified breakdown of the election criteria. Look in the Windows NT Resource Kit for detailed information about the election criteria.

Directory Replicator

In any network environment, it is a challenge to maintain consistent logon scripts and user profiles across multiple servers. In Windows NT Server, this process is handled with the Directory Replicator service. You can configure the Directory Replicator service to synchronize an entire directory structure across multiple servers.

In configuring the directory service, you must select the export server and all the import servers. The export server is the computer that holds the original copy of the directory structure and files. Each import server receives a complete copy of the export server's directory structure. The directory structure on the export server is monitored by the Directory Replicator service. If the contents of the directory change, the changes are copied to all the import servers. The file copying and directory monitoring is completed by a special service account you create. You must then configure the Directory Replicator service to use this service account.

You can use the Directory Replicator service to maintain consistent logon scripts, system policies, or data files across the distributed network environment.

In the following sections, you will review the procedures and components required to configure the Directory Replication service. The sections are

◆ Directory Replicator Service Account

◆ Installing Directory Replicator Service

  • Configuring the Export Server

  • Configuring the Import Server

◆ Managing Directory Replication

Directory Replicator Service Account

The Directory Replicator service account must have proper access on all the servers participating in the directory replication process. All export servers and import servers need to assign the access to this service account. The following access is required for your Directory Replicator service account:

◆ The account should be a member of the Backup Operators and Replicators groups.

◆ There should be no time or logon restrictions for the account.

◆ The Password Never Expires option should be selected.

◆ The User Must Change Password At Next Logon option should be turned off.

Installing and Configuring Directory Replicator Service

The Directory Replicator service is installed during the installation of Windows NT Server. To get the Directory Replicator Service to function, all you need to do is configure the service. Prior to

---

WARNING

Potential Problems with Replication Accounts If you are not running the service packs for Windows NT Server, this replication account does not work properly. To fix this problem, apply the Windows NT service packs or assign the Administrators group membership to the service account.

configuring the service, be sure your Directory Replicator service account has been created and assigned the appropriate permissions. Open Control Panel and double-click the Services icon. You then see a list of all the services installed on your Windows NT Server. Locate the Directory Replicator service, as shown in Figure 3.24.

You should notice that the Directory Replicator service is set to a manual startup, as shown in Figure 3.24. The service is not started at this time, and you should not start the system until all configuration is complete. Perform the tasks outlined in Step by Step 3.2 to configure the directory replication service.

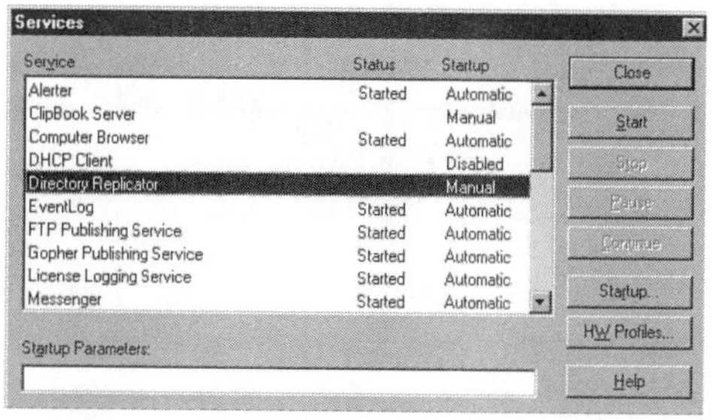

FIGURE 3.24

To get the Directory Replicator Service to function, all you need to do is configure the service.

STEP BY STEP

3.2 Configuring the Directory Replication Service

1. To change the properties for the Directory Replicator service, make sure it is selected in the Service list and then click Startup (refer to Figure 3.24).

   You see the current settings of your Directory Replicator service (see Figure 3.25).

2. To configure the service to work with the Directory Replicator service account, you must change the Startup Type to Automatic. Then, you must fill in the Log On As This Account option with the name and password of your service account. Figure 3.26 shows the screen completed to use a service account named `repluser`.

FIGURE 3.25

You see the Directory Replicator service configuration.

Once you configure the Directory Replicator service, you still need to configure the entire process. The export and import servers have to be selected and prepared before you start the Directory Replicator service. Make sure all the Directory Replicator service settings you completed are saved, but do not start the service.

Configuring the Export Server

To configure the export server, start Server Manager and double-click on the export server. Clicking Replication in the Server Properties dialog box results in the dialog box shown in Figure 3.27.

FIGURE 3.26

The Directory Replicator service account.

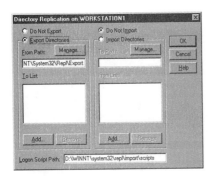

FIGURE 3.27
Configuring the export server for directory replication.

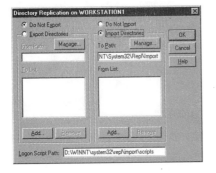

FIGURE 3.28
Configuring the import computer for directory replication.

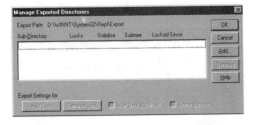

FIGURE 3.29
These options are available for managing the directory replication of the export server.

When configuring the export server, you have the option to specify the export directory. The default export directory is

```
C:\WINNT\system32\repl\export\
```

All subdirectories and corresponding files are sent to all the computers listed as import computers in the Export Directories section of the Directory Replication dialog box.

Unless computers are specified in the import section, the export server only sends the contents of the export directory to computers in its own domain. Therefore, it is critical that you include all systems requiring the files. It is possible for your own computer to act as both an export and import computer.

Configuring the Import Server

You also configure the import computer in the Server Manager | Properties dialog box. To configure the import computer, click Replication to open the Directory Replication dialog box. The import computer can be the same computer as the export server.

In the Import Directories section of the Directory Replication dialog box (see Figure 3.28), you can select the import directory. The default import directory is

```
C:\WINNT\system32\repl\import
```

Remember that the default directory for executing logon scripts in a Windows NT system is

```
C:\WINNT\system32\repl\import\scripts
```

The netlogon share points to the same directory.

You must also select which export server the import computer should receive the directories from. Make sure your import computer does not receive updates from multiple export servers, or you might have difficulty maintaining consistency across your servers.

Managing Directory Replication

You can control directory replication from both the export and import servers. You can place locks on certain directories to exclude them from the replication process. You also can designate a stabilization time to ensure that the files in your directories are not modified during a replication. This can be important while updating files that will be replicated to all your import servers. In Figure 3.29, you can see the options available for managing the directory replication of the export server.

The import server has similar options, as shown in Figure 3.30. You can manage directory locking from either the export server or the import server. This feature is handy because each server might need to manage the replication process.

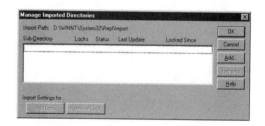

FIGURE 3.30
These options are available for managing the directory replication of the import server.

Directory Replicator Service

The directory replicator service can be a fairly finicky process. When reviewing this section, the key points to verify are

- The directory replicator service account must have appropriate access privileges (Backup Operators and Replicators groups). The account should have no time restrictions, and the password should not expire.

- The service should be installed but not started until all configuration is complete. The configuration includes the service account, export server, import server, and the service itself.

CONFIGURING HARD DISKS TO IMPROVE PERFORMANCE AND TO PROVIDE REDUNDANCY

Configure hard disks to meet various requirements. Requirements include providing redundancy and improving performance.

The hard disk is one of the busiest components in a server. All the information for your network is stored on the hard drives. In Windows NT Server, various hard disk options and fault tolerance options are available to help you improve disk performance. In this section, you will look at configuring your system to use the disk options available in Windows NT Server. All hard disk configuration can be done using the Disk Administrator tool. The different disk configurations you need to understand for the Enterprise exam are

◆ Stripe set

◆ Volume set

◆ Disk mirroring

◆ Stripe set with parity

The tool used for configuring and viewing your hard disk configuration is the Disk Administrator (see Figure 3.31). To start the Disk Administrator, choose Administrative Tools (common) from the Programs submenu of the Start menu, and then select Disk Administrator from the list. When the program is first started, you see a progress bar initializing your hard disk configuration.

Configuring a Stripe Set

Implementing a stripe set helps you achieve improved disk performance. The information is written across multiple physical disks, which greatly increases your disk reads and writes.

A stripe set is created from free space on your hard disks. You cannot create a stripe set on the boot or system partitions. They are existing partitions, and a stripe set is created using free disk space across multiple physical disks. A stripe set must use equal amounts of disk space across each physical disk. A stripe set requires a minimum of two disks and is limited to a maximum of 32 disks.

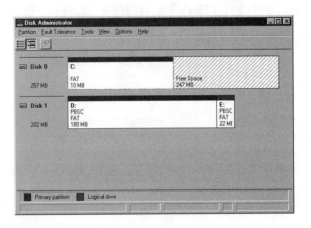

FIGURE 3.31

The tool used for configuring and viewing your hard disk configuration is the Disk Administrator.

To create a stripe set, perform the tasks outlined in Step by Step 3.3.

STEP BY STEP

3.3 Creating a Stripe Set

1. Start the Disk Administrator and select the free space from each of the disks to be used in the stripe set. To select multiple disks, hold down Ctrl and click with the mouse on each section.

2. When all the sections are selected, select Create Stripe Set in the Partition menu (see Figure 3.32).

The stripe set is created, and the partitions are all treated as one drive letter.

FIGURE 3.32
Setting up a stripe set.

Configuring a Volume Set

A volume set enables you to extend your drive letters across multiple partitions. The partitions can be on multiple physical disks or on the same physical disk. To set up a volume set, perform the tasks outlined in Step by Step 3.4.

STEP BY STEP

3.4 Setting Up a Volume Set

1. Select the free space from all the drives you want to include.

2. Select Create Volume Set command in the Partition menu (see Figure 3.33).

3. After the volume set has been created, you must format it as you would any disk partition. To format the drive, select Format from the Tools menu of the Disk Administrator, as shown in Figure 3.34. If you format the partition with the NTFS file system, you can extend the volume set if necessary.

EXAM TIP

Volume Sets on Enterprise Exam
Volume sets are discussed on the Windows NT Server exam. They also might be mentioned on the Enterprise exam, however, especially as a question involving extending a volume set. Only an NTFS partition can be extended in a volume set. If the file system is FAT, it cannot be extended.

FIGURE 3.33
Setting up a volume set.

continues

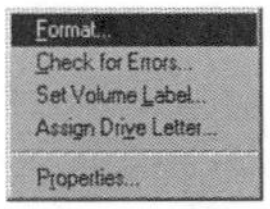

FIGURE 3.34
Formatting a drive using the Disk Administrator.

FIGURE 3.35
Extending a volume set.

FIGURE 3.36
Select Establish Mirror from the Fault Tolerance menu.

continued

4. To extend a volume set, select the volume set and the free space to be added to it. Then, select Extend Volume Set in the Partition menu, as shown in Figure 3.35.

The volume set can be extended across the entire disk space, or it can be spread across multiple physical disks and treated as one partition. The volume set has now been set up.

Configuring Disk Mirroring

To establish a disk mirror, you are required to have two physical disks in your NT system. With disk mirroring, you can use an existing disk partition—including the system and boot partitions. Disk mirroring provides a duplicate set of your data on a spare disk. To establish a disk mirror, you first must select the drive to mirror. You then select the free space to use on a second physical disk. Next, select Establish Mirror from the Fault Tolerance menu, as shown in Figure 3.36. The mirror set begins to duplicate all existing information from the first drive onto the mirror copy. Any new data is written to both drives by FTDISK.SYS.

After the disk mirror is created, you might need to break the mirror. This process is discussed in greater detail in Chapter 12, "Troubleshooting Installation, Setup, Configuration, and Printing Problems." As part of configuration, however, you should know how to break a mirror set.

As shown in Figure 3.37, the stripe set is split across two physical disks. Both partitions, however, are labeled E:.

To remove or break a mirror set, select the mirror set and then select Break Mirror from the Fault Tolerance menu (see Figure 3.38).

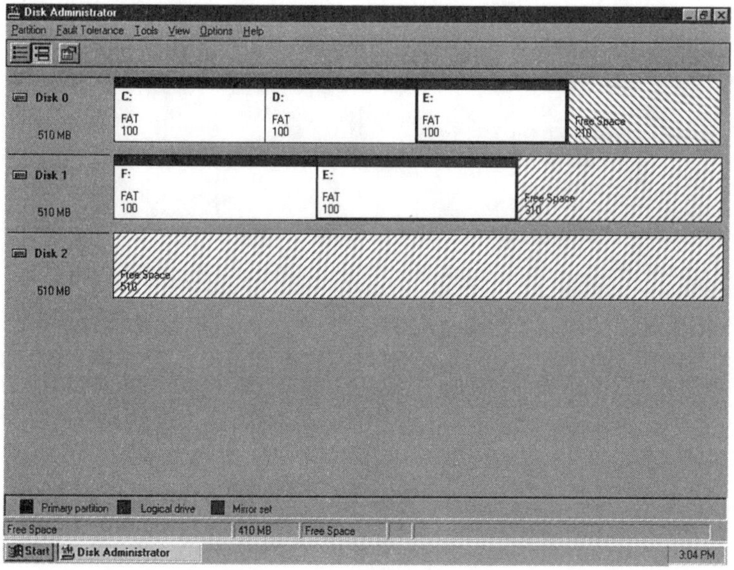

FIGURE 3.37
The stripe set is split across two physical disks; both are labeled E:.

Configuring a Stripe Set with Parity

A stripe set with parity is the best supported fault tolerance method available. It writes the data and parity information across a minimum of three physical disks. If any one of the disks fails, the data can be regenerated from the remaining data and the parity. To configure a stripe set with parity, you must have a minimum of three physical disks and a maximum of 32 physical disks. As with a stripe set, you cannot create a stripe set with parity from an existing partition.

A stripe set with parity is created by combining a minimum of three sections of free space across physical disks. By holding down the Ctrl key, you can select multiple sections of free space. Only after the three sections are selected can you select Create Stripe Set with Parity in the Fault Tolerance menu, as shown in Figure 3.39.

After you select Create Stripe Set with Parity, you are prompted to enter the size of the stripe set with parity. By default, the value shown is the maximum size available. The minimum size also is listed for your information in Figure 3.40.

The stripe set is then configured. In the Disk Administrator, you can see the stripe set written across multiple physical disks (see Figure 3.41). The legend across the bottom of the Disk Administrator shows which partitions belong to the stripe set with parity.

FIGURE 3.38
To remove or break a mirror set, select the mirror set and then select Break Mirror from the Fault Tolerance menu.

FIGURE 3.39
Only after the three sections are selected can you select Create Stripe Set with Parity in the Fault Tolerance menu.

FIGURE 3.40
Here you configure a stripe set with parity.

FIGURE 3.41

In the Disk Administrator, you can see the stripe set written across multiple physical disks.

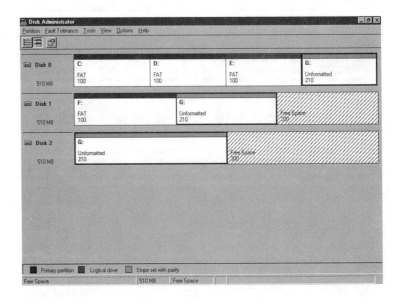

After the creation of any new partition, you also have to format your drive. To format, select the stripe set with parity and then select Format under the Tools menu.

REVIEW BREAK

Configuring Hard Disks

When selecting the fault tolerance solution to implement, review the planning chapters to ensure that you select the best solution for your needs. The solution that supplies the best redundancy and optimization mix is the stripe set with parity. In the following list are a few quick points to help you review each of the fault tolerance and disk options available:

- *Stripe set.* A stripe set gives you improved disk read and write performance; however, it supplies no fault tolerance. A minimum of two disks is required, and it can stripe up to 32 physical disks. The system partition cannot be included in a stripe set.

- *Volume set.* A volume set allows you to extend partitions beyond one physical disk; however, it supplies no fault tolerance. You can extend a volume set only with the NTFS file system.

- *Disk mirroring.* A mirror set uses two physical disks and it provides full data redundancy. Often referred to as RAID level 1, disk mirroring is a useful solution to assigning redundancy to the system partition, as well as any other disks in the system.

- *Stripe set with parity.* A stripe set with parity enables fault toler-ance in your system. A minimum of three physical disks is required, and a maximum of 32 physical disks can be included in a stripe set with parity. A stripe set with parity cannot include the system partition of your Windows NT system.

CONFIGURING PRINTERS

Configure printers. Tasks include adding and configuring a printer, implementing a printer pool, and setting print priorities.

When you set up a network printer in Windows NT, you are guided by a wizard that prompts you for each printer option. In this section, you will examine the options available for configuring a printer. You will also follow the installation steps required to configure a network printer.

You can reach all the settings for installing and configuring printers by clicking the Printers icon in Control Panel or by selecting Start | Settings | Printers. The Printers dialog box contains all your installed printers as well as an icon for installing new printers (see Figure 3.42).

To configure an existing printer, right-click the selected printer and select Properties from the pop-up menu. The printer Properties dia-log box contains all the options available for setting up your printer (see Figure 3.43). If you cannot view these properties, you might not have sufficient access privileges.

In the upcoming subsections, you will look into

- ◆ Adding a printer
- ◆ Connecting to an existing network printer
- ◆ Implementing a printer pool

FIGURE 3.42
The Printers dialog box contains all your installed printers and an icon for installing new printers.

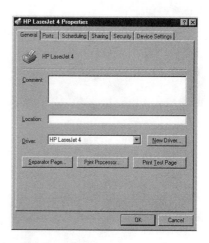

FIGURE 3.43
The printer Properties dialog box contains all the options available for setting up your printer.

Adding a Printer

Adding printers in Windows NT Server is simplified by the Add Printer Wizard. To access the Add Printer Wizard, double-click the Add Printer icon in the Printers dialog box.

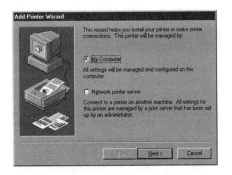

FIGURE 3.44
Select whether you are installing a printer on your computer or connecting to a network printer server.

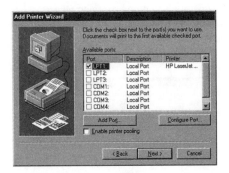

FIGURE 3.45
Select the port where you are installing your printer.

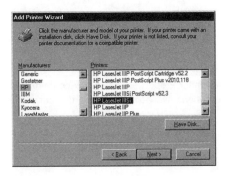

FIGURE 3.46
Select the manufacturer and model of your printer.

When adding a printer, you perform the following basic steps:

1. Make sure the printer is on the Hardware Compatibility List or have the driver for your printer available.

2. Log on to the system as a user with Print Operator, Administrator, or Server Operator access privileges.

3. Run the Add Printer Wizard and follow all prompts.

When installing a printer in a Windows NT system, you can either connect to an existing network printer or install your own printer and share it with other computers.

To add a new printer to your computer, follow the steps in Step by Step 3.5.

STEP BY STEP

3.5 Installing a Printer on an NT System

1. Double-click the Add Printer icon to start the Add Printer Wizard.

2. Select whether you are installing a printer on your computer or connecting to a network printer server (see Figure 3.44). For this example, select the My Computer option and click Next.

3. Select the port you are installing your printer on and then click Next (see Figure 3.45).

4. You are then prompted to select the manufacturer and model of your printer from the list boxes, as shown in Figure 3.46. You can click Have Disk if your printer is not listed but you have the printer driver for the computer. After your printer is selected, click Next to continue.

5. Assign a printer name for your printer, as shown in Figure 3.47. Then, specify whether you want your Windows programs to use this printer as the default printer.

6. If you want to share your printer with other users on the network, assign a share name and select which client operating systems can access your shared printer (see Figure 3.48). If you are not sharing the printer, select Not Shared. After the screen is complete, click Next to continue.

7. Finally, you get the option to print a test page to verify that your printer is communicating properly with your system (see Figure 3.49). Select the appropriate test option and then click Finish.

   The printer driver is now installed. You might be prompted to enter the location of your Windows NT Server source files. If you are prompted, enter the directory that contains the printer driver.

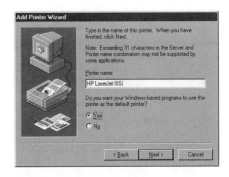

FIGURE 3.47
Assign a printer name for your printer.

Connecting to an Existing Network Printer

If you are adding an existing network printer to your system, you can use the Add Printer Wizard to configure the printer.

To add an existing network printer to your system, follow the steps in Step by Step 3.6.

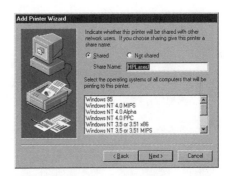

FIGURE 3.48
If you want to share your printer with other users on the network, assign a share name and select which client operating systems can access your shared printer.

STEP BY STEP

3.6 Adding an Existing Network Printer

1. Start the Add Printer Wizard by double-clicking the Add Printer icon.

2. Select the Network printer server option and click Next (see Figure 3.50).

continues

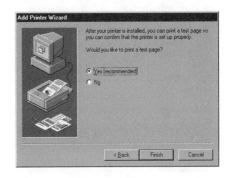

FIGURE 3.49
Print a test page to verify that your printer is communicating properly with your system.

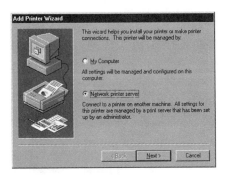

FIGURE 3.50
Add an existing network printer.

FIGURE 3.51
Find the network printer.

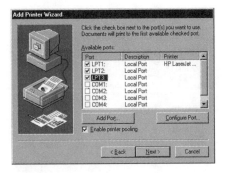

FIGURE 3.52
Enable the printer pooling option.

continued

3. Enter the network path to the network printer or select it from the Shared Printers list, as shown in Figure 3.51. When you locate the network printer, click OK to continue.

4. Select whether to use this printer as your default Windows printer and then click Next.

5. Click Finish, and the printer driver is installed. You also can assign a name to this printer.

You will see a printer icon that allows you to automatically redirect print jobs to the network printer.

Implementing a Printer Pool

By implementing a printer pool, you can have multiple printers handling one print queue. There are a few restrictions on setting up a printer pool. The main issue is that all the printers must use the same printer driver. You can combine up to eight printers to use the same printer driver and print spooler. This method can help to meet your organization's printing needs and speed up the printing process.

To implement a printer pool, follow the steps in Step by Step 3.7.

STEP BY STEP

3.7 Implementing a Printer Pool

1. Double-click the Add Printer icon.

2. Select My Computer for the location or management of the printer pool and then click Next.

3. When selecting the port for your printer pool, you must select all ports to be managed by this printer. Make sure you enable the printer pooling option, as shown in Figure 3.52.

If you need to configure a jet-direct printer or other network-based printers not connected to your physical computer, click the Add Port option. Select the appropriate printer port to establish your connection, as shown in Figure 3.53.

After all the ports are configured and selected, click Next to continue with the installation.

4. Select the printer driver to be used by all the printers in your printer pool and then click Next.

5. Assign a printer name to the printer pool. Specify whether this printer pool should be your default Windows printer and click Next.

6. Share the printer with clients. Make sure all operating systems that can connect are selected. If you select all the operating systems, your clients do not need to load the driver locally. When they first make a connection to the network printer, the printer driver is copied locally to their computer system.

7. After all the wizard dialog boxes are complete, click Finish.

The printer driver is now loaded, and your printer is ready for use.

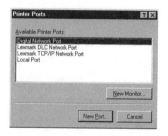

FIGURE 3.53
Select the appropriate printer port to establish your connection.

WARNING

Printer Pool Rules Remember that in a printer pool, you can combine a maximum of eight printers. All the printers, however, must be able to function with the same printer driver.

Configuring Printers

R E V I E W   B R E A K

The installation of a printer is a fairly simplistic procedure that is not tested heavily on the exam; however, the printer pool is a key point. The items to remember about printer pools are as follows:

- All printers in a printer pool must be able to function using the same printer driver.

- A printer pool may have a maximum of eight printers in the pool.

CONFIGURING WINDOWS NT SERVER FOR VARIOUS TYPES OF CLIENTS

Configure a Windows NT Server computer for various types of client computers. Client computer types include Windows NT Workstation, Windows 95, and Macintosh.

Your Windows NT Server is the selected server for various client operating systems. In this section, you look at the configuration requirements for

- Windows NT Workstation clients

- Windows 95 clients

- Macintosh clients

Windows NT Server automatically handles all the requests from each of these clients. The Windows NT Workstation and Windows 95 clients use Windows NT logon security and provide complete functionality as a Windows NT client right out of the box. To enable connectivity with Apple Macintosh computers, you must install the services for the Macintosh on the Windows NT Server computer.

To install the various operating systems supported by Windows NT Server, you can use a program installed on your Windows NT Server computer. The Network Client Administrator can simplify the installation of your client computers (see Figure 3.54).

The Network Client Administrator is in the Administrative Tools group. You can use the Network Client Administrator program to

- **Make a network installation startup disk.** This option creates an MS-DOS boot disk that contains commands required to connect to a network server and that automatically installs Windows NT Workstation, Windows 95, or DOS network clients.

- **Make an installation disk set.** This option enables the creation of installation disks for the DOS network client, LAN Manager 2.2c for DOS, or LAN Manager 2.2c for OS/2.

FIGURE 3.54
The Network Client Administrator can simplify the installation of your client computers.

◆ **Copy client-based network administration tools.** This option enables you to share the network administration tools with client computers. The client computers that can use the network administration tools are Windows NT Workstation and Windows 95 computers.

◆ **View remoteboot client information.** This option enables you to view the remoteboot client information. To install remoteboot, go to the Services tab of the Network dialog box.

Windows NT Workstation Clients

To set up a Windows NT Workstation computer to use your Windows NT Server, you might have to create a computer account for the Windows NT Workstation computer. The computer account is then used by the Remote Procedure Calls (RPC) service to make a secure communication. This account, which verifies when the computer is started, also can be used for monitoring services on your NT Workstation computer. To install the Windows NT Workstation computer, you can install it as a standalone system and then, in the Network dialog box, have your NT Workstation computer join the domain. During the joining process, you can automatically create a computer account in the domain. You must, however, have Server Operator or Administrator access to create this computer account. If you want to create the computer account in the Windows NT Server computer, you can use Server Manager.

After you have a Windows NT Workstation client configured, the users and the client computer can use the Windows NT security, and all user properties apply.

You can also install the client-based Network Administration tools. These tools enable you to manage your Windows NT Server from your Windows NT Workstation client computer.

The system requirements for installing the Windows NT Workstation server tools are

◆ Windows NT Workstation must be installed.

◆ It must have a 486DX/33 or higher processor.

◆ A minimum of 12MB RAM is needed.

◆ There must be 2.5MB of free disk space in the system partition.

◆ The Workstation and Server services must be installed on the NT Workstation computer.

Table 3.3 illustrates the tools found in the Windows NT Workstation Server tools.

TABLE 3.3

WINDOWS NT WORKSTATION SERVER TOOLS

Tools	Use This Tool to...
Server Manager	Manage Windows NT-based computers and domain controllers.
User Manager for Domains	Manage users, groups, and user rights for Windows NT domains.
WINS Manager	Administer the WINS servers.
DHCP Manager	Administer the DHCP servers.
Remote Access Administrator	Administer the remote access service on a computer running Windows NT.
Service for Macintosh	Share Windows NT resources with Macintosh clients.
System Policy Editor	Modify and maintain user and system policies.

Windows 95 Clients

You can install windows 95 as a client on your Windows NT Server. Using the Network Client Administrator program, you can create an automated installation from a floppy disk. You can configure any installation of Windows 95 with a Microsoft Network client loaded to log on to a Windows NT domain. You perform this configuration in the Network properties of your Windows 95 computers.

Windows 95 also has server tools available to enable Windows 95 computers to administer a Windows NT system. The system requirements for the Windows 95 computer to use the server tools are

- Windows 95 must be installed.

- A 486DX/33 or higher processor is required.

- A minimum of 8MB of RAM is required.

- There must be 3MB of free disk space available at the system partition.

- The client for Microsoft networks must be installed.

Macintosh Clients

For Windows NT to enable integration with Apple Macintosh clients, you must first install Services for Macintosh on your Windows NT Server. Services for Macintosh is a group of programs and utilities that enable the two operating systems to communicate. Services for Macintosh enables file and print sharing between the Macintosh clients and the Windows NT Server. The Windows NT Server also is able to share Macintosh printers with the other clients of the Windows NT Server.

When Services for Macintosh is installed, the AppleTalk protocol gets installed onto the Windows NT Server. This protocol is required for connectivity with the Macintosh computers.

Server and Client Requirements

A few requirements must be met prior to installing Services for Macintosh onto your network. The requirements for the Windows NT Server computer are

- 2MB of free disk space

- An NTFS partition to be used as the Macintosh volume

Requirements for the Macintosh computer are

- Version 6.0.8 or later of the Macintosh operating system

- Version 2.0 of the AppleTalk filing protocol

- Network cards that enable connectivity into the same network as the Windows NT Server system

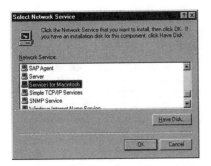

FIGURE 3.55
Installing Services for Macintosh.

Installing the Services for Macintosh

To install Services for Macintosh, perform the tasks outlined in Step by Step 3.8.

STEP BY STEP

3.8 Installing the Services for Macintosh

1. Open the Network dialog box of your Windows NT system. Change to the Services tab and click Add to add a new service (see Figure 3.55).

2. Select Services for Macintosh in the list of available services and click OK.

3. Services for Macintosh is installed automatically, and you are prompted to restart your system.

   Once the services for the Macintosh are installed, your system is ready for connectivity with a Macintosh client.

REVIEW BREAK

Configuring NT Server for Client Computers

When installing a client computer, you must ensure that your Windows NT system is prepared for and configured for the client. The Windows clients are able to connect to Windows NT Server without any configuration required on the server; however, some configuration is required on the client computers. For the Apple Macintosh client, NT Server must install the Services for Macintosh, which includes the AppleTalk protocol. It is this protocol that enables the seamless connection between the Windows NT system and the Apple clients.

CASE STUDY: CONVERTING TO AN NT ENVIRONMENT

ESSENCE OF THE CASE

Here are the essential elements of the case. The textile plant needs to install and configure the following:

- One Windows NT Server to act as a Primary Domain Controller that includes the Services for Macintosh and TCP/IP and NWLink IPX/SPX protocol for connectivity.

- TCP/IP for Internet connectivity and the majority of connections between clients.

- NWLink IPX/SPX-compatible protocol for connectivity with NetWare servers until they can be phased out with new NT servers.

- Windows NT Server installed as a member server to host email and applications as required.

SCENARIO

JPS Consulting has been hired to propose a network solution for a large textile plant in Winnipeg. The plant is currently using Novell NetWare 3.12 as its network environment. In the near future, the plant would like to incorporate all the desktop workstations, 500 users and computers, into a single centrally administered Windows NT network. The desktop computers are a mix of Windows 95 and Windows NT Workstation computers with the odd Macintosh used for desktop publishing and graphic layouts. The network requires a number of application servers to run the custom software the company has, as well as servers to handle logon and security for the network. The employees understand how to install the servers but require direction on the server roles and requirements to handle each of the desktop clients. Internet access and email are also mandatory requirements for this organization.

ANALYSIS

A conversion from a Novell NetWare to Windows NT environment is common. To facilitate the conversion, it is recommended that you leave the NetWare system up and running until the Windows NT domain is stabilized using a PDC for all desktop client access. The PDC should have NWLink and TCP/IP installed to simplify connections with the clients, as well as the Services for Macintosh to facilitate the Macintosh computers. For the application servers, depending on the application, install each of the additional servers as member servers to reduce the network and computer load of those systems. One domain is adequate in this environment because it maintains only 500 users, and in a single domain, the system can be centrally managed and administered.

CHAPTER SUMMARY

KEY TERMS

• subnet mask

• printer pool

• remote procedure calls (RPC)

This chapter covers the installation and configuration of common components and services in a Windows NT server environment. To be fully prepared for this portion of the exam, it is recommended that you gain some hands-on experience in the installation and configuration of each of the components covered. The main points to understand are

◆ The various server roles available in NT Server:

• Primary Domain Controller

• Backup Domain Controller

• Member server

◆ Installation and configuration of the networking protocols:

• TCP/IP

• NWLink IPX/SPX compatible

• DLC

• AppleTalk

◆ Windows NT core services:

• Server

• Workstation

• Computer Browser

• Directory Replication

◆ Configuring hard disks for fault tolerance and performance:

• Disk mirroring. Full disk duplication; may also be called disk duplexing if a second disk controller is used.

• Stripe sets. No fault tolerance; however, can improve disk performance.

• Stripe set with parity. Fault tolerance through the use of parity bits to regenerate the data in the case of a faulty disk.

CHAPTER SUMMARY

- Volume sets. Used to extend NTFS partitions beyond a physical disk or partition.

◆ Installation and configuration of printers

- Installing, configuring, and sharing a printer.

- Implementing a printer pool—all printers must use the same print driver.

◆ Configuring Windows NT Server for various types of clients

This list outlines the areas of focus on the exam. Having strong knowledge of the procedures required to implement these items is the key to being successful in this section of the exam.

APPLY YOUR LEARNING

This section allows you to assess how well you understood the material in the chapter. Review and exam questions test your knowledge of the tasks and concepts specified in the objectives. The exercises provide you with opportunities to engage in the sorts of tasks that compose the skill sets the objectives reflect.

For more review and exam questions, see the Top Score test engine on the CD-ROM that came with this book.

Exercises

The following exercises provide you with an opportunity to apply what you've learned in this chapter.

3.1 Installing Windows NT Server 4 as a Primary Domain Controller

In this exercise, you step through the process of installing Windows NT Server 4 as a PDC. The setup also includes some additional services and protocols. Your system should have at least 150MB of free disk space to complete this exercise.

Time Estimate: 45 minutes

1. Access the Windows NT Server 4 source directory from a CD-ROM, or copy all the source files for Windows NT Server onto the local hard drive. The I386 directory contains the files you use to install the Intel-based software.

> **NOTE**
> **SMARTDRV.EXE** Make sure SMARTDRV.EXE is loaded prior to starting the installation of Windows NT because it dramatically reduces the time required to complete the first stage of the setup.

2. From the Windows NT Server directory, enter the command line **WINNT /B**. This starts Windows NT Setup and enables you to complete the setup without creating the three boot disks.

3. The setup program copies the Windows NT Server 4 software into temporary directories on your computer. When you are finished copying the files, it prompts you to restart the system.

4. After the system has been restarted, you should notice that the Windows NT boot menu is configured to autostart Windows NT. At this time, you should prepare to start the DOS-based portion of the Windows NT setup. Read the Welcome to Windows NT Setup screen, and press Enter to start the setup of Windows NT.

5. The program then attempts to detect all mass-storage devices in your system. Review the selection and, if it is correct, press Enter to continue.

6. The End User Licensing Agreement screen is displayed for you to review. Read the screen, pressing Page Down to view the entire document. When you reach the bottom, press F8 to accept the terms of the agreement.

7. You then are prompted for the type of installation to complete. If this is the first occurrence of Windows NT on this system, press Enter to install Windows NT. If an existing installation of Windows NT is still on this system, pressing Enter upgrades the installation. If you want a new installation of Windows NT, press N to cancel the upgrade.

8. You see a list of the hardware and software on your computer. Press Enter to continue with installation.

APPLY YOUR LEARNING

9. Select the drive onto which you want to install Windows NT Server. Make sure it has at least 120MB of free disk space to complete the installation. You also want to make sure the current file system is left intact, so FAT is the file system for your Windows NT system.

> **NOTE**
>
> **NTFS** If you want to use NTFS as the file system, this screen enables you to convert your file system to NTFS.

10. Press Enter to use the default directory, \WINNT.

11. Press Enter to have the setup program examine your hard disks.

12. The system then prompts you to restart. When the system is restarted, it is in the graphical portion of the setup.

13. When the Windows NT Server Setup Wizard appears, click Next to start using it.

14. Enter your name and organization information and click Next.

15. Type your CD key, located on the Windows NT Server CD-ROM, and click Next.

16. Select the licensing mode you want to use. For this exercise, select Per Server with 10 concurrent connections and click Next.

17. Enter the computer name for your Windows NT Server computer. For this exercise, enter **Comp1** as the computer name and click Next.

> **NOTE**
>
> **Computer Name** The computer name can have a maximum of 15 characters, and it must be unique on the network it is attached to.

18. Select the Primary Domain Controller option and click Next.

19. Enter a password for the Administrator account. For this exercise, use **password** as the password. Make sure you confirm the password and then click Next.

20. You might get a prompt regarding a floating point workaround. Select Do Not Enable The Floating Point Workaround and click Next to continue.

21. Click Yes, create an emergency repair disk, and then click Next.

22. Click Next to select the default components. You are then presented with Phase 2 of the setup, "Installing Windows NT Networking."

23. Click Next to begin Phase 2.

24. Make sure Wired to the network is selected and click Next.

25. Clear the Install Microsoft Internet Information Server check box and click Next.

26. Click Start Search to have the setup program automatically detect your network cards. If you have multiple cards, click Find Next until all of them are located. If your card is not located automatically, click Select from list and choose your network card manually. When the proper network adapters are selected, click Next to continue.

APPLY YOUR LEARNING

27. Select TCP/IP and NetBEUI as your protocols and click Next.

28. All the default network services should be used, so click Next to continue.

29. Click Next to install the network components.

30. If you are prompted to confirm the settings for your network adapter, make sure they are displayed correctly and click Next to continue.

31. You next are prompted to use DHCP. If you have a DHCP server, click Yes. If you do not have a DHCP server, click No.

32. Click Next to accept the default bindings for your system.

33. Click Next to start the network.

34. If you did not use DHCP, when you are prompted for your TCP/IP settings, use `131.107.2.100` for your IP address and `255.255.255.0` for a subnet mask. No default gateway is required for this exercise.

35. When prompted for your domain name, enter **DomainA** and click Next.

36. Phase 3 of the setup starts. Click Finish to start the last phase of the setup.

37. When prompted, enter the date, time, and time zone information for your location and click Next.

38. You must then configure your video adapter. Click OK to confirm the detected video adapter.

39. Click Test to verify the settings for your video adapter.

40. If the settings appear correctly, click Yes. Then, click OK to continue with the installation.

41. The system then prepares to create the emergency repair disk. Get a blank high-density floppy disk, insert it into drive A: when prompted, and click OK.

42. When the emergency repair information has been written to disk, the system removes the temporary files and prompts you to restart.

43. When the system restarts, Windows NT Server has been installed successfully.

3.2   Configuring the TCP/IP Protocol

In this exercise, you modify the TCP/IP protocol to use a DHCP server and then to manually input an IP Address.

Time Estimate: 15 minutes

1. Select Start | Settings | Control Panel and then double-click the Network icon.

2. Select the Protocols tab.

3. Highlight TCP/IP Protocol and then click Properties.

4. On the IP Address tab of the Microsoft TCP/IP Properties dialog box, enable Obtain an IP address from a DHCP server.

5. Click OK to close the Microsoft TCP/IP Properties dialog box and then click OK to close the Network dialog box.

6. The system prompts you to restart the system for the new settings to take effect. Restart the system.

7. When the system restarts, open a command prompt and enter **IPCONFIG /ALL** to view your current TCP/IP settings.

APPLY YOUR LEARNING

> **NOTE**
>
> **DHCP Server**   If there's not a DHCP server available when you run the IPCONFIG command, all the addresses should be set to 0.0.0.0. If these are already the current settings, all is configured properly and you are only missing the DHCP server.

8. Next, you will reset the IP address back to a manual IP address. Right-click the Network Neighborhood icon and select Properties. This opens the Network dialog box.

9. Select the Protocols tab.

10. Highlight TCP/IP Protocol and click Properties.

11. In the Specify an IP address section, enter **131.107.2.100** as the IP address.

12. For the subnet mask, enter **255.255.255.0**.

13. For the default gateway, enter **131.107.2.1**.

14. Next, select the WINS Address tab.

15. Enter **131.107.2.2** for the primary WINS server.

16. Change to the DNS tab. Click the Add button.

17. Enter **131.107.2.2** in the list of DNS servers.

18. Click OK to save all settings.

19. Click Close in the Network properties dialog box. You are using your new settings.

20. Start a command prompt and enter **IPCONFIG /ALL**. Note that your current IP information has been changed to the settings you just entered.

3.3   Configuring Directory Replication on a Windows NT Server

In this exercise, you configure the Directory Replicator service to automatically replicate logon scripts.

Time Estimate: 30 minutes

1. Before you can configure directory replication, you must create a Directory Replicator service account. Start User Manager for Domains and create a new user named replacct. This account should be a member of the Replicator and Backup Operators groups. Make sure there are no password or time restrictions on this account. When the user has been created, click Add and then close the User Manager.

2. Click Start | Settings | Control Panel and double-click the Services icon.

3. Highlight Directory Replicator in the Services dialog box and click Startup.

4. In the Service dialog box, select Automatic in the Startup Type section.

5. In the Log on As section, click This Account and select replacct. Click Add to add the account. If you created a password for this account, make sure you enter it in the password fields. Click OK, and the Services dialog box is displayed again.

6. Click Close to exit the Services dialog box.

7. Click Start | Programs | Administrative Tools | Server Manager.

8. Locate your computer in the list and double-click to view the properties of your computer.

9. Click Replication.

10. The Directory Replication dialog box is presented.

11. Enable the Export Directories radio button.

12. Click Add to add a new computer for exporting. Select your computer name in the list and then click OK to add it to the list.

13. Next, enable the Import Directories radio button.

14. Click the Add button in this section, select your computer name, and then click OK.

15. Click OK to close the Directory Replication dialog box. The Directory Replicator service should start when you click OK to close the dialog box.

16. Start the Windows NT Explorer and locate the \WINNT\System32\Repl\Export\scripts directory.

17. Create a text file called LOGIN.TXT in this directory.

18. Open the \WINNT\System32\Repl\Import\ Scripts directory. Watch this directory until the LOGIN.TXT file appears. This process might take a few minutes, so be patient.

19. When you see the file in the directory, close Explorer.

20. Click Start | Programs | Administrative Tools | Server Manager.

21. Locate your computer and double-click to view its properties.

22. Click Replication.

23. In the Export Directories section of the Directory Replication dialog box, click Manage. You should see status information about your directory replication.

24. Click Manage in the Import Directories section to view the status from the import computer.

At the completion of this exercise, you might want to set the Directory Replicator service back to a manual start.

3.4   Adding a Printer in a Windows NT Server 4 Environment

In this exercise, you add a printer and share it so others in your domain can access it as a network printer.

Time Estimate: 15 minutes

1. Click Start | Settings | Printers.

2. Double-click the Add Printers icon.

3. Enable the My Computer radio button and click Next.

4. Under Available ports, select the LPT1 check box. Click Next to continue.

5. Under Manufacturers, select HP (Hewlett-Packard).

6. Under Printers, select the HP LaserJet 4. Click Next to continue.

7. In the Printer name box, enter **HP LaserJet 4** and click Next.

8. Enable the Shared radio button.

9. In the Share Name box, enter **Laser** and then click Next.

APPLY YOUR LEARNING

10. When asked if you want to print a test page, select No and then click Finish.

11. You should see the HP LaserJet 4 icon in the Printers dialog box.

12. To view the print queue for the HP LaserJet 4 printer, double-click the printer's icon.

13. This dialog box is where all print jobs are transferred. The printer also can be paused from this screen. Close the Printers dialog box.

3.5 Creating a Printer Pool in Windows NT Server 4

In this exercise, you install and configure a printer pool on your Windows NT Server.

Time Estimate: 15 minutes

1. Click Start | Settings | Printers.

2. Double-click the HP LaserJet 4 printer icon.

3. Under the Printer menu, select Pause Printing.

4. Close the HP LaserJet 4 dialog box.

5. Right-click the HP LaserJet 4 printer icon and select Properties.

6. Select the Ports tab.

7. Turn on the Enable Printer Pooling option.

8. Click LPT2, but make sure LPT1 is still selected.

9. Click OK.

With printer pooling enabled, the print jobs can be redirected to any of the ports configured in the printer pool. Remember, all the printers in a printer pool must be able to use the same printer driver.

Review Questions

Answers to the following questions are found in the section "Answers and Explanations," later in the chapter. At the end of each of those answers, you are informed of where (that is, in what section of the chapter) to find more information.

1. Your company currently is running Windows NT Server in a single-domain model. You are finding that logon request processing is slow, and you want to install a new server into your network to help handle logon requests. What type of server should you install in your environment?

2. What is the name of the setup program for Windows NT Server? What is the name if you are installing from a 32-bit operating system?

3. Can you upgrade Windows NT Server installed as a member server to a domain controller?

4. What action do you take if your Primary Domain Controller is down for repairs, and you want to set up one of your Backup Domain Controllers to act as the PDC?

5. What service is used to send a copy of the SAM database from the PDC to the BDCs?

6. What network protocols are supported by Windows NT Server?

7. What network protocol can you use to connect to the Internet?

8. What configuration options are mandatory when installing TCP/IP?

9. What is the function of the default gateway?

10. What service enables automatic configuration of IP addresses for client computers?

11. What service must be installed to configure the AppleTalk protocol?

12. What is the function of the Server service?

13. What is the default export directory for the Directory Replicator service?

14. You have three computers you want to put into a printer pool. The printers are an HP LaserJet 4, an IBM Lexmark, and a dot matrix. Can these printers be placed into a printer pool together?

15. How many disks are required to create a stripe set with parity?

Exam Questions

The following questions are similar to those you will face on the Microsoft exam. Answers to these questions can be found in the section "Answers and Explanations," later in the chapter. At the end of each of those answers, you are informed of where (that is, what section of the chapter) to find more information.

1. In the Directory Replicator service, which types of computers can act as export computers? Choose all that apply.

   A. Windows NT Server computers (domain controllers only)

   B. Windows NT Workstation computers

   C. Windows NT Server computers

   D. Windows 95 computers

2. To enable Macintosh users to store files on a Windows NT Server computer, what must be installed?

   A. GSNW

   B. Services for Macintosh

   C. WINS

   D. DNS

3. What is the disk-partitioning scheme that enables equal areas of disk space from 2 to 32 physical drives to be combined into one logical drive?

   A. Volume set

   B. Stripe set with parity

   C. Stripe set

   D. Mirror set

4. What type of disk system makes an exact copy of all data from one disk onto another disk?

   A. Stripe set with parity

   B. Stripe set

   C. Volume set

   D. Mirror set

5. Select the types of disk systems that are fault tolerant. Select all correct answers.

A. Volume sets

B. Disk striping

C. Disk striping with parity

D. Disk mirroring

6. What is the name of the utility used to implement fault tolerance in Windows NT Server?

A. User Manager for Domains

B. Server Manager

C. Disk Administrator

D. Control Panel

7. You installed Windows NT Server 4, but during the installation process, you selected Server as the type of installation. You now want to make the server a Backup Domain Controller. What must you do to convert the server?

A. Run the Convert command.

B. Do nothing; the member server also can act as a domain controller.

C. Reinstall Windows NT Server as a domain controller.

D. Under Control Panel | Network, change the server type to Backup Domain Controller.

8. What is the main difference between an NT Server installed as a domain controller and an NT Server not installed as a domain controller?

A. A domain controller maintains a copy of the domain directory database; a non-domain controller does not.

B. A non-domain controller validates user logons; a domain controller does not.

C. A domain controller is best suited to an application server role in the network.

D. There is no difference between the domain controller and the non-domain controller.

9. To set up a printer pool, which of the following criteria must be met? Select all correct answers.

A. All printers should be in the same general area.

B. The printers should be the same make and model and use the same printer driver.

C. The printers must be connected to the same print server.

D. The printer must be connected to the same type of port.

10. How do you install a new printer? Select all that apply.

A. From the Start menu, select Settings | Printers. Click the Add Printers icon.

B. Start Print Manager and add the printer from the Printer menu.

C. Open Control Panel and click the Printer icon. Then, double-click the Add Printer icon.

D. Run the Windows NT Setup program and install the printer under the Configuration menu.

11. How do you configure a network protocol in Windows NT Server? Select all that apply.

    A. From the Start menu, select Settings | Control Panel. Double-click the Network icon.

    B. Right-click Network Neighborhood icon and select the Properties.

    C. From Server Manager.

    D. From the Network Client Administrator.

12. What is the default export directory in the Directory Replicator service?

    A. C:\WINNT\System

    B. C:\WINNT\System32\etc

    C. C:\WINNT\System32\Repl\Import

    D. C:\WINNT\System32\Repl\Export

Answers to Review Questions

1. Backup Domain Controller. See the section "Defining Server Roles in Windows NT Server" earlier in this chapter for more information.

2. WINNT.EXE, WINNT32.EXE. See the section "Installing Windows NT 4 Server in Various Server Roles" for more information.

3. No, you must reinstall to change server roles. See the section "Changing Server Roles" for more information.

4. Use the Server Manager and promote the BDC to a PDC. See the section "Changing Server Roles" for more information.

5. Netlogon service. See the section "Defining Server Roles in Windows NT Server" for more information.

6. TCP/IP, NWLink IPX/SPX compatible, NetBEUI, AppleTalk, and DLC. See the section "Configuring Networking Protocols and Protocol Bindings" for more information.

7. TCP/IP. See the section "TCP/IP" for more information.

8. IP address, subnet mask. See the section "TCP/IP" for more information.

9. To route TCP/IP packets outside of your physical network to other TCP/IP computers. See the section "TCP/IP" for more information.

10. DHCP. See the section "TCP/IP" for more information.

11. Services for Macintosh. See the section "Configuring Windows NT Server for Various Types of Clients" for more information.

12. Handle outgoing network communication. See the section "Configuring Windows NT Server Core Services" for more information.

13. C:\WINNT\System32\Repl\Export. See the section "Configuring Windows NT Server Core Services" in this chapter for more information.

14. No, printers in a printer pool must use a common printer driver. See the section "Configuring Printers" in this chapter for more information.

15. Three physical disks. See the section "Configuring Hard Disks to Improve Performance and to Provide Redundancy" for more information.

APPLY YOUR LEARNING

Answers to Exam Questions

1. **A. B. C.** To play the role of an export server in the directory replication process, the operating system must be a Windows NT computer, NT server, or NT workstation. See the section "Installing Windows NT Server 4 in Various Server Roles."

2. **B.** The Services for Macintosh must be loaded for Macintosh clients to connect to a Windows NT Server. See the section "Configuring Protocols" in this chapter.

3. **C.** You can use a stripe set to combine equal areas of space across 2–32 physical disks into one logical partition. See the section "Configuring Hard Disks to Improve Performance and to Provide Redundancy."

4. **D.** A mirror set makes an exact duplicate of all of the contents of the mirrored drive onto a backup mirror drive to ensure complete redundancy of data. See the section "Configuring Hard Disks to Improve Performance and to Provide Redundancy."

5. **C. D.** Disk mirroring and stripe set with parity are the only options that have fault tolerance. See the section "Configuring Hard Disks to Improve Performance and to Provide Redundancy."

6. **C.** The Disk Administrator is the utility that manages all of the aspects of the physical hard disks, including fault tolerance options. See the section "Configuring Hard Disks to Improve Performance and to Provide Redundancy."

7. **C.** To change the server role in an NT Server environment, you must do a complete reinstall of the NT Server software. See the section "Installing Windows NT Server 4 in Various Server Roles."

8. **A.** The difference between a domain controller and a member server is that the domain controller has a copy of the domain account database, whereas a member server has only a local account database. See the section "Installing Windows NT Server 4 in Various Server Roles."

9. **A. B. C.** To set up a printer pool, the printers must all be controlled through a single print server, they must be the same or similar model, and they should be kept in close proximity to one another to eliminate the confusion to the users. See the section "Implementing a Printer Pool."

10. **A. C.** Printers can be installed from the Control Panel printers icon or from the printers option in the Start menu. See the section "Adding a Printer."

11. **A. B.** A network protocol is configured from the Network Properties dialog box. You can access this dialog through Control Panel or through the Network Neighborhood icon. See the section "Installing Protocols."

12. **D.** The default directory for the export server in the directory replication process is C:\WINNT\SYSTEM32\REPL\EXPORT. See the section "Directory Replicator."

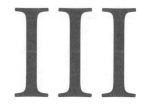

PART

MANAGING RESOURCES

This chapter helps you to prepare for the Microsoft exam by covering the following objectives within the "Managing Resources" category:

Manage user and group accounts. Considerations include

- ◆ **Managing Windows NT user accounts**

- ◆ **Managing Windows NT user rights**

- ◆ **Managing Windows NT groups**

- ◆ **Administering account policies**

- ◆ **Auditing changes to the user account database**

▶ This objective covers all the tasks and options available in creating and managing user and group accounts in a Windows NT Server environment. The user and group management is the cornerstone of your environment. Without a logical process for this component, your network will not succeed in meeting the needs of your users.

Create and manage policies and profiles for various situations. Policies and profiles include

- ◆ **Local user profiles**

- ◆ **Roaming user profiles**

- ◆ **System policies**

▶ This objective defines each of the types of policies and profiles available, as well as the procedures used to implement policies and profiles in your environment. The policies and profiles are gaining in popularity within the administrative world. By gaining experience in this area, you will be able to apply this knowledge in your environment and simplify your day-to-day tasks.

CHAPTER 4

Managing User and Group Accounts

AGLP—use it; live by it. Throughout this chapter, you'll see the acronym AGLP defined and used. This is a process that Microsoft lives by and tests fairly extensively on the Enterprise exam. In every question you face relating to user accounts and permissions, ensure that you follow the Accounts, Global groups, Local groups, Permission strategy of AGLP.

Managing resources is one of the major tasks facing Windows NT administrators, especially when dealing with an enterprise system. Good management leads to better network design and implementation. By maintaining and managing your user and group accounts and utilizing the policies and profiles in your Windows NT Server environment, you can greatly reduce your administrative overhead in your environment.

In this chapter, the following areas of managing resources are discussed:

◆ Managing user and group accounts

◆ Creating and managing system policies and user profiles

Managing User and Group Accounts

Manage user and group accounts. Considerations include managing Windows NT user accounts, managing Windows NT user rights, managing Windows NT groups, administering account policy, and auditing changes to the user account database.

Creation of a good SAM database is essential to a well-designed network. Your environment can run only as smoothly as you allow it. By establishing a strong process for creating and managing your user and group accounts, you will maintain a functional NT environment. Managing user and group accounts is best understood when broken down into the following parts:

◆ Managing Windows NT user accounts

◆ Managing Windows NT group accounts

◆ Managing Windows NT user rights

◆ Administering account policies

◆ Auditing changes to the user account database

The main topics to be discussed in this section are the following:

◆ Creating Windows NT user accounts

◆ Defining your account policy

◆ Template accounts

◆ Managing global and local groups

◆ User rights

Creating Windows NT User Accounts

Windows NT user accounts, with their unique identifiers commonly referred to as security identifiers or SIDs, enable users to log on to the Windows NT network. Their user account/password combination is their access ticket to all resources on the NT network. Creation of user accounts is an important task because it is duplicated with the creation of each user in your environment. Ideally, you want to reduce the individual configuration required when creating a large group of users.

Windows NT user accounts are created in User Manager for Domains. This utility enables all user and group management within the domain. To create a new account, the user running User Manager for Domains must be a member of either the Administrators local group or the Account Operators local group.

The following sections delve deeper into the accounts options available for your user accounts. The sections that will be addressed are

◆ User properties

◆ Group properties

◆ User Environment dialog box

◆ Logon hours properties

◆ Logon workstations

◆ Account information

◆ Dial-in information

Review each of the sections to gain a firm understanding of all the options.

User Properties

Each user has several property boxes for configuration. When you create a new user, the first dialog box, the New User dialog box, applies individual settings. The New User dialog box displays such items as the user's name and the user's password and lets you handle the changing of that password. See Figure 4.1 for an example.

> **NOTE**
>
> **Member Servers' User Manager**
> Windows NT Workstation and Windows NT Server installed as member servers have their own utility called User Manager. You use it to manage the local account database rather than the domain's account database.

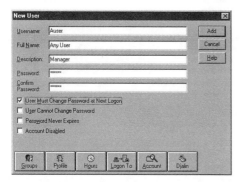

FIGURE 4.1
Entering a new user account forces a password
change at next logon.

The top section of the dialog box sets the user's name and password for accessing the network. Specifically, each setting is set as follows:

◆ **User name.** Each user has an individual user name for logging on to the network. This name must be unique within the domain. The name can be no longer than 20 characters and cannot contain "/\[]:;|=,+*?<>" as characters. The goal of enterprise networking is for each user in the enterprise to have only *one* user account, as defined in the planning chapter of this book.

◆ **Full name.** This enables you to display the user's full name. You can use the full name as a sort setting by selecting Sort by Full Name from the View menu.

◆ **Description.** This setting is copied from account to account if you use a template. It further describes a user or the user's role in the network. An example is to describe the user as an assistant or manager.

◆ **Password/Confirm password.** The password for the user can be up to 14 characters long. If the user is working at an NT-class system, the password is case sensitive.

Of the five properties at the top of the dialog box, only the description is copied from account to account. You must reenter all the other settings for a copied user.

The remaining settings in the User Properties dialog box relate to how passwords are handled. The settings are

◆ **User Must Change Password at Next Logon.** This approach forces the user to change his password when he next logs on to the network. This procedure is commonly used for new user accounts and when resetting a password for a user who has forgotten his original password.

◆ **User Cannot Change Password.** This selection is used in higher-security networks in which the users are assigned passwords for their accounts. Setting this option prevents users from changing their passwords. This option also is useful in working with temporary employees or guest accounts.

WARNING

Guard Against Selection Combination Be sure not to select the account policy Users Must Log On in Order to Change Password if you have already selected User Must Change Password at Next Logon. This combination causes the user to be prompted to change his password during the logon, but then he is informed he is not allowed to change the password at this time.

◆ **Password Never Expires.** This setting overrides the account policy of password expiration. You should use this setting only for service accounts in Windows NT or the Microsoft BackOffice products.

◆ **Account Disabled.** The Account Disabled setting prevents the user from using the account. It is used primarily when a new account is created but not yet activated. Another use is to disable an account to determine whether it should ultimately be deleted or re-enabled at a later date.

◆ **Account Locked Out.** This setting becomes active only when a user's account is locked out by the operating system for failing the Account Lockout settings. To reactivate an account, clear the check box for this setting.

> **NOTE**
>
> **Lockout Limitation** Note that only the operating system can lock out an account. To prevent an account from being used, members of the Administrators or Account Operators group can only disable an account. The Administrator account can appear to be locked out, but it will still be accessible.

Group Properties

The Group Memberships dialog box (see Figure 4.2) is where you assign a particular user to various groups. Generally, users are assigned to global groups. In this dialog box, you can assign users to global and local groups only in the same domain as the user. To assign a user to a group in a different domain, you must use that domain's local group properties.

The primary group option at the bottom of the Group Memberships dialog box is used by Services for Macintosh. You can designate a primary global group for the account. When permissions are assigned in Services for Macintosh, you can assign more rights to members of a specific primary group. Normally, you would not change this from the Domain Users global group.

> **WARNING**
>
> **Stay with Default** By default, users are assigned to the Domain Users global group. It is best not to remove any users from this group because it is used for most default security assignments.

User Environment Profile Dialog Box

The User Environment Profile dialog box (see Figure 4.3) is one of the main configuration boxes in an enterprise network.

This dialog box enables the administrator to configure the following to be centrally located:

◆ User profile path

◆ Logon script

◆ Home directory

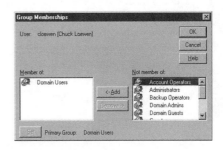

FIGURE 4.2
The Group Memberships dialog box is where you assign a particular user to various groups.

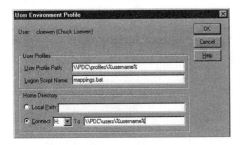

FIGURE 4.3
The User Environment Profile dialog box lets the administrator configure items to be centrally located.

> **WARNING**
>
> **Configure Roaming Profiles Separately**   Windows NT roaming profiles are exclusive to Windows NT systems. They are configured differently than Windows 95 roaming profiles. If a user is running both operating systems, he needs to configure each roaming profile separately.

> **WARNING**
>
> **Synchronize Clocks**   Any users configured for the roaming profile option should have a logon script that synchronizes its clock to the clock of the server containing the user's profile. If they are not synchronized, the user initially receives a message that the current version of the profile is newer than the server-based profile. This could lead to a loss of the configuration stored in the roaming profile.

The main purpose in centrally locating these options is to store all these items on a central server. Having users centrally store their profiles and home directories makes the process of backing up their data more manageable. Rather than install backup agents at each client machine, you can back up a centralized directory structure. In addition, Windows NT users can log on to different Windows NT workstations on the network, and their settings will follow them with roaming profiles.

User Profile Path

The User Profile Path designates the specific location on a server where the user's profile is stored. Figure 4.4 shows the typical directory structure.

As the directory structure reveals, the profile path contains the user portion of the Registry in the file NTUSER.DAT. The directory structure itself also contains a user's Start menu, desktop layout, and recently used file listing. By using this profile path, users can make their desktop and personal configuration settings follow them to whichever NT computer they use. These traveling settings include the shortcuts on the desktop but not added icons.

The most common path entered for the user profile path is \\SERVER\PROFILESHARE\%USERNAME%. Note that this location is server specific. You should attempt to locate the user's profile on a server in the same subnet as the client to limit WAN traffic.

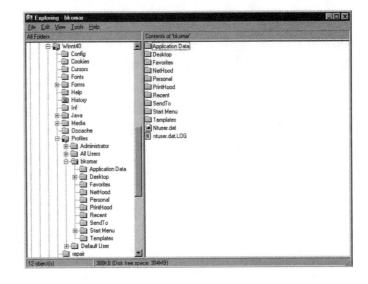

FIGURE 4.4
Here is a typical profile directory structure.

Logon Script

The logon script enables an administrator to configure common drive mappings, to run central batch files, and to configure the system. Although profiles only work on Windows NT clients, the logon script works on all versions of Microsoft Networking. When configuring a logon script, enter the name of the *.BAT or *.CMD file that you want to execute. The logon scripts are stored by default in the directory:

```
\%SYSTEMROOT%\SYSTEM32\REPL\IMPORT\SCRIPTS
```

This directory is shared as the netlogon share.

The main purpose of the logon script is to present a common network layout to all clients on the network. One of the most common errors is when two users save to the same area of the network, but one client sees the data stored as drive X: and the other calls it drive Y:. Although this does not seem to be a problem at first glance, it can lead to the following types of problems:

◆ The users can have difficulty finding common documents. One will say it is on the X: drive; the other might not even have an X: drive mapped out.

◆ Advanced features such as Object Linking and Embedding (OLE) will fail because the embedded link is path specific. Because the second user does not have a file called X:\SNAPS\PICTURE.PCX, he will not be able to see the complete document.

Some of the more common logon script commands appear in the following sample logon script:

```
@echo off
net time \\pdc /set /yes
net use h: /home
net use s: \\pdc\pubdata
call ..\smsls.bat
```

The command `net time \\PDC /set /yes` synchronizes the clock of the computer that the user is logging on to with the clock on the computer named PDC. The option `/set` changes the time of the local host, and the `/yes` option verifies that you do want the time change to take place.

The command `net use h: /home` sets drive letter H: to map out to the share defined in the Profiles tab as the user's home directory. The setting works for all Microsoft clients.

NOTE **The Logon Script**   The logon script is executed from the netlogon share of the domain controller that authenticated the user's logon. It is essential that all domain controllers have the same copy of the logon script. This is best accomplished by using the Directory Replicator service.

NOTE **Intuitive Naming**   Use an intuitive drive letter assignment in your logon scripts. Using H: to represent the home directory, P: for common programs used on the network, and S: for a shared directory assists your users in remembering where data is stored on the network.

NOTE **KiXtart95**   The Windows NT 4 Server Resource Kit includes a utility called KiXtart95, which provides more advanced logon script capabilities. Some of the enhancements include logic flow, looping, and messaging options. The version shipped with the resource kit supports Windows 95 and NT clients. Another version supports DOS and Windows for Workgroups clients. Check out the resource kit documentation for more information about using KiXtart95.

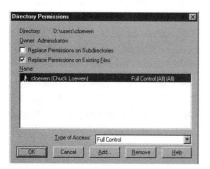

FIGURE 4.5
These permissions are automatically assigned on a user's home directory.

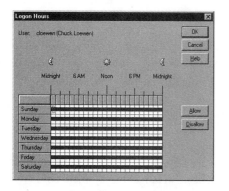

FIGURE 4.6
The Logon Hours dialog box enables the administrator to set what hours the user account is allowed access to the network.

Setting Drive Letter Manually
For Windows 95, Windows for Workgroups, and DOS clients, you must set up a logon script with the command net use x:/home in which x: is the desired drive letter for the home directory. This maps the home directory to the same drive letter as that for Windows NT clients. This setting automatically sets the drive letter only if the client is using a Windows NT client.

The command net use s: \\pdc\pubdata sets drive letter S: to point to the shared folder shared as pubdata. Using this line in a logon script ensures that every user has a consistent drive letter assigned to a share. This consistency avoids confusion for the users.

Home Directory

The home directory setting in the user's profile creates a personal directory in which the user can store data on a network server. If you configure the home directory to be connected to a network location, a Windows NT client automatically maps out the drive to the letter assigned in the dialog box.

The most common entry used for creating home directories is a common share called USERS. Assuming this share has been created, you enter that path for each home directory as \\COMPUTER\USERS\%USERNAME%. If the home directory share is located on an NTFS volume, the permissions are set as shown in Figure 4.5. Note that only the user for whom the directory is created has access to the directory. Even the administrator is not allowed to see into the directory unless he takes ownership of the directory.

The user's home directory actually maps out as a subdirectory under drive letter H: in this example. If you want it to appear as a root directory, then you must create a share for each user's home directory. Although this takes some time, it is preferable because it prevents users from scanning other user's home directories.

Logon Hours Properties

The Logon Hours dialog box (see Figure 4.6) enables the administrator to set what hours the user account is allowed access to the network. If the user attempts to log on during nonallowed hours, he sees a dialog box stating that he is not allowed to log on during these hours.

If the user is already logged on when his logon hours restriction goes into effect, he is not able to connect to any further net shares. Likewise, he is not able to use any of his current shares. He gets the dialog box shown in Figure 4.7.

If the user actually logs out, he is not allowed to log on to the network again until the next block of time when he has permission.

If the user is connecting to your network through Dial-Up Networking, you can forcibly disconnect him from the network. To do this, enable the Account Policy option to forcibly disconnect remote users from the server when logon hours expire. The user will be disconnected from the network. This option does not affect local users.

You must be careful when you set time restrictions on users. If the users work from 9 a.m. to 5 p.m., give them some leeway in their logon hours. Never set logon hours exactly the same as work hours because users will never be able to start earlier or work late at any time. The most common usage of this restriction is for employees working shifts or to prevent logons during backup times.

Logon Workstations

The Logon Workstations dialog box is used to restrict users to working at specific workstations (see Figure 4.8). You use this only when you require a user to log on to a specific computer or group of computers. Most commonly, you require this because a specific software application is installed locally on those systems. This prevents a user from logging on to a computer that does not have the software installed. You can specify up to eight computer names. They are entered as the computer name, not UNC format. For example, you type in INSTRUCTOR not \\INSTRUCTOR.

Account Information

You use the Account Information dialog box, shown in Figure 4.9, to define two things:

◆ An account's expiration date

◆ Whether the account is a global or local account

Account Expiration Date

The account expiration date can be used for term employees if the administrator knows when the account should stop being accessible. If you enter a date, the account is rendered unusable when that date is reached.

This is preferable to immediately deleting the account because you might want to ultimately assign another user to start using the same account at a later date. You also might forget to disable the account manually when the date approaches.

> **NOTE**
>
> **Set to Change**   Some administrators feel that assigning users the Full Control permissions gives them excessive rights on the network. If you share this concern, you might want to change the user permissions to Change so they cannot change the permissions on the directory.

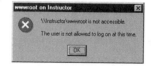

FIGURE 4.7
The Notice dialog box indicates that logon hours have expired.

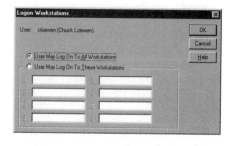

FIGURE 4.8
The Logon Workstations dialog box where you restrict users to working at specific workstations.

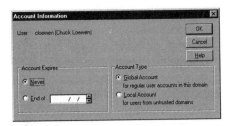

FIGURE 4.9
The Account Information dialog box where you define an account's expiration date as well as whether the account is a global or local account.

Account Type

Very rarely would you ever change the account type from a global account. If a trust relationship exists between two domains, the global account can be assigned permissions to resources in the trusting domain. In other words, a global account can cross domain trust boundaries.

A local account, on the other hand, can exist only in the domain where it is created. It is not available in a trusting domain for assignment of permissions. You use the local account to create an account and password that a user from a non-trusted domain could use to access local resources.

A common usage, for example, might be granting printer access to users in a non-trusted domain. If they use the account THEM with password XYZZY, this matches the local account name and password that you set up to give them access to the printer.

Dial-In Information

The Dial-In Information dialog box enables the administrator to determine which users are granted dial-in access to the network (see Figure 4.10). If the user can dial in to connect, you have several options for implementing call-back security.

If you select No Call Back, the user immediately is able to use network resources. This option is commonly used in low-security networks and for users working out of hotel rooms.

If you use Set By Caller, the user is prompted to enter the phone number where he is located; the Remote Access Server calls him back at that number. This option is most commonly implemented when the user calls in from various offices with direct phone lines. If extensions are involved, however, you cannot set this feature. This feature is commonly used in medium-security networks.

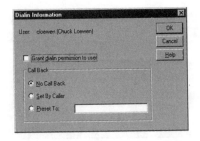

FIGURE 4.10
The Dial-In Information dialog box enables the administrator to determine which users are granted dial-in access to the network.

If Preset To is configured, the user dials in to the office network. Upon connecting, the line is dropped and the user is called back at a predefined phone number. Many companies with people who work at home use this option so the bulk of the phone charges are carried by the office. This provides a higher security level than the other options because the user must be located at a specific phone number for a full transaction to take place.

To create a sample user name John Smith, and to set several of the
options just discussed, perform the tasks outlined in Step by
Step 4.1.

STEP BY STEP

4.1 Creating a Sample User

1. Start the User Manager for Domains.

2. From the User menu, select New User.

3. Create a user with the name _John Smith. The account
   should have the User Must Change Password at Next
   Logon option enabled.

4. In the User Environment Profile dialog box, make the following two entries:

   - The User Profile Path should be \\SERVER\
     PROFILES\%USERNAME%.

   - The home directory should be entered in Connect
     To as \\SERVER\USERS\%USERNAME%.

5. In the Logon Hours dialog box, set the logon hours to
   Mondays through Fridays from 8 a.m. to 6 p.m.

6. In the Logon Workstations dialog box, set the allowed
   workstations to Comp1, Comp2, Instructor, and Server.

7. In the Account Information dialog box, set the account
   expiration date to December 31, 1999.

   An NT user account, with specific settings, has now been
   created and established.

Defining Your Account Policy

Before you start implementing your user accounts, one of the most
important policies to set is your account policy. This policy affects
every account in the domain; there is no picking and choosing
which accounts are affected. The account policies define how

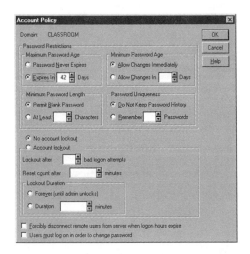

FIGURE 4.11
The Account Policy dialog box; the account policy affects every account in the domain.

password changes are handled and how to react if a user improperly enters his password (see Figure 4.11).

The password portion of the Account Policy dialog box determines your rules for password security. Options within the dialog box include

◆ Maximum password age

◆ Minimum password age

◆ Minimum password length

◆ Password uniqueness

◆ Account lockout

◆ Lockout duration

◆ Forcibly disconnect remote users from server when logon hours expire

◆ User must log on in order to change password

The Maximum Password Age determines the length of time a user can use his current password before the system prompts him to change it. Depending on the level of security you want on your network, Table 4.1 presents some suggested guidelines.

TABLE 4.1

SUGGESTED PASSWORD AGES

Type of Network Password Age	Suggested Maximum
Low security	No password expire required
Medium security	45–90 days
High security	14–45 days

The Minimum Password Age prevents the user from performing a quick change of his password. In other words, if the system tells a user to change his password, this option prevents him from immediately changing it back to his original password. This encourages the user to switch over to a brand-new password. In a high-security network, you could set the Minimum Password Age to one day less than the Maximum Password Age.

The Minimum Password Length designates the fewest number of characters allowed in a password. Some industry guidelines for password lengths are outlined in Table 4.2.

TABLE 4.2

SUGGESTED PASSWORD LENGTHS

Type of Network Length	Suggested Password
Low security	0–6 characters
Medium security	6–8 characters
High security	8–14 characters

Password Uniqueness determines how often a user can reuse a password. The time span for reuse is determined by a combination of the Minimum and Maximum Password Ages.

WARNING

Don't Set Age Too Low Be very careful in your implementation of password ages. If you set the age too short, you increase the number of help desk calls for lost passwords.

RESTRICTING PASSWORDS FURTHER

Service Pack 2 for Windows NT 4 introduced a new security DLL named PASSFILT.DLL that allows the administrator to further restrict passwords. Under this new security DLL, users must use passwords that meet the following requirements:

- Passwords must be at least six characters long.
- Passwords cannot contain your user name or any part of the user's full name.
- Passwords must contain three of the following four types of characters:
  - English uppercase letters
  - English lowercase letters
  - Numbers 0–9
  - Special characters such as punctuation

Account Lockout sets how many chances a user gets before the operating system locks out the account. It also sets how frequently the operating system resets the bad logon attempt counter. Be sure to keep the number of minutes between resets low. The account lockout counter increases by one each time an incorrect password is entered for a user. When the lockout counter reaches the threshold you set, the account is locked out and must be reset by an administrator. You should reset the account lockout counter frequently so that bad logon attempts over a period of time do not cause the account to be locked out.

Lockout Duration determines how long the account remains locked out. It is advisable to leave this setting at Forever. This means an administrator or account operator has to reset the account to grant access to the network. This helps the administrator keep track of bad logon attempts and potential attacks on the network.

If you select Forcibly Disconnect Remote Users from Server when Logon Hours Expire, dial-in users lose their connection when their logon hours expire. This setting does not affect users directly logged on to the network.

If you select Users Must Log On in Order to Change Password, users can change their passwords only when logged on to the network. Be cautious when using this setting. If you also set the user property User Must Change Password at Next Logon, users cannot change their passwords *or* log on to the network. You have set up an endless circle in which they must change their password to log on but they must log on to change their password.

Template Accounts

As an administrator, you should consider creating template accounts for the various types of users that you create regularly. Templates enable you to quickly create new user accounts when required. These template accounts should be disabled to prevent their use for network access.

To use template accounts to your advantage, select the preferred template in User Manager for Domains and select Copy from the User menu (or press F8). This copies the template with all properties except the following:

◆ User name

◆ Full Name

◆ Password

◆ Confirm password

Template accounts also work best when you use the %USERNAME% environment variable for both the User Profile Path and the Home Directory. This also enables the option User Must Change Password at Next Logon while disabling the Accounts Disabled box in the User Properties dialog box.

ADDUSERS.EXE

The resource kit includes a utility called ADDUSERS.EXE that lets you add users in batch mode from a comma-separated value file. The syntax of this command is

```
addusers [\\computername] {/c¦/d¦/e} filename /s:x
```

\\computername is the name of the computer to which you want to add the users and groups.

/c signifies that you want to create the users, global groups, and local groups specified in filename.

/d signifies that you want to dump all the accounts, global groups, and local groups to the file filename. This does not dump the passwords of the users.

/e signifies that you want to erase the accounts, global groups, and local groups specified in filename.

/s:x sets the separator character that you want to use. If not specified, it defaults to the comma character.

The syntax of the text file used for the input and output of the addusers command is

```
[Users]
<User Name>, <Full Name>, <Password>, <Home Drive>,
<Home Path>, <Profile>, <Script>
[Global]
<Global Group Name>, <Comment>, <Username>,...
[Local]
<Local Group Name>, <Comment>, <Username>,...
```

NOTE

Setting Priorities Simultaneously
If you want to implement the same account property change for a group of existing accounts, select all the accounts by holding down the Ctrl key and clicking each account you want to change. Then, select Properties from the User menu. This enables you to change the properties of multiple users simultaneously. See Figure 4.12 for an example of setting multiple account properties.

FIGURE 4.12
Setting multiple account properties.

Managing Global and Local Groups

The use of global and local groups in an enterprise Windows NT environment is one of the key concepts tested in the exam. This section looks into the following areas:

◆ Differences between global and local groups

◆ Creation of global groups

◆ Built-in global groups

◆ Creation of local groups

◆ Built-in local groups

◆ Special groups

◆ Management of global and local groups in a multidomain environment

Differences Between Global and Local Groups

One of the most difficult enterprise technology topics to understand is the difference between global and local groups. In an enterprise network, the acronym AGLP defines the use of global and local groups.

AGLP stands for Accounts, Global groups, Local groups, Permissions. When you want to assign permissions to any resource, you should follow a few simple rules. All user accounts are placed into global groups; global groups get assigned into local groups. The local groups have the resources and permissions assigned to them. To see an example of how this applies, check out the following steps:

1. Make sure user accounts exist for each user who needs access to the resource.

2. Assign all user accounts to a common global group. If the users are spread across multiple domains, you have to create a global group in each domain. Global groups can contain users only from the domain in which they are located.

3. Assign the global groups from each domain to a local group in the domain where the resource exists. If the resource is on a

Windows NT domain controller, the local group is created on a domain controller. If the resource is on a Windows NT workstation or Windows NT member server, the local group is created on that system's local account database.

4. Assign necessary permissions to the local group.

The toughest part of working with global and local groups is realizing that you use global groups simply for putting together a set of users who have a common interest. That could include all the people in the accounting department, all the users who need to use a color laser printer, or all the people who serve as editors of the company's policies manual.

Local groups are the only groups that should be assigned permissions. When assigning local groups permissions, the administrator should always determine whether there is an existing local group with the appropriate permissions. If you want to grant a user the capability to create new users or to change group memberships, for example, the account operators local group might already have these permissions. There would be no reason to create a new local group to perform these tasks.

Creation of Global Groups

You create global groups with the User Manager for Domains utility. When a global group is created, it is initially written to the SAM database on the Primary Domain Controller. It is then synchronized with the Backup Domain Controllers during the synchronization process. The global groups are accessible from any domain controller. Perform the tasks outlined in Step by Step 4.2 to create a global group.

STEP BY STEP

4.2 Creating a Global Group

1. Select User | New Global Group from the User Manager for Domains menu.

continues

> **NOTE**
>
> **Limitless Group Membership** A user can be a member of any number of global groups. For example, he can be a member of the accounting global group and also of the managers global group.

> **NOTE**
>
> **Prechoosing** You can prechoose the members of a new global group by Ctrl-clicking each member in the User Manager for Domains and then creating the new global group. This is why the user you have selected in User Manager for Domains is often made a member of any new global groups that you create.

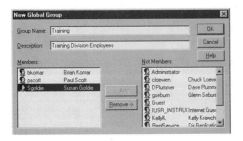

FIGURE 4.13
The New Global Group dialog box enables you to add and remove users from the current domain as members of the global group.

continued

2. The New Global Group dialog box appears (see Figure 4.13). This dialog box enables you to add and remove users from the current domain as members of the global group.

3. After you have added all users, click OK to complete the creation of the global group.

Built-In Global Groups

When you first install an NT domain, there are three predefined global groups, as listed in Table 4.3.

TABLE 4.3

INITIAL GLOBAL GROUP MEMBERSHIPS

Global Group	*Initial Membership*
Domain Admins	Administrator
Domain Guests	Guest
Domain Users	All user accounts except for Guest

Creation of Local Groups

You create local groups when you don't have an existing local group with the appropriate permissions to access a resource. Depending on the access levels required for each resource, you might need multiple local groups to best define the access levels required.

To create a new local group, select User | New Local Group from the menu of User Manager for Domains or User Manager. This displays the New Local Group dialog box (see Figure 4.14).

To add a global group to the local group, click Add in the New Local Group dialog box. This brings up a list of global groups and global accounts that could be made members of the local group. Note that the drop-down list at the top enables you to add global accounts and global groups from trusted domains to the local group.

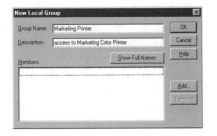

FIGURE 4.14
The New Local Group dialog box.

Built-In Local Groups

The built-in groups that you find will vary, depending on what version of Windows NT you are running: Windows NT workstation, Windows NT member servers, or Windows NT domain controllers.

Local groups found only on domain controllers include

◆ Account Operators

◆ Print Operators

◆ Server Operators

The local group found only on Windows NT workstations or member servers is the Power Users group.

Local groups found on all Windows NT systems include

◆ Administrators

◆ Backup Operators

◆ Guests

◆ Replicator

◆ Users

The Account Operators local group has the capability to create and manage users and groups within the domain. They cannot modify membership in the following groups:

◆ Administrators

◆ Account Operators

◆ Backup Operators

◆ Print Operators

◆ Server Operators

◆ Domain Admins

If Account Operators were able to modify the membership of these groups, they ultimately could increase their own rights on the network beyond those of an Account Operator. Only administrators can change the membership of these groups. Account Operators cannot modify users who are members of the operator groups, either.

NOTE **Assigning Local Group to a Resource on a Domain Controller**   If you want to assign the local group to a resource on a domain controller, you need to add the local group to the domain account database using User Manager for Domains. If the resource is on a Windows NT workstation or a Windows NT member server, you must add the local group to the local account database of that computer.

NOTE **"Shortcut" Local Group Creation**
You do not have to physically visit the Windows NT workstation or Windows NT member server to create the new local group. All you have to do is choose Select Domain from the User menu and type in the NetBIOS name of the computer where you want to create the local group. This opens that computer's SAM database for you to create the new local group. This shortcut is possible because the Domain Admins group from the domain was automatically added to the Administrators local group of the Windows NT workstation computer when it joined the domain.

NOTE

Apply Only Global Groups to Local Groups   Use only global groups as members of local groups. Although it is possible to add a user directly to a local group, it is not desirable in an enterprise network. The use of global groups helps greatly as a network grows from a single-domain model to a multidomain model. It also facilitates the management of the enterprise network.

NOTE

Add the Domain Admins Global Group   If your network is set up in a Master Domain Model, it is a good idea to add the Domain Admins global group from the Master Domain to each Resource Domain's Administrators local group. This gives any member of the Domain Admins in the Master Domain the capability to manage the entire enterprise network.

WARNING

Administration Rights   Any time a Windows NT workstation or Windows NT member server is added to a domain, the Domain Admins group from the domain they have joined is automatically added to the local group Administrators of the joining system. This means any members of the domain's Domain Admins group can administer the system.

The Print Operators group can create new printers in the domain and maintain existing printers. These maintenance activities include sharing printers and managing all the jobs in a printer queue.

Members of the Server Operators group are able to create shared directories on a domain controller. Other capabilities include

◆ Locking or unlocking the server console

◆ Formatting a disk on a server

◆ Backing up and restoring a file to a server

◆ Managing all facets of printing

◆ Shutting down servers

◆ Modifying the system date and time

The Power Users group basically combines the rights of the Account Operators, Print Operators, and Server Operators groups. Remember that this group exists only on Windows NT workstations and Windows NT member servers.

The Administrators group appears on all Windows NT-class computers. This group can manage any and all aspects of the Windows NT domain. The initial membership in the Administrators group is the precreated Administrator account and the Domain Admins global group.

The Backup Operators local group's members have the right to back up and restore any files on the system. This right supersedes any permissions assigned to these files and directories. Backup Operators also can shut down a server.

The Guests local group provides the capability to grant guests of the domain access to specific resources. The initial membership in the Guests local group is the Domain Guests global group from the domain.

The Replicator group is used by the Directory Replicator service. Membership in this group enables a member to be involved in the process of maintaining a directory structure and its contents on multiple domain controllers.

The Users local group contains the global group Domain Users. You will most often use this group when increasing the security on a Windows NT domain. Rather than keep the default share and NTFS permissions, use the local group Users instead of Everyone.

Special Groups

In addition to the predefined local and global groups preinstalled in Windows NT 4, some special groups exist in Windows NT. Membership in these groups is not based as much on user names as on how the user is functioning on the network.

The special groups implemented in Windows NT 4 are

◆ **Everyone.** The Everyone group includes absolutely everyone who can connect to your network. The Everyone group includes users who are not defined in the Accounts database. Use this group wisely.

◆ **Creator/Owner.** The Creator/Owner group applies to every object created in Windows NT. The user or the group (the case of any member of Administrators) that creates an object is automatically a member of the Creator/Owner group. If you take ownership of a file or directory, you are automatically a member of the Creator/Owner group. The most common use of the Creator/Owner group is implementing printer security. The default print permissions give Creator/Owner members the capability to manage documents. You can reorder your jobs, pause your jobs, or delete your jobs in the queue. You cannot do this to anyone else's jobs in the queue.

◆ **Network.** Network group membership is based on whether the user is connecting remotely to a resource. If data is handled remotely on another Windows networking system, assigning permissions to the Network group affects any remote users working with that data. It does not affect local users of the data.

◆ **Interactive.** Interactive group membership is based on whether the user is sitting locally at the server where the data is stored. If the data is stored on a local drive, assigned permissions to the Interactive group affect any users working with that data.

◆ **System.** This special group never includes users. It refers to the Windows NT operating system itself when it has to access resources on the network.

Management of Global and Local Groups in a Multidomain Environment

The real art and functionality of using global and local groups emerges in a multidomain environment. When working with groups across trust relationships, the following guidelines are useful:

◆ Always gather users into global groups. Remember that global groups can contain user accounts only from the same domain. You might have to create the same named global group in multiple domains.

◆ If you have multiple account domains, use the same name for a global group that has the same types of members. Remember that when multiple domains are involved, the group name is referred to as DOMAIN\GROUP.

◆ Before the global groups are created, determine whether an existing local group meets your needs. There is no sense in creating duplicate local groups.

◆ Remember that the local group must be created where the resource is located. If the resource is on a domain controller, create the local group in the Domain Account database. If the resource is on a Windows NT workstation or Windows NT member server, you must create the group in that system's local account database.

◆ Be sure to set the permissions for a resource before you make the global groups a member of the local group assigned to the resource. That way, security is set for the resource.

To test yourself on applying global and local group memberships, see the exercises at the end of the chapter.

EXAM TIP

Group Implementation Question, Domains Whenever you are faced with a group implementation question, remember that global groups can contain user accounts only from the same domain. If any of the suggested answers places users from one domain into a global group in another domain, you can eliminate the answer as a possible correct answer.

EXAM TIP

Group Combinations Remember that the only allowable group within a group membership is that of a global group as a member of a local group. Any other combinations are impossible.

EXAM TIP

Trust Relationship Questions Remember that in trust relationship questions, only global groups from the trusted domain can be members of local groups in the trusting domain. Global groups cannot cross domain boundaries in the other direction.

User Rights

Typically, Windows NT security is based on protecting a specific object found in Windows NT. User rights define security when the activity to be performed by a user cannot be associated with one particular object. Several predefined user rights can grant these nondiscretionary levels of access to the system. An example is the capability to log on to a system or to shut down the system. The User Rights policy is implemented through the User Manager for Domain's User Rights option in the Policy menu (see Figure 4.15).

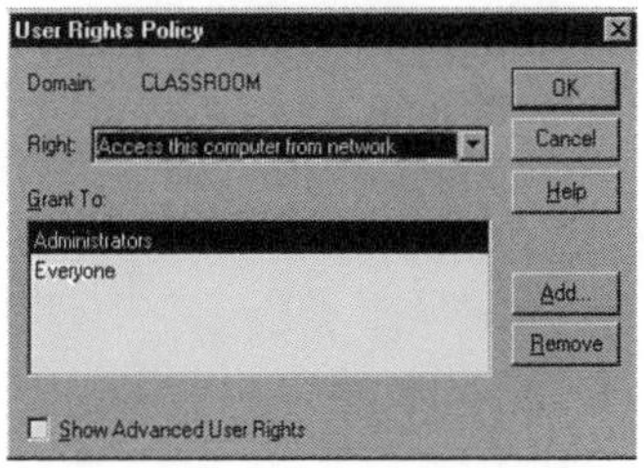

FIGURE 4.15
The User Rights Policy dialog box.

The Default User Rights

User rights are automatically implemented in Windows NT 4. The actual user rights are stored in the SAM account database, which is in the `Security` hive of the `HKEY_LOCAL_MACHINE` subtree in the Registry. Table 4.4 describes each of the basic and advanced user rights as defined in Windows NT Workstation and Windows NT Server.

> **NOTE**
>
> **Set Rights for NT 4** In Windows NT 4, the set of user rights is defined by the system and cannot be modified. There is talk that future versions of Windows NT will allow developers to define new user rights applicable to their applications.

TABLE 4.4

USER RIGHTS ASSIGNMENTS IN WINDOWS NT 4

User Right	This Right Allows	Initially Assigned to
Access this computer from the network	Those assigned this right can connect to the computer through the network.	Administrators, Everyone, Power Users*
Act as part of the operating system	Allows a process to perform as a secure, trusted part of the operating system. An example of this is the Microsoft Exchange 5.0 Server Service account. It requires this right to handle POP3 mail requests from clients.	(None)
Add workstations to the domain	Allows a user to add workstations to the domain so that it can recognize the domain's user and global accounts.	None, but this is a predefined right for all members of the Administrators and Server Operators local groups that cannot be revoked

continues

TABLE 4.4	*continued*

USER RIGHTS ASSIGNMENTS IN WINDOWS NT 4

User Right	*This Right Allows*	*Initially Assigned to*
Backup files and directories	Allows a user to back up files and directories on the computer, no matter what their file and directory permissions are.	Administrators, Backup Operators, and Server Operators
Bypass traverse checking	Allows a user to change directories and traverse the directory structure, even if the user has no permissions for the traversed directory structures.	Everyone
Change system time	Allows a user to set the time of the computer's internal clock.	Administrators, Server Operators, Power Users*
Create a pagefile	Determines which users are able to create a pagefile for the Virtual Memory Manager to use.	Administrators
Create a token object	Gives the right to create access tokens.	None; this is a predefined right of the Local Security Authority
Create permanent shared objects	Allows a user to create special shared objects, such as \\DEVICE, that are used within Windows NT. This has nothing to do with creating file or printer shares.	(None)
Debug programs	Allows a user to debug various low-level objects such as threads.	Administrators
Force shutdown from a remote system	This right is not currently implemented in Windows NT 4 but has been reserved for future use.	Administrators, Server Operators, Power Users*
Generate security audits	Allows a process to generate security audit logs.	(None)

User Right	This Right Allows	Initially Assigned to
Increase quotas	This right is not currently implemented in Windows NT 4 but has been reserved for future use. Products such as Disk Quota Manager might use this right.	Administrators
Increase scheduling priority	Allows a user to boost the execution priority of a process using the Task Manager.	Administrators, Power Users*
Load and unload device drivers	Allows a user to install and remove device drivers.	Administrators
Lock pages in memory	Allows a user to lock pages in memory so the pages cannot be paged out to the paging file.	(None)
Log on as a batch job	This right is not currently implemented in Windows NT 4 but has been reserved for future use.	(None)
Log on as a service	Allows a process to register with the systems as a service. This right is automatically granted to any account set up as a service account.	(None)
Log on locally	Allows users to log on to the system by typing their user names and passwords into the User Authentication dialog box.	Account Operators, Administrators, Backup Operators, Everyone, Print Operators, Server Operators, Power Users*, Guests*, Users*
Manage auditing and security log	Allows a user to specify which files, groups, and printers to audit. This does not allow the user to change the audit policy, only to work within the framework defined by a member of the Administrators group. This right also allows the user to view and to clear the security log in the Event Viewer.	Administrators

continues

TABLE 4.4	*continued*

USER RIGHTS ASSIGNMENTS IN WINDOWS NT 4

User Right	*This Right Allows*	*Initially Assigned to*
Modify firmware environment variables	Allows a user to modify system environment variables stored in nonvolatile RAM on RISC-based systems.	Administrators
Profile single process	Allows a user to performance sample a process.	Administrators, Power Users*
Profile system performance	Allows a user to performance sample a computer.	Administrators
Replace a process-level token	The system uses this right to modify a process's security access token. This is used by the process of impersonation.	(None)
Restore files and directories	Allows a user to restore backed-up files and directories no matter what the permissions are on these files and directories.	Administrators, Backup Operators, Server Operators
Shut down the system	Allows a user to shut down the Windows NT computer system.	Account Operators, Administrators, Backup Operators, Print Operators, Server Operators, Everyone*, Users*, Power Users*
Take ownership of files or other objects	Allows users to take ownership of any object on the computer, even if they do not have sufficient permissions to access the object.	Administrators

*Only in Windows NT Workstation.

Modifying User Rights

When modifying user rights, there are generally two issues:

◆ Can I further restrict user rights?

◆ When should I modify user rights?

You generally do not want to adjust the default user rights. Changing the user rights could possibly render the server unusable. There are some suggested guidelines to further secure your system's user rights. Two of the rights that have been granted default excess rights are

◆ **Log on locally.** The default membership includes the Everyone and Guest groups on Windows NT Workstation. It is recommended that you remove these two groups and replace them with the Users local group from the local account database. Be sure that the domain's Domain Users global group is a member of the Users local group.

◆ **Shut down the system.** The default membership in Windows NT Workstation includes the Everyone group. This group should not be assigned this privilege. You might also want to consider revoking this right from the Everyone group if you want all systems to be left running during the night.

WARNING

Limited Prevention Remember, revoking the right to shut down a computer only prevents the user from selecting Shutdown from the Shut Down Windows dialog box. This does not prevent users from turning off the power to the computer. One of the key security concerns for a server is making sure the server itself is located in a secure location such that only people with appropriate security clearance can actually physically touch the server.

Example: Application of User Rights When Implementing the Directory Replication Service

As discussed in previous chapters, the Directory Replication service requires a service account, which it uses to perform its tasks of maintaining a consistent netlogon share on all domain controllers. To ensure that the service account is configured properly while implementing the user account and group properties, review the following steps to see an example of the importance of user management. You follow the tasks outlined in Step by Step 4.3 to configure the Directory Replication service with a service account.

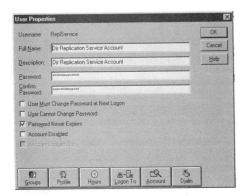

FIGURE 4.16

Setting up the Directory Replicator service account in User Manager for Domains.

FIGURE 4.17

Configuring the Directory Replicator service to use your precreated service account.

NOTE

Dynamic Configuration When you want to configure all your domain controllers to participate in directory replication, it is best to do it centrally by using the Server Manager utility. You can manage the services for each server using this utility rather than make these changes at each primary and backup domain controller.

STEP BY STEP

4.3 Creating a Service Account for Directory Replication

1. Create an account in the User Manager for Domains to be used as the service account.

2. Set the account properties as shown in Figure 4.16. Be sure to deselect User Must Change Password at Next Logon and to select Password Never Expires. All service accounts should be set this way so they are never prompted to change their passwords.

3. Make the user a member of the Replicator local group and the Backup Operators group. These groups grant the service account the necessary rights to perform its predetermined tasks. The Replicator local group allows the account to perform the directory replication task. The Backup Operators group allows the account to read all files in the REPL$\SCRIPTS directory of the export server, no matter what the permissions are on the share. It also allows this account to write these files to the netlogon share of all import servers, no matter what permissions exist on these directories.

4. From the Policies menu, select User Rights. Grant the newly created account the Log On as a Service user right. This right is displayed only when you select the Show Advanced User Rights check box.

5. Open Control Panel.

6. Open the Service applet.

7. From the list of services, select the Directory Replicator service and click the Startup button.

8. Fill in the dialog box as shown in Figure 4.17. Change the startup type to Automatic. Also be sure to change the Log On As option to use the account you have set up. Use the … button to select the account name from the list, as it must be the full domain\user name. Finally, enter the password you set for the account.

9. Click Start to start the service. The next time you restart the system, the service will start automatically due to the Automatic start setting.

Once you complete all of these steps, you have fully configured the directory replication process. Refer to Chapter 3, "Installing and Configuring Windows NT in the Enterprise," for additional information on the use and functionality of the directory replicator service.

User and Group Management

The chapter up to this point has offered a review of all the options available in user and group management. The exam does not focus a great deal on the actual steps required; however, the process is a foundation for all other procedures within your enterprise environment. Ensure that you fully understand the AGLP procedure; remember that accounts are placed into global groups, global groups are placed into local groups, and the local groups have the resource and permissions assigned to them.

Building on your user and group management, using system policies and user profiles can be an excellent administrative tool.

CREATING AND MANAGING SYSTEM POLICIES AND USER PROFILES

Create and manage policies and profiles for various situations. Policies and profiles include local user profiles, roaming user profiles, and system policies.

System policies and user profiles assist in the centralization of management in a Windows NT enterprise network. System policies help an administrator implement common Registry settings across the enterprise. User profiles store the user portion of the Registry. You can implement profiles as either local or roaming. A roaming profile enables users to make the user portion of their configuration

> **NOTE**
>
> **Move a Shortcut**   Most types of software place their shortcuts into the All Users directory structure if installed by the Administrator. If the software was installed by a user not belonging to the Domain Admins global group, you can move the shortcut to the All Users directory structure so it will be available to all users of the local system.

> **NOTE**
>
> **Add to the Default User Directory Structure**   If you want specific shortcuts on the desktop or special items in the Start menu, add the necessary shortcuts to the Default User directory structure. Any users who log on to the system inherit this directory structure if they are using local profiles and logging on for the first time.

> **NOTE**
>
> **ODBC Driver Settings**   ODBC driver settings are stored in user profiles. If users connect to an ODBC database source from various computers and with different levels of security, using roaming profiles assists in reducing the amount of configuration required.

follow them wherever they log on in the Windows NT network. The main topics discussed in this section are as follows:

◆ User profiles—local profiles versus roaming profiles

◆ System policies

Local Profiles Versus Roaming Profiles

Whenever a user logs on to a system, he creates a local profile on that system. The local profile is implemented as a set of directory structures (see Figure 4.18). This directory structure includes the Desktop folder and the Start Menu folder. The user portion of the Registry is stored in the file NTUSER.DAT.

When a user logs on to the network, his desktop and Start menu are based on the local system he is logging on to. The desktop is based on the user's Profiles directory and the All Users directory. The same is true for the Start Menu directory.

The problem with local profiles is that every workstation you log on to has its own version of the local profile. You must set user configuration settings at each workstation you log on to.

To overcome this problem, implement roaming profiles. Roaming profiles download the user portion of the Registry from a designated system to the system that the user is currently logged on to. Any changes to the settings are copied back to the central location so they can be retrieved at the next workstation they log on to.

The following three subsections cover roaming profiles in greater detail.

FIGURE 4.18
The local profile is implemented as a set of directory structures.

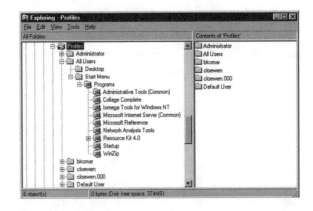

Configuring Roaming Profiles in Windows NT

If you want to configure a user account to use a roaming profile, the first thing to do is set the profile path in the User Manager for Domains to that account. If you are configuring a block of users, the best method is to do a group property change. First, select all the users you want to have roaming profiles; then, select Properties from the User menu. See Figure 4.19 for the necessary settings.

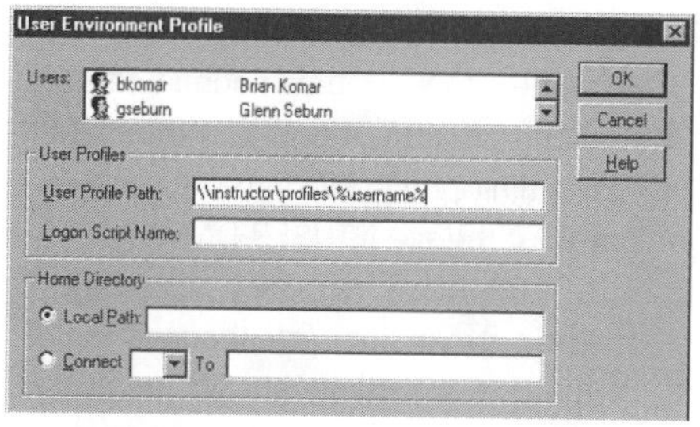

The most common setting is to share a directory with a share name such as profiles. It should allow the local group Users the permission of Full Control. With this share, you can set the user's profile path to \\SERVER\SHARE\%USERNAME%. The next time the user logs on, his profile information can be saved to this profile directory.

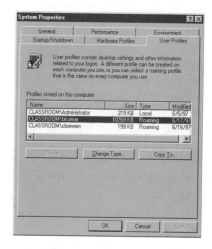

FIGURE 4.19
Use of %USERNAME% in the profile path.

Tuning Roaming Profiles

An administrator can determine whether the user profiles stored on the local system are roaming or local profiles. You view the User Profiles tab in the System Properties dialog box in the Control Panel (see Figure 4.20).

The dialog box shows all the profiles currently stored on the system and whether they are roaming or local profiles. You can change the profile between a roaming and local profile by clicking Change Type. This opens the Change Type dialog box, as shown in Figure 4.21.

You also use this dialog box also to configure how to handle roaming profiles when the user logs on to the network over a slow WAN link. This is an extremely useful setting for laptop users who log on to the enterprise network from various locations. Remember that the roaming profile is stored on a specific server, even though the user can be authenticated on any domain controller within the domain.

For roaming profiles to work without user intervention, synchronize all workstation clocks with the domain controller that will be storing the user profile. This prevents the local version of the profile from showing a more recent date/time stamp than the version stored on the server.

Implementing Roaming Profiles in Windows 95

Windows 95 users also can have roaming profiles configured so their user-based configurations can follow them from workstation to

FIGURE 4.20
The User Profiles tab in the System Properties dialog box.

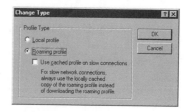

FIGURE 4.21
You change a profile between local and roaming in the Change Type dialog box.

NOTE **NTUSER.MAN** You can configure a roaming profile to become a mandatory roaming profile by changing the name of the file NTUSER.DAT to NTUSER.MAN. This makes the profile a read-only version. Any changes made to the user's settings are not saved to the central server location. The next time the user logs on to the network, the profile is reset to the original settings. You can make this change when you want a group of users to share the same roaming profile.

NOTE **Store Profiles on a Different Server** You do not have to store all the profiles on the same server. Put the profile for each user on the server nearest to that user. This arrangement helps reduce WAN traffic because profiles can grow quite large if a lot of data is stored in the user's profile directory.

NOTE **Make the User Profile Path Setting in Template Accounts** If you plan to use roaming profiles, make the User Profile Path a setting in all your template accounts. It might be best to set up template accounts based on server proximity so that the nearest server houses the user's roaming profile.

workstation. Implementing roaming profiles in Windows 95 differs from Windows NT in the following ways:

◆ Separate user profiles are not implemented automatically in Windows 95 as they are in Windows NT.

◆ The user portion of the Registry is saved in the file USER.DAT in Windows 95, whereas it is stored in NTUSER.DAT in Windows NT.

◆ The User Profile Path setting in the user's properties has no effect on Windows 95 clients. Their roaming profile information is stored in their Windows NT home directory.

To change Windows 95 from using shared user profiles to using separate profiles, perform the tasks in Step by Step 4.4.

STEP BY STEP

4.4 Configuring User Profiles in Windows 95

1. Open the Control Panel.

2. Open the Password icon in the Control Panel.

3. Select the User Profile tab. You must change the setting to Users Can Customize Their Preferences and Desktop Settings. Be sure to also enable the options to Include Desktop Icons and Network Neighborhood Contents in User Settings and Include Start Menu and Program Groups in User Settings.

4. Restart the computer for this change to take effect.

Users who log on for the first time are informed that they have not logged on to this computer before. They are asked whether they want to maintain this user's settings in their own personal profile.

This profile change in configuration causes the My Briefcase desktop icon to change to a folder icon. Each user must create a new instance of the briefcase.

System Policies

System policies help the network administrator restrict what configuration changes the user can make to his profile. By combining roaming profiles and system policies, the administrator does not force a consistent desktop on the users, but he can control what the user can do to that desktop. The administrator can ensure that the user cannot modify certain settings.

System policies work much like a merge operation. You can think of system policies as a copy of your Registry. When you log on to the network and the NTCONFIG.POL file exists on the domain controller, it merges its settings into your Registry, changing your Registry settings as indicated in the system policy.

You implement system policies using the System Policy Editor. The System Policy Editor is automatically installed with any Windows NT domain controller. You can configure system policies to

◆ Implement defaults for hardware configuration—for all computers using the profile or for a specific machine.

◆ Restrict changing specific parameters that affect the hardware configuration of the participating system.

◆ Set defaults for all users in the areas of the personal settings that they can configure.

◆ Restrict users from changing specific areas of their configuration to prevent tampering with the system. An example is disabling all Registry editing tools for a specific user.

◆ Apply all defaults and restrictions on a group level rather than a user level.

The rest of this chapter explores system policies and how you can use them to manage your system.

Implementing System Policies

To create computer, user, and group policies, you must use the System Policy Editor. The System Policy Editor is automatically installed on all domain controllers in the Administrative Tools group of the Start menu. When you create a new policy file, it presents you with two default icons within the policy (see Figure 4.22).

NOTE

Mix Roaming Profiles and System Policies You can only use roaming profiles to limit what users can do if you implement Mandatory Profiles. If you want to allow users to modify some of their personal settings, but you want to restrict other areas, you must implement a mix of roaming profiles and system policies.

NOTE

"Re-Log On" to Activate Some Settings Some settings that you can configure do not take effect until the next time you log on to the network. This happens when the event that the policy is set for has already passed. An example is a policy creating a Logon Banner dialog box.

NOTE

System Policy Editor Uses You can also use the System Policy Editor to change settings in the Registry of the system it is being executed on. Many times, it is easier to use the System Policy Editor because it has a better interface for finding common restrictions you might want to place on a Windows NT workstation.

FIGURE 4.22
The System Policy Editor with two default icons.

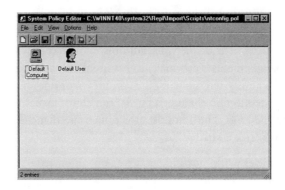

These two default icons represent the following:

◆ Default Computer

◆ Default User

You use Default Computer to configure all machine-specific settings. All property changes within this section affect the HKEY_LOCAL_MACHINE subtree of the Registry. Default Computer applies to any client that uses the policy but does not have a specific machine entry created for itself in the policy file.

Default User specifies default policy settings for all users who will use the policy. Default User affects the HKEY_CURRENT_USER subtree of the Registry. If the user is configured to use a roaming profile, this information is stored in the centralized version of NTUSER.DAT in the profile directory.

Creating a New System Policy

Creating a system policy is outlined in Step by Step 4.5.

NOTE

Windows 95 System Policy Editor The Windows NT System Policy Editor does include a template file called WINDOWS.ADM that is supposed to work with Windows 95 system policies. The currently shipped version does not work with Windows 95 system policies. If you need to work with Windows 95 system policies, be sure to perform all creation and editing using only the Windows 95 System Policy Editor. Although this problem might be fixed in future updates, it is still better to use the Windows 95 System Policy Editor for setting Windows 95 policies because it offers greater flexibility.

STEP BY STEP

4.5 Creating a System Policy

1. From the Start menu, choose Programs | Administrative Tools (Common) | System Policy Editor.

---

2. Verify that the proper template files are loaded by choosing Policy Template from the Options menu. The default templates that should be loaded are

   - C:\%WINNTROOT%\INF\COMMON.ADM

   - C:\%WINNTROOT%\INF\WINNT.ADM

3. From the File menu, select New Policy.

4. To adjust settings affecting the HKEY_LOCAL_MACHINE sub-tree, double-click the Default Computer icon. To adjust settings affecting each user's HKEY_CURRENT_USER subtree in the Registry, double-click the Default User icon.

5. After you make all the setting changes, you must save the file. The location where all Windows NT clients will look for the file is the netlogon share of the domain controller that authenticates the user. The best location to save this file is

   `\\CENTRAL SERVER\REPL$\SCRIPTS\NTCONFIG.POL`

   NTCONFIG.POL is the name you use to save your policy file. This file is available only if you set up directory replication between your domain controllers. The Directory Replication service ensures that an up-to-date version of the policy is stored in each domain controller that the export server has been configured to replicate to.

> **NOTE**
>
> **Three Changes** You can implement three possible changes for each option in the System Policy Editor. Each option has a check box that can be set as follows:
>
> - **Clear.** This changes the client's Registry to not implement the Registry setting. If it was previously enabled in the client's Registry, it is disabled after the policy is implemented.
>
> - **Shaded.** This leaves the client's Registry exactly as it is. If the option is enabled in the client's Registry, it remains enabled. If the option is disabled, it remains disabled.
>
> - **Checked.** This changes the client's Registry to match exactly what the system policy has configured. The client has no choice.

Configuring Computer Policies

You can configure computer policies to lock down common machine settings that affect all users of a Windows NT system (see Figure 4.23).

Common settings to configure include

◆ Programs to automatically run at the startup of the computer system, such as virus scans. Clicking the System | Run option in the Default Computer Properties dialog box sets this.

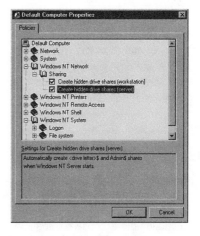

FIGURE 4.23
The Default Computer Properties dialog box enables you to configure computer policies.

E X A M   T I P

Where a Policy Is Stored For questions about where a policy should be stored, the answer they are after is where the client expects to find the file. The answer is always the netlogon share of the domain controller that authenticates the user. The file must always be named NTCONFIG.POL for Windows NT policies.

E X A M   T I P

System Policy Files and NetWare If the network operating system in question is Novell NetWare, the system policy files are stored in the SYS:PUBLIC directory in Novell NetWare 4.x and in the individual user's mail directory in Novell NetWare 3.x.

E X A M   T I P

Scripts and Directory Replication If you are ever presented with a question about a policy or logon script that executes only some of the time when the user logs on to the network, the best answer is that this scenario occurs when directory replication is not set up between the servers. Directory replication ensures that each domain controller in the domain contains the exact same files and versions of the files in its netlogon share.

◆ Ensuring that all Windows NT clients have the administrative shares automatically created upon startup of the systems. This enhances the capability of the administrator to centrally manage the network. Clicking the Windows NT Network | Sharing option in the Default Computer Properties dialog box sets this.

◆ Implementing customized shared folders, including the Desktop folder, Start Menu folder, Startup folder, and Programs folder. You can set these folders to point to an actual network share location so that multiple machines can have common desktops or Start menus. Clicking the Windows NT Shell | Custom shared folders option in the Default Computer Properties dialog box sets this.

◆ Presenting a customized dialog box, called the Logon Banner, that can be used to inform users of upcoming maintenance to the network or for other network information. Clicking the Windows NT System | Logon option in the Default Computer Properties dialog box sets this.

◆ Removing the last logged-on user from the Authentication dialog box. Because many users have ineffective passwords, knowing the user's logon name can lead to guessing the password. You set this option by clicking the Windows NT System | Logon option in the Default Computer Properties dialog box.

You can implement computer policies on a computer-by-computer basis by selecting Add Computer from the Edit menu. This adds a new icon to the policy with the computer's name. Figure 4.24 shows the NTCONFIG.POL file after a computer policy was added for the computer named BKOMAR. To change the policy for this computer, just double-click the icon for that computer.

When a user logs on to the network, the network processes its machine-specific policy. If it has no machine-specific policy, the default computer policy is merged into the user's HKEY_LOCAL_MACHINE Registry subkey.

The following example shows you how you can modify the NT environment to enable or disable additional options. In the upcoming example, the shutdown option will be enabled in the logon screen.

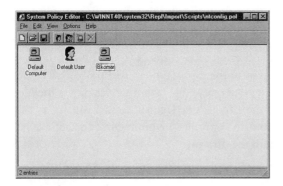

FIGURE 4.24
NTCONFIG.POL after the BKOMAR computer
was added.

Example: Enabling a Shutdown Button in the Authentication Dialog Box

In Step by Step 4.6, you create a system policy for enabling the shutdown button in the Windows NT Authentication dialog box.

> **NOTE**
>
> **Reversing a Policy** It is a tricky process to reverse a system policy. After a system downloads a computer policy, it becomes part of the Registry on that computer. Just deleting NTCONFIG.POL does not allow the system to return to its previous setting. You first must configure the policy to do the reverse of your previous setting. After all users have logged on and downloaded the policy file, you can delete it. Remember, if any other policies have been set, you cannot delete the NTCONFIG.POL file.

STEP BY STEP

4.6 Enabling the Shutdown Button in the NT Authentication Dialog Box

1. Start the System Policy Editor. Assuming you have already implemented system policies, open your existing system policy file. (It should be named NTCONFIG.POL.)

2. Double-click the Local Computer icon. The Local Computer Properties dialog box appears.

3. Click the plus sign (+) next to Windows NT System. This displays the subkeys under Windows NT System, as shown in Figure 4.25.

4. Click the plus sign next to Logon. This displays the options available under the Logon setting.

5. Click the check box next to Enable Shutdown from Authentication dialog box. If you want to make the shutdown option available to all users, make sure this option is checked. If you want to leave the option available on all systems using the policy, make sure the check box is grayed out. Finally, if you want to never have the Shutdown button available on the network, ensure the check box is cleared.

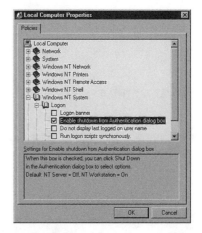

FIGURE 4.25
Configuring the computer policy to allow shutdown from the Authentication dialog box.

continues

continued

NOTE **Shutdown Button Defaults** The default for Windows NT Server is to disable the Shutdown button in the Authentication dialog box. The Windows NT Workstation default is to enable the Shutdown button. By using this policy setting, you can have a consistent dialog box across the enterprise. It is generally set to disabled on all systems so that only users with the proper rights can shut down any Windows NT-class system.

6. Save the file. Remember, if you are using the Directory Replication service, the NTCONFIG.POL file should be saved to the export server's REPL$\SCRIPTS directory. The Directory Replication service moves the file to all the import server's netlogon shares. If you are in a single domain controller environment, you can save it directly into the directory

```
\%WinNTRoot\system32\repl\import\scripts
```

The next time users log on to the network, the system policy downloads and merges with their current Registry settings. Depending on how you configured Step 5 and the previous setting for the shutdown button, users might not notice this change until the *next* time they log on to the network. The policy is loaded only after a successful logon to the network. Because the Authentication dialog box is presented before users have logged on, they cannot see this change until their next logon.

Configuring User Policies

You can implement user policies through the System Policy Editor's Default User Properties dialog box (see Figure 4.26). These policies affect the HKEY_CURRENT_USER Registry subtree. Each user is affected individually by these settings.

You can also implement user policies on a user-by-user basis. To create an individual user policy, select Add User from the Edit menu. When a user logs on, the system checks NTCONFIG.POL for a policy for the specific user. If there is no policy, the system uses the default user policy for the logon process.

Some common implementations of user profiles are

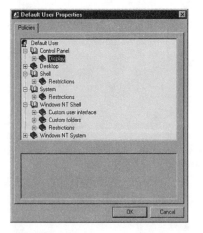

FIGURE 4.26
The Default User Properties dialog box enables you to configure user policies.

◆ Locking down display properties to prevent users from changing the resolution of their monitors. Display properties can be locked down as a whole or on each individual property page of display properties. This setting is adjusted by clicking the Control Panel | Display | Restrict Display option of the Default User Properties dialog box.

◆ Setting a default color scheme or wallpaper. This can be set by clicking the Desktop option of the Default User Properties dialog box.

◆ If you want to restrict access to portions of the Start menu or desktop, you click the Shell | Restrictions option of the Default User Properties dialog box.

◆ If you need to limit what applications can run at a workstation, click the System | Restrictions option of the Default User Properties dialog box. You can also use this option to prevent the user from modifying the Registry.

◆ You can prevent users from mapping or disconnecting network drives by clicking the Windows NT Shell | Restrictions option of the Default User Properties dialog box.

NOTE

For NetWare If your primary network operating system is Novell NetWare, the NTCONFIG.POL file must be stored in the SYS:PUBLIC directory if you are running Novell NetWare 4.x and in each user's mail directory if you are running Novell NetWare 3.x or earlier.

Implementing Group Policies

If you need user settings to affect multiple users, you can implement group policies. Group policies, however, add another level of complexity to the processing of the policies. Some of the additional considerations include

◆ The System Policy Editor uses global groups for group membership. You must implement appropriate trust relationships to see the necessary global groups.

◆ Because a user can belong to multiple global groups, the order in which the groups are processed is important. One group's settings could be the opposite of another group's. Group order is set in the Group Priority option of the Options menu.

Processing Order for System Policies

Figure 4.27 shows the processing order of a system policy.

When a user logs on to a network in which system policies have been implemented, the following steps occur:

1. The user successfully logs on to the network.

2. The user profile is read from the netlogon share of the authenticating domain controller.

EXAM TIP

Key Concepts Tested with System Policies The key concept that will be tested is what files are used for implementing system policies and where the system policies are stored. Remember that Windows NT system policies are stored in the file NTCONFIG.POL and Windows 95 policies are stored in CONFIG.POL.

FIGURE 4.27

The order of processing for system policies.

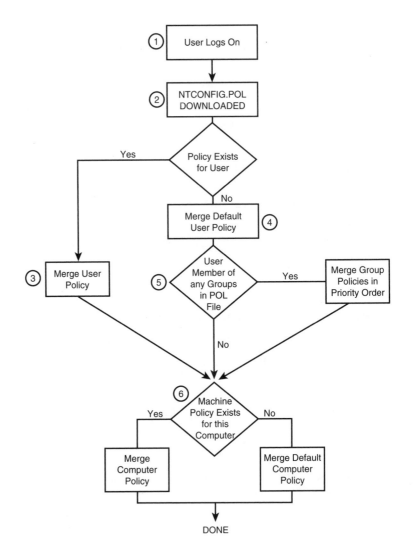

3. If a predefined policy exists for a user, that policy is merged into the HKEY_CURRENT_USER Registry subtree. The processing then moves to step 5.

4. If no predefined user policy exists, the default user policy is processed.

5. The group priority list is examined. If the user is a member of any of the global groups for which a policy exists, he or she is processed according to the group priority order. The priority is ordered from bottom to top of the group priority list. Each of the group policies is applied to the HKEY_CURRENT_USER Registry subtree.

6. After the user and group policies are processed, the machine policies are determined. If there is a predefined machine policy, that policy is merged with the HKEY_LOCAL_MACHINE Registry subtree. If there is no predefined machine policy for the system that the user is logging on from, the default machine policy is merged with the HKEY_LOCAL_MACHINE subtree.

Differences Between Windows NT and Windows 95 Profiles

Although Windows NT automatically implements system policies in its clients, more configuration is necessary for Windows 95 if you want it to recognize group policies. First, you must configure the Windows 95 clients individually to recognize group policies. This configuration is outlined in Step by Step 4.7.

STEP BY STEP

4.7 Configuring Windows 95 for Group Policies

1. Open the Windows 95 Control Panel.

2. In Control Panel, click the Add/Remove Programs icon.

3. Change to the Windows Setup tab and click Have Disk.

4. The system policy installation files are located on the Windows 95 CD in the directory \ADMIN\ APPTOOLS\POLEDIT. Select this directory using the Browse button.

5. When the options to install are presented, be sure to select Group Policies.

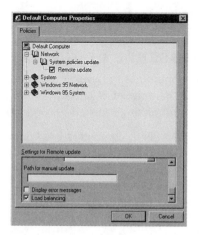

FIGURE 4.28
Configuring a Windows 95 client to search for CONFIG.POL on all domain controllers.

After the client is configured to use system policies, one more change is recommended in a Windows 95 network environment. By default, the Windows 95 client looks for the file CONFIG.POL only on the Primary Domain Controller's netlogon share. If you want the Windows 95 client to be able to process the system policy from any domain controller, as in Windows NT, you must enable the Load Balancing option by clicking the Network | System policies update | Remote update option, as shown in Figure 4.28.

Profiles and Policies

Profiles and policies can be powerful tools to assist in the administrative tasks in your environment. The following list reviews the main topics covered in this section for the noted objective:

- **Roaming profiles.** The user portion of the Registry is downloaded from a central location, allowing the user settings to follow the user anywhere within the network environment.

- **Local profiles.** The user settings are stored at each workstation and are not copied to other computers. Each workstation that you use will have different desktop and user settings.

- **System policies.** System policies enable the administrator to restrict user configuration changes on systems. This allows the administrator to maintain the settings of the desktop of systems without the fear that a user can modify them.

- **Computer policies.** Computer policies allow the lockdown of common machine settings that affect all users of that computer.

CASE STUDY: RESTRICTING ACCESS

ESSENCE OF THE CASE

- You need to develop a solution to restrict the amount of network browsing without restricting required network connections.

- All client computers are Windows NT Workstation with numerous Windows NT servers placed throughout the environment.

SCENARIO

JPS Consulting was asked whether it is possible to restrict the access to additional network systems in an environment. The available network bandwidth is being dramatically reduced due to an excessive amount of browsing through the Network Neighborhood. The organization tried to implement a higher level of security; even though it limited what the users can access, they can still use the Network Neighborhood to attempt the connections. All the client computers are using NT Workstation as the operating system, and the organization has six NT servers playing various roles throughout the environment.

CASE STUDY: RESTRICTING ACCESS

ANALYSIS

In this scenario, you can create a user policy to restrict access to the Network Neighborhood icon on the desktop. This new policy could restrict users to precreated network shares and reduce network-browsing traffic. Start the System Policy Editor. Assuming you have already implemented system policies, open your existing system policy file (recall that it should be named NTCONFIG.POL). Double-click the Default User icon. The Default User Properties dialog box appears. Click the plus sign (+) next to Shell to display the subkeys. Click the plus sign next to Restrictions to display all the available settings for this option. If you want to remove the Network Neighborhood icon from the desktop entirely, click the check box next to the option Hide Network Neighborhood. If you just want to prevent users from seeing any portion of the network other than their workgroups, click the check

box next to the option No Entire Network in Network Neighborhood. Finally, if you want to prevent users from seeing the servers in their workgroups that have sharing enabled, click the No Workgroup Contents in Network Neighborhood option. Save the file. Remember, if you are using the Directory Replication service, the NTCONFIG.POL file should be saved to the export server's REPL$\SCRIPTS directory. The Directory Replication service moves the file to all the import server's netlogon shares. If you are in a single domain controller environment, you can save it directly into the following directory:

```
\%WINNTROOT\SYSTEM32\REPL\IMPORT\SCRIPTS
```

The next time a user logs on to the network, the user policy downloads and merges with his or her current Registry settings. Depending on how you configured the previous setting for the display of the Network Neighborhood, the user might immediately notice the implemented changes.

CHAPTER SUMMARY

KEY TERMS

- logon script
- account policy
- AGLP
- user rights
- policies
- roaming profiles
- local profiles

For a thorough understanding of the concepts involved in managing user and group accounts and implementing profiles and policies, and to be successful on the exam, focus on the following:

◆ Always use the AGLP order when assigning permissions to user and group accounts.

◆ Use a template account to simplify the mass creation of user accounts.

◆ You use the global group to hold users with similar task requirements.

◆ You assign the local groups permissions and place the global groups into the appropriate local group.

◆ Whenever possible, use a built-in local or global group. Never create a group to replace a built-in group.

◆ Ensure that proper user rights are assigned to each group, and maintain consistency in assigning user rights.

◆ You can use policies and profiles to simplify administration and add an extended level of administrative control over the users' desktops. Use them wisely and effectively to manage your user and group accounts.

The Windows NT Server 4.0 Enterprise exam does not weigh heavily on this area; however, you need strong knowledge of user and group accounts with policies and profiles to be successful in other areas of the exam relating to managing resources.

APPLY YOUR LEARNING

This section allows you to assess how well you understood the material in the chapter. Review and exam questions test your knowledge of the tasks and concepts specified in the objectives. The exercises provide you with opportunities to engage in the sorts of tasks that compose the skill sets the objectives reflect.

For more review and exam questions, see the Top Score test engine on the CD-ROM that came with this book.

Exercises

The following exercises provide you with an opportunity to apply what you've learned in this chapter.

4.1   Creating a Template User Account

In this exercise, you create a Template User account to use for a base account. You want each user to have the following properties:

◆ The users are all signed to term contracts that expire on December 31, 1998.

◆ The users should be able to access computers only from Monday through Friday between the hours of 8 a.m. and 6 p.m.

◆ The users are able to use only the computers named Elm, Fir, Oak, and Birch.

◆ All users require roaming profiles stored on the server named DOC in a share named PROFILES.

◆ The users must change passwords the next time they log on to the network.

◆ All users store their data in a personal directory on the server named DOC in a share named USERS.

Time Estimate: 15 minutes

1. Start the User Manager for Domains.

2. From the User menu, select New User.

3. Create a user with the name _Template. The account should have the User Must Change Password at Next Logon option enabled and the Account Disabled option enabled. (This does not copy to the other accounts.)

4. In the User Environment Profile dialog box, make the following two entries:

   • The User Profile Path should be \\DOC\PROFILES\%USERNAME%.

   • The home directory should be entered in Connect To as \\DOC\USERS\ %USERNAME%.

5. In the Logon Hours dialog box, set the logon hours to Mondays through Fridays from 8 a.m. to 6 p.m.

6. In the Logon Workstations dialog box, set the allowed workstations to Elm, Fir, Oak, and Birch.

7. In the Account Information dialog box, set the account expiration date to December 31, 1998.

4.2   Using the Template Account to Create Accounts

In this exercise, you use your _Template account to create accounts for Bob Smith, Mary Jones, and Larry Wilkes. This exercise demonstrates the ease of creating accounts using a template account.

APPLY YOUR LEARNING

Time Estimate: 10 minutes

1. In User Manager for Domains, select the _Template account created in Exercise 4.1.

2. From the User menu, select Copy (or press the F8 key).

3. Enter the user name BOB for Bob Smith, his full name, and his position as Accounting Clerk as the description. Set his initial password to Banter8. Click Add to complete the copy.

4. In the copy of _Template dialog box, enter the user name MARY for Mary Jones, her full name, and her position as Accounting Manager as the description. Set her initial password to Banter8. Click Add to complete the copy.

5. Add Larry Wilkes the Sales Manager using the same defaults.

4.3 Modifying User Rights

In Exercise 4.3, you investigate the user rights assigned to a Windows NT domain controller. You can better protect the domain controller by implementing more secure user rights than those implemented by default. This exercise shows you how to do just that.

Time Estimate: 15 minutes

1. Start the User Manager for Domains.

2. Create two new local groups. Name them Backup and Restore.

3. From the Policies menu, select User Rights.

4. For the right Access This Computer From Network, select the group Everyone and click Remove.

5. Click Add and select the local group Users. This limits access to the computer to only known members of the domain, not everyone who has access to the network segment.

6. For the right Back Up Files and Directories, select the group Backup Operators and click Remove.

7. Click Add and select the new local group called Backup you created in step 2.

8. For the right Restore Files and Directories, select the group Backup Operators and click Remove.

9. Click Add and select the new local group called Restore you created in step 2. Many organizations prefer to separate the functions of Backup and Restore. Steps 7 and 9 have replaced the default local group named Backup Operators with two local groups named Backup and Restore. To make them fully functional, you had to modify the default user rights.

4.4 Creating a Roaming Profile

This exercise takes a user account and transforms it into a roaming profile.

Time Estimate: 15 minutes

1. Start the Windows NT Explorer.

2. Create a new folder named Profiles on an NTFS partition.

3. Share the newly created folder as Profiles. Set the share permissions to only allow the Users group Change permissions.

4. Start User Manager for Domains.

APPLY YOUR LEARNING

5. Select the account you created for Mary Jones in Exercise 4.2, and select Properties from the User menu.

6. Click Profiles to open the User Environment Profile dialog box.

7. In the User Profile Path, type

   `\\SERVERNAME\PROFILES\%USERNAME%`

   where SERVERNAME is the name of the Primary Domain Controller you are working on.

8. To enable Mary Jones to log on to a domain controller, select User Rights from the Policies menu.

9. Select the user right Logon Locally.

10. Click Add.

11. Click Show Users to show user names and group names.

12. Select Mary Jones's account from the list and click Add.

13. Log off.

14. Log on as Mary with password Banter8.

15. Right-click the My Computer icon and select Properties from the pop-up menu.

16. Click the User Profiles tab. Note that the profile type for Mary is now Roaming.

The following three exercises are based on Figure 4.29. These examples investigate the use of global and local groups in gaining access to resources in a master domain model.

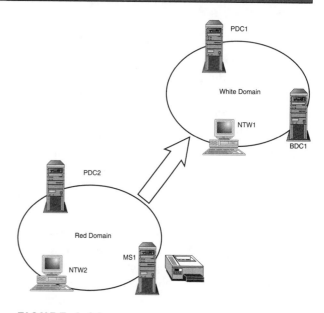

FIGURE 4.29
A sample enterprise domain structure.

4.5 Using Existing Local Groups

In Figure 4.29, the White Domain is the master domain and the Red Domain is functioning as the resource domain. If the users Susan, Paul, Brian, and Chuck all have accounts in the White Domain, the group assignments in the upcoming list must be implemented to enable them to modify or create shares in either domain.

Time Estimate: 15 minutes

1. Is there a global group that contains just these four users? This is probably not the case, so create a new global group in the White Domain that contains these four users. In this example, use the name SHARERS.

APPLY YOUR LEARNING

2. Next, you must establish whether an existing local group gives the users sufficient rights to create shares in the domain. The Server Operators group has this permission. Because you want to provide the capability to create shares in either domain, you must use the Server Operators Group in both domains.

3. Now, assign the SHARERS global group in the White Domain as a member of the Red Domain's Server Operators local group and the White Domain's Server Operators group.

4. If it is necessary to let the users create shares on the NTW1, NTW2, and MS1 computers, you need further group assignments. Because these computers are not domain controllers, you must add the global group to a local group that has these permissions on Windows NT workstations and Windows NT member servers. The local group with these permissions is the Power Users local group. Thus, you must add the WHITE\SHARERS global group to NTW1\Power Users, NTW2\Power Users, and MS1\Power Users.

4.6 Having to Create New Local Groups

Using the network configuration shown in Figure 4.29, say that the Human Resources database is stored on PDC2 in the Red Domain. If Paul and Chuck need access to this database, what group memberships do you need to implement?

Time Estimate: 10 minutes

1. Is there a global group that contains just these two users? No. Create a new global group in the White Domain that contains Paul and Chuck. In this example, use the name HumanResources.

2. Next, you must establish whether an existing local group gives the users sufficient rights to use the Human Resources database. Because there is no predefined Windows NT local group for using file resources, you have to create a new local group. Call it HRDATA. Because the resource exists on a domain controller, this local group must be created in the Domain Account database.

3. You must assign permissions to the HRDATA local group to give appropriate access rights to any members of the group.

4. Finally, make the WHITE\HumanResources global group a member of the RED\HRDATA local group.

4.7 Working with Pre-Existing Global and Local Groups

Using the network configuration shown in Figure 4.29, say that all users in the White Domain need to use the printer attached to MS1. What group memberships do you need to implement?

Time Estimate: 10 minutes

1. Is there a global group that contains just the domain users? Yes, the Domain Users global group in the White Domain contains all regular users of the domain. Remember that the only account not included is Guest. This account, however, is disabled by default.

2. Next, you must establish whether an existing local group gives the users sufficient rights to use the printer. Because the printer is attached to a Windows NT Member Server, you must use that server's local account database. You can use the Users local group to handle this scenario by adjusting the properties on the printer.

3. It is best to adjust the printer's properties to change the permissions from giving Everyone the print permission to giving the Users local group print permissions. Figure 4.30 shows how the permissions for the printer should ultimately be set.

4. Finally, make the WHITE\Domain Users global group a member of the MS1\Users local group.

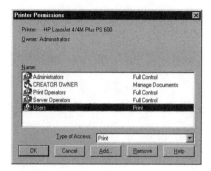

FIGURE 4.30
These settings are your suggested print permission settings.

Review Questions

1. What environment variable do you use to create multiple home directories all at one time?

2. The Blue domain trusts the Red domain. If Bill has an account in the Red domain, what group memberships do you use to enable Bill to perform backups in both the Blue domain and the Red domain?

3. What groups have the built-in right to create accounts in User Manager for Domains?

4. How can you use system policies to restrict access to the Network Neighborhood?

5. What is the name of the file that contains system policies? Where is it stored in a Windows NT network? Where is it stored in a Novell NetWare Network?

Exam Questions

1. The Red Domain trusts the Blue Domain. If Pasquale, a user in the Blue Domain, is required to create shares and set permissions on folders on the Red Domain's Primary Domain Controller, which group should he belong to?

   A. Blue Domain's Account Operators group

   B. Red Domain's Account Operators group

   C. Blue Domain's Server Operator group

   D. Red Domain's Server Operators group

2. The Group Domain trusts the Systems Domain. Irene's account is located in the Systems domain. If Irene needs to perform backups in the Group domain, which group memberships must be implemented?

   A. Create a new local group in the Systems Domain called Backups. Make Irene a member of the Backups group. Make the Backups group a member of the Backup Operators group in the Group domain.

   B. Create a new local group in the Group domain called Backups. Make Irene a member of the Backups group. Make the Backups group a member of the Backup Operators group in the Group domain.

C. Create a new global group in the Systems domain called Backups. Make Irene a member of the Backups group. Make the Backups group a member of the Backup Operators group in the Group domain.

D. Create a new global group in the Group domain called Backups. Make Irene a member of the Backups group. Make the Backups group a member of the Backup Operators group in the Group domain.

3. What groups are allowed the user right to change the system time on an NT domain controller?

   A. Account Operators

   B. Administrators

   C. Backup Operators

   D. Power Users

   E. Server Operators

4. Windows NT system policies are stored in the file named

   A. NTCONFIG.POL

   B. SYSTEM.POL

   C. CONFIG.POL

   D. SYSTEM.DAT

5. To create a mandatory user profile, you must complete the following step:

   A. In the Control Panel, click the System icon. On the User Profile tab in the System Properties dialog box, change the Roaming Profile type to Mandatory.

   B. In User Manager for Domains, double-click the User name, and on the User Environment Profile dialog box, change the Profile type to Roaming.

   C. Rename the file NTUSER.DAT in the user's profile directory NTUSER.MAN.

   D. Rename the file USER.DAT in the user's profile directory USER.MAN.

6. Which files are used as templates for Windows NT system policies?

   A. ADMIN.ADM

   B. COMMON.ADM

   C. WINNT.ADM

   D. WINDOWS.ADM

7. A Windows 95 user only occasionally has his or her system policy downloaded to the system in a Windows NT domain environment because _____ has not been enabled in the system policy.

   A. Load balancing

   B. Manual update

   C. Distributed processing

   D. Automatic update

8. What entry for home directories is used to auto-generate home directories in User Manager for Domains?

   A. \\SERVER\%USERS%

   B. \\SERVER\%USERNAME%

C. \\SERVER\USERS\%USERS%

D. \\SERVER\USER\%USERNAME%

9. Minimum password lengths are set in the
_____.

A. User rights policy

B. User's property page

C. System policies

D. Account policy

Answers to Review Questions

1. %USERNAME%. See the section "Template Accounts," earlier in this chapter for more information.

2. You must first place Bill first in a user-created global group. Create this global group in the Red domain where Bill's account resides. This global group then must be a member of the Backup Operators local group in both the Red and Blue domains. See the section "Managing Global and Local Groups" for more information.

3. Administrators and Account Operators. See the section "Creating Windows NT User Accounts" for more information.

4. The administrator could set a system policy that restricts access to the Network Neighborhood through user settings (refer to Figure 4.27). See the case study, "Restricting Access," earlier in this chapter for more information.

5. The file is called NTCONFIG.POL for Windows NT systems and CONFIG.POL for Windows 95 systems. It is stored in the netlogon share on all Windows NT domain controllers and in the SYS:PUBLIC directory on NetWare servers. See the section "System Policies" for more information.

Answers to Exam Questions

1. **D.** To create shares and assign permissions, the user must be a member of the Server Operators group, or higher, in the required domain. See the section "Built-In Local Groups."

2. **C.** To do backups in a trusting domain, the user must be placed in a global group; you must then place that global group in the local Backup Operators group of the trusting domain. See the section "Built-In Local Groups."

3. **B. E.** Only a member of the Administrators group or the Server Operators group can change the system time. See the section "Built-In Local Groups."

4. **A.** The file that contains the systems policies in Windows NT is NTCONFIG.POL See the section "System Policies."

5. **C.** A mandatory user profile is created in a similar fashion to any other user profile. The only difference is in the file extension used by the profile. Mandatory profiles have the *.MAN extension. See the section "Configuring Roaming Profiles in Windows NT."

APPLY YOUR LEARNING

6. **B. C.** The two files that you can use as a template for a system policy are COMMON.ADM and WINNT.ADM. See the section "Creating a New System Policy."

7. **A.** If load balancing is not enabled on the system policy, the Windows 95 client will only download the policy when the Windows NT server is available. See the section "System Policies."

8. **D.** You use the %USERNAME% variable to create a directory based on the user name. See the section "User Profile Path."

9. **D.** The minimum password length is set up in the account policy. See the section "Defining Your Account Policy."

This chapter helps you to prepare for the Microsoft exam by covering the following objectives within the "Managing Resources" category:

Administer remote servers from various types of client computers. Client computer types include:

- ◆ **Windows 95**

- ◆ **Windows NT Workstation**

▶ This objective requires that you have an understanding of the remote administration tools available, and the processes involved to administer your NT server from other client operating systems.

Manage disk resources. Tasks include:

- ◆ **Creating and sharing resources**

- ◆ **Implementing permissions and security**

- ◆ **Establishing file auditing**

▶ Securing your resources is the main theme involved in managing the disk resources. Ensure that you can create, share, and secure all disk resources in a Windows NT environment. This would include using user and group permissions, as well as, enabling the auditing features of Windows NT.

CHAPTER 5

Managing Resources: Remote Administration and Disk Resources

In preparing for the Managing Resources objectives, the best method to prepare yourself for the exam is to review the material in this chapter, and then apply each of the options and procedures listed to ensure that you have some hands-on experience with securing your disk resources. This section is not weighted heavily on the exam; however, it is a critical component to the integrity of your networked data.

Managing resources encompasses much more than just user and group accounts and system policies and user profiles. In order to completely manage your network environment you must look at the remote administration options available as well as applying the administration tools into your network resources. You also need to know how to manage your disk resources and use the Windows NT permissions to maximize your network security. You need a strong understanding of auditing in Windows NT.

In this chapter, the following areas of managing resources are discussed:

◆ Remote administration of Windows NT

◆ Managing disk resources, including:

• Configuring share-level permissions in Windows NT

• Configuring NTFS permissions in Windows NT

• Combining share and NTFS permissions to give your network the best level of security

◆ Implementing auditing in Windows NT

Your knowledge of managing user and group accounts as well as setting system policies and user profiles will be strengthened in this section to ensure that you understand how to apply the AGLP procedures into the network resources in your environment.

REMOTE ADMINISTRATION OF WINDOWS NT

Administer remote servers from various types of client computers. Client computer types include Windows 95 and Windows NT Workstation.

A common initial misconception is that you must be located at a Windows NT Domain Controller to manage a Windows NT domain. Several versions of the Remote Administration Tools for Windows NT enable Windows NT domains to be administered from Windows 95 and from Windows NT Workstation. This section also explores a new utility that comes with the Windows NT Server Resource Kit—the Web-based administration tools.

Remote Administration Tools for Windows 95

The Windows 95 Remote Administration Tools enable a client running Windows 95 to manage the following aspects of a Windows NT Server domain:

◆ Users in a domain can be managed with User Manager for Domains.

◆ Servers in the domain can be managed using Server Manager.

◆ Troubleshooting of servers can be done using the Event Viewer to view system, application, and audit logs.

◆ Extensions to the Windows 95 Explorer enable management of NTFS permissions, auditing, and print permissions through the Network Neighborhood.

◆ Servers running File and Print Services for NetWare can be managed from the Windows 95 system through the FPNW tab of any drive on that server.

To install Remote Administration for Windows NT Server on a Windows 95 system, the tasks in Step by Step 5.1 must be performed.

STEP BY STEP

5.1 Installing the Remote Administration Tools for Windows 95

1. Open the Windows 95 Control Panel.

2. Click on the Add/Remove Programs icon in the Control Panel.

3. On the Windows Setup tab, click on Have Disk.

4. Insert the Windows NT Server CD and, using the Browse button, select the \CLIENTS\SRVTOOLS\WIN95 directory in which the SRVTOOLS.INF file is located.

continues

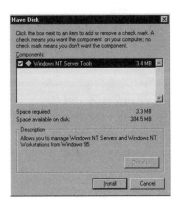

FIGURE 5.1
Adding Windows NT Server Tools to a Windows 95 system.

continued

5. In the dialog box that appears after clicking on OK, select the Windows NT Server Tools option and click on Install (see Figure 5.1). This by default installs the Server tools into the c:\srvtools directory using about 3MB of disk space.

6. You must manually adjust the path statement in AUTOEXEC.BAT to include the directory C:\SRVTOOLS.

7. After the path has been adjusted in AUTOEXEC.BAT, the system must be rebooted for all changes to take place.

After all steps have been completed you have successfully installed the remote administration tools on your Windows 95 machine. To view these tools you can click the Start button, move to programs, and then locate the Windows NT Admin group in the list.

> **NOTE**
>
> **Include the Directory**   If you do not include the C:\SRVTOOLS directory in the path, the Explorer extensions for Windows NT Server tools do not function. The necessary *.DLL files are stored in this directory and cannot be found without the inclusion of this directory in the path.

Whenever a user tries to administer an NT domain using the Windows NT Remote Administration tools, the user is asked to enter his password before running the utility. This ensures that the user has sufficient privileges to run the Administration tools.

Remote Administration Tools for Windows NT

The Windows NT Server tools for Windows NT Workstation enable the management of a Windows NT domain from either a Windows NT Workstation or a Windows NT Member Server. The Windows NT Server tools for Windows NT Workstation include the following utilities:

◆ DHCP Manager

◆ System Policy Editor

◆ Remote Access Admin

◆ Remote Boot Manager

◆ Server Manager

> **EXAM TIP**
>
> **Client Management Questions**
> The exam deals primarily with what kind of management can be done from a specific client. Another possible question is to enumerate what clients Windows NT domains can be managed from. This is referring to running the actual management utilities such as User Manager for Domains.

◆ User Manager for Domains

◆ WINS Manager

◆ Extensions for Managing Services for Macintosh

To install the Server tools for Windows NT Workstation, the tasks in Step by Step 5.2 must be performed.

STEP BY STEP

5.2 Installing Remote Admin Tools on Windows NT

1. Insert the Windows NT Server 4 CD.

2. Run SETUP.BAT from the \clients\srvtools\winnt folder. This copies all the necessary files to the NT Workstation and makes the necessary Registry setting changes to enable management of Windows NT domains.

3. The installation program does not automatically create the Windows NT Server tools icons in the Start menu. You must create the icons manually in the Start menu.

   At the end of these steps the files have all been installed onto your Windows NT machine. To locate the files you can use the explorer and change to the %systemroot%\system32 directory.

N O T E

Windows 3.x   Windows NT domains also can be administered from Windows 3.x. The Server tools for Windows 3.x are included on any Windows NT Server 3.5x CD in the directory \CLIENTS\SRVTOOLS\WFW. Because Windows 3.x was a 16-bit operating system, this also installs a version of Win32s to enable running of 32-bit applications in a 16-bit environment. Both the Windows 95 and Windows for Workgroups Server tools do not give you all the tools included with Windows NT. Due to this, there are some limitations in what can be administered on your Windows NT network when administering from a Windows 95 or Windows for Workgroups client.

Web-Based Administration Tools

The Windows NT Server Resource Kit includes a new utility that enables Windows NT Servers to be remotely administered from Windows, Macintosh, and UNIX hosts running Web-browser software. This utility is also available for download from the Microsoft Web site. The Web Administration tool is implemented as an Internet Information Server extension, so be sure to have IIS installed prior to implementing the Web administration tool. The only caveat is that the person connecting to the NT Administration page must be a member of the domain's Administrators local group.

To install the Web Administration tools on a domain controller, perform the tasks in Step by Step 5.3.

STEP BY STEP

5.3 Installing the Web Administration Tools

1. Insert the Windows NT Server Resource Kit CD into the CD drive of the domain controller to be managed.

2. From the Autorun screen presented when the CD was inserted, select the Web Administration link.

3. On the next screen, select the Install Now link.

4. You have to agree to the End User License Agreement by clicking on Yes to continue the installation.

5. Click on Continue to start the actual installation.

6. To complete the installation, click on Exit to Windows. The Readme file for the Web Administration tools is displayed to finalize the installation.

7. To access the Web-based Administration tools, start up your Web browser and go to the following address (see Figure 5.2):

   http://<your_server_name>/ntadmin/ntadmin.htm

   The Web Administration tools are now installed.

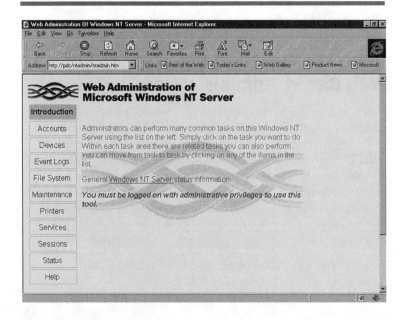

FIGURE 5.2
The Web-based Windows NT administration tools.

The Web Administration tools are intended for an experienced NT administrator. These tools enable limited administration of a Windows NT Domain Controller using HTML forms. Management tasks that can be performed from the Web-based Administration tools include:

- Managing user accounts.

- Managing global and local accounts.

- Stopping and starting devices on the system.

- Viewing the system, audit, and application logs.

- Managing shared directories and their permissions.

- Managing NTFS file and directory permissions.

- Sending a broadcast message to all users with open sessions to the server.

- Setting up the server to run the Windows NT Resource Kit Remote Console utility.

- Rebooting the server using the Web page.

- Setting the preferences for the Web Administration tools.

- Managing any printers hosted by the server.

- Stopping, starting, and configuring services running on the server.

- Managing all active sessions. This includes disconnecting all or specific sessions.

- Viewing the server configuration. This makes use of the WINMSDP utility from the resource kit. This utility gives the same information as the graphical WINMSD utility but in straight-text format.

- Viewing a report format on selected performance counters.

- Viewing server statistics.

To gain some additional insight and experience using the Web-based administration tool, see the example in the following subsection.

NOTE

Added Scripts The Web-based administration install program added several scripts to the directory c:\inetpub\scripts\NTAdmin and installed the actual Web for this site to c:\inetpub\wwwroot\NTAdmin by default. This site does not use the default.htm page, so that the administrator must type in the actual Web page ntadmin.htm to open this Web site.

WARNING

Take Care When Stopping Services Be careful which services you attempt to stop. If you stop the World Wide Web Publishing service or the Server service, you will not be able to restart them remotely.

Example: Adding a New User Using the Web Administration Tools

Step by Step 5.4 guides you through the process of adding a new user to the domain using only the Web Administration tools.

STEP BY STEP

5.4 Adding a New User Using the Web Administration Tools

1. Start Internet Explorer.

2. Open the site **http://*Your Server*/ntadmin/ntadmin.htm.**

3. Click on the Accounts link on the left edge of the screen.

4. Click on the Users link.

5. Click on the Create New User button.

6. Figure 5.3 shows the input required on the Create New User Account form that the Web Administration presents. After all necessary information is entered, click on Create.

7. The final screen should give a successful result, and you should now see the new user's name in the list of user accounts.

   The Web administration tools offer many of the day to day tasks available through a convenient Web link. In the above example the creation of a new user was accomplished from a remote location through the Internet.

The Web Administration tool enables you to quickly create a new user, but you will note that you cannot set all properties of the user account from within the tool. You are, however, able to set up a basic user account. This tool enables you to perform quick and dirty administration of the network. To determine whether this helps your organization, play with the utility and try to perform what you consider your day-to-day tasks using the Web Administration tool.

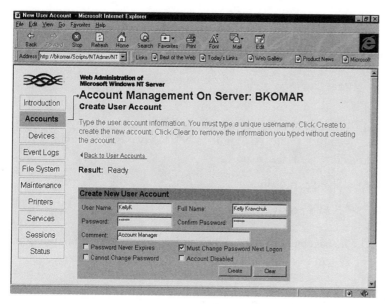

FIGURE 5.3
Adding a new user with the Web Administration tool.

Remote Administration

The chapter up to this point has focused on the remote administration tools available for your Windows NT Server. The following list summarizes the key tools:

- **Remote Administration Tools for Windows 95**. Allows User Manager, Server manager, Event Viewer, and NTFS file permissions to be executed from the Windows 95 computer.

- **Remote Administration for Windows NT**. Allows User Manager, Server manager, DHCP Manager, System Policy Editor, Remote Access Admin, Remote Boot Manager, WINS Manager, and NTFS file permissions to be executed from a Windows NT machine.

- **Web-Based Administration**. Allows for common tasks to be completed via an Internet connection into the Windows NT Server.

MANAGING DISK RESOURCES

Manage disk resources. Tasks include creating and sharing resources, implementing permissions and security, and establishing file auditing.

In Managing your disk resources the main theme encompasses securing your disk resources. Windows NT has two levels of security for protecting your disk resources:

◆ Share permissions

◆ NTFS permissions

The management of both sets of permissions protects your Windows NT system from inappropriate access to your disk resources.

Share-Level Security

Share-level security enables a Windows NT administrator to protect his resources from network users. Not only do shares have a level of security, they also are used as the entry point into the system for Windows NT users.

There are four explicit share permissions that can be implemented. They are:

◆ Read

◆ Change

◆ Full Control

◆ No Access

The Read permission enables a user to connect to the resource and run programs. Users also can view any documents that are stored in the share, but they cannot make any changes to the documents.

The Change permissions setting enables a user to connect to a resource and run programs. It also allows users to create new documents and subfolders, to modify existing documents, and to delete documents.

The Full Control permission enables users to do anything they want in the share. It also enables them to change the share permissions to

> **EXAM TIP**
>
> **Heavy Testing Here** The Windows NT Server Enterprise exam tests extensively about the capability to apply this security in a Windows NT multidomain environment.

> **NOTE**
>
> **Access Denied** There is also an implicit permission of Access Denied. This occurs when a user does not belong to any of the groups that have been assigned permissions to use a share. In this case, the user has an implicit Access Denied permission. Users are not able to use the resource, but can gain access if they are assigned permissions to the resource directly or are added to a group that has access to the resource.

affect all users. The Full Control permissions generally are not required for most users. Change is sufficient for most day-to-day business needs.

The No Access permission is the most powerful permission. When it is implemented, the user that has been assigned this permission has no access to that resource. It does not matter what other permissions have been assigned. The No Access permission overrides any other assigned permissions.

In the following sections you will cover the following topics as they relate to share permissions:

◆ Determining Effective Share Permissions

◆ Creating a Shared Folder

Determining Effective Share Permissions

When users, through group membership, have been assigned varying levels of share permissions, their effective shared permissions are the accumulation of their individual shared permissions. Susan is a member of the TrainingDocs local group, for example, and it has been assigned the share permissions of Change to the Training share. Susan herself, however, has been assigned the share permissions of Full Control to the Training share (see Figure 5.4). Susan's effective rights to the share, then, are Full Control.

The only time this is not the case is when the user, or a group the user belongs to, has been assigned the explicit permission of No Access. The No Access permission always takes precedence over any other permissions assigned.

Creating a Shared Folder

To create a shared folder, perform the tasks in Step by Step 5.5.

STEP BY STEP

5.5 Creating a Shared Folder

1. Right-click on the folder you want to share in either My Computer or the Windows NT Explorer. Remember that this folder will be an artificial root directory for all users who access the share.

continues

NOTE **FAT Volume** Windows NT share permissions are the only security that can be assigned to data on a FAT volume.

NOTE **No Separate Permissions** Windows NT share permissions do not allow for separate permissions to be set at the file level. After share-level permissions are set, they remain the same for all files and subfolders within the shared folder.

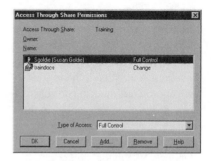

FIGURE 5.4
Share-level permissions for a resource; here, the effective rights to the share are Full Control.

FIGURE 5.5
The Sharing tab of the Properties dialog box enables you to name the share and to set limits on how many users can access the share simultaneously.

continued

2. From the pop-up menu, select the Sharing… option.

3. As shown in Figure 5.5, the Sharing tab of the Properties dialog box enables you to name the share and to set limits on how many users can access the share simultaneously.

4. Click on Permissions.

5. You should first determine if there is an existing local group that can be used to grant access to the resource. If there is, you can grant access to the share by clicking the Add… button and selecting the local group from the list of groups. If no local group exists, you might need to switch briefly into User Manager for Domains and add the local group to the appropriate accounts database. To remove a group from the list, select the group you want to remove and click on Remove.

6. Click on OK to finalize the permissions for the share.

7. Click on OK to close the Properties dialog box.

By following the preceding steps you can create a share and assign permissions to the share. This process will probably become second nature to you as you setup your NT environment.

In Windows NT Workstation, the maximum number of users that can connect to a share is ten. It does not matter if you set the number higher in the Sharing tab of the Properties dialog box. This number is hard-coded into the operating system. To be more specific, Windows NT Workstation supports only a maximum of 10 inbound connections, and that may limit the number of users into a share.

NTFS Permissions

NTFS permissions enable you to assign more comprehensive security to your computer system. NTFS permissions are able to protect you at the file level. Share permissions, on the other hand, can only be applied to the directory level. NTFS permissions can affect users logged on locally or across the network to the system where the NTFS permissions are applied. Share permissions are only in effect when the user connects to the resource through the network.

N O T E   **Creating a Local Group**   Remember that local groups must be created in the accounts database where the resource is located. If the resource is located on a domain controller, the local group must be created in the domain's accounts database. If the resource is located on a Windows NT Workstation or a Windows NT Member Server, the local group must be created in that system's accounts database.

NTFS permissions, when applied at the directory level, can be applied as one of the default assignments shown in Table 5.1.

No Sharing for Global Groups
Although you can add a global group to the groups with access to the share, this will never be a correct answer on the exam. The only groups that should be assigned permissions to a share are local groups. Even in practical experience, a global group should not be assigned permissions to a share. This is because if you move to a multidomain environment, you need to come to the share itself to grant users from a new domain access to the resource. If you had assigned the permissions to a local group initially, all you would need to do is add a global group from the new domain to the local group in the existing domain using User Manager for Domains. This is far simpler than having to regrant permissions to the share.

TABLE 5.1

NTFS DIRECTORY PERMISSIONS

NTFS Permission	*Meaning*
No Access (none)(none)	The No Access NTFS permission means the user has absolutely No Access to the directory or its files. This overrides any other NTFS permissions assigned through other group memberships.
List (RX) (Not Specified)	The List NTFS permission enables users to view the contents of a directory and to navigate to its subdirectories. It does not grant them access to the files in these directories unless specified in file permissions.
Read (RX) (RX)	The Read NTFS permission enables users to navigate the entire directory structure, to view the contents of the directory and any files therein, and to execute programs.
Add (WX) (Not Specified)	The Add NTFS permission enables the user to add new subdirectories and files to the directory. It does not give the user access to the files within the directory unless specified in other NTFS permissions.
Add & Read (RWX) (RX)	The Add & Read NTFS permission enables a user to add new files to the directory structure. After the file has been added, the user now only has Read Only access to the files. This permission also enables the user to run programs.
Change (RWXD) (RWXD)	The Change NTFS permission enables users to do the most data manipulation. They can view the contents of directories and files, run programs, modify the contents of data files, and delete files.
Full Control (All) (All)	The Full Control permission gives the user all the capabilities of the Change permission. In addition, the user can change the permissions on that directory or any of its contents. The user also can take ownership of the directory or any of its contents.
Special Directory...	The NTFS permissions can be set as desired to any combination of (R)ead, (W)rite, E(X)ecute, (D)elete, Change (P)ermissions, and Take (O)wnership.

NTFS permissions also can be applied to individual files in directories. The NTFS file permissions are shown in Table 5.2.

TABLE 5.2

NTFS FILE PERMISSIONS

NTFS Permission	*Meaning*
No Access (none)	The No Access NTFS file permission means the user has absolutely No Access to that file. This overrides any other NTFS directory and file permissions that might have been assigned to the user through other group memberships.
Read (RX)	The Read NTFS file permission enables the user to view the contents of files but to make no changes to the contents. The user also can execute the file if it is a program.
Change (RWXD)	The Change NTFS file permission enables users to make any editing changes they want to a data file, including deleting the file.
Full Control (All)	The Full Control file permission gives the user all the capabilities of the Change permission. Users also can change the permissions on the file and take ownership of the file if they are not the owner presently.
Special File...	The NTFS file permissions can be set as desired to any combination of (R)ead, (W)rite, E(X)ecute, (D)elete, Change (P)ermissions, and Take (O)wnership.

The upcoming sections will take you into more detail of the NTFS permissions and how you can utilize them to your advantage. The sections that are upcoming include:

◆ Determining Effective NTFS Permissions

◆ The effects of Moving and Copying on NTFS Permissions

◆ Setting NTFS Permissions

Determining Effective NTFS Permissions

As with share permissions, NTFS permissions are based on the cumulative permissions from all group memberships. Again, the only wildcard is the No Access permission. If a user, or a local group the user belongs to, is assigned the No Access permission, it does not matter what any other permissions assigned are. The user has no access. The following two examples give you some additional insight into how NTFS permissions are combined, and the effects of the No Access permission.

EXAM TIP

Levels of Access If you are ever required to give more than one level of access to a share, you need a separate local group for each level of access required. An example would be a request to have most users able to connect to the share and read any of the documents located in the share. Another group of users would need to manage the share and modify the contents of the share. The first group of users would need to be made members of a global group that is added to a local group, and that group would be granted READ permissions to the share. The managing users would need to be made members of a separate global group that is added to a local group, and that group would be granted Change permissions to the share.

Example: Combining NTFS Permissions

Here's an example of combining NTFS permissons. Scott is a member of the AccountingDocs local group and a member of the Administrators local group. What would Scott's effective NTFS permissions be if the following permissions have been assigned for the Accounting Data directory in an NTFS volume?

◆ AccountingDocs is assigned Add & Read permissions.

◆ Administrators have been assigned Change permissions.

◆ Scott himself is assigned Read permissions.

The effective permissions for Scott would be Change permissions. This is because the combination of all of his individually assigned NTFS rights would be (RWXD) (RWXD), which equals Change permissions.

Example: The Effect of the No Access NTFS Permissions

In a second example, Scott is still a member of the same local groups (AccountingDocs and Administrators). What would Scott's effective NTFS permissions be if the following NTFS permissions assignments were made?

◆ AccountingDocs is assigned Add & Read permissions.

◆ Administrators have been assigned Full Control permissions.

◆ Users have been assigned Read permissions.

◆ Scott himself is assigned the No Access permission.

In this case, Scott would have no access to the NTFS resource. This is because he himself was assigned the No Access permission. No Access could have been assigned to any of the groups that Scott belonged to with the same result. No Access permissions always result in no access to the NTFS resource.

How Moving and Copying Affect NTFS Permissions

If a file is moved or copied to a new directory, this could change the permissions on an NTFS file. It depends on whether the file is moved or copied and on whether the target directory is on the same NTFS volume.

If a file is copied from one directory to another on a single NTFS volume, the file inherits the directory permissions for new files of the target directory. If a file is moved from one directory to another directory on the same NTFS volume, it retains the same NTFS permissions it had from the originating directory.

It gets confusing when moving or copying files from one NTFS volume to another NTFS volume. When you copy a file from an NTFS volume to another NTFS volume, the file always inherits the permissions of the target directory. This is also the case when you move a file between NTFS volumes. This is because the file is not actually moved between NTFS volumes. The actual process is as follows:

1. The file is copied to the target directory. This causes the file to inherit the permissions of the target directory.

2. The file in the target directory is compared to the originating file to verify that they are identical.

3. The original file is deleted from the originating directory.

Setting NTFS Permissions

NTFS permissions are set from the Security tab of an NTFS file or directory object's Properties dialog box. To set NTFS permissions, a user must meet one of the following criteria:

◆ Be a member of the Administrators local group.

◆ Be a member of the Server Operators local group.

◆ Be a member of the Power Users local group in a Windows NT Workstation or Windows NT Member Server environment.

◆ Be assigned the NTFS Change permission (P) for a directory or file resource.

◆ Be the Owner of a file or directory object. The owner of any object can change the permissions of that object at any time.

◆ Have permission to Take Ownership so that he can become the owner of the file or directory object and change the permissions of that object.

To set the NTFS permissions on a directory or file object, the tasks in Step by Step 5.6 must be performed.

STEP BY STEP

5.6 Setting NTFS Permissions

1. Right-click on the NTFS Resource.

2. Select Properties from the pop-up menu for the object.

3. Switch to the Security tab of the object's Properties dialog box. This only appears if the resource is on an NTFS volume.

4. Click on Permissions.

5. Click on Add… to add new groups and users and to assign NTFS permissions to them (see Figure 5.6).

6. Click on the local group or user that you want to assign permissions to, and choose the NTFS permission you want to assign from the type of Access drop-down list.

7. Click on OK to return to the Directory Permissions dialog box. From the top of the dialog box, choose whether you want to replace the permissions on all subdirectories and on all existing files in the directory (see Figure 5.7).

8. Click on OK to make your changes to NTFS permissions take effect.

9. Answer Yes to the dialog box that questions whether you want the change in security information to replace the existing security information on all files in all subdirectories (see Figure 5.8).

10. Click on OK to exit the directory's properties dialog box.

    The NTFS permissions have been set.

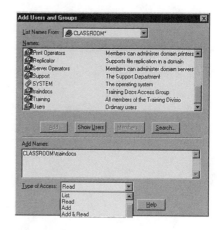

FIGURE 5.6
Setting NTFS permissions for a group.

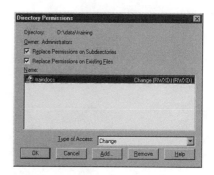

FIGURE 5.7
Setting permissions to replace all existing permissions in the current directory and all subdirectories.

FIGURE 5.8
Verifying the changes to all subdirectories.

USING THE CACLS COMMAND

Although the graphical interface allows for easy changes to the NTFS permissions on a directory, it is lacking in that it replaces all existing security information on a subdirectory. What happens if you simply want to add the Administrators group to have full control of a directory structure? The problem is that the current directory has varying security information throughout the directory tree. The only command that can work for you in this situation is the CACLS.EXE command. CACLS stands for Change the Access Control Lists.

The syntax of the CACLS command is:

```
CACLS filename [/T] [/E] [/C] [/G user:perm] [/R user]
[/P user:perm] [/D user]
```

The syntax elements are defined in the following table:

Option	*Meaning*
filename	The name of the file that you want to change the NTFS permissions of. Wildcards are allowed in place of a file name.
/T	Changes the NTFS permissions for all files in the current directory and all subdirectories.
/E	Edits the existing NTFS permissions rather than replacing the NTFS permissions.
/C	Continues processing the command, even if errors occur during the change of NTFS permissions due to insufficient rights.
/G user:perm	Grants the user (or group) specified the permission. Permissions can include: (R)ead, (C)hange, or (F)ull Control.
/R user	Revokes any rights assigned to the user currently.
/P user:perm	Replaces the user's current NTFS permissions with the PERM specified in the command. Permissions can include: (N)one, (R)ead, (C)hange, or (F)ull Control.
/D user	Denies the specified user access to the NTFS resource by assigning him the No Access permission.

Combining Share and NTFS Permissions

The combination of Windows NT share permissions and NTFS permissions determines the ultimate access a user has to a resource on the server's disk. When combining share permissions and NTFS permissions, no preference is given to one or the other. The key factor is which of the two effective permissions is the most restrictive.

If the shared permissions for a directory are more restrictive than the NTFS permissions, the shared permissions are the effective permissions for the directory when connected to the network. If the NTFS permissions for a directory are more restrictive than the shared permissions, the NTFS permissions are the effective permissions for the directory.

The directory tree shown in Figure 5.9 shows the data folder has been shared as data; the local group Users is assigned the share permission Change. The local group Accounting has been assigned the NTFS permission Change to the Accounting subdirectory. Likewise, the Marketing folder has been assigned two sets of NTFS permissions. The Users local group has been assigned Read permissions, and the Marketing local group has been assigned the Full Control permission.

In this example, the effective share permissions for the entire directory structure are Change for all users of the network. This includes all users except the Guest account from the domain database.

For the Accounting folder, the only group that has access is the Accounting local group. Because the NTFS and share permissions are the same, their effective permissions are Change for the directory. All other users are not able to access the directory because their NTFS effective permissions are not listed. This is different than No Access because if users are made members of the Accounting local group, they then have access to the Accounting directory.

For the Marketing folder, the Marketing local group has effective permissions of Change. This is because the share permission of Change is more restrictive than the Full Control NTFS permission. All other users have an effective permission of Read. This is because the NTFS permission Read, assigned to the local group Users, is more restrictive than the share permissions of Change.

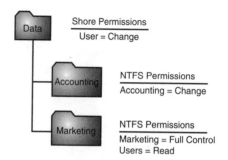

FIGURE 5.9
The data directory's share and NTFS permissions.

The Windows NT Security Model

In the Windows NT security model, users are associated with resources. Each resource has an Access Control List (ACL) that contains Access Control Entries (ACEs). When it is determined whether a user should be granted access to a resource, the user's access token is compared to the ACL for the resource he is trying to access.

When a user logs on to the system, he receives an access token that will be attached to any processes he runs during the logon session. This access token contains his security ID (SID) and all his group memberships. This access token serves as the process's credentials for the logon session. Whenever the user tries to access an object, he presents the access token as his credentials. Because the access token is built during the logon process, group membership is not modified until the next user logon.

When the user attempts to open a resource, the user's access token is compared to the Access Control List for the resource. The Access Control Entries within the Access Control List are, by default, sorted with all No Access permissions at the top of the list. The evaluation of whether the user should be granted access to the resource goes as follows:

1. If the user, or any group he belongs to, is explicitly denied access (assigned the No Access permission), access to the resource is denied.

2. The ACEs are checked next to see if any of the entries explicitly assign the user, or a group the user belongs to, the type of access they are attempting. If there is such an entry, access is granted to the resource.

3. Each entry in the ACL is investigated to see if the accumulated permissions allow the user to have the access he has attempted.

4. If the necessary rights cannot be accumulated from the ACL, the user is denied the access he has attempted.

When a user has opened the object successfully, the user's process is given a handle to the object. This handle is used to identify which user is accessing the object. The system also creates a list of granted access rights to the object. This way, if the user attempts different transactions with the object, only the list of granted rights needs to be evaluated. The entire process of checking the object's ACL does not have to be performed on every transaction attempt.

This is both good and bad. It is good in that subsequent actions on a resource do not require a check against the ACL every time the user attempts to manipulate the data. This ultimately reduces network traffic because the Windows NT Challenge/Response transaction does not have to be performed over and over again. It is bad in that the user has the same access to the object as he did when he opened it, even if the ACL is modified for the object after access has occurred. The list of granted rights to the object that is stored in the user's process table for that handle is not modified. The user has the same level of access until he closes the object and, ultimately, closes the handle to the object.

IMPLEMENTING AUDITING IN WINDOWS NT

Manage disk resources. Tasks include creating and sharing resources, implementing permissions and security, and establishing file auditing.

Auditing features in Windows NT enable the administrator to collect information about how the system is being utilized. All auditing is recorded to the audit log in the Event Viewer. Using the auditing feature, the administrator can find security holes in the network. Auditing can be adjusted to the level required by your organization. Some organizations need intensive auditing to determine usage of the network; others might only require information about logon failures.

An administrator establishes what areas can be audited in a Windows NT domain. Setting the Audit Policy in the User Manager for Domains (see Figure 5.10) accomplishes this.

When setting the Audit Policy, the administrator must determine whether to audit successes and/or failures. The events that can be set for audit are shown in Table 5.3.

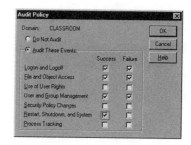

FIGURE 5.10
The Audit Policy dialog box is used to establish what areas can be audited in an NT domain.

TABLE 5.3

AUDIT EVENTS

Category	Meaning
Logon and Logoff	This category charts the successes and/or failures of a single logon/logoff attempt. This includes interactive, network, and service logon/logoff attempts.
File and Object Access	This category charts successes and/or failures of accesses to protected objects. This category must be set to enable auditing of printers and file-level access on NTFS volumes.
Use of User Rights	This category reports on successes and/or failures of a user's attempt to make use of his assigned user rights. This also records when a change is made to the User Rights Policy.
User and Group Management	This category audits any attempts to change the account database, including creating a new account or group and changing the membership of groups. Creating a new user also can lead to file and object-access audit events as the account database is accessed and modified.
Security Policy Changes	This category records any attempts to change the User Rights, Audit, or Trust Relationship Policies.
Restart, Shutdown, and System	This category records, then restarts or shuts down attempts. It also audits trusted logons to the Local Security Authority that affect the system's security.
Process Tracking	This category enables auditing of programs that were executed and closed on the system. This also includes handle duplication and indirect object access.

In the coming sections we will look at auditing for a number of components. The sections are:

◆ Auditing changes to the user account database

◆ Implementing file level auditing

◆ Implementing Print Auditing

◆ Auditing Logons and Logoffs

Auditing Changes to the User Account Database

When an organization implements decentralized administration of the Windows NT account database, it might be desirable to audit all changes to the Accounts database. Remember, only members of the local groups Administrators and Account Operators can add, modify, and delete users in User Manager for Domains.

To enable auditing of changes to the account database, a member of the Administrators group must enable auditing User and Group Management. If you want to know exactly which files are being updated, File and Object Access should also be enabled (see Figure 5.11).

The addition of File and Object Access helps you determine when an Account Operator attempts to add a member to one of the Operator or Administrators local groups. When this attempt is made, the Account Operator faces a dialog box stating that the attempt is unsuccessful. Auditing only User and Group Management does not capture this error. You must enable File and Object Access so you can see the unsuccessful attempt to write to the SAM database (see Figure 5.12).

This Event Viewer security entry shows that Pscott tried to make a change to the object DOMAINS\Builtin\Aliases\00000220. Although, at first look, this does not really explain what Pscott attempted to do, if you look at the SAM hive of the Registry (see Figure 5.13), it begins to make more sense.

If you look at the Domains\Builtin subtree, you can see that the 00000220 folder is the first folder under the Aliases folder. Next, looking in the Names subfolder of the Alias subfolder, you can see that this is the alias for the Account Operators local group. So this failure audit is a result of Pscott attempting to add a new member to the Account Operators local group. This is not possible because Pscott is not a member of the Administrators local group, the only group that can modify operator accounts.

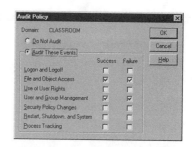

FIGURE 5.11
Settings to audit user and group management; here, File and Object Access is enabled.

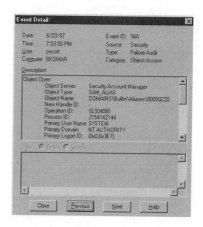

FIGURE 5.12
An object access failure event.

FIGURE 5.13
The HKEY_LOCAL_MACHINE\SAM\SAM\
Domains\Builtin hive.

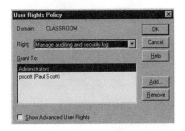

FIGURE 5.14
Setting the Manage auditing and security log
user right.

Implementing File-Level Auditing

File-level auditing enables an administrator to review the security log to determine who might have created, deleted, or modified a specified file or directory. This can help identify problems in the security model implemented in a domain. To set up file-level auditing, two separate steps are required:

1. Enable File and Object Access auditing in the domain's Audit Policy.

2. Enable the detail of file-level auditing that you want to employ on specific file and directory objects on an NTFS volume.

A member of the Administrators local group must enable File and Object Access auditing (refer to Figure 5.10). After this has been enabled, administrators and any users or groups assigned the user right Manage auditing and security log (see Figure 5.14) can set auditing on specific directories and review the security log for audit successes and failures.

To set up auditing on a specific directory or file on an NTFS volume, the person assigned the task of setting up auditing must bring up the properties for that directory or file object. After selecting the Security tab of the object's Properties dialog box, the person can click on Auditing to set the auditing levels for that object (see Figure 5.15).

Setting the Permissions to Audit

Figure 5.16 provides an example of the Directory Auditing dialog box of an object's Security properties.

The administrator has to set the following items:

◆ Who are you going to audit?

◆ What actions are you going to audit?

◆ Do you want to apply this auditing to files and subfolders?

When determining who you are going to audit, remember that you are more likely to determine who was performing a task by auditing the Everyone group rather than a smaller local group. The Everyone group is preferred when auditing because it includes all users that connect to the network (whether they are known users is not important). If you know, however, that only members of the local group Accounting_Users have access to a folder and its subfolders, then it is fine to just audit this group.

After you have selected who you are going to audit, you now must select what actions you are going to audit. Auditing is always based on either successes or failures. Be careful what you choose here. The actions that can be audited for a file or folder directly match the six different NTFS permissions. You must choose the correct combination of permissions being used to determine who is performing the task that has caused the need for an audit. Remember, if you are trying to determine who has been deleting the General Ledger, you must audit delete successes (as they have been very successful in deleting the file). Actions that can be audited include the following:

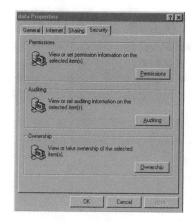

FIGURE 5.15
The Security tab of an NTFS directory.

◆ By enabling the Read event, it can be determined whether an attempt was made to open a file.

◆ By enabling the Write event, it can be determined when a user attempted to modify the contents of a file.

◆ By enabling the Execute event, it can be determined when a user has attempted to run a program.

◆ By enabling the Delete event, it can be determined when a user has attempted to delete a file object.

◆ By enabling the Change Permissions event, it can be determined when a user has tried to change the permissions on a file or directory.

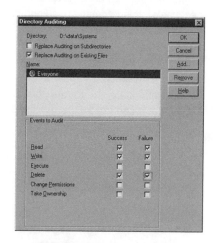

◆ By enabling the Take Ownership event, it can be determined when a user has attempted to take ownership of a file or directory object.

FIGURE 5.16
Setting auditing on a folder.

After auditing has been set, the Event Viewer's security log can be checked to determine whether there has been access to the file or directory on which auditing was enabled. Figure 5.17 shows an event in which BKOMAR attempted to delete the file named SECRET.DOC. It is recorded as a failure event in the Event Viewer. The event shows that BKOMAR from the Classroom domain was denied when attempting to delete the file D:\DATA\SYSTEMS\SECRET.DOC. If you scroll further down in the dialog box, it reveals that the access tried was Delete.

N O T E **Auditing Different Groups for Same Resource** If you want to audit different groups for the same resource, you can set different areas to audit for each group. Just select the group in the Name section of the Directory Auditing dialog box and set the events you want to audit for that group. Each group can have its own audit settings.

N O T E **Don't Crowd the Security Log File** When auditing, you need to be careful because all this information is kept in the NT security log file. This file can fill up quickly if you are auditing too many things. Be selective in the events that you audit. Also be sure to set an appropriate size for the audit log so that it can handle the number of events that will be recorded.

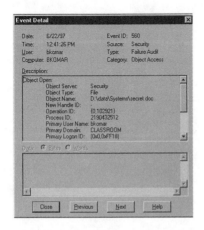

FIGURE 5.17
Security failure event for an attempt to delete a file; BKOMAR attempted to delete SECRET.DOC.

How Moving and Copying Files Affects Auditing

As with NTFS permissions, the task of copying and moving files directly affects the auditing of files. If you copy a file from one NTFS directory to another NTFS directory, the new copy of the file inherits the auditing set on the target directory.

If you move a file from one NTFS directory to another NTFS directory on the same logical volume, the file maintains the same auditing settings it had in the first directory.

If you move a file from one NTFS directory to another NTFS directory, but they reside on different NTFS logical volumes, the file inherits the audit settings of the new folder. This is because anytime a file is moved between volumes on Windows NT, the actual chain of events is a copy, verify, and delete. That is, a copy of the original file is placed in the new directory. This copy is verified against the original copy of the file. If they match, the original file is deleted.

Implementing Print Auditing

Like file and directory auditing, print auditing is also available under Windows NT. Auditing printing enables you to monitor the following areas of printing:

◆ Who attempted to print a document to a specific printer?

◆ Who attempted to manage documents that have been sent to a printer? This includes changing the order of documents in the printer or halting the printer itself.

◆ Who attempted to delete a document in the printer?

◆ Who attempted to change the permissions assigned to the printer?

◆ Who attempted to take ownership of the printer?

The Printer Auditing dialog box is accessed by clicking on the Auditing button in the Security tab of the printer's Properties dialog box (see Figure 5.18).

Auditing a printer is set up exactly the same as auditing folders. You must determine who you want to audit and which events the audit monitors. Be careful which groups you perform auditing on. This list should match the local groups that have been assigned permissions to use the printer.

After auditing settings have been established, the administrator—or a user with the user right to Manage auditing and the security log—can view the auditing events in the security log of the Event Viewer.

Auditing Logons and Logoffs

If you feel your network has been compromised and unwanted users are accessing it, auditing logons and logoffs can help determine what account they are using to access the network and what computer they are accessing the network from.

Auditing the successes and failures of the Logon and Logoff audit category can determine where the access point to your network might be. It is recommended that you monitor both successes and failures—you not only want to know where the attempts to access the network are taking place, you want to know whether they are successful.

Figure 5.19 shows a security log entry for an unsuccessful logon attempt. The figure shows that someone attempted to log on to the CLASSROOM domain using the account named BKOMAR. The workstation where the logon was attempted was also named BKOMAR. Does this mean that someone tried to log on to the network using BKOMAR's account? Not necessarily. This could also just be a mistyped password. The key is to watch for trends in logon attempts.

> **EXAM TIP**
>
> **Auditing Questions** Most questions ask you to determine what level of auditing needs to be established for a directory. Know the six different events that can be audited for a directory and what each event means. Also, be looking for a trick question that asks you to audit a file on a FAT volume. Auditing can only be performed on NTFS volumes.

> **EXAM TIP**
>
> **Transferring Files** You can expect a question that involves copying or moving a file and the effect on its compression settings, NTFS permissions, or auditing settings. Watch out for the trick question that transfers the file to a FAT volume. FAT does not support any of these features, so it would remove all settings established for the file.

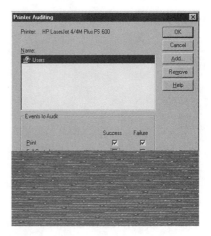

FIGURE 5.18
The Printer Auditing dialog box is used to set auditing on a printer.

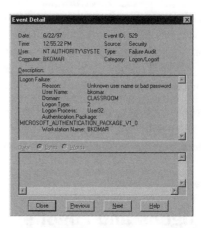

FIGURE 5.19
A logon attempt failure event in the security
log; someone attempted to log on to the
CLASSROOM domain using the account named
BKOMAR.

CASE STUDY: IMPLEMENTING SECURITY

ESSENCE OF THE CASE

Here are the essential elements in this case:

- Require a process to secure each individual file on the Windows NT Servers.

- Require auditing of access usage of select files on the Windows NT server.

- Need an advanced level of security for the files, both network and local.

SCENARIO

A legal firm has been noticing that valuable client information has been leaked out of confidential reports that are located on their corporate server. They believe that the information is secured, but wanted to increase the security to the files located on their Windows NT Servers. They currently use network share permissions for securing access and resource permissions. The Windows NT Servers are physically located in a locked room with only select individuals with the keys for the server room. They want to absolutely secure their environment and implement the auditing the accessing of confidential files.

ANALYSIS

In developing a solution for their needs, the first step was to convert all disk drives on the Windows NT servers to the NTFS partition. With NTFS as the file system, they were able to assign

CASE STUDY: IMPLEMENTING SECURITY

access permissions to each file and directory, in addition to the network permissions assigned by the network share. Due to the integrated auditing features of Windows NT and the NTFS file system, they were also able to enable the file auditing features which enabled them to maintain a log of file and directory usage. The legal firm found that the implementation of these features was the correct answer to their security needs.

CHAPTER SUMMARY

There will be several questions on the exam that test your ability to assign NTFS and share permissions. Most cases involve a multidomain model. Remember the following tips:

- ◆ Users can only be assigned to global groups in the same domain.

- ◆ Only global groups from trusted domains can become members of local groups in trusting domains.

- ◆ NTFS permissions are only assigned to local groups in all correct test answers.

- ◆ Only NTFS permissions give you file-level security.

Understanding the auditing options available for file, directory, and print auditing are the main items to remember for the exam. There is not a large focus on questions regarding the implementation of auditing, rather they are directed towards what information auditing can gather, and where the audit logs are kept.

KEY TERMS
- IIS
- NTFS
- FAT
- CACLS

APPLY YOUR LEARNING

This section allows you to assess how well you understood the material in the chapter. Review and Exam questions test your knowledge of the tasks and concepts specified in the objectives. The Exercises provide you with opportunities to engage in the sorts of tasks that comprise the skill sets the objectives reflect.

For more Review and Exam type questions, see the Top Score test engine on the CD-ROM that came with this book.

Exercises

5.1   Implementing Web Administration

This exercise requires the WEBADMIN.EXE utility found on this book's CD-ROM. It reviews the steps necessary to install the Web Administration tools and creates a new user using the web tools. This exercise assumes IIS is presently installed on your system.

Time Estimate: 30 minutes

1. On the CD, double-click on the WEBADMIN.EXE program.

2. The installation starts by asking you to agree to the End User License Agreement. Click on I agree.

3. The software installs itself. At completion, it displays the Readme.doc for the program.

4. Start Internet Explorer.

5. Go to the address **http://localhost/ntadmin/ntadmin.htm**.

6. Click on the Accounts option.

7. Click on the Users hyperlink.

8. Click on Create New to create a new user account.

9. Enter the following information:
   - User Name: **smann**
   - Full Name: **Sandra Mann**
   - Password: **welcome**
   - Confirm Password: **welcome**
   - Comment: Office Manager

10. Only select Must Change Password Next Logon.

11. Click on Create. The follow-up web page should state Successfully able to create user "smann."

5.2   Determining NTFS and Shared Permissions

This is a paper-based exercise based on the domain structure shown in Figure 5.20.

Time Estimate: 30 minutes

Dianne, Lynn, Chris, Claire, Shelley, Kerri, and Maureen all have accounts in the central Head Office Accounts domain. The following responsibilities have been assigned to the users:

◆ Claire, Chris, and Dianne need to back up and restore all files in the BOSTON, TORONTO, and HEADOFFICE domains.

◆ Shelley is assigned the task of creating new user accounts for new employees.

◆ All seven users require access to the programs share on the PRODUCTION computer. The PRODUCTION computer is a PDC in the BOSTON domain.

APPLY YOUR LEARNING

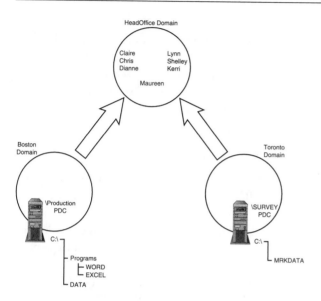

FIGURE 5.20
A multidomain trust example.

◆ Maureen and Kerri are completing a market survey and need appropriate access to the MRKDATA share on the SURVEY server in the TORONTO domain. The SURVEY server is a PDC in the TORONTO domain.

◆ The DATA share requires the capability for only the user who stored a document on the share to be able to modify the document. All other users should be able to view the document but not make modifications. The DATA share is located on the PRODUCTION server in the BOSTON domain.

Based on these specifications, answer the following questions:

1. What local group can provide the backup capabilities needed by Claire, Chris, and Dianne?

2. What group memberships are required to allow Claire, Chris, and Dianne to perform their backup and restore tasks?

3. Which domain should Shelley be creating new user accounts in?

4. What group memberships should be performed to grant Shelley the necessary rights to created new user accounts?

5. What NTFS permissions need to be set to enable all users to use the programs directory?

6. What directory should be shared to enable access to the Word and Excel programs?

7. What permissions should be set on this share?

8. What group assignments are required to make this share accessible to all seven users?

9. What directory needs to be shared to grant Maureen and Kerri access to the market survey data?

10. What group memberships are required to grant Maureen and Kerri access to the market survey data?

11. What share and NTFS permissions need to be set to grant the desired level of access?

12. Which directory should be shared to grant users an access point to the central data share?

13. What permissions and group assignments are required to grant the desired levels of access to the data share? Keep in mind there are two levels of access required to the share.

APPLY YOUR LEARNING

Solutions:

1. Backup Operators

2. In the HEADOFFICE domain, you must create a global group to contain Claire, Chris, and Dianne's accounts. Say you named the global group BACKUPS. Next you assign the HEAD-OFFICE\BACKUPS global group as a member of the BOSTON\BACKUP OPERATORS, TORONTO\BACKUP OPERATORS, and HEADOFFICE\BACKUP OPERATORS local groups.

3. HEADOFFICE

4. Because the accounts only need to be created in the Master domain of the model, you have two choices. The 100-percent Microsoft solution has you create a global group in the HEADOFFICE domain called ACCOUNTS. This global group then is made a member of the HEADOFFICE\ACCOUNT OPERATORS local group. Because there is only one account, you also could just assign Shelley's user account as a member of the HEADOFFICE\ACCOUNT OPERATORS local group.

5. The NTFS permission READ should be assigned to the local group BOSTON\USERS. This NTFS permissions assignment should be applied to the programs directory and all its subdirectories.

6. The c:\programs directory on the PRODUC-TION server should be shared as PROGRAMS.

7. The share permissions should be set with BOSTON\USERS having the READ share permission. To run programs, no greater permissions than READ are required.

8. The global group HEADOFFICE\DOMAIN USERS should be made a member of the local group BOSTON\USERS. This enables all the users in the HEADOFFICE domain to have access to the PROGRAMS share in the BOSTON domain.

9. C:\MRKDATA on the SURVEY server in the TORONTO domain

10. A global group must be created in the HEAD-OFFICE domain that includes only the accounts for Maureen and Kerri. Assume this group is named SURVEYORS. Next, a local group has to be created in the TORONTO domain to grant access rights to the MRKDATA share. Assuming this local group is called MRKDATUSERS, the HEADOFFICE\SURVEYORS global group is assigned as a member of the TORONTO\MRKDATUSERS local group.

11. The following share and NTFS permission assignments would be performed:

    • Set the share permissions on the MRKDATA share so only the TORONTO\MRKDATUSERS local group has Change permissions.

    • Set the NTFS permissions on C:\MRKDATA as TORONTO\MRKDATUSERS having Change permissions.

12. The C:\DATA directory on the PRODUCTION server should be shared as DATA to grant access to the data share.

13. The following group assignments, and share and NTFS permission assignments would be made:

    • The HEADOFFICE\DOMAIN USERS global group was already made a member

APPLY YOUR LEARNING

of the BOSTON\USERS local group in answer 8.

- The Data directory's share permissions should be set so BOSTON\USERS has Change permissions.

- The C:\DATA NTFS permissions should be set so the BOSTON\USERS local group has ADD & READ permissions to the directory. Also, the special group CREATOR/OWNER should be assigned Change permissions. This combination enables any user to add a document to the data share, but only the author of the document is able to modify or delete the document.

5.3 Determining an Audit Policy

This is a paper-based exercise to determine an Audit Policy for your domain.

Time Estimate: 15 minutes

The following criteria are used to make your decision:

- ◆ The XYZ Corporation needs to know whenever a user is not able to log on to the network successfully. Management feels the network has slowed down and needs proof that it is affecting logon authentication.

- ◆ Due to some security breaches, several users have been given access to the accounts database. The company wants to know who has been modifying the accounts database.

- ◆ The server has been shut down on several mornings. Management wants to know which user has been shutting down the server.

- ◆ To prevent tampering with the Audit policies determined in this exercise, management wants every change to audit policies to be tracked.

Based on these specifications, answer the following questions:

1. What Audit Policy should you set for the domain?

2. Which users can set up this auditing policy?

3. How do you give the Managers global group the capability to review the audit logs for the domain?

Solutions:

1. The following Audit Policy could be implemented:

   - Failure of Logon and Logoff

   - Success and Failure of User and Group Management

   - Success and Failure of Restart, Shutdown, and System

   - Success and Failure of Security Policy Changes

2. Only members of the Administrators local group can set Audit Policy.

3. You first create a local group called Auditors in your domain. Next add the Managers global group as a member of the Auditors local group. Finally, you assign the Auditors local group the user right Manage auditing and security log. This enables them to review the audit logs. By using a local group for this assignment, you allow for

growth if another trusted domain needs the same level of access. A global group from this domain could be added to the local group Auditors.

Review Questions

1. What operating systems can be used to remotely administer Windows NT domains using the standard utilities included with Windows NT?

2. What auditing settings do you use to determine which account was being used to attempt access to the LAN?

3. Can Windows NT be administered from a Macintosh computer system?

4. A file is currently stored in a directory on an NTFS partition with the current permissions of Change. If the file is moved to a new directory on the same partition with Full Control permissions, what are the permissions of the moved file?

5. A file is currently stored in a directory on an NTFS partition with the current permissions of Change. If the file is moved to a new directory on a different NTFS partition with Full Control permissions, what are the permissions of the moved file?

Exam Questions

1. The XYZ Corporation has decided to implement auditing in the domain. The decision to implement auditing was based on a hacker's attempt to access accounting information on the network. The goals that the XYZ corporation wants to achieve are:

Primary Objective

The XYZ Corporation wants to keep track of all logons and logoffs to the network so it can better determine who is logging on to their network and when.

Secondary Objectives

The XYZ Corporation fears that someone on the inside is granting unwanted access to resources. Due to this, they want to monitor all changes to the Accounts in their organization; and

The XYZ Corporation wants to determine actual usage of its accounting database. It is located on the server named ACCOUNTS in the share named DATA.

Proposed Solution

The auditing policy for the domain was set as the following:

- Audit both Success and Failure for Logon and Logoff

- Monitor Success and Failure for File and Object Access

- Monitor Success and Failure for User and Group Management

No other configuration was performed to implement these audit policies.

This implementation answers:

A. The primary objective and the two secondary objectives

B. The primary objective and only one of the secondary objectives

C. Only the primary objective

D. None of the objectives

APPLY YOUR LEARNING

2. Which client operating systems can the Server Tools for Windows NT be installed to?

   A. Windows 95

   B. Windows NT Workstation

   C. OS/2

   D. Windows for Workgroups

   E. DOS

3. To monitor users attempts to change their passwords, the following auditing category must be enabled:

   A. File and Object Access

   B. Security Policy Change

   C. Use of User Rights

   D. User and Group Management

4. What utilities from the following list are available to a Windows 95 system running the Window NT Server Tools?

   A. User Manager for Domains

   B. DHCP Manager

   C. WINS Manager

   D. Event Viewer

   E. Server Manager

5. To determine who has been changing the account policy for a domain, you would enable which audit category?

   A. Logon and Logoff

   B. User and Group Management

   C. Security Policy Changes

   D. Process Tracking

6. The data directory is shared with the following permissions:

   Group1 : Read

   Group3 : Full Control

   The Accounting subdirectory of the data directory has been assigned the following NTFS permissions:

   Allen : Add

   Group2 : Change

   Group3 : Change

   If Allen is a member of Group1 and Group2, what are his effective permissions in the Accounting folder when he connects through the network?

   A. Read

   B. Add

   C. Change

   D. Full Control

Answers to Review Questions

1. Windows for Workgroups, Windows 95, Windows NT Workstation, and Windows NT Member Servers. See the section "Web-Based Administration Tools" for more information.

2. Enable auditing for Logons and Logoffs. Be sure to enable logging for both successes and failures. See the section "Auditing Logons and Logoffs" for more information.

APPLY YOUR LEARNING

3. Yes. If you had enabled Services for Macintosh to allow the Macintosh user to authenticate with the NT Network, you then could use the Web Administration tools that ship with the NT Server Resource Kit. See the section "Web-Based Administration Tools" for more information.

4. The permissions remain Change permissions in the case of moving a file to a new directory on the same partition. See the section "How Moving and Copying Affect NTFS Permissions" for more information.

5. The file now has Full Control permissions. This is because whenever a file is moved between partitions, it is actually copied, verified, then deleted. This prevents a loss of data if the move did not occur correctly. See the section "How Moving and Copying Affect NTFS Permissions" for more information.

Answers to Exam Questions

1. **B.** Just adding file and object access does not audit changes to the actual Accounting database. The actual data directory has to have auditing configured to audit Read and Write events to note changes to the accounting database. See the section "Implementing File-Level Auditing."

2. **A. B. D.** The server tools for Windows NT server are available on Windows 95, Windows NT Workstation, and Windows for Workgroups. See the section "Remote Administration of Windows NT."

3. **D.** The User and Group Management category should be enabled to audit success and failure in order to monitor the password changing attempts. See the section "Auditing Changes to the User Account Database."

4. **A. D. E.** A windows 95 system that has the server tools installed would have User manager for domains, event viewer, and the server manager utilities available. See the section "Remote Administration Tools for Windows 95."

5. **C.** Enabling success and failures to the Security Policy Changes in the audit would allow you to monitor changes and attempted changes to the account policies. See the section "Auditing Changes to the User Account Database."

6. **A.** When Allen connects through the network, he would have the read permissions to that share. See the section "Combining Share and NTFS Permissions."

CONNECTIVITY

This chapter helps you to prepare for the Microsoft exam by covering the following objective within the "Connectivity" category:

Install and configure multiprotocol routing to serve various functions. Functions include

- ◆ **Internet router**

- ◆ **BOOTP/DHCP Relay Agent**

- ◆ **IPX Router**

▶ This objective focuses on the connectivity protocols available in Windows NT Server and how they can be configured to enable multiprotocol routing in your Windows NT Server environment.

CHAPTER 6

Connectivity:
Multiprotocol Routing

Connectivity in Windows NT is one of the strongest points of the operating system. By allowing the connectivity between Windows NT and almost all other network operating systems, the multiprotocol routing is a critical piece of the enterprise environment. To prepare for this component of the exam, you must read and reread this chapter, paying close attention to the benefits and flexibility and the routing capabilities of each protocol. Hands-on experience would be helpful in your preparations; however, the exam does not focus on the procedures of these topics. The exam focuses more on the reasons and benefits of multiprotocol routing in a Windows NT Enterprise environment.

Microsoft Windows NT 4 was designed with the enterprise customer in mind; therefore, it has the capability to interoperate in heterogeneous environments. In this chapter, you are introduced to the connectivity tools built into Windows NT. The enterprise exam contains various questions relating to Windows NT's heterogeneous connectivity solutions. Answering these questions successfully requires a strong working knowledge of the built-in utilities as well as experience in implementing these tools.

This chapter discusses various networking protocols and how they are used to achieve interconnectivity. The benefit of interconnectivity and specifically the use of protocols and services to achieve a multiprotocol routed environment are critical in any Windows NT environment. This chapter covers the following main topics:

◆ Communication protocols in Windows NT Server 4.0

◆ Configuring the enterprise protocols

◆ Installing and configuring multiprotocol routing

COMMUNICATION PROTOCOLS IN WINDOWS NT SERVER 4.0

Microsoft distributes Windows NT with support for these popular protocols:

◆ TCP/IP

◆ IPX or NWLink

◆ NetBEUI

◆ DLC

◆ AppleTalk

The following sections overview each protocol; then, the chapter explains how to configure these protocols.

TCP/IP

The Transmission Control Protocol/Internet Protocol (TCP/IP) is an industry-standard suite of protocols designed for wide area network (WAN) environments. TCP/IP was developed in 1969 by the U.S. Department of Defense Advanced Research Projects Agency as a resource-sharing experiment called ARPAnet. Its purpose was to provide high-speed communication links using packet-switched networks. Since 1969, ARPAnet has grown into a worldwide community of networks known as the Internet. TCP/IP also is a popular protocol in academic environments because it is freely available and the source code is widely distributed. Hence, it has become accepted as the de facto communication protocol for UNIX-type hosts as well.

Although called TCP/IP, this acronym actually refers to a whole suite of protocols. Figure 6.1 summarizes the protocol suite.

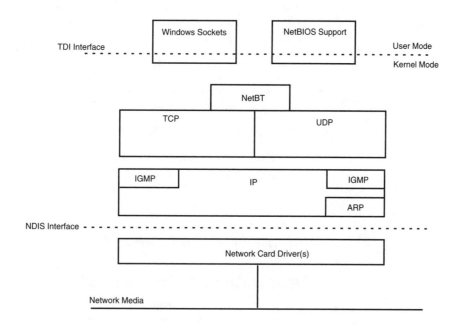

FIGURE 6.1

A graphical representation of the TCP/IP protocol suite.

To gain an understanding of these protocols, you need to take a quick tour of the different modules, or subprotocols, of the suite. The following sections cover the most important aspects:

- ◆ TCP
- ◆ UDP
- ◆ IP
- ◆ ICMP
- ◆ ARP
- ◆ Other IP protocols
- ◆ API interfaces

Transmission Control Protocol (TCP)

TCP is a reliable, connection-oriented delivery service that provides much of the same functionality as User Datagram Protocol (UDP). TCP views data as a stream of bytes, rather than frames. The data transmits in segments.

Connection-oriented means that

- ◆ For each segment sent, the receiving host must return an acknowledgment (ACK) within a specified period.
- ◆ If an ACK is not received, the data is retransmitted.
- ◆ If the segment arrives corrupted, the receiving host discards it. Because an ACK is not sent, the sender retransmits the segment.

Examples of applications that use the TCP transport mechanism are File Transfer Protocol (FTP) and any HTTP Web client.

User Datagram Protocol (UDP)

The User Datagram Protocol (UDP) provides a connectionless datagram service that offers unreliable, best-effort delivery. The arrival of datagrams is not guaranteed, nor is the correct sequencing of delivered packets.

Applications that do not require an acknowledgment of data receipt use UDP. The Domain Name Resolver (DNR), the NetBIOS over TCP/IP (NBT) driver, Simple Network Management Protocol (SNMP), and other sockets-based applications use UDP.

Internet Protocol (IP)

The Internet Protocol (IP) is the second of two primary TCP/IP protocols. Unlike the reliable, connection-oriented delivery that the TCP protocol provides, the Internet Protocol is an unreliable, best-effort, connectionless delivery service. Delivery is not guaranteed; a packet might be lost, delivered out of sequence, duplicated, or delayed.

Connectionless means that

◆ IP packets are independent from other packets.

◆ An acknowledgment is not required when data is received.

◆ The sender and receiver aren't informed when a packet is lost or sent out of sequence.

IP assumes delivery might be difficult. It always makes a best-effort attempt to deliver a packet. The IP protocol provides routing of information from one host to another (routing is its primary function). It also provides a mechanism for fragmentation and reassembly of packets by setting rules that tell routers what to do with packets. If a router cannot transfer the entire datagram, the router can fragment the packet into smaller pieces before continuing. The IP protocol also defines how data is transferred throughout the internetwork.

The implementation of IP in Microsoft TCP/IP does not fragment packets. Because a router could fragment the IP packet, however, Microsoft TCP/IP does handle reassembly.

Internet Control Message Protocol (ICMP)

The Internet Control Message Protocol (ICMP) is a mechanism for reporting errors that result from delivery problems. A connectionless system means that datagrams are delivered without any coordination between the originating and destination workstations. If the time-to-live counter expires due to network congestion or the unavailability of a destination workstation, IP fails to deliver the datagram. ICMP must be implemented in all TCP/IP implementations.

Table 6.1 shows the most common ICMP messages.

TABLE 6.1

COMMON ICMP MESSAGES

Message	Use
Echo request and echo reply:	Used in the ping utility
Source quench:	Indicates congestion on a port
Destination unreachable:	Indicates a route or host is down

ICMP messages are contained in IP datagrams to ensure that the messages can find their way to the appropriate hosts.

Address Resolution Protocol (ARP)

Before computers can communicate on a network, they must know each other's physical addresses, or Media Access Control (MAC) address. ARP obtains the physical address of a TCP/IP host and maps it to the host's logical IP address. TCP/IP uses the IP address to identify a host as part of a TCP/IP Internet. Obtaining the physical address is known as *address resolution*. Address resolution occurs when the requesting host sends a request broadcast on the local network using the target host's destination IP address. The target host responds by sending a broadcast reply of its physical address and adding the physical address to the sender's hardware address field.

Other IP Protocols

Two common line protocols are Serial Link Internetwork Protocol (SLIP) and Point-to-Point Protocol (PPP). These protocols are used for communication between two TCP/IP-based host machines through asynchronous or synchronous modems and telephone lines.

API Interfaces

API stands for Application Programmers Interface. Windows NT 4 provides two APIs for application developers to access the IP protocol stack:

◆ The NetBIOS API

◆ The Windows Sockets API

The NetBIOS API

IBM originally created the NetBIOS set of API calls to provide a
simple way for developers to write network-aware applications. The
original API set had a few limitations, such as a connection limitation of 255 sessions. Microsoft extended this API set to form the
NetBIOS interface available in Windows NT today. Almost all the
Microsoft applications that ship with Windows NT are based on this
NetBIOS API set. You can see this in the interfaces of almost all the
administrative tools, such as Explorer and Performance Monitor, in
which NetBIOS machine names are used to uniquely identify the
systems. (Many legacy and new third-party applications, such as
Lotus Notes, use the NetBIOS interface as well.)

To overcome the limitations of NetBIOS API, Windows NT also
currently supports Windows Sockets (or Winsock, as it is more commonly known).

The Windows Sockets API

The Winsock API originally was developed for Berkeley UNIX and
was called Berkeley Sockets API. The UNIX community widely
adopted it, and then, Microsoft adapted it for the Windows platforms.

The benefit of using this API as opposed to the NetBIOS interface is
scalability. The Winsock API's scalability stems from the addressing
structure that IP uses.

The IP Address Mechanism

This section overviews IP's address mechanism. For more in-depth
coverage, see the Microsoft Authorized Technical Education Center
(ATEC) document "Supporting TCP/IP on Windows NT." You can
find these documents on the Microsoft Web site at
`http://www.microsoft.com/train_cert`.

TCP/IP hosts are identified by logical IP addresses. The IP address
identifies a computer's location on the network, similar to the way a
street address identifies a house on a city block. Just as a street
address must identify a unique residence, an IP address must be
globally unique and have a uniform format.

An IP address is 32 bits long and consists of four 8-bit fields. The
fields are separated by periods. Each field can represent a decimal

number from 0 through 255. This format is called dotted decimal notation:

```
240.24.2.3
```

Each IP address defines the network address and the host address. The network address identifies the network as a whole. All computers on a given network must have the same network address. That network address, however, must be unique on the Internet.

The host address identifies a workstation, server, or router within a network. The address for each host must be unique to the network address.

Address Classes

The Internet community has defined five classes of addresses to accommodate networks of varying sizes. LAN Manager supports class A, B, and C networks. The address class defines the fields used for the network address and the host address. It also determines the number of networks and the number of hosts per network. If you plan to use Internet resources, you must obtain one or more unique network addresses from the Network Information Center (NIC).

Table 6.2 shows the network address and host address fields for class A, B, and C IP addressing.

TABLE 6.2

CLASSES AND ADDRESSING

Class	IP Address	Network Address	Host Address
A	w.x.y.z	w	x.y.z
B	w.x.y.z	w.x	y.z
C	w.x.y.z	w.x.y	z

Class A Addresses

Class A addresses are assigned to networks that have many hosts. The high-order bit in a class A address is always set to zero. The next seven bits (the first field) represent the network address. The remaining 24 bits (the last three fields) represent the host address. This enables 126 networks and approximately 17 million hosts per network.

Class B Addresses

Class B addresses are assigned to medium-sized networks. The high-order bits in a class B address are always set to 1–0. The next 14 bits (the first two fields) represent the network address. The remaining 24 bits (the last two fields) represent the host address. This enables 16,384 networks and approximately 65,534 hosts per network. Refer to Table 6.2 to see an example of Class B addresses.

Class C Addresses

Class C addresses usually are used for small LANs. The high-order bits in class C addresses are always set to 1–1–0. The next 21 bits (the first three fields) represent the network address. The remaining eight bits (the last field) represent the host address. This enables approximately 2 million networks and 254 hosts per network. As shown in Table 6.2, a class C address can have 254 hosts.

IP Addressing Guidelines

This section describes guidelines for a number of IP addressing areas:

- ◆ Network address
- ◆ Valid private Internet network address range
- ◆ Host address
- ◆ Subnet masks
- ◆ DHCP (automatic IP address assignment)
- ◆ Address translation

Understanding each of the guidelines associated with each of these areas is crucial to understanding the IP addressing scheme for an enterprise network.

Network Address

The following guidelines apply to the network address:

◆ The network address must be unique. If you are on the Internet, the network address must be unique to the Internet. If you are not on the Internet, the network address must be unique to your intranet.

◆ The network address cannot begin with the number 127. The number 127 in a class A address is reserved for internal loop-back functions.

◆ The first field in a network address cannot be zero (all bits set to 0). Zero indicates that the address is a local host and cannot be routed.

◆ The first field in a network address cannot be 255 (all bits set to 1). The number 255 acts as a broadcast.

Valid Private Internet Network Address Range

Table 6.3 provides the valid private Internet network address ranges.

TABLE 6.3

VALID PRIVATE INTERNET ADDRESSES

Class	Beginning	Ending
Class A	001.x.y.z	126.x.y.z
Class B	128.0.y.z	191.255.y.z
Class C	192.0.0.z	223.255.255.z

Host Address

The following guidelines apply to the host address:

◆ The host address must be unique to the network address.

◆ The host address cannot be all 1 bits. If all bits are set to 1 (or an address of 255), the address is interpreted as a broadcast address rather than a host address.

◆ The host address cannot be all 0 bits. If all bits are set to 0, the address is interpreted to mean "this network only."

Subnet Masks

A subnet is used to define your local network segment, which is used to group your physical network addresses within your range of IP addresses. To implement subnet addressing, some bits from the host address are used for the network address of the subnet. The purpose of the subnet mask is to inform TCP/IP hosts which bits of the 32-bit IP address correspond to the network address and which bits correspond to the host address. It accomplishes this function by masking the network address. Bits corresponding to the network address are set to 1. Bits corresponding to the host address are set to 0.

If you do not use subnets, Windows NT 4 requires that you use a default subnet mask. In a default subnet mask, all bits corresponding to the network address are set to 1. The decimal value is 255.

Table 6.4 shows the default subnet masks that Windows NT 4 uses.

TABLE 6.4

SUBNET MASKS

Address Class	Bits Used for Subnet Mask	Dotted Notation
Class A	11111111 00000000 00000000 00000000	255.0.0.0
Class B	11111111 11111111 00000000 00000000	255.255.0.0
Class C	11111111 11111111 11111111 00000000	255.255.255.0

To implement subnet addressing, you must define a subnet mask for your intranet. The number of host bits set to 1 varies, depending on the total number of subnets.

Table 6.5 provides examples of class A and class B subnet masks using four bits from the host address.

TABLE 6.5

CLASS A AND B SUBNET MASKS

Address Class	Bits Used for Subnet Mask	Dotted Notation
Class A	11111111 11110000 00000000 00000000	255.240.0.0
Class B	11111111 11111111 11110000 00000000	255.255.240.0

The number of bits used for the subnet mask determines the possible number of subnets and hosts per subnet. Before you define a subnet mask, you should have a good idea of the number of subnets and hosts you'll have in the future. Using more bits than required for the subnet mask can save you the time and trouble of having to reassign IP addresses in the future.

If you use a class B address and have 7 subnets, for example, you need 4 bits for your subnet mask (3 bits only allow for 6 subnets). This leaves 4 bits for the host address, allowing 4,094 possible hosts. If you know that the number of hosts per subnet will never exceed 1,000, but that the number of subnets could increase to as many as 60, you should use 6 bits for the subnet mask to allow for up to 62 subnets, with 1,022 hosts per subnet.

To define a subnet mask, perform the tasks outlined in Step by Step 6.1.

STEP BY STEP

6.1 Defining a Subnet Mask

1. Determine the number of subnets required; based on this number, determine the number of bits to use for the subnet mask.

2. Evaluate the possible number of hosts per subnet.

3. Use additional bits for the subnet mask if either of the following applies to your situation:

- You expect never to require as many hosts per subnet as the remaining bits allow.

- You expect the number of subnets to increase in the future, requiring additional bits from the host address.

Defining your subnets can be somewhat tricky if you do not analyze your current and future needs appropriately. Ensure that you break down each subnet so the correct number of hosts are assigned to each subnet.

Table 6.6 lists the subnet masks for class A networks.

TABLE 6.6

SUBNET MASKS FOR CLASS A NETWORKS

Required Number of Subnets	Number of Hosts per Subnet	Number of Bits	Subnet Mask
0	Invalid	1	Invalid
2	4,194,302	2	255.192.0.0
6	2,097,150	3	255.224.0.0
14	1,048,574	4	255.240.0.0
30	524,286	5	255.248.0.0
62	262,142	6	255.252.0.0
126	131,070	7	255.254.0.0
254	65,534	8	255.255.0.0

Table 6.7 lists the subnet masks for class B networks.

N O T E

Number of Bits for Subnet Mask
You can use more than eight bits for the subnet mask. Remember, the more bits you use for the subnet mask, the fewer hosts per subnet.

Usually, you should consult the IP address administrator (or Internet service provider) to obtain a subnet mask; otherwise, you should leave it at the default setting.

TABLE 6.7

SUBNET MASKS FOR CLASS B NETWORKS

Number of Subnets	Number of Hosts per Subnet	Required Number of Bits	Subnet Mask
0	Invalid	1	Invalid
2	16,382	2	255.255.192.0
6	8,190	3	255.255.224.0
14	4,094	4	255.255.240.0
30	2,046	5	255.255.248.0
62	1,022	6	255.255.252.0
126	510	7	255.255.254.0
254	254	8	255.255.255.0

DHCP (Automatic IP Address Assignment)

The major headache of using IP addresses is the administration. The administrator must make sure every machine has a unique IP address. On a network of fewer than 40 machines, that's no big deal. When the administrator must look after several thousand machines, however, it becomes a nightmare. Figure 6.2 sketches a typical scenario.

In this scenario, the administrator must visit every Windows NT workstation in the network and configure the IP address manually through the Network icon in Control Panel. (See "Configuring Enterprise Protocols," later in this chapter for details.)

The other option is automatic address assignment—the best option for large networks. In this scenario, you need one Windows NT server with the Dynamic Host Configuration Protocol (DHCP) server service installed.

Now look at the scenario shown in Figure 6.3. The only difference is that the pool of IP addresses is set up on the server. The clients are configured as DHCP clients, which means they automatically obtain their IP addresses from this pool of addresses on the server.

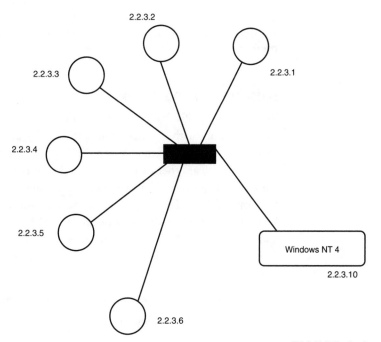

FIGURE 6.2
Manually configuring an IP address assignment.

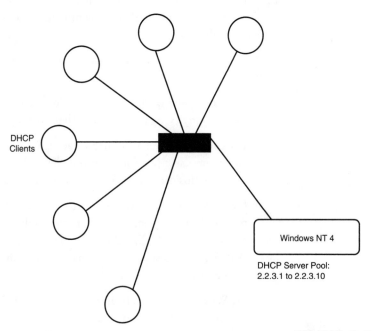

FIGURE 6.3
Automatic IP address assignment using DHCP.

The end result is the same; every machine on the network has been assigned a unique IP address. Only the implementation differs; using DHCP is much simpler.

Address Translation

TCP/IP under Windows NT enables a computer to communicate over a network with another computer by using an IP address, a host name, or a NetBIOS name. When one computer attempts to communicate with another computer using one of these three naming conventions, however, that name ultimately must be resolved to a hardware address. The following commands provide an example of how TCP/IP resolves a host name and a NetBIOS name to a MAC address. The machine name the user specifies must be resolved to an IP address. Here are a few examples of commands using a machine name:

```
ping Server where Server refers to the remote machine

NET USE * \\Server\Share

Event Viewer—Select Computer
```

In each of these examples, a machine name references a particular machine; in the world of IP, this machine name must be translated into an IP address.

Windows NT employs six methods to resolve a host name to an IP address:

◆ Broadcast. The workstation does a local broadcast to determine whether any system responds to that host name.

◆ Looking in the NetBIOS name cache. Windows NT caches any names already resolved in the NetBIOS name cache. (You can view this cache by using the NBTstat -c command.)

◆ Using WINS. The Windows Internet Naming Service (WINS) resolves NetBIOS names to IP addresses dynamically. To use WINS, you need a Windows NT Server system with the WINS service installed. After that, the system operates mostly automatically, as follows:

1. When a client boots up, it notifies the WINS server of its NetBIOS name and IP address.

2. The server builds a database of all clients.

3. When a client wants to resolve a NetBIOS name, it contacts the WINS server for the information. The WINS server looks up the name in its database and resolves the name to an IP address.

◆ Looking up the host name in the \%SYSTEMROOT%\ SYSTEM32\DRIVERS\ETC\HOSTS file. This file takes exactly the same format as the /ETC/HOSTS file on any UNIX-type system.

◆ Looking up the host name in the \%SYSTEMROOT%\ SYSTEM32\ DRIVERS\ETC\LMHOSTS file.

◆ Using DNS. Domain Name Services is used on the Internet to resolve host names. This system uses DNS servers that have been supplied with the necessary information to resolve the host names. The DNS client sends a query to the DNS server, which responds with the IP address.

> **NOTE**
>
> **DNS with NT 4 Versus NT 3.51**
> Windows NT 3.51 users had to obtain the Windows NT Resource Kit before they could implement a DNS server on NT. Windows NT 4 is distributed with the DNS server software. Setup and configuration are covered later in this chapter in the section "Configuring Enterprise Protocols."

Upper-Layer Services and Applications

In addition to installing the TCP/IP protocol itself, Windows NT provides a host of applications for the IP environment. The following sections discuss several of these.

TCP/IP Printing Support

TCP/IP printing support (basically the lpr and lpd daemons) is a set of applications that enables bidirectional printing to and from other IP hosts, such as UNIX and MVS. You can use the line printer remote (lpr) utility to send print jobs to an IP host. You execute it from the command line, and it follows UNIX command syntax. To send a file named CONFIG.SYS to an IP host named UNIX using a printer called P1, for example, you can use the following command:

```
lpr -S UNIX -P P1 config.sys
```

Rather than print a file manually, as in the preceding example, you can set up a printer on Windows NT and spool all jobs for that printer to the IP host. Perform the tasks in Step by Step 6.2 to set up such a printer.

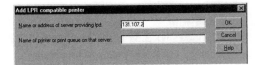

FIGURE 6.4
The Add LPR-Compatible Printer dialog box is where you install the LPR printer port.

STEP BY STEP

6.2 Installing a TCP/IP printer

1. Install a printer in Windows NT in the usual fashion (using Control Panel | Printers | Add Printer), but instead of choosing a normal printer port such as LPT1, select OTHER and choose LPR printer. Supply the IP address of the remote IP host and the printer name. Figure 6.4 shows the Add LPR-Compatible Printer dialog box.

2. Share the printer by right-clicking the Printers icon and choosing the Sharing option.

3. Start the TCP/IP Print Server from Control Panel | Services. The IP hosts now can print to the printer using the lpr command.

   Once the printer is set up, you can print from the UNIX server to the Windows NT server through the shared printer.

IPX/SPX

Originally standardized by Xerox as the XNS protocol, Novell's NetWare made this protocol popular in the form of Internetwork Packet Exchange/Sequenced Packet Exchange (IPX/SPX). The protocol provides an enterprise solution as a routable and scalable protocol, without the overhead involved with the TCP/IP protocol. (It is also lacking in some of the features of the IP stack, such as fragmentation and reassembly, congestion control, and so on.)

The IPX protocol offers the benefit of automatic configuration, cutting out the administrative overhead involved in IP. Instead of the administrator assigning every workstation a unique address, IPX takes the 6-byte MAC (or network adapter) address to identify the system. Windows NT also automatically picks a unique 4-byte network address, resulting in a unique 10-byte address per system. For example:

```
Network:MAC address = ff010002:0080aac556D3
```

If Windows NT detects that an IPX address has already been assigned to a segment, it adopts the same address. Figure 6.5 describes how IPX network addresses are assigned.

When using different frame types on the Ethernet or Token Ring network, you must assign an IPX network address to each frame type. Frames refer to the packets on the physical medium in a network. One frame type varies from another frame type in the number of fields in the packet and the function of the different fields in the packets. The following list summarizes frame types:

◆ **Ethernet 802.2.** Official IEEE 802.3 specification; use with versions of Novell NetWare 3.12 and later.

◆ **Ethernet 802.3.** Novell's modification on the IEEE frame type, dropping the LLC header in the packet; use with versions of Novell NetWare earlier than and including version 3.1.

◆ **Ethernet Type II.** The standard frame type for UNIX, VMS, and other operating systems.

◆ **Ethernet SNAP.** Frame type used on EtherTalk networks.

◆ **Token Ring.** Official IEEE 802.5 specification.

◆ **Token Ring SNAP.** Use on TokenTalk networks.

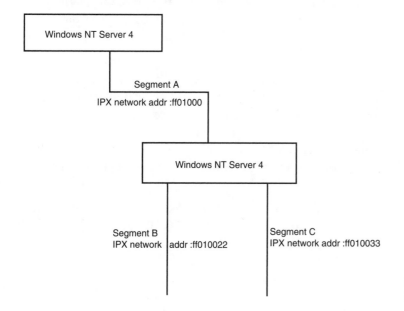

FIGURE 6.5
IPX network address assignment.

Windows NT automatically detects different frame types on the network, and if an IPX address hasn't already been assigned to the segment, the operating system assigns one. In Figure 6.5, for example, an IPX address might have been assigned to segment A on frame type 802.2. Adding the 802.3 frame type requires a second IPX network address on segment A (for example, FF01044).

This addressing scheme converts IPX literally into a plug-and-play protocol. Adding workstations to a network does not require careful planning as far as addressing is concerned.

An exception to the "No configuration necessary" rule of IPX is the internal IPX address. Some software packages (such as Btrieve server) require an internal IPX address to be assigned to the Windows NT system. The process for this is covered in the section "Configuring Enterprise Protocols" later in this chapter. To give you an in-depth understanding of the NWLink IPX/SPX protocol and its uses in an Windows NT environment, the following section introduces the upper-layer services available in NWLink IPX/SPX protocol.

NWLink Upper-Layer Services

The most important upper-layer service that relies on the installation of NWLink IPX/SPX-compatible protocol is the Gateway/Client Service for NetWare. For Novell people, this service is equivalent to Novell's NETX or VLM utilities. It provides a NetWare Core Protocol (NCP) redirector to enable file and print sharing off a Novell server.

This service is now Novell Directory Service aware (NDS-aware) so that you can browse NDS objects and run NDS utilities such as Novell's NWADMIN. The Gateway Service is distributed only with Windows NT Server. You can use the Gateway Service for NetWare to provide Microsoft SMB (non-Novell) clients with access to Novell file and print services. Figure 6.6 shows a typical application for this service.

In this scenario, the clients can share files and printers off the Novell file server without requiring that NWLink IPX/SPX protocol or Novell client software be installed.

WARNING

Watch for Bottleneck   You should use this scenario only for occasional file and print access because the single licensed connection to the Novell server can impose a bottleneck on performance.

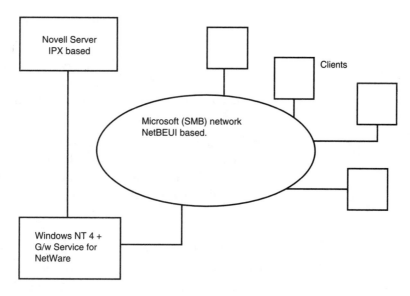

FIGURE 6.6
Using the Gateway Service for NetWare.

NetBEUI

NetBEUI stands for NetBIOS Extended User Interface. When IBM originally developed the NetBIOS protocol standard for LANs, the specification covered both API and the transport protocol. Because the transport protocol has a few limitations, however, Microsoft decided to extend the protocol part of the specification. The result is that the NetBIOS API remains essentially untouched, but the transport protocol has been extended to what is now known as NetBEUI.

NetBEUI is a small, fast, self-tuning protocol, suitable for small networks, generally between 2 and 200 nodes on the network. It isn't a routable protocol, however, which makes it unsuitable for most enterprise environments (unless employed as a firewalling mechanism in the Internet).

DLC (Data Link Control)

IBM designed the DLC protocol for its Systems Network Architecture (SNA) networks. Originally available as Synchronous Datalink Control (SDLC), then upgraded to HDLC, and even later adopted by IEEE in the Logic Link Control (LLC) format, this protocol is nonroutable, which makes it unsuitable as a general, everyday networking protocol. The two main reasons for using this protocol with Windows NT are as follows:

◆ Setting up the workstation or server to act in an SNA environment. This could be a server in the role of a Microsoft SNA server gateway or a workstation directly on the same ring as an IBM AS/400, running a 5250 terminal-emulation package.

◆ Connecting the Windows NT system to a LAN-attached printer (such as HP JetDirect) that can only interpret DLC. (Many of the later printer models are now able to communicate through IP or IPX as well.)

AppleTalk

The term AppleTalk refers to the Apple network architecture. It is actually a collection of protocols that correspond roughly to the OSI model and are implemented and included in the Macintosh hardware (through a LocalTalk port) and operating system software. The AppleTalk protocols support LocalTalk, EtherTalk (Ethernet), and TokenTalk (Token Ring).

Table 6.8 summarizes the types of networks supported by AppleTalk protocols.

TABLE 6.8

NETWORKS SUPPORTED BY APPLETALK PROTOCOLS

Hardware	Number of Nodes	Speed
LocalTalk	32 nodes	230.4KB/sec
EtherTalk	254 nodes	10MB/sec
TokenTalk	N/A	16 or 4MB/sec

At its most basic level, AppleTalk running on LocalTalk provides printer sharing for Macintoshes to an Apple LaserWriter.

The two versions, or phases, of AppleTalk are Phase I and Phase II.

Phase I

AppleTalk Phase I was the first implementation of AppleTalk.
The following statements summarize Phase I:

◆ The LocalTalk protocol is limited to 32 addresses on the
network.

◆ The Ethernet/PhoneNet protocol limit is 254 addresses on the
network.

◆ Each network has its own network number and zone.

◆ Each node on a network must belong to the same zone.

◆ Phase I supports 16 hops.

◆ Phase I fails to consider several popular protocols.

Phase II

Apple created Phase II as a way to interconnect to more popular protocols across networks. The addressing under Phase II now is limited
only by the topology, not by the AppleTalk addressing. Phase II is
backward-compatible to Phase I.

The following statements summarize Phase II—LocalTalk:

◆ It still is limited to a single network zone and a single network
number.

◆ It is limited to 250 addresses.

The following statements summarize Phase II—Ethernet and
Token Ring:

◆ The EtherTalk/PhoneNet limit is 16 million addresses.

◆ It uses the network number range.

◆ It supports 216 hops.

◆ It can have up to 256 zones per user (EtherTalk/TokenTalk).

◆ Zones can cross network numbers.

◆ It implements spanning tree.

AppleShare

AppleShare is the Apple file-server software that provides file sharing. The client-side software is included with every copy of Finder and System Software version 6.0 or greater. The AppleShare Print Server is a server-based print spooler.

The preceding sections gave you the background information on each of the available protocols in Windows NT. The upcoming sections introduce the configuration of these protocols for enterprise uses.

CONFIGURING ENTERPRISE PROTOCOLS

In this section on configuring your Windows NT system for enterprise connectivity, you will cover the following topics:

- ◆ Configuring TCP/IP
- ◆ Configuring DHCP Server Service
- ◆ Configuring the DNS Service
- ◆ Configuring the WINS Server Service

In each of these sections, you will review the installation and configuration procedures and gain an understanding about where you could utilize them in your enterprise environment.

Configuring TCP/IP

This section begins by showing you how to configure basic TCP/IP information, and then, it moves on to more advanced configuration information, such as DNS, WINS, and routing.

Basic TCP/IP Setup

To configure a system with the minimum information necessary for enterprise connectivity with TCP/IP, you need to define at least the following parameters:

◆ IP address

◆ Subnet mask

◆ Default gateway

The IP address of the system must follow the rules set out earlier in this chapter. For example, a valid address and subnet mask are 195.24.43.3 and 255.255.255.0, respectively. To see an example of configuring TCP/IP, follow the tasks outlined in Step by Step 6.3.

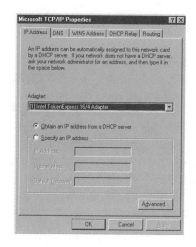

FIGURE 6.7
TCP/IP configuration.

STEP BY STEP

6.3 Configuring TCP/IP Protocol

1. In Control Panel, click the Networks icon and select the Protocols tab.

2. Select TCP/IP and click Properties.

3. Click OK and you get the configuration screen shown in Figure 6.7.

4. If Windows NT Server has been configured to supply the address through the DHCP mechanism, choose the Obtain an IP Address from a DHCP Server option. If no DHCP server is available, choose the Specify an IP Address Option and fill in the IP Address and Subnet Mask fields.

5. If the station is connected to other networks or segments through a router, also fill in the address of that router in the Default Gateway field. If the system isn't connected to another network, this field can remain blank.

6. You now can click Advanced to open the Advanced IP Addressing dialog box (see Figure 6.8).

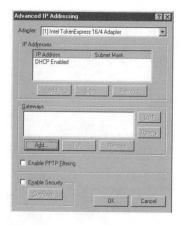

FIGURE 6.8
The Advanced IP Addressing dialog box.

continues

continued

7. In this dialog box, you can add IP addresses and more default gateways to the adapter. In this example, you do not require any of these options; however, the two options are

- **Enable Point-to-Point Tunneling Protocol (PPTP) filtering.** PPTP is a new networking technology that supports multiprotocol virtual private networks (VPNs), enabling remote users to access corporate networks securely across the Internet. When enabled, this effectively disables the network adapter for all other protocols. Only PPTP packets are allowed in.

- **Enable TCP/IP security.** TCP/IP security enables you to control the type of TCP/IP network traffic that reaches your computers running Windows NT Server. This security mechanism typically is used on Internet servers.

Configuring TCP/IP is a fairly straightforward process; ensure that all required information is entered properly. If you need connections to a network segment outside of your subnet, ensure that the default gateway has been configured.

> **WARNING**
>
> **Take Care When Setting Parameters** Incorrectly setting these parameters can adversely affect your server's internetwork functionality. If in doubt, contact your administrator or leave the default settings.

This concludes the basic IP setup information. Next, you will examine each of the other tabs in the Microsoft TCP/IP Properties dialog box (refer to Figure 6.7).

DNS Setup

You set up information concerning Domain Name System (DNS) servers on the DNS tab (see Figure 6.9). The first two entries, Host Name and Domain, are optional. You can use the Domain field to identify your computer on a smaller local network, such as one within your company. By default, this is your Windows NT computer name, but your network administrator can assign a different host name to your computer. The host name is combined with a domain name or suffix to create your Internet address.

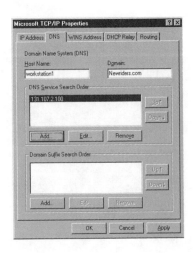

FIGURE 6.9
You set up information concerning Domain Name System (DNS) servers on the DNS tab.

The next entries are more important, especially if your machine is connected to the Internet. The DNS Service Search Order section lists the DNS servers containing a database that Windows NT searches for the name assigned to your computer or other hosts on the internetwork. Servers are searched in the order listed.

Note that this information can be supplied by a DHCP server as well. If a DHCP server supplies the DNS server information, you should still make sure the host name and domain name are set for your system.

WINS Address

The most important fields on the WINS Address tab are the Primary WINS Server field and the optional Secondary WINS Server field (see Figure 6.10). These addresses specify the WINS servers that collect and keep databases of WINS clients so that NetBIOS names can be resolved to IP addresses on demand.

Optional parameters include the Enable DNS for Windows Resolution and Enable LMHOSTS Lookup check boxes. This last parameter provides backward compatibility with LAN Manager servers, in which the LMHOSTS file in the %SYSTEMROOT\ SYSTEM32\DRIVERS\ETC\ directory serves to resolve host names. Look at the LMHOSTS.SAM file in this directory for an example.

The last parameter, the Scope ID field, is an optional NetBIOS scope ID. To communicate, all computers on a TCP/IP internetwork must have the same scope ID. It provides information to use if a DNS server is not found for name recognition. Usually, this value is left blank. The network administrator should provide the correct value for this parameter. It is used to segregate large networks into groups when the WINS servers and groups overlap. More than anything else, it limits the capability to resolve host addresses.

DHCP Relay

The DHCP Relay tab enables a Windows NT system to relay DHCP messages to clients across an IP router (see Figure 6.11). IP routers usually are configured not to forward broadcasts, so a client asking (broadcasting) for an IP address on a local segment when the DHCP server is located somewhere else goes unanswered. You also can specify optional timeout parameters here.

Add the address of any DHCP servers here so that DHCP requests (IP packets) can be directed there.

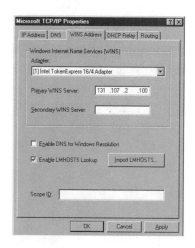

FIGURE 6.10
The most important fields on the WINS Address tab are the Primary WINS Server field and the optional Secondary WINS Server field.

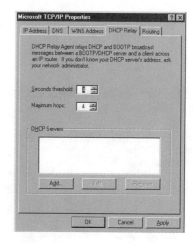

FIGURE 6.11
The DHCP Relay tab enables a Windows NT system to relay DHCP messages to clients across an IP router.

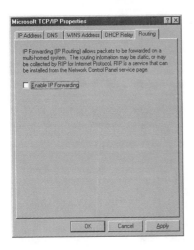

FIGURE 6.12
Use the Routing tab to make the Windows NT
system act as a router.

Routing

Use the Routing tab (see Figure 6.12) to make the Windows NT
system act as a router (also referred to as a multihomed machine).
This usually entails a Windows NT system that has more than one
network adapter. IP packets can now be forwarded through the various network interfaces. Disable this option if you do not want the
NT system to route and forward packets across the various segments
connected to it.

Configuring the DHCP Server Service

Using a DHCP server can reduce your configuration time dramatically. DHCP is used to automatically distribute TCP/IP information
to any DHCP clients on your network.

Setting up the DHCP Server service requires Windows NT Server
with DHCP installed as a service. To install the DHCP Server
service, add the service under Control Panel | Networks, as in Figure
6.13.

After you install the DHCP Server service, you can configure the
service by clicking Start | Administrative Tools | DHCP Manager.

The local machine always appears on the list, but you can remotely
administer other servers by adding a server using the Servers menu
option. After clicking the local machine (or any other server appearing in the list), you then set up the DHCP scope by performing the
tasks in Step by Step 6.4.

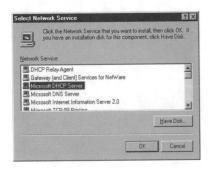

FIGURE 6.13
The DHCP Server service.

STEP BY STEP

6.4 Configuring a DHCP Scope

1. Click the Scope menu and select Create Scope. The
   Create Scope dialog box appears (see Figure 6.14).

2. Fill in the Start Address and End Address of the IP address
   pool being handed out. For example, you might enter
   177.22.34.100 in the Start Address field and
   177.22.34.200 in the End Address field.

3. You also have the option to exclude a set of addresses. You usually do this when the network consists of machines that are not DHCP-aware, such as printers or legacy operating systems.

4. You generally should give the scope a name; this identifies the batch of systems to which this pool of addresses will be dished out.

5. Specifying the lease duration, which indicates how long a client machine can keep an address before it must reapply, is an important step. Keep the lease period short (a few days) when users are highly mobile. Conversely, lengthen the lease period to several months or years if you want the workstations to keep the IP addresses for a long time. You also can set the period to unlimited, in which case the workstations keep their assigned addresses forever.

By following these steps, you configure the scope for your clients to use. Any client configured to receive TCP/IP information from the DHCP server is leased an address from within your range.

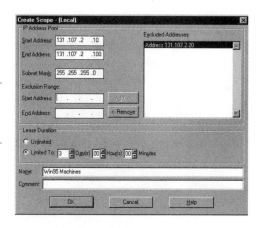

FIGURE 6.14
The Create Scope dialog box.

The DHCP database is created in JET format (MS Access) and stored in the \%SYSTEMROOT%\SYSTEM32\DHCP subdirectory. You should back up the database occasionally using the JETPACK command, which also clears out deleted records. To back up and pack the database, perform the tasks in Step by Step 6.5.

STEP BY STEP

6.5 Backing Up and Packing the Database

1. Stop the DHCP Server service via Control Panel | Services. You must stop the service because it holds the files open and prevents closing the files for backup.

continues

continued

2. Execute the following command from the DHCP subdirectory to check database consistency and to back up the database in the C:\BACKUP.DIR directory:

       JETPACK DHCP.mdb C:\backup.dir\dhcp.mdb

3. Restart the DHCP Server service.

   By completing the backing up and packing of the database, you clean up any old records and recover any disk space used for this database.

Configuring the DNS Service

You primarily use the Domain Name Server service on the Internet and on UNIX-based systems to resolve host names. You install the service by clicking the Networks icon in Control Panel. This installs the service into the service database and, after rebooting, starts the service automatically. The service is configured using the DNS Manager, which appears in the Administrative Tools menu.

After you install the service, you set up records in the DNS database. Follow Step by Step 6.6 to see how this works. Figure 6.15 shows a sample domain structure.

In this figure, the two systems are situated in the `imaginary.com` domain. The two host names are referred to as `www.imaginary.com` and `ftp.imaginary.com`, and the relevant IP addresses are provided. To set this up in the DNS Manager, perform the tasks in Step by Step 6.6.

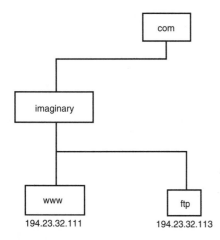

FIGURE 6.15
A sample domain structure.

STEP BY STEP

6.6 Configuring DNS in Windows NT Server 4.0

1. Create the top domain structure first (in this case, com). You do this by selecting the DNS menu and adding the server. Enter the IP address of the DNS server. You can use the loopback address of `127.0.0.1` for the current system.

2. Select the server, and then from the DNS menu, select New Zone. Select Primary and type **com** for the zone name. A tab automatically fills in the zone file name (in this case, com.dns). Then, click Next and Finish (see Figure 6.16).

3. Create the subdomain, imaginary, using the same approach; that is, select New Zone from the DNS menu and step through the wizard.

4. Create the two hosts, ftp and www, in the domain by selecting New Host and entering the host name (for example, ftp or www) and the IP address for the host. Be sure to enable the Create PTR Record option to ensure that reverse lookups also work.

5. Enable the Update Server Data Files option to refresh the server records, and then, you are done. To test the DNS setup, open a command prompt and try the following command:

```
ping ftp.imaginary.com
```

The command should return the proper IP address for the server if the DNS entries are filled in.

6. The last step is to update all clients with the IP address of the new DNS server. You can do this manually on every client by clicking the Networks icon in Control Panel, or you can insert the address into the DHCP configuration on the DHCP server.

continues

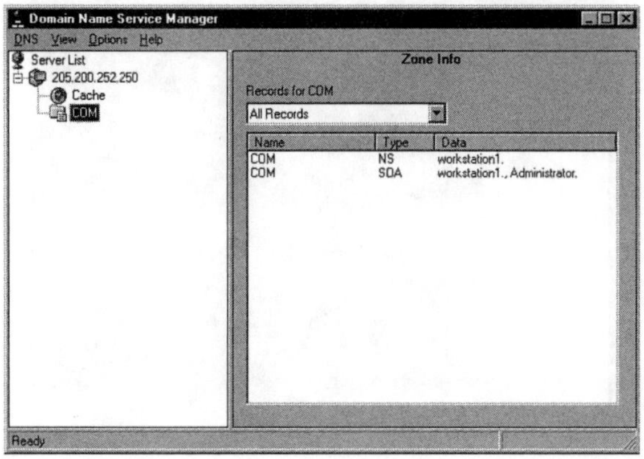

FIGURE 6.16
The DNS Manager program.

continued

Once each step has been completed, your DNS has been configured and tested. To add additional hosts in this database, follow Step 4 for each additional host.

Configuring the WINS Server Service

You install the Windows Internet Name Server service by clicking Networks in Control Panel. After installing it, you can maintain the service by using the WINS Manager accessible via the Administrative Tools menu (see Figure 6.17).

In a regular server environment, you usually can leave the WINS server running with the default parameters, so it requires little, if any, configuration. In the enterprise environment, however, the WINS server replicates its WINS database with other servers in the system so that WINS servers eventually carry all the database entries. This requires some configuration. To do this, select the Replication Partner option under the Server menu to see the dialog box shown in Figure 6.18.

As you can see, you must add and then configure WINS server addresses for push and/or pull replication. Push partners push their data down on other WINS servers, and pull partners request (or pull) the databases from remote servers.

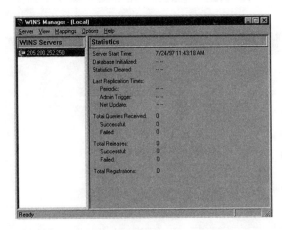

FIGURE 6.17
You can maintain the WINS Server service by using the WINS Manager application on the Administrative Tools menu.

The WINS database is created in JET format (MS Access) and is stored in the \%SYSTEMROOT%\SYSTEM32\WINS subdirectory. You should back up the database occasionally using the JETPACK command, which also clears out deleted records. To back up and pack the database, perform the tasks in Step by Step 6.7.

FIGURE 6.18
The Replication Partners options.

STEP BY STEP

6.7 Backing Up and Packing the Database

1. Stop the WINS Service using Control Panel | Services. You must stop the service first because it holds open the files, preventing you from closing the files for backup.

2. Execute the following command from the WINS subdirectory:

```
JETPACK WINS.mdb C:\backup.dir\wins.mdb
```

3. Restart the WINS Service.

   By following all these steps to back up and pack the database, you can ensure that it is clean and that it uses the minimal amount of disk space for the data.

This process checks database consistency and also backs up the database in the C:\BACKUP.DIR directory. You also can carry out this procedure by choosing Mappings | Back Up Database.

INSTALLING AND CONFIGURING MULTIPROTOCOL ROUTING

Install and configure multiprotocol routing to serve various functions. Functions include Internet router, BOOTP/DHCP Relay Agent, and IPX router.

This section discusses installing and configuring multiprotocol routing, including Internet routing and IPX routing. Multiprotocol routing gives you flexibility in the connection method used by your clients and maintaining security. In the coming sections, you will examine the following:

◆ Internet router

◆ IPX router

Each of these routing tools can be handy when maintaining connectivity between your Windows NT network and other network operating systems and protocols.

Internet Router

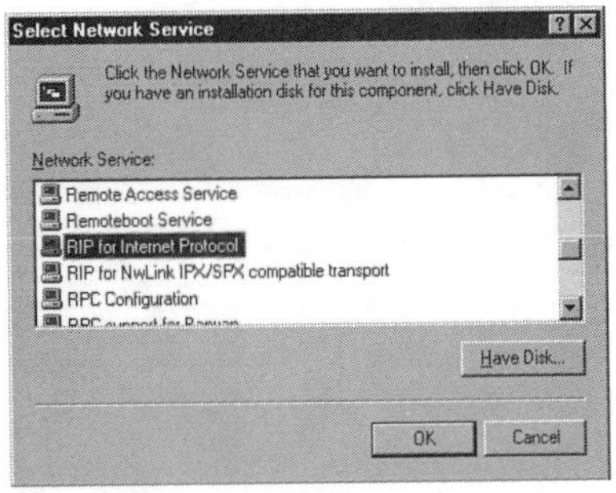

Windows NT can act as a router and as a firewall between the Internet and the internal network. With a router, all incoming packets from the Internet are forwarded into the network. With a firewall, clients typically do not run the IP protocol. This means packets coming in from the Internet (IP packets) cannot get past the server.

FIGURE 6.19
The RIP routing software.

> **Route RIP** Without the RIP protocol, you must manually set up router tables using the ROUTE ADD command.

Setting up Windows NT as an Internet router is as simple as installing two network adapters in the system and then enabling IP routing in the TCP/IP protocol configuration. This option enables Windows NT to act as a static router. Note that it cannot exchange Routing Information Protocol (RIP) routing packets with other IP RIP routers unless the RIP routing software is installed (see Figure 6.19).

To enable IP RIP routing, the service must be installed from the Networks dialog box in Control Panel.

This enables Windows NT to send out RIP packets once every 60 seconds to exchange routing information with other dynamic RIP routing routers.

IPX Router

You enable the IPX router by installing the IPX RIP router software via Control Panel | Networks | Services (see Figure 6.20).

After installing the IPX RIP router, Windows NT can route IPX packets over the network adapters installed. It uses the RIP to exchange its routing table information with other RIP routers. The default sending interval is once every 60 seconds, so you must be careful in deploying hundreds of RIP routers in an enterprise environment. These packets can consume a big chunk of network

FIGURE 6.20
The IPX RIP router.

bandwidth (especially on WANs, where the bandwidth usually is limited to 64Kbps).

The configuration screen for the IPX RIP router is quite straightforward. It only prompts for whether the administrator wants to propagate NetBIOS broadcasts (type 20) packets over the router (see Figure 6.21).

You have to do this only if both sides of the Windows NT router contain Microsoft clients (such as Windows 95 or Windows for Workgroups) that need to communicate browsing information over the router.

The RIP router for IPX can be fine-tuned in the Registry (REGEDT32.EXE) under the following key:

```
HKEY_LOCAL_MACHINE/SYSTEM/CurrentControlSet/Services/
➥NWLinkRIP/Parameters
```

See the Windows NT Resource Kit for more details.

FIGURE 6.21
The configuration screen for the IPX RIP router is quite straightforward.

> **N O T E** **LSP** Third-party products that plug into Windows NT 4 can provide more advanced forms of IPX routing in the form of Link State Protocol (LSP).

CASE STUDY: MANIPULATING INTERNET ACCESS

ESSENCE OF THE CASE

Here are the essential elements in this case:

- Require that all clients be automatically assigned TCP/IP configuration settings.

- Share the Class C addresses across 270 workstations.

- Must allocate two dedicated IP addresses for the static Internet systems.

SCENARIO

As the Internet grows in popularity, the number of available IP address ranges is getting smaller and smaller. A college is having a small problem with TCP/IP configuration of the desktop computers. They have 270 computers in their facility and only a Class C address. They do not require that all machines be connected to the Internet at all times; however, each system must be able to support the Internet connection when required. At any one time, they may have 200 computers accessing the Internet, and they have two dedicated servers used for Internet-related mail and a Web site. They require a solution that would automate the allocation of TCP/IP configuration settings to their computers, allow the IP addresses to be shared across the 270 computers to

continues

CASE STUDY: MANIPULATING INTERNET ACCESS

potentially allow all systems to access the Internet, and still be able to manually configure the IP address for their two Internet-related servers.

ANALYSIS

This problem will continue to arise as the number of address ranges for the Internet dwindles. Lowering the lease duration to four hours would allow the IP addresses to be shared by numerous computers. The solution of lowering the

lease duration will cause some additional network traffic on the line due to the constant regenerating of IP addresses to clients; however, it solves the client's needs in spreading the IP addresses across the 270 computers. DHCP Server and the configuration options available are flexible and effective in allocating the TCP/IP configuration information to your desktop clients. In the DHCP scope configuration, the static IP addresses can be excluded to ensure that they are not used in a classroom computer.

CHAPTER SUMMARY

KEY TERMS

- TCP
- UDP
- ARP
- IP
- ICMP
- DHCP
- DNS
- NetBIOS
- host name
- subnet mask
- MAC
- multiprotocol routing

It should now be obvious that Windows NT Server 4.0 was designed specifically for networking in an enterprise environment. The inclusion of the industry-standard protocols and tools to simplify the configuration and extension of your NT network into other environments makes this operating system a powerful piece of your heterogeneous environment. The main factors to consider in this chapter are

◆ A strong understanding of the functionality of each of the Windows NT protocols—with a strong lean toward TCP/IP and the configuration options available. Understanding the configuration of DHCP Server is also tested on this exam.

◆ The services used to resolve the IP addresses and names of hosts in a TCP/IP environment: the DNS service, WINS Service, the Hosts file, and the LMHosts files.

◆ The routing mechanisms available in Windows NT are powerful and largely unknown to the vast majority of NT administrators. Ensure that you review the configuration and functionality of Internet or IP routing, as well as the IPX routing tools available.

APPLY YOUR LEARNING

This section allows you to assess how well you understand the material in the chapter. Review and exam questions test your knowledge of the tasks and concepts specified in the objectives. The exercises provide you with opportunities to engage in the sorts of tasks that compose the skill sets the objectives reflect.

For more review and exam questions, see the Top Score test engine on the CD-ROM that came with this book.

Exercises

The following exercises provide you with an opportunity to apply what you've learned in this chapter.

6.1   Installing and Configuring the DNS Service in Windows NT Server 4

This exercise steps you through the installation and configuration of the DNS service under Windows NT Server 4.

Time Estimate: 15 minutes

1. Get the IP address of your computer. You need it to complete these steps.

2. Right-click Network Neighborhood and select Properties.

3. Select the Services tab.

4. Click Add.

5. In the Network Services list, select Microsoft DNS Server and click OK.

6. Enter the path to the Windows NT Server source directory and click Continue.

7. Click Close in the Network dialog box.

8. Click Yes to restart the computer.

9. After the system restarts, log on.

10. Click Start | Programs | Administrative Tools, and then click DNS Manager.

11. In the DNS menu, click New Server.

12. In the DNS server box, type your computer name and click OK.

13. Highlight your computer name in the DNS Manager window.

14. In the DNS menu, click New Zone.

15. Click the Primary check box and then click Next.

16. In Zone Name, enter **newriders.com** and then press Tab to move to the Zone File box. The Zone File is automatically filled in.

17. Click Next and then finish.

18. To add a computer to your DNS server, right-click the Zone Name and then click New Host.

19. In the Host Name, enter the computer name.

20. In the Host IP Address, enter the IP address for the new computer.

21. Click Add Host.

22. Click Done.

6.2   Installing and Configuring the DHCP Server Service in Windows NT Server 4

This exercise steps you through the installation and configuration of the DHCP Server service under Windows NT Server 4.

Time Estimate: 15 minutes

APPLY YOUR LEARNING

1. Right-click Network Neighborhood and select Properties.

2. Select the Services tab.

3. Click Add.

4. In the Network Service list, select Microsoft DHCP Server Service and click OK.

5. Enter the path to the Windows NT Server source directory and click Continue.

6. Click Close in the Network dialog box.

7. Click Yes to restart the computer.

8. After the system restarts, log on.

9. Click Start | Programs | Administrative and Tools, then click DHCP Manager.

10. Once the DHCP Manager utility has started, select the Scope menu and click create scope.

11. Move to the Start address and enter `200.190.180.20`, and then move to the end address and enter `200.190.180.50`. The subnet mask to be used is `255.255.255.0`.

12. The exclusion range can remain blank for both start and end addresses; move to the Lease Duration options.

13. Limit the lease duration to 8 hours, and then click OK.

14. You have configured your DHCP server. When a DHCP client boots up on your network, it is assigned an IP address within the specified range of `200.190.180.20` to `200.190.180.50`.

Review Questions

1. Where can you enable IP routing in Windows NT Server 4?

2. What service is needed to enable IPX routing in a Windows NT Server computer?

3. List all the subprotocols used to make up the TCP/IP protocol suite.

4. Which of the subprotocols in the TCP/IP suite use a connection-oriented delivery method?

5. What are the minimum required parameters needed in configuring TCP/IP for an enterprise environment?

6. What service can you use to automatically allocate IP addresses to clients' machines?

7. What is the function of the scope ID in the TCP/IP configuration settings?

Exam Questions

1. What protocol is responsible for routing information between TCP/IP-based networks?

   A. TCP

   B. IP

   C. ICMP

   D. UDP

APPLY YOUR LEARNING

2. What is the main function of the Address Resolution Protocol in TCP/IP?

   A. It is responsible for maintaining routing tables on an IP internetwork.

   B. It is responsible for traffic control between routers on an IP internetwork.

   C. It is responsible for resolving host names into IP addresses.

   D. It is responsible for resolving IP addresses into hardware addresses.

3. Which service that runs on Windows NT Server computers enables you to assign IP address information dynamically instead of configuring each computer manually?

   A. WINS

   B. DHCP

   C. IPConfig

   D. SNMP

4. Which service typically is used on the Internet to resolve the host name of a computer into an IP address?

   A. WINS

   B. DNS

   C. DHCP

   D. LMHosts

5. To configure DHCP to lease out IP addresses, what must first be configured using the DHCP Server Manager?

   A. A DHCP scope

   B. A NetBIOS scope ID

   C. A subnet mask

   D. An IP address range

Answers to Review Questions

1. Control Panel | Networks | TCP/IP Properties. See the section "IPX Router" for more information.

2. RIP for NWLink IPX/SPX-compatible transport. See the section "IPX Router" for more information.

3. The subprotocols are TCP, IP, UDP, ICMP, and ARP. See the section "TCP/IP" for more information.

4. Transmission Control Protocol, TCP, uses connection-oriented delivery. See the section "TCP/IP" for more information.

5. The IP address, subnet mask, and default gateway are the required parameters for configuring TCP/IP. See the section "Basic TCP/IP Setup" for more information.

6. The DHCP Server service. See the section "Configuring a DHCP Server Service" for more information.

7. The scope ID is used to segregate a physical network into smaller groups. See the section "WINS Address" for more information.

Answers to Exam Questions

1. **B.** The IP, or Internet protocol, is responsible for the routing between TCP/IP-based networks. See the section "TCP/IP."

2. **D.** ARP is used to resolve the IP addresses into the MAC, or hardware, address of a network card. See the section "TCP/IP."

3. **B.** The DHCP server service is used to automatically allocate IP addresses in a Windows NT network. See the section "DHCP (Automatic IP Address Assignment)."

4. **B.** The DNS service is used to resolve the host name into an IP address. See the section "Configuring the DNS Service."

5. **A.** A DHCP scope is the first step in configuring the DHCP server service. See the section "Configuring the DHCP Server Service."

This chapter helps you to prepare for the Microsoft exam by covering the following objectives within the "Connectivity" category:

Configure Windows NT Server for interoperability with NetWare servers by using various tools. Tools include

- ◆ **Gateway Service for NetWare**

- ◆ **Migration Tool for NetWare**

▶ This objective focuses on the configuration and functionality required for connectivity between Windows NT and Novell NetWare. The Gateway Services for NetWare and the NWCONV utility make up the majority of the discussion.

Install and configure Internet Information Server.

▶ Internet Information Server is an integrated component of Windows NT Server. To be fully prepared for this objective, you must understand the installation and configuration settings required to allow your Windows NT system to function as an Internet server using Internet Information Server.

Install and configure Internet services. Services include

- ◆ **World Wide Web**

- ◆ **DNS**

- ◆ **Intranet**

▶ This objective ensures that you fully understand the Internet services available in a Windows NT server. The services included in this objective are subsets of the Internet Information Server, and you must fully understand the use and configuration options available for these Internet services.

CHAPTER 7

Additional Connectivity Utilities

Install and configure Remote Access Services (RAS). Configuration options include

- ◆ **RAS communications**
- ◆ **RAS protocols**
- ◆ **RAS security**

▶ This objective covers all the installation and configuration requirements for the remote access service in Windows NT. RAS is used to allow remote, or dial-in, connectivity in your Windows NT environment.

STUDY STRATEGIES

The connectivity services in Windows NT are fairly straightforward in the installation and configuration processes; however, ensure that you fully understand all of the settings available. A large component of connectivity will rely on securing each of the connection methods listed throughout this chapter. In preparing for the exam, ensure that you have fully read each of the sections, and install and configure each of the utilities discussed in this chapter.

In the selection of your enterprise protocol, you must ensure that all other network systems in your environment offer support for the chosen protocol and connectivity method. In this chapter, you will work through various services and tools used to maintain your heterogeneous environment within a Windows NT network.

This chapter discusses various networking connectivity tools and how they are used to achieve interconnectivity between systems. This chapter covers the following topics:

◆ Interoperability with NetWare servers

◆ Installation and configuration of Internet Information Server (IIS)

◆ Installation and configuration of Remote Access Service (RAS)

INTEROPERABILITY WITH NETWARE

Configure Windows NT Server for interoperability with NetWare servers by using various tools. Tools include Gateway Service for NetWare and Migration Tool for NetWare.

Although organizations continue to rapidly deploy Windows NT in the enterprise, many organizations still have legacy NetWare systems that must be able to interoperate with Windows NT. It is important to completely understand the tools and utilities available for this NetWare connection as well as know how to properly implement these tools under Windows NT Server.

Microsoft ensured compatibility with NetWare servers by including the NWLink IPX/SPX-compatible protocol, but it did not stop there. Microsoft also bundles the Gateway Service for NetWare (GSNW) and includes a utility to help smooth the conversion from NetWare to Windows NT Server. In the following sections, you will examine the following:

◆ Gateway Service for NetWare (GSNW)

◆ NWCONV: Migration Tool for NetWare

Gateway Service for NetWare

Gateway Service for NetWare performs the following functions:

◆ GSNW enables Windows NT Servers to access NetWare file and print resources.

◆ GSNW enables the Windows NT Servers to act as a gateway to the NetWare file and print resources. The Windows NT Server enables users to borrow the connection to the NetWare server by setting it up as a shared connection.

GSNW can provide Windows NT networks with convenient access to NetWare resources. GSNW enables one single connection to be shared by multiple Windows NT clients. This connection sharing is convenient. It also, however, causes a significant performance loss for the NetWare resource. The GSNW is ideal for occasional NetWare resource access, but it is not recommended for heavy traffic routing because it could bottleneck your system.

Installing the GSNW

GSNW is a network service, and you install it using the Services tab of the Network dialog box accessed through Control Panel. For the tasks necessary to install the Gateway Service for NetWare, see Step by Step 7.1.

STEP BY STEP

7.1 Installing the GSNW

1. Click the Services tab of the Network dialog box (accessed through Control Panel).

2. Click Add to view a list of available services (see Figure 7.1).

3. In the list, select the Gateway Services for NetWare and then click OK. You might be prompted for the location of your Windows NT source files; give the location.

4. You are prompted to restart your system.

   By completing each of these steps, you will successfully install the GSNW service.

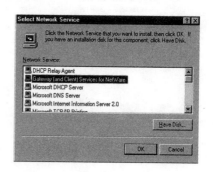

FIGURE 7.1
GSNW is installed through the Services tab of the Network dialog box.

Later in this chapter, you will review the configuration options available for this service.

Configuring GSNW

After the system is restarted, you can configure GSNW to act as a gateway to the NetWare resources. To enable GSNW to act as a gateway for your Windows NT clients, perform the tasks in Step by Step 7.2.

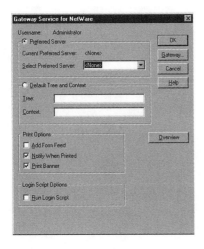

FIGURE 7.2
The Gateway Service for NetWare dialog box.

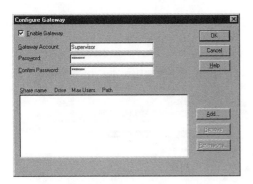

FIGURE 7.3
The Configure Gateway dialog box.

STEP BY STEP

7.2 Configuring a NetWare Gateway

1. On the NetWare server, create a group called NTGATEWAY.

2. Create a user account on the NetWare server for the gateway to use and add the account to the NTGATEWAY group.

3. From Control Panel, double-click the GSNW icon to open the Gateway Service for NetWare dialog box (see Figure 7.2).

4. To configure the gateway options, click Gateway in the upper-right corner of the dialog box.

5. You see the Configure Gateway dialog box (see Figure 7.3).

6. Click the Enable Gateway check box. In the Gateway Account and Password fields, enter the name of the gateway account and the password for the account you created on the NetWare server.

7. You can create shares to the NetWare resources in the bottom section of the Configure Gateway dialog box. Click Add to create a share to the NetWare resources (see Figure 7.4).

8. After you create the share, you can apply the standard Windows NT share permissions to the NetWare share. Click Permissions to assign specific permissions to your Windows NT users.

9. When you complete the Configure Gateway dialog box, click OK to close it. You can select your preferred NetWare server, default tree and context, and print options for your Windows NT Server to connect to the NetWare server.

10. When all configuration settings are established, click OK to close the Gateway Service for NetWare dialog box.

   By completing these steps, you enabled your Windows NT Server to function as a gateway into the NetWare server that was selected. Users within your Windows NT environment will be able to connect through the Windows NT system into the NetWare server's resources.

FIGURE 7.4
Use the Add button to create a share to NetWare resources.

NWCONV: Migration Tool for NetWare

The Migration Tool for NetWare transfers file and directory information and user and group account information from a NetWare server to a Windows NT domain controller. The Migration Tool can preserve the directory and file permissions if it is being transferred to an NTFS partition. Table 7.1 displays the corresponding NetWare and Windows NT NTFS rights that are being converted.

TABLE 7.1

CONVERSION OF RIGHTS

Novell NetWare Permission	*Windows NT Permission*
Supervisor (S)	Full Control (All)
Read (R)	Read (RX)
Write (W)	Change (RWXD)
Erase (E)	Change (RWXD)
Modify (M)	Change (RWXD)
Create (C)	Add (WX) custom right
File scan (F)	List (RX) custom right
Access control (A)	Change permission (P)

If the partition you are migrating to is a FAT partition, no rights or permissions are maintained.

To start the Migration Tool for NetWare, you must run the NWCONV.EXE file. There is no icon for this utility, so you must execute it from a command prompt or from Start | Run. This utility is located in the %systemroot%\system32\ directory on your Windows NT server.

Steps for Migrating from NetWare

When the Migration Tool for NetWare is first started, a dialog box enables you to select the NetWare server and Windows NT Server domain controller that you will be working with (see Figure 7.5).

To accomplish the migration from the NetWare server to your Windows NT Server, you must have Supervisor access to the NetWare system, and you must be an Administrator in the Windows NT domain to which you are migrating.

To complete the migration from a NetWare server to a Windows NT server, perform the tasks in Step by Step 7.3.

STEP BY STEP

7.3 Migrating from NetWare Server to Windows NT Server

1. From the Start menu, select Run, enter **NWCONV**, and press Enter.

2. Click Add, select your NetWare server and Windows NT domain controller, and then click OK.

3. You have the option of configuring the User Options or the File Options. After each of these sections is configured, either you can click Start Migration or you can do a trial migration first to verify your settings.

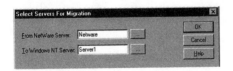

FIGURE 7.5
Using the NetWare Migration Tool.

The NWCONV utility can be powerful, and when you
configure the user and file options, it will enable you to
transfer the NetWare server's contents to your Windows
NT Server.

In the following section, you will examine the configuration settings
available in the NWCONV utility. The sections cover the user and
group options available, specifically:

◆ Passwords

◆ User names and group names

◆ Defaults

User and Group Options

All the user accounts from your NetWare server are migrated by
default to the Windows NT domain controller. To disable the transfer of users and groups, deselect the Transfer Users and Groups
check box located at the top of the User and Group Options dialog
box (see Figure 7.6).

The User and Group Options dialog box holds all the available
options on four tabs:

◆ Passwords

◆ User names

◆ Group names

◆ Defaults

Passwords

For security reasons, the passwords from the NetWare server cannot
migrate. You can use the Migration Tool, however, to specify how
the passwords for the migrated users should be handled:

◆ **No password.** The migrated users have no passwords
assigned to them.

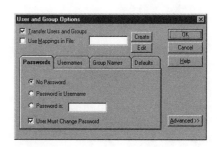

FIGURE 7.6
To disable the transfer of users and groups,
deselect the Transfer Users and Groups
check box.

◆ **Password is user name.** The migrated users have passwords that are the same as their user names.

◆ **Password is.** Assigns a single password to all migrated users.

◆ **User must change password.** Forces the migrated users to change their passwords the first time they log on to the Windows NT Server.

User Names and Group Names

The Migration Tool needs to be configured in case it runs into a duplicate user name or group name during migration. The User Names tab enables you to select how the Migration Tool should react in that circumstance:

◆ **Log error.** Adds an error to the ERROR.LOG file.

◆ **Ignore.** Causes the account to be skipped with no error messages or warnings.

◆ **Overwrite with new information.** The existing account is overwritten with the new NetWare user information.

◆ **Add prefix.** Includes a prefix with the user account to enable you to distinguish the difference between the existing account and the migrated account.

Defaults

The Defaults tab contains two options:

◆ **Use supervisor defaults.** You can use the Supervisor account restrictions for the migrated users instead of using the account policies in Windows NT Server.

◆ **Add supervisors to the administrators group.** The migrated users that have Supervisor-equivalent access are added to the Windows NT domain's Administrators group. By default, the Supervisors from the NetWare system are not added to this group.

REVIEW BREAK

Connectivity with NetWare

Connectivity between Windows NT and a NetWare server requires the use of the Gateway Services for NetWare. You use the NetWare conversion utility, NWCONV, to transfer the user and file information from NetWare to a Windows NT Server. The following list items summarize the main points in this section on NetWare connectivity:

- GSNW can be used as a gateway between Windows NT clients and a NetWare server.

- GSNW acts as a NetWare client to the Windows NT Server, allowing the NT Server a connection to the NetWare server.

- GSNW is a service in Windows NT, and it is installed using Control Panel.

- For GSNW to be used as a gateway into a NetWare server, you must create a gateway user account and place it in a NetWare group called NTGATEWAY.

- In configuring the GSNW as a gateway, you can assign permissions to the gateway share by accessing the GSNW icon in Control Panel.

- For GSNW to be functional, you must install and configure the NWLink IPX/SPX protocol.

- To convert user and file information from a NetWare server to a Windows NT server, you use the NWCONV.EXE utility.

- NWCONV requires that GSNW be installed prior to any conversion being carried out.

- To maintain the NetWare directory and file-level permissions in the NWCONV utility, you must convert to an NTFS partition on the Windows NT system.

Install and Configure Internet Information Server

Install and configure Internet Information Server.

Microsoft went to a great deal of trouble to provide strong interoperability between Windows NT and other systems available on the market. Microsoft did not stop there; it also includes excellent applications for communicating via the Internet. Internet Information Server is bundled with Windows NT 4 and can be installed automatically during the initial installation of your Windows NT Server system.

Internet Information Server (IIS) serves primarily as a World Wide Web (WWW) server, but it also offers FTP and Gopher support. Because this software is included with Windows NT Server software, it makes perfect sense to learn a little bit about what IIS can do for you. The Enterprise exam will have a few questions relating to the installation and configuration of IIS. Before you can look into the installation and configuration of IIS, you must understand the different components and functions of IIS.

Overview of IIS

Internet Information Server uses Hypertext Transfer Protocol (HTTP), File Transfer Protocol (FTP), and the Gopher service to provide Internet publishing services to your Windows NT Server computer.

Hypertext Transfer Protocol (HTTP)

HTTP is a client/server protocol used on the World Wide Web. HTTP Web pages enable the client and server machines to interact and be updated quickly using Windows Sockets. HTTP is pervasive on the Internet; more information about this standard appears at http://www.ics.uci.edu/pub/ietf/http/.

File Transfer Protocol (FTP)

FTP is the protocol used to transfer files from one computer to another using TCP/IP. In any FTP file transfer, each computer must play a role in the connection. One system must be the FTP server, and the other is the FTP client. The FTP client does all the work in the transfer; the FTP server is only a depository. This protocol is handy for transfer of files across the Internet.

Gopher Service

Gopher provides a means to create a set of hierarchical links to other computers or to annotate files or directories. This service is not as

common as FTP or HTTP, but it is included with IIS for backward
compatibility with older Internet technology.

Installation Steps for IIS

Installing IIS is simple. During the initial installation of your
Windows NT Server software, you might remember being prompted
about whether you wanted to install IIS at that time. Even if you
said no, you still have the opportunity to install it at any time from a
working installation of Windows NT Server.

To install Internet Information Server, perform the tasks in Step by
Step 7.4.

STEP BY STEP

7.4 Installing IIS

1. From the desktop, double-click the Install Internet
   Information Server icon, if available. Otherwise, choose
   Start | Programs | Microsoft Internet Server (Common) |
   Internet Information Server Setup.

2. You see the Internet Information Server Setup dialog box.
   Click OK to continue.

3. The setup displays a list of all the components available
   for you to install (see Figure 7.7). Make sure all the correct
   options are selected and click OK.

> **NOTE**
> **Alternative Install** As an alternative,
> you can add IIS from the Services tab
> of the Network dialog box.

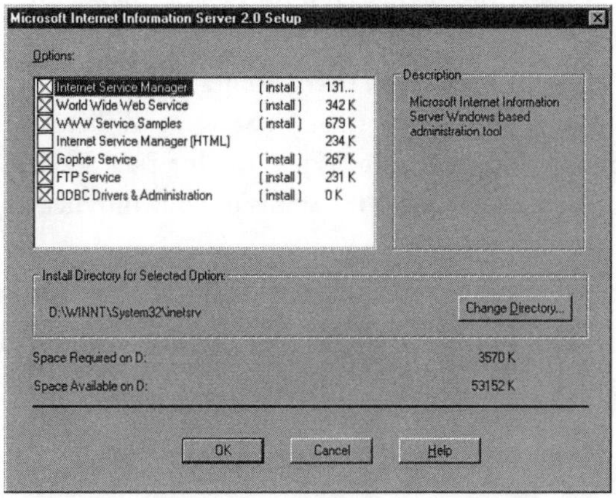

FIGURE 7.7
Setup displays the available IIS components.

FIGURE 7.8
Creating publishing directories.

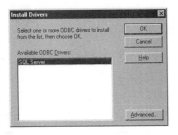

FIGURE 7.9
The OBDC connectivity drivers.

4. A dialog box verifying the installation directory appears. Click Yes to verify the directory creation.

5. The Publishing Directories dialog box appears (see Figure 7.8). Click OK to accept the default directories. Then, click Yes to verify the creation of the publishing directories.

6. A dialog box prompting for the type of ODBC connectivity drivers might appear; click the database type, such as SQL Server, and then click OK (see Figure 7.9).

7. When setup is complete, click OK.

When all these steps are complete, Windows NT Server is ready to host your Internet publications. If you want to test your IIS installation, enter `http://your_computername` from a Web browser and verify that you can see the default Web page installed with IIS. If you can see this Web page, your installation and all the Internet services are functional.

Installing Internet Information Server is the easy part. You might need to configure the system based on your specific needs. Each of the services can be configured, and in the following sections, you learn the configuration options for each of the IIS services.

Internet Information Server provides a graphical administration tool called the Internet Service Manager. With this tool, you can centrally manage, control, and monitor the Internet services in your Windows NT network. The Internet Service Manager uses the built-in Windows NT security model, so it offers a secure method of remotely administering your Web sites and other Internet services. To start the Internet Service Manager, select Programs from the Start menu, select Microsoft Internet Information Server, and then click the Internet Service Manager icon. When the Internet Service Manager is started, you're able to view the status of your Internet services (see Figure 7.10).

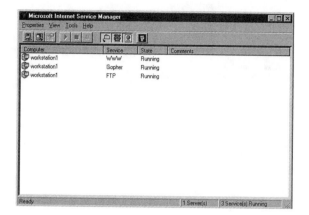

FIGURE 7.10
The Internet Service Manager displays the Internet services installed on this machine.

The Internet Service Manager has three views you can use to monitor the information you need a little more easily. The three main views are

◆ **Report view.** This is the default view. The Report view lists each computer alphabetically with each Internet service shown on a separate line in the screen (see Figure 7.11).

◆ **Servers view.** This view groups all the services on each server and only lists each computer with an Internet service loaded on it. You can then expand the servers to display the services loaded (see Figure 7.12).

◆ **Services view.** Each Internet service is listed with the corresponding servers grouped by service (see Figure 7.13).

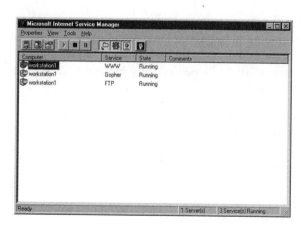

FIGURE 7.11
The Report view is the default view.

FIGURE 7.12
The Servers view groups all the services on each server and only lists each computer with an Internet service loaded on it.

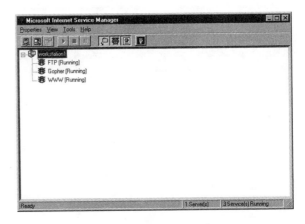

FIGURE 7.13
The Services view.

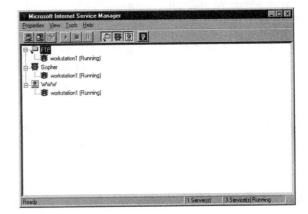

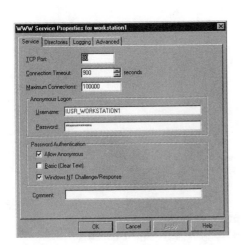

In each of the views, you can double-click an entry to view the Properties dialog box for the selected item. In these dialog boxes, you can perform the configuration of the servers and services. Figure 7.14 displays a sample Properties dialog box for the WWW service on the computer.

In the next several sections, you look into the configuration options of each of the Internet services.

FIGURE 7.14
The Properties dialog box for the WWW service.

Configuring WWW Service

Install and configure Internet services, including World Wide Web service.

To view the configuration selections for your WWW service, double-click the WWW service in the Internet Service Manager.

In the Properties dialog box for the WWW service, you will notice the tabs across the top of the dialog box. These tabs contain the configuration options.

The Services Tab

The Services tab enables you to set user logon and authentication requirements, as well as provide port and connection information for the service (refer to Figure 7.14).

The Directories Tab

The Directories tab shows you the location of your home directories and where to place all your Internet publications. This tab also sets the name of the default document and whether directory browsing is enabled (see Figure 7.15).

The Logging Tab

The Logging tab enables you to log the activities of the services (see Figure 7.16). You can select a log file name and log format. You also can specify how often to start a new log file. A nice feature of this logging is the option to log to a SQL/ODBC database. This option is only available if the ODBC drivers are installed on your system.

The Advanced Tab

The Advanced tab enables you to prevent access to the service, based on IP addresses (see Figure 7.17). This enables you to secure an intranet by selecting an IP address range and then limiting the access allowed to the site. You can also use this tab to limit the network bandwidth for outbound traffic from the server.

FIGURE 7.15

The Directories tab shows you the location of your home directories.

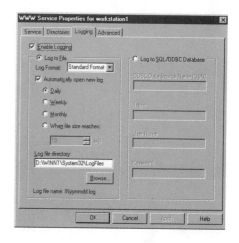

FIGURE 7.16

The Logging tab enables you to log the activities of the services.

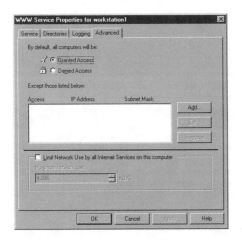

FIGURE 7.17
The Advanced tab enables you to prevent
access to the service, based on IP addresses.

Configuring FTP Service

The properties of the FTP service are similar to those of the WWW
services. The only difference is the Messages tab (see Figure 7.18).
This tab enables you to enter welcome and exit messages for users of
your FTP service.

Configuring Gopher Service

The Gopher service has four basic tabs in its Properties dialog box
(see Figure 7.19). These tabs are similar to those found in the
WWW service, and you can refer to that section for more detailed
information.

NT and IIS

Internet Information Server is an integrated component in Windows
NT Server 4.0. The IIS services are installed using the Control Panel
or Network icon or during the installation phase. The following bul-
lets summarize the key points in installing and configuring IIS:

- The three Internet services included in IIS are HTTP, FTP,
  and Gopher.

- HTTP is used to host Web pages from your Windows NT
  Server system.

- FTP is a protocol used for transferring files across the Internet
  using the TCP/IP protocol.

- Gopher is used to create a set of hierarchical links to other
  computers or to annotate files or directories.

- The Internet Service Manager is the utility used to manage and
  configure your Internet services in IIS.

- The Internet Service Manager has three views you can use to
  view your services. The three views are Report, Servers, and
  Services.

REMOTE ACCESS SERVICE (RAS)

Install and configure Remote Access Service (RAS). Configuration options include configuring RAS communications, protocols, and security.

The Enterprise exam contains a few questions about the use of RAS. To be successful with these questions, you must have a solid understanding of RAS, including its installation and configuration.

Windows NT Remote Access Service extends the power of Windows NT networking to anywhere you can find a phone line. Using RAS, a Windows NT computer can connect to a remote network through a dial-up connection and can fully participate in the network as a network client. RAS also enables your Windows NT computer to receive dial-up connections from remote computers.

RAS supports SLIP and PPP line protocols and NetBEUI, TCP/IP, and IPX network protocols. Because so many Internet users access their service providers using a phone line, RAS often serves as an Internet interface.

The Dial-Up Networking application, which you can locate by selecting Start | Programs | Accessories, enables you to create phonebook entries. A phonebook entry is a preconfigured dial-up connection to a specific site. The Control Panel Telephony application (discussed in more detail later in this chapter) enables the remote user to preconfigure dialing properties for different dialing locations.

RAS can connect to a remote computer using any of the following media:

◆ **Public Switched Telephone Network (PSTN).** (Also known as the phone company.) RAS can connect using a modem through an ordinary phone line.

◆ **X.25.** A packet-switched network. Computers access the network through a Packet Assembler Disassembler (PAD) device. X.25 supports dial-up or direct connections.

◆ **Null modem cable.** A cable that connects two computers directly. The computers communicate using their modems (rather than network adapter cards).

◆ **ISDN.** A digital line that provides faster communication and more bandwidth than a normal phone line. (It also costs more, which is why not everybody has it.) A computer must have a special ISDN card to access an ISDN line.

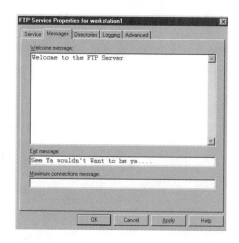

FIGURE 7.18
The Messages tab enables you to enter welcome and exit messages for users of your FTP service.

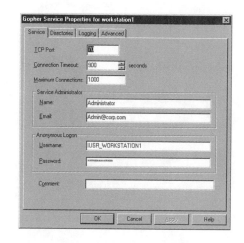

FIGURE 7.19
The Properties dialog box of the Gopher service.

Windows NT also includes a new feature called Multilink. Using Multilink, a Windows NT computer can form an RAS connection using more than one physical pathway. One Multilink connection, for example, could use two modems at once (or one modem line and one ISDN line) to form a single logical link. By using multiple pathways for one connection, Multilink can greatly increase bandwidth. The computer has to have access to more than one pathway (that is, it must have two modems installed).

The following sections will introduce you to the various components and standards the RAS has incorporated, as well as the installation and configuration settings.

RAS Security

Like everything else in Windows NT, RAS is designed for security. The following are some of RAS's security features:

◆ **Auditing.** RAS can leave an audit trail, enabling you to see who logged on when and what authentication they provided.

◆ **Callback security.** You can enable RAS server to use callback (hang up all incoming calls and call the caller back), and you can limit callback numbers to prearranged sites that you know are safe.

◆ **Encryption.** RAS can encrypt logon information, or it can encrypt all data crossing the connection.

◆ **Security hosts.** In case Windows NT is not safe enough, you can add an extra dose of security by using a third-party intermediary security host—a computer that stands between the RAS client and the RAS server and requires an extra round of authentication.

◆ **PPTP filtering.** You can tell Windows NT to filter out all packets except ultra-safe PPTP packets (discussed later in this chapter).

RAS Line Protocols

Remote Access Service supports the SLIP, PPP, and PPTP line protocols. The following sections define these protocols in detail.

SLIP

Serial Line Interface Protocol (SLIP) is a standard protocol for serial line connections over TCP/IP networks. SLIP is relatively old for the computer age—it was developed in 1984—and although it is not yet completely obsolete, it does lack some of the features available in PPP. Each node in a SLIP connection must have a static IP address; that is, you can't use nifty Windows NT features such as DHCP and WINS. Unlike PPP, SLIP does not support NetBEUI or IPX. You must use TCP/IP with SLIP. Also, SLIP cannot encrypt logon information.

PPP

Point-to-Point Protocol (PPP) was originally conceived as a deluxe version of SLIP. Like SLIP, PPP is an industry standard for point-to-point communications, but PPP offers several advantages over SLIP. Most notably, PPP isn't limited to TCP/IP. PPP also supports IPX, NetBEUI, and several other network protocols, such as AppleTalk and DECnet.

Because PPP supports so many protocols, it provides more flexibility in configuring network communications. Windows NT automatically binds PPP to TCP/IP, NetBEUI, and IPX if those protocols are installed at the same time as the RAS service.

PPTP

Point-to-Point Tunneling Protocol (PPTP) is related to PPP, but it is different and important enough to deserve separate discussion. PPTP is a protocol that enables you to transmit PPP packets over a TCP/IP network securely. Because the Internet is a TCP/IP network, PPTP enables highly private network links over the otherwise highly public Internet. PPTP connections are encrypted, making them nearly impenetrable to virtual voyeurs.

In fact, PPTP is part of an emerging technology called Virtual Private Networks (VPNs). The point of VPNs is to provide corporate networks with the same (or close to the same) security over the Internet that they would have over a direct connection.

Another exciting advantage of PPTP (and another reason that it fits nicely into the scheme of the virtual private network) is that PPTP does not discriminate among protocols. Because PPP supports NetBEUI, IPX, and other network protocols and because PPTP operates on PPP packets, PPTP actually enables you to transmit non-TCP/IP protocols over the Internet.

Because PPTP provides intranet privacy over the open Internet, it can significantly reduce costs in some situations. Networks that once would have depended on extravagant direct connections now can hook up through a local Internet service provider.

We now turn to discussion on how to install, configure, and use RAS server and Dial-Up Networking.

Installing a RAS Server

The Remote Access Service is installed using the Services tab of the Network dialog box. Prior to installation, you should gather some basic information to be used during the installation of RAS. You need to know the following:

- ◆ The type of modem to be used by RAS
- ◆ Whether the device is used for outgoing RAS communication, incoming RAS communication, or both
- ◆ The protocols to be used by RAS
- ◆ Whether the callback security feature needs to be configured

After you have all the required information, you are ready to begin the installation of RAS. To complete the RAS installation, perform the tasks in Step by Step 7.5.

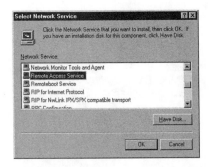

FIGURE 7.20
The Remote Access Service is added through the Select Network Service dialog box.

STEP BY STEP

7.5 Installing RAS

1. In Control Panel, double-click the Network icon.

2. In the Network dialog box, select the Services tab. Click Add to display the Select Network Service dialog box.

3. In the Select Network Service dialog box, choose Remote Access Service from the Network Service list and click OK (see Figure 7.20). Windows NT prompts you for the path to the Windows NT Installation CD-ROM.

4. Windows NT prompts you for the name of a RAS-capable device and an associated communications port

(see Figure 7.21). A modem installed on your system typically appears as a default value. Click OK to accept the modem, or click the down arrow to choose another RAS-capable device on your system. You also can install a new modem or an X.25 Pad using the Install Modem and Install X25 Pad buttons.

5. The Remote Access Setup dialog box appears (see Figure 7.22).

   Click Configure to specify whether to use the port for dial-out connections, dial-in connections, or both. The Port Usage options in Figure 7.23 apply only to the port. In other words, you could configure COM1 for Dial out only and COM2 for Receive calls only. In the Remote Access Setup dialog box, you also can add or remove a port entry from the list. The Clone button enables you to copy a port configuration.

6. Click the Network button in the Remote Access Setup dialog box to specify the network protocols for your Remote Access Service to support.

   The Server Settings options in the lower portion of the Network Configuration dialog box appear only if you configure the port to receive calls (see Figure 7.24). Select one or more of the dial-out protocols. If you want RAS to take care of receiving calls, select one or more of the server protocols and choose an encryption setting for incoming connections. You also can enable Multilink. Multilink (described earlier in this chapter) enables one logical connection to use several physical pathways.

   Note in Figure 7.24 that a Configure button follows each of the Server Settings protocol options. Each Configure button opens a dialog box that enables you to specify configuration options for the protocol, as follows:

   • The RAS Server NetBEUI Configuration dialog box enables you to specify whether the incoming caller has access to the entire network or to only the RAS server.

     By confining a caller's access to the RAS server, you improve security (because the caller can access only one PC), but you reduce functionality because the caller cannot access information on other machines.

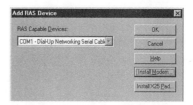

FIGURE 7.21
Windows NT prompts you for the name of a RAS-capable device and an associated communications port.

FIGURE 7.22
The Remote Access Setup dialog box.

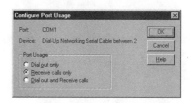

FIGURE 7.23
The Network Configuration dialog box.

FIGURE 7.24
Server protocol and encryption settings are selected in the Network Configuration dialog box.

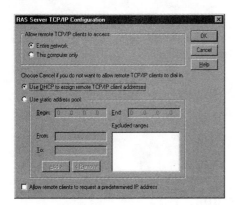

FIGURE 7.25
The RAS Server TCP/IP Configuration dialog box enables you to define how the RAS server assigns IP addresses to dial-up clients.

- The RAS Server TCP/IP Configuration dialog box enables you to define how the RAS server assigns IP addresses to dial-up clients (see Figure 7.25). You can use DHCP to assign client addresses, or you can configure RAS to assign IP addresses from a static address pool. If you choose to use a static address pool, enter the beginning and ending addresses in the range. To exclude a range of addresses within the address pool, enter the beginning and ending addresses in the range you're excluding in the From and To boxes and then click Add. The excluded range appears in the Excluded Ranges list box.

  The RAS Server TCP/IP Configuration dialog box enables you to specify whether a client can access the entire network or only the RAS server. By confining a caller's access to the RAS server, you improve security (because the caller can access only one PC), but you reduce functionality because the caller cannot access information on other machines.

- The RAS Server IPX Configuration dialog box enables you to specify how the RAS server assigns IPX network numbers (see Figure 7.26).

You can specify whether a client can access the entire network or only the RAS server. By confining a caller's access to the RAS server, you improve security (because the caller can access only one PC), but you reduce functionality because the caller cannot access information on other machines.

7. After you define the RAS settings to your satisfaction, click OK.

8. The Network Services tab appears in the foreground. You should see Remote Access Service in the list of services. Click Close.

9. Windows NT asks whether you want to restart your computer. Click Yes.

Once you complete all the steps, you will have successfully installed RAS. At this time, you have selected the port and modem to use, the port usage available for your RAS server, the supported protocols, and how each protocol can be used to access the network.

You are now ready to begin the configuration of your RAS server; the following section covers the options available to you.

Configuring RAS

In configuring the Remote Access Service, you need to configure the communication ports, the network protocols, and the encryption settings required for remote users when dialing into your Windows NT Server using the RAS as a server.

The RAS server is configured using the Services tab in the Network dialog box, which is found by clicking the Network icon in Control Panel. Locate the Remote Access Service and click Properties. This opens the Remote Access Setup dialog box, as shown in Figure 7.27.

A number of configuration options are available from this dialog box:

* ◆ **Add.** Used to add a port to be used by RAS. Can be accessed by a modem or X.25 pad.

* ◆ **Remove.** Removes a port being used by RAS.

* ◆ **Configure.** Changes the settings for a port being used by RAS.

* ◆ **Clone.** Copies the settings being used from one port to another.

* ◆ **Network.** Configures the network protocols and encryption to be used by RAS.

To make configuration changes to an existing port being used by RAS, click Configure (see Figure 7.28).

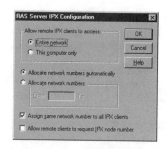

FIGURE 7.26
The RAS Server IPX Configuration dialog box enables you to specify how the RAS server assigns IPX network numbers.

FIGURE 7.27
The Remote Access Setup dialog box.

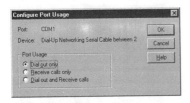

FIGURE 7.28
To make configuration changes to an existing port being used by RAS, click Configure.

FIGURE 7.29
The Remote Access Setup dialog box.

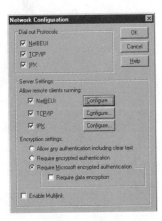

FIGURE 7.30
The Network Configuration dialog box.

The following list describes each of the options:

◆ **Dial out only.** Port is used only for outgoing RAS connections.

◆ **Receive calls only.** Port is used for receiving calls from RAS clients.

◆ **Dial out and receive calls.** Port is used for both outgoing and incoming RAS connections.

Each port listed in the Remote Access Setup dialog box can be configured for different roles. COM1 can be configured to only dial out, whereas COM2 is only used for receiving calls. By allowing each port to be configured separately, you have a great deal of flexibility with Remote Access Service.

After the ports are configured, you next have to configure the network settings. Perform the tasks outlined in Step by Step 7.6 to do so.

STEP BY STEP

7.6 Configuring the Network Settings

1. Start from the Remote Access Setup dialog box (see Figure 7.29).

2. Click Network to view the Network Configuration dialog box (see Figure 7.30).

3. Configure network settings....

The network configuration settings apply to all the ports enabled in RAS. Notice in the top section of the dialog box that you can select which protocols to use for dial-out calls. By clicking the check box beside the required protocols, you can enable or disable each of the protocols. For the RAS server settings, you must configure the middle section of the dialog box. As a RAS server, you can control how far each selected protocol can go or if it is accepted by RAS clients at all. Again, the check box directly beside each protocol enables or disables the protocol. Clicking Configure, located to the right of each listed protocol, also can restrict the protocols. Each protocol can be configured slightly differently, as described here:

- **Configuring a RAS server to use the NetBEUI protocol.** Configuring the NetBEUI protocol to be available for RAS clients enables remote clients to access either the entire network or just the RAS server, as shown in Figure 7.31.

- **Configuring a RAS server to use the TCP/IP protocol.** The TCP/IP Configure button in RAS has the same access options as the NetBEUI option. As shown in Figure 7.32, the RAS clients can be either restricted to this computer or allowed to access the entire network. The TCP/IP settings, however, also enable the configuration of IP addresses for the RAS clients. You can use the DHCP server on the network to assign an IP address, or you can create a static address pool controlled by the RAS server. By using these settings, you can allocate specific IP addresses to be used for the RAS clients.

- **Configuring a RAS server to use the IPX protocol.** In Figure 7.33, you can see that the IPX protocol also has the capability to control whether remote clients can access the entire network or just this computer. You also have the option to allocate a network number for the IPX client. The alternative is to let the RAS server automatically allocate network numbers.

FIGURE 7.31
Configuring a RAS server to use the NetBEUI protocol.

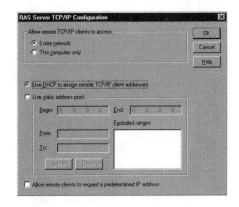

FIGURE 7.32
Configuring a RAS server to use the TCP/IP protocol.

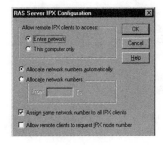

FIGURE 7.33
Configuring a RAS server to use the IPX protocol.

Dial-Up Networking

Dial-Up Networking can be referred to as the process in using the RAS server. Most of the user configuration is done in the Dial-Up Networking sections.

Dial-Up Networking enables you to establish remote connections with other computers. The most common uses for Dial-Up Networking are as follows:

◆ Accessing an Internet service provider

◆ Accessing a remote Windows NT computer or domain

You can reach Dial-Up Networking by performing the tasks in Step by Step 7.7.

STEP BY STEP

7.7 Configuring Dial-Up Networking

1. Select Programs from the Start menu.

2. Select Accessories from the Programs list.

3. Click the Dial-Up Networking icon. Figure 7.34 shows the Dial-Up Networking main screen.

   After you launch Dial-Up Networking, you enter a phone number to connect with. Additional configuration options can be set to ensure that you will have a secured connection through Dial-Up Networking. The upcoming sections will cover many of the configuration options.

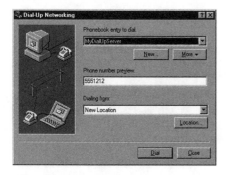

FIGURE 7.34
The Dial-Up Networking main screen.

Dial-Up Networking maintains a list of phonebook entries. A phonebook entry is a bundle of information that Windows NT needs to establish a specific connection. You can use Dial-Up Networking to create a phonebook entry for your access provider, your Windows NT domain, or any other dial-up connection. When it is time to connect, select a phonebook entry from the drop-down menu at the top of the screen and click Dial. If you access the phonebook entry often, you can create a desktop shortcut to access the phonebook entry directly.

You can create a new phonebook entry by performing the tasks in Step by Step 7.8.

STEP BY STEP

7.8 Creating a New Phonebook Entry

1. Click New in the Dial-Up Networking main screen to open the New Phonebook Entry dialog box (see Figure 7.35).

2. In the Basic tab of the New Phonebook Entry dialog box, specify a name for the entry and the phone number you want Windows NT to dial to make the connection. Adding a descriptive comment is optional. The Alternates button next to the phone number box enables you to specify a prioritized list of alternative phone numbers. You also can specify a different modem or can configure a modem from the Basic tab.

3. In the Server tab of the New Phonebook Entry dialog box (see Figure 7.36), specify the communications protocol for the dial-up server (in the drop-down menu at the top of the screen) and the network protocol.

   If you select the TCP/IP network protocol, click TCP/IP Settings to bring up the PPP TCP/IP Settings dialog box (see Figure 7.37).

4. The Script tab of the New Phonebook Entry dialog box defines some of the connection's logon properties (see Figure 7.38). You can tell Windows NT to pop up a terminal window after dialing or to run a logon script after dialing. A terminal window enables you to interactively log on to the remote server in terminal mode. The Run this script option automates the logon process. For more information about dial-up logon scripts, click Edit script. The Edit script button places you in a file called SWITCH.INF that provides instructions and sample logon scripts. The Before dialing button enables you to specify a terminal window or a logon script to execute before you dial.

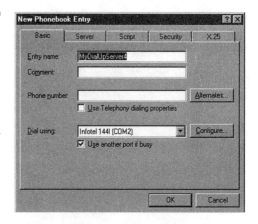

FIGURE 7.35
The New Phonebook Entry dialog box.

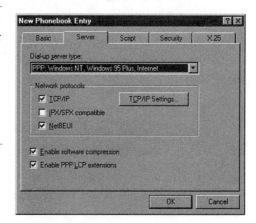

FIGURE 7.36
Specify the communications protocol for the dial-up server and the network protocol in the Server tab of the New Phonebook Entry dialog box.

continues

continued

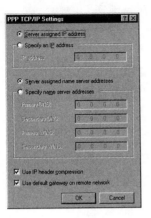

FIGURE 7.37
The PPP TCP/IP Settings dialog box.

5. The Security tab of the New Phonebook Entry dialog box offers some encryption options (see Figure 7.39). You can require encrypted authentication, or you can elect to accept any authentication including clear text. You also can specify data encryption.

6. The X.25 tab of the New Phonebook Entry dialog box (see Figure 7.40) is only for X.25 service (described previously in this chapter). Select an X.25 access provider from the drop-down menu and enter the requested information.

7. After you make changes to the New Phonebook Entry dialog box, click OK. The new phonebook entry appears in the drop-down menu at the top of the Dial-Up Networking screen.

Once you have created and configured the settings for your remote servers in the phonebook, you can use those entries to make connections to the remote servers. The flexibility of the phone book allows you to configure each entry to varying levels of security and connection methods; to add additional entries in the phonebook, refer back to step 1.

R E V I E W   B R E A K

RAS

Remote Access Server can be a very powerful and useful tool in allowing you to extend the reaches of your network to remote and traveling users. The following list summarizes RAS main points.

- RAS supports SLIP and PPP line protocols.

- With PPP, RAS can support NetBEUI, NWLink, and TCP/IP across the communication line.

- RAS uses the following media to communicate with remote systems: PSTN, X.25, null modem cable, and ISDN.

- The RAS security features available are auditing, callback security, encryption, PPTP filtering.

- To install RAS, use the network icon in the Control Panel.

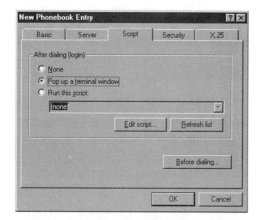

FIGURE 7.38
The Script tab of the New Phonebook Entry dialog box defines some of the connection's logon properties.

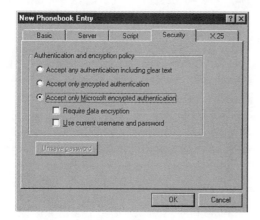

FIGURE 7.39
The Security tab of the New Phonebook Entry dialog box offers some encryption options.

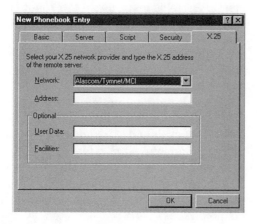

FIGURE 7.40
The X.25 tab of the New Phonebook Entry dialog box is only for X.25 service.

CASE STUDY: INCORPORATING NETWARE INTO NT

ESSENCE OF THE CASE

Here are the essential elements in this case:

- Needs to connect existing NetWare environment with Windows NT servers.

- Requires some RAS servers to handle incoming calls into the Windows NT network.

- Dial-in users need to access the NetWare servers, so they must be allowed to pass through the Windows NT Server into the NetWare application.

- For legal documents and reference material, they require a simple, quick method of transferring information and holding information for remote users.

SCENARIO

In many corporations today, it is common to see a mix of network operating systems running the required applications of the users. A legal firm needs some assistance in connecting its existing NetWare environment with Windows NT servers. It runs NetWare 3.12 servers to host a custom application that the users need access to; however, the main system is being upgraded to numerous Windows NT servers. Many of the employees travel across the country to investigate details for their clients, and when they are on the road they require access to the network systems and corporate information. At times, they would like to dial in and connect to the Windows NT networks and run the custom NetWare application. Other times, they may just require legal documents or additional reference material.

ANALYSIS

To ensure that dial-up connectivity is available, Remote Access Service is installed on one of the Windows NT servers. With RAS on this machine, DigiPort is installed to allow multiple users to dial in at one time. This solves the problem of users connecting to the NT network remotely. To allow these dial-in users access to the NetWare systems, GSNW is installed on the Windows NT server and shared off the NetWare system to users. This allows complete network access for remote users. The only remaining problem then is developing a simple solution for transferring internal information quickly and efficiently to remote users without requiring them to search all over the corporate network. To accomplish this, IIS is installed, and FTP and HTTP services are enabled. An intranet of reference information is established; and for quick transfer of documents, a secured FTP site is used to allow for the secured download and upload of documents remotely.

CHAPTER SUMMARY

The Enterprise exam has a major focus on connectivity with external systems and remote clients. Connections with Novell NetWare and allowing compatibility with Internet standards can be powerful features. In addition to the remote access features and service available in Windows NT, the connectivity options are numerous within Windows NT. With this in mind, you must surely realize that Microsoft focuses a great deal of the exam on the connectivity of Windows NT. The main points to understand to be successful with this section of the exam have been broken down in the following list:

◆ GSNW enables Windows NT Server to act as a gateway to NetWare file and print resources. The Windows NT Server that has GSNW installed can also use GSNW to function as a NetWare client allowing complete connectivity and functionality.

◆ For GSNW to be installed, the NWLink IPX/SPX protocol must be installed on the Windows NT Server.

◆ To enable the GSNW to act as a gateway through to the NetWare resources, a group called NTGATEWAY must be created on the NetWare server.

◆ NWCONV is the utility used to migrate your NetWare servers to a Windows NT environment.

◆ NWCONV can transfer file and directory information and preserve permissions if migrating to an NTFS partition on a Windows NT Server.

◆ NWCONV can transfer user and group account information into the Windows NT Server SAM database. This tool can be configured to handle duplicate entries in the directory database in one of the following ways: log error, ignore, overwrite with new information, or add a prefix.

◆ Internet Information Server supports HTTP, FTP, and Gopher connections.

KEY TERMS

- GSNW
- NWCONV
- gateway
- IIS
- HTTP
- FTP
- Gopher
- SLIP
- PPP
- PPTP
- PSTN
- Multilink

CHAPTER SUMMARY

◆ IIS can be installed during the installation of your Windows NT software or can be added as a service at any time.

◆ The administrative tool used for managing your IIS system is called the Internet Service Manager.

◆ The Internet Service Manager allows you to view the information in one of three selected views: Report, Servers, or Services.

◆ To enable remote users to connect to your Windows NT network using a telephone connection, you should install Remote Access Service.

◆ RAS supports SLIP and PPP line protocols.

◆ With the SLIP line protocol, RAS supports only the TCP/IP protocol.

◆ With the PPP line protocol, RAS supports NetBEUI, NWLink IPX/SPX, and TCP/IP protocols.

◆ RAS can connect using the following media: PSTN (Public Switched Telephone Network), X.25, ISDN, or a null modem cable.

The use of Windows NT in heterogeneous networks is increasing daily due to the power and built-in capabilities of the communication tools discussed in this chapter. Ensure that you have a strong understanding of each of the utilities and services explained throughout this chapter to be fully prepared for the Enterprise exam.

APPLY YOUR LEARNING	

Exercises

The following exercises provide you with an opportunity to apply what you've learned in this chapter.

7.1 Installing the Gateway Service for NetWare

This exercise steps you through the process of installing the Gateway Service for NetWare. It also helps you set up a gateway from the Windows NT Server to the NetWare server.

Time Estimate: 15 Minutes

1. Right-click Network Neighborhood and select the Properties option.

2. Select the Services tab.

3. Click Add, and then select the Gateway (and Client) Services for NetWare option.

4. Click OK.

5. You might be prompted for the location of your Windows NT Server source directory. Enter the location of the source files and then click Continue.

6. Click Close to close the Network dialog box. The network is reconfigured.

7. The system then prompts you to restart your computer. Click OK to restart.

8. When the system restarts, log on to the Windows NT domain. You are then prompted for the NetWare server to log on to. Select the NetWare server available and then click OK to log on to the NetWare server.

9. After the system has completed the logons, click Start | Settings | Control Panel.

10. When Control Panel is open, locate the GSNW icon and double-click it to launch the Gateway Services for NetWare dialog box.

11. In the Select Preferred Server drop-down box, select your NetWare server.

12. Click Gateway. The Configure Gateway dialog box opens.

13. Click the Enable Gateway check box.

14. Enter the gateway Account name and Password. Remember that the gateway account must be a valid account on the NetWare server, and it must be a member of the NetWare NTGATEWAY group.

15. Click Add to create a NetWare share to the NetWare server.

16. Enter the Share Name. For this example, enter `NetWare` as the share name.

17. In the Network Path, enter the UNC path to the NetWare server SYS volume. Type `\\NWSERVER\SYS`.

18. Click Z: in the Use Drive box and then click OK.

19. Click OK to close the Configure Gateway dialog box.

20. Click OK to close the Gateway Service for NetWare dialog box.

APPLY YOUR LEARNING

7.2 Running a Trial Migration from a NetWare Server to a Windows NT Domain Controller

This exercise steps you through the configuration settings for the migration process. Then you perform a trial migration.

Time Estimate: 20 minutes

1. To start a NetWare migration, select Run from the Start menu.

2. In the Run dialog box enter NWCONV.EXE and press Enter.

3. When the NWCONV utility starts, you are prompted to select the NetWare and Windows NT servers to be used for the migration. After the servers have been selected, click OK.

4. Click User Options.

5. Make sure the Transfer Users and Groups check box is selected in the User and Group Options dialog box.

6. In the Passwords tab, select No Password.

7. Click the User Names tab, select Add Prefix, and enter NW for the prefix.

8. Click the Group Names tab, select Add Prefix, and enter NW for the prefix.

9. Click OK on the User and Group Options dialog box.

10. Click File Options, and then select the files and directories to transfer.

11. When the files and directories are selected, click OK to close the File Options dialog box.

12. When the User and File Options have been configured, click Trial Migration.

13. When the trial migration is complete, view the log files to see if there are any potential problems in your migration.

14. After the trial migration is complete and you have reviewed the log files, click Exit to close the Migration Tool.

7.3 Installing Internet Information Server

This exercise steps you through the installation of IIS, with the services for the WWW, FTP, and Gopher enabled.

Time Estimate: 15 minutes

1. Right-click Network Neighborhood and select Properties.

2. Select the Services tab.

3. Click Add and then click the Microsoft Internet Information Server 2.0 option. Click OK.

4. The Internet Information Server Welcome dialog box displays. Click OK to continue.

5. Review the installation options, make sure all are selected, and then click OK.

6. You might be prompted to create the installation directory for IIS. Click Yes to create the directory.

7. The Publishing Directories dialog box appears. Click OK to select the default publishing directories.

8. Again, you might be prompted to create the directories. Click Yes to create them.

APPLY YOUR LEARNING

9. When the Internet domain name warning dialog box appears, click OK.

10. Select the SQL Server entry on the ODBC Drivers dialog box, and click OK.

11. The setup is now complete. Click OK when finished.

7.4 Installation of Remote Access Service on a Windows NT Server

This exercise installs RAS service and configures it to receive calls only.

Time Estimate: 15 minutes

1. Right-click Network Neighborhood and select the Services tab.

2. Click Add.

3. Select Remote Access Service and then click OK.

4. Enter the location of the source files for your Windows NT Server software.

5. The Remote Access Setup dialog box opens, prompting you to allow the setup wizard to detect your modem. Click Yes.

6. Click the Don't Detect My Modem, I Will Select It From The List option and then click Next.

7. Select Dial-Up Networking Serial Cable between 2 PCs and then click Next.

8. Select COM1 as the selected port and click Next.

9. In the Location Information dialog box, enter the appropriate country.

10. Enter your area code in the What Area (or City) Code Are You In Now? box.

11. Click Next.

12. Click Finish.

13. Click OK to add the modem into your Remote Access Setup dialog box.

14. Click Configure.

15. Enable the Receive calls only option.

16. Click OK to close the Port Configuration dialog box.

17. Click OK to close the Remote Access Setup dialog box.

7.5 Configuring RAS to Dial Out and Receive Communication

This exercise enables you to configure your RAS settings to allow your RAS server to dial out and to receive RAS calls.

Time estimate: 15 minutes

1. In Control Panel, double-click the Network icon.

2. Select the Services tab.

3. Locate the Remote Access Service and then click Properties.

4. In the Remote Access Setup dialog box, click Configure.

5. Enable the Dial out and Receive calls option and then click OK.

6. Click Network in the Remote Access Setup dialog box.

7. In the Dial out Protocols section of the Network Configuration dialog box, disable all protocols except TCP/IP.

APPLY YOUR LEARNING

8. In the Server Settings section, go to the Allow Remote Clients option and disable all protocols except TCP/IP.

9. Click the TCP/IP Configure button.

10. Make sure the remote clients can access the entire network through TCP/IP.

11. Click to Allow Remote Clients to use the DHCP server.

12. Click OK to close the TCP/IP settings.

13. Click OK to close the Network Configuration dialog box.

14. Click OK to close the Remote Access Server Setup dialog box.

Review Questions

1. What is the name of the service that enables your Windows NT Server computer to connect to a NetWare server?

2. What functionality does the Gateway Service for NetWare offer?

3. What is the purpose of the NWCONV.EXE utility?

4. What is the name of the service that enables Internet publications to be accessed on a Windows NT Server computer?

5. What Internet services does IIS support?

6. What are the available line protocols that RAS supports?

7. What communication lines does RAS support?

8. What is the name of the line protocol that enables encryption across a PPP connection?

Exam Questions

1. Which service enables users from a Windows NT network to access file and print resources on a NetWare server?

   A. TCP/IP

   B. Gateway Service for NetWare

   C. Services for the Macintosh

   D. NWLink IPX/SPX-Compatible protocol

2. What Internet services are installed as part of the Internet Information Server? Select all that apply.

   A. WWW

   B. Finger

   C. Gopher

   D. FTP

   E. PPTP

3. After installing IIS, what is the name of the program used to configure and monitor the Internet services?

   A. Server Manager

   B. Internet Service Manager

   C. Control Panel, Services, IIS

   D. User Manager for Domains

APPLY YOUR LEARNING

4. What are the three views used by the Internet Service Manager? Select all that apply.

    A. Report

    B. Services

    C. Servers

    D. Web

5. What is the name of the service that enables users to access the Windows NT network through a telephone line and a modem?

    A. Remote Control Service

    B. Remote Access Service

    C. Remote Network Service

    D. The Internet

6. What type(s) of communications does RAS support? Select all that apply.

    A. Public Switched Telephone Network (PSTN)

    B. X.25

    C. IEEE X.400

    D. Null modem cable

    E. ISDN

    F. Radio LAN

7. What is the name of the feature that enables RAS to use more than one communication channel at a time for the same connection?

    A. Multinet

    B. Multilink

    C. ISDN

    D. Multichannel

8. Identify the two serial protocols that RAS supports:

    A. Ethernet and Token Ring

    B. IPX and TCP/IP

    C. SLIP and PPP

    D. ESLIP and PPTP

9. Which of the serial protocols support NetBEUI, IPX, and TCP/IP over RAS?

    A. SLIP

    B. ESLIP

    C. PPP

    D. TCP/IP

10. You want to enable users to connect to your local area network using RAS. You are concerned, however, about security in your RAS connection. What security features does RAS support? Select all that apply.

    A. PPTP

    B. Callback to a fixed number

    C. Callback to a variable number

    D. Microsoft Authenticated Logons

11. What is the name of the utility used to help the migration of your NetWare system to a Windows NT Server?

    A. NWMIGRATE.EXE

    B. NWCONV.EXE

    C. NWMIG.EXE

    D. NETCONFIG.EXE

APPLY YOUR LEARNING

12. When using the Migration Tool from a NetWare server to a Windows NT domain controller, what information can be migrated across? Select all that apply.

    A. User accounts

    B. Group accounts

    C. Files and directories from the NetWare server

    D. Logon scripts

13. What must be in place to keep the file and directory permissions during a migration from NetWare to Windows NT?

    A. The user running the migration must have Administrator privileges.

    B. The Windows NT computer must have an NTFS partition.

    C. The Windows NT computer must have a FAT partition.

    D. The NetWare computer must have an NTFS partition.

Answers to Review Questions

1. The service that functions as a NetWare client software and also allows the users to use it as a gateway to the NetWare servers is the Gateway Services for NetWare. See the section "Interoperability with NetWare" for more information.

2. Connectivity with NetWare servers for file and print access and sharing of a gateway through the Windows NT server into the resources of the NetWare server. See the section "Interoperability with NetWare" for more information.

3. To migrate the users, groups, and directory information from a NetWare server. See the section "NWCONV: Migration Tool for NetWare" for more information.

4. Internet Information Server. See the section "Install and Configure Internet Information Server" for more information.

5. Gopher, FTP, and HTTP (WWW). See the section "Install and Configure Internet Information Server" for more information.

6. PPP and SLIP. See the section "RAS Line Protocols" for more information.

7. ISDN, X.25, Public Switched Telephone Network/Modem. See the section "Installing and Configuring Remote Access Service (RAS)" for more information.

8. PPTP. See the section "RAS Line Protocols" for more information.

Answers to Exam Questions

1. **B.** The Gateway Service for NetWare is used to enable users from a Windows NT network to access NetWare file and print resources. See the section "Gateway Service for NetWare."

2. **A. C. D.** IIS supports HTTP, FTP, and Gopher services for connectivity. See the section "Overview of IIS."

3. **B.** The Internet Service Manager is the graphical tool used to manage your IIS services. See the section "Installation Steps for IIS."

APPLY YOUR LEARNING

4. **A. B. C.** The Internet Service Manager displays the IIS services in Report view, Servers view, and Services view. See the section "Installation Steps for IIS."

5. **B.** Remote Access Service, or RAS, enables remote users to dial in to a Windows NT system. See the section "Installing and Configuring Remote Access Service (RAS)."

6. **A. B. D. E.** RAS supports the following communication media: PSTN, X.25, ISDN, and null modem cable. See the section "Installing and Configuring Remote Access Service (RAS)."

7. **B.** Multilink is the feature that allows the use of multiple communication channels for a RAS session. See the section "Installing and Configuring Remote Access Service (RAS)."

8. **C.** RAS supports SLIP and PPP line protocols. See the section "RAS Line Protocols."

9. **C.** PPP supports NetBEUI, TCP/IP, and IPX protocols, whereas SLIP supports only TCP/IP. See the section "RAS Line Protocols."

10. **A. B. C. D.** RAS supports all of the listed features as security options. See the section "RAS Security."

11. **B.** NWCONV is the utility used to migrate your NetWare server information into a Windows NT server. See the section "NWCONV: Migration Tool for NetWare."

12. **A. B. C.** NWCONV allows you to migrate user and group accounts and file and directories into a Windows NT server. See the section "NWCONV: Migration Tool for NetWare."

13. **A. B.** To maintain the file and directory permissions from NetWare in the Windows NT server, an NTFS partition must be used as the receiving partition, and the user must have Administrator privileges to the servers. See the section "Steps to Migrating from NetWare."

MONITORING AND OPTIMIZATION

This chapter helps you to prepare for the Microsoft exam by covering the following objective within the "Monitoring and Optimization" category:

Establish a baseline for measuring system performance. Tasks include creating a database of measurement data.

▶ This objective is focused on ensuring that you understand the need for creating a baseline and maintaining the database of measurement. The idea is not to force you to use a specific type of database; this topic is more of an overview of analysis and optimization terms and standards.

CHAPTER 8

Analysis and Optimization Overview

OUTLINE

The main purpose of this chapter is to supply you with the background knowledge required to analyze and then optimize your Windows NT network. This chapter introduces you to the tools used for analysis and optimization, and it explains the purpose of a baseline for measurement and the use of a database for tracking the analyzed components. As you read the information in this chapter, the best method for preparing yourself for the exam is to apply these strategies to the procedures of the following two chapters: Chapter 9, "Using Performance Monitor," and Chapter 10, "Using Network Monitor."

Almost anyone can install Windows NT; the trick is to get the system to operate at the highest level of performance possible, which is not always a simple task. One reason is that most people don't know what is causing their systems to perform poorly.

To make your systems operate better, you have to know what is happening internally. You use monitoring tools to gather information about your systems and the network.

This chapter discusses the following topics:

◆ Defining analysis and optimization

◆ Resources to be monitored

◆ Tools for monitoring

In addressing each of these topics, this chapter introduces many terms and strategies for locating bottlenecks in your computer systems and on your network. After building your foundation of knowledge for analysis, the next two chapters focus on some of the tools mentioned in this chapter and turn the strategies into practical procedures that you can use to analyze your Windows NT system.

DEFINING ANALYSIS AND OPTIMIZATION

This chapter deals with the strategies and utilities used for server analysis of the Microsoft Windows NT 4 system. The process of monitoring and optimizing a system must include a thoughtful and organized process of record keeping. You keep records for analyzing current resource usage and projecting future demands on resources. This involves looking for an overuse of resources and determining how it causes a decrease in system performance. Analysis, however, is not limited to finding such bottlenecks. You can detect underused resources as well.

To conduct analysis and optimization, you do the following:

◆ Create a baseline of current use.

◆ Monitor the use over a period of time.

◆ Analyze data to determine non-optimum system use.

◆ Determine how the system should be used.

◆ Determine whether you should add resources to the system or whether the system needs to be upgraded.

The upcoming two sections discuss establishing a baseline and establishing a database. The creation and maintenance of these two components are critical in performing any analysis on your Windows NT system. Without both of these components, you cannot fully optimize your environment.

Establishing a Baseline

Establish a baseline for measuring system performance.

Whenever you analyze a system's performance, you must first create a baseline to measure from. If you do not have a standard to compare to, you cannot tell whether performance is good, bad, or somewhere in between.

If you have an established baseline, you can always compare system performance to that baseline whenever you make any changes to the system, whether they are good or bad. If you add a new disk controller, for example, you could monitor disk performance to see if file transfer rates improve. If there is no baseline, you cannot tell.

The reason you monitor a system is to see whether a resource is overused or underused or operating at its maximum capacity. When you purchase components (hard disks, CDs, modems, and so on), the manufacturers provide specifications regarding the maximum rate of performance. After you add components to a system, it is rare that they actually perform at their advertised maximum rates. Each component has an effect on the others, creating additional loads that were not present when you made a benchmark of the components.

Knowing how data is collected can provide a wide variety of information. Taking a measurement, for example, adding all the components, and then measuring again displays the effect of all the components working together. Another way of measuring is to take a separate measure as each component is added. This provides data about how each individual component affects the performance of the system. Yet another way is to add components one at a time, but in different combinations. This provides a better understanding of how each different component affects the performance of the others.

To obtain further understanding of system performance, you need to build a baseline for each server system and then use it to measure the performance of different resources. In the coming chapters, you will use various Windows NT utilities to create a baseline of your system.

Establishing a Database

Create a database of measurement data.

The second step in preparing for analysis is to take the collected data and put it into a database so it can be analyzed. This involves collecting the information over a period of time and adding all of it to a database. Once in a database, the information can be used to identify bottlenecks and trends.

Bottlenecks are the problem areas that need addressing to improve the performance of the system, and trends are useful for capacity planning and preparing for future needs.

After the information is in a database, it is then accessible, measurable, and manageable. The database utilities complement the data collection utilities. The collection utilities gather great quantities of data, and the database utilities enable you to organize the information into meaningful and manageable groups.

You can use numerous database utilities to analyze the data collected. Some of the databases Microsoft provides are

- ◆ Performance Monitor
- ◆ Microsoft Excel
- ◆ Microsoft Access
- ◆ Microsoft FoxPro
- ◆ Microsoft SQL Server

In addition to the utilities listed, many other applications are developed by other vendors.

Regardless of what application you use to analyze the data, the most important step is to collect the data over a significant period of time.

RESOURCES TO BE MONITORED

Analysis and optimization of the server start with determining the maximum throughput of each resource in use on the system and the network. You should monitor the throughput of each resource individually both during installation and after installation is complete with all resources in use. This way, you can determine how the use of each resource affects the others. You should monitor a number of system resources. Of all the resources that can be monitored, the following four have the greatest impact on the performance of the server:

◆ Memory

◆ Processor

◆ Disk

◆ Network

When monitoring a server system, it is important to monitor each resource individually as well as the system as a whole. By monitoring each resource, you can determine how you need to configure that resource for optimum performance. At the same time, it is important to monitor the system as a whole to see how each resource affects the others. The tuning of an individual resource can adversely affect the performance of other resources. Poor performance of one resource can cause the poor performance of another. An example of this is disk access. Disks can be extremely busy and can fail to perform at an expected level. This poor performance, however, might be due to the system not having enough RAM. When the system doesn't have enough RAM, disk performance is diminished due to excessive paging, which results in poor response to user requests. Monitoring the four resources (memory, processor, disk, and network) simultaneously shows the effects the resource combinations have on one another and the server system.

Memory

You need to consider two main types of memory when analyzing server performance:

◆ Physical random access memory (RAM)

◆ Virtual memory cache (paging file)

The rule of thumb for memory seems to be that you can never have too much, especially physical memory. In other words, the more memory you have, the better.

Another factor affecting the pagefile is its location. You can optimize the system, for example, by moving the pagefile from the system partition to another partition. This can greatly decrease disk access time, especially if the two partitions are on different hard drives and there is a separate disk controller for each drive. This recommendation comes from Microsoft. If you move the pagefile from the system partition, however, the Crashdump utility is disabled. The Crashdump utility writes whatever was in memory to a file called MEMORY.DMP if the system crashes. This file is used by Microsoft to determine the cause of the crash.

If you have a stable system that never crashes, move the pagefile to a different partition. All Windows NT's virtual drivers constantly request to read from the system partition. By moving the pagefile to another partition, you distribute the disk request load.

If the server system exhibits intermittent instability, it is best to leave the pagefile in its default location and to create a large secondary pagefile on another drive. The large secondary pagefile gets most of the accesses and still allows the crash dump, so it can determine the cause of the instability.

Processor

The type and number of processors greatly affect the performance of the system. There is no comparison, for example, between the performance of a system with an Intel 80486 processor and a system with a Digital Alpha XP 4 processor.

Windows NT Server supports symmetric multiprocessing. If multiple applications are running simultaneously on a multiprocessor system, the processing is shared among processors. Likewise, if a single multithreaded application is running on a system, the processing of the threads can be shared among the processors. Windows NT Server 4 can scale up to 32 processors.

Disk

A number of factors affect disk performance, and all of them should be taken into account when you analyze and optimize the system.

The factors include

◆ Type and number of controllers

◆ Types of drives implemented

◆ Controllers that support RAID

◆ Busmaster controllers

◆ Caching

◆ Type of work being performed

Type and Number of Controllers

The type and number of controllers can greatly affect the disk performance of the system when responding to requests to read information from or write information to the disks. If you increase the number of controllers, the system can write to the disks simultaneously. This increases throughput. If the system has only one drive, choosing a different type of drive or a different type or make of controller can increase throughput. Table 8.1 contains examples of the throughput of different drive types. Remember that these values are approximate, and with the constant improvement of hardware, the values might be upgraded by the time that you read this; so for accurate values for these components, check the product specifications.

| TABLE 8.1 |

THROUGHPUT OF DIFFERENT DRIVE TYPES

Drive Type	Transfer Rate
IDE controllers	About 2.5MB/sec
Standard SCSI controllers	About 3MB/sec
SCSI-2 controllers	About 5MB/sec
Fast SCSI-2 controllers	About 10MB/sec
Ultra Wide SCSI/SCSI-3	Up to 40MB/sec on a PCI bus

In addition to the type of controller, the number of controllers also can make a difference in performance. With software-implemented RAID (redundant array of inexpensive disks), such as a stripe set, you can improve performance substantially. For a stripe set over six hard drives, for example, with a controller for every two drives, the performance is much better than for the six drives controlled by a single controller.

Types of Drives Implemented

The performance of a disk drive is almost always measured in disk access time. This refers to how long it takes a disk to react to a read or write request. The times for different drives and different drive types can vary greatly; some react as quickly as seven or eight milliseconds. In addition to access rate, you should consider rotation speed and maximum data transfer rates.

Use drives that complement the rest of the system architecture. Choose the fastest drive to work with the fastest controller. There is no point in using a fast controller to control a slow disk.

Controllers That Support RAID

Controllers that support hardware-implemented RAID can provide better performance than Windows NT Server's software implementation of RAID. Implementing Windows NT Server's striping or striping with parity also can improve performance. This depends greatly on the number of controllers. In one test, writing a 200MB file to a stripe set was 20 percent faster than writing to a single drive in the same system. This same result might not occur in all tests on all systems, so you must test and analyze each system individually.

Busmaster Controllers

Busmaster controllers have a processor that handles interrupts. It also transfers data to memory locations until the data is ready to be processed by the CPU. This reduces the number of interrupts the CPU must handle.

Caching

Read and write caching can help improve disk response time because data is held in cache on the controller instead of being written directly to the disk. This cache does not require RAM or internal cache. This cache can cause problems with certain applications, however, depending on how they have been written. Some applications are written for access by a single user, whereas others are written assuming multiple users will access and update the file simultaneously. The latter scenario can be a nightmare if the application is not written properly.

Here is an example: Two people have a file open at the same time, and the first person saves a change to the file. That change is not immediately written to the disk; instead, it is written to the cache. If the second person makes a change to the same area (such as a record in database) and saves the change before the first person's change was written, then there is potential for data loss.

Caching is a great way to improve the performance of disk access. The one situation to watch is a custom application. If the programmer is not aware of how Windows NT handles information being written to and read from the disk, you can encounter the problem previously described in the example. In the majority of cases (especially software out of the box), however, there is no problem with caching, and it is highly recommended.

Type of Work Being Performed

As mentioned in the previous section, if the application is disk-bound (many read and write requests), implementing the fastest disk system provides the best performance.

For a single-processor system, Microsoft recommends implementing the Fast SCSI-2 disk controller as the minimum.

Network

The performance of networking components on the server, as well as the performance of the overall network, can depend on a number of factors. Often, you must examine each component individually to see how it affects network capacity and server performance. This section covers the following items relating to network performance and components:

◆ Type of network adapter

◆ Multiple network adapters

◆ Protocols in use

◆ Additional network services

◆ Applications in use

◆ Number of users

◆ Other physical network components

◆ Directory services

Type of Network Adapter

Use an adapter that has a high bandwidth, and avoid those that use programmed input/output. The programmed I/O cards use the CPU to move data between the network adapter and the RAM, thus using processing time and reducing performance.

Table 8.2 shows examples of the speeds of transfer that you can expect from different network adapter cards.

TABLE 8.2

TRANSFER SPEEDS FOR VARIOUS NETWORK ADAPTER CARDS ON AN ETHERNET 10BaseX NETWORK

Type of Adapter	Transfer Speed
8-bit network adapter	Up to 400KB/sec
16-bit network adapter	Up to 800KB/sec
32-bit network adapter	Up to 1.2MB/sec

Multiple Network Adapters

Installing multiple adapters in a server can be beneficial because it enables the server to process network requests simultaneously. Generally, the processor works at a rate much higher than the rate at which the network adapter can transfer requests. If you place additional network adapters in the server, the system can use the processor more efficiently. If multiple protocols are used on the network, another possibility is to assign a specific protocol for each network adapter. It is common to assign all server-based traffic to one adapter and assign all hosting (using a protocol such as SNA) to another adapter.

Protocols in Use

Most protocols have fairly similar performance, depending on the function. Some functions can be performed only with certain types of protocols. Reducing the number of protocols installed or even disabling protocols for certain services can increase performance.

Additional Network Services

Each additional service installed demands more memory and increases processor overhead. These services commonly include

- ◆ DHCP
- ◆ WINS
- ◆ RAS
- ◆ Services for Macintosh

These are some of the most common services installed on a server, but by no means are they all the services that you can install. Reducing the number of services on the server improves performance, but at what cost? Without services such as DHCP or WINS, network administration overhead increases. Without RAS, remote users cannot access the network.

Applications in Use

Each application running on the server requires additional memory and increases processor overhead. These applications commonly include

- ◆ Internet services
- ◆ Messaging applications such as Exchange Server

◆ Microsoft System Management Server

◆ Microsoft SQL Server

◆ Microsoft SNA Server

◆ Antivirus software

Number of Users

As the number of users accessing a server at the same time increases, the quality of the server's performance decreases. Another factor is the number of inactive connections. Mapped drives to the server, or from the server to another system, require processing time to monitor each connection.

Other Physical Network Components

Routers, bridges, printers, modems, and other physical network components all affect the performance of the network and, thus, the performance of the server. If a router can relay broadcast messages, for example, it can increase the network traffic. Older routers with smaller buffers lose more packets if there is a lot of traffic and TCP/IP is not optimized properly.

Directory Services

The implemented domain model and structure have a direct effect on the performance of the server. Table 8.3 shows how the network can be affected.

TABLE 8.3

EFFECTS OF VARIOUS FACTORS ON NETWORK
PERFORMANCE

Factor Affecting Performance	*Considerations*
Number of users	Consider not only the number of users in the domain, but also the number of simultaneous logon requests that need to be handled by the domain controllers.

Factor Affecting Performance	*Considerations*
Number of BDCs (backup domain controllers)	The more domain controllers in a domain, the more account synchronization traffic.
Location of users and domain controllers	Across a WAN, domain account validation can be very slow. If the domain controllers are on separate legs of the WAN, domain account synchronization can use a large percentage of the WAN bandwidth. Changing the `ReplicatorGovernor` parameter can improve the performance of the synchronization across the WAN.

Analyzing Your System

In analyzing your computer and network, you should focus on the following key points:

- Establish a baseline measurement of your system when it's functioning at its normal level. You can use the baseline in comparative analysis at a later point.

- Establish a database to maintain the baseline results, any subsequent analysis results on the system to compare trends, and potential pitfalls in your system.

- The main resources to monitor are the memory, processor, disk, and network.

TOOLS FOR MONITORING

A number of tools that come with Windows NT 4 Server enable you to monitor and analyze the system.

Some of the tools that Microsoft provides are

- ◆ Server Manager
- ◆ Windows NT Diagnostics
- ◆ Response Probe

◆ Task Manager

◆ Performance Monitor

◆ Network Monitor

All these tools come with Windows NT 4 (Network Monitor must be installed) except Response Probe, which comes with the Resource Kit.

Server Manager

You can perform basic analysis of a server using Server Manager. You can monitor the number of users currently connected, the amount of idle time for each of the connections, and the share names in use. Server Manager also can monitor other servers on the network, enabling the analysis of all servers from a single, centralized location.

The items viewed in Server Manager can help you determine peak operating times for a server and can indicate what resources are most commonly used. Through analysis of what is used, an administrator can determine whether resources should be moved to different systems to better balance the load.

Windows NT Diagnostics

You can perform simple performance analysis tasks using NT Diagnostics. It displays the current configuration for the processor, memory, disk, and network. NT Diagnostics can be an excellent tool for viewing resource information and general settings from within your Windows NT Server. You cannot modify settings using Windows NT Diagnostics; however, it can be an efficient tool for locating conflicts and other hardware problems.

Response Probe

Response Probe is a utility used to apply controlled stress on a system and monitor the response. This tool is useful for determining a resource's capacity before placing it in a "live" production environment.

Task Manager

Task Manager enables the viewing, stopping, and starting of applications and processes. It also contains the Performance Monitor capabilities that enable you to view memory and CPU utilization. The Task Manager is an excellent starting point for any NT system troubleshooting or optimization. At any time, you can launch the Task Manager and view the list of services running and the memory and CPU utilization used for each service. Sometimes you can locate a bottleneck simply by using the Task Manager.

Performance Monitor

Performance Monitor is an administrative tool for monitoring NT workstations and servers. It uses a series of counters to track data for different objects installed on the system. These data can include the number of processes waiting for disk time, the number of threads waiting for processor time, the number of packets transmitted over the network per second, and so on. You can view data in real time (see Figure 8.1) or log it for use at a later date. You can display the data in charts or logs and set alerts to warn when a threshold value is exceeded. The Performance Monitor tool is examined in more depth in Chapter 9.

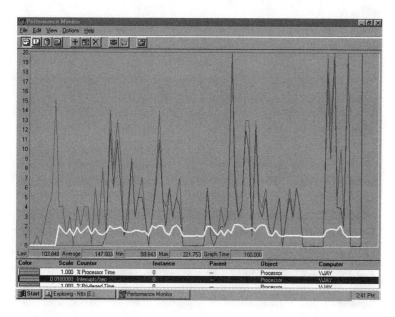

FIGURE 8.1

Data can be viewed in real time, as it is here in the Performance Monitor.

Network Monitor

Network Monitor captures and views the network traffic going in and out of the system on which Network Monitor is running. The information being monitored includes the number of broadcasts, the size and contents of the packets, and network statistics (see Figure 8.2). After capturing network traffic, you can analyze the data to resolve traffic problems.

Microsoft also offers a "promiscuous" version of Network Monitor with the Systems Management Server software. This version enables you to view and capture network traffic across the entire network.

Network Monitor is covered in more detail in Chapter 10.

R E V I E W   B R E A K

Monitoring Tools

The tools that you can use to monitor your Windows NT server may include one or more of the tools listed in this chapter. The following list is a summary of the tools available that are built in to Windows NT Server 4.0:

- Server Manager

- Windows NT Diagnostics

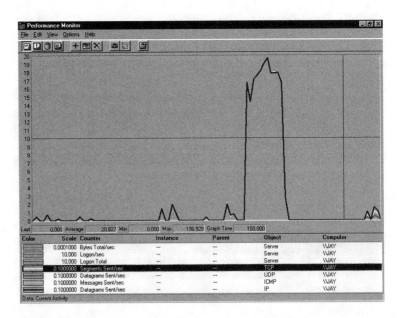

FIGURE 8.2
Network Monitor captures and views the number of broadcasts, the size and contents of the packets, and network statistics.

- Response Probe

- Performance Monitor

- Network Monitor

You can use each of these tools for troubleshooting and optimizing your Windows NT systems. In the coming chapters, these tools are explained in more detail.

CASE STUDY: ANALYZING AND OPTIMIZING A NETWORK

ESSENCE OF THE CASE

Here are the essential elements in this case:

- Need to gain an understanding of the tools and utilities available for monitoring a Windows NT system.

- Need to understand what resources must be monitored to prepare for optimization.

SCENARIO

A common complaint within a network environment is that the network is too slow. To combat this problem, the network must be optimized; a number of systems and resources must be analyzed. JPS Consulting is one such company in need of analysis and optimization. Unfortunately, the individuals responsible for this analysis and optimization—as is the case in many companies—have little experience in this area because they were always told that Windows NT is a self-optimizing operating system. They need to become acquainted with the types of tools available for optimizing Windows NT, and they to know how their system can be optimized.

ANALYSIS

In Windows NT, you can use a number of utilities and tools integrated into the operating system to monitor your Windows NT system. The tools that are useful for monitoring are

- Windows NT Diagnostics

- Task Manager

CASE STUDY: ANALYZING AND OPTIMIZING A NETWORK

- Performance Monitor

- Network Monitor

- Server Manager

By using these tools, the individuals at JPS Consulting will monitor the hardware of their system to ensure that no hardware conflicts exist—because they would be a major cause of bottlenecks to the system. These utilities will also monitor the key resources of the system to ensure that it is running at its full potential and that it is not restricted by minimal resources or

other potential problems. The key resources to monitor are

- Memory

- Disk

- Network

- Processor

Using the tools for monitoring, you can quickly locate any problem areas and then work toward a resolution to increase your system's performance.

CHAPTER SUMMARY

KEY TERMS

- baseline

- Response Probe

- Task Manager

- Performance Monitor

- resource

In this chapter, you focused on gaining an understanding of the purpose of analysis and optimization in your Windows NT system. When you are preparing for the exam, ensure that you know each of the utilities available to assist in analyzing your system and that you understand the need for a baseline and a database to maintain your measurements.

The main points to reinforce for this chapter are as follows:

◆ The utilities available for analysis of your Windows NT system are Server Manager, Windows NT Diagnostics, Response Probe, Task Manager, Performance Monitor, and Network Monitor.

◆ The four main resources to monitor in performance analysis are the memory, processor, disk, and network.

◆ A baseline is a normal level of the resources in your system.

◆ Some common tools that you can use to maintain your database of system measurements are Microsoft SQL Server, Microsoft Access, Microsoft FoxPro, Microsoft Excel, and Performance Monitor.

APPLY YOUR LEARNING

This section allows you to assess how well you understand the material in the chapter. Review and exam questions test your knowledge of the tasks and concepts specified in the objectives.

For more review and exam questions, see the Top Score test engine on the CD-ROM that came with this book.

Review Questions

1. As a network administrator, Alice has received many complaints about disk access time on the server. The server, which is a PDC, is a DHCP server. Should she get a faster disk drive? What should she check to find the disk access problem?

2. Chuck has complained to you that the server seems to be operating slower than it used to. He doesn't have any hard facts, but he insists something has made it slower. How can you prove or disprove his belief?

3. Peter is supporting a network with 5 Windows NT servers and 70 Windows 95 systems as workstations in a single subnet. Access anywhere in the network is quite slow. He took over the network from an expert who said they should have TCP/IP, NWLink, and NetBEUI installed on all the systems. What impact does the use of multiple protocols have on the network? If it is necessary to have all three protocols on the network, what can Peter do to reduce the network traffic?

4. Steve is administering a network that uses NWLink as its protocol and has 200 users running a combination of Windows NT 4 Workstation and Windows 95 on their desktops. One main file server is running Windows NT Server with Service Pack 3 installed. Access to files on the server is slow. He checked the disk access speed, and it is one of the fastest on the market. What can Steve do to improve access to the server's disks?

5. You want to create a baseline of your Windows NT servers. Which resources should you monitor to ensure that you have statistics that cover the most common resources in your system?

Exam Questions

1. A network has a large number of Windows 95 and Windows NT Workstation 4 systems. Select every option that could help reduce network traffic:

   A. Reduce the number of protocols used at the workstations and servers.

   B. Increase the number of network cards in the servers.

   C. Turn off file and print sharing on the desktop systems.

   D. Install SNMP.

APPLY YOUR LEARNING

2. Which bottleneck makes the access time to a disk seem slow to a user logged on locally?

   A. Memory

   B. Processor

   C. Disk

   D. Network

3. Jack is administering a network that has three distinct groups. There are approximately 200 users, and most of them are complaining that network response time is slow. What could be done to increase performance?

   A. Subnet the network and put each of the groups onto its own subnet.

   B. Move the pagefile to a different directory.

   C. Remove file and print sharing from the workstations and have all access go through a server.

   D. Add another network card to the server.

4. To view the performance of your pagefile in a Windows NT system, which two resources would you need to monitor?

   A. Disk

   B. Processor

   C. Network

   D. Memory

Answers to Review Questions

1. She could monitor both the disk and the pagefile. If there are a lot of page faults, the server might be running out of memory. This would cause the disk drives to thrash and would slow overall disk access. See the section "Memory" in this chapter for more information.

2. If a baseline was created when the system was first installed, monitor the system and compare the results to the baseline. Otherwise, you should make a baseline and then perform monitoring. See the section "Establishing a Baseline" in this chapter for more information.

3. Whenever a message is sent out on the network, the message must be repeated for each protocol. Three protocols triples the amount of traffic a single protocol creates. Disable the services of protocols that are not needed. See the sections "Network" and "Protocols in Use" for more information.

4. Because the slow access is not the disk itself, you must assume the network access is slow. Check whether the adapter is a 16-bit or 32-bit card. If it is a 32-bit card, install a second network card into the system. Also, there might be a lot of network traffic. Disabling the Server service on any computers that do not share folders and printers reduces network traffic. See the section "Network" in this chapter for more information.

5. The most common resources to be monitored that affect the performance of your Windows NT system are the disk, memory, processor, and network. See the section "Resources to Be Monitored" in this chapter.

Answers to Exam Questions

1. **A. B. C.** To reduce the amount of traffic on your network, you can reduce the number of network services that are running and reduce or limit the number of protocols loaded in your environment. See the section "Network" for more information.

2. **C.** The disk is the most common resource to cause a bottleneck on the disk of a user logged on locally. See the section "Disk" in this chapter for more information.

3. **A. C. D.** To increase performance, you could subnet the network into smaller networks, remove or reduce all additional network services, and add an additional network card to handle some of the requests. See the section "Network" for more information.

4. **A. D.** The two resources that need to be monitored in assessing the performance of the pagefile are the memory and disk resources. See the section "Resources to Be Monitored" in this chapter for more information.

This chapter helps you to prepare for the Microsoft exam by covering the following objectives within the "Monitoring and Optimization" category:

Monitor performance of various functions by using Performance Monitor. The resources you monitor include

- ◆ **Processor**
- ◆ **Memory**
- ◆ **Disk**
- ◆ **Network**

▶ This objective requires you to fully understand how to use the Performance Monitor as a utility that can assist you in monitoring the common resources within your system. The common resources used in this objective are the processor, memory, disk, and network.

Identify performance bottlenecks.

▶ By using the Performance Monitor, you must be able to analyze the resources being measured and be able to identify system and resource bottlenecks based on the analyzed data.

Optimize performance for various results. Results include

- ◆ **Controlling network traffic**
- ◆ **Controlling server load**

▶ Once you complete the monitoring and analysis of bottlenecks using the Performance Monitor, you should be able to optimize the Windows NT Server system. The network load and network traffic are the main areas of optimization you address to meet this objective.

C H A P T E R 9

Using Performance Monitor

The Performance Monitor utility can be a powerful tool in analysis and optimization of your Windows NT network. In addition to the information in the body of this chapter, you are required to gain a great deal of hands-on experience with this tool to be fully prepared for the exam. Work through the exercises at the end of this chapter and also monitor some of your everyday tasks to analyze your own system and resource consumption.

This chapter continues with the monitoring and optimization objectives in the enterprise exam. In this chapter, we focus on one of the tools used to analyze your Windows NT system, the Performance Monitor. The Performance Monitor is a powerful utility, and you must have a strong understanding about what it can do for you and how it functions. This chapter covers the following sections:

◆ Overview of Performance Monitor

◆ Objects in Performance Monitor

◆ Counters in Performance Monitor

◆ Views in Performance Monitor

◆ Creating a baseline using Performance Monitor

◆ Performance analysis

Performance Monitor is a useful tool for analyzing the server system. It helps you to better plan for future use and, at the same time, to optimize its current performance.

OVERVIEW OF PERFORMANCE MONITOR

One of the utilities integrated within Windows NT Server is the Performance Monitor. The Performance Monitor is a graphical tool that allows you to view system resources and components of your computer system. In viewing these resources—or objects, as they are called within the Performance Monitor—you can enable various counters that allow you to monitor your system and locate any potential problems or bottlenecks with your computer.

Performance Monitor is designed to show a broad view of computer performance. Viewing the correct objects and counters might indicate the cause of a problem. In most cases, the tool enables you to completely resolve the problem, or at least it suggests which specialized tool you should use next. Such tools can include a profiler, a network analyzer or sniffer, a working set monitor, or some other tool.

This section identifies some of the options available in Performance Monitor for monitoring, analyzing server performance, and gathering specific data.

The options available in Performance Monitor let you accumulate a complete set of data for analysis. Some of the options include

◆ Viewing data from multiple computers simultaneously

◆ Seeing how changes affect the computer

◆ Changing charts of current activity while viewing them

◆ Starting a program or procedure automatically or sending a notice when a threshold is exceeded

◆ Exporting Performance Monitor data to spreadsheets or database programs or using it as raw input for programs

◆ Saving different combinations of counter and option settings for quick starts and changes

◆ Logging data about various objects from multiple computers over time

◆ Creating reports about current activity or trends over time

As shown in Figure 9.1, you can monitor different counters for the processor object in a chart format.

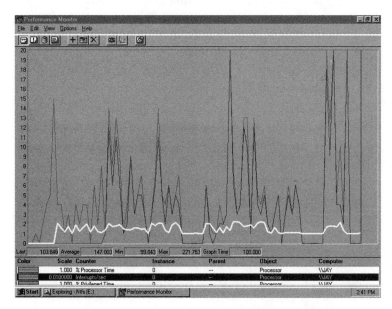

FIGURE 9.1
A Chart view of the %Processor Time, Interrupts/Sec., and %Privileged Time of a single computer.

A number of other factors can adversely affect the data gathered using Performance Monitor. The user, for example, has control over the frequency with which data is gathered. If the interval is too short, the log file can unnecessarily become very large. The values of certain counters might become skewed due to the increased burden on the processor. If the frequency interval is too long, the counters might miss significant changes in data. Another example of inaccurate data can occur if monitoring takes place too soon after system startup. During startup, all processes and services are initiated, which creates a burden on the processor.

If you do not want the network itself to be monitored, you should take the computer off the network during monitoring. While monitoring disk activity and responsiveness, for example, the computer might respond to a network request or simply monitor a connection to a network resource. The data you gather at that point might indicate a problem where there is none.

Objects in Performance Monitor

What you really monitor in a computer system is the behavior of its objects. An *object* is a standard mechanism for identifying and using a system resource. Objects are created to represent individual threads, processes, physical devices, and sections of shared memory. Performance Monitor groups counters by object type. Each object has a unique set of counters assigned to it. Certain objects and their respective counters are available on all systems; others are available only when the computer is running the associated software or service. If the system is acting as a DHCP server, for example, it has specific objects that are not available on a non-DHCP server (see Figure 9.2).

Each object type can have more than one component installed in the computer. These components are referred to as instances; they are displayed in the Instance box of any Add to dialog box (see Figure 9.3). The Instance box also can contain the _Total instance. This instance represents the total of all instances.

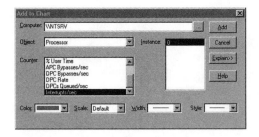

FIGURE 9.2
The Processor object is selected and displayed within the Performance Monitor.

A system with more than one disk drive has a specific instance for each drive plus the _Total instance. It might be necessary to monitor objects and counters from each drive to see if one is not responding as well as another. Other cases of multiple instances include network cards, processors, processes, threads, and page files. Notice that the PhysicalDisk object of this computer shows two disks (two instances, 0 and 1).

Some objects are dependent on or a part of another object. This type of object also can be referred to as a *child object*. An object that has one or more dependent objects can be referred to as a *parent object*.

In most cases, the parent object is a process and the child object is a thread. A process can be an application (Word for Windows), a service (browser, netlogon), or a subsystem (Win32 subsystem). Each process consists of an executable program, virtual memory addresses, and at least one thread.

A *thread* is an object with a process that executes program instructions. By having multiple threads, a process can carry out different parts of its program on different processes concurrently. Threads dependent on a process or parent object are indicated by an arrow from parent object to child object (see Figure 9.4).

Microsoft designed Performance Monitor to have as little impact on Windows NT as possible. It still, however, has an effect on the system. Therefore, when monitoring anything other than network performance, it is recommended that you monitor the server system from a remote computer. When monitoring for network performance, it is best to do so in Log mode.

The core objects that you can monitor on any Windows NT 4 system are described in Table 9.1.

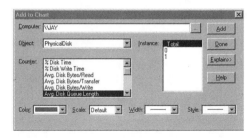

FIGURE 9.3
The Add to Chart dialog box showing objects and instances.

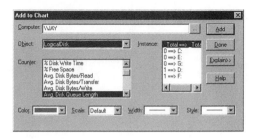

FIGURE 9.4
Logical drives C, E, and G are shown as assigned to physical disk 0.

TABLE 9.1

CORE OBJECTS CAPABLE OF BEING MONITORED

Core Object Name	Description of Object
Cache	An area of physical memory that holds recently used data.
LogicalDisk	Partitions and other logical views of disk space.

continues

| TABLE 9.1 | *continued* |

CORE OBJECTS CAPABLE OF BEING MONITORED

Core Object Name	Description of Object
Memory	Physical and paged random access memory used to store code and data.
Objects	Certain system software objects and application process objects.
Paging File	File used to expand virtual memory locations to increase memory.
PhysicalDisk	A single spindle-disk unit or RAID device.
Process	Software object that represents a running program.
Processor	Hardware unit (CPU) that executes program instructions.
Redirector	File system that diverts file requests to the network servers. It is also sometimes referred to as the Workstation service.
System	Contains counters that apply to all system hardware and software.
Thread	The part of a process that uses the processor.

COUNTERS IN PERFORMANCE MONITOR

A *counter* defines the type of data available from a type of object. Performance Monitor can display, collect, and average data from counters using the Windows NT Registry and the Performance Library DLLs.

Performance Monitor uses counters to track the functions an object can execute. With a disk drive, for example, you might want to track how many times per second a disk is asked to write information. In another case, you might want to see what percentage of the processor's time is spent carrying out user requests. Adding it to the chart or log activates each counter.

Counters display in the order they were selected and added. If you select and add multiple counters at the same time, they appear in alphabetical order (see Figure 9.5).

There are three types of counters:

◆ **Instantaneous.** Instantaneous counters always display the most recent measurement. The Process:Thread count displays the number of threads in the last measurement.

◆ **Averaging.** Averaging counters measure a value over a period of time and display the average of the last two measurements.

◆ **Difference.** Difference counters subtract the last measurement from the preceding measurement and display the difference if it is a positive value. A negative value is shown as zero.

Other performance monitoring applications can read the data gathered from Performance Monitor and can display and use the negative values.

Another way to look at the data counters provide is to ask, what type of data is being gathered? Is it absolute or relative information?

The basic difference between the two is that an *absolute* value is exactly the duration taken or the amount reached, whereas a *relative* value is one measurement compared to another. Look at the transfer rates of a disk using absolute values with different intervals, as shown in Table 9.2.

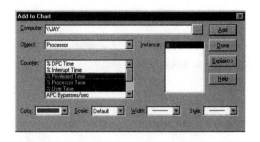

FIGURE 9.5
Three of the processor's objects counters are selected and ready to be added.

TABLE 9.2

ABSOLUTE TRANSFER RATES

Counter	5-Second Interval	5-Minute Interval
Disk time	4.652 seconds	263.89 seconds
Bytes transferred	82,524 bytes	4,978,335 bytes

It is difficult to tell which measurement is showing a faster rate of transfer. If you look at the same information in Table 9.3 using relative counters, however, it is easier to compare the results. Although the results are similar, a slightly higher rate of bytes were transferred per second during the 5-minute interval, plus the disk was active for a smaller percentage of time.

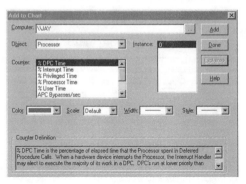

FIGURE 9.6

Brief descriptions of counters appear in the Counter Definition box.

<table>
<tr><td colspan="3">**TABLE 9.3**</td></tr>
<tr><td colspan="3">**RELATIVE TRANSFER RATES**</td></tr>
</table>

Counter	5-Second Interval	5-Minute Interval
Disk time	93.04%	87.96%
Bytes transferred	16504.8 bytes/sec	16594.45 bytes/sec

If you are unsure what a counter's function is (there are a tremendous number of counters), select the counter in question and then click Explain in the Add to dialog box. A brief description displays at the bottom of the dialog box. Figure 9.6 shows an example of a description.

VIEWS IN PERFORMANCE MONITOR

Performance Monitor offers various ways to view data. The Chart, Report, Log, and Alert views are described in Table 9.4.

TABLE 9.4

VARIOUS WAYS TO VIEW DATA IN PERFORMANCE MONITOR

View	Description
Chart	A chart is a graphical display of the value of a counter over a period of time. You can display many counters at the same time.
Log	The selected data is stored in a file on a disk for future analysis. You can open a log file in Performance Monitor to create charts, reports, or alerts.
Alert	You can set an alert on an individual counter. This causes an event to display if the counter attains the specified value. You can set many alerts at the same time.
Report	A report shows the value of the counter. You can create a report of all the counters.

The four views are always available, but only one can be viewed at a time. The default view is the Chart view. The following sections explore each of the views in greater detail.

Chart View

You use charts to monitor the current activity of the selected computer. A chart is especially useful for displaying an intermittent problem or for discovering why an application is slow or inefficient. Figure 9.7 shows the Chart view and the Chart Options dialog box. The default Chart view shows that the vertical scale always starts as 0 to 100. Notice that changing the vertical scale makes it easier to get an accurate reading on small value counters.

You can also set the scale for a single counter.

After you add a counter, a vertical red line moves across the chart from left to right. This is the Time Line, and it is positioned just past the last result. When it reaches the far right, it wraps to the left and rewrites the screen. Other monitoring applications do not wrap and rewrite the screen. Instead, they scroll the screen to the right. This method enables you to keep a visual record of what has happened more than 100 units beforehand. This method, however, is much more resource-intensive than those that do wrap, so it can cause skewed results.

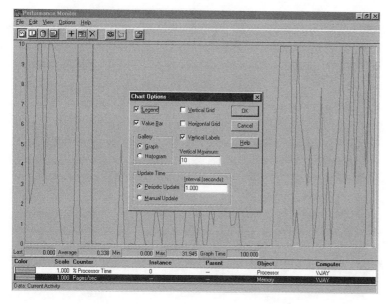

FIGURE 9.7

You can use the Chart Options dialog box to adjust the Chart view to your specific settings.

As mentioned, the vertical scale at the left is always 0 to 100 by default. The scale itself can be adjusted, but it always starts at zero. If you want to view from any other value, export the data to a spreadsheet and then analyze it. You can set the maximum value from the Chart Options dialog box, and it can be any positive number up to 1.4 billion. You can also add horizontal and vertical gridlines, but they increase the resource overhead. At the bottom of the screen is a color-coded legend. You can move this legend to another location by changing the setting in the Chart Options dialog box.

Depending on what options are selected, the chart might not be easy to read. Some measurements might be very large or very small. In these cases, you should adjust the scale of the chart. In addition to adjusting the scale, you can also customize the color, width, and style of line for each counter. To make it easier to compare a small value counter to a large value counter, you can also change the scale of the individual counter.

At the bottom of the chart is a value bar. This line provides the selected counter's last, average, maximum, and minimum values. Pressing the Delete key removes the selected line from the chart.

N O T E

Highlighting a Line To highlight an individual chart line, select the line in the legend and press Ctrl+H. This turns the corresponding line white and makes it much wider than the other lines, as shown in Figure 9.8. After the highlight is enabled, it can be moved from one chart line to another using either the up/down arrow keys or the mouse. To disable the highlight, press Ctrl+H again.

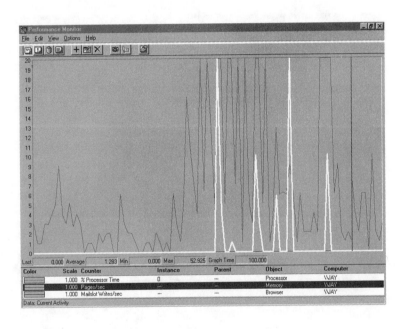

FIGURE 9.8
Pressing Ctrl+H highlights the selected counter; in this figure, it is the pages/sec counter.

The average, maximum, and minimum values are calculated using the values of the line on the screen. After the time line has wrapped, the last 100 observations are used. This reflects real-time analysis. If you need more history, however, you should keep a log.

To view the value bar, you must display the legend. The value bar reflects the data for the line selected in the legend. If you cannot see the legend, you cannot select a line; therefore, the value bar is not shown. If the Performance Monitor window is too small, the legend is not displayed (see Figure 9.9).

Selecting Clear Display from the Edit menu clears the data in the chart. This is useful for removing unwanted data when you start to capture new data.

When you initially add a line to the chart, there is a slight delay. This delay might be longer or shorter, depending on the interval, but by default, it is approximately 10 seconds. The reason for the delay is that most counters are displayed as a rate or a percentage. To display a percentage or rate, the chart must read data snapshots before displaying values.

Another way to look at a chart is to look at a histogram. A *histogram* is a vertical bar chart used to display many instances of a given counter at one time (see Figure 9.10).

Although the histogram does not provide any history, it is useful for directly comparing many similar counters.

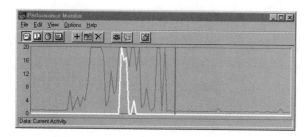

FIGURE 9.9
When the window becomes too small, the legend and value bar are not displayed.

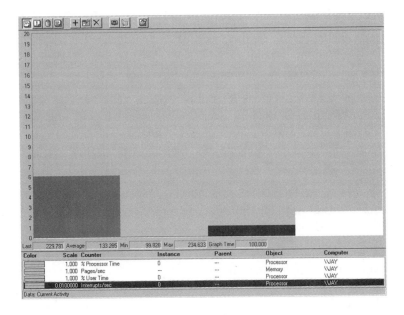

Log View

You use the Log view to perform serious analysis of the system. It is only through extensive logging of data over a period of time in different situations that you can discover bottlenecks or consider capacity planning accurate (see Figure 9.11).

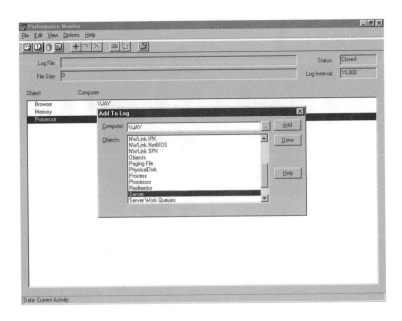

FIGURE 9.11
Only the objects are selected when you set up the log; you can monitor all the counters within these objects.

The process works like this: Data is collected about current activity for added objects and is saved to a log file for future viewing. After creating these log files, you can analyze the data for performance problems. For a server, the log provides information that you can use for capacity planning by showing trends over a long period of time. A log file can be charted, reported, or exported and can contain data from multiple computers.

While a log is being created, a log symbol appears and a Changing Total File Size indicator appears at the right side of the status bar.

A log file can be a lot more useful if you add bookmarks during the logging. Because you do not have the luxury of the real-time view, you can add bookmarks to the time an event is to take place. When viewing the file later, you can access the different bookmarks to see how the system was affected by those events.

> **NOTE**
>
> **Viewing a "Running" Log**   If you want to view the contents of the log while it is still collecting data, open a second instance of Performance Monitor. Switch to the desired view (Chart or Report) and set the data values displayed to the name of the running log file (see Figure 9.12).

When configuring what is to be logged, do not worry about selecting counters. You can only select which objects are to be monitored—and all counters for the specified objects are recorded. After the file is created and opened for analysis, then you can choose which counters to view.

When data is being logged, you cannot view it from another view such as Chart or Report. If you try to open the log file while it is collecting data, the log is stopped and the counter settings all are cleared.

You should remember a few things when setting up a log:

◆ If you specify an existing log file when you create a new log, the logged data is appended to the existing file. It *does not* overwrite the file. This is a useful feature.

◆ By default, the time interval for logging is 15 seconds, not 5 seconds. The reason is that, generally, a log is run for longer periods of time. If the time interval is too short, the log file could become enormous.

FIGURE 9.12
You can select the log file in the Data From... dialog box.

◆ You must remember to click the Start Log button. If you forget to click Start Log and just click Save, you are returned to the Log view but the status is closed. You then have to return to the Log Options dialog box and click Start Log.

◆ If the Start Log button is grayed out (not available), make sure you specified a name for the log file. Also make sure that you added at least one object to the log.

◆ You can change the time interval to capture more detail during logging of a significant event—without stopping the log. The smaller the time interval, however, the larger the file. You probably want to increase the time interval after the event has taken place.

◆ Select Stop Logging when you feel sufficient data has been gathered. Otherwise, you might end up creating a file as big as your hard drive.

WARNING

Space Considerations The log file can grow in size and fill a disk drive very quickly, depending on how many objects are being monitored and what the interval is set to. Be sure to place the log on a large drive and to check its status regularly.

Although the Log view does not provide real-time viewing of what is taking place, it is useful for analyzing the performance of the computer and each of its resources. The data gathered by the log can be viewed in a chart or report. It also can be exported to a spreadsheet or database for analysis.

Alert View

The Alert view is a low-overhead type of monitor. It enables you to keep track of many events on many computers with a minimum amount of attention spent watching the Performance Monitor window. You can set up the Alert view to log the performance of selected counters and instances for objects. You can notify a person or computer when events take place (see Figure 9.13).

The counters are added in much the same way as in charts and reports, except that when you add a counter or instance in Alert view, you must provide a threshold value.

Examples of thresholds you might want to monitor include %Free Space and %Processor Time. With %Free Space, you want to be notified when the free space on the logical disk drops below a certain value. For the %Processor Time, you want to know when the processor is being used for more than a certain percentage of time. You set these thresholds in the Add to Alert dialog box (see Figure 9.14).

The alert is set to %User Time greater than 90%. When a counter exceeds the set threshold, the date and time of the event is recorded in the Alert view. Entries are added one after another, up to 1,000 entries. At that time, as new entries are added, the oldest entries are removed.

The alert condition applies to a counter value over the period of time of the interval. If the interval is 5 seconds and the alert is set for %Processor Time over 80, then the average %Processor Time must be greater than 80% over a 5-second interval to merit an alert. Figure 9.15 shows an example of the %Processor Time set to 90%, which has been exceeded twice.

The processor twice exceeded the threshold of 90%. Only one alert condition can be set for a counter for the same instance. You cannot, for example, set one alert to trigger when the %User Time exceeds 75% and again when it drops below 40%.

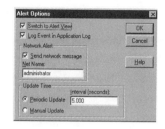

FIGURE 9.13
The Alert options dialog box.

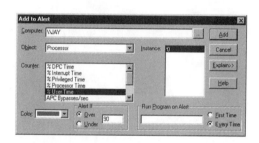

FIGURE 9.14
The Add to Alert dialog box; use the Alert If section of this dialog box to set the threshold values for your alert.

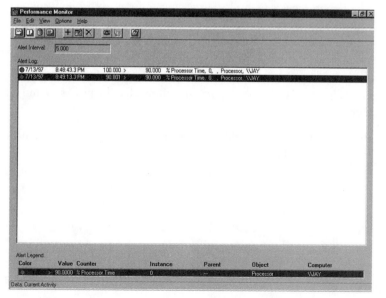

FIGURE 9.15
The alert log for an exceeded %Processor Time.

When an alert occurs, you can run a program every time or only the first time that event takes place. You have many options for what this program can be. It can be a batch file that exports data to a database, or it can start another instance of Performance Monitor using settings that permit a closer look at specific counters and instances.

As mentioned, you can monitor numerous computers from a single computer across the network. This decreases the resource overhead on the computers being monitored, but it can greatly increase the amount of network traffic. At each interval for each item added to the specified views, a message is sent from the monitored system to the monitoring computer. If you add many counters with short intervals, you can significantly reduce the network bandwidth.

One way to reduce network traffic is to set Performance Monitor to run as a service. There is no graphical display when Performance Monitor runs as a service. It is controlled by MONITOR.EXE, and a workspace settings file created in Performance Monitor specifies the settings to monitor. The MONITOR.EXE file is on the Windows NT Server 4.0 Resource Kit CD.

Report View

The Report view is useful for displaying constantly changing counter and instance values of objects. The values are displayed in separate columns for each instance. Reports of averaged counters show the average values during the time window, and reports of instantaneous counters show the value of the counter at the end of the time window. Figure 9.16 shows a report on counters for the processor and memory.

As with charts, you can add multiple counters and multiple instances for a report. Unlike charts, however, there are no special display features such as the scale-factor or line-color options. The only option that you can modify in reports is the time interval. The default interval is five seconds, but you can change it to any value you want.

FIGURE 9.16
A report of counters for the processor and
memory resources.

The Report view helps you understand object behavior. You can gain a better understanding of the system by setting up a report with specific objects and counters and then watching the values change as different loads are added to the system.

Objects added to a report are grouped together by the computer to which they belong. Choosing the same counters for two computers enables you to make comparisons under similar network stress. Figure 9.17 shows how you can compare the counters from two computers.

As objects are added to the report, they appear directly below each other until they go off the screen. At this time, a scroll bar appears at the right side of the window so you can scroll up or down through the report. If too many instances are added for the width of the window, a scroll bar appears at the bottom of the window to permit horizontal scrolling.

If there are too many counters and too many instances to be viewed conveniently at one time, start another instance of Performance Monitor. This enables you to view a different set of data at the same time. Each set has the same counters and instances selected, but the view is scrolled to a different area. This works, but it does create more overhead on the system performing the monitoring. Another option is to either log or export the data. This option works well, but it does not allow for real-time monitoring.

FIGURE 9.17
The same counters for two separate computers
for a comparison in Report view.

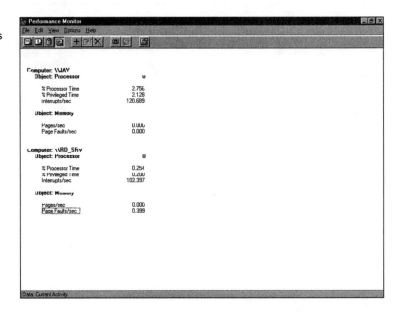

If you want to remove a counter from the Report view, select it and
then select Delete from the Edit menu, or highlight the object and
press the Delete key on the keyboard. To remove multiple counters
from a report, either delete them one-by-one or delete the object and
then add the desired counters back again. It is not possible to select
and delete multiple counters with a single command.

R E V I E W   B R E A K

Performance Monitor Views

In the previous sections, you have been introduced to the components and views of the Performance Monitor. For a summary of the
main views in the Performance Monitor, review the following list:

- Chart view—This view is useful for viewing the objects and
  counters in a real-time mode. This mode allows you to view
  the data in a graphical format. You can also use the Chart view
  to view the contents of a log file.

- Log view—This view allows you to set all the options required for creating a log of your system resources or objects. Once this log is created, it can be viewed with the Chart view.

- Alert view—The Alert view is where you configure warnings or alerts for your system resources or objects. In this view, you can configure threshold levels for counters and then launch an action based on the threshold values being exceeded.

- Report view—The Report view allows you to view the object and counters as an averaged value. This view is useful for comparing the values of multiple similarly configured systems.

Now, you will dive into the use of the Performance Monitor and gain insight into how to analyze the information and then optimize your Windows NT system.

CREATING A BASELINE USING PERFORMANCE MONITOR

A computer system's baseline is a collection of data that indicates how an individual system resource, a collection of system resources, or the system as a whole performs. You compare this information to later activity to monitor system usage and system response to usage.

It is important to remember that when setting up the baseline, you should carefully choose the resources to be monitored. Expect demands on a server to increase. Choose all the objects and counters that are important now and that you expect to be important in the future. If you do not choose objects for the initial baseline that become important after the system is in production, you have nothing to compare data with.

Although all systems are unique (few have identical hardware, software, and services installed), you should always include memory, processor, disk, and network objects in the baseline. In Step by Step 9.1, you can get an idea of how to configure your log file to create your baseline.

STEP BY STEP

9.1 Configuring a Log File to Create a Baseline

1. Start the Performance Monitor and change to the Log view.

2. Select the Add to Chart button, and then add the Memory, Processor, Physical Disk, Server, and Network Adapter. Select the Done button.

3. Select the Chart | Chart Options command.

4. Set the time interval to 600 seconds (10 minutes).

5. Set the name of the file to NTLOG.

6. Start the log.

7. Leave this log running for an extended period while your system continues to run normal activities.

   Always include memory, processor, disk, and network objects in the baseline.

After the initial set of data is captured, use the same settings and capture data on a regular basis. Place this information in a database and analyze the performance of the system. Has it become more efficient? Has it become slower? Are trends developing as more users, more services, or more applications are added to the server? With a good set of data, you can analyze a system and optimize its performance.

To create a baseline measurement, you must use the Log view. This is the only way to create a log of activity. While measuring, you will log, relog, and append logs to get a complete set of information.

As previously mentioned, make an educated choice about what should be selected before logging is started. Any kind of analysis should include the four basic objects mentioned earlier. When monitoring a server, however, you might want to include other objects:

◆ Cache

◆ Logical disk

- ◆ Memory

- ◆ Network adapter

- ◆ Network subnet activity on at least one server in the subnet

- ◆ Physical disk (if using a RAID system)

- ◆ Processor

- ◆ Server

- ◆ System

When relogging, increase the time interval to reduce the file size. In most cases, the extra data that is lost is not critical. As a rule of thumb, you might multiply the time interval by 10. For an initial time interval, you might use 60 seconds. Then when relogging, use a time interval of 600 seconds. For most servers, this provides plenty of data.

Another option to consider is appending successive logs to the original log file. This way, all logs are kept together in a "master" log file or archive. No data is lost. To prevent confusion about where one set of data ends and another begins, bookmarks are automatically inserted to separate the logs.

You should take measurements for a full week at different times of the day so that information can be recorded at both peak and slow times of each day. As is often mentioned, it is important to record activity during peak periods of the day. It also is important to record activity during slow periods to check the level of activity at those times. Ideally, you should have enough data to know whether there is any significant change in the different counters during different times of the day.

To automate the collection of data, Windows NT 4 is capable of starting Performance Monitor as a service. When started as a service, it has less impact on the system because there is no graphical display to use valuable resources. To use Performance Monitor as a service, you must use the MONITOR.EXE file located on the Windows NT Server Resource Kit. To see the tasks required, review Step by Step 9.2.

N O T E **Activate Disk Counters** When monitoring the disk, remember to activate the disk counters using the command `diskperf -y`. If you do not use this command, the counters can be selected but no activity is displayed.

In the case of a software RAID system, start `diskperf` with the `-ye` option.

N O T E **Monitoring TCP/IP Counters** When you want to monitor TCP/IP counters, make sure that SNMP is installed. Without the SNMP service installed, the TCP/IP counters are not available.

N O T E **Space Considerations** Performance Monitor log files can grow to be quite large. Set up monitoring on a system that is not itself being monitored and that has a large amount of free disk space. Practice taking logs using different time intervals to get a feel for how large a file can become.

STEP BY STEP

9.2 Using Performance Monitor as a Service

1. The easiest method is to use the Log view and select the objects to monitor. As recommended, the minimum objects to include are memory, disk, processor, and network.

2. Set the time interval to the desired frequency. This depends on how long you require the logging to take place and how much free disk space is available for the log file. Remember that if the logging interval is too short, the log file can grow quickly.

3. Name the log file and save the settings in a Performance Monitor workspace settings file.

4. Configure Performance Monitor, or the MONITOR.EXE utility, to start as a service when it reboots.

PERFORMANCE ANALYSIS

Monitor performance of various functions by using Performance Monitor. The resources you monitor include processor, memory, disk, and network.

Now that the process for creating a baseline has been established, analysis of the system and resource requirement forecasting can begin.

Overview

There are four basic steps to performing analysis on a system. Depending on who is doing the analysis, there can be more or fewer steps, but these are the basics:

◆ Determine what is normal for the system and how to deal with the non-normal.

◆ Set expectations of how the system or resource should respond under specific conditions.

◆ Help plan for upgrades and additions.

◆ Provide better input into system budgeting requirements.

Following proper collection of data, analysis of the data, and optimization of the server, the system should perform in a satisfactory manner. With the system operating well, users are likely to be satisfied with the server.

When you want to analyze a system, you should first determine what functions the server performs. The three types of Windows NT servers are described in Table 9.5.

TABLE 9.5

WINDOWS NT SERVERS

Server Type	Description
File and print server	Users generally access a file and print server for data storage and retrieval. It also can be used for loading application software over the network.
Application server	Users in a client/server environment access the server to run their application. The server runs the application engine that users access using a local version of the application front end.
Domain server	A domain server validates user account logons. In addition, it also generates data transfer between itself and other domain controllers to synchronize the account database.

To set expectations, you must know what is expected of a system. This is referred to as *workload characterization*. A *workload unit* is a list of requests made on the system or a resource. An example of a workload unit might be the number of bytes transferred per second.

To determine workload characterization, you must understand what is taking place in each environment. With a file and print server, the biggest concern is disk I/O or the number of users accessing the server. With an application server, the area of concern is how much memory an application server is using. It's not that memory isn't important on a file and print server; it is a matter of deciding what device could become a system bottleneck.

NOTE **Computer Limitations** Not everyone has the luxury of a separate computer for each type of server. Many Windows NT installations have servers acting in one, two, or all three of the server roles. In these situations, you might have to sacrifice or reduce the performance of one server role to bring the performance of another role up to a satisfactory level and get the best overall performance.

NOTE **Don't Jump to Conclusions** Don't jump to conclusions about what is causing a bottleneck. Sometimes, one resource appears to be the problem when it is actually a different resource. A computer can appear to have poor disk access time, and when you look at the drive light, it appears to be "thrashing." On closer inspection, you find that you are working on large files and there is not enough memory. Therefore, the page-file has grown to a very large size, and there is constant swapping between the physical and virtual memory.

During the process of determining workload characterization, it is common to find a resource that is not performing properly. Because this resource is not performing properly, the system does not perform properly. This symptom is referred to as a *bottleneck*.

A bottleneck restricts the workflow, for example, when too many users access a server at the same time. File access becomes slow because the server is trying to respond to all the user requests.

After one bottleneck is discovered and resolved, another bottleneck often appears. It is not necessarily true that you created a new bottleneck by addressing the first one. It could be that there were always two bottlenecks, but one was more noticeable than the other. Sometimes, however, solving a bottleneck problem does create another bottleneck.

The following list offers an example of what could occur when you analyze and optimize a server that was providing poor response time to users:

1. You might discover that the network card is an 8-bit instead of a 32-bit network card. To increase performance and remove the bottleneck, you replace the card. After monitoring, you discover that performance has improved only minimally, but the processor utilization jumped from 65 percent to 95 percent.

2. This time, the processor is too slow to respond to all the incoming requests. You replace the P75 with a P200, and there still is no improvement in performance. The processor utilization drops to 40 percent, but the disk time exceeds 90 percent.

3. Further monitoring shows that disk access is slow. There are multiple disks with a single controller. You install additional controllers and enable disk striping. Disk times are still high, but paging accounts for 75 percent of the disk accesses.

4. The performance is still poor, and the disk drives are still thrashing. You add memory, and finally, the system performs up to expectations.

Because Windows NT is self-tuning to a certain degree, a good percentage of optimization involves upgrading hardware, not changing Registry settings. It is important, however, to know what needs to be upgraded and what doesn't.

In the following sections, you will review the Performance Monitor settings used to monitor the various server roles that are available in Windows NT server and then to locate various bottlenecks in each of the four main resources. The following sections cover

◆ Analysis of a file and print server

◆ Analysis of an application server

◆ Finding memory bottlenecks

◆ Finding processor bottlenecks

◆ Finding disk bottlenecks

◆ Finding network bottlenecks

In each of these sections, you will be introduced to the objects and counters used to analyze these types of systems, as well as some considerations for each that enable you to locate a bottleneck or problem based on the results of your analysis.

Analysis of a File and Print Server

Identify performance bottlenecks.

File and print servers generally are accessed for data storage and retrieval and sometimes for loading applications across the network. Therefore, the largest load applied comes from users who access the server at the same time and the resource requirements they demand.

Events that you monitor for this type of server appear in Table 9.6.

TABLE 9.6

FILE AND PRINT SERVER MONITORING

Workload Unit	Performance Monitor Counter
Concurrent user sessions	Server: Server Sessions
The number of open files	Server: Files Open
Average transaction size	PhysicalDisk: Avg. Disk Bytes/Transfer
Amount of disk activity	PhysicalDisk: %Disk Time
Type of disk activity	PhysicalDisk: %Disk Read TimePhysicalDisk: %Write Time
Network use	Network Segment: %Network Utilization

In addition to the items in the table, you might find that additional resources (such as memory) are being consumed and should also be monitored.

All four of the main system components are important in any server. It is just that some resources are more important than others, depending on the type of server being analyzed. For a file and print server, the order of importance is explained in Table 9.7.

TABLE 9.7

ORDER OF COMPONENT IMPORTANCE IN A FILE AND PRINT SERVER

Priority	*Resource*	*Implications*
1	Memory	Memory is used for caching opened files in a file and print server system. If there is insufficient RAM for caching, performance takes a big hit.
2	Processor	The processor is used for each network connection. This means all network traffic must pass through the processor. The implementation of busmastering network cards and disk controllers helps to reduce the processing that must take place at the CPU and, thus, frees the CPU to respond to requests.
3	Disk	The disk drive is the primary resource users are going to access. The speed of the disk drives affects the general perception of how the server operates.
4	Network	A number of factors affect the network system (adapter type, number of adapters, protocols used, and so on). It does not matter, however, how fast the disk drive is, how much RAM there is, or how many processors there are if the network adapter is slow. The data cannot be transferred efficiently from the network to the computer memory.

In analyzing your results from the recommended counters, you may also want to review the forecasting considerations in the next section. These considerations can be helpful as you extend the use of your system into a larger environment.

Forecasting Considerations and Recommendations for a File and Print Server

When forecasting resource requirements for a file and print server, keep the following in mind:

◆ Monitor the number of user sessions and the effect each session has on the four main system resources. The most common areas for bottlenecks are disk usage and network performance.

◆ If the server is used to retrieve and update data files, monitor the disk and network resources.

◆ If the server is used for data files and loading applications, you should monitor memory, disk, and network resources. When files are opened off the server, Windows NT tries to cache the open files and could cause memory to bottleneck.

◆ Make sure you select Maximize Throughput for File Sharing in the Server dialog box (see Figure 9.18).

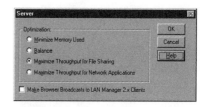

FIGURE 9.18
Choose the proper option for a file and print server.

Analysis of an Application Server

Identify performance bottlenecks.

Workload units are key when analyzing an application server. The main difference between a file and print server and an application server is that file and print servers are generally accessed with fewer requests. Each request to a file and print server is usually quite large in size. An application server has more frequent, smaller requests from the client computer.

In addition to the more frequent requests, the application server also has the additional overhead of running the application. Because the application is run at the server, there is a greater demand for memory and processor resources.

Workload units that you need to monitor appear in Table 9.8.

TABLE 9.8

MONITORING WORKLOAD

Workload Unit	Performance Monitor Counter
Concurrent user sessions	Server: Server Sessions
Processor usage	Processor: %Processor Time
Average disk transaction size	PhysicalDisk: Avg. Disk Bytes/Transfer
Amount of disk activity	PhysicalDisk: %Disk Time
Network use	Network Segment: %Network Utilization
Average network transaction	NetBEUI: Frame Bytes/sec (similar size counter for each protocol)
Available memory	Memory: Available Bytes
Amount of paging	Memory: Pages/sec
Usage of cache	Cache: Copy Read Hits %

In addition to the counters Performance Monitor provides, certain applications (such as Microsoft Exchange Server) provide additional counters and predefined charts. If application-specific counters are available, be sure to use them when analyzing the server.

Table 9.9 lists the four main resources in order of importance and briefly describes their roles in an application server.

TABLE 9.9

RESOURCES AND THEIR ROLES IN AN APPLICATION SERVER

Priority	Resource	Roles
1	Processor	Applications run on the server instead of the client side of the network. If a large number of users access the server, upgrading to a high-end processor or adding processors can improve performance. If a computer is capable of symmetric multiprocessing, then using multiple, less-powerful processors might be a better solution than using a single, more-powerful processor.

Priority	Resource	Roles
2	Memory	Memory is needed at the server to support both the server needs and the application needs. The amount of additional RAM needed depends on the number of users accessing the server and the application requirements.
3	Disk	Client/server applications typically access large amounts of data. Therefore, they demand more of the disk drives. Carefully consider both the disk controller and the type of disk.
4	Network	Client/server applications transfer many requests across the network. These requests often are queries or commands that are very small in size. Therefore, it is important to get the data in and out quickly.

Forecasting Considerations and Recommendations for an Application Server

If analysis has revealed the following sources as bottlenecks, follow these recommendations:

◆ If the applications are disk bound and the disk is the bottleneck, consider whether the application is mainly reading or writing to the disk. If the application is mainly reading from the disk, consider implementing a hardware RAID or controller caching, both of which can improve performance or replace the existing drives with faster ones. If multiple drives are necessary, additional controllers might improve performance. If the application is mainly writing to the disk and the disk is the bottleneck, consider implementing a hardware RAID. Whether fault tolerance is important determines what level of RAID is required.

◆ If memory-intensive applications are the bottleneck, add RAM or increase internal caching. One common problem is a secondary cache size that is too small. Also consider moving applications to other servers. Some applications, such as Systems Management Server, either can have all the server

NOTE

Memory and Cache When memory is the bottleneck, check what the internal cache is set to if it has been set. Secondary cache is used to provide read-ahead access to RAM. If you add RAM without increasing the secondary cache, lower cache usage can result. This causes the secondary cache to attempt to provide caching for a larger amount of RAM. General recommendations for secondary cache are 256KB for 16–32MB of RAM and 512KB for systems above 32MB of RAM. These specs are available from OEM specifications, not from Performance Monitor.

functions on one computer or can keep specific components on other servers for a more balanced load of system hardware resources.

◆ If applications generate a high amount of network traffic, monitor the network to determine if it is the bottleneck. If it is, consider upgrading to a 32-bit network card, adding additional network cards, isolating traffic by subnetting, and upgrading the network components of cabling, bridges, routers, and so on.

◆ If the applications are CPU-bound and the processor is the bottleneck, you have two options. If the application is large and multithreaded, consider switching to a symmetric multiprocessing computer or upgrading the processor in the existing system.

◆ Make sure you choose the proper option for an application server in the Server dialog box, as shown in Figure 9.19.

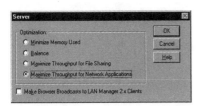

FIGURE 9.19
Server memory is optimized for network applications.

Finding Memory Bottlenecks

Optimize performance for various results. Results include controlling network traffic and controlling server load.

The most common resource bottleneck in a Windows NT Server is memory. Adding more RAM almost always increases the performance of a server.

The reason memory has the greatest impact on the system is that a shortage of memory causes the system to read and write from the disk more often. Accessing the disk is much slower than just executing from the processor.

The following sections explain the different types of memory used within Windows NT, as well as some of the common objects and counters to monitor in locating memory bottlenecks.

Non-Paged and Paged RAM

The RAM in Windows NT is broken down into two categories:

◆ Non-paged

◆ Paged

Non-paged RAM is data placed directly into a specific memory location that cannot be written to or retrieved from disk. Certain data structures must be mapped to physical memory to support interrupt routines or to prevent multiprocessor conflicts.

Paged RAM is virtual memory, in which all applications believe they have a full range of memory addresses available. Windows NT gives each application a virtual memory space and then maps that memory space to physical memory.

Virtual Memory

The virtual memory of Windows NT 4 is actually a system that combines physical memory, file system cache, and a disk for information storage and retrieval. Program code and data are stored on disk until they are needed; then, they move into physical memory. The least recently used (LRU) code and data are written back to the disk because new space in physical memory is required for new code and data. If a system does not have enough memory, the code and data must be written to and retrieved from the disk more often. Because the writing to and reading from the disk is a slower, more resource-intensive process, it can become the system bottleneck.

Page Faults

The best indicator that memory is the bottleneck is when there is a sustained, high rate of hard page faults. These occur when the data a program needs is not found in its working set or in physical memory. The data must be retrieved from the disk. If the level of hard page faults remains at a level of more than five per second, memory is definitely a bottleneck.

Table 9.10 shows some of the counters to watch and the range that is acceptable.

TABLE 9.10

PAGE FAULT COUNTERS

Counter	*Description*
Pages/sec	This is the number of requests that had to access the disk because the requested pages were not available in RAM. This value can average anywhere from 0 to 20, but if it has an extended period over 5, you should add RAM.
Available bytes	This is the amount of available physical memory. It is normally low because the Windows NT Disk Cache Manager uses extra memory for caching until requests for memory occur. If this value is consistently below 4MB, excessive paging is probably occurring and you should add RAM.
Committed bytes	This is the amount of virtual memory allocated either to physical RAM for storage or to the pagefile. If the amount of committed bytes is greater than RAM, then you should add RAM.
Pool Nonpaged Bytes	This is the amount of RAM in the pool nonpaged memory area, where space is used by operating system components as they carry out their tasks. If the value has a steady increase without an increase in activity, an application or process might have a memory leak. Check with the software developer to see if there are any known problems with the application. If there are, is there a patch for the application?

Figure 9.20 shows an example of these counters.

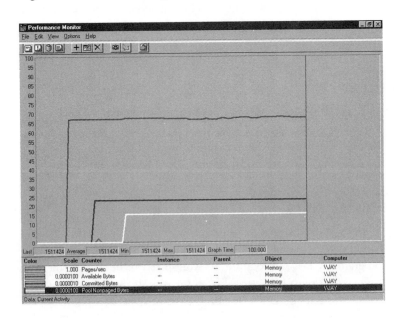

FIGURE 9.20
This system has 32MB of RAM and easily passes desired specifications.

Finding Processor Bottlenecks

Optimize performance for various results. Results include controlling network traffic and controlling server load.

Everything that occurs on a server involves the processor. Because the CPU on an application server is generally more active than on a file and print server, the normal level of activity is different between the two types of servers.

The two most common problems when the processor is a bottleneck are CPU-bound applications and drivers and excessive interrupts generated by inadequate disk or network components.

Table 9.11 shows the counters to watch and the kinds of values to look for.

Figure 9.21 shows an example of the monitoring of the processor. Notice the vertical scale; the values are within the specifications in Table 9.11.

> **WARNING**
>
> **Try Offloading First** Just because the processor is a bottleneck doesn't mean you should run out and replace it with the latest and greatest. Sometimes, people ask their servers to do too much. Look at offloading some of the processes to another server, if possible. Through careful planning and distributing the load, all resources are better utilized.

TABLE 9.11

BOTTLENECK INDICATORS

Counter	Description
%Processor Time	This is the amount of time the processor is busy and is the %Privileged Time plus the %User Time. When the processor is consistently above 75–80%, it has become a bottleneck. Before replacing the processor, analyze what is using the processor to see if something else is causing the high usage.
%Privileged Time	This is the amount of time the processor spends performing operating system services. Like %Processor Time, this value should average below 75%.
%User Time	This is the amount of time the processor spends running user services such as desktop applications. Again, this value should average below 75%.
Interrupts/sec	This is the number of interrupts the processor is handling from applications and hardware devices. Windows NT Server can handle thousands of interrupts/second. If the number is much higher than the baseline, however, there might be a hardware error.
System: Processor	This is the number of requests the Queue Length processor has in its queue. Each of these requests is a thread waiting to be processed. Normally, this value is zero, but if the queue length is consistently two or greater, there is a problem. Check each of the processes to see if one is causing the congestion.
Server Work Queues:Queue Length	This is the number of requests in the queue for a particular processor. Again, if the queue length is two or greater, there is a problem. If only one processor is exceeding the limits, replace the processor. For multiprocessor systems, the queue length should never be more than n + 1, in which n is the number of processors.

FIGURE 9.21
Monitoring the processor; the values are within specifications here.

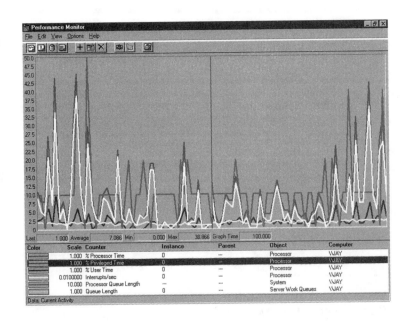

Activate Disk Counters Remember to activate Performance Monitor disk counters before monitoring the disk drives. By default, the counters are not enabled and do not show any activity when added to Performance Monitor.

Type **diskperf -y** at a command prompt to enable the counters on the local computer.

Type **diskperf -y\\servername** at a command prompt to enable the counters on a remote computer.

Type **diskperf -ye** at a command prompt to enable the counters on the local computer with a RAID implementation (see Figure 9.22).

Finding Disk Bottlenecks

Optimize performance for various results. Results include controlling network traffic and controlling server load.

Disks are used to store programs and the data that programs process. Frequently, the disk bottlenecks a system because disk response time is greater than that of other resources. The disk also can hide other problems, such as a lack of memory.

Performance Monitor has counters for both the PhysicalDisk and LogicalDisk objects. The LogicalDisk monitors the logical partitions of physical drives that indicate when a service or application is making excessive requests. The PhysicalDisk is used to monitor the physical disk drive as a whole.

Table 9.12 shows some of the counters to use and what values to watch for when monitoring the disk. The examples shown are for the physical disk. Similar counters are available for logical disks. A *logical disk* is a partition that can be part of a single disk or span a number of disks.

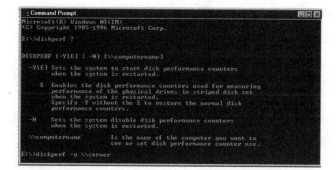

TABLE 9.12

DISK MONITORING

Counter	Description
%Disk Time	This is the amount of time the disk is busy with reads and writes. If this value is consistently near 100%, the disk is heavily used. A more acceptable value is around 50%. Check to see which processes are causing the most activity and offload some activity.
Disk Queue Length	This is the number of waiting disk I/O requests. If this value is consistently two or higher, upgrade the disk.
Avg. Disk Bytes/Transfer	This is the average number of bytes transferred to or from the system during read and write operations. The larger the size, the more efficient the system. Due to the different types of systems and the processes being run, you have no specific values to watch. Depending on the system, you might need to upgrade the drives.
Disk Bytes/Sec	This is the rate at which bytes are transferred to or from the disk during read and write operations. The higher the average, the more efficient the system. Depending on the system, you might need to upgrade the drives.

Figure 9.23 shows a monitor of the counters mentioned in the table. Although some counters appear to have exceeded the specifications (disk queue length), what you notice are only spikes. The counters actually averaged much lower values.

FIGURE 9.23

Disk activity during the copying of files from the monitored computer to a remote computer.

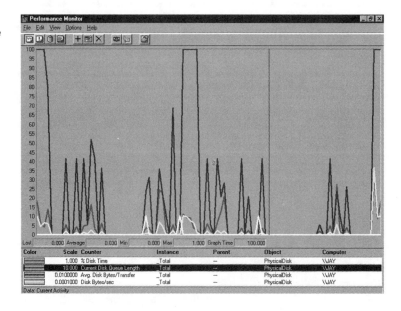

If the disk is the bottleneck, you have a number of possible solutions:

◆ Offload some of the processes to another system.

◆ Add a faster controller or an on-board caching controller.

◆ Add more memory to permit more caching by Windows NT.

◆ Add more disk drives in a RAID environment. This spreads the data across multiple physical disks and improves performance.

Finding Network Bottlenecks

Optimize performance for various results. Results include controlling network traffic and controlling server load.

Due to the complexity of most networks today, finding a network bottleneck can be difficult. A number of factors can affect network performance. In addition, you can monitor a number of objects and counters. Determining which ones should be monitored depends on the environment.

Table 9.13 shows some counters to monitor and some values to watch for when a lot of activity from the network is at the server.

TABLE 9.13

FINDING BOTTLENECKS

Counter	Description
Server: Bytes Total/Sec	This is the number of bytes the server has sent and received over the network. It indicates how busy the server is for sending and receiving data. If this value is low, add an adapter.
Server: Logon/Sec	This is the number of logon attempts for local, across-the-network, and service-account authentication in the last second. This counter is useful to watch for domain controllers. If this value is low, add domain controllers.
Server: Logon Total	This is the number of logon attempts for local, across-the-network, and service-account authentication since the server was started. Again, this is a valuable counter for a domain controller. If this value is low, add domain controllers.
Network Segment:%Network utilization	This is the percentage of bandwidth in use for the local network segment. This is used to monitor the effects of different network operations, such as account synchronization and logon validation. Limit the number of protocols if this number is high.
Network Interface: Bytes Sent/Sec	This is the number of bytes sent using the selected adapter. Upgrade the network adapter if there is a problem.
Network Interface: Bytes Total/Sec	This is the number of bytes sent and received using the selected adapter. Upgrade the network adapter if there is a problem.

Figure 9.24 shows some of the network traffic on a member server while monitoring the activity on the TCP/IP segments.

FIGURE 9.24
Only the TCP/IP objects are active on this member server.

If the network is the bottleneck, you can do a number of things.

◆ On the server, add an adapter, upgrade to a better adapter, or upgrade to better routers and bridges.

◆ Add more servers to the network to distribute the load.

◆ Segment the network to isolate traffic to appropriate segments.

CASE STUDY: MONITORING BACKUP

ESSENCE OF THE CASE

Here are the essential elements in this case:

· Monitor each of the servers locally.

· Use the Performance Monitor from a remote server.

· The objects to log are disk, memory, processor, network, and process.

SCENARIO

Several IT professionals in a large power company experienced some undesired functionality with a backup operation. The organization has two main systems that automate backup each evening; every second night, one of the servers completes the backup, interchanging so that each night the backup is completed. When backup server 1 is used, the backup is completed in 2.5 hours; however, when the same data is backed up with backup server 2, it takes more than 8 hours to complete. In terms of computer hardware, the systems are identical in make and

CASE STUDY: MONITORING BACKUP

model, and they run the same software. To monitor this situation, the Performance Monitor was enabled on both systems to check out the backup process. The systems were monitored for two nights to establish logs to be used as a baseline for additional analysis. The following two days, the backups were left to run. Again, backup server 2 took 8 hours to complete. The situation became obviously troublesome, so diagnostic tests were run on all the components of both backup servers. Everything tested okay. The problem needed solving, and it needed solving with monitoring and optimization utilities.

ANALYSIS

The Performance Monitor was used to remotely create a log of the following key objects for several days:

- Disk
- Memory
- Processor
- Network
- Process

In analyzing the log files, it was noticed that every day at approximately 6:15 PM, backup server 2 showed a dramatic increase in the Processor: %Processor Time and %DPC Time. This increase in the processor then stopped the following morning at 8:03 AM on day one and 9:35 AM of day two. The times may seem completely random from an outside analyzer; however, on day one, the server was approached at approximately 8:00 AM, the usual starting time, and it was noticed that the 3D pipes screen saver was on. On day two, the server wasn't checked until approximately 9:30AM; again, the 3D pipe screen saver was noticed. Upon investigation, it was found that backup server 1 had no screen saver running and that backup server 2 had a screen saver set to launch after 15 minutes of inactivity, and it happened to be a screen saver that used the OpenGL video language that uses numerous processor cycles when activated. Such a screen saver might look nice; however, it is not a wise selection for a server.

CHAPTER SUMMARY

KEY TERMS

- Performance Monitor
- object
- counter
- thread
- diskperf

The Performance Monitor is a graphical utility that you can use for monitoring and analyzing your system resources within Windows NT. You can choose objects and counters within the Performance Monitor; it is these elements that let you log and view system data.

This chapter introduced numerous objects and counters in the Performance Monitor. To prepare for the exam, review the following the key topics:

• paged RAM

• non-paged RAM

◆ The four views available in the Performance Monitor are the Report view, the Log view, the Chart view, and the Alert view.

◆ The main resources to monitor in any system are the disk, memory, network, and processor.

◆ Each of the main resources are grouped as separate objects; within each object are counters. A counter is the type of data available from a type of resource or object. Each counter may also have an multiple instances. An instance is available for multiple components in a counter.

◆ To make the disk counters active, you must run the diskperf utility.

Work through the review questions to test your understanding of the concepts. The hands-on exercises in this chapter are an excellent tool for building your experience with the Performance Monitor. Beyond each of these exercises, ensure that you do some monitoring on your own to fully understand each of the monitoring and optimization options available through the Performance Monitor.

This section allows you to assess how well you understand the material in the chapter. Review and exam questions test your knowledge of the tasks and concepts specified in the objectives. The exercises provide you with opportunities to engage in the sorts of tasks that compose the skill sets the objectives reflect.

For more review and exam questions, see the Top Score test engine on the CD-ROM that came with this book.

Exercises

The following exercises provide you with an opportunity to apply what you've learned in this chapter.

9.1 Monitoring the Memory Performance

This exercise is intended to reinforce learning about the monitoring capabilities of Performance Monitor specifically relating to memory counters.

Time Estimate: 10 minutes

1. Start Performance Monitor.

2. Click Edit | Add to Chart to open the dialog box.

3. Add the counters of Pages/sec and Page Faults/sec for the Memory object.

4. Open the Chart Options dialog box and change the time interval to one second.

5. Open Disk Administrator, and then open Server Manager. Open three other applications that you have installed on your computer.

6. Switch back to Performance Monitor and view the results.

7. Take notice of the counters that you added to the monitor. Did they change once you launched additional programs? You may notice some page faults as you change from program to program. (However, this depends on the size of the programs that you launched.)

9.2 Monitoring the Processor Performance

This exercise is intended to reinforce learning about the monitoring capabilities of Performance Monitor specifically relating to processor counters.

Time Estimate: 10 minutes

1. While viewing Performance monitor, press Delete until all the counters are removed from the legend.

2. Click Edit | Add to Chart to open the dialog box.

3. Add the counters of %Processor Time, %Privileged Time, Processor Queue Length, and Interrupts/sec.

4. Open Disk Administrator, and then open Server Manager.

5. Switch back to Performance Monitor and view the results.

9.3 Monitoring the Disk Performance

This exercise is intended to reinforce learning about the monitoring capabilities of Performance Monitor specifically relating to disk counters.

Time Estimate: 10 minutes

1. Remove all the counters from the chart by pressing Delete.

APPLY YOUR LEARNING

2. Because the disk counters are not activated by default, activate them now. To do this, you must run the `diskperf -Y` command from a command prompt. Then, restart your system to enable the disk performance counters.

3. After you restart your system, start Performance Monitor.

4. Click Edit|Add to Chart to open the dialog box.

5. Add the counters of Avg. Disk Bytes/Write, Avg. Disk Bytes/Read, %Disk time, and Avg. Disk Queue Length for both the PhysicalDisk and LogicalDisk objects.

6. Open Explorer.

7. Create a directory called Temp in the root directory of the C: drive.

8. Copy the WinNTRoot directory to the new Temp directory.

9. While the files are being copied, open User Manager for Domains.

10. Switch back to Performance Monitor and view the results.

9.4 Monitoring the Network Performance

This exercise is intended to reinforce learning about the monitoring capabilities of Performance Monitor specifically relating to network counters.

Time Estimate: 10 minutes

1. Delete all the counters from the chart.

2. Add all the counters for the Workstation object.

3. Open Server Manager.

4. Open Explorer to the Temp directory.

5. Map a drive to a computer share on the network.

6. Copy the files from the Temp directory to the mapped drive.

7. While the files are being copied, switch to Server Manager and open the properties of a computer on the network.

8. Switch back to Performance Monitor to view the results.

Review Questions

1. As network administrator, Alice has received many complaints about disk access time on the server. The server is a PDC and a DHCP server. Should she get a faster disk drive? What should she check to find the disk access problem?

2. An application server is running a custom application written specifically to run on Windows NT 4. How can you check whether you are getting optimum performance from your current server?

APPLY YOUR LEARNING

3. Mary is working from a remote site, and she wants to monitor the disks in her server. The disks are about two years old, and she wants to check their access time. When she adds the disk counters to Performance Monitor, however, nothing registers. What is wrong with Mary's server?

4. Erin's network seems to be running slower than normal. Her network has direct Internet access using a DHCP server. When she goes to Performance Monitor to check the counters for the different protocols that make up the TCP/IP protocol, she can't find them. What does Erin need to do?

5. What are the four different views available in the Performance Monitor?

6. What are the various items that you can view in the Performance Monitor? Specifically, what are the names of the various groups of resources and the specific items within the groups?

7. In analyzing a file and print server, list the resources to monitor in order of importance.

8. In analyzing an application server, list the resources to monitor in order of importance.

Exam Questions

1. You can use Performance Monitor to monitor the activity of the disk. To activate the disk counters, you must first run `diskperf -y`. What must be run if you want to monitor a disk system that is part of a RAID system?

A. `diskperf -yr`

B. `diskperf -y stripe`

C. `diskperf -ye`

D. `diskperf -raid`

2. You suspect your processor is the bottleneck of your system. What two counters should you check?

A. %DPC Time, %User Time

B. %Processor Time, Avg. Disk Queue Length

C. Interrupts/sec, Processor Queue Length

D. Processor Queue Length, %Processor Time

3. In configuring a Windows NT Server to function as an application server, which of the following server settings should you select?

A. Minimize memory used

B. Balance

C. Maximize throughput for file sharing

D. Maximize throughput for network application

4. In configuring a Windows NT Server to function as a file and print server, which of the following server settings should you select?

A. Minimize memory used

B. Balance

C. Maximize throughput for file sharing

D. Maximize throughput for network application

APPLY YOUR LEARNING

5. A server is functioning slowly on disk read and writes. You have a fast hard drive; however, even when you are not accessing the disk, you notice that the hard drive light is lighting up and the disk is thrashing. When you monitor this with the Performance Monitor, which two resources could be causing the bottleneck?

A. Disk

B. Processor

C. Network

D. Memory

Answers to Review Questions

1. She could monitor both the disk and the pagefile. If there are a lot of page faults, the server might be running out of memory. This would cause the disk drives to thrash and would slow overall disk access. See the sections "Performance Analysis" and "Overview" in this chapter.

2. Use Performance Monitor to check processor activity. The factors that you can investigate include Processor Queue Length, %Processor Time, and %Privileged Time. If the processor is averaging more than 80% usage or if the queue length is two or more, you might need to upgrade the processor or you might need a dual processor system. See the section "Finding Processor Bottlenecks" in this chapter.

3. There is nothing wrong with Mary's server. She just needs to run `diskperf -y` to activate the disk counters. See the section "Finding Disk Bottlenecks" in this chapter.

4. To activate the counters for TCP/IP, she needs to install SNMP first. See "Creating a Baseline Using Performance Monitor" in this chapter.

5. The four views available in the Performance Monitor are the Chart view, Report view, Log view, and Alert view. Each of these views can be used for viewing specific information on the objects and counters. See the section "Views in Performance Monitor" in this chapter.

6. The Performance Monitor groups resources by objects; within each object are counters, and within each counter are instances. See the section "Objects in Performance Monitor" in this chapter.

7. In a file and print server, the resources in order of importance are memory, processor, disk, and network. See the section "Analysis of a File and Print Server" in this chapter.

8. In an application server, the resources in order of importance are processor, memory, disk, and network. See the section "Analysis of an Application Server" in this chapter.

APPLY YOUR LEARNING

Answers to Exam Questions

1. **C.** To monitor the disk performance of a physical disk in a RAID system, you must execute `diskperf -ye`. See the section "Finding Disk Bottlenecks" in this chapter.

2. **D.** In locating a bottleneck with your processor, the two counters to monitor are the Processor Queue Length and the %Processor Time. See the section "Finding Processor Bottlenecks" in this chapter.

3. **D.** To optimize the server settings for an application server, you should select Maximize Throughput for a Network Application in the Server dialog box. See the section "Analysis of an Application Server" in this chapter.

4. **C.** To optimize the server settings for a file and print server, you should select Maximize Throughput for File Sharing in the Server dialog box. See the section "Analysis of a File and Print Server" in this chapter.

5. **A. D.** You should monitor the disk and the memory for a bottleneck. The disk access time is the problem; however, if you notice that the drive is active without your direct request, it may be caused by a memory requirement due to insufficient physical memory. The page file may be constantly accessed to supplement the RAM. See the section "Finding Memory Bottlenecks" in this chapter.

This chapter helps you to prepare for the Microsoft exam by covering the following objectives within the "Monitoring and Optimization" category:

Monitor network traffic using Network Monitor. Tasks include

- ◆ **Collecting data**

- ◆ **Presenting data**

- ◆ **Filtering data**

▶ To meet this objective, you must have a strong working knowledge of the Network Monitor. Using Network Monitor to collect data, view the data, and use filters to focus on specific network traffic is essential.

Identify performance bottlenecks.

▶ Using the Network Monitor, you must be able to spot performance bottlenecks specifically relating to network traffic. This objective was also covered in the previous chapter: using the Performance Monitor to identify the performance bottlenecks.

Optimize performance for various results. Results include

- ◆ **Controlling network traffic**

- ◆ **Controlling server load**

▶ This objective requires you to apply the Network Monitor in isolating performance bottlenecks and make solid recommendations to improve the performance of your system, specifically dealing with the network traffic.

CHAPTER 10

Using Network Monitor

STUDY STRATEGIES

In preparing for the objectives relating to the Network Monitor, you need a firm understanding of the utility and its various features. The exam does not focus on the details of the Network Monitor data; however, you must fully understand how to use this tool and optimize the Windows NT network for each of the different sections of network traffic. To prepare for these objectives, read the material in this chapter and then spend some time using the Network Monitor tool itself.

Network Monitor is a network packet analyzer that comes with Windows NT Server 4. There are actually two versions of Network Monitor available from Microsoft. The first version comes with Windows NT Server 4 (simple), and it is capable of monitoring the packets (frames) sent or received by a Windows NT Server 4 computer (see Figure 10.1). The second version comes with Microsoft Systems Management Server (full version), and it is capable of monitoring all traffic on the network.

The advantage of the full version of Network Monitor is that any system can be monitored on the network.

This chapter covers the following sections relating to Network Monitor:

◆ Overview of network services

◆ Traffic analysis

◆ Installing Network Monitor

◆ Using Network Monitor

◆ Analyzing data

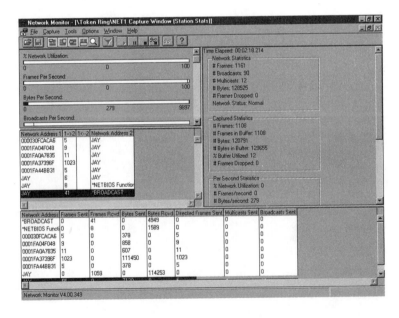

FIGURE 10.1
Network Monitor capturing network traffic.

OVERVIEW OF NETWORK SERVICES

Windows NT 4 provides a number of network services that enable users to carry out specific requirements on their network. Some of the services are automatically installed with Windows NT Server; others can be added later, depending on what you need to accomplished. In general, all services impact the capacity and performance of the network.

Table 10.1 lists some of the more commonly installed network components. Some are installed by default; others are not.

TABLE 10.1

NETWORK COMPONENTS

Component	*Description*
Computer Browser	Enables users to find or "browse" resources on the network without having to remember specific paths or the correct syntax.
DHCP	The automatic distribution and administration of TCP/IP addresses and related parameters to DHCP clients.
Directory Replicator	The automatic duplication of directories among Windows NT computers.
Domain Name System (DNS)	The resolution of TCP/IP host names to IP addresses.
Internet Explorer	An Internet browser that provides access to the World Wide Web (WWW) to view and download files.
Netlogon	This service performs user account logon validation and synchronization of user accounts in a domain.
Server	Enables network clients to access shared resources.
WINS	A centralized database that resolves computer names, or NetBIOS names, to TCP/IP addresses for browsing and resource access.
Workstation	Provides network access to shared resources. Its requests are processed by the Server service on the resource computer.

When analyzing network traffic, you must be aware of the activated network services because they each put a load on the network. Many of the services in Table 10.1 are common services and will be analyzed throughout this chapter. By no means are these the only services available; this list is simply the most common services used within a Windows NT network.

TRAFFIC ANALYSIS

In any office network environment, end users expect the network to be fast and reliable (without any data loss). Department managers expect their servers to be efficient and to adapt to the changing needs of users and the latest versions of software. Typically, administrators need to optimize their networks or plan for the effects on an ever-changing network.

To optimize or capacity-plan your network, as with the optimization of a server, you must know what traffic is currently being generated. Analysis involves determining what effect each Windows NT Server service has on the network. This analysis is performed with a network analyzer. A number of third-party programs can perform this function to varying degrees, and the Network Monitor is a useful built-in tool. The Network Monitor can be run on a corporate network for optimization purposes or on an isolated network for prediction purposes.

There are two methods for optimizing network traffic. One is to provide users with better response time by implementing network services that can speed up network traffic. The Computer Browser, for example, is a service installed by default that makes the user's life simpler (and therefore better). The Computer Browser enables users to access Network Neighborhood to view the available shared resources on the network. This can be a great service to users. By enabling browsing on the network, however, you increase network traffic. Browsing is accomplished through broadcast packets. Each computer that creates a share broadcasts to the rest of the network that it has a resource available for others to use. If the computer has more than one protocol installed, a broadcast message is sent for each of the protocols installed. As you can imagine, if you have 500 computers with two or three protocols installed and they all create a share, a lot of traffic is generated.

The second method is to provide the user with more bandwidth on the network by reducing network traffic generated by services. The administrator, for example, might decide to reduce network traffic by stopping the browser service and by disabling the capability to create a share on all computers (except for servers). This definitely reduces traffic, but it makes things more difficult for the end user. To connect to the server's shares, the user must know the exact name of the server, the share, and the syntax to connect to the share.

If a user wants to share a file with another user, that first user must perform the following steps:

1. Connect to the server using the proper syntax. Generally, you use a UNC path such as \\Server\share.

2. Create a directory in which to place the file; this can be any name that you choose.

3. Copy the file to the directory on the server.

4. Tell the other user where to find the file; ensure that he has the full UNC path and directory because no browsing is enabled in this scenario.

5. The other user must connect to the server using the correct syntax.

6. The other user then can copy the file to his own computer.

The end user must have greater knowledge of how the network operates and the naming conventions used throughout the network environment. With the browser service, a user can search the Network Neighborhood to locate the proper server and share required.

Each method is valid and deserves consideration, but a properly optimized network is going to strike a compromise between the two methods.

Network traffic analysis also is important for predicting the future demands on the network. By testing and establishing the capacity of the network, management can plan and budget for necessary upgrades. *Capacity planning* is the method of analyzing the network as one or more factors are increased. As the network grows, different services are added; you should be able predict what effect each service will have on the network. Then, you can make changes to stabilize the network when the services are added.

When analyzing traffic, you have to focus your attention on a number of key points. The upcoming sections address each one of these points in greater detail to give you a strong foundation in the components to include in your network traffic analysis. The sections covered include

◆ Classifying services

◆ Frame types

◆ Contents of a frame

◆ Network protocols and frames

Classifying Services

Classifying services enables an administrator to better predict the effects on a network as changes are made. Each of the Windows NT Server services can be classified with three simple questions:

◆ What kind of traffic does this service generate?

◆ How often is this traffic generated?

◆ What impact does this traffic have on the network?

There are some basic guidelines for classifying services on the server:

1. Isolate a network segment. This helps to prevent other network traffic from skewing the results of monitoring. In other words, stop all network traffic not related to the service you want to monitor.

2. Use Network Monitor or some third-party program to monitor the network traffic.

3. Capture the appropriate traffic by initiating the service to be classified. If analyzing the network traffic generated by the DHCP service, for example, you could create DHCP traffic by releasing and renewing a TCP/IP lease from a DHCP client computer.

4. Identify each captured frame to ensure that all the traffic is generated by the service and not by some other function.

Following these steps provides a baseline of how this service generates network traffic. It is recommended, however, that you perform these steps a number of times for each service to ensure the data is accurate. Each time the test is run, make sure the computer is set up the exact same way to ensure no other variables are involved. Carry out each step for each service separately, and then monitor them together to see how they affect each other.

Frame Types

Captured network traffic is displayed in segments called frames. The *frame* is the addressing and protocol information, as well as the data sent from one computer or host (routers, bridges, and so on) to another.

The three types of frames are broadcast, multicast, and directed. Table 10.2 provides a description of each frame type.

TABLE 10.2

FRAME TYPES

Frame Type	Description
Broadcast	Broadcasts are sent with the destination of FFFFFFFFFFFF. No host can be configured with this address, but all hosts on the network (subnet) accept this frame and process it. The frame is passed up the stack until it is determined whether the frame is meant for that computer.
Multicast	Multicasts are sent to a portion of the computers on the network. Like broadcast frames, multicast frames are not sent to a specific Media Access Control (MAC) address, but to a select few addresses on the network. Each host on the network must register its multicast address to become a member of a multicast set. NetBEUI and some TCP/IP applications use multicasting.
Directed	Directed frames are the most common type of frame. Each of these frames has a specific address for a host on the network. All other hosts disregard this frame because it does not contain the host's MAC address.

FIGURE 10.2

The analyzed frame from a browser announcement; the hexadecimal pane at the bottom also includes all the information within the frame.

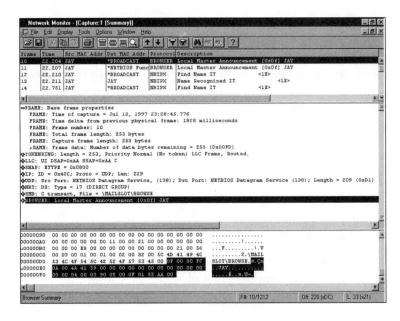

Each protocol shipped with Windows NT 4 implements broadcasting in different ways. NWLink and TCP/IP use broadcasts, for example, whereas NetBEUI use multicasts. Figure 10.2 shows a broadcast frame used for browsing.

Contents of a Frame

All frames are broken down into different pieces, or fields, that can be analyzed. Some contain addressing information, others contain data, and so on. By analyzing the addressing portion of the frame, you can determine whether the frame was a broadcast type. This helps you determine which service created the frame and whether it can be optimized.

Table 10.3 describes some of the fields of an Ethernet 802.3 frame.

TABLE 10.3

ETHERNET FRAME FIELDS

Frame Field	Description
Preamble	This is eight bytes in size and is not seen in a trace. It is used to notify the transceiver that data is coming.
Destination address	This specifies the MAC address of the host to receive the frame. It is six bytes in length.
Source address	This specifies the MAC address of the host that is the sender of the frame. It also is six bytes in length.
Type or length	This specifies the protocol that originated the frame or the amount of data in the frame. It is two bytes in length.
Data	This is the portion of the frame that can actually contain data or additional protocol headers and descriptions. It can be up to 1,500 bytes in length.
Cyclic Redundancy Check (CKC)	This is used as a checksum on the entire frame contents to see if it was delivered intact. It is four bytes in length and is not seen in a trace.

The address fields in Network Monitor can display both MAC addresses and NetBIOS names. Network Monitor automatically displays the NetBIOS name for systems it recognizes.

Figure 10.3 shows the fields displayed by default in Network Monitor. Notice the source and destination addresses, as well as the protocol and the description of each frame.

Network Protocols and Frames

The type of network traffic generated often depends on the protocol used to send the frames. Although all protocols use both broadcast and directed frames, some rely on one method more than the other. TCP/IP, for example, uses directed traffic more often than broadcasts; NetBEUI and NWLink use broadcasts more than directed traffic.

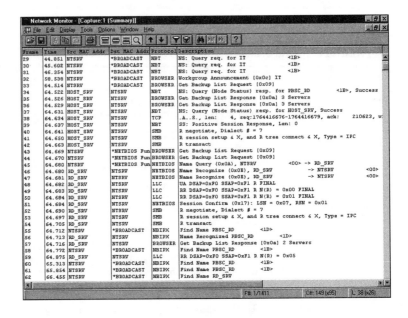

To understand why protocols use one method more often than
another, you have to look at their original implementation. TCP/IP
was originally designed to enable communication between computers of different types and different operating systems. To communicate over a WAN, you cannot broadcast; you have to send directed
frames for any kind of reliable connectivity. NetBEUI was developed
as a protocol for use in LANs; NWLink was meant for both LANs
and WANs. LANs were initially on single segments and, therefore,
broadcasts could be used. Because they are able to communicate
with broadcasts, the packets being sent can be much smaller. The
frame doesn't need to include as much information . This is a big
limitation in larger networks. If the network has a number of segments, the routers connecting the segments must be able to either
forward broadcast frames or use a different protocol. If the routers
do forward broadcast frames, there is a tremendous impact on the
network because of the increased network traffic.

As more companies want connectivity over WANs and more people
want access to the Internet, TCP/IP has become the protocol of
choice. Table 10.4 gives examples of frame size and speed differences
between TCP/IP and NWLink (802.2) for some basic transactions.

TABLE 10.4

TCP/IP NWLINK COMPARISON

Network Function	TCP/IP	NWLink (802.2)
PDC startup	81 frames 11,765 bytes 56.6 sec	148 frames 22,410 bytes 86.6 sec
Windows 95 client startup	58 frames 8,729 bytes 22.2 sec	32 frames 5,904 bytes 15.0 sec
User logon validation	41 frames 6,715 bytes 2.5 sec	28 frames 5,488 bytes 2.3 sec
Transferring a 2MB file	1,870 frames 2,186,572 bytes 12.5 sec	1,873 frames 2,225,630 bytes 11.3 sec

As you can see in the table, TCP/IP does not always send the smallest amount of frames or bytes, nor does it use the least amount of time. In most cases, it is expected to be slower because of its size. This table was created to show that it can operate in a range close to the other protocols. Because of its capability to link computers over a WAN, TCP/IP can be the protocol of choice for both a LAN and a WAN.

Traffic Analysis

REVIEW BREAK

If you fully understand the various components found while analyzing traffic, you will be more successful in locating potential network bottlenecks and offering relevant optimization recommendations. The main components to monitor with your network traffic analysis follow:

- Locate and classify each service. Analyze the amount of traffic generated from each individual service, the frequency of the traffic, and the overall effect it has on the network segment.

- Understand the three different types of frames: broadcast, multicast, and directed.

- Review the contents of a frame and ensure that you can find the destination address, source address, and data located in each frame.

In the upcoming sections, you will be introduced to the Network Monitor in greater detail. The following topics are discussed:

◆ Installing the Network Monitor

◆ Capturing and displaying data with the Network Monitor

◆ Analyzing data with the Network Monitor

It is these areas that will supply you with all the information necessary to use the Network Monitor as an analysis tool and to be successful on the enterprise exam with the Network Monitor objectives.

INSTALLING NETWORK MONITOR

You can install Network Monitor on machines running Windows for Workgroups, Windows 95, Windows NT Workstation, or Windows NT Server. Network Monitor does not require special hardware other than a network adapter supported by the system on which it is installed.

Windows NT 4 supports a new version of Network Device Interface Specification, NDIS 4.0, which enables a new mode for capturing network traffic. This new mode is called *local only*, and it provides better performance while running Network Monitor because it only accepts frames destined for that computer. With previous versions of NDIS, the monitoring computer always had to go into *promiscuous mode*. This meant the network adapter had to accept all frames on the network cable, whether directed for it or not. Accepting all frames has a huge impact on the CPU.

Most network adapters support promiscuous mode. However, some do not. Check with the hardware manufacturer to see whether promiscuous mode is supported.

Network Monitor consists of two components:

◆ Network Monitor application

◆ Network Monitor Agent

The Network Monitor application enables a system to capture and display network data, to display network statistics, and to save the captured data for future analysis.

NOTE

Network Monitor and NDIS 4.0
Running Network Monitor on a system whose operating system supports NDIS 4.0 provides a big performance gain. In any case, you want to run Network Monitor on a system that is not directly involved in your daily production. If this is not possible, make sure it is installed on a system whose operating system supports NDIS 4.0.

The Network Monitor Agent enables a computer to capture all network traffic and to send it over the network to the computer running the Network Monitor application. This capability is automatically installed on any computer running Network Monitor. You can run it on a Windows 95 system not running the Network Monitor application just to gather network traffic. The information that the Windows 95 system gathers can then be sent to a system running Network Monitor for viewing and analyzing the data. A Network Monitor Agent is available for both Windows 95 and Windows NT. You can also configure the Network Monitor Agent by setting capture and display passwords, as well as by specifying which network card is monitored if there are multiple cards (see Figure 10.4). The display passwords can be configured to include an additional level of security for your environment. Only users who know the configured password can view the contents of your network capture. You can set the display passwords upon the first launch of the Network Monitor or by using Control Panel.

To install the simple version of Network Monitor, perform the tasks outlined in Step by Step 10.1.

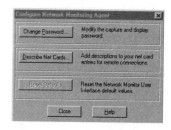

FIGURE 10.4
The Configure Network Monitoring Agent dialog box enables you to set passwords for capturing and displaying network traffic.

STEP BY STEP

10.1 Installing a Simple Version of Network Monitor

1. Open Control Panel.

2. Click the Network icon to open the Network dialog box.

3. Select the Services tab and then click Add.

4. Select Network Monitor Tools and Agent (see Figure 10.5) and then click OK or Close until you return to Control Panel.

   You might have to restart your system after the final step; however, it will depend on the services that were previously loaded on your system. Later in this chapter, we use the Network Monitor to capture and analyze the data.

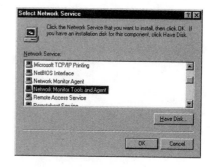

FIGURE 10.5
Selecting the Network Monitor Tools and Agent to be installed on your Windows NT system.

You can install the full version of Network Monitor by running SETUP.EXE from the \NMEXT\DISK1 directory of the Systems Management Server 1.2 CD.

USING NETWORK MONITOR

Monitor network traffic by using Network Monitor. Tasks include collecting, presenting, and filtering data.

The Capture Window is the default view of Network Monitor. This window provides four views of the data being captured on the network. The window areas are

◆ **Graph.** Located in the top-left corner.

◆ **Session Statistics.** Located directly below the graph.

◆ **Total Statistics.** Located on the right side of the window.

◆ **Station Statistics.** Located across the bottom of the window.

Figure 10.6 shows the different areas of the window.

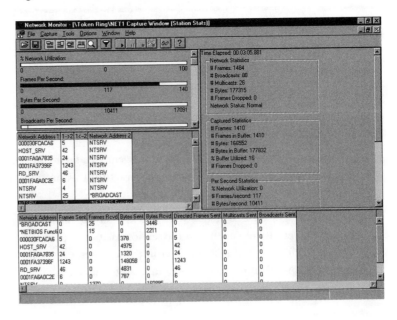

FIGURE 10.6
The areas of the Network Monitor window.

Table 10.5 describes each area of the Network Monitor window.

TABLE 10.5

NETWORK MONITOR WINDOW AREAS

Window Area	Description
Graph	This is a horizontal bar chart that displays the current activity as a percentage of network utilization. The bars displayed are Frames Per Second, Bytes Per Second, Broadcasts Per Second, and Multicasts Per Second.
Session Statistics	This is a summary of the transactions between two hosts and a display of which host initiated the broadcasts or multicasts.
Total Statistics	These are statistics for the traffic on the network as a whole, the frames captured, the per-second statistics, and the network adapter statistics.
Station Statistics	This is a summary of the number of frames and bytes sent and received, the number of frames initiated by a host, and the number of broadcasts and multicasts.

Using the Network Monitor involves capturing data, displaying data and then analyzing the data based on function and services. In the upcoming sections, you will cover the following topics in preparing to use the Network Monitor as an analysis tool:

◆ Capturing and displaying data in the Network Monitor

◆ Analyzing data with the Network Monitor

Capturing and Displaying Data

Capturing data using Network Monitor is quite simple and can be initiated in one of three ways:

◆ Select Capture | Start from the menu bar.

◆ Click the Start Capture button in the toolbar.

◆ Press F10, the function key.

After you start the capture, information is displayed in all four areas of the Network Monitor window. This is current statistical information about the network as well as statistical information about the captured data. A single broadcast message, for example, could be 425 bytes in size (captured data information), and there could be 10 broadcasts in a 10-second interval (network information).

Stopping the capture of data is just as simple as starting it:

◆ Select Capture | Stop from the menu bar.

◆ Click the Stop Capture button in the toolbar.

◆ Press F11, the function key.

◆ Click the Stop and View button in the toolbar.

If you start both Network Monitor and a capture, absolutely all traffic is recorded. This can generate a tremendous amount of information. If you do not know exactly what you are looking for, it can be quite intimidating to sift through all the information.

To control the amount of data captured, you can set a capture filter. A *filter* describes what type of data should be captured and displayed. All data must pass through the filter before it can be captured. The most common items to filter are either the protocol (NetBEUI, IPX, TCP/IP, and so on) or the destination or source address (MAC address, IP address, and so on). Figure 10.7 shows the Capture Filter dialog box.

Figure 10.8 shows how you can add parameters or addresses to accomplish filtering.

Captured data can be displayed or saved to a capture file (*.CAP) for analysis later.

After the data is captured, you need to analyze it. To do this, you must display the data in one of three ways:

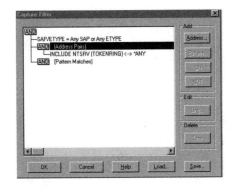

FIGURE 10.7
By default, nothing is filtered in Network Monitor, allowing all network traffic to be captured.

◆ Select Capture | Display Captured Data from the menu bar.

◆ Click the Display Captured Data button in the toolbar.

◆ Press F12, the function key.

As with capturing data, you can apply filters while viewing the data. This enables the capture of numerous types of information, but it also permits you to filter for frames of particular interest during analysis. Perhaps, for example, you captured using a filter that only caught broadcasts. Then, during analysis, you want to see how many of those broadcasts were sent by a particular network card (MAC address).

The following three areas make up the display window for Network Monitor (see Figure 10.9):

◆ The Summary pane

◆ The Detail pane

◆ The Hexadecimal pane

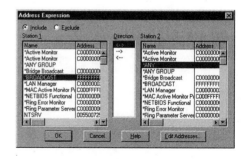

FIGURE 10.8

Include or exclude whatever needs to be filtered from the captured data, and focus your analysis on a specific protocol or service.

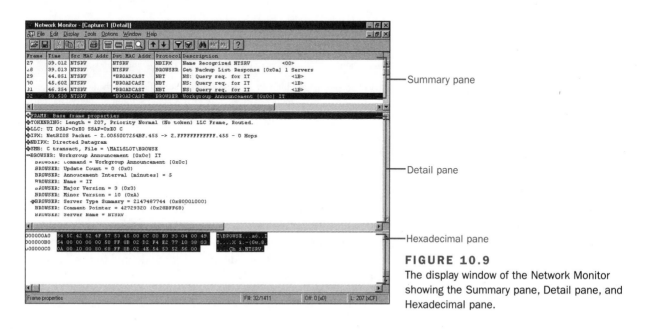

Summary pane

Detail pane

Hexadecimal pane

FIGURE 10.9

The display window of the Network Monitor showing the Summary pane, Detail pane, and Hexadecimal pane.

Summary Pane

The Summary pane displays by default when displaying captured data. This pane shows a list of all the frames that were captured and information about each of them. This pane is always either the full size of the window or appears at the top of the window. The nine columns can be sorted, moved, and resized. Table 10.6 provides a description of each of the columns available.

TABLE 10.6

SUMMARY PANE COLUMNS

Column	Description
Frame	This is the number assigned to the frame. All frames captured during one session are sequentially numbered.
Time	By default, this is the time when the frame was captured in relation to when the capture was started. This can be configured to show either the time of day or the elapsed time since the previous frame was captured.
Src MAC Addr	The hardware address of the computer that sent the frame.
Dst MAC Addr	The hardware address of the recipient computer.
Protocol	This is the protocol used to send the frame.
Description	This is a description or summary of the frame's contents.
Src Other Addr	This is an additional address identifier other than the MAC address (such as an IP or IPX address) from the source computer.
Dst Other Addr	Like Src Other Addr, this is an additional address for the recipient computer.
Type Other Addr	This specifies which type of address is displayed in the preceding two columns.

As previously mentioned, the Summary pane displays either in the full window or in the top of the window. To switch to a detailed view of an individual frame, double-click the desired frame. Then, all three panes are displayed.

Detail Pane

The Detail pane displays in the middle of the window, and it shows protocol information for the frame selected in the Summary pane. If there are several protocol layers to a frame, the topmost or outermost layer is displayed first.

When a protocol is selected in the Detail pane, the equivalent hexa-decimal information is highlighted in the Hexadecimal pane at the bottom of the window. Plus (+) and minus (–) signs indicate whether a protocol has additional information to be displayed. Double-click an item with a + to expand the information. Likewise, double-click an item with a – to collapse the information.

Hexadecimal Pane

The Hexadecimal pane displays the contents of the frame in hexa-decimal format and in an ASCII format. The corresponding infor-mation selected in the Detail pane is highlighted in the same color in the Hexadecimal pane (see Figure 10.10). Analysis often takes place in this area. Looking closely at this area can reveal some detailed information. In many circumstances, the actual contents of data or a document (such as an email message) can be viewed in this area and provide a good argument for encrypting sensitive data, user names, and passwords.

By using the Network Monitor to capture and display data, you can begin to analyze the network frames and the corresponding data within your network. In the next section, you will look at various services and tasks that Windows NT executes across the network and examine the number of frames and total network traffic generated by each of the tasks.

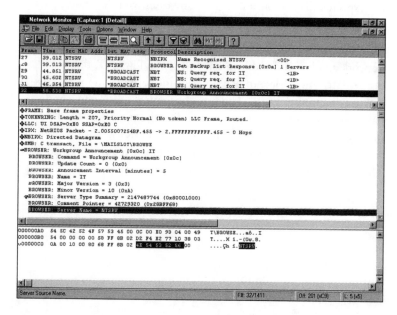

FIGURE 10.10

Server name is selected in the Detail pane, and the corresponding information is highlight-ed in the Hexadecimal pane.

ANALYZING DATA

Identify performance bottlenecks.

As with any kind of monitoring and analysis, the monitoring is the easy part. The data analysis is the tricky part. You have to decide which components have what type of impact on the system and the network.

To get an idea of the different types of traffic (and traffic analysis), look at three basic services or functions of Windows NT:

◆ Client traffic

◆ Client-to-server traffic

◆ Server-to-server traffic

Client Traffic and Optimization

Optimize performance for various results. Results include controlling network traffic and controlling server load.

When you think of client traffic, you probably think of file session traffic; however, there is more to client traffic then just accessing and downloading files. In this section, you will analyze logon traffic and the expected file session traffic. In many cases, you may find that these client traffic frames can put a heavy load on your network.

One of the first provisions to a user is the capability to log on to the network and be validated by a server. In Windows NT, the user presses Ctrl+Alt+Delete to halt any real-mode applications and display the logon dialog box. The user then enters a user name and password and ensures that the proper domain or workgroup name is displayed for validation. After the user clicks OK, one of the domain controllers for the selected domain validates the request for logon. The domain controllers are referred to as logon servers.

The first thing the user's computer needs to do is find a logon server. After a logon server is located, an exchange takes place to validate the user, check the system time, run logon scripts if they exist, set up profiles if they exist, carry out policies if they exist, and so on.

The amount of traffic generated by a single logon is minimal. When a number of users all log on to the network at the same time, however, the demand on the logon server can increase substantially. The question about logon traffic is, how many logon servers are required to support logons? The minimum amount of logon traffic generated is 24 frames and 3,105 bytes. This amount is generated by a default user without logon scripts, policies, profiles, and so on. You must determine how much traffic a single user generates, including any scripts, policies, and so on that might be incorporated.

Some other considerations are

◆ When do people log on? Are they all logging on at 8 a.m. or randomly over an hour during the morning from 7:30 a.m. to 8:30 a.m.?

◆ Are all the users logging on from a local network computer, or are there users logging on from remote sites?

Locating a Logon Server

The first action that must take place for a user to log on is finding the logon server. In a Windows NT network, that can be done in two ways, depending on what is implemented:

◆ Send a broadcast message across the network to the netlogon mail slot (only located on domain controllers).

◆ Send a query to the WINS server for all registered domain controllers in the selected domain. If it is found, send a request through directed frames.

When you use the broadcast method, you need a minimum of two frames to locate the netlogon mail slot. The computer sends the request to the NetBIOS name of the domain name being logged into with <00> as the 16th character.

If you want to log on to DOMAIN10, for example, the request is sent to DOMAIN10   <00> with spaces in the middle to fill up the places. If this was captured in Network Monitor, it would look similar to the following:

```
45 62.352 CLIENT *BROADCAST NETLOGON LM1.0/2.0 LOGON
➥Request from client
```

By looking at the details of the captured frame, you can then find which domain is being requested. This request is about 260 bytes for Windows 95 and about 300 bytes for Windows NT, depending on the computer name.

Each domain controller running the netlogon service in the segment responds to the request, stating that they all can accommodate the request. The response sent by the domain controllers is a directed message because the original request contains the requester's computer name and address. The following is an example of what the reply might look like:

```
57 64.869  BDC10 CLIENT NETLOGON LM2.0 Response to LOGON
➥Request
```

The response sent by the logon contains the source address and computer name of the server. This frame is about 230 bytes for Windows 95 and about 270 bytes for Windows NT.

When you use a WINS server, the network traffic is a little different:

1. The requesting computer sends a directed message to the WINS server for the domain name with <1C> as the 16th character. This standard request is about 92 bytes in size, and it basically asks for a return of all IP addresses for the logon servers in the domain. The following is an example of the request:

```
25 37.624 CLIENT WINS-SRV NBT NS: Query req. for
DOMAIN10       <1C>
```

2. The WINS server responds to the request with a frame that contains the IP address of all registered domain controllers in the WINS database, up to a maximum of 25. This frame can vary greatly in size, depending on the number of domain

controllers in the domain. For two domain controllers, the frame size is 116 bytes. The following is an example of the reply from a WINS server:

```
32 44.324 WINS-SRV CLIENT NBT NS: Query (Node Status) resp.
➥for DOMAIN10      <1C>, Success
```

3. After the client computer receives the frame from the WINS server, it sends a directed message to each of the servers (IP addresses) listed in the frame, asking for logon validation. The client ignores any response it receives from a logon server until it has sent out requests to all logon servers listed by the WINS server. The following is an example of the request the client might send:

```
39 44.968 CLIENT PDC10 NETLOGON SAM LOGON request from
➥client
```

4. Each server then responds in the manner mentioned when broadcasting was discussed earlier in the "Locate a Logon Server" section.

Logon Validation

After the requests for a logon server are all sent out, the client computer then accepts the first logon server response to that request. It does not matter whether the request was generated from a broadcast or from a directed message.

Four factors are involved in validating the logon:

◆ The amount of traffic generated by establishing the session

◆ The amount of traffic generated if the client is at a Windows 95 computer

◆ The amount of traffic generated if the client is at a Windows NT computer

◆ The termination of the session

Establishing a Session

The traffic generated to establish a session with TCP/IP takes 11 frames. It generates about 1,300 bytes of traffic for a Windows 95 system and about 1,400 bytes for a Windows NT system.

These actions need to take place:

◆ The client must resolve the NetBIOS name of the selected logon server. This can be done through broadcast or WINS.

◆ A TCP session is established with the logon server, using the three-way handshake.

◆ A NetBIOS session is established with the logon server.

◆ The Server Message Block (SMB) protocol negotiation takes place.

◆ An SMB tree connection to the logon server's IPC share is established:

```
\\logonserver\IPC$
```

Interprocess Communications (IPC) is the means by which all systems establish a communication link with each other. When a system connects to a share, it also connects to the IPC$ share.

Validating Windows 95

After the session is established, the Windows 95 client starts communicating with the logon server using two remote Application Programming Interface (API) calls to validate the logon:

1. The first API call is NetWkstaUserLogon. This API requests logon validation, and the server responds with either a success or failure message. The following are examples of the request and response.

   Request:

   ```
   103 20.763 CLIENT PDC10 SMB C transact, Remote API
   ```

   Response:

   ```
   104 20.858 PDC10 CLIENT SMB R transact, Remote API
   ```

2. The second API call is NetRemoteTOD. This second API retrieves the server's time information to determine any time zone difference. This happens so the file date and time stamping can be calculated correctly. The server responds with the correct time as kept by the domain controller. The response appears as shown here:

Request:

```
105 20.883 CLIENT PDC10 SMB C transact, Remote API
```

Response:

```
106 20.891 PDC10 CLIENT SMB R transact, Remote API
```

As indicated, calling these two remote APIs and receiving their responses uses four frames and about 765 bytes.

Validating Windows NT

A Windows NT client has three unique steps when asking for logon validation:

1. The first step is to get a list of trusted domains if trusts have been established. This generates about 12 frames and about 2,000 bytes of traffic. Each time a user logs on, this process occurs unless a user logs on, logs off, and then logs on again within five minutes (otherwise, the information is cached) or unless there is a large list of trusted domains.

2. Secondly, a secure channel must be established between the Windows NT client and the logon server. This process takes place during Windows NT initialization and creates 8 frames and about 1,400 bytes of traffic. This process verifies that a valid account for the computer exists in the domain.

3. The third step is the validation itself. With Windows 95, two remote APIs are called; with Windows NT systems, there is only one API call and response. The two frames are about 900 bytes in size, depending on the names of the computers and domains involved. If the named pipes to netlogon have been closed, an additional four frames that are about 700 bytes combined are generated. The following is an example of the single request and response:

```
140 30.308 NTW1   BDC10 R_LOGON RPC Client call
➥logon:NetrLogonSamLogon(..)

141 30.378 BDC10 NTW1   R_LOGON RPC Server response
➥logon:NetrLogonSamLogon(..)
```

After the user is validated, policies, profiles, and scripts can execute. All of these items add to the network traffic.

Terminating the Session

After the user is validated, you can terminate the session with the validation server. To do so, the connection to IPC$ is disconnected, and the TCP and NetBIOS sessions also are terminated. This whole process takes 5 frames and generates about 360 bytes of traffic.

Optimizing Logon Traffic

To achieve the optimum response time for logon validation, you must install the proper number of domain controllers. As well as providing enough domain controllers in the network, you should configure each domain controller for better performance and should place them in an area close to the users. This creates four things to consider when optimizing the logon validation:

◆ Determine the hardware required for better performance.

◆ Configure the domain controllers to increase the number of logon validations.

◆ Determine the number of domain controllers needed.

◆ Determine the best location for each of the domain controllers.

Hardware Requirements

To determine the hardware requirements for domain controllers, you must look at the number of accounts in the Security Accounts Manager (SAM). Look at the size of the SAM file in the directory WINNTROOT\SYSTEM32\CONFIG.

The following is some basic information about how much space is used by different accounts:

◆ Each global group is 512 bytes with an additional 12 bytes per member.

◆ Each local group is 512 bytes with an additional 36 bytes per member.

◆ Each computer account is 512 bytes.

◆ Each user account is 1,024 bytes (about 1KB).

Microsoft makes the following recommendations for setting up a domain:

◆ The amount of RAM in a domain controller should be about 2.5 times the size of the SAM.

◆ The SAM should never be more than 40MB in size.

◆ The maximum number of entries (objects) in the SAM should be no more than 40,000.

Table 10.7 provides some rough recommendations, according to the number of users.

TABLE 10.7

SAM DATABASE RECOMMENDATIONS

No. of Users	SAM Size	RAM Size	Page File Size
3,000	5MB	16MB	32MB
10,000	10MB	32MB	64MB
15,000	15MB	48MB	96MB
30,000	45MB	64MB	128MB

When you implement a domain controller for logon validation, the processor type makes little difference. When a domain controller plays a dual role, however, such as a validation logon server and a file and print server, a lot more is required of the processor.

Also, if the domain is very large, it is recommended that you keep domain controllers strictly for logon validation and set up different servers for file and print services.

Maximizing the Throughput

In Windows NT Server, the Maximize Throughput for File Sharing option is configured by default in the Server dialog box. This means the maximum amount of resources are set aside for file and print requests from across the network. This is the proper setting for a file and print server. For a domain controller, however, this setting does not provide the best performance for logon validation. A domain controller should have the Maximize Throughput for Network

Think It Through First Before running to your network room and reconfiguring all your domain controllers, remember to ask yourself, "Are these domain controllers used only for logon, or are they also used for file and print sharing?" If they are also used for file and print sharing, you must decide which service needs the biggest boost.

Say you have a smaller company of about 150 employees, for example, and you have two domain controllers. Each domain controller also controls printers and shares files. There is only a brief period when people are logging on. After that, they use the servers for accessing files and printers. If you change the configuration of the Server service in this situation, you will hinder the server instead of optimizing it.

Applications option enabled instead. If you change just this one setting, most domain controllers can triple the number of simultaneous logons.

Number of Domain Controllers

It is often difficult to nail down an actual figure for how many domain controllers should be in a domain. Microsoft gives a rough recommendation of one domain controller for every 2,000 user accounts. This value should be enough for normal logon validation, but to verify those assumptions, you can track Performance Monitor counters. Table 10.8 describes the counters that can help determine whether the correct number of domain controllers are installed.

TABLE 10.8

COUNTERS AND CONTROLLERS

Object/Counter	Description
Server: Logon/sec	This is the number of logon attempts per second. It includes both failed and successful logons for interactive, network, and service accounts.
Server: Logon Total	This counter monitors the total number of logon requests (interactive, network, and service), both failed and successful, since the server last started.

Logon Server Location

The fourth major item to consider when optimizing the performance of the logon server is where the users are located. Generally speaking, the closer the domain controller is to the users, the faster the user are validated. Any time the request must pass over a WAN (slow link), the validation process is going to be slow.

If there are remote users logging onto the domain, you must consider whether it would be beneficial to place a domain controller at the remote site. There are advantages and disadvantages to having the logon server in each location.

First, look at the advantages of having the domain controller at the remote site:

◆ The users at the remote site will be validated quickly because the communication between the client and the logon server is fast.

◆ If there are multiple users at the remote site, there is a reduced cost because you don't have a lot of people using up the bandwidth of the WAN when logging on.

Now, look at the disadvantages of having a domain at the remote site:

◆ Even though logon traffic is decreased, you still have the traffic of the domain controllers talking to each other to synchronize the account database. If a user is added or removed, it might take more than an hour before the controller is synchronized with the other domain controllers if they are across a WAN.

◆ For just one remote user, putting a domain controller at that site is expensive and hard to justify. As the number of users at the remote site increases, however, the cost can be justified. There is no special figure for when that justification occurs, however, because it depends on the company, the locations, the hardware being used, and so on.

◆ Because synchronization cannot occur as often as it normally would on a LAN, there might be users who cannot gain the access they should have. There also might be users who shouldn't have access because their rights were removed, yet they do have access because the account database has not been synchronized from the primary domain controller.

The following sections review the logon traffic generated from client logons, the client traffic generated from file sessions, the frames involved in file sessions, and some optimization recommendations.

> **NOTE**
>
> **More Is Not Always Better** When you're deciding how many domain controllers you need for logon validation, remember to consider that the more domain controllers there are, the more network traffic is generated. Each domain controller responds when a logon request is sent. In many cases, more is not always better.

File Session Traffic

Almost all communication between computers requires the establishment of a session before the communication actually takes place. DHCP, WINS, and DNS are a few of the communications in a Windows NT network that do not require an established session before communication starts.

The amount of traffic generated to create a session is not large. An average session normally falls in the range of 10 to 14 frames and about 1,500 bytes. After a session is established, you can set up a number of connections to different shares between the two computers, but they still use the same session. It is not the establishment of the session that tends to create network traffic; the traffic is created by what is done after the session is established. In addition, throughout the day, a user can establish multiple sessions that increase network traffic.

Even with multiple sessions established, the amount of traffic is light compared to the traffic generated after the session is established. It helps to look at the traffic as a part of or the starting point for other traffic.

There are five major steps in establishing a session:

1. Resolve the NetBIOS name (computer name) to an IP address.

2. Resolve the IP address to the MAC address (hardware address) of the computer.

3. Establish a TCP session.

4. Establish a NetBIOS session.

5. Negotiate the computer's SMB protocols.

Resolving the IP Address

Most communication between computers using Microsoft Windows products uses NetBIOS names (computer names). Because the hardware layer does not work with computer names, a few resolutions must take place.

First, the systems must find the corresponding IP address for the computer name. There are a number of ways to do this:

- ◆ Broadcast to all computers on the segment.

- ◆ Query the WINS server for the IP address.

- ◆ Parse the LMHosts file if one exists.

- ◆ Parse the Hosts file if one exists.

- ◆ Query a DNS server for the IP address.

Other methods are used as well; these are just a few of the more common ones used in Microsoft networks.

Although you are not going to examine this traffic generation in depth, asking for the address from a WINS server generates about 195 bytes. If resolved by broadcasting, it is substantially more.

Resolving the Hardware Address

After the NetBIOS name is resolved to an IP address, the IP must be resolved to the hardware address. As previously mentioned, network cards know how to talk to hardware addresses, not IP addresses. The Address Resolution Protocol (ARP) is used to resolve the IP address to the MAC address.

The process is simple. The source computer broadcasts a 60-byte message that serves as a request to the target computer with its MAC address. The following is an example of such a request:

```
10 4.445 WINNT *BROADCAST ARP_RARP ARP: Request,
➥Target IP: 131.107.2.200
```

When the target computer receives the ARP request, it replies to the source computer with its MAC address. The reply also is 60 bytes in size.

```
14 4.622 NTSRV WINNT ARP_RARP ARP: Reply,
➥Target IP: 131.107.2.100 Target Hdwr Addr: 00055AF323
```

These lines generate 120 bytes of traffic. Because the ARP cache entries are flushed after every 2 minutes of nonuse and after 10 minutes even with constant use, this process takes place all the time.

Establishing a TCP Session

After the computer name is resolved to an IP address and the IP address is resolved to a MAC address, a TCP session can be established. Because TCP is connection-oriented or directed communication, a TCP session must first be established. Because TCP is connection-oriented, it offers guaranteed delivery, which is why a session must be established. This type of communication is required for file sessions. It is also sometimes referred to as the *three-way handshake.*

The three-way handshake generates about 180 bytes of traffic and generally only needs to occur once between the client and server.

With one TCP session, you can set up multiple file connections. The following is an example of the handshake:

```
19 5.323 WINNT NTSRV TCP .S, seq: 446756-446759, ack:0
22 5.655 NTSRV WINNT TCP .A..S., seq: 54763465-54763468,
➡ack: 446757
23 5.697 WINNT NTSRV TCP .A,  seq: 446757-446757,
➡ack: 54763466
```

NetBIOS Session

After the TCP session is established, you can start a NetBIOS session. As with the TCP session, you must start a NetBIOS session before two hosts can have any further communication. The target server must validate both the computer name and the fact that it can establish another NetBIOS session.

This takes two frames and 186 bytes:

```
24 5.697 WINNT NTSRV NBT SS: Session Request, dest: NTSRV,
➡Source: WINNT
25 5.699 NTSRV WINNT NBT SS: Positive Session Response
```

The NetBIOS session between a client and a server only needs to be established once; multiple file connections are serviced by the one session.

SMB Protocol

After the NetBIOS session is accepted, the two computers can then negotiate their server message block (SMB) protocols. Each SMB protocol is like a dialect, and each computer can understand a number of different dialects. The client sends a frame to the server, informing it of which SMB protocols it understands. The server then compares the list of SMBs to its own and chooses the highest level of SMB common to both the client and the server. It then informs the client which SMB it has chosen:

```
28 5.702 WINNT NTSRV SMB C negotiate, Dialect = NT LM 0.12
29 5.707 NTSRV WINNT SMB R negotiate, Dialect # = 5
```

Different dialects support different features, such as long file names, unicode, and so on. All the Microsoft client systems (Windows for Workgroups, Windows 95, and so on) support different levels of SMB dialects.

The two frames in the example generate a total of about 350 bytes, depending on the level of SMBs they understand. As with the NetBIOS session, this only needs occur once per client and server.

Connecting and Disconnecting

After all the sessions are established and the SMB protocol is chosen, the client can actually connect to the server through a share point. It is through this connection that the transfer of files across the network takes place.

There are three distinct components to transferring files:

◆ Connection sequence

◆ Data transfer

◆ Terminate session

The client first needs to connect to the server, so it sends an SMB session and tree-connect request. It indicates the share name it wants to connect to and the user name and password of the user requesting the connection:

```
46 8.774 NTWRK SRV1 SMB C session setup & X, Username =
➥USER5, AND c TREE CONNECT & x
```

The server then validates the user name and password, and if able to accept another tree-connect request, it responds with a success message:

```
47 8.933 SRV1 NTWRK SMB R session setup & X, and R tree
➥connect & X, Type = A:
```

Depending on the names of the user, server, share, and SMB, these two messages can vary from 350 bytes for a Windows 95 system to more than 500 bytes for a Windows NT system.

In the examples given so far, it would have taken 11 frames and more than 100 milliseconds for the client to connect to a Windows NT 4 server. After the connection is completed, the transfer of files can take place. This is where the vast bulk of network traffic actually happens.

Analyzing the traffic on the network that is generated from data transfer can be difficult. You must choose a standard file size must, and then try transfers at different times of the day with different protocols.

After a user completes the transfer of files, the session can be terminated. This is as simple as the client requesting that the connection be terminated. The server then responds with a success message:

```
47 18.554 NTWRK NTSRV SMB C tree disconnect
48 18.557 NTSRV NTWRK SMB Ctree disconnect
```

In the preceding example, the client would have provided the tree ID (TID) that was to be disconnected.

These two frames would generate 186 bytes and would be repeated for each disconnection request.

After the last file connection to a server is disconnected, some additional traffic is generated because the TCP session also is terminated:

```
50 18.600 NTWRK NTSRV TCP.A...F, seq: 448452-448452,
➥ack: 55893877
51 18.602 NTSRV NTWRK TCP.A...F, seq: 55893877-55893877,
➥ack: 448453
52 18.603 NTWRK NTSRV TCP.A...., seq: 448453-448453,
➥ack: 55893878
```

The three frames needed to disconnect generate 180 bytes of network traffic.

Optimizing File Session Traffic

Although file session traffic is minimal when compared to the amount of traffic generated during the transfer of a file, you can still do a few things to reduce traffic:

◆ Remove any excess protocols, or at least disable them for functions or services where they are not needed. As an example, if you install TCP/IP, NWLink, and NetBEUI on all your computers and then create a share, you are creating unnecessary traffic. Your computer broadcasts to the master browser that it has a resource to share. Because it has three protocols installed that are enabled, it broadcasts all three protocols to make sure everyone can hear it.

◆ Make sure the servers are in a location close to the people who use them most, especially if they can be kept on the same subnet. If a server is on one segment and the majority of users who access it are on another segment, a lot of unnecessary traffic is generated. Match users and the servers they use the most on the same subnet.

Client-to-Server Traffic and Optimization

Optimize performance for various results. Results include controlling network traffic and controlling server load.

Client-to-server traffic is the communication a client has with a server. Some of the types of traffic it can be beneficial to monitor are browser, intranet browsing, and DNS. This section focuses on browsing and intranet browsing traffic.

Browser Traffic

Browser traffic is all the traffic generated during the browser process, both in announcing available resources and in retrieving lists of available resources. The entire process is as follows:

1. Servers (any computer with a share) are added to the browse list by announcing themselves to the master browser.

2. The master browser shares the list of servers with the backup browsers and the master browsers of other domains.

3. The client computer retrieves a list of backup browsers from the master browser.

4. The client retrieves a list of servers from a backup browser.

5. The client retrieves a list of shared resources from the server.

The function of browsing is automatic and is implemented through broadcasts. This makes it a simple task on a single subnet. In a network with multiple subnets, the broadcasts are restricted to each subnet unless either the routers are able to forward browser packets or WINS has been implemented. Without either of these two options enabled, full network browsing is not available with multiple subnets.

Depending on how many computers are in each subnet and how many computers have shares enabled, a tremendous amount of traffic can be generated by all the computers announcing themselves to the master browser.

Each frame is usually between 200 and 300 bytes in size and broadcasts use UDP Port 138.

NOTE **Subnetting** In previous chapters, it was mentioned that subnetting your network is a good way to reduce network traffic. If you add a router that can forward broadcasts, you defeat one of the purposes of subnetting. Network traffic is greatly increased by enabling broadcast forwarding, and the router can become a bottleneck. Don't implement broadcast forwarding at the router unless absolutely necessary.

Server Announcements

A computer with resources available on the network announces itself once a minute for the first five minutes after it is started. After that, it announces itself once every 12 minutes. Each announcement is 243 bytes in size and can look like this:

```
31 21.534 WIN95 *BROADCAST BROWSER Host Announcement [0x01]
➥WIN95
```

These announcements occur whether there is a share on the computer or not. When you start the Server service or enable the file and print service, the announcements are sent automatically.

After the master browser receives the announcements from the servers, it creates a browse list and distributes the browse list to all the backup browsers through broadcasts.

Get the Backup List

The client needs two frames to get the list of backup browsers from the master browser.

First, the client sends a Get Backup List Request to the domain name with <1D> as the 16th character. This request is about 215 bytes in size:

```
142 54.210 NTWRK *BROADCAST BROWSER Get Backup List Request
➥[0x09]
```

When the local master browser receives the request, it responds with a Get Backup List Response. Included in the response is the list of available backup browsers. This frame can vary in size, depending on how many backup browsers there are. A list with two backup browsers is about 230 bytes, and each additional backup browser adds 27+ bytes:

```
145 54.218 PDCNT NTWRK BROWSER Get Backup List Response
➥[0x0a]   2 Servers
```

The client then communicates with one of the backup browsers in the list.

If there is no response from a master browser, the client assumes no master browser is available and forces an election by sending an election frame of 255 bytes:

```
65 28.734 NTWRK *BROADCAST BROWSER Election [0x08] [Force]
```

Get the Browse List

After the client gets a list of the backup browsers, it connects with one of them. It gets the list of servers (browse list) from the backup browser. Getting the browse list can take up to 19 frames and about 2,200 bytes total, depending on the number of backup browsers in your environment.

Get the Share List

After the client has the list of servers, it can connect to the desired server. After the client has connected to the server, it gets a list of shares available from that particular server. The amount of frames and bytes this takes varies greatly. It depends on how many shares are in the list and whether the server is in the same domain.

Optimizing Browser Traffic

Browsing is provided to enable efficient use of network resources by a typical end user. When you make it easy for users to access resources on the network, the efficiency of the network is sacrificed due to the increase in network traffic.

You can do a few things to help reduce the network traffic generated by browsing.

Disable the Server Component

Most users, and even many administrators, do not realize how much additional traffic is generated by enabling file and print sharing on workstations. If a computer does not need to have shares on it, disable that function. On Windows for Workgroups and Windows 95 systems, this means removing file and print sharing. On a Windows NT Workstation system, it means disabling the Server service.

If users need to share files, it is better to make common space available on a server they can read from and write to, rather than let them create their own shares.

If there are many servers in your environment, you can also reduce frames by removing the computer comments.

Potential Browsers

The software automatically determines the number of backup browsers in a network. There is one backup browser for every 32 computers on the subnet. If an additional backup browser is needed, the master browser notifies a potential browser and promotes it to the role of backup browser.

If there are computers that you never want to be a browser for some reason, such as processor speed or limited memory, you can disable that option:

◆ To disable the option on a Windows NT system, set the `HKEY_LOCAL_MACHINE\SYSTEM\CurrentControlSet\ Services\Browser\Parameters\MaintainServerList` value to `No`.

◆ For Windows 95 systems, click the Network icon in Control Panel. Set the Properties for the File and Print Sharing Browse Master parameter to Disabled.

◆ In Windows for Workgroups systems, add `MaintainServerList=No` to the `[network]` section of the SYSTEM.INI file.

This stops these systems from registering, renewing, and releasing the <1E> NetBIOS names with WINS or through broadcasts.

Reduce Protocols

The browsing system depends on the protocol. This means the traffic is repeated for each protocol installed. If three protocols are installed on a computer, then each announcement, renewal, release, and so on is repeated three times. To reduce traffic, disable the server component for certain protocols. For example, if you have a Windows NT Workstation running TCP/IP and NetBEUI for Internet access and local communication, you might decide to use only NetBEUI internally and only TCP/IP to surf the Internet. In this case, disable the server for TCP/IP so announcements are only sent by NetBEUI. If everyone else is running TCP/IP as well, remove the NetBEUI protocol altogether.

Intranet Browsing Traffic

With companies now creating their own internal Web sites to share information, fewer users are establishing file connections to servers to retrieve static information. Two main benefits are that it is a graphical means of browsing information and that information can be shared with users outside the confines of the company.

Intranet browsing can generate a large percentage of network traffic. Searching for and connecting to a Web site does not create this traffic. It is created by the amount of information downloaded. Web sites often contain large graphics that use a lot of bandwidth.

Connecting to a Web Site

Connecting to a Web site is a simple process. The first step in intranet browsing is resolving the Web server's name. This can be done in many ways, such as through broadcasting (if on the same subnet), WINS, or a DNS name lookup.

After the Web server name is resolved, you must establish a TCP session using TCP Port 80.

After the connection to the server is established, the server can start making requests for information. The requests for pages from the Web server are usually made through Hypertext Transfer Protocol (HTTP) commands. These HTTP commands are actually GET commands that request the page (or file) specified. After the page is downloaded, there might be other pages (graphics or images) as part of the first page that also must be downloaded. These additional HTTP GET commands are initiated automatically.

When you visit a Web page, you generate the following number of requests:

```
27 5.398 WIN95 WEBSRV HTTP GET Request (from client using
port 1076)
```

This frame can vary greatly, depending on the length of the host name and the size of the file to be downloaded. An average size is around 350–400 bytes.

After the Web server receives the request and the file in question is available, it responds with the appropriate number of HTTP response frames. If the file is larger than 1,238 bytes, at least two response frames are sent to transfer the file. If additional frames need to be sent, they are 1,450 bytes because the HTTP header information is not included.

If a page has many graphics, many TCP sessions and HTTP GET commands can be issued for each page. A separate TCP session and TCP Port is used for each requested file. A single page, for example, can have 10 graphics that average 4,000 bytes. Downloading just that one page can consume more than 50,000 bytes.

> **NOTE**
>
> **Use Small Graphics**   When creating pages for your internal Web server, make sure the graphics are relatively small, possibly in a GIF format. This keeps your intranet operating more efficiently.

Intranet Security

By default, Microsoft Internet Information Server 2.0 enables anonymous connections. This means users are allowed to access the site without validation of user names and passwords. This makes using the site easy, but it also leaves the server open to security violations. You can enable security on most Web servers, including MS Internet Information Server 2.0. This security could be basic encoding of user account information or encrypting the user account information.

Windows NT uses a security feature called Challenge/Response on the Web server. It is enabled each time a file download request is received.

The client makes a request to the server, where it sends its unencoded information. The server then responds to the client with the appropriate encryption code to use.

The client then sends its authentication information (using the encryption key specified by the server) to the server. The server then processes the request and sends the file to the client.

Optimizing Intranet Browsing

The single most important thing to remember about Web pages on an intranet is keep them small in size. The following are a few ways you can keep page size down and minimize intranet browsing traffic:

◆ **Keep the Web pages small.** The less scrolling needed to view a page, the better. If you need to provide more information than what can fit on one page, insert links to other small pages.

◆ **Limit the size of graphics, images, or AVIs.** Each image placed in a Web page must be downloaded when that page is opened. If possible, reuse graphics throughout the site to reduce downloads.

◆ **Increase the cache at client computers.** As files are downloaded from the intranet pages, they are temporarily placed in a directory called Cache. When the amount of disk space designated for the cache is used up and more files are downloaded, files already in the cache must be deleted. If previous pages are viewed again, those associated files must be downloaded again.

◆ **Is security a big concern at your site?** If your network is a closed and secure environment, removing the need for authentication reduces network traffic.

Server-to-Server Traffic and Optimization

A large amount of traffic is generated between the various servers in your environment. In this section, you examine the traffic generated by server browsing and trust relationships.

Server Browser Traffic

As previously discussed, browsing is enabled by default in a Microsoft network.

Just as browser traffic exists between client and server, several different types of browser traffic are generated between servers. The basics of server browsing follow:

1. At startup, the PDC assumes the role of domain master browser for its domain.

2. At startup, each BDC becomes either a backup browser or the master browser of its subnet if there is no PDC on the subnet.

3. Each master browser announces itself every 15 minutes to the master browsers of other domains on the local subnet.

4. Every 15 minutes, each domain master browser contacts the WINS server for a listing of all domains.

5. Every 12 minutes, each master browser contacts the domain master browser for an update of the browse list.

6. Each backup browser contacts its local master browser to retrieve an updated list every 15 minutes.

Along with the announcement traffic a server generates, it also can create additional traffic by taking part in other browser traffic:

◆ Browser elections take place if a client cannot find a master browser, if the master browser announces it is being shut down, or if a domain controller is being initialized.

◆ Master browsers in different domains share their browse lists to permit servers and resources to be accessed throughout the network.

◆ Backup browsers retrieve updated browse lists from their local master browser.

The impact that browsing has on the network is relative. Yes, browsing definitely increases the amount of traffic and, in turn, can slow the entire network down. If you increase the amount of traffic generated by browsing, however, users can have more up-to-date browse lists.

Optimizing server browsing can mean reducing or increasing network traffic, depending on the situation.

Browser Announcements

All computers with a Server service enabled announce themselves every 12 minutes to the master browser. This keeps the server included in the browse list. Along with this announcement, any other browsing capabilities are also included. Depending on the browser capabilities of the computer, the announcement is about 245 bytes in size:

```
20 12.456 NTSRV *BROADCAST BROWSER Host Announcement [0x01]
```

If the host that is announcing is capable of being the master browser, it must first determine whether it should be the master. To do this, it must find out the identity of the master browser. The Announcement Request frame is a broadcast used to establish this identity. It is about 20 to 250 bytes in size, depending on the computer name.

If there is a master browser on the subnet, it responds with a Local Master Announcement. This announcement is the same size as its announcement frame.

If there is no master browser or if the requesting server thinks it should be the master browser (PDC or BDC for example), it forces an election. An election frame is about 220 to 230 bytes:

```
60 17.522 NTBDC *BROADCAST BROWSER Election [0x08] [Force]
```

All browsers (backup and master) and potential browsers respond to the election after a random period of time by broadcasting their announcements. The random wait period is used to enable the system with the highest priority to respond first. The sequence in which the different operating systems respond is Windows NT first, then Windows 95, and then Windows for Workgroups. After the initial response, the computer waits a time period before sending its election criteria to see who has the highest criteria.

After four election responses, the computer with the highest criteria wins the election and becomes the master browser. It sends a Local Master Announcement to inform the other computers that it is becoming the master browser.

The master browser then determines which potential browsers should become backup browsers. By default, all BDCs are backup browsers unless they are on a subnet without a PDC. Then, they are the master browser. If there are not enough BDCs for the number of computers on the subnet, the master browser requests that a potential browser become a backup browser.

Browse List Updates

In a routed TCP/IP network, there is a domain master browser for each domain throughout the entire enterprise. In most cases, the domain master browser also is the primary domain controller, unless it is not running. One role of the domain master browser is to retrieve a browse list from the other domains in the enterprise. This can be done in two ways:

◆ Every 15 minutes, the master browser announces itself to the other master browsers using a Workgroup Announcement frame. This frame is directed to the special NetBIOS name of <01><02>_MSBROWSE_<02><01>. All master browsers register this name. If the announcement ID is for a new domain, the master browser adds it to its list. This updated list is exchanged with the domain master browser every 12 minutes.

◆ The domain master browser contacts the WINS server every 15 minutes and queries all registered domain names. These domains are added to the list and exchanged with the master browsers every 15 minutes.

After the domain master browser has an updated list, it must distribute the list to the master browsers on all the subnets.

When the local master browser has received the updated list, it provides the list to the backup browsers. Backup browsers retrieve the list every 12 minutes from the local master browser. The process of the backup browser retrieving the list from the master browser is exactly the same as how a client retrieves the browse list from the backup browser.

After the backup browser has the updated browse list, the client can retrieve the list when needed.

Optimize Server Browser

Most of the traffic generated by browsing takes place automatically at intervals that cannot be configured. There are, however, three ways that you can reduce server browser traffic:

- ◆ Reduce the number of protocols.
- ◆ Reduce the number of entries in the list.
- ◆ Increase the amount of time between browser updates.

Reduce Protocols

Browsing takes place separately on each installed and bound protocol. If three protocols are installed, each frame must be sent three times. By removing one or two of the protocols, you can reduce browser traffic.

Reduce Entries

If there is only one protocol installed, or the protocols installed are needed, disable the Server service for protocols that do not need to act as a server. Without the Server service running, the computer does not announce itself to the master browser. Therefore, there are fewer entries in the browse list.

Modify the Registry

Most of the intervals involved in the browse cannot be modified. You can change two Registry settings, however, for the master and backup browsers at HKEY_LOCAL_MACHINE\SYSTEM\Current ControlSet\Services\Browser\Parameters.

`MasterPeriodicity` is used to set the frequency with which a master browser contacts a domain master browser. By default, this time interval is 12 minutes (720 seconds), with a minimum of five minutes (300 seconds) and a maximum of 4 million seconds. To modify the interval, you must add this parameter as a `REG_DWORD` on the master browsers. You can change this parameter on-the-fly without rebooting to enable the changes.

`BackupPeriodicity` is used to set the frequency with which a backup browser contacts the master browser. By default, this time interval is 12 minutes. This parameter also is a `REG_DWORD`, but it does require that the system be rebooted. You could try a value of 25 to 30 minutes initially to see how browsing is affected. You should perform this configuration on all systems that could be a browser.

Trust Relationship Traffic

In organizations in which the administration of domains is central, it makes sense to have one domain as an account domain and other domains strictly for resources. Trust relationships between domains enable a user from one domain to access resources in another domain.

A *trust* occurs when one domain permits users from another domain to have access to its resources. After the trust is established, the administrator of the resource (trusting) domain can assign permissions to local resources to users and groups from the account (trusted) domain.

When a user from a trusted domain tries to access a resource on the trusting domain, the trusting domain passes the account authentication to the trusted domain.

The three areas that generate traffic are

- ◆ Creating the trust creates a lot of traffic (about 16,000 bytes), but the traffic only occurs at the time the trust is created.

- ◆ Using trusted accounts creates traffic. If the administrator of the trusting domain assigns permissions to an account from the trusted domain, a lot of traffic is generated. This occurs each time permissions are being assigned.

- ◆ Passthrough authentication creates additional traffic. Additional traffic is generated each time a user tries to access resources from a trusting domain. Traffic is also generated when a user tries to log on at a Windows NT Workstation using a trusted account, and the computer is a member of the trusting domain.

Establishing a Trust

A trust relationship is created only once between two domains unless the trust has been broken for some reason. Creating a trust is a two-step process.

First, the trusted domain permits itself to be trusted by another domain. No network traffic is generated by this unless there are BDCs in the domain. If there are, then the PDC makes an announcement and creates a hidden account in the SAM, which then must be synchronized with the BDCs.

The second part occurs when the trusting domain adds the first domain as the trusted domain. This sequence of events generates the majority of the network traffic and could be in excess of 20,000 bytes of traffic. Briefly, what happens is this:

◆ The trusting domain controller determines the name and address of the primary domain controller.

◆ The TCP and NetBIOS sessions are established with the primary domain controller.

◆ The trusting domain controller tries to connect to the IPC$ share of the primary domain controller, but it fails because it uses its own trusting account. This happens to validate that the account is created in the trusted domain.

◆ The session with the PDC is terminated.

◆ The browse list is retrieved from the trusted domain using normal methods.

◆ A connection is established to a domain controller in the trusted domain, where it makes a number of calls to the LSA (Local Security Authority) to get the domain name of the trusted domain.

After information is gathered from the domain, the domain updates its own LSA database and synchronizes it with the BDCs.

Finally, the trusting domain tries to find all the domain controllers for the trusted domain and attempts to log on to the trusted domain. It uses a special account referred to as the Interdomain Trust User Account. If the logon attempt is successful, the trust is complete.

Trust Accounts

After a trust is established, you can assign permissions to users from the trusted domain or add the user from the trusted domain to a local group.

When this occurs, traffic is generated by the trusting domain PDC as it connects to the IPC$ share of the trusted domain PDC to query the LSA and SAM. The amount of traffic generated can vary, depending on the size of the databases, but it could be in excess of 18,000 bytes.

Each time you display a member of a trusted account when assigning permissions, additional traffic is generated. The trusting domain must enumerate the SID of the trusted account.

Pass-Through Authentication

Whenever a user tries to log on or to access a resource, the account must first be validated. If the user account is from a trusted domain instead of the domain in which the computer or resource is located, a process called *pass-through authentication* takes place.

Pass-through authentication is the most common form of network traffic generated from a trust.

When a request to validate a trusted account occurs, the domain controller of the trusting domain must contact a domain controller from the trusted domain. The domain controller of the trusting domain then establishes a named-pipe connection with the domain controller of the trusted domain. After the named pipe is established, three APIs are directed to the netlogon service of the trusted domain controller.

These APIs set up challenge and authentication of the trusted domain and then request logon validation. They also provide the user name, computer name, and domain name of the client.

The entire process of pass-through authentication can take up to 4,500 bytes initially. On later attempts, however, it can take less than 1,000 bytes.

Optimizing Trust Relationship Traffic

Normally, trust relationships do not create a lot of network traffic. There are two ways, however, to reduce traffic from a trust relationship.

Less Trusts

Obviously, if you want to reduce the amount of traffic generated by trust relationships, reduce the number of trust relationships.

Sometimes, when a network starts to grow, not a lot of thought is given to how the network is organized. Sometimes, too many people want to maintain control of their particular area. In these cases, what generally happens is that a number of domains are created with their own accounts, and everybody trusts everybody. This is known as the full-trust model. It works okay if there is support staff (administrators) at each location.

To reduce traffic, sometimes the entire network must be restructured so that, rather than user accounts in each domain and two one-way trusts between all domains, you set up one one-way trust between the resource domains and the master domain. All the user accounts are in one location, and there is a reduction in the number of trusts.

Group Accounts

Trusted user accounts generate additional traffic. The best way to reduce traffic is also a good organizational strategy:

◆ You should never give user accounts permission to a resource directly. Permissions to a resource should always be assigned to a local group.

◆ You should always add user accounts to global groups. In turn, you add the global groups to the local groups.

As an example, Microsoft did some tests. For looking up the SID for two user accounts from a trusted domain, the frame size was 636 bytes. Looking up the SID of a global group from a trusted domain took 552 bytes. Because the frame size to look up a global group does not increase with the number of users added to the group, you can greatly reduce network traffic.

CASE STUDY: MONITORING NETWORK BANDWIDTH

ESSENCE OF THE CASE

Here are the essential elements in this case:

- A utility is required to monitor the network bandwidth being used.

- The captured data must be stored so it can be analyzed to resolve any potential problems.

- The utility should be integrated within the system or have a low price.

SCENARIO

A common theme in any network environment is a concern regarding the amount of network bandwidth available. On many occasions, we have been asked to evaluate the actual load in a corporate network. In one particular analysis, we were assisting a public school board who was looking at computer-based training (CBT) solutions as a supplement to their classrooms. The CBT used sound and graphics and required a fair amount of available bandwidth. The problem was they had no idea how much bandwidth was currently being used. They needed a tool that could measure the current bandwidth usage, and also capture the data, so they could analyze high usage to find methods to optimize and then reduce the bandwidth usage. The client wanted to keep the costs down as much as possible and did not want to purchase specialized equipment for this analysis.

ANALYSIS

To meet the analysis needs of this client, we used the Network Monitor that is bundled with the MS BackOffice suite, the full SMS version. This utility allowed us to monitor the network and view the current usage statistics from the Statistics window of the Network Monitor, and it also stored all the captured frames in a file that we could analyze at a later point. In this specific circumstance, we found that the network utilization was running at approximately 22 percent of available bandwidth, and the additional load required for the CBT was an extra 10 percent. With the combination of these bandwidth requirements, we were able to properly assess the validity of this CBT solution for the school district.

CHAPTER SUMMARY

KEY TERMS

- frame
- broadcast
- multicast
- directed frame
- MAC—Media Access Control
- IPC—Interprocess Communication
- API—Application Programming Interface

This chapter reviewed the Network Monitor as a tool for monitoring and optimizing your Windows NT network. The following points summarize the key items to understand in using the Network Monitor as a monitoring tool:

◆ Two versions of the Network Monitor are available: the scaled-down version built-in to the Windows NT Server operating system and the full version that is a component of Microsoft Systems Management Server.

◆ The Network Monitor window has four sections: Graph, Session Statistics, Station Statistics, and Total Statistics.

◆ Once the Network Monitor has captured some data, you use the display window to view the frames. The three sections of the display window are the Summary pane, the Detail pane, and the Hexadecimal pane.

◆ To optimize the logon traffic in your Windows NT network, you should consider four main points:

   1. Determine the hardware required to increase performance.

   2. Configure the domain controllers to increase the number of logon validations.

   3. Determine the number of domain controllers needed.

   4. Determine the best location for each of the domain controllers.

◆ The following are a few good points for optimizing file session traffic:

   1. Remove any excess protocols.

   2. Reduce the number of WAN links required for file transfer.

◆ Consider three points when attempting to optimize server browser traffic:

   1. Reduce the number of protocols.

   2. Reduce the number of entries in the browse list.

   3. Increase the amount of time between browser updates.

CHAPTER SUMMARY

◆ Trust relationships generate a large amount of network traffic; in optimizing your system, keep the number of trusts low.

These points mention some of the items on the enterprise exam. By no means is it a complete list; you should fully review the entire chapter on the Network Monitor.

| APPLY YOUR LEARNING |

This section allows you to assess how well you understand the material in the chapter. Review and exam questions test your knowledge of the tasks and concepts specified in the objectives. The exercises provide you with opportunities to engage in the sorts of tasks that compose the skill set the objectives reflect.

For more review and exam questions, see the Top Score test engine on the CD-ROM that came with this book.

Exercise

The following exercise provides you with an opportunity to apply what you've learned in this chapter.

10.1 Monitoring Network Traffic

The purpose of this exercise is to illustrate how you can use Network Monitor to capture and recognize the frames of data being sent and received from the local computer. The first thing you do is install Network Monitor.

Time Estimate: 20 minutes

1. Open Control Panel and double-click the Network icon.

2. Select the Services tab and click Add.

3. Select Network Monitor Tools and Agent and then click OK. You may be prompted for the location of the Windows NT source files; direct your system to the appropriate directory and close all other dialog boxes.

4. Restart your computer as prompted.

5. Open Network Monitor and view the different areas of the window.

6. Click the Capture button in the toolbar.

7. Open a command-prompt window.

8. Type **PING** and then the name of a computer on your network.

9. Type **NET USE X: ***computername**sharename* to manually map a drive to a share on the network.

10. Switch back to Network Monitor and click Stop Capture and Display (the button with the glasses).

11. Find the following frames: MAC address resolution, NetBIOS name resolution, the PING command, the NET USE command.

12. Identify what types of commands were used for each of the resolutions. Are you using WINS?

Review Questions

1. John implemented a number of Windows NT 4 Servers at his company. Some are file servers, some are application servers, one is a PDC, and two are BDCs. The access to file and application servers is fine, but it is slow to log on. What could he change to improve the logon time?

2. Mike heard it is good practice to monitor your network traffic using Network Monitor. He clicked the Network icon in Control Panel and

APPLY YOUR LEARNING

installed the Network Monitor Agent, but nothing happens. What else does Mike need to do?

3. Paul is a contractor who was called in to optimize the performance of a company's Windows NT network. The company is running a master domain model with five domains trusting a single master domain. Paul looked at some of the permissions on the resources in the trusting domains and found that only users were added to the list, no groups. What impact does this have on the network?

4. What are the three different types of frames that you can monitored across the network?

5. Which two fields contained in a frame cannot be displayed in a trace?

6. When using the Network Monitor, what function key can you use to start a capture?

7. List the three areas that make up the display window in the Network Monitor?

8. What file extension would you use to save a capture file for later viewing?

9. When establishing a TCP/IP session, how many frames are generated?

Exam Questions

1. What are the areas of the Network Monitor window when it is capturing data?

    A. Network Statistics, Session Statistics, Counters

    B. Graph, Session Statistics, Total Statistics, Station Statistics

    C. Objects, Counters, Instances

    D. Sessions, Real Time, Transfer Statistics

2. How should you arrange users and groups when assigning permissions across domain trusts?

    A. Assign the users to local groups, and then assign the local groups to global groups in the appropriate domain.

    B. Create a global group in the resource domain and add the users from the account domain to the global group. Assign the global group to the local group and then assign the permissions to the local group.

    C. Users from an account domain do not have access to resources in a resource domain.

    D. Assign users to a global group in their domain and add that global group to a local group in the resource domain. Assign permissions to the local group.

3. What areas can you display while viewing the captured data in Network Monitor?

    A. Resource pane, Data pane

    B. Summary pane, Detail pane, Hexadecimal pane

    C. Report pane, Alert pane, Detail pane

    D. None of the above

APPLY YOUR LEARNING

4. Which of the following services helps to reduce network traffic?

   A. WINS

   B. DHCP

   C. Remote Access Service

   D. SNMP

5. A user says he cannot connect to a resource displayed for a remote system in Explorer. Why would a resource be displayed if it is not available?

   A. The Browser service has been disabled.

   B. The WINS server is providing an old list of resources.

   C. The system is down or has removed the share, but the browse list has not been updated.

   D. Browsing was enabled before the browse list was updated.

6. How can you speed up logon validation over a slow link?

   A. Add another WINS server.

   B. Install a proxy server.

   C. Add more resource domains.

   D. Put a BDC at each of the remote sites.

7. Why is TCP/IP the default protocol for Windows NT?

   A. It was designed for use on LANs and WANs.

   B. It reduces the number of bytes sent across the network.

   C. TCP/IP is the fastest protocol.

   D. It is the simplest to set up.

8. What are the two versions of the Network Monitor?

   A. Real mode and Protected mode

   B. Local-only mode and Promiscuous mode

   C. Promiscuous mode and Server mode

   D. LAN mode and WAN mode

9. What is the total size of a global group in the SAM database?

   A. Each global group is 512 bytes with an additional 12 bytes per member.

   B. Each global group is 512 bytes with an additional 36 bytes per member.

   C. Each global group is 512 bytes.

   D. Each global group is 1024 bytes.

Answers to Review Questions

1. Check the properties of the Server service in the Network dialog box. By default, Windows NT is optimized as a file and print server. See the section "Maximizing the Throughput" in this chapter.

2. The Network Monitor Agent enables you to monitor your system. If you want to monitor network traffic in and out of a system, you must install Network Monitor Tools and Agent. See the sections "Installing Network Monitor" and "Software" in this chapter.

APPLY YOUR LEARNING

3. By adding users instead of groups to the permission list across the domain trust, you greatly increase network traffic. See the section "Group Accounts" in this chapter.

4. The three types of frames that you can monitor on a network are broadcast frames, multicast frames, and directed frames. See the section "Frame Types" in this chapter.

5. The Preamble, at eight bytes, and the Cyclic Redundancy Check (CRC), at four bytes, are not displayed when you use the Network Monitor to trace. See the section "Contents of a Frame" in this chapter.

6. The F10 function key is one option you can use to start a capture using the Network Monitor. See the section "Capture and Display Data" in this chapter.

7. The three display areas in the Network Monitor are the Summary pane, Detail pane, and Hexadecimal pane. See the section "Capture and Display Data" in this chapter.

8. Captured data can be displayed or saved to a capture file (*.CAP) for analysis later. See the section "Capture and Display Data" in this chapter.

9. When you establish a TCP/IP session, the three-way handshake generates about 180 bytes of traffic and generally only needs to happen once between the client and server. See the section "Establishing a TCP Session" in this chapter.

Answers to Exam Questions

1. **B.** The four sections of the Network Monitor window that is displayed when capturing data are Graph, Session Statistics, Total Statistics, and Station Statistics. See the section "Using Network Monitor" in this chapter.

2. **D.** When assigning permissions across trusts, you should always follow AGLP—accounts into global groups, global groups into local groups, and local groups assigned permissions. See the section "Optimize Trust Relationship Traffic" in this chapter.

3. **B.** The three areas available to display data in the captured file are the Summary pane, the Detail pane, and the Hexadecimal pane. See the section "Capturing and Displaying Data" in this chapter.

4. **A.** The WINS service helps reduce traffic by reducing the need to locate servers using broadcast frames. See the section "Client Traffic and Optimization" in this chapter.

5. **C.** At times, computer names may be displayed in the browse list after they have been shut down or removed from the network. This situation will resolve itself in the browse list updating that is a continuous process. See the section "Browser Traffic" in this chapter.

6. **D.** You can optimize logon validation by making a domain controller available at each remote site, ensuring that logon traffic does not need to cross a slow WAN link. See the section "Optimizing Logon Traffic" in this chapter.

APPLY YOUR LEARNING

7. **A.** The TCP/IP protocol is the most widely used protocol for LAN and WAN connectivity. See the section "Network Protocols and Frames" in this chapter.

8. **B.** The two versions of the Network Monitor are Local mode, included in Windows NT Server, and Promiscuous mode, which is included with Systems Management Server. See the section "Overview" in this chapter.

9. **A.** Each global group is 512 bytes with an additional 12 bytes per member. See the section "Optimizing Logon Traffic" in this chapter.

VI

TROUBLESHOOTING

No specific objectives are directly addressed in this chapter. Rather, this chapter serves as the foundation for Chapters 12 through 15, each of which covers one or more of the objectives in the "Troubleshooting" category.

CHAPTER 11

Troubleshooting Tools

STUDY STRATEGIES

Use the tools introduced in this chapter to assist in troubleshooting your Windows NT system. A strong knowledge of the available utilities can be a great addition to your troubleshooting tool belt.

This chapter prepares you for the Enterprise exam by introducing troubleshooting utilities for your Windows NT system. This chapter gives you the background knowledge for the next chapters relating to troubleshooting various processes in Windows NT. This chapter is intended to give you instruction in the troubleshooting techniques and tools that are covered on the Enterprise exam. The following tools are covered throughout this chapter:

◆ Event Viewer

◆ Network Monitor

◆ REGEDT32

◆ NTBackup

◆ The emergency repair process

A large variety of troubleshooting tools are included with Windows NT. Understanding the features of these tools is essential to identifying—and solving—various problems in a Windows NT environment. A large variety of third-party utilities that are not listed here are also available for troubleshooting Windows NT.

EVENT VIEWER

You use the Event Viewer in Windows NT to record errors, warnings, and informational messages from the operating system and from applications. These messages are an important part of troubleshooting because they form a record of your system's activity. Figure 11.1 shows an Event Viewer screen.

A series of three event logs are maintained by Windows NT:

◆ **The system event log.** The system log is used to record events generated by Windows NT system components such as drivers and services.

◆ **The security event log.** The security log records events related to system security. With the security log, the system audit policy determines which events will be logged. You create and maintain system audit policies with User Manager.

◆ **The application event log.** The application event log is used to record messages generated by applications.

FIGURE 11.1
The Windows NT Event Viewer is an excellent reference tool for locating system errors and warnings, otherwise known as events.

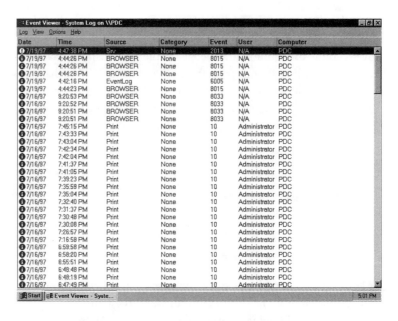

Each event has a number of fields containing a variety of information. Depending on the event, some of these fields are not used. When you view event details, the screen shown in Figure 11.2 displays event information.

The fields shown represent the various types of information described in the following list.

FIGURE 11.2
The Event Detail screen displays (as one might guess) the details of an event from the Event Viewer.

◆ **Date.** The date the event message was logged.

◆ **Time.** The time the event message was logged.

◆ **User.** The user who caused the event.

◆ **Computer.** The name of the computer where the event occurred.

◆ **Event ID.** A numeric value for a specific message as defined by the source of the message.

◆ **Source.** The application or system component that logged the event.

◆ **Type.** A classification of the event, as defined by Windows NT, such as an error, warning, or information message.

◆ **Category.** A classification of the event, as defined by the source of the message.

- ◆ **Description.** A textual explanation of the event.

- ◆ **Data.** Hexadecimal and ASCII data specific to an event, shown either as a series of byte or word values.

NETWORK MONITOR

You can use the Network Monitor application to examine network traffic and to monitor network performance. Although a more complete discussion of this utility is provided in Chapter 10, "Using Network Monitor," the application is relatively straightforward. Essentially, the Network Monitor is a network sniffer, and you can use it to check for the following:

- ◆ Bad packet CRC (cyclic redundancy checks). A packet with a bad CRC value indicates that the packet itself is corrupted.

- ◆ Network saturation, which may be caused by a network card that is constantly sending broadcast packets.

- ◆ Network utilization and performance problems. Using Network Monitor to monitor these items can be handy when you want to locate any potential problems with new applications in your environment.

REGEDT32

The Registry is perhaps the most complex part of Windows NT. It is an internal database containing Windows NT configuration information. Effectively, the Registry is a replacement for Windows 3.x .INI and other configuration files. Because the Registry contains a great deal of critical information, Microsoft did not intend for it to be accessed by users. It is possible to cause a great deal of damage to Windows NT unless you use extreme caution when modifying the Registry. With that in mind, be very careful when modifying the Registry. The Registry Editor screen is shown in Figure 11.3.

FIGURE 11.3
The Registry Editor; here, it displays the
HKEY_LOCAL_MACHINE tree and the keys.

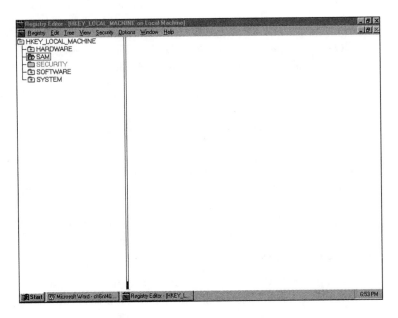

The Registry is a structured database of hierarchical trees. The five trees within the Registry are HKEY_LOCAL_MACHINE, HKEY_USERS, HKEY_CURRENT_CONFIG, HKEY_CLASSES_ROOT, and HKEY_CURRENT_USER. Each tree has a series of keys, subkeys, and value entries. Using a Registry editor tool such as REGEDT32 or REGEDIT, you can modify a system's configuration to solve system problems and conflicts.

NTBACKUP

Windows NT includes a tape backup utility called NTBackup, which provides a graphical interface for backing up and restoring files from either NTFS or FAT partitions. Using the NTBACKUP utility, it can be easy to recover from any system problems that can be caused by many sources. In preparing to use this utility, you should also be aware of a few restrictions. The NTBackup utility cannot back up the following types of files:

◆ **Files you do not have permissions to read.** The only time you can back up files without having read permissions is if you have backup permissions.

◆ **Paging files.** These are used for virtual memory and cannot be backed up. You do not need to back up the information in paging files.

◆ **Registries on remote computers.** You can back up your local Registry, but not remote Registries.

◆ **Files that are locked open by application software.** An example is a database file opened by a user in a locked state (either exclusive or shared).

The Windows NTBackup screen is shown in Figure 11.4.

To back up files, the first step is to select the files, directories, or volumes to back up. Once all the appropriate items are selected, the next step is to click the Backup button and specify options for the backup set. Restoring files follows the same process, beginning with selecting files from a tape and then clicking Restore.

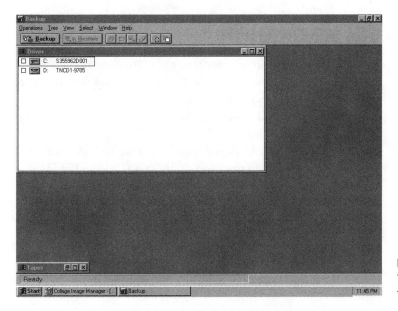

FIGURE 11.4
The NTBackup main screen; here, it displays the two disks located in the computer.

EMERGENCY REPAIR PROCESS

When a Windows NT installation is damaged, a recovery procedure called the emergency repair process is used to fix it. Using the emergency repair process, you can save yourself a great deal of grief in system recovery and repair. To perform an emergency repair, you need the original CD-ROM, setup disks (Intel platforms only), and a recovery disk.

To use the emergency repair process, you need a number of required items updated and available. The following sections introduce the required tools and the process:

◆ The RDISK utility

◆ Creating a boot disk

◆ Performing an emergency repair

The RDISK Utility

When performing an emergency repair of a Windows NT system, you must have a recovery disk. The RDISK utility is what you use to create and maintain recovery disks (see Figure 11.5). (If you have not created recovery disks yet, put down this book and create recovery disks for all your Windows NT servers. Although they may never be needed, recovery disks are a form of insurance.) RDISK is a straightforward utility in the \%SYSTEMROOT%\SYSTEM32 directory.

You use the Create Repair Disk button for the initial creation of a recovery disk, which requires a blank floppy disk. Note that the disk need not be formatted (or even blank) because RDISK will format it for you.

A recovery disk has copies of a Windows NT system's configuration files. Thus, you cannot use a recovery disk created for one specific computer on a different computer. Also, you should update recovery disks whenever your system configuration changes.

The recovery disk contains the following files, as shown in the directory listing:

```
Volume in drive A has no label.
Volume Serial Number is 9C13-B5CD

Directory of A:\

07/23/97   07:59p                   51,618  setup.log
07/25/97   01:27p                  212,092  system._
07/25/97   01:28p                  206,551  software._
07/14/97   11:01p                    5,827  security._
07/14/97   11:01p                    4,992  sam._
07/14/97   11:01p                   15,425  default._
07/25/97   01:28p                   14,687  ntuser.da_
08/09/96   01:30a                      438  autoexec.nt
07/14/97   10:56p                    2,510  config.nt
9 File(s)            514,140 bytes
941,568 bytes free
```

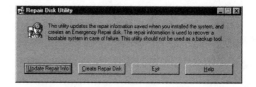

FIGURE 11.5
The RDISK utility is what you use to update the emergency repair data.

The following list provides an overview of the information contained in these files:

- ◆ **SETUP.LOG.** A log of files installed and CRC (cyclic redundancy check) checksums for each file. This file is read only, hidden, and system.

- ◆ **SYSTEM._.** The contents of the HKEY_LOCAL_MACHINE\SYSTEM Registry key in compressed format.

- ◆ **SOFTWARE._.** The contents of the HKEY_LOCAL_ MACHINE\SOFTWARE Registry key in compressed format.

- ◆ **SECURITY._.** The contents of the HKEY_LOCAL_ MACHINE\SECURITY Registry key in compressed format.

- ◆ **SAM._.** The contents of the HKEY_LOCAL_MACHINE\SAM Registry key in compressed format.

- ◆ **DEFAULT._.** The contents of the HKEY_LOCAL_MACHINE\DEFAULT in compressed format.

- ◆ **NTUSER.DA_.** The contents of %SYSTEMROOT%\PROFILES\DEFAULT USER\NTUSER.DAY in compressed format.

- ◆ **AUTOEXEC.NT.** A copy of %SYSTEMROOT%\SYSTEM32\AUTOEXEC.NT (configuration file for the MS-DOS environment under Windows NT).

- ◆ **CONFIG.NT.** A copy of %SYSTEMROOT%\SYSTEM32\CONFIG.NT (configuration file for the MS-DOS environment under Windows NT).

Creating the Boot Disks

An integral component of the emergency repair process comes from an NT boot disk. If you do not have the Windows NT setup boot disks handy, you can create them using the Windows NT CD-ROM. Prior to creating boot disks, you need three blank, formatted 1.44MB floppy disks. If your system is equipped with a 2.88MB floppy disk, it is recommended that you format the disks as 1.44MB anyway; problems have been reported with 2.88MB recovery disks. Also note that the floppy disks must be blank because the utility will not create boot disks on media that already contain files.

To create a Windows NT boot disk for an Intel-based system, perform the tasks outlined in Step by Step 11.1.

STEP BY STEP

11.1 Creating an NT Boot Disk for an Intel-Based System

1. Place the Windows NT CD-ROM into a system running Windows NT or any other operating system.

2. Locate either WINNT.EXE or WINNT32.EXE (WINNT for 16-bit operating systems, WINNT32 for 32-bit operating systems). Execute the appropriate file using the /OX command-line parameter.

---

3. You are prompted to insert blank floppy disks. You will provide them in the order of disk 3, disk 2, and disk 1. Ensure that you mark the disks correctly to simplify your emergency repair process if it's ever required.

RISC systems, unlike Intel systems, do not require boot disks. Instead, you use the firmware to provide a series of boot options.

Finally, for systems that support the El Torrito (non-emulation) CD-ROM format, you can boot the computer directly from the CD-ROM.

Performing an Emergency Repair

The emergency repair process is quite straightforward and requires little in terms of preparation. If you have not yet made recovery disks for all your Windows NT servers, do so now. Intel and RISC systems share the same basic emergency repair process. Some differences, however, do exist:

◆ Intel systems require boot disks in order to execute the emergency repair process, whereas RISC systems do not.

◆ Intel systems with FAT partitions can be booted from an MS-DOS system disk. Any Intel system using NTFS partitions and RISC systems cannot be booted using an MS-DOS system disk.

Once you have the boot disks (if required), Windows NT CD-ROM, and the recovery disk, the emergency repair process can begin. The tasks outlined in Step by Step 11.2 apply to the standard emergency repair on an Intel-based machine. The tasks are similar, however, for other systems.

STEP BY STEP

11.2 Performing an Emergency Repair

1. Insert the Windows NT Server disk 1 and boot the computer.

2. When prompted, insert disk 2 and proceed until you see the screen shown in Figure 11.6.

3. Select R to begin the recovery process.

You will see the following four options for your emergency repair process:

◆ Inspect Registry files

◆ Inspect startup environment

◆ Verify Windows NT system files

◆ Inspect boot sector

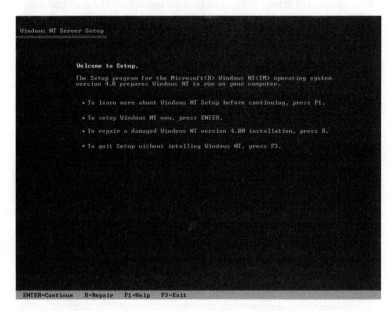

FIGURE 11.6

This setup screen provides you with the option to perform an emergency repair of your system.

By default, all four tasks are selected, but you can deselect tasks as required. Note that to select or deselect items, you must use the cursor keys because there is no mouse driver loaded at this point. These four tasks perform the operations discussed in the following four sections.

Inspect Registry Files

You can use the Inspect Registry Files option to repair Registry keys. When this option is selected, you are provided with a list of Registry files to restore. A warning also indicates that information can be lost. Proceed until you are prompted with a list of information that can be restored:

```
[ ] SYSTEM (System Configuration)
[ ] SOFTWARE (Software Information)
[ ] DEFAULT (Default User Profile)
[ ] NTUSER.DAT (New User Profile)
[ ] SECURITY (Security Policy)
[ ] SAM (User Accounts Database)
    Continue (perform selected tasks)
```

Select the Registry keys you want to restore and then select Continue.

Inspect Startup Environment

The Inspect Startup Environment option will verify that the Windows NT files in the system partition are not missing or corrupt. If required, the emergency repair will replace these files from the Windows NT Server CD-ROM. On Intel-based systems, the repair will ensure that Windows NT is listed in BOOT.INI. If this is not the case or if BOOT.INI is missing, the repair will change or create the file as required. On RISC systems, startup information in NVRAM is inspected and repaired if required.

Verify Windows NT System Files

The Verify Windows NT System Files option verifies that the Windows NT system files are not corrupt or missing. The file SETUP.LOG on the recovery disk contains a list of every file installed and also has a cyclic redundancy check (CRC) checksum for every file. The checksums are computed for each file present on the system and compared with SETUP.LOG. If the checksums don't match, the repair process asks whether it should replace the files from the Windows NT Server CD. If you have applied service packs to your system, you might need to reinstall these packs once the repair process is complete.

Inspect Boot Sector

On Intel systems, the Inspect Boot Sector option verifies that the boot sector on the system partition is configured to load NTLDR on startup. If this is not the case, the boot sector is repaired. This part of the recovery process is not required for RISC systems.

Once the entire process is complete, your system will be configured as a bootable system, and all errors encountered will have been repaired.

CHAPTER SUMMARY

KEY TERMS

- Event Viewer
- REGEDT32
- NTBackup
- emergency repair process
- RDISK utility
- boot disks
- boot sector

This chapter introduced you to several tools for the troubleshooting techniques in the next four chapters on troubleshooting the Windows NT processes. The tools covered are

- ◆ Event Viewer
- ◆ Network Monitor
- ◆ REGEDT32
- ◆ NTBACKUP
- ◆ The emergency repair process

Make sure these tools are installed in your Windows NT system; the next chapters have you using these tools to assist in the trouble-shooting process.

APPLY YOUR LEARNING

This section allows you to assess how well you understand the material in the chapter.

For more review and exam questions, see the Top Score test engine on the CD-ROM that came with this book.

Review Questions

1. What tools can you use to view security audit logs?

2. From a server console, can you back up a remote Registry?

3. If a service does not start when you boot Windows NT, where should you look to see what caused the problem?

Exam Questions

1. Under Windows NT version 4, which command can you use to create the setup boot disks?

   A. WINNT /OX

   B. WINNT /B

   C. WINNT32 /OX

   D. WINNT32 /B

   E. None of the above

2. What purposes does the SETUP.LOG file on a recovery disk serve?

   A. Maintains a list of service startups when the system boots

   B. Provides licensing information for Windows NT Server

   C. Provides the information necessary for CRC checks of Windows NT system files

   D. Contains a list of all service packs installed on your system

   E. None of the above

3. Which of the following information is available within the Event Viewer?

   A. Error messages from services and devices

   B. Informational messages from applications

   C. Security messages from the operating system

   D. Date and time of system startup

   E. All of the above

4. Which of the following operations is not performed as part of the recovery process?

   A. Verifying Windows NT startup files

   B. Verifying startup information in NVRAM on RISC systems

C. Verifying startup information in NVRAM on Intel systems

D. Verifying Registry files

E. None of the above

5. From REGEDT32, which of the following tasks can you complete? Choose all that apply.

A. Backing up Registry keys

B. Adding Registry values

C. Modifying Registry values

D. Restoring the entire Registry

E. Deleting Registry keys

6. Which of the following statements regarding a recovery disk are incorrect?

A. A recovery disk is bootable.

B. Recovery disks contain copies of Registry information.

C. Recovery disks can be created on one computer system and used to perform the recovery process on other computer systems.

D. NTLDR is copied onto a recovery disk by the RDISK utility.

E. Recovery disks never need to be updated.

Answers to Review Questions

1. You can use the Event Viewer to view system errors and events that are caused by a service not starting properly. See the sections "Troubleshooting Tools" and "Event Viewer."

2. No, it is not possible to back up a Registry remotely using the NTBACKUP utility. See the section "NTBackup."

3. You should check the Event Viewer system log. Locate the EventLog entry and work up the series of events to see what failed first and what other errors were caused by the failure. See the section "Event Viewer."

Answers to Exam Questions

1. **A. C.** You can use the /OX switch with either WINNT.EXE or WINNT32.EXE. See the section "Creating the Boot Disks" in this chapter.

2. **C.** The SETUP.LOG file contains a list of files and the CRC checksum of each file installed. See the section "The Emergency Repair Process."

3. **E.** You can view all of the information in the Event Viewer. See the section "Event Viewer" in this chapter.

4. **C.** The recovery process does not verify the start-up information in NVRAM for Intel-based systems; this is only done on a RISC-based system. See the section "Inspect Startup Environment" in this chapter.

APPLY YOUR LEARNING

5. **A. B. C. E.** All can be completed except for restoring the entire Registry. See the section "REGEDT32" in this chapter.

6. **A. C. D. E.** The recovery disks do not contain copies of the Registry information; that must be backed up using NTBackup. See the section "The RDISK Utility" in this chapter.

This chapter helps you to prepare for the Microsoft exam by covering the following objectives within the "Troubleshooting" category:

Choose the appropriate course of action to take to resolve installation failures.

▶ You need a strong understanding of the installation procedure and solutions to solve any potential problems encountered.

Choose the appropriate course of action to take to resolve boot failures.

▶ The startup or boot phase of Windows NT server is the starting point for your server; with a thorough understanding of the boot process, you can easily resolve any potential boot failures.

Choose the appropriate course of action to take to resolve configuration errors. Tasks include

◆ **Backing up and restoring the Registry**

◆ **Editing the Registry**

▶ To meet this objective, you must be able to successfully troubleshoot and resolve configuration errors; this may include using the control panel or the Registry editor for resolution.

Choose the appropriate course of action to take to resolve printer problems.

▶ This objective is pretty self-explanatory. You need a practical approach to this topic. Take the information offered in this chapter and apply it to real situations for hands-on experience.

CHAPTER 12

Troubleshooting Installation, Setup, Configuration, and Printing

To build your knowledge of troubleshooting, you need experience. Roughly 75 percent of all problems are fixed based on previous experience with the software package. One method that can be helpful in gaining experience is to cause problems to your system in a controlled environment. Remove some of the system files, and then monitor how the system reacts. Once you see the reaction of the system when a problem occurs, you will be able to quickly diagnose problems based on your experience when it is needed. Many of the questions on the enterprise exam relate to troubleshooting; however, to correctly prepare for these questions, gaining a thorough knowledge of each process used by Windows NT is the best study method.

This chapter is intended to give you instruction in the troubleshooting techniques and tools that are covered on the enterprise exam, focusing on installation, startup, configuration, and printing. The following sections are included:

◆ Installation errors

◆ Startup errors

◆ Configuration problems

◆ Printer problems

During the installation of Windows NT, a number of errors can occur and prevent a successful install. The following section discusses some of the likely problem areas.

INSTALLATION ERRORS

Choose the appropriate course of action to take to resolve installation failures.

As with other operating systems, Windows NT Server has minimum hardware requirements for installation. By ensuring that your system meets these requirements before you install Windows NT Server, you can avoid many problems. The upcoming list describes these requirements, along with "recommended" hardware. Note that although Windows NT Server will install on a system with "minimum" hardware, performance and functionality are limited on a system equipped with the bare minimum. For instance, although a network interface card (NIC) is not required, network functions are not available unless a NIC is installed.

Unlike other operating systems, Windows NT has specific hardware requirements. In addition to the minimum hardware requirements (minimum configuration details follow), it is also essential to consider the Windows NT Hardware Compatibility List (HCL); this file appears in the \SUPPORT\HCL.HLP directory on the Windows NT Server CD-ROM. If your system and all its installed components are on the HCL, you can avoid many potential difficulties. Following are the requirements and recommendations:

- ◆ **CPU.** For Intel-based systems, any 486, Pentium, or Pentium Pro processor. For RISC-based systems, any supported RISC processor (for example, MIPS 4x00 or Alpha).

- ◆ **Video adapter.** VGA or better.

- ◆ **Hard disk drive.** A minimum of 110MB of free space.

- ◆ **Floppy disk drive.** A 3.5-inch or 5.25-inch floppy drive for Intel systems (used for setup boot disks).

- ◆ **CD-ROM drive.** A supported CD-ROM drive is necessary either in the system on which NT Server is being installed or in another computer connected via a network.

- ◆ **Memory.** At least 16MB is recommended for Intel or RISC systems (although 12MB is sufficient for installation of NT Workstation on an Intel platform). Because the price of memory has decreased dramatically, using a larger quantity of memory is advisable (32MB being a reasonable minimum) because it will significantly increase system performance.

- ◆ **Network adapter.** Although a network adapter is not strictly necessary, networking will not be available unless a network adapter is installed.

- ◆ **Pointing device.** A mouse or other pointing device is not strictly necessary but is highly recommended.

Microsoft publishes a Hardware Compatibility List (HCL) for Windows NT Server. If your system and all its installed components are on the HCL, you can avoid many problems during installation and also in operation. Another way you can ensure that your system components are supported is by using the NT hardware qualifies, NTHQ.EXE from the Windows NT Server CD-ROM in the \SUPPORT\HQTOOL directory.

Before installing Windows NT, you should make a list of all the components in your system along with the resources they use. For instance, network cards usually require interrupts and I/O ports, as do sound cards. Having this information available can greatly simplify the installation process.

Problems can occur during setup that will prevent the installation from completing. The upcoming subsections outline some of the possible problems as well as some solutions.

Media Errors

Magnetic and optical media are not immortal. Heat, magnetic fields, coffee, and other environmental factors can damage media. Clearly, if the installation media are damaged, it is impossible to install Windows NT. For the distribution CD-ROM, there is little that can be done other than replace the disk. The boot floppies can also be damaged; however, you can easily re-create them. (The procedure for creating boot disks is described in the section "Creating the Boot Disks" in Chapter 11, "Troubleshooting Tools.")

Hardware Problems

Hardware devices can cause problems during the installation of Windows NT. If all your hardware devices are on the Hardware Compatibility List, you can avoid many of these problems. Some other concerns are covered in the following upcoming sections:

◆ Hard disk problems

◆ Unsupported CD-ROM

◆ Network adapter problems

◆ Other hardware

Hard Disk Problems

If a hard disk error occurs during setup (or after the initial reboot), check the following:

◆ Scan each of your hard drives for viruses. Boot sector viruses affecting the master boot record can cause many problems with Windows NT (or any other operating systems).

◆ If you are using SCSI (Small Computer System Interface) drives, ensure that your SCSI chain is properly terminated. Also ensure that the BIOS on the boot SCSI adapter is enabled and that the BIOS on all other SCSI adapters is disabled. Finally, ensure that all SCSI devices have unique SCSI IDs.

◆ If using EIDE (Enhanced Integrated Drive Electronics) drives, make sure that the system drive is on the first controller on the motherboard. In addition, make sure that the file I/O and disk access are set to standard.

◆ For IDE/EIDE or ESDI drives, make sure that the controller is functional before undertaking the installation of Windows NT. Also, ensure that if drives are larger than 1024 cylinders, Windows NT supports the disk configuration utility you are using.

◆ If you are using IDE, EIDE, or ESDI drives, make sure that the jumpers are set correctly for master or slave drives.

Unsupported CD-ROMs

If Windows NT does not support your CD-ROM drive, it is still possible to perform the installation. With the command WINNT /b, the files that are normally placed on the setup disks are placed on your hard drive. Additionally, you can copy the files from the CD-ROM onto your hard drive. This process enables you to copy files from a DOS-accessible CD-ROM drive and to access these files from Windows NT setup. The WINNT /T:<pathname> command enables you to place the Windows NT distribution files onto a hard drive, thereby avoiding the requirement to load files from a CD-ROM drive. Alternately, you can install Windows NT from another computer on the network.

Network Adapter Problems

Network adapters and their associated hardware can also cause problems during installation. Prior to starting the installation of Windows NT, you should obtain a list of which resources are used by your network adapter cards and ensure that no conflicts will occur within your system. Typically, a network adapter requires an interrupt (IRQ) and an I/O port, and it may require other resources such as a DMA channel. Make sure that these resources are not in use by other components within your system before starting the installation of Windows NT. In addition, you should check the following:

◆ For 10-Base-2 (or thinwire) Ethernet networks, make sure that your cable is terminated properly. In other words, both ends of the segment must be terminated properly. Also make sure that your cabling does not run next to (or over) electrical conduits.

◆ For 10-Base-T (twisted pair) Ethernet networks, make sure that connectors are properly crimped (the RJ-45 connectors are making solid contact with the wires within the unshielded twisted pair cable). A repeater (concentrator) is necessary, commonly referred to as a hub. A large variety of cable test equipment can accurately diagnose problems. Note that 10-Base-T equipment has a link light that will indicate whether you have a connection to your concentrator. Finally, ensure that you have not exceeded the recommended cable length (usually 100 meters from the repeater to your computer, including all path cables or cross-connects).

◆ For 10-Base-F networks (or FDDI or any other fiber optic networks), you must pay special care to the cabling. Fiber optic cable is extremely fragile and can easily be broken. Make sure that the cable has not been bent or broken. Also, when diagnosing any faults with fiber optic cables, never look directly into the end of a live cable. With networks such as 10-Base-F or FDDI, signal strength is not high enough to be harmful, but this is not the case when dealing with single-mode fiber optic connections. Even low-level emissions can cause damage after prolonged exposures. Retinas can easily be damaged, and they are quite difficult to replace. Please, be careful.

◆ ATM networks (asynchronous transfer mode) have very strict requirements for cabling. Please ensure that you follow all the manufacturer recommendations for your cabling plant.

◆ For token-ring networks, make sure that your cabling connections are reliable. As with 10-Base-T, a concentrator is required for correct operation (in this case, referred to as a MAU, Media Access Unit), and your link to the concentrator must be functional. As with 10-Base-T, a large variety of diagnostic tools are available to diagnose and resolve problems.

This list does not mention all the possible problem areas with network interface cards and other related equipment. Indeed, we could write a complete encyclopedia discussing nothing other than problems with networks. Any issue from the trivial to the obscure can cause problems. As a general rule of thumb, read all the manuals and specifications for your network interface card and all other associated devices before installing Windows NT, and make sure that you follow all proposed recommendations.

Other Hardware

A large variety of hardware is supported under Windows NT. As such, a large variety of problems can also occur with these hardware devices. Some of the likely problem areas are

◆ **Sound adapters.** Ensure that you have the correct values for interrupts, I/O ports, and DMA channels prior to installing Windows NT.

◆ **SCSI devices.** Make sure that each device on your SCSI chain has a unique SCSI ID and that your host adapter is configured to operate with each device. Also ensure that your SCSI bus is correctly terminated.

◆ **PCMCIA cards.** If your system supports PCMCIA cards and you want to use these cards under Windows NT, make sure that the cards are present in your system during installation.

Naming Problems

During the installation of Windows NT, you are asked for a computer name. This name must be unique within your domain. If it is not, a large number of problems can occur.

With Windows NT Server, you are also asked for a domain name (or workgroup name for small installations). For PDCs (Primary Domain Controllers), the domain name need not exist yet because the PDC will be the major part of your domain. For BDCs (Backup Domain Controllers) and member servers (servers that are part of your domain but do not validate logon requests), the domain specified must already exist (that is, a PDC must already be installed with the same domain name). Note that for BDCs and member servers, installation will not complete successfully unless the PDC is already installed and accessible via the network. Finally if NT is installed as a server (that is, no domain in place), you will also have the option of entering a workgroup name.

Windows NT has a series of rules for computer names. Generally, the names do not cause a problem. Avoid the following characters, however, because they are not allowed in a Windows NT computer name: / \ [ ] " : ; | < > + = , ? *. Also, a computer name cannot exceed 15 characters (this is a NetBIOS limitation).

Installation Errors

This last main section covered various potential problems with the installation process and how you can avoid them. The main task to remember with installation problems is to verify that all of your system components are supported by Windows NT. Check the Hardware Compatibility List, or obtain a driver from the manufacturer of the component.

STARTUP ERRORS

Choose the appropriate course of action to take to resolve boot failures.

The startup process for Windows NT Server is straightforward, and you can fix errors relatively painlessly. The startup sequence is similar on both Intel and RISC platforms. The following sections review the boot process and then discuss some possible boot errors and the resolution for these problems.

Overview of the Booting Process

The boot sequence in Windows NT is composed of a series of five distinct phases:

1. Bootup
2. Kernel Load
3. Kernel Initialization
4. Services Load
5. Windows 32 Subsystem Start

These phases are the same on both Intel- and RISC-based computers; however, there are some differences in implementation.

The main differences between the Intel boot process and the RISC boot process are hardware detection and the boot menu. On Intel systems, hardware detection is done by NTDETECT, and the boot menu is provided by NTLDR. On RISC systems, hardware information is taken directly from NVRAM, and the computer provides the boot menu itself.

The Boot Process

The entire boot process is a series of operations that load, initialize, and start the various subsystems, services, and device drivers required to operate Windows NT. The process differs slightly on Intel and RISC platforms.

The Intel Boot Process

An Intel system has two portions to the boot process. The first occurs before Windows NT begins to load. In this part of the boot process, the problems that may occur are typically related to hardware errors, boot sectors, or partition tables. Although this first phase of the boot process is not technically part of the Windows NT boot process, the following areas may cause problems:

◆ **Viruses.** Many viruses can infect an Intel system and prevent Windows NT from booting. You should check any diskettes you insert into your system with a virus scanner.

◆ **New hardware or new drivers.** If you have installed new hardware or changed device drivers, these drivers may prevent your system from booting. Always keep track of what changes you make to your system, and become familiar with the recovery process and the last known good set (discussed later in this chapter).

◆ **Hardware failures.** Hard drives, memory chips, disk controllers, and other components can fail. Although little can be done other than replace faulty components, ensuring that spare parts are available can be a lifesaver.

Once an Intel system displays the boot loader screen, the Windows NT boot process begins. The sequence of events is listed here:

1. NTLDR runs and initializes the system. The CPU is switched to a flat memory model, and mini file system drivers are loaded to enable the system to read the disk.

2. The BOOT.INI file is read, and the menu is presented to the user.

3. NTDETECT runs and detects installed hardware components.

4. NTOSKRNL.EXE executes and begins the actual startup of Windows NT. Four separate phases occur in sequence: kernel load, kernel initialization, services load, and Windows 32 subsystem start.

The four phases controlled by NTOSKRNL.EXE load the Hardware Abstraction Layer functionality, initialize drivers, and start all services marked as "automatic" startup. Once all these phases are complete, you are presented with the standard logon screen.

The RISC Boot Process

On RISC computers, the process is similar but somewhat simpler. As with Intel systems, a boot process occurs before Windows NT starts. It is much simpler, however, and tends to cause fewer problems. The usual causes of problems on RISC computers are missing or corrupt files or incorrect firmware revisions.

Once a RISC system displays the boot loader screen, the Windows NT boot process begins. The sequence of events is as follows:

1. Hardware configuration is downloaded from NVRAM (nonvolatile RAM). NTDETECT is not required.

2. The boot menu is displayed by the RISC system. Note that NTLDR is not required; instead, the system uses an OSLOADER.EXE file.

3. Once Windows NT is selected as the operating system, NTOSKRNL.EXE executes. The rest of the boot process is identical to that of an Intel system's.

Creating a Boot Diskette

You can create a boot diskette for a Windows NT system. This preventive action enables you to boot your system if the startup files are damaged or missing. The procedure to create a boot diskette is quite straightforward. An unusual caveat applies, however; the boot diskette must be formatted with Windows NT. You can do this from either the My Computer applet or a command prompt. The disk must be formatted if you want to copy the Windows NT partition boot sector. To create a Windows NT boot diskette, follow the tasks outlined in Step by Step 12.1.

STEP BY STEP

12.1 Creating a Windows NT Book Diskette

1. Format a floppy diskette within Windows NT.

2. For Intel systems: Using either My Computer, Windows NT Explorer, or a command prompt, copy the following files to the diskette: NTLDR, BOOT.INI, NTDETECT.COM, BOOTSECT.DOS, and NTBOOTDD.SYS (if required).

3. For RISC systems: Copy the following files to the newly formatted disk: OSLOADER.EXE, HAL.DLL, and *.PAL (for Alpha systems only).

   Note that with RISC systems, a few more steps are required. To boot from a diskette, you have to add an alternate boot selection in your system firmware. Refer to your system's documentation for information on how to add a boot selection.

Boot Errors

Many errors can occur during the booting of a Windows NT system. Basically, two distinct areas can cause problems:

- The computer itself (hardware failures, for example)

- The operating system

The options available for BOOT.INI can help isolate the specific problem. With a standard BOOT.INI, you might not be able to determine where the error is occurring. By making some changes, you can increase the chance of finding the source of the error.

Within BOOT.INI, you can add a series of options to entries for troubleshooting and debugging purposes. You can use the following options:

◆ **/SOS.** This option will display kernel and driver names during system startup. If you suspect that a driver is missing or corrupted, append the /SOS switch to the BOOT.INI line that loads Windows NT.

◆ **/MAXMEM.** This option enables you to specify the quantity of memory Windows NT will use. If you suspect a problem with a faulty memory chip, for instance, this option will enable you to boot your system using less than the total quantity of available RAM. You should never specify a value less than 12MBbecause Windows NT Workstation requires at least 12MB for normal operation, whereas NT Server requires 16MB.

◆ **/BASEVIDEO.** This option forces Windows NT to use the standard VGA display driver. If your display no longer appears correctly or if a driver upgrade has made your display unreadable, you can add this option to BOOT.INI.

You exercise these options by appending the appropriate switch to a line in BOOT.INI. For instance, if you were to add the /SOS switch to your BOOT.INI, the file would appear as shown in the following listing:

```
[boot loader]
timeout=30
default=multi(0)disk(0)rdisk(0)partition(1)\WINNT40
 [operating systems]
multi(0)disk(0)rdisk(0)partition(1)\WINNT40="Windows NT
➥Server Version 4.00 (with SOS)"  /sos
multi(0)disk(0)rdisk(0)partition(1)\WINNT40="Windows NT
➥Server Version 4.00 [VGA mode]" /basevideo /sos
```

Correcting Boot Problems

Many problems can prevent a Windows NT system from booting. These problems range from hardware failures to software problems. To a large extent, however, you can overcome these problems. As with any other operating system, it is essential to have known good backups and other information necessary to recover your system. With Windows NT, having an up-to-date recovery disk can be an invaluable asset when your NT system no longer boots. As mentioned previously, make recovery disks and keep these disks up to date. The following sections cover some possible processes that can be helpful in troubleshooting boot problems. The sections include

◆ Using the last known good

◆ Using the boot diskette

◆ Using the emergency repair process

Using the Last Known Good

The Last Known Good option is available when you start your Windows NT system. Basically, the last known good option enables you to boot your system using the Registry settings that were in effect the last time you successfully booted your system and logged on. If your system configuration is changed and you are no longer able to boot your computer, this option reverts your configuration to the settings that were in effect the last time you successfully booted your computer. To use the last known good option, restart your system and when prompted, press the space bar for the last known good option.

Using the Boot Diskette

You can create a boot diskette for your Windows NT system as discussed earlier in this chapter. Using a boot diskette is handy under many of the following circumstances:

◆ Your master boot record or your partition boot sector is damaged or corrupted.

◆ The disk where Windows NT is installed is damaged or corrupt, and the boot partition is on another disk.

◆ You are adding or removing hard disks from your system and may need a boot disk in order to boot the system in case of problems.

Using the Emergency Repair Process

You can use the emergency repair process to recover a previously bootable Windows NT system. See Chapter 11 for more information on the emergency repair process.

CONFIGURATION PROBLEMS

Choose the appropriate course of action to take to resolve configuration errors. Tasks include backing up and restoring the Registry and editing the Registry.

Many configuration problems can occur, and they are often related to services, device drivers, or startup control data. This information is stored in the Registry under the HKEY_LOCAL_MACHINE key. The following sections offer a review of the various tools and procedures you will use in resolving configuration problems using the Registry.

◆ Registry overview

◆ Editing the Registry

◆ Using NTBackup to back up and restore the Registry

Registry Overview

The Registry stores most of the configuration information for Windows NT. The Registry is organized as a series of keys, subkeys, and values. A file system is similar in organization; a file is stored with a file name made up of a drive letter, a directory, and a file name (that is, C:\USERS\MYFILE.TXT), and the file can contain data. In much the same way, the Registry stores information as a key, subkey, and value (that is, HKEY_LOCAL_MACHINE\MySubkey\MyValue).

Several subkeys within the Registry store configuration information. Generally, information related to system configuration is stored in HKEY_LOCAL_MACHINE. This subkey contains configuration information relating to your system's hardware, installed software, and all the installed services on your computer.

Editing the Registry

Many of your configuration problems can only be resolved by editing the Registry directly. You can edit the information stored in the Registry using standard tools included with Windows NT. Exercise extreme caution when editing the Registry. Making a backup of the Registry prior to editing any values is a prudent idea. (The procedure for backing up the Registry is discussed later in this section.)

Using REGEDT32

You can edit the Registry using REGEDT32, a tool provided with Windows NT. This tool provides a graphical interface to examine and modify Registry information on either local or remote computers. All the information in the Registry can be edited using this tool. Much of the key information, however, can also be changed using standard administrative tools such as Control Panel. Using standard tools to modify the Registry is preferable because this reduces the likelihood of accidental changes or deletions.

Values

Within the Registry, information is stored as a series of values. An analogy to the Registry is a standard file system. Whereas a file is referenced as a drive letter, directory name, and file name (that is, C:\USERS\DEFAULT\TEXT.TXT), Registry information is referenced as a Registry key, subkey, and value (that is, `HKEY_LOCAL_MACHINE\SYSTEM\Setup\Setup Type`). Files that contain data, such as text and Registry values, also contain data of specific value types.

Value Types

Each value in the Registry has data contained as a specific value type. Each value type differs in the type of data it can contain. The value types used in Windows NT are as follows:

◆ **REG_BINARY.** Binary information, entered either as a sequence of binary digits or hexadecimal digits.

◆ **REG_SZ.** A string value (human-readable text).

◆ **REG_EXPAND_SZ.** A string value that also contains a variable, such as `%SystemRoot%`.

◆ **REG_DWORD.** A four-byte hexadecimal value.

◆ **REG_MULTI_SZ.** A large string value (multiple lines of text, such as a paragraph).

Adding a Value

You can add values at any point in the Registry by selecting the desired key and selecting Edit/Add Value from the REGEDT32 menu. You are then asked for the name of the new value, its data type, and the data itself (see Figure 12.1).

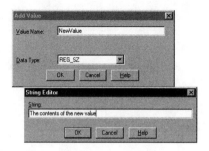

FIGURE 12.1

When adding a value to the Registry, you are asked for the name, the type, and the data for the value.

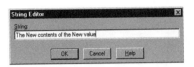

FIGURE 12.2
Values within the Registry can be edited and resaved.

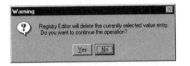

FIGURE 12.3
You are asked to confirm the deletion of the value you have selected.

FIGURE 12.4
Saving a Registry Key in REGEDT32.

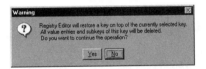

FIGURE 12.5
The Restore Registry Key warning dialog box appears before the Registry values are restored.

Editing a Value

Locating the desired Registry key and double-clicking the desired value can modify existing Registry values. Depending on the value type of the selected value, you are presented with an appropriate editor. Once the desired modifications are complete, click OK to save the new value (see Figure 12.2).

Deleting a Value

You can easily delete any Registry value from REGEDT32. The usual caveat applies: Make sure you have a backup copy before deleting Registry values. To delete a Registry value, simply select the desired value and press the Delete key. You are asked whether you really want to delete the selected value (see Figure 12.3).

Backing Up and Restoring Registry Keys

You can back up and restore Registry keys and the values they contain. The RDISK utility creates a complete copy of the Registry, and the recovery process can restore selected Registry keys. You can use other utilities to make either partial or complete backups of the Registry. In addition, it is possible to restore the entire Registry, a selected key, or a subkey.

From REGEDT32, select Registry/Save key and enter a file name (see Figure 12.4). A binary file is created with the selected Registry information.

Selecting Registry/Restore can restore this information. You are prompted to select a file to be restored. Note that because the Registry is open when Windows NT is running, you cannot restore the entire Registry from REGEDT32 because some of the keys are opened by the operating system. Once a file is selected, a warning message is displayed before the Registry values are restored (see Figure 12.5).

If you choose to proceed, all existing Registry keys and values are deleted before the restore operation begins. If you have made any changes to the Registry since the backup was completed, this information is deleted.

Using REGEDIT

REGEDIT is an alternate tool that you can use to edit the Windows NT Registry. Although it is quite similar to REGEDT32, REGEDIT provides slightly better search capabilities (see Figure 12.6). With REGEDIT, you can search for information by strings, values, keys, and subkeys, whereas REGEDT32 enables searching only on keys and subkeys.

Permissions

As with file access under Windows NT, access to the Registry is also restricted on the basis of permissions. Note that these permissions only apply when the Windows NT system root is installed on an NTFS volume. You can also use file permissions to restrict access to REGEDT32 and REGEDIT to reduce the likelihood of unauthorized access to the Registry.

Windows NT defines a series of Registry permissions that you can set for users and groups. The following list describes the permissions:

◆ **Read.** Users/groups are allowed to read the Registry key but cannot change the information.

◆ **Full control.** Users/groups have permission to read, modify, delete, or take ownership of a key.

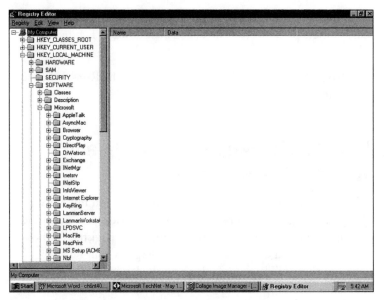

FIGURE 12.6
The REGEDIT window, viewing the contents of the Windows NT Registry.

◆ **Special access.** Enables fine-tuning of access permissions and is broken down as follows:

- **Query value.** Permission to read a value.

- **Set value.** Permission to modify a value.

- **Create subkey.** Permission to create a subkey under an existing key.

- **Enumerate subkey.** Permission to list the subkeys of a Registry key.

- **Notify.** Permission to open a key with notify access.

- **Create link.** Permission to create a symbolic link (a "shortcut") for a Registry key.

- **Delete.** Permission to delete a Registry key.

- **Write DAC.** Permission to modify permissions (Discretionary Access Control—see the NSA Orange Book for a collection of acronyms) for a key.

- **Write owner.** Capability to take ownership of a Registry key.

- **Read control.** Permission to read the security information for a key.

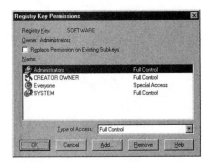

FIGURE 12.7

The Registry Key Permissions dialog box enables you to change permissions settings.

Selecting Security/Permissions from the REGEDT32 menu can change these permissions. The dialog box shown in Figure 12.7 appears.

The "special access" permissions dialog box for the Registry keys is shown in Figure 12.8.

Using NTBackup to Back Up and Restore the Registry

Any time you make any changes to the Registry, you must ensure that you have good backups. You can use NTBackup to make backup copies of the Registry and also to restore the Registry. As mentioned earlier, you can back up the local Registry but not remote registries using NTBackup. To back up the Registry, start a backup, and when presented with the Backup Information dialog box, select the Back Up Local Registry check box as shown in Figure 12.9.

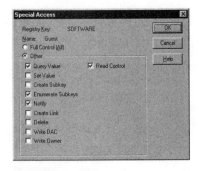

FIGURE 12.8

Special access settings are available for the Registry.

TROUBLESHOOTING PRINTER PROBLEMS

Choose the appropriate course of action to take to resolve printer problems.

The Windows NT print model attempts to provide a seamless environment where clients using a wide range of operating systems can print with ease. To provide this appearance of a seamless environment, Windows NT utilizes an intricate printing process. Due to the complexity of the print model, a number of problems can occur.

Overview of the Printing Process

Before examining the print model, it is necessary to cover the vocabulary used by Microsoft to explain the model. A somewhat baffling collection of terminology describes the print model. The following list covers, in general terms, most of the vocabulary of the print model:

◆ Print devices are the actual "hardware" devices that produce hard-copy output. Print devices can be touched; they are actual physical entities.

◆ Logical printer (or printer) is the term used to describe the software interface between the operating system and the print device. Logical printers (or printers) cannot be touched because they don't exist physically. The printer determines how output is sent to a print device (such as a parallel port or a share on a remote computer). A single printer can send output to multiple print devices, and multiple printers can send output to a single print device.

◆ A print spooler is a collection of DLLs that are responsible for receiving, distributing, and processing print jobs.

◆ A print job is either data or printer commands that are destined for a print device. Print jobs can be classified into data types, depending on what processing, if any, the spooler must perform to produce a printed copy. A simple example of processing is whether a form feed needs to be added to the end of a print job.

FIGURE 12.9
Select Back Up Local Registry in the Backup Information dialog box.

◆ A queue is a series of print jobs waiting to be printed.

◆ Rendering is synonymous with creating a print job. The graphics interface device (GDI) calls the printer driver and creates a print job in the appropriate data type. For instance, consider an MS Write file destined for a PostScript printer. The rendering process creates a PostScript print job that is sent to the print device.

◆ Job types refer to the content of the print job. Examples of job types are EMF (enhanced metafile—a print device independent data type), RAW (a job that needs no processing by the spooler), and RAW—FF appended (a job that needs a form feed added by the spooler).

These terms describe the print model of Windows NT. A typical example of the print model in action is as follows: A client computer wants to send a print job to a print device connected to a Windows NT Server. The sequence of events that takes place appears in the following list:

1. The application (MS Word, for example) makes a series of GDI calls. The GDI uses the printer driver to perform rendering of the print job.

2. The print job is sent to the print spooler on the workstation that generated the print job.

3. The print job is sent via a remote print provider that connects the workstation to the remote print device.

4. The print spooler on the NT system receives the print job and performs whatever processing is required (if any).

5. Finally, the print job is sent to the actual print device, and if everything is in working order, a paper copy is generated.

To fully understand the print process, you must also review the following two topics:

◆ Files involved in printing

◆ Directories

Files Involved in Printing

A series of files are involved in the printing process. Although client computers using operating systems other than Windows NT use different files, the following list shows the major files used under Windows NT:

- ◆ The print spooler uses WINSPOOL.DRV, SPOOLSS.EXE, and SPOOLSS.DLL.

- ◆ Local print providers (used for printers connected to a local port, such as LPT1 or COM1) use LOCALSPL.DLL.

- ◆ Remote print providers (used for printers that are not connected to a local port—such as a printer equipped with a network interface card) use WIN32SP.DLL for NT print servers. NetWare print servers use NWPROVAU.DLL instead.

- ◆ Print monitors (used to send jobs from the spooler to the print device) can use one of a series of files, depending on how the printer is connected. For local printers, the print monitor uses LOCALMON.DLL. For network-connected printers, the print monitor uses a DLL specific to the network connection (for example, HPMON.DLL or LPRMON.DLL).

Directories

By default, most of the files involved in printing are stored in the %SYSTEMROOT%\SYSTEM32 directory. One notable exception is the spooler's workspace that can be placed on any given drive or directory. However, by default, it is located in %SYSTEMROOT%\SYSTEM32\SPOOL\PRINTERS.
Also note that users require change permissions on the spool area.

Basic Printer Troubleshooting

Printer troubleshooting procedures revolve around determining which part of the printer model failed and finding a solution to the underlying problem. Some basic steps are given in the following list:

- ◆ Ensure that the print device is properly connected and online and has paper.

◆ Print as an administrator. If you are able to print when logged on as an administrator, but not when logged on as a user, the problem lies with permissions.

◆ Make sure that all the required files are present on the print server.

◆ For network-connected printers, ensure that the network cabling is connected properly.

Within the NT print model, problems can occur at any of the stages discussed in this list. Seven processes are involved in a network print job:

1. A print share is created on the print server. Usually, this does not cause any problems.

2. A client system connects to the print share. Problems in this area are not likely to be limited to printing and can indicate a failure of a networking component or a client software configuration problem.

3. The client creates a print job. Problems in this part of the print process are typically related to a specific application. If another application works fine, the problem is likely with the application itself.

4. The print job is sent to the print share. If problems occur at this level, they are likely related to network hardware failures or client networking software problems.

5. The server receives the print job. The print job is spooled, or kept in a queue, and the print server performs any processing that may be required. At this point, errors are typically related to a lack of disk space for the print spooler or an incorrect printer definition.

6. The print server sends the print jobs to the appropriate print device, either via a local port or a network connection. Problems at this part of the process could be related to hardware problems, such as a failed parallel port.

7. The print device generates paper output. At this point in the print process, the printer itself may be malfunctioning or could be configured incorrectly.

The basic rule of thumb for troubleshooting print problems is to walk through the print model. Once you discover the likely point of failure, change the configuration of that process and verify whether the problem has been solved.

Troubleshooting Network Printers

Unlike locally connected printers, network printers are not necessarily connected directly to a computer. This adds an extra layer to the printing process and an extra dimension to troubleshooting.

Two common areas that cause problems with printers are

◆ Permissions

◆ Drivers

If improper permissions are set for the printers, your users will encounter a number of problems. Review the following section on permissions to ensure that you fully understand how each is used and set up.

Permissions

As with any other resource on a Windows NT network, you can configure printers with permissions to restrict access. You can use the following permissions to control access to print devices under Windows NT:

◆ **Full control.** Enables full access and administrative control.

◆ **Manage documents.** Enables a user or group to change the status of any print job.

◆ **Print.** Permits a user to send print jobs to a print device and to pause, resume, or delete any of her own jobs.

◆ **No Access.** Denies all access to a print device.

The dialog box shown in Figure 12.10 shows how you can assign permissions to a printer.

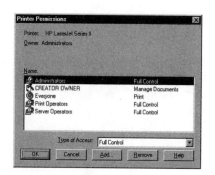

FIGURE 12.10
The Printer permissions dialog box enables you to assign permissions to a printer.

When a printer is created under Windows NT, the following permissions are assigned:

◆ Administrator, Server Operator, and Print Operator groups are granted Full Control.

◆ The Creator Owner group is granted Manage Documents permissions.

◆ All users are granted Print permissions.

You can add separator pages to any printer. One separator page is generated between each print job. These pages are generally used to identify the user who created the print job, the date and time the print job was created, and so forth. These files are stored in %SYSTEMROOT%\SYSTEM32 by default, and three separator page files are provided with Windows NT. You can adapt the separator page files included with NT for your specific requirements.

You can perform basic print administration functions such as pausing printers and deleting print jobs using Print Manager.

Drivers

If you have an invalid or corrupt driver, you will encounter numerous problems with your printers. Corrupt printer drivers are caused by your system modifying or possibly removing a driver file. Printer drivers are used as part of the rendering process. The GDI calls print drivers to perform the rendering of a print job. All print drivers under Windows NT are implemented as Dynamic Link Libraries (.DLLs).

As a part of the Windows NT print model, clients using Windows NT do not need print drivers installed manually. Instead, the driver is automatically downloaded to the client workstation as required. This process does not work correctly if the client is running Windows NT 4 and the print server is running an earlier version of Windows NT.

The LPD Server

If you improperly configure the TCP/IP print service, you can encounter numerous problems with network printing. TCP/IP print service is usually referred to as LPD (UNIX-speak for Line Printer

Daemon). LPD accepts and processes print jobs from Line Printer Remote (LPR) clients. Most UNIX systems provide LPR clients. The LPR protocol is a part of the TCP/IP protocol suite and is defined in RFC1179. Most implementations of LPR differ slightly from one another, and features are not necessarily consistent across different versions.

Within Windows NT, an LPR command-line utility is available, as is an LPR print monitor. Both of these programs perform as clients and send print jobs to an LPD service running on another computer. Windows NT also includes an LPD service, the Microsoft TCP/IP Print service that can accept print jobs from LPR clients.

The LPR command is shown here, and the options are explained immediately following:

```
Usage: lpr -S server -P printer [-C class] [-J job]
➥[-o option] [-x] [-d] filename
```

◆ **-S.** The server name or IP address of the computer providing lpd service.

◆ **-P.** The printer name on the host that you want to use.

◆ **-C.** Job class, appears on the separator page.

◆ **-J.** Job name, also appears on the separator page.

◆ **-o.** Type of file, the default is a text file, use -o l for binary (formatted).

◆ **-x.** Needed for compatibility with SunOS 4.1.x and prior versions.

◆ **-d.** Send data file first.

The LPR print monitor fits into the Windows NT print model and enables you to access an LPR printer through the standard Windows NT printing process. To install an LPR port monitor, select the Add Port option from the Add Printer application and enter the required information, as shown in Figure 12.11.

You can add the TCP/IP print service to a Windows NT Server, and it acts as an LPD service. This service enables Windows NT to provide print services to any LPR client. To install this service, perform the tasks outlined in Step by Step 12.2.

Prerequisites For LPR printing to be available, you must create an LPR printer through Print Manager. For Windows NT Server to act as an LPD server, you must install TCP/IP printing.

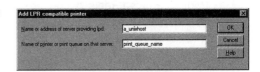

FIGURE 12.11
To install an LPR port monitor, select the Add Port option from the Add Printer application and enter the required information.

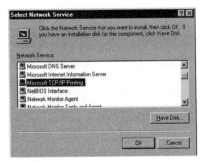

FIGURE 12.12
Adding the TCP/IP printing service.

STEP BY STEP

12.2 Installing TCP/IP Print Service

1. Select the Control Panel | Network application.

2. In the Network dialog box, select the Microsoft TCP/IP printing option (see Figure 12.12).

3. Click the OK button and then close the Network dialog box.

REVIEW BREAK

Printing Problems

The main problems that may occur with printing are usually based on permission problems or an invalid or corrupt printer driver. If a problem does occur, print from various users. If certain user are able to access the printer, verify the permissions. If none of the users can access the printer, check or replace the printer driver.

CASE STUDY: CREATING BACKUPS

ESSENCE OF THE CASE

Here are the essential elements in this case:

- Modifications to the Registry must be done manually using the Registry editor.

- Prior to making Registry changes, the administrator must back up the Registry as well as all of the data.

- The installation instructions for the new software must be followed closely.

Scenario

Protech Investments has a Windows NT network environment. They recently purchased some new custom-developed software. The installation instructions for the new software require that some Registry changes be made manually. The administrator must make these changes using the Registry editor. Before making any modifications, however, the administrator must back up the system to have a recovery option available. Protech Investments uses the NTBackup utility to run backups of its system on a regular schedule. The administrator must use this utility to create Registry backups as well as data backups prior to making any modifications.

CASE STUDY: CREATING BACKUPS

ANALYSIS

The administrator used the Registry editor REGEDT32 to back up any keys that would be modified based on the installation instructions for the new software product. Once the Registry was backed up, the administrator ran a system backup for emergency retrieval if anything went wrong with the Registry changes. The administrator then used REGEDT32 to modify and add the new values into the Registry. After the Registry changes were made, the system was restarted to verify that the new settings were valid. All the settings were verified, and the installation of the new software was completed without any problems. Protech Investments was happy with the results. If anything had gone wrong, however, the company was fully prepared to restore the Registry to its original settings with the Registry backups.

CHAPTER SUMMARY

KEY TERMS
- HCL (Hardware Compatibility List)
- NTHQ (NT Hardware Qualifier)

Troubleshooting a Windows NT system requires a strong understanding of the processes and tools available to you. To be an effective troubleshooter, first and foremost you must have experience. Take time to review each of the main processes listed in this chapter:

◆ The types of installation problems.

- Hard disk problems.

- Unsupported CD-ROMS.

- Network adapter problems and conflicts.

- Naming problems: Each computer must be uniquely named, following the NetBIOS naming conventions.

◆ Startup errors.

- Missing files that are involved in the boot process—NTLDR, NTDETECT.COM, BOOT.INI, and NTOSKRNL.EXE.

- Modifying the BOOT.INI for options.

- Creating an NT boot disk.

- Last Known Good option.

◆ Configuration problems.

- Use the Registry for configuration and troubleshooting.

- Always back up the Registry prior to editing the contents.

- Back up and restore the Registry.

◆ Troubleshooting printers.

- Understand and review the overview of the printing process.

- Understand the files involved in the printing process.

- Always verify the printer is on and online as a first step in troubleshooting a printer.

The troubleshooting of any process must be completed by an individual who is competent in the installation and an overview of the process. This competence can only be gained through experience. In preparing for this section of your exam, you should review the chapters that correspond to each of the troubleshooting areas.

APPLY YOUR LEARNING

This section allows you to assess how well you understand the material in the chapter. Review and exam questions test your knowledge of the tasks and concepts specified in the objectives. The exercises provide you with opportunities to engage in the sorts of tasks that compose the skill sets the objectives reflect.

For more review and exam questions, see the Top Score test engine on the CD-ROM that came with this book.

Exercises

The following exercises provide you with an opportunity to apply what you've learned in this chapter.

12.1 Boot File Errors

In this exercise, you will get a chance to see some of the errors that can occur when you start NT. If your boot or system partition is an NTFS partition, it is critical that you create the boot floppy. Make sure that you can still boot to your previous operating system.

Time Estimate: 25 minutes

Creating a Boot Floppy: In this first step, you will create a boot floppy that will enable you to start the operating system. This will enable you to recover from the errors you will create.

1. Format a 1.44MB floppy disk under NT. (If your A: is a 5.25-inch, format a 1.2MB floppy.) In NT Explorer, right-click drive A: and choose format from the context menu.

2. Copy the files required for booting your platform to the floppy. You can find the following files in the root directory of the startup drive:

Intel Platform

NTLDR

NTBOOTDD.SYS (only appears on systems that require it)

BOOT.INI

NTDETECT.COM

RISC Platform

OSLOADER.EXE

HAL.DLL

*.PAL (only for Alpha machines)

3. With the floppy in the A: drive, shut down and restart the system to verify that the boot disk works.

Important note: Do not proceed if the floppy does not work.

Missing Loader File: In this step, you will rename the main operating system startup file. This lets you see the sort of errors that can occur on a corrupted disk.

1. In the root of the system partition, locate the file NTLDR (for Intel) or OSLOADER.EXE (for RISC).

2. Rename the file so the system will not find it when it tries to start (NTLDR.GOOD, for example).

3. Remove the floppy if it is in the drive. Shut down and restart the system.

4. You should get an error saying the system could not find NTLDR or OSLOADER.EXE (as appropriate).

5. Restart the computer with the boot floppy in drive A:.

APPLY YOUR LEARNING

6. When the operating system restarts, rename NTLDR or OSLOADER.EXE back to the original name.

7. Restart the system without the floppy to ensure it is functioning.

Missing NTDETECT.COM (Intel Only).
Unfortunately, this exercise only works on Intel platforms. Rename the NTDETECT.COM to see the error that occurs when this file is missing.

1. In the root of the system partition, locate the file NTDETECT.COM.

2. Rename the file so the system won't find it when it tries to start (NTDETECT.GOOD, for example).

3. Remove the floppy if it is in the drive. Shut down and restart the system.

4. You should get an error saying NTDETECT V1.0 Checking Hardware…, NTDETECT failed.

5. Restart the computer with the boot floppy in drive A:.

6. When the operating system restarts, rename NTDETECT.COM back to the original name.

7. Restart the system without the floppy to ensure it is functioning.

12.2 Saving and Restoring Registry Keys

In this exercise, you will back up a Registry key and then restore it. This exercise will work with non-critical areas of the Registry.

Time Estimate: 15 minutes

1. Start the Registry Editor (Start | Run REGEDT32).

2. Open the HKEY_CURRENT_USER window, and then open the Control Panel key.

3. Click Desktop in the Control Panel key.

4. If you don't have a Wallpaper entry, minimize enough windows to see the desktop and add a wallpaper. Return to the Registry Editor and verify the change is reflected.

5. Choose Registry | Save Key. Enter the name **DESKTOP.REG**, and click Save.

6. Switch to the HKEY_USERS window in the Registry Editor.

7. Open the .DEFAULT key and then the Control Panel key under that.

8. Click Desktop under Control Panel.

9. Choose Registry | Save Key and enter **OLDDESKTOP.REG** as the file name. Click Save.

10. Choose Registry | Restore from the menu and select DESKTOP.REG as the file name.

11. You will receive a warning. Click Yes after you have read it.

12. Log off. The wallpaper you had should now be shown in the logon screen.

13. Log on and open the Registry Editor.

14. Switch to the HKEY_USERS window in the Registry Editor.

15. Open the .DEFAULT key and then the Control Panel key under that.

APPLY YOUR LEARNING

16. Choose Registry | Restore from the menu and select OLDDESKTOP.REG as the file name. This will restore the original configuration.

12.3 Printer Errors

In this last exercise, you will see the errors that can occur due to errors in printer setup and the files that are used for printing.

Time Estimate: 15 minutes

1. From the Start button, choose Settings | Control Panel. Double-click the Services icon.

2. Locate the Spooler service and stop it.

3. In the Windows NT directory under SYSTEM32, locate the SPOOLSS.DLL and rename it.

4. Restart the system. You will receive the Service Control Manager message, and the system will appear to hang for a few minutes.

5. Use Event Viewer to locate and view the effect.

6. Rename the file back to the original name. Then, attempt to start the Spooler service manually.

7. In the Windows NT directory, open the SYSTEM32\SPOOL directory. This is the main directory for printer files.

8. Open the PRTPROCS directory. Under this directory, you will see a W32xxx directory (where xxx is the platform you are running on). Open this directory.

9. Rename the WINPRINT.DLL. Stop and start the Spooler service.

10. Attempt to print. You should get an error saying no printers exist. Name the file back to WINPRINT.DLL.

11. Can you print? No, the WINPRINT.DLL is loaded in memory when the Spooler service starts.

12. Stop and restart the Spooler service and make sure you can print again.

Review Questions

1. If you had to install Windows NT from a non-supported CD-ROM drive, what methods would be suitable?

2. List the Windows NT boot process files used on a RISC computer.

3. What procedures enable you to boot a Windows NT system after installing a new video driver that resulted in a blue screen error message on startup?

4. List the ways in which you can back up the Registry.

5. If a user cannot print to a network printer connected as a share, what could be the cause?

6. What files are required for system startup on an Intel platform?

7. What BOOT.INI switch can you add to set your video resolution to VGA 640×480, 16 colors?

Exam Questions

1. Which of the following files cannot be backed up using NTBackup?

   A. The local Registry

   B. A remote paging file

   C. NTLDR

   D. A Registry on a remote computer

   E. CONFIG.NT

2. Which of the following information is not stored in the Registry?

   A. User accounts and passwords

   B. Keyboard configuration

   C. Network interface card configuration

   D. The computer name

   E. None of the above

3. If a new print device is created on your system, which of the following statements is true?

   A. Administrators will be granted Full Control permissions by default.

   B. No users will be able to send print jobs unless they are granted permissions.

   C. Any user will be able to delete print jobs submitted by other users.

   D. Administrators will not be able to pause the printer.

   E. Users can pause the printer.

4. From REGEDT32, which of the following tasks can be completed? Choose all that apply.

   A. Backing up Registry keys

   B. Adding Registry values

   C. Modifying Registry values

   D. Restoring the entire Registry

   E. Deleting Registry keys

5. Which of the following files are required on a Windows NT boot diskette for a RISC system? Choose all that apply.

   A. BOOT.INI

   B. NTDETECT.COM

   C. HAL.DLL

   D. BOOTDD.SYS

   E. OSLOADER.EXE

6. Which of the following computer names cannot be used for a Windows NT system?

   A. MYCOMPUTER

   B. [MYCOMPUTER]

   C. MY:COMPUTER

   D. MYCOMPUTER+VCR

   E. MyComputer

7. Which of the following statements are incorrect?

    A. The Last Known Good set is updated every time a Windows NT system boots.

    B. The Last Known Good set can be used to boot a Windows NT system using a previously working configuration.

    C. The Last Known Good set is only updated when you successfully log on to a Windows NT system.

    D. The Last Known Good set is automatically copied onto a recovery disk by RDISK.

    E. All of the above.

8. On a RISC system, which of the following components is responsible for determining what hardware is installed?

    A. NTDETECT

    B. NTLDR

    C. OSLOADER.EXE

    D. BOOT.INI

    E. None of the above

9. If you are able to print a document when you are logged on as DaveA but are unable to print a document when you are logged on as DonnaB, which of the following is likely the cause?

    A. The print driver is not installed on the workstation.

    B. DonnaB does not have sufficient permissions on the printer.

    C. The printer has been deleted.

    D. The application is not configured correctly for the printer.

    E. The print spooler is not started.

10. When installing a backup domain controller named PARIS02 on the MYCORP domain, which of the following situations will prevent installation from succeeding?

    A. The PDC for the MYCORP domain is not available.

    B. Another BDC named PARIS02 already exists in the domain.

    C. There are no other BDCs in the domain.

    D. A Windows NT workstation named PARIS02 already exists in the domain.

    E. All of the above.

11. If you want to make a complete backup of the Registry on a remote computer, which of the following procedures can you use?

    A. Using NTBackup, select the appropriate computer and check the Backup Registry option.

    B. From REGEDT32, connect to the computer and save each of the Registry keys to separate files.

    C. Connect the ADMIN$ share and copy the CONFIG directory.

    D. This cannot be done.

12. Your computer has a CD-ROM drive that is not supported by Windows NT. Which of the following procedures can you use to install Windows NT?

   A. Install Windows NT from another computer elsewhere on the network.

   B. Use the /T:<path> option with WINNT to specify an alternate path for the setup files.

   C. Install Windows NT using the /OX option to create boot disks.

   D. Replace the CD-ROM drive with a supported CD-ROM drive.

   E. All of the above.

13. You have made a backup of the HKEY_LOCAL_MACHINE Registry key using REGEDT32, and you want to restore these values. Which of the following statements are correct?

   A. Any changes made to the Registry since the backup was made will be deleted before the restore process begins.

   B. Any changes made to the Registry since the backup was made will not be deleted, and the backed-up information will only overwrite existing values.

   C. Any changes made to the Registry since the backup was made will not be deleted, and the restore process will prompt you if any information will be lost.

   D. Any changes to the Registry since the last backup was made will be deleted, and the restore process will warn you before the restore process begins.

   E. None of the above.

14. A client is unable to send a print job to a remote printer. Other clients can send print jobs without any difficulty. The client is able to send a print job to the printer using Notepad. Which of the following is the likely cause of the problem?

   A. The user does not have adequate permissions to send jobs to the print device.

   B. The printer is disconnected from the network.

   C. The spooler does not have enough disk space to spool print jobs.

   D. The client's application is not configured correctly.

   E. The printer has been paused.

Answers to Review Questions

1. Copying the required files from the CD-ROM to your hard drive or running WINNT /B with an appropriate path name. See the section "Unsupported CD-ROMs."

2. The files used for the boot process on a RISC system are OSLOADER.EXE and NTOSKRNL.EXE See "The RISC Boot Process."

APPLY YOUR LEARNING

3. Booting your NT system from an NT boot disk and selecting the BASEVIDEO option, using the last known good option on startup, or booting the system using the recovery disk. See "Correcting Boot Problems."

4. REGEDT32 from a remote computer, REGEDT32 from the local computer, or RDISK. See "Backing Up and Restoring Registry Keys" and "Using NTBackup to Back Up and Restore the Registry."

5. The printer is not turned on, the printer is out of paper, or the user does not have sufficient permissions to use the printer. See "Basic Printer Troubleshooting."

6. The files for Intel startup are NTLDR, NTBOOTDD.SYS, BOOT.INI, NTDE-TECT.COM and the system files in the WINNT\SYSTEM32 directory. See "The Intel Boot Process."

7. You would add the /BASEVIDEO switch. This has already been added to the entry that is marked [VGA Only]. See "Boot Errors."

Answers to Exam Questions

1. **B. D.** The paging file and remote registries cannot be backed up using the NTBackup utility. See the section "Using NTBackup to Back Up and Restore the Registry" earlier in this chapter.

2. **E.** All of the Windows NT configuration and user account information is located in the Registry. See the section "Registry Overview" in this chapter.

3. **A.** When a printer is created under Windows NT, Administrators and Print Operators are granted full control by default. See the section "Troubleshooting Network Printers."

4. **A. B. C. E.** REGEDT32 cannot restore the entire Registry; it can only restore select keys. See the section "Editing the Registry" in this chapter.

5. **C. E.** HAL.DLL and OSLOADER.EXE are the only files required on the RISC-based NT boot disk. See the section "Creating a Boot Diskette" in this chapter.

6. **B. C. D.** A computer name must follow the NetBIOS naming conventions. See the section "Naming Problems" in this chapter.

7. **A. D.** See the section "Correcting Boot Problems" in this chapter.

8. **E.** A RISC-based system does not use a Windows NT boot file to determine the hardware components; it is done by the firmware. See the section "The RISC Boot Process."

9. **B.** The user does not have sufficient privileges to access the printer. See the section "Troubleshooting Network Printers" in this chapter.

10. **A. B. D.** When you install a computer in a Windows NT domain, the PDC must be available and the name must be unique on the network. See the section "Naming Problems" in this chapter.

11. **B.** To back up a remote Registry, you must back up each individual key using the REGEDT32 utility. See the section "Editing the Registry" in this chapter.

12. **A. B. D.** If the CD-ROM is not supported, you must either place the files elsewhere for the installation or replace the CD-ROM. See the section "Unsupported CD-ROMs" in this chapter.

13. **A. D.** All modified Registry entries will be deleted and the backup copy will remain. See the section "Using NTBackup to Back Up and Restore the Registry" in this chapter.

14. **D.** The logical solution is that the client's application is not configured to use that printer. See the section "Basic Printer Troubleshooting" in this chapter.

This chapter helps you to prepare for the Microsoft exam by covering the following objectives within the "Troubleshooting" category:

Choose the appropriate course of action to take to resolve RAS problems.

▶ Troubleshooting Remote Access Service requires an in-depth knowledge of the functionality of RAS and the various configuration options available. This objective deals with solving any potential problems in an orderly fashion.

Choose the appropriate course of action to take to resolve connectivity problems.

▶ This objective covers all additional connectivity utilities and tools included in Windows NT and ensures that you understand the processes involved. With this knowledge, you must then be able to resolve any connectivity problem to meet the objective.

CHAPTER 13

Troubleshooting RAS and Connectivity Problems

Being an effective troubleshooter requires hands-on experience with a wide variety of problems. In reading through this chapter, you should use a few systems to build your hands-on experience. Try out the processes that this chapter introduces and ensure that you understand each of the procedures listed in the chapter.

Connectivity in a Windows NT network is the cornerstone of your entire network structure. In previous chapters, you looked at the installation, configuration, and connectivity options available to you. This chapter focuses on common troubleshooting issues relating to the connectivity of your systems.

The Remote Access Service (RAS) is the starting point, and is a very common area for trouble in a Windows NT system. The chapter then discusses the networking services and protocols within Windows NT. Follow through this chapter and then complete the questions and exercises at the end to obtain a thorough understanding of the troubleshooting of the processes involved in Windows NT connectivity.

This chapter is split into two main sections:

◆ Remote Access Service

◆ Connectivity issues

REMOTE ACCESS SERVICE

Choose the appropriate course of action to take to resolve RAS problems.

One of the many challenges that face network administrators today is that of the requirement for users to dial in to the network. The prevalence of laptops and telecommuters makes this process necessary. Windows NT comes with the dial-in service known as Remote Access Service (RAS). This section looks at RAS and discusses some of the problems that you might encounter as you attempt to implement Dial-Up Networking.

Overview of RAS

Essentially, RAS enables users to connect to your network and work as if their systems are physically connected to it. RAS has two main components:

◆ The server (RAS)

◆ The client (Dial-Up Networking)

The RAS server, which can be Windows NT Server, Workstation, or Windows 95 (either through Service Pack 1 or OEM Service Release 2), enables users to connect to the network from a remote location. The Microsoft RAS server always uses the PPP (Point-to-Point Protocol) when users are dialing in to the network.

PPP VERSUS SLIP

When clients connect to a server using a modem, they must do so through something other than the frames that usually traverse a network. Some other transport method is needed. In the case of dial-up servers (or terminal servers), there are two popular line protocols. Serial Line Internet Protocol, or SLIP, is used frequently in UNIX implementations. SLIP is the older of the two line protocols and is geared directly for TCP/IP communications. Windows NT can use the services of a SLIP server. However, it does not provide a SLIP server. Because SLIP requires a static Internet Protocol (IP) address and does not provide a facility for logging on securely (passwords are sent as clear text), Microsoft's RAS server uses PPP.

PPP was developed as a replacement for SLIP and provides several different advantages over the earlier protocol. PPP can automatically provide the client computer with an IP address and other configuration. It provides a secure logon and can transport protocols other than TCP/IP (such as AppleTalk, IPX, and NetBEUI).

There are two important extensions to PPP: the Multilink Protocol (MP) and Point-to-Point Tunneling Protocol (PPTP). Windows NT supports both of these protocols.

Multilink Protocol enables a client station to connect to a remote server using more than one physical connection. This capability provides better throughput over standard modems. You will, however, need multiple phone lines and modems to enable this protocol. Using Multilink Protocol can be an easy interim solution if you need to connect to offices temporarily and do not have the time or budget to set up a leased line or other similar connection.

PPTP facilitates secure connections across the Internet. Using PPTP, users can connect to any Internet service provider (ISP) and to the office network. During the session initialization, the client and server negotiate a 40-bit session key. This key is then used to encrypt all packets that will be sent back and forth over the Internet. The packets will be encapsulated into PPP packets as the data.

In addition to connecting to a Microsoft RAS server, Windows Dial-Up Networking can connect with other forms of RAS (other dial-in servers such as UNIX terminal servers, for example) using either SLIP or PPP. All that is required is a communications device.

Modems

No remote access connection would be possible without the installation and configuration of a modem. Modems have been around for years and provide a cheap and relatively reliable method of communications over the Public Switched Telephone Network (PSTN.) Installing a modem in a computer is a straightforward process. This section covers the configuring and testing of modems and explains what can go wrong with them.

There are two main types of modems:

◆ Internal

◆ External

Internal modems are slightly cheaper, but require you to open the computer to install them and require a free interrupt (IRQ). If you elect to go with an external modem, you should check that you have a communications (COM) port available. The upcoming subsections cover ports, then modem installation and configuration, and then dialing properties (and the troubleshooting issues that might come up for each).

Ports

Whether you have an internal or external modem, you will need to install the modem as a communications port. Usually this installation is no problem. However, in some cases (notable with internal modems, but also with external modems), you will need to change the settings for the port. If you cannot talk to the modem, you should also check the port settings. Step by Step 13.1 walks you through the process of verifying the port settings of a modem.

STEP BY STEP

13.1 Verifying the Port Settings

1. Open the Control Panel (Start, Settings, Control Panel).

2. Double-click the Ports icon. This brings up the Ports dialog box (see Figure 13.1).

3. Select the port for which you want to check the settings and click Settings. Another dialog box appears, showing you the settings for the port (see Figure 13.2).

   Again, if you cannot talk to the modem, check the port settings.

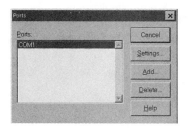

FIGURE 13.1
You configure the port for your modem through the Ports dialog box.

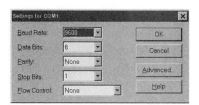

FIGURE 13.2
This dialog box displays the settings for COM1.

Five settings are available. These are general settings, however, and affect only applications that don't set these parameters. The following list provides a brief description of the parameters:

◆ **Baud Rate.** This is the rate at which the data will flow. Serial communications moves your data one bit at a time. In addition, for every byte that is sent, there are (normally) four bits of overhead. Therefore, to find the transfer rate in bytes, divide this number by 12.

◆ **Data Bits.** Not all systems use eight bits to store one character. Some systems use only seven. This setting enables the computer to adjust the number of bits used in the transfer.

◆ **Parity.** Parity is used to verify that information that is being transferred is getting across the line successfully. The parity can be Even, Odd, Mark, or Space, or you can choose No Parity (the most commonly used setting).

◆ **Stop Bits.** In some systems, these are used to mark the end of the transmission.

◆ **Flow Control.** You can set this option to Xon/Xoff, Hardware, or None. Flow control, as the name implies, is used to control the movement of the data between the modem and your computer. Hardware flow control uses Request to Send (RTS) and Clear to Send (CTS). Through the RTS wire in the cable, the system sends a signal telling the modem that it wants to send data. When the modem finishes transmitting what is in its

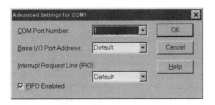

FIGURE 13.3
The advanced settings for COM1.

WARNING
Take Care When Making Changes in the Advanced Dialog Box If you make changes in this dialog box, the system is no longer a standard system. You can affect many applications if you make changes here.

buffer and has space, it will signal the computer that it can send the data using the CTS wire. Xon/Xoff is a software form of Flow Control where the modem sends Xon (ASCII character 17) when it is ready for data from the computer, and Xoff (ASCII character 19) when the modem has too much data. (This type of flow control does not work well with binary transfers, as the Xon and Xoff characters can be part of a file.)

In most cases, you can ignore these settings. The application that you are using will set and reset them. If you click the Advanced button, however, you will find some settings that you need to be aware of (see Figure 13.3).

The options that you can set in the Advanced dialog box affect all applications that use the communications port. The following list provides an overview of the options that you can set:

◆ **COM Port Number.** Here you select the port that you want to configure.

◆ **Base I/O Port Address.** When information is received from a hardware (physical) device, the BIOS places the information in RAM. This setting changes where in RAM the BIOS will place the information. Unless your hardware requires a different address, do not change this setting.

◆ **Interrupt Request Line (IRQ).** After the BIOS places the information in RAM, it alerts the CPU to the presence of the data. The BIOS does so by using a hardware interrupt. Interrupts are a prime source for conflicts and one of the main causes of system failures. As previously stated, unless your hardware requires you to do so, do not change this option.

◆ **FIFO Enabled.** This setting enables the on-chip buffering available in 16550 UARTs. Note that on some of the older revisions of the 16550, there were problems with random data loss when using FIFO. If you are experiencing unexplained problems, try disabling FIFO. With FIFO enabled, a slight increase in throughput can occur.

When you are attempting to troubleshoot a serial problem, you should always check that these settings are correct. Making sure that the port options are correct will enable you to communicate with the modem.

Modem Installation and Configuration

Installing a modem is simple in Windows NT. After connecting the hardware, go to the Control Panel and double-click the Modems icon.

If no modem is installed, the Modem Installer Wizard starts automatically (see Figure 13.4). This wizard guides you through the installation of the modem.

If you have already used the installer once and it could not detect the modem, you probably have one of two problems. Either the modem cannot be detected and you will have to install it manually, or the system can't see the modem, in which case you should check the port. If you need to install the modem manually, check the box "Don't detect my modem, I will select it from a list." This selection brings up a screen that enables you to select the modem (see Figure 13.5).

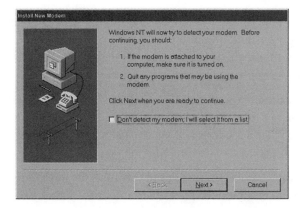

FIGURE 13.4
The Install New Modem Wizard assists you in configuring your new modem.

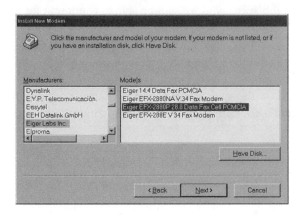

FIGURE 13.5
You can manually select your modem in the Install New Modem dialog box.

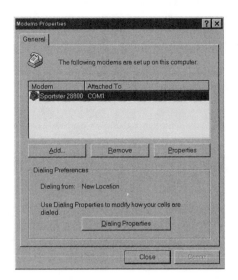

FIGURE 13.6

In this case, the Modem Properties dialog box lists one Sportster 28800 modem.

FIGURE 13.7

The General properties tab for a modem; several different options are of interest for troubleshooting.

After installing the modem, you can check modem properties by clicking the Modems icon in the Control Panel. After you click the icon, you see the Modem Properties dialog box, which lists all the available modems (see Figure 13.6).

In this dialog box, you can check and set the properties for the modems that are installed in the computer. Several different options are of interest for troubleshooting. Select Modem, Properties to bring up the General Properties tab for the modem (see Figure 13.7).

You need to check only a couple of settings on the General Properties tab. The following list provides the properties and describes what you should check for:

◆ **Port.** Displays the port on which the modem was installed. You should check this setting if the hardware has been changed, and also check the port settings if the modem is not working.

◆ **Speaker Volume.** Determines the volume of the speaker during the connection phase. This should be turned up to enable you to verify that you are getting a dial tone and that the receiver on the other end is in fact a modem.

◆ **Maximum Speed.** Sets the fastest rate at which the system will attempt to communicate with the modem. If this is set too high, some modems will not be able to respond to the system. If this is the case, try lowering the rate.

◆ **Only Connect at This Speed.** Instructs the modem that it must connect to the remote site at the same speed you set for communications with the modem. If the other site cannot support this speed, you will not be able to communicate with that site.

The other tab in the Modem Properties dialog box is the Connection tab (see Figure 13.8). The Connection tab enables you to control how the modem will connect. There are a couple of settings that you can check here when you attempt to troubleshoot modems.

The Connection tab has two sections: the Connection preferences and the Call preferences. The Connection preferences are the communications settings (which were discussed in the "Ports section" earlier in this chapter). These settings override the port settings. The three items from the Call preferences are as follows:

◆ **Wait for dial tone before dialing.** Usually, you should not select this option; however, some phone systems still do not have a dial tone. Make sure that this option is set correctly for your area.

◆ **Cancel the call if not connected within.** This option sets the maximum amount of time that it will take to establish the call. If the line conditions are poor, you might have to increase this number to allow the modem more time to establish a connection and negotiate the line speed that will be used.

◆ **Disconnect a call if idle for more than.** This option enables you to set the maximum amount of time that a call can sit idle. Windows NT 4 provides an autodial service. This provision automatically calls back a server if you have become disconnected and then attempts to use a network service. This feature reduces the amount of time a user can tie up a line and can prevent massive long distance charges.

The final thing to check when doing modem configurations and when troubleshooting is the information in the Advanced Connection dialog box (see Figure 13.9). These settings can adversely affect communications.

There are a few options that you will want to verify in the advanced modem options. The following list describes the different options and things that you should look for:

◆ **Use error control.** This option turns on or off some common settings that affect the way the system deals with the modem. The specific options are as follows:

    • **Required to connect.** This option forces the modem to establish that an error-correcting protocol (such as MNP class 5) be used before the connection is established. You should not use this setting by default. If the modem on the other end of the connection does not support the same class of error detection, the connection will fail.

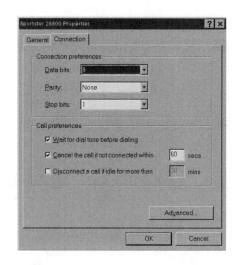

FIGURE 13.8
The Connection tab in the Modem Properties dialog box enables you to control the way that the modem will connect.

NOTE

Time Limit Users need to be made aware of the time limit. If they are required to enter information for a terminal logon, they should be informed about the time limit. Otherwise, the terminal screen will appear unexpectedly when the system tries to auto-connect.

Another item of which the user is typically not aware is that when using an ISP for email, setting the email program to check for new mail at periodic intervals will cause the system to dial the server automatically to check for mail physically, possibly using up the number of hours that the user's ISP allows.

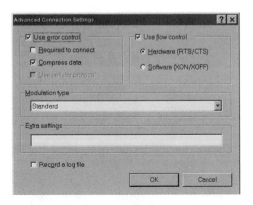

FIGURE 13.9
The settings in the Advanced Connection Settings dialog box can adversely affect communications.

NOTE

Added Security You might notice that in Figure 13.10 the phone number is not shown as the modem called it. This feature provides added security.

- **Compress data.** This option tells the modem to use data compression. Microsoft RAS automatically implements software compression between the client and workstation if both are Microsoft products. You should turn on this option only if you will be talking to a non-Microsoft server; otherwise, the modem will try and compress data that is already compressed.

- **Use cellular protocol.** This option tells the system that you will be using a cellular modem.

◆ **User flow control.** This option overrides the flow control setting for the port. Both types of flow control are available. In most cases, you should choose to use hardware flow control. Using flow control enables you to set the speed of the transmission between the computer and the modem. The choices are Xon/Xoff and hardware.

◆ **Modulation type.** This option enables users to set the type of frequency modulation for the modem to that of the phone system they are using. The modulation is either standard or Bell, and deals with the sound frequency that will be used for the send and receive channels for the communicating hosts.

◆ **Extra settings.** This option enables you to enter extra modem initialization strings that you want to send to the modem whenever a call is placed.

◆ **Record a log file.** This probably is the most important setting from the perspective of troubleshooting. This setting records a file that enables you to see the communications that take place between the modem and the computer during the connection phase of the communications. An example of the log is shown in Figure 13.10.

Dialing Properties

From the Modem Properties dialog box (refer to Figure 13.6), you can also click the Dialing Properties button. This displays a dialog box that enables you to configure the system so that it knows where you are dialing from. This information is used with Dial-Up Networking to enable the system to determine whether your call is long distance, whether it should use a calling card, how to disable the call-waiting feature, and so forth.

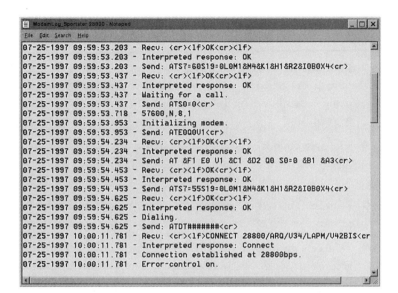

FIGURE 13.10
The modem log as shown in Notepad.

When you click the Dialing Properties button, the Dialing Properties dialog box shown in Figure 13.11 appears. You can create a single location or multiple locations.

Several different options are available, and if you do not set them correctly, the client computer might attempt to connect to a local server as a long distance call (or vice versa).

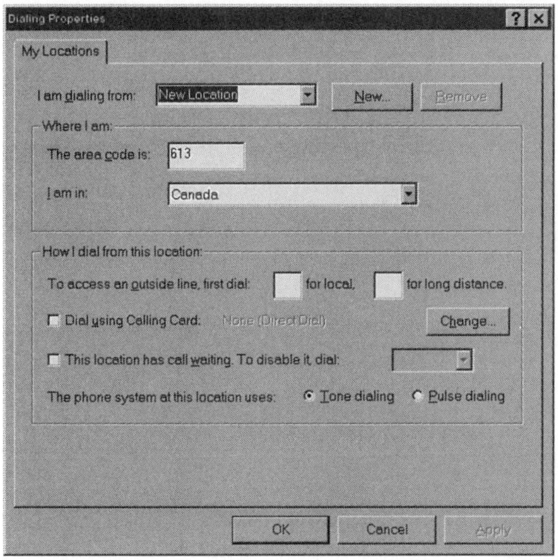

FIGURE 13.11
The Dialing Properties dialog box.

The following list describes the options that you can select in this dialog box:

- ◆ **I am dialing from.** This setting specifies the name of the location. To create a new entry, click the New button and enter a name in this box. The user needs to know which entry to use when dialing.

- ◆ **The area code is.** The computer can use this information to determine whether it must dial the number as a long distance number or a local number.

- ◆ **I am in.** This setting specifies the country code for dialing purposes so the system can connect to international numbers.

- ◆ **To access an outside line, first dial.** This setting specifies the access code for dialing out from a location. There is an entry for local calls and one for long distance.

- ◆ **Dial using Calling Card.** In this setting, you can specify that the computer enters the Calling Card information to make the connection with the remote host. Click the Change button to review or change the Calling Card information.

- ◆ **This location has call waiting.** The call-waiting tone often causes a connection to be dropped. You can enter the information here to disable call waiting for the location from which you are dialing.

- ◆ **The phone system at this location uses.** This option enables you to select whether the system from which you are calling uses tone or pulse dialing.

If you have problems trying to connect, you should always verify the information in the Dialing Properties dialog box.

Other Communications Technologies

As stated previously, there are other ways in which you can connect to the Windows NT Server. There are two principal ways that you can connect: ISDN (Integrated Services Digital Network) and X.25 (which is a wide area networking standard).

ISDN

One of the best choices for connecting remote sites, or even for individuals or small organizations to connect to the Internet, ISDN is becoming a very common communications method.

Whereas a standard phone line can handle transmission speeds of up to 9,600 bits per second (compression makes up the rest of the transmission speed in most modems such as those that transfer data at 33.6 or 56 kilobytes per second, or Kbps), ISDN transmits at speeds of 64 or 128 Kbps —depending on whether it is one or two channel.

ISDN is a point-to-point communications technology, and you must install special equipment at both the server and at the remote site. You must install an ISDN card (which acts as a network card) in place of a modem in both computers. ISDN connections are more expensive than modems. If there is a requirement for higher speed, however, the cost will most likely be justified. Be aware, though, that in some parts of the world, this is a metered service; the more you use, the more you pay.

X.25

The X.25 protocol is not an actual device, but rather a standard for connections. This packet-switching communication protocol was designed for wide area network (WAN) connectivity.

RAS supports X.25 connections using Packet Assemblers/Disassemblers (PADs) and X.25 smart cards. You install these smart cards as network cards, just like you install ISDN.

Dial-In Permissions

As with all other aspects of Windows NT, there is security built into the RAS server. At a minimum, a user must have an account in Windows NT, and that account must have dial-in permissions set.

You can grant users dial-in permissions using the User Manager (or User Manager for Domains) or through the Remote Access Admin program. If you are having problems connecting to the RAS server, these permissions are one of the first things you should check. Perform the tasks outlined in Step by Step 13.2 to set or check dial-in permissions.

STEP BY STEP

13.2 Enabling Dial-In for a User

1. Open the User Manager (Start, Programs, Administrative Tools, User Manager).

2. Select the account that you are using and choose User, Properties. You will see the User Properties dialog box shown in Figure 13.12.

3. Click the Dialin button. This brings up the Dialin Information dialog box (see Figure 13.13).

4. Check the "Grant dialin permission to user" box to enable the user to dial in.

   By completing these steps, you can enable, or at least ensure, dial-in permission for your users. Without this access, users cannot use the Dial-Up Networking utilities.

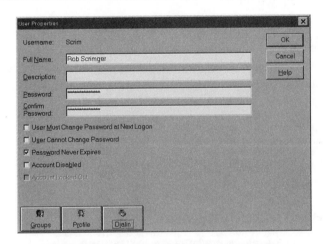

FIGURE 13.12
The User Properties dialog box.

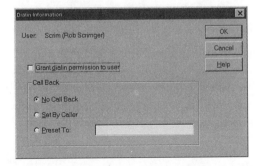

FIGURE 13.13
You configure the port for your modem in the Dialin Information dialog box.

You can also check the permissions from the Remote Access Admin utility. Perform the tasks outlined in Step by Step 13.3 to check permissions this way.

STEP BY STEP

13.3 Verifying Dial-In Permissions Using the RAS Admin Utility

1. Start the Remote Access Admin (Start, Programs, Administrative tools, RAS Admin).

2. From the menu, choose Users, Permissions.

3. In the Remote Access Permissions dialog box, select the user and ensure that Dialin permission is granted (see Figure 13.14).

By following the steps, you can verify that the dial-in permissions are enabled for each user. This can be very helpful when troubleshooting a failed user connection.

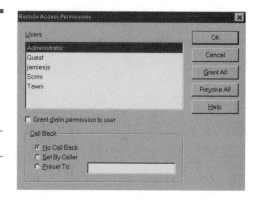

FIGURE 13.14
You can set Dialin permission in the Remote Access Admin.

Call Back Security

You probably noticed in both of the methods that there is a setting for Call Back. Call Back means that the server will do just that—call the user back. You can set Call Back to one of three options:

◆ **No Call Back.** This default setting disables the Call Back feature.

◆ **Set By Caller.** Using this option, the user can set the number that should be used when the server calls back. This is useful if you have a large number of users who will be traveling and want to centralize long distance.

◆ **Preset To.** This setting enhances the security of the network by forcing the user to be at a set phone number. If this option is set, the user can call only from that one location.

PPP Problems

As was mentioned earlier, Windows NT acts as a PPP server. This means that the client station and the server undergo a negotiation during the initial phase of the call.

During the negotiation, the client and server decide on the protocol to use and the parameters for the protocol. If there are problems attempting to connect, you might want to set up PPP logging to watch the negotiation between the server and client.

You set up PPP logging on the server by changing the Logging option under the following:

```
HKEY_LOCAL_MACHINE\SYSTEM\CurrentControlSet\Services\
➥RASMAN\PPP\Parameters
```

The log file will be in the system32\RAS folder and, like the modem log, can be viewed using any text editor.

Some of the problems that you might encounter are given in the following list:

◆ You must ensure that the protocol you are requesting from the RAS client is available on the RAS server. Unless there is at least one common protocol, the connection will fail.

◆ If you are using NetBEUI, ensure that the name you are using on the RAS client is not in use on the network to which you are attempting to connect.

◆ If you are attempting to connect using TCP/IP, you must configure the RAS server to provide you with an address.

Troubleshooting the Client

Probably the most common problem you will encounter is a configuration error on the client end. This section goes through the configuration of the client computer and points out those areas that cause problems.

The component that is used to connect to the RAS server is Dial-Up Networking. Before you can configure Dial-Up Networking, you must install a modem or another means of communications.

Using Dial-Up Networking, you create a phonebook entry for each of the locations that you will call. The steps that are required to create an entry are outlined in Step by Step 13.4.

STEP BY STEP

13.4 Creating a Phonebook Entry for Dial-Up Networking

1. Click the My Computer icon, then click Dial-Up Networking. (If you do not have an entry, a wizard appears that guides you through creating a phonebook entry.)

2. Click the New button to create an entry. You can also select an entry in the list, click More, and choose Edit the Entry.

   If you click New, the New Entry Wizard appears. You can choose to enter the information manually. Because this chapter is concerned with troubleshooting, this section covers the manual entries, as they provide more options.

3. The New (or Edit) Phonebook entry dialog box appears (see Figure 13.15). By default, it opens to the Basic tab; the options available on this tab are as follows. Enter or verify the information.

   - **Entry name.** Specifies the name of the entry.

   - **Comment.** Enables you to enter any comment you want to make about the entry.

   - **Phone number.** Specifies the phone number for the entry; you should verify this number. You can enter multiple entries by selecting the Alternates button. These numbers will be attempted in the sequence in which you enter them, and you have the option to move the successful number to the top of the list.

   - **Use Telephony dialing properties.** Tells the system to use the properties that you set for your location when dialing the number. When you are troubleshooting, you should try turning this off.

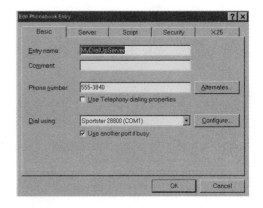

FIGURE 13.15
The Basic tab for a phonebook entry.

continues

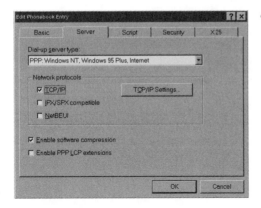

FIGURE 13.16
The Server tab for a phonebook entry.

continued

- **Dial using.** Informs the system which modem you want to use when dialing. Verify that the modem exists. If Multilink is selected, choose Configure and verify that the phone numbers are entered for each of the modems listed.

- **Use another port if busy.** Tells the system to dial using another modem if the modem specified is busy.

4. Select the Server tab and enter or verify the information (see Figure 13.16). The entries are as follows:

   - **Dial-up server type.** Tells the system the type of server to which you are trying to connect. There are three different types of servers that you can use: PPP (such as Windows NT), SLIP, and Windows NT 3.1 RAS. Make sure the correct type is selected or your computer will attempt to use the wrong line protocol.

   - **Network protocols.** Enables you to select the protocols you want to be able to use. If the client computer will be using the Internet, you must select TCP/IP. If the client is going to use the services of a remote NetWare server, you must select IPX/SPX. If you will be using only the services from a Windows NT network, you can choose any of the protocols (remembering that the server must also use the selected protocol).

   - **Enable software compression.** Turns on the software compression. If you are working with a Windows NT Server, you can select this option. For troubleshooting purposes, you should turn this option off.

   - **Enable PPP LCP extensions.** Tells the system that the PPP server will be able to set up the client station and to verify the user name and password. You should also turn off this option when you are troubleshooting.

5. If you are using TCP/IP for this connection, you should also set or verify the TCP/IP settings. The TCP/IP setting screen appears; the screen differs depending on the type of server you select. Shown in Figure 13.17 are the PPP settings. The available options are as follows:

- **Server assigned IP address.** Tells the computer that the server will assign the IP address for this station. For this option to have an effect, the server must have some means of assigning an IP address.

- **Specify an IP address.** Enables you to give the station an IP address. The address must be unique, and must be correct for the server's network. The server must also enable the client to request an IP address.

- **Server assigned name server addresses.** Tells the system that the server will assign the IP addresses for DNS and WINS servers.

- **Specify name server addresses.** Lets you set the addresses for DNS and WINS servers. This option enables you to see whether the server is giving you correct addresses.

- **Use IP header compression.** Using IP header compression reduces the overhead that is transmitted over the modem. For troubleshooting, you should disable this option.

- **Use default gateway on the remote network.** If you are connected to a network and dialed in to a service provider, selecting this option tells NT to send information that is bound for a remote network to the gateway on the dial-in server.

6. Set the script options on the Script tab (see Figure 13.18).

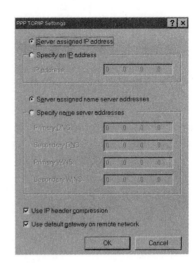

FIGURE 13.17
The PPP TCP/IP settings dialog box.

continues

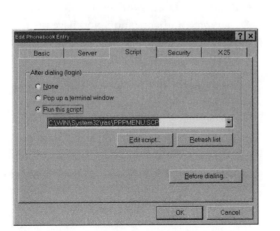

FIGURE 13.18
The Script tab for a phonebook entry.

continued

The options on the Script tab are as follows:

- **After dialing (login).** There are three different settings that you can choose here. Make sure that you choose the correct one. For NT-to-NT communications, you can select None. For other connections, you might have to enter information. For troubleshooting, you should try the terminal window. In this window, you can enter the information manually rather than using the script. If this works, you should verify the script.

- **Before dialing.** If you click this button, you are presented with basically the same options as with the preceding button. With these options, you can bring up a window or run a script before you dial the remote host.

7. Select or enter the security information on the Security tab (see Figure 13.19). Unless you set the security to the same level as that on the server, the connection will probably fail. The options are as follows:

- **Authentication and encryption policy.** Here you can set the level of security that you want to use. For troubleshooting, you can try Accept any authentication including clear text. This setting should match the setting on the server.

- **Require data encryption.** If you are using Microsoft encrypted authentication, you have the option to encrypt all data that is being sent over the connection. This setting should be the same as that on the server.

- **Use current user name and password.** This option enables Windows to send the current user name and password as your logon information. If you are not using the same name and password on the client as you do on the network, do not select this option. You will be prompted for the user name and password to log on as when you attempt to connect (see Figure 13.20).

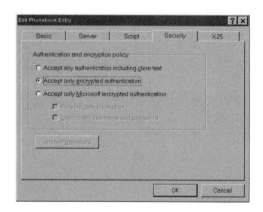

FIGURE 13.19
The Security tab for the phonebook entry.

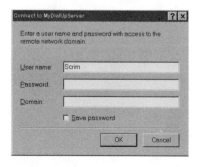

FIGURE 13.20
The prompt for logon information.

- **Unsave password.** If you told the system to save the logon password for a connection, you can clear it by clicking this button. You should do this in the case of a logon problem.

8. Finally, you can enter or check the information for X.25 connections (see Figure 13.21).

    At the completion of the preceding steps, you will have successfully created a phonebook entry that will be used to connect to a remote RAS server. If you set all settings correctly, no problems should occur.

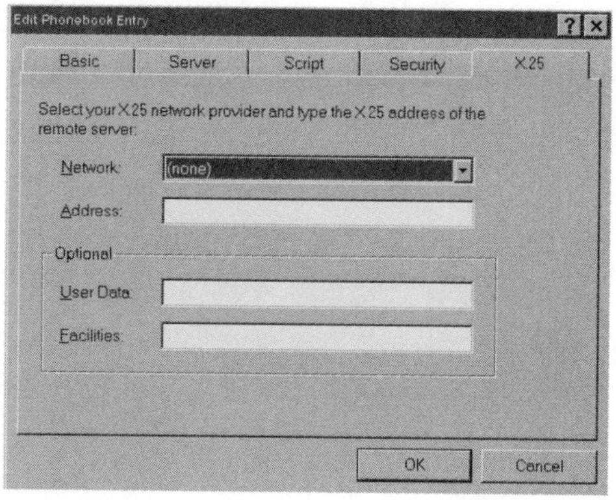

FIGURE 13.21
The X.25 tab for a phonebook entry.

You can configure many different options, and therefore a great potential exists for errors. Client errors tend to be either validation problems or errors in the network protocols. Remember that you might need to check the configuration of the server.

Troubleshooting the Server

This section covers the RAS server and the configuration of that server (and the problems that might arise therein). Probably the best place to start is the installation of the RAS server. After a short description of the installation, this section moves on to the server's configuration.

Installing the RAS Server

The tasks outlined in Step by Step 13.5 describe the process of installing RAS.

STEP BY STEP

13.5 Installing RAS

1. Open the Network settings dialog box (Start, Settings, Control Panel, Network).

2. From the Services tab, choose Add.

continues

continued

3. From the list that appears, choose Remote Access Service, then click OK.

4. When prompted, enter the path to the Windows NT source files.

5. RAS asks you for the device that it should use at that point. (This device includes ISDN and X.25.) Enter the device.

6. The Remote Access Setup dialog box appears (see Figure 13.22). Click Continue (the following section discusses the options for this dialog box).

7. From the Network settings dialog box, click Close.

8. When prompted, shut down and restart your system.

   At the completion of these steps, RAS is installed on your system. Usually you should not encounter any problems during installation, unless you have not properly configured your modem.

Configuring the RAS Server

If several users are all having problems connecting to your RAS server, you should check the modem first, then check the configuration of the server. This section covers the basic configuration for a RAS server. This configuration is done when you install RAS or when you verify it after installation by going to the Network settings dialog box and double-clicking on Remote Access Service from the Services tab.

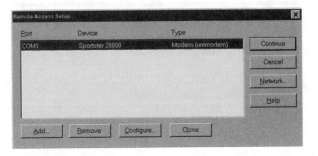

FIGURE 13.22
The Remote Access Setup dialog box.

You then see the dialog box shown in Figure 13.22. You can configure each port and set the network preferences overall. Four buttons affect the port settings:

FIGURE 13.23
Configuring port usage; check this information if no users can dial in.

◆ **Add.** Enables you to add another port to the RAS server. This port can be a modem, an X.25 PAD, or a PPTP Virtual Private Network.

◆ **Remove.** Removes the port from RAS.

◆ **Configure.** Brings up a dialog box (see Figure 13.23) that will enable you to configure how this port is to be used. You should click this button if no users can dial in.

◆ **Clone.** Lets you copy a port. Windows NT Server has been tested with up to 256 ports.

> **NOTE**
> **Limitations** Windows NT Workstation and Windows 95 (with service pack 1 or the OSR2 release) enable only one client to dial in.

After configuring the ports, you must configure the network settings. These affect what users can see, how they are authenticated, and what protocols they can use when they dial in to the network. When you click the Network button, you see a dialog box like the one shown in Figure 13.24.

This dialog box includes three main sections. The first is Dial out Protocols. In this section, you set which protocols you can use to dial in to another server. Then there are the dial-in protocols that set the protocols with which users can connect to you.

Finally, there are the Encryption settings. The level of security that you choose must also be set on the client computer. If the client cannot use the same level of security, the server will not be able to validate the client.

For each of the server-side protocols, there is a configuration button. The following sections discuss the configuration of each. Before you can use a protocol with RAS, it must be installed on the server.

Configuring NetBEUI on the RAS Server

Very little configuration is required for the NetBEUI protocol. As you can see in Figure 13.25, the options deal only with what clients can see. They can see this computer only or the entire network.

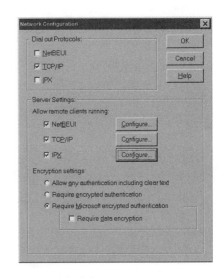

FIGURE 13.24
The network configuration dialog box.

FIGURE 13.25
The NetBEUI configuration options deal only with what clients can see.

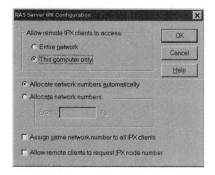

FIGURE 13.26
IPX configuration on the RAS server is fairly straightforward.

NetBEUI is the fastest of the dial-in protocols and can be used to enable connections to any Windows NT-based system on the network, even ones that are running other protocols. This can occur because of the NetBIOS gateway that is included in NT RAS. The NetBIOS gateway can take your requests bound for a server that does not speak NetBEUI and forward them on your behalf.

Configuring IPX for RAS Server Connections

If your environment is a mix of both NT and NetWare, you will probably want to enable the IPX protocol on the RAS server. This will enable the clients to communicate with the NetWare servers over the RAS connection. The configuration dialog box is fairly straightforward (see Figure 13.26).

Again there is the option of enabling the clients to see this computer only or the entire network. The other options deal with the IPX node numbers that identify a station that is using IPX. Usually you will not need to change the defaults, but if you are having problems, try resetting the dialog box to the default.

The only case where you might have a problem is a secure package that reads the node number. In this case, do not assign the same node number to all clients. If the numbers need to be entered in the software, either assign a group of node numbers that you will be able to enter, or enable the client to request a specific number.

Configuring TCP/IP on the RAS Server

If you run a mixed network that includes UNIX-like hosts, then you should enable the TCP/IP protocol on the RAS server. This will also enable your clients to use an Internet connection on your network. The RAS Server TCP/IP Configuration dialog box, as seen in Figure 13.27, again includes the capability to restrict network access to the RAS server.

The other options all deal with the assignment of TCP/IP addresses to the clients that are dialing in. By default, the RAS server uses the services of a Dynamic Host Configuration Protocol (DHCP) server to assign the addresses. If your DHCP server has a long lease period, you might want to assign the numbers from a pool of addresses that are given on the server. If you enable the client to request an address, you must configure the client stations for all the other parameters.

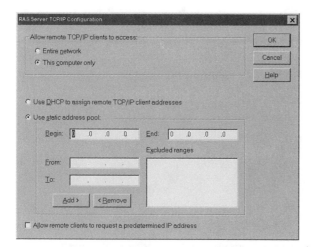

FIGURE 13.27
The RAS Server TCP/IP Configuration dialog box enables you to restrict network access to the RAS server.

If your clients are having problems connecting, assign a range of addresses to the RAS server. This will eliminate any problems that are related to the DHCP server and still enable you to prevent clients from requesting specific IP addresses.

Monitoring the RAS Connection

After making the RAS connection, you can monitor the connection. There is a tool for both the client side and the server side. This section looks at both sides as you can use them to see what is happening with the connection and to help discover what might be going wrong.

Monitoring from the RAS Server

From the server, you can use the Remote Access Admin tool to monitor the ports as well as active connections. From the Start menu, choose Programs, Administrative tools, RAS Admin. This brings up the Admin tool (see Figure 13.28).

Select the server that you want to look at and double-click the server. Figure 13.29 shows a list of the communications ports that will appear. For every port that is available on the server, you see the users who arecurrently connected and the time that they connected.

FIGURE 13.28
The Remote Access Admin tool.

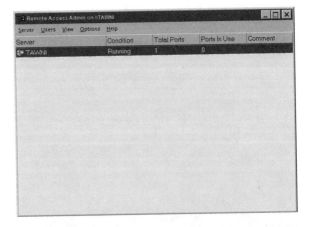

FIGURE 13.29
Communications ports on a RAS server.

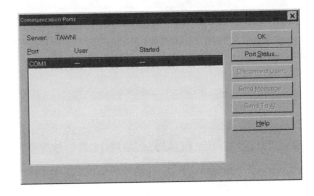

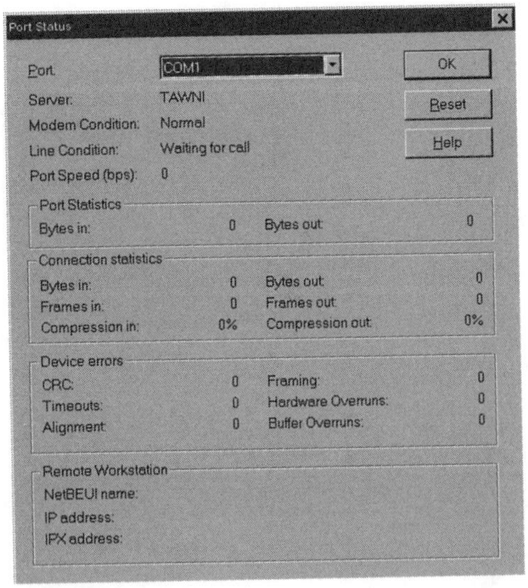

From here you can disconnect users or send a message to a single user or all the users who are connected to the server. You can also check the port status. The Port Status dialog box shows you all the connection information for the port (see Figure 13.30).

Dial-Up Networking Monitor

On the client side, the Dial-Up Networking Monitor is an application you can use to check the status of the communications and look for any possible problems. There are three tabs in the monitor.

The Status Tab

The Status tab provides you with basic information about the connection (see Figure 13.31). From here you have the option to hang up the connection or to view the details about the connection.

FIGURE 13.30
The Port Status dialog box.

Clicking the Details button brings up another screen (see Figure 13.32) that gives you the details about the clients' names on the network.

The Summary Tab

The Summary tab summarizes all the connections that the client currently has open (see Figure 13.33). This tab is really useful only when you have multiple connections.

The Preferences Tab

The Preferences tab, shown in Figure 13.34, enables you to control the settings for Dial-Up Networking. There are several options that you should be aware of on this tab.

The options that you can set break down into two main areas. You can control when a sound is played and how the Dial-Up Networking monitor will look.

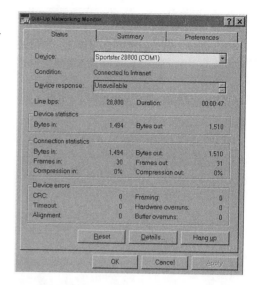

FIGURE 13.31
The Status tab from the Dial-Up Networking monitor provides you with basic information about the connection.

Common RAS Problems

Clients experience two common problems with RAS. This section describes these problems.

Authentication

There are two areas where authentication can be a problem. The client can attempt to connect using the incorrect user name and password. This can easily happen if the user is dialing from a home system. The RAS client can be set to attempt the connection using the current user name and password.

The other authentication problem occurs if the security settings on the server and the client do not match. You can get around this problem by using the Allow any authentication setting or possibly by using the After Dial terminal window.

Call Back with Multilink

There is currently no way in which you can configure Call Back security with a Multilink setup. If you attempt to do this, the initial connections are made and then the server hangs up. The server only has one number for the client and only calls back to one port.

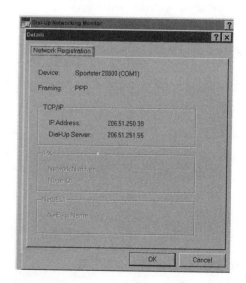

FIGURE 13.32
Connection Details shows the clients' network identification.

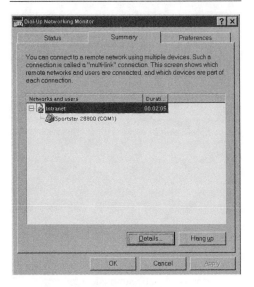

FIGURE 13.33
The Summary tab summarizes all the connections that the client currently has open.

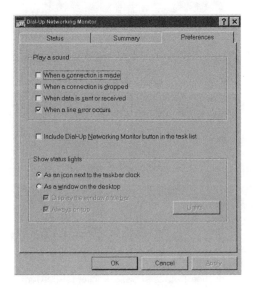

FIGURE 13.34
The Preferences tab enables you to set Dial-Up Networking preferences.

RAS Troubleshooting

Numerous RAS settings can cause some problems with your RAS connections. Ensure that you have an understanding of the installation process, as well as any configuration settings required to enable your RAS server. You can avoid some of the common problems that can occur by doing the following:

- Ensuring that the modem and communication medium are configured and functional prior to installing RAS. Modifying settings after installation can be difficult, so you should have all hardware tested and working first.

- Verifying that dial-in permissions have been enabled for the required users. This issue is commonly forgotten in your RAS configuration.

CONNECTIVITY ISSUES

Choose the appropriate course of action to take to resolve connectivity problems.

This section examines the various issues that arise when you connect a system to the network. This section deals primarily with the problems that are created during configuration of the various network protocols and services. You should always remember to check the obvious things first, such as the network cabling.

Naming Problems

Microsoft networking has been based on NetBIOS for many years. Therefore, each of the services that you will run on your computer must register as that service at your computer name.

You can imagine what sort of problems you might have if every street in your town were to be called First Street. That same sort of confusion results if two or more computers on your network have the same name.

NetBIOS names are 16 characters long. You enter the first 15 as you install the system. You use the other character to identify the services that you are running on the computer. Each service registers on the computer with the computer name and uses the 16th character as a code that describes the service.

One of the most common problems on a network is a computer of the same name. The system will warn you as it starts up that a computer with the same name already exists. You need to go to the Network dialog box's Identification tab and change the computer name (see Figure 13.35).

The name that you enter for your computer must be unique on the network; otherwise, you will not be able to communicate. If you make any changes to your computer name, you are prompted to restart the computer so that the new name is registered.

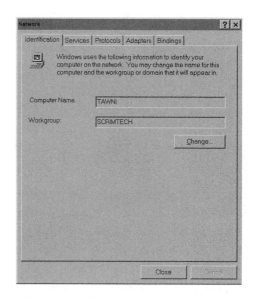

FIGURE 13.35
You can change the name of the computer on the Identification tab of the Network dialog box.

Domain Validation

Windows NT is designed to use a domain model for network administration. Therefore, as a computer starts up, a domain controller must validate the user. You need to be aware of several potential problems involving domain validation. Those problems are touched on in the upcoming two subsections.

The Logon Process

There are actually a fair number of steps that are involved in the logon process. The following list details the steps that take place:

1. The user presses Ctrl+Alt+Del. This brings up the Windows NT Logon dialog box that is handled by the Winlogon process. All user mode activity stops at this point and the user enters his or her logon ID and password.

2. The Winlogon process passes the request to the Local System Authority (LSA). The LSA then uses a broadcast to locate a domain controller.

3. The LSA creates a secure connection with the domain controller and passes the user name, password, and logon domain to the domain controller.

4. On the domain controller (if it is a domain controller for the logon domain), the Security Accounts Manager verifies the user name and password with Windows NT Directory Services.

5. Information about the user is gathered and an Access Token is generated. The domain controller passes the Access Token back through the secure connection to the LSA on the client computer.

6. The LSA passes the Access Token to the Winlogon process that now creates a user process and attaches the Token to it.

7. Windows NT now loads the user's shell.

The single most common logon problem, other than typing mistakes, is the inability of the system to find a domain controller. You must ensure that the system can see the domain controller. That is, the system must be able to talk to the network and find a domain controller.

The problem is worse if you use the TCP/IP protocol for your network protocol. As previously mentioned, the search for a domain controller requires that the system perform a broadcast. This NetBIOS-based broadcast is not forwarded by TCP/IP routers that require the availability of a WINS server or LMHOSTS file to resolve the name for the client computer.

Pass-Through Authentication

Windows NT domains can be logically joined together. This enables a user who has an account on one domain to log on to a system that is in a completely different domain. Such domains are joined using a trust relationship.

This type of authentication is referred to as pass-through authentication. The process is basically the same as the one previously described, only the domain controller now uses its Netlogon service to create a secure connection with a domain controller in the trusted domain. It can then ask the trusted domain controller to verify the user.

Further, any time the users attempt to use the services of the domain they are currently in, the Netlogon process again verifies that the user is a valid user in the remote domain.

There are two main issues to be aware of in using pass-through authentication. First, a domain controller from the domain in which the user's account resides must be available. If no controller is available, the process fails. Second, the trust relationship must exist and be intact.

NetBEUI

NetBEUI is a very simple protocol. Relatively little will go wrong with it. The only major point that you must bear in mind is that NetBEUI is not a routable protocol. Therefore, if your network is broken into segments, there must be some way for broadcast traffic to pass among the segments.

NWLink

NWLink is Microsoft's 32-bit implementation of the IPX/SPX protocol standard. Using NWLink provides the common protocol that enables Windows NT to interconnect with Novell networks. You must have a client installed on the computer as well as the protocol.

By default, the NWLink enables you to interact with client/server class applications. Therefore, you can run a SQL server that a NetWare client can use. (The client must be running NetBIOS, which is optional in NetWare.) If you are running a Lotus Notes server on a Novell server, you can use the Lotus Notes server from your Windows NT workstation if you use NWLink.

If you want to be able to work with the file and print services of a Novell system, you must add either Client Services for NetWare (on Workstation) or Gateway (and Client) Services for NetWare (on Server). These services enable your Windows NT system to function as a Novell client.

The only configuration that needs to be done for NWLink is the frame type. Novell servers use different frame types, depending on the network topology and the version of NetWare in use. If you are having problems communicating with a Novell server, check that the frame types are compatible.

You can set the frame type in the Network settings dialog box by choosing the NWLink protocol and clicking the Properties button. A screen similar to the one shown in Figure 13.36 appears. From the drop-down list, choose the frame type.

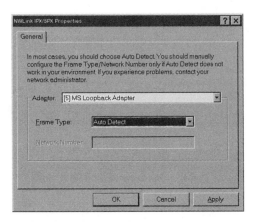

FIGURE 13.36
Setting the frame type in the NWLink protocol.

If you are running multiple NetWare servers, you might have to set more than one frame type on the Windows NT workstation. To do so, you must use REGEDT32. You can add the setting in the Registry under the following:

```
HKEY_LOCAL_MACHINE\SYSTEM\CurrentControlSet\Services\MWlnkIpx\
➥NetConfig\Card_Driver_Name.
```

The setting is a REG_MULTI_SZ, which means that you can enter more than one frame type. The following list gives you the available entries for the different frame types:

◆ 0—Ethernet II

◆ 1—Ethernet 802.3

◆ 2—Ethernet 802.2

◆ 3—Ethernet SNAP (Sub Network Access Protocol)

◆ 4—ARCnet

TCP/IP

TCP/IP (Transmission Control Protocol/Internet Protocol) has become the standard protocol for most networks. The TCP/IP protocol is designed for wide area networking and is routable.

Most of the problems that you encounter using the TCP/IP protocol deal with the actual configuration of the system. TCP/IP uses a 32-bit binary address to identify uniquely each host that is connected to a network. The address consists of two pieces. The first portion is the network address and the second portion is the host on that network.

The number of bits that are used to identify the network is variable, and this is where the subnet mask comes in. A subnet mask is used to tell the system which portion is which. The network portion is set to all ones and the host portion is set to all zeros. This subnet mask is used to extract the network ID from the IP address so that the computer can determine whether a given address is local or remote. If the network IDs match, the address is local. Otherwise, the address is remote.

People usually do not view the IP address as a string of 32 ones and zeros but rather as four decimal numbers between 0 and 255, separated by dots (hence the name *dotted decimal notation*).

There are two ways to configure TCP/IP. You can enter all the information manually, or you can use a DHCP server that will provide all the configuration information automatically for the host.

After configuring your TCP/IP settings, you must then test or verify that the settings are functional. The following sections introduce some utilities you can use to verify your TCP/IP settings.

TCP/IP Testing

Whenever you configure a host to use TCP/IP, you should test the host to ensure that it can communicate properly over the protocol. At a bare minimum, the TCP/IP configuration must have a TCP/IP address and a subnet mask. If you communicate with hosts that are on other networks, you also need a default gateway that tells the system where to send the information that needs to go to other networks. The default gateway, in Microsoft terms, is a router.

To test and verify your TCP/IP settings, you can use the following utilities:

◆ IPCONFIG

◆ PING

These utilities are discussed in the following two subsections to ensure that you understand how these tools can assist you.

IPCONFIG

To verify that the configuration has been entered, you can use IPCONFIG. If you simply type IPCONFIG at a command prompt, the screen will display the IP address, subnet mask, and default gateway for you. There are also three switches that you can use with IPCONFIG. These switches are as follows:

◆ **/ALL.** You will normally use this switch to view all of the configuration information for a computer. An example is shown in Figure 13.37.

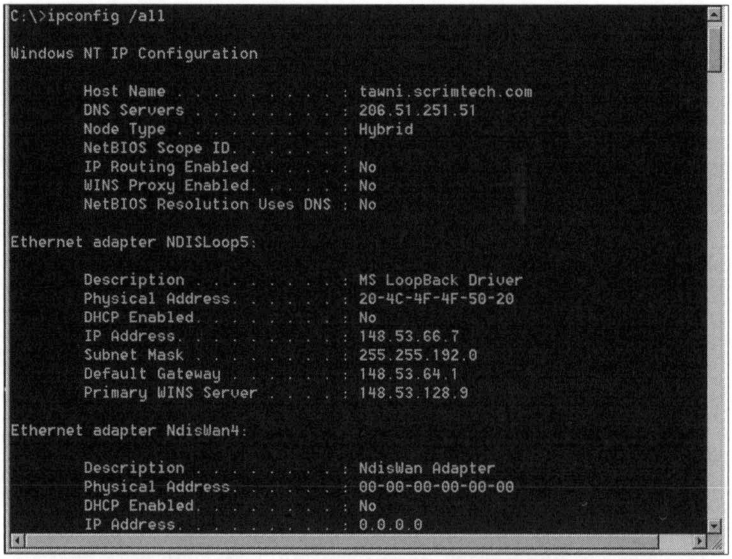

FIGURE 13.37
A command window showing the output of the IPCONFIG /ALL command.

```
C:\>ipconfig /all

Windows NT IP Configuration

        Host Name . . . . . . . . . . : tawni.scrimtech.com
        DNS Servers . . . . . . . . . : 206.51.251.51
        Node Type . . . . . . . . . . : Hybrid
        NetBIOS Scope ID. . . . . . . :
        IP Routing Enabled. . . . . . : No
        WINS Proxy Enabled. . . . . . : No
        NetBIOS Resolution Uses DNS : No

Ethernet adapter NDISLoop5:

        Description . . . . . . . . . : MS LoopBack Driver
        Physical Address. . . . . . . : 20-4C-4F-4F-50-20
        DHCP Enabled. . . . . . . . . : No
        IP Address. . . . . . . . . . : 148.53.66.7
        Subnet Mask . . . . . . . . . : 255.255.192.0
        Default Gateway . . . . . . . : 148.53.64.1
        Primary WINS Server . . . . . : 148.53.128.9

Ethernet adapter NdisWan4:

        Description . . . . . . . . . : NdisWan Adapter
        Physical Address. . . . . . . : 00-00-00-00-00-00
        DHCP Enabled. . . . . . . . . : No
        IP Address. . . . . . . . . . : 0.0.0.0
```

FIGURE 13.37
A command window showing the output of the IPCONFIG /ALL command.

◆ **/RELEASE.** If you are using DHCP, this switch drops the IP address that you got from the DHCP server. You should use this switch before you move a client to a different network. When the computer next attempts to initialize the TCP/IP stack, it will request a new address from a DHCP server.

◆ **/RENEW.** DHCP works by leasing an address. The /RENEW option forces the computer to attempt to renew the lease on the address. You can use this switch to verify that the client can see the DHCP server, as well as bring down any changes that the DHCP server made to the configuration.

PING

Using IPCONFIG, you can ensure that the client has an IP address. The next step is to ensure that the client can connect to the network. In TCP/IP, you use a utility called PING (Packet Internet Grouper) to check the capability to connect to the network. There are a series of addresses that you should PING to verify the communications (see Figure 13.38).

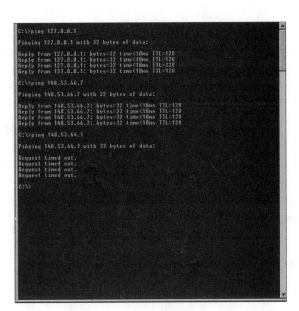

FIGURE 13.38
A command prompt showing the PING command being used to diagnose a problem.

Step by Step 13.6 provides the series of steps that you should follow to check the connection using PING.

STEP BY STEP

13.6 Using PING to Check the Connection

1. PING 127.0.0.1. This special address, commonly referred to as the loopback address, checks the protocol and verifies that the protocol is installed correctly.

2. PING *your_IP_address*. This address verifies that the TCP/IP protocol is correctly bound to the network card. You should substitute the IP address of the host for *your_IP_address*.

3. PING *default_gateway_IP_address*. This address checks that you can connect to the network. You can use the *default_gateway* or any valid host ID that you know is on the same network as you are. This command also checks that the subnet mask is not using too many bits for the network ID.

continues

continued

4. PING *remote_host_IP_address.* This address checks to see that you can connect to the router, or default gateway, and that you are in fact able to go past it. This address also ensures that the subnet mask is not using too few bits.

If you receive a response on each of these PINGs, you have successfully proven your TCP/IP connection.

After verifying that you can communicate using these steps, you should attempt to PING other computers using their names.

Configuration Errors

As previously was stated, the primary problem you encounter using the TCP/IP protocol is a configuration error. Because of the many numbers involved in TCP/IP, you need to be careful entering the information. Beyond the basic IP address error, there are other configuration errors that prevent a system from being able to communicate properly.

The following sections cover the different parts of the configuration and tell you where to change the configuration. Changing the configuration always requires opening the Network settings dialog box, choosing the Protocols tab, and going to the TCP/IP properties.

Subnet Masks

Normally only one subnet mask should be in use on a network (at least for the client computers). This means that if you see a different subnet mask being used in your configurations, you should recognize it as an error.

If the subnet mask is incorrect, the client computer might be able to communicate with some hosts, only remote systems, or only local systems. In all cases of problems communicating over TCP/IP, you should verify that the subnet mask is correct.

You set the IP address on the IP Address tab of the TCP/IP Properties dialog box (see Figure 13.39). You need to enter configuration information for each network card in your system. It is important to note that each network card requires its own TCP/IP configuration settings.

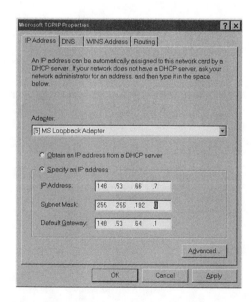

FIGURE 13.39
The IP Address tab's configuration settings.

You can also choose to have the system pick up an IP address automatically from a DHCP server. You can also select this setting on a card-by-card basis.

Name Resolution

Another problem that occurs is incorrect information being entered for name resolution. There are two types of name servers: DNS servers resolve names of non-NetBIOS systems (such as Web servers or FTP servers), and WINS (Windows Internet Naming Service) servers resolve NetBIOS names. In both cases, the name resolves to a TCP/IP address.

You set the information for the DNS server on the DNS tab (see Figure 13.40). The host name defaults to the computer name. You can also enter the domain information. This information pertains to the Internet domain name, not the Windows NT domain. The Internet domain name is added to the host name to create a Fully Qualified Domain Name (FQDN). This name must also be in your DNS server if you want other Internet users to be able to find your computer.

Enter the IP address of the DNS server that you want to use and click Add. You can enter more than one DNS server. The Domain Suffix search order enables you to enter domain suffixes. When you attempt to connect to a host, your system attempts to resolve the name as you enter it. If it cannot, your system will try again to append the suffix that you enter here. If you enter many suffixes, you might find that it takes a long time to find a computer on your network.

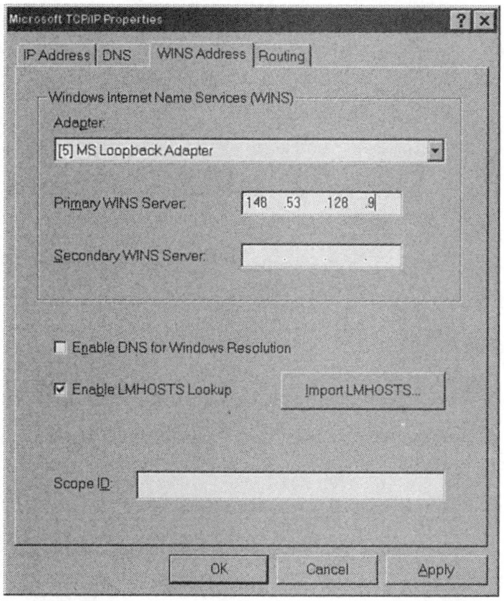

When you are attempting to connect to a NetBIOS name (using the Windows NT Explorer), you must resolve it. This requires that you enter a WINS server address on the WINS Address tab (see Figure 13.41).

The WINS Address tab includes a couple of settings that you need to be aware of. The following list describes the items found on the tab:

◆ **Windows Internet Name Services.** This area enables you to enter both a primary and secondary WINS server IP address for each network card in your system.

◆ **Enable DNS for Windows Resolution.** If you check this box, the DNS server is used to resolve NetBIOS names.

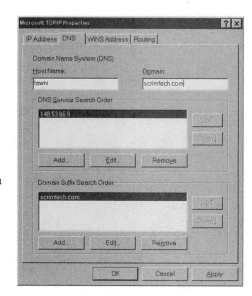

FIGURE 13.40
Configuring the use of a DNS server.

FIGURE 13.41
The WINS Address tab.

◆ **Enable LMHOSTS Lookup.** If this option is selected, your system can use the LMHOSTS file (a text file located at \%systemroot\system32\drivers\etc—see LMHOSTS.SAM in that folder for more information). If you require LMHOSTS, ensure that this setting is turned on.

◆ **Scope ID.** The scope ID can prevent hosts from being able to communicate. Only computers that have the same scope ID can communicate using NetBIOS over TCP/IP.

If you can successfully PING by IP address but not by name, you should check that the servers that perform name resolution are entered in the appropriate spots. IPCONFIG's /ALL switch can provide this information for you.

DHCP

DHCP is a powerful tool that enables you to configure the clients on your network automatically. You need to be aware of two main problems that you could have using DHCP. DHCP servers do not share information about addresses that they have leased. This means that if multiple DHCP servers are not configured correctly, they might lease out the same address to more than one client at the same time.

The other problem to be aware of is that if the DHCP server is not available, the client computers cannot obtain or renew leases for IP addresses. The client displays a warning message and tries again in five minutes. The message, however, gives the user the opportunity to hide further messages. In this case, the computer on the network would not have an address, and when the user attempts to connect, he or she cannot use TCP/IP.

Advanced Configuration

Several other configuration options are available. From the main IP address tab, you can enter the Advanced IP configuration screen (see Figure 13.42).

In this dialog box, you can enter multiple IP addresses for each of the network cards in your system. You can also add other gateway addresses. This dialog box is also where you can enable PPTP filtering that enables you to use the PPTP Virtual Private Network with the RAS server.

NOTE

Service Pack 3 Fix This problem has been addressed in service pack 3. The server now PINGs the address to ensure that it is not already in use.

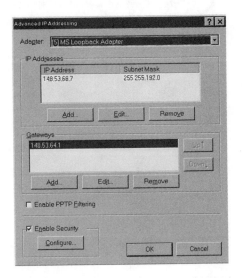

FIGURE 13.42
The Advanced IP Addressing dialog box.

The last option is to enable TCP/IP security. When troubleshooting, you should disable this setting. When it is enabled, you can configure the TCP/IP protocol to accept only certain TCP or UDP ports and IP protocols (see Figure 13.43).

Sessions

After verifying that you can communicate with the remote host using IPCONFIG and PING, you should then move on to test the capability to create a session.

There are two types of sessions:

◆ Regular Windows NT sessions

◆ Winsock or TCP/IP sessions

To test Winsock sessions, you need to use a Winsock application, such as FTP or Internet Explorer. The one you choose to use depends on the service that is running on the server.

Windows NT comes with a utility that will enable you to verify the status of TCP/IP connections called NETSTAT. Figure 13.44 shows the output of the command.

Testing the capability to create a NetBIOS session is simply a matter of trying to connect to the system. You can use the Windows NT Explorer to do this. If you open the Network Neighborhood and can see the system, click it and see if you get a list of shares. If not, you probably have a name resolution problem because your system cannot resolve the computer name to an IP address. Check the WINS information.

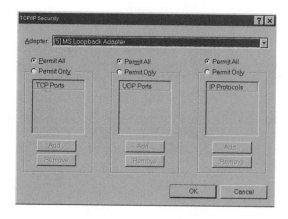

FIGURE 13.43
Security settings for TCP/IP.

FIGURE 13.44
Use the NETSTAT command to check session status.

FIGURE 13.45
Use the NBTSTAT command to check the connection to a remote host.

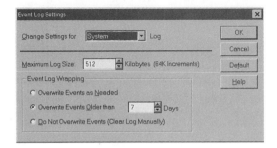

Like NETSTAT, there is a utility to check the status of NetBIOS over TCP/IP connections. In Figure 13.45, the NBTSTAT command is used to check the connection to a remote host.

Network Services

You might see several services on your system. This section covers each of them so you are aware of what they do. This discussion will help you figure out which service could be the problem in a given situation. The services are as follows:

❖ **Messenger Service.** This service listens to the network and receives pop-up messages for you. These are messages such as printer notifications that are sent without a session to a name on the network.

◆ **Alerter Service.** The Alerter service sends the notifications that are received by the messenger service.

◆ **Browser Service.** The Browser service is responsible for putting the list of domains (and workgroups) together and for your domain (or workgroup) dealing with the list of servers that are available. The Browser service on most systems simply broadcasts its presence to the network every 12 minutes (this broadcast happens on all systems that can share files and printers).

◆ **Workstation Service.** A computer's Workstation service is responsible for connecting to a remote computer using NetBIOS and accessing the services of the computer. In some networks, this service is referred to as the redirector because it takes requests to read a file and redirect it over the network.

◆ **Server Service.** When you connect to another computer, that computer must be running a service that will accept your connection and act on the instructions that you provide. The Server service is the Windows NT service that provides the network with access to the resources on a computer.

Connectivity Troubleshooting

REVIEW BREAK

The most effective method for troubleshooting connectivity is to have a thorough understanding of the installation and configuration options of each of the network protocols. If you understand the options available, you can narrow down the possible problem areas very quickly. Also ensure that you use utilities such as IPCONFIG and PING to test your connections.

CASE STUDY: TROUBLESHOOTING RAS

ESSENCE OF THE CASE

Here are the essential elements in this case:

- A log of the local modems in the field representatives' laptops must be recorded.

- A log of the RAS service is required to isolate the problem.

SCENARIO

A large national training company is running RAS on a Windows NT server to enable the field representatives to dial in to the corporate network. The company needs to maintain a high level of security and has enabled the call-back feature in the RAS. Several of the field representatives are complaining that they cannot maintain a connection to the RAS server. The problem might be due to the modem settings of the field representatives' laptops, or the problem might exist with the RAS server. The company is looking for a method that enables users to view a record of the incoming calls and any problems that occur with each call.

ANALYSIS

In attempting to determine the problem, the first action to take is to implement a log file of all communications between the field representatives' modems and the RAS server. To enable the log for the field representatives' modems, you must enable the Record a log file option found in the Advanced Connection Settings dialog box for the field representatives' modems. After you enable this option, a modem log is created on each of the laptops during the connection process. The modem log must also be enabled on the RAS server to ensure that the process is documented from both connecting systems. Enable the Record a log file option in the Advanced Connection Settings dialog box of the RAS server. You should also use the RAS Admin program to view the live connections, and you can check the port status while the users are attempting the connections. The best method available for troubleshooting a RAS connection is to enable the modem logs and review these documents.

CHAPTER SUMMARY

This chapter reviewed many of the processes involved with RAS and with connectivity in general within a Windows NT environment. The easiest (and most feasible) method for troubleshooting in this area is to gain experience in all of the processes in your system. Numerous processes are involved and there is no quick method for troubleshooting potential problems. The main areas to focus on are as follows:

◆ **RAS.** The installation and configuration are critical components in understanding and being able to troubleshoot RAS effectively. Also ensure that you have verified all modem settings prior to configuring your RAS software.

◆ **Networking protocols.** Previous chapters have discussed networking protocols in detail; for troubleshooting this process, ensure that you have a thorough understanding of all the configuration options available, and how each one can affect the system.

KEY TERMS

- PPP
- SLIP
- PTP
- PSTN
- Multilink
- NETSTAT
- NBTSTAT

This section enables you to assess how well you understood the material in the chapter. Review and exam questions test your knowledge of the tasks and concepts specified in the objectives. The exercises provide you with opportunities to engage in the sorts of tasks that comprise the skill sets that the objectives reflect.

For more review and exam type questions, see the Top Score test engine on the CD-ROM that comes with this book.

Exercise

The following exercise provides you an opportunity to apply what you've learned in this chapter.

13.1 Creating and Reviewing a Modem Log

This exercise steps you through the procedure to create and review a modem log. You need a modem for this exercise, which assumes that you have the modem and Dial-Up Networking installed.

Time Estimate: 30 minutes

Preparing to Record the Log. These steps set up Windows NT to record the log of the modem activity.

1. From the Start button, choose Setting, Control Panel.

2. Double-click the Modem icon. This should bring up the Modem dialog box.

3. Choose the modem to work with and then click the Properties button.

4. From the Connection tab, click the Advanced button.

5. Check the Record a log box and choose OK. Choose OK again to return to the Modem dialog box.

6. Make a note of the modem type that you are using. Click Close. You can also close the Control Panel.

Recording the Log. In this step, you dial a number and let NT record the log.

1. Double-click the My Computer icon.

2. Open Dial-Up Networking.

3. Choose a dialing entry and dial.

   If you have not already created an entry, create one with a phone number that will not work. This provides an example of a problem connecting. Try 555 as the first three numbers. This exchange is not valid in most areas. Alternatively, you can enter your own number to create a busy signal.

4. Connect as usual.

5. Disconnect from the remote system.

Reading the Modem Log. Now that you have created a modem log, you can read it.

1. Start NT Explorer. Choose the Windows installation folder (winroot) and look for a file starting with *ModemLog*.

2. Confirm the remainder of the name is the name of the modem and double-click the file to open it.

3. Scroll through the log.

APPLY YOUR LEARNING

Review Questions

1. If you have tested a modem on the client and server but still cannot connect, what actions can you take?

2. What is the series of steps that you should take to verify network connectivity using TCP/IP?

3. What line protocol does RAS use when dialing in to the network?

4. What three communications technologies can RAS use for connections?

5. What are the three different call-back security options available in RAS?

6. What are the three port configuration settings available for your RAS server?

7. What utility can you use to view the TCP/IP settings for your Windows NT Server?

8. What utility can you use to verify a NetBIOS over TCP/IP connection?

Exam Questions

1. The NT RAS Server accepts which line protocol?

   A. NetBEUI

   B. PPTP

   C. TCP/IP

   D. PPP

   E. SLIP

2. What is the maximum number of inbound RAS connections on Windows NT Server?

   A. 1

   B. 16

   C. 64

   D. 128

   E. 256

3. Which of the following types of connections does RAS support?

   A. PSTN

   B. X.25

   C. IEEE X.500

   D. RadioLan

   E. ISDN

APPLY YOUR LEARNING

4. Does Multilink work with call-back security?

   A. Yes

   B. No

   C. It depends on the configuration

5. Which of these network protocols does RAS support?

   A. NWLink

   B. NetBIOS

   C. CSLIP

   D. Winsock

   E. TCP/IP

6. A user calls up and complains that he or she cannot dial in. After further discussion, you find that the user receives a message saying something about not being allowed to dial in. What should you check?

   A. Restart the Windows NT Server. One of the modems must be disabled.

   B. Change the security options on the RAS server to enable any authentication including clear text.

   C. Tell the user to restart his or her system and try again.

   D. Check the user's permissions in the User Manager for Domains.

   E. Tell the user that he or she cannot call in while talking to you.

7. What does the user need in addition to RAS to connect to a NetWare server through the RAS connection?

   A. Novell NetWare

   B. Nothing, this is automatic

   C. NWLink

   D. A NetWare client and protocol

   E. This is not possible

8. Which of the following protocols is available for NT?

   A. NetBEUI

   B. UDP

   C. NWLink

   D. All of the above

Answers to Review Questions

1. The next step is to verify that the security settings and dial-in permissions are valid. Failing this, you can create a log of the PPP handshake by setting the Logging option to 1 in the Registry under HKEY_LOCAL_MACHINE\System\CurrentControlSet\Services\RASMAN\PPP. See "Dial-In Permissions" and "PPP Problems."

2. The steps are as follows:

   a. Verify that you have an address by using IPCONFIG.

   b. PING 127.0.0.1 to check that the protocol is in and functioning properly.

APPLY YOUR LEARNING

c. PING your_IP_address to verify that the protocol is bound to the card correctly.

d. PING local_computer to check that you are on the network, and that your subnet mask is correct.

e. PING the remote_host to ensure that you can see your router, and can pass through the router.

See "IPCONFIG" and "PING."

3. The Microsoft RAS server always uses PPP when users are dialing in to the network. See the section "Overview of RAS."

4. RAS uses the PSTN (Public Switched Telephone Network), ISDN (Integrated Services Digital Network), and X.25 communications technologies for connectivity. See the section "Other Communication Technologies."

5. The three settings for callback security are No Call Back, Set By Caller, and Preset To. See the section "Call Back Security."

6. The RAS server port can be configured as Dial Out Only, Receive Calls Only, or Dial Out and Receive Calls. See the section "Configuring the RAS Server."

7. You can use the IPCONFIG utility to view your TCP/IP settings on a Windows NT Server. See the section "IPCONFIG."

8. You can use the NBTSTAT utility to verify a NetBIOS over a TCP/IP connection to a remote host. See the section "Sessions."

Answers to Exam Questions

1. **D.** Windows NT RAS servers accept inbound calls using the PPP line protocol. See the section "Overview of RAS."

2. **E.** The maximum number of inbound connections that can be supported by a RAS server is 256. See the section "Configuring the RAS Server."

3. **A. B. E.** RAS supports PSTN, ISDN, and X.25 communications technologies for connections. See the section "Other Communications Technologies."

4. **B.** No. Call Back security does not work with Multilink, as the call back cannot be configured to dial multiple lines. See the section "Call Back with Multilink."

5. **A. E.** RAS supports TCP/IP, NWLINK, and NetBEUI protocols. See the section "Configuring the RAS Server."

6. **D.** If a user is getting a message stating that he or she cannot dial in, the connection is being made; however, the user most likely lacks adequate permissions to dial in. See the section "Dial-In Permissions."

7. **D.** If the user has a NetWare client and protocol, he or she can route through the RAS server and access a NetWare server. See the section "Configuring the RAS Server."

8. **A. D.** Windows NT supports the TCP/IP, NetBEUI, and NWLINK protocols. See the section "Connectivity Issues."

This chapter helps you to prepare for the Microsoft exam by covering the following objectives within the "Troubleshooting" category:

Choose the appropriate course of action to take to resolve resource access and permission problems.

▶ Connecting to resources within your network environment is one of the most common tasks carried out by users. To be successful with this objective, you must be able to resolve resource connection problems and solve any permission conflicts that are encountered.

Choose the appropriate course of action to take to resolve fault-tolerance failures. Fault-tolerance methods include the following:

◆ **Tape backup**

◆ **Mirroring**

◆ **Stripe set with parity**

▶ To implement fault tolerance within your Windows NT system, you must ensure that you fully understand how it is installed and configured, and also how to recover from the fault-tolerance settings in case of a disk drive failure. The use of backups is critical as a safety net for any data recovery.

CHAPTER 14

Troubleshooting Resource Access and Fault-Tolerance Problems

STUDY STRATEGIES

The best way to prepare for these types of questions, as well as any troubleshooting objective, is to gain real-world experience. For this chapter, working with resources—specifically share permissions, NTFS permissions, and the hard-disk fault-tolerance options available within Windows NT—is the only way of building your knowledge to the level required for the exam.

This chapter prepares you for the exam by introducing utilities used in troubleshooting resource access and the fault-tolerance solutions implemented within your Windows NT system. It is intended to give you instruction in the troubleshooting techniques and tools that are covered on the Enterprise exam. The chapter is split into two main sections:

◆ Sharing problems

◆ Fault-tolerance problems

SHARING PROBLEMS

Choose the appropriate course of action to take to resolve resource access and permission problems.

One of the key uses of a network is to enable the users of the network to share files. Although sharing is relatively straightforward, problems occasionally arise, causing grief to the users involved.

A very common problem occurs when users search for but cannot find a resource. This is an issue that normally is related to connectivity; moreover, it is an issue of the browser service. The browser service creates and distributes a list of the servers that are on the network. This problem normally resolves itself as the list is updated, and is a matter of educating users. The following sections review the most common problems associated with sharing resources. The areas in which sharing problems arise include the following:

◆ Share permissions

◆ Combined permissions

Share Permissions

One of the most common problems is that of permissions. The key issues are the ability of a user to access a share and to save files to it and the problem of keeping the users out of shares that they are not supposed to be in. There are two types of permissions that you can use in Windows NT.

Share-level permissions describe the permissions that users have if they connect across the network. This type of permission is applied to the folder that is shared, and the same level of access is given to all of the folders under it. This differs from Windows 95, where you can use the share permissions to change the rights of unshared sub-folders.

The other type of permissions is NTFS permissions. NTFS permissions are applied both to the folders and to files. A folder, can have many different files, each of which has its own different permissions. In any system, the results of permissions are a common source of problems, either because security is too open or because improper permission settings have been granted to a user or group.

You should keep in mind two main issues about permissions:

◆ The default permissions for both share and NTFS give the Windows NT group Everyone full control over the files and folders. Whenever you format a drive as NTFS or when you first share a folder, you should remove these permissions. The Everyone group contains everyone, including a guest or any other user who, for one reason or another, can connect to your system.

◆ The NTFS folder permission Delete takes precedence over any file permissions. In all other cases, the file permissions take precedence over the folder permissions.

Combined Permissions

The one thing that can complicate matters is that you can assign a folder to both NTFS permissions and share permissions. The files in a share could also have NTFS file permissions.

Usually, you should leave the share permissions fairly open (Users—Full Control) and lock the files and folder up with NTFS permissions. This is not because the NTFS permissions take precedence, but because Windows NT will compare the share and NTFS permission and will apply whichever is more restrictive.

That means if you tighten up the share permissions, all the users will have is Read permission, even a user whose home folder is under the share.

Another point to remember is always to follow the AGLP process for assigning permissions to users. Remember that you should group similar users into global groups. This enables the user to be used on other computers in the domain. On the local machine that has the information or resource, create a local group. Give the local group the full control (or less control if the group members don't need full control) and permissions (rights) to the share. Set the NTFS permissions to the exact permissions that are required.

At this point, all you need to do is take the global group from the domain and add it to the local group on the computer that has the information, which can be a domain controller.

> **EXAM TIP**
>
> **Not Heavy on the Exam**
> The Enterprise exam has very few questions regarding troubleshooting the resources; however, ensure that you have a strong understanding of the permissions—both share and NTFS—and that you fully understand how the permissions combine. Chapter 5, "Managing Resources: Remote Administration and Disk Resources," covers these topics in greater detail.

FAULT-TOLERANCE PROBLEMS

Choose the appropriate course of action to take to resolve fault-tolerance failures.

In any Windows NT system, hard drives might fail, and users might lose both precious data and time. Much time and energy has been spent in trying to make computers, and notably hard disks, last longer. But there will always be that day when you come into the office and the server is down with a failed hard disk. Ensure that you have a backup strategy in place to assist you in recovering files in case of any emergencies.

As a supplement to your backup strategy, you might also implement one of the Windows NT fault-tolerance options. The following sections review the supported fault-tolerance options available, and assist you in preparing to recover by using each of these options in case of hard disk failure.

Fault-Tolerant Methods

Two levels of fault tolerance are built into Windows NT server: disk mirroring and duplexing and disk striping with parity. Both of these methods are sound ways to protect your data if one disk fails. Remember that if you lose more than one disk, you will lose your data. You still need to perform backups.

NOTE

FTDISK.SYS The driver that is used for fault-tolerant disk sets is FTDISK.SYS.

The upcoming sections cover in more detail the procedures and processes involved in troubleshooting your fault-tolerant options. The topics covered are the following:

◆ Tape backups

◆ Disk mirroring

◆ Disk stripe set with parity

Tape Backup

Backing up data is very important. Windows NT comes with a backup utility—NT Backup. This utility might not necessarily provide the best system for meeting your needs, but it does provide a built-in system that you can use to provide those crucial backups.

Types of Backups

The primary thing that you need to do is to determine the frequency and type of backup that you will do. There are three main types of backups that you might want to perform:

◆ **Full.** This backs up all the files that you mark and marks the files as having been backed up. This is the longest of the backups because it transfers the most data.

◆ **Differential.** This backs up all the files that have changed since the last backup. A differential does not mark the files as being backed up. As time passes since the last full backup, the differentials will become increasingly larger. However, you have to reload only the full backup and the differential to return to the position of the last backup.

◆ **Incremental.** This backs up any files that have changed since the last backup and then marks them as having been backed up. If your system crashes, you need to start by loading a full backup and then each incremental backup since that full backup.

Backup Strategy

How often you back up depends on the amount of data that is created or changed, and how much of the created or changed data you are willing to lose. If your data changes frequently, you need to back up often, using incremental backups.

Remember that the Windows NT backup program can't back up a file that is open. If you require this facility, you need a program that can perform backup operations while a file is in use; numerous third-party utilities offer additional backup features.

Mirroring

Mirroring is vastly less efficient than a stripe set with parity. A major advantage to using mirroring over a stripe set with parity is that mirroring can be done on the system and boot partitions, whereas a stripe set with parity cannot.

The basics of mirroring are very simple. Every write that is performed on one disk is performed on another disk. This means that if the first disk goes, you can recover using the mirrored copy.

Disk duplexing is the same as mirroring, only in the case of disk duplexing, each disk drive has its own disk controller, which offers complete duplication of all components used in a disk configuration. In the following sections, you review the following topics:

◆ Mirroring a drive

◆ Creating a fault-tolerance boot disk

◆ Using the boot disk

> **WARNING**
>
> **Must Be Identical** If you are mirroring the system partition, the disks and partitions should be absolutely identical. Otherwise, the MBR/DBR (master boot record/disk boot record) that contains the driver information will not be correct.
>
> Remember that any time you update the disk configuration, you must update the Emergency Repair Disk. This update copies the disk configuration changes so that you can recover the fault-tolerant set in case of Registry problems.

Mirroring a Drive

Creating a mirror is very simple. You need to have another drive that has at least the same or more free space as the drive you want to mirror. From the Disk Administrator, perform the tasks outlined in Step by Step 14.1 to create a mirrored drive.

STEP BY STEP

14.1 Creating a Mirrored Drive

1. In the Disk Administrator, click the drive that you want to mirror.

2. Holding the Ctrl key, click an area of free space of equal or greater size on another physical disk in your system.

3. From the Fault Tolerance menu, choose Mirroring.

4. Choose Partition, Commit changes now.

5. You receive an informational warning that you must restart. Restart the computer.

6. The mirror set initializes. Check the Event Viewer to ensure that the driver FTDISK has started this process.

   By following each of the preceding steps, you will successfully implement a mirror set. This set can be very helpful in ensuring that your system can recover completely from any problems with the hard disks in your computer.

Creating a Fault-Tolerant Boot Disk

If you are mirroring the system partition, you should create a fault-tolerant boot disk and test it.

Creating the disk is described in previous chapters. After you have the basic disk, you need to edit BOOT.INI to point at the other member of the mirror set. The following sections assist you in understanding the BOOT.INI file so your modifications are correct. The topics to be covered include the following:

◆ Understanding ARC naming

◆ Editing BOOT.INI

Understanding ARC Naming

When you edit BOOT.INI, your entry is the ARC (Advanced RISC Computing) name of the system partition. You need to point this at the other copy of the system partition.

Although ARC naming looks complicated, it is really rather simple. The name is in four parts, of which you use three. The syntax is as follows:

```
multi/scsi(#)disk(#)rdisk(#)partition(#)
```

The following list outlines the parts of this syntax:

◆ **multi/scsi.** You will either use multi or scsi, not both. Use multi in all cases except when using a SCSI controller that cannot handle int13 (hard disk access) BIOS routines. This is uncommon. The number following either multi or scsi is the logical number of the controller, with the first controller being 0, the second being 1, and so forth.

◆ **disk.** When you use a SCSI disk, you use the disk parameter to indicate which of the drives on the controller is the drive you are specifying. Again, the numbers start at 0 for the first drive, 1 for the second, and so on.

◆ **rdisk.** You use this parameter for the other controllers in the same way you use the disk parameter for SCSI.

◆ **partition.** This is the partition on the disk to which you are pointing. The first partition is 1, the second is 2, and so forth. Remember that you can have up to four primary partitions or three primary and one extended partitions. The extended partition is always the last partition, and the first logical drive in the partition has the partition's number. Other drives in the extended partition are numbered successively in increments of one.

As an example, the second primary partition on the third drive of the second EIDE controller could be described as follows:

```
multi(1)disk(0)rdisk(2)partition(2)
```

Although you do not use the disk variable, you must include it.

Editing BOOT.INI

Before you edit the BOOT.INI file on the floppy (not the hard disk), make sure you remove the attributes from the file. They will be Read Only and System.

To remove the attributes, enter the following command:

```
ATTRIB -s -r a:\boot.ini
```

Using the Boot Disk

If you are lucky, you will never need to use the boot floppy. If you do, however, several steps are required after booting from the floppy. The upcoming sections step you through the process used to troubleshoot a broken mirror set. The topics covered include the following:

◆ Breaking the mirror set

◆ Restoring the drive

Breaking the Mirror Set

The boot floppy gets the operating system up and running. You should immediately back up the mirrored copy of the mirror set. To back up the drive, you must break your mirror set. To do this, perform the tasks outlined in Step by Step 14.2.

STEP BY STEP

14.2 Breaking the Mirror Set

1. Run the Disk Administrator.

2. From the Disk Administrator, click the remaining fragment of the mirrored set.

3. Choose Fault Tolerance, Break Mirror Set from the menu.

   At the end of these three steps, you should notice that the mirror set has been broken, and you can now back up the drive.

Restoring the Drive

After backing up the remaining members of the mirror set, replace the drive that is defective and restart the system from the boot floppy.

You can now use the Disk Administrator to create and format the new partition on the drive that you have replaced.

After replacing and restoring the drive as part of the mirror set, restore the backup to this new drive. If this new drive is the boot drive (where the Windows NT files are), make sure you restore the Registry from the backup. Now boot from the recovered disk. Your system should now be functional once more, with all data fully recovered.

Stripe Set with Parity

Although the mirror set is useful for providing fault-tolerant methods that work for the boot and system partitions, the stripe set with parity is a more efficient system. You should use this system instead of a mirror set for data areas that exist on your systems.

Overview

There are two concepts that make a stripe set with parity work. First there is the concept of striping. What a normal stripe set (and one with parity) does is take the information that you want to write to the disk in 64K chunks and splits the information into smaller parts. These smaller parts are then written to separate disks.

In a regular stripe set, the smaller parts result in increased performance. The system achieves this increase by reducing the distance the physical drive heads need to move to do their job. For instance, if a drive must cover half the surface of a disk to write a large file, splitting the file into two and writing it to two disks at the same time increases the performance, because the head needs to cover only a fourth of the drive instead of half. Because a stripe set can have up to 32 parts, you could reduce the travel to as little as 1/64 from one-half.

The following sections cover the following topics:

◆ Creating a stripe set with parity

◆ Regenerating data on-the-fly

◆ Regenerating the stripe set

Creating a Stripe Set with Parity

Creating a stripe set with parity is very simple. Make sure that you have free space on at least three different drives. Remember that the maximum number of disks that can be used in a stripe set with parity is 32 drives. To create a stripe set with parity, perform the tasks outlined in Step by Step 14.3.

STEP BY STEP

14.3 Creating a Stripe Set with Parity

1. From the Disk Administrator, click the first drive that you want to use.

2. Holding down the Ctrl key, click all the other drives to include in the stripe set with parity.

3. Choose Fault Tolerant, Stripe Set with Parity.

4. The system asks you for the size and suggests the largest possible. This suggested size is that of the smallest free space you choose times the number of disks. All the areas used must be of the same size. Choose OK and commit the changes.

   Now that you have created the structure for your stripe set with parity, you must restart for the changes to take effect to your drives. After restarting the system, you can format the partition and begin to use your stripe set with parity. Note that you cannot quick-format the partition and that the formatted size is the total space of all drives minus the one drive used for parity.

Regenerating Data On-the-Fly

This concept is relatively simple, yet very handy. A stripe set with parity has a check mechanism that enables the system to re-create the data when it is needed. This means that the system will need to store some information on the disks as well. The system, however, can then recover the data automatically.

Every stripe set with parity requires at least three drives. This is because one drive, whether you use 3 or 32, will be used to hold the parity information. The parity is actually moved from disk to disk. Consider Table 14.1.

TABLE 14.1

EXAMPLE OF A STRIPE SET WITH PARITY

Disk 1	Disk 2	Disk 3	Disk 4
1	0	0	1
0	1	1	0
1	1	1	1
0	0	1	1
0	1	1	0
1	1	0	0
1	0	0	1

The example in Table 14.1 is oversimplified. Simple binary adding has been used in place of the more complicated calculations the system will do.

Now picture disk number 3 failing. This system can (and will) regenerate the information that was on the disk in memory. The process goes like this: 1 (disk 1) + 0 (disk 2) = 1 + 1 (disk 4) = 10 (binary). The last bit is used for the parity in this case, and the data is recovered. Try the other lines for yourself to make sure.

If the information that was on the stripe set has to be regenerated in memory, system performance will suffer. Therefore, you need to fix the stripe set quickly before another drive dies.

Regenerating the Stripe Set

Unlike repairing a mirror set, fixing a stripe set with parity is simple. Perform the tasks outlined in Step by Step 14.4 to regenerate your stripe set with parity.

STEP BY STEP

14.4 Regenerating the Stripe Set

1. Physically replace the faulty disk drive.

2. Start the Disk Administrator.

3. Select your stripe set with parity that you need to repair and then Ctrl+click the free space of the drive you added to fix the stripe set.

4. From the menu, choose Fault Tolerant, Regenerate. Note that this process can take some time, although the process takes less time than restoring from tape.

   The drives regenerate all the required data from the parity bits and the data bits. When you complete your stripe set with parity, the drives will be completely functional.

R E V I E W   B R E A K

Fault-Tolerance Problems

Most problems that you will encounter with fault tolerance in Windows NT will be the result of a hard disk failure. Ensure that you have a solid backup schedule and that you have up-to-date emergency repair disks and boot disks. For recovering from a faulty disk drive in a fault-tolerance configuration, ensure that you understand the process to break a mirror set, and can regenerate your stripe set with parity.

CASE STUDY: DESIGNING A FAULT-TOLERANCE SOLUTION

ESSENCE OF THE CASE

Here are the essential elements in this case:

- The client requires a fault-tolerance solution that enables the company to duplicate the data files.

- The solution must be able to function with the loss of one of the disks— to autoregenerate the data.

- Currently the Windows NT Server has two disk drives.

SCENARIO

JPS Consulting has been approached to assist with the design of a fault-tolerance solution for an accounting firm. The data on the company's disk drives is very critical, so the company requires a method to ensure duplication of the data. The server that JPS Consulting is using is a Windows NT Server with two disk drives—one that holds the system files and one that contains the data files—and the company currently follows a backup strategy each night. The main concern is that if the disk drive fails, the company's employees will not be able to complete any work on that day. The company needs a solution that enables the system to keep functioning and enables the employees to resolve the problem efficiently and limit downtime.

ANALYSIS

The accounting firm must purchase two additional disk drives and then configure the system to use these disks. Using the Disk Administrator, the client then sets up a stripe set with parity encompassing the existing data disk and the two new disks. The stripe set with parity enables the client to autoregenerate the data in case of a faulty disk drive and also gives the client an efficient solution for repairing the stripe set with parity, by replacing any faulty drives and using the regenerate command in the Disk Administrator. The client will maintain its current backup strategy and use it as an additional security measure for the recovery of any data.

CHAPTER SUMMARY

KEY TERMS

- NTFS
- AGLP
- disk mirroring
- disk duplexing
- disk stripe set with parity
- BOOT.INI
- ARC

The easiest way to summarize this chapter is to list each of the main topics covered and list a few common points that are required for each for you to succeed on the exam.

◆ **Share permissions.** A common problem when troubleshooting share resources is in the share permissions. Ensure that the minimum functional permissions have been assigned. Make sure that the Everyone group does not have full control of a share.

◆ **Combining NTFS and share permissions.** When combining these permissions, remember that NT will use the most restrictive of the combined permissions. As a rule, use the NTFS permissions as the highest level of permissions, and use the share permissions mainly for access to the folder or share.

◆ **Tape backups.** In any system that you are using, ensure that you have a good backup strategy. Any component in your system can be faulty, and it is your responsibility to have a recovery plan in case of emergencies.

◆ **Disk mirroring.** If you are implementing disk mirroring in your system, ensure that you have created a fault-tolerant boot disk that you can use in case of drive failure. By having this disk preconfigured and handy, you can break the mirror set and replace the drive with very little downtime for your server.

◆ **Stripe set with parity.** This system allows the data to be automatically regenerated if a drive is faulty. Although the system performance will dramatically decline, a stripe set with parity is still a functional box and you risk no possibility of losing any data. If you find that a drive in your stripe set is faulty, replace the drive and use the Regenerate command from the Disk Administrator.

APPLY YOUR LEARNING

Exercises

14.1 Mirroring a Partition

In this exercise, you mirror a partition. This exercise requires that you have NT Server installed and that you have a disk available with some free space on as few as two physical drives.

Time Estimate: 15 minutes

1. Start the Disk Administrator (Start, Programs, Administrative tools).

2. Select a drive to mirror. (If you don't have a drive, or don't want to work with one of the ones that you have, select an area of free space and create a small partition.)

3. Select an area of free space on another drive by holding the Ctrl key and clicking.

4. Choose Fault Tolerance, Mirror from the menu.

5. Choose Partition, Commit Changes Now.

6. The system warns you that the change you have requested will require you to restart the computer. Acknowledge this.

7. The system will give you a warning about updating the emergency repair disk. Acknowledge this.

8. You will now be asked whether you want to restart your system. Go ahead and restart. (Even if you are not asked, restart your system anyway; this will initiate the mirroring.)

9. After restarting the system, go to the Event Viewer and observe the FTDISK entries.

10. Go back to the Disk Administrator and click the mirrored partition.

11. Choose Fault Tolerance, Break Mirror Set. Shut down and restart your computer. (If you created a small partition for this exercise, you can delete it now.)

Review Questions

1. If a member of a stripe set with parity fails, what must you do to recover the data?

2. Why does NT support both disk mirroring and stripe sets with parity?

3. When you are working with share and NTFS permissions, which takes precedence?

4. What are the three types of backups available in the NTBACKUP utility?

5. What is the difference between disk mirroring and disk duplexing?

6. What utility is used to set up the fault-tolerance options in Windows NT?

APPLY YOUR LEARNING

Exam Questions

1. If a user connects to a shared file source across a network, which of the following takes place?

   A. The share permissions are applied, and then the NTFS permissions are applied.

   B. The NTFS permissions are applied, and then the share permissions are applied.

   C. Both sets of permissions are evaluated, and the more restrictive permissions are used.

2. How many disks can be used when mirroring?

   A. Two

   B. Between 2 and 32

   C. Between 3 and 32

   D. Up to 256

3. How many disks can be used when creating a disk stripe set with parity?

   A. Two

   B. Between 2 and 32

   C. Between 3 and 32

   D. Up to 256

4. What command is used to regenerate a stripe set with parity in the Disk Administrator?

   A. Fault Tolerant, Create Stripe Set

   B. Disk, Regenerate

   C. Fault Tolerant, Regenerate

   D. File, Disk Repair

5. If a disk fails in a mirror set, can the data be autoregenerated?

   A. Yes.

   B. No.

   C. It depends on the configuration settings.

Answers to Review Questions

1. When a member of a stripe set with parity fails, you replace the disk and restart the system. You can then use the Fault Tolerance menu in the Disk Administrator to regenerate the stripe set with parity. See "Regenerating the Stripe Set."

2. The disk mirroring enables you to place the system and boot partition on a fault-tolerant partition even though they cannot be placed on a stripe set with parity. See "Mirroring."

3. Neither. The system uses whichever permissions are more restrictive. See "Share Permissions."

4. The three types of backups available through NTBACKUP are Full, Differential, and Incremental. See the section "Types of Backups."

5. Disk mirroring uses two physical disks and one common disk controller, whereas disk duplexing uses two physical disks and two physical disk controllers to provide complete duplication. See the section "Mirroring."

6. The Disk Administrator is the utility used to create the fault-tolerant options available in Windows NT. See the section "Mirroring a Drive."

APPLY YOUR LEARNING

Answers to Exam Questions

1. **C.** When permissions are combined, the most restrictive are used. See the section "Combining Permissions."

2. **A.** A mirror set consists of two physical disks. See the section "Mirroring."

3. **C.** A stripe set with parity can use a minimum of three disks and a maximum of 32 disks. See the section "Stripe Set with Parity."

4. **C.** The command Fault Tolerant, Regenerate is used to regenerate a stripe set with parity. See the section "Regenerating the Stripe Set."

5. **B.** If a drive fails in a mirror set, the data cannot be regenerated. See the section "Breaking the Mirror Set."

This chapter helps you to prepare for the Microsoft exam by covering the following objectives within the "Troubleshooting" category:

Perform advanced problem resolution. Tasks include the following:

- ◆ **Diagnosing and interpreting a blue screen**

- ◆ **Configuring a memory dump**

- ◆ **Using the event log service**

▶ This objective involves having a strong understanding of the tools available to you while diagnosing system problems within Windows NT. The Event Viewer is a utility that contains any system errors that occur while your system is still operable. When the system crashes and cannot recover, you must analyze blue screens. Understanding tools available to assist in interpreting blue screens and viewing memory dumps are requirements for fully meeting this objective.

CHAPTER 15

Advanced Troubleshooting

STUDY STRATEGIES

The advanced troubleshooting and the utilities used are probably new to you. Try each of the utilities and review each of the processes listed throughout this chapter to ensure that you have a strong understanding of advanced troubleshooting. The blue screen analysis can be somewhat daunting at first, but ensure that you are familiar with the various components of the blue screen and can pull out the required information from them. The way to succeed on this section of the exam is to have real, hands-on experience with these tools.

As the operating systems get more advanced, so does the complexity of troubleshooting serious system errors. Although Windows NT is normally extremely stable once the operating system is running, there will be times when the operating system doesn't work. Much of this trouble is configuration related or requires reloading of an application.

Even Windows NT, from time to time, will not want to work. Solving the problem when you can start the operating system is relatively easy. When you are faced with a blue screen filled with hexadecimal code, the problem gets more complex.

This chapter deals first with the Event Viewer that enables you to fix problems that occur after the operating system is up. Then it moves on to troubleshooting the blue screen or stop errors that can be very frustrating. The following are the main topics covered in this chapter:

◆ The event log

◆ Blue screen errors

◆ Memory dump files

THE EVENT LOG

One of the best features of Windows NT is the capability of the operating system to start to load even if there are problems that will prevent the system from being fully functional. This capability usually at least enables you to get to the Event Viewer to see where the problem with the system lies. The Event Viewer is in the Administrative tools group under Start, Programs. This section on the event log addresses the following topics:

◆ Examining the parts of the Event Log

◆ Configuring the Event Logs

◆ Using the Event Log

◆ Finding more information

Examining the Parts of the Event Log

The Event Viewer takes care of the three main event logs. The logs that are recorded are the system log, the security log, and the application log. Each of the logs handles different events that occur in NT:

◆ **System log.** All the device drivers, services, and other system-related components are tracked in the system log. You examine this log if you get the "At least one driver or service has failed" message when you start Windows NT.

◆ **Security log.** This log tracks events that deal with the security of the system. The events that are logged depends on the settings that you select in the User Manager under Policies, Auditing. Be aware that excessive auditing of events will reduce your system performance.

◆ **Application log.** Any 32-bit application that is written to use Microsoft API calls can record information in the application log. This log often tells you why Exchange Server is not working or the SQL server could not start.

The first place you should usually look for information is the Event Viewer. The Event Viewer can help you direct your troubleshooting based on the system events. Jumping into the configuration of the TCP/IP protocol might not fix a problem with another host that has the same computer name.

Configuring the Event Logs

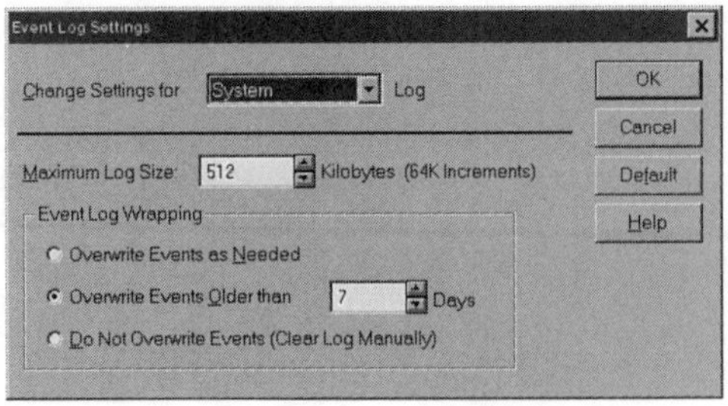

The event logs store a good deal of information, and the more services and applications that are on a system and the more auditing that you require, the larger the amount of information you will receive. To prevent the event logs from filling up, thus causing other problems, you should configure the logs to the size that you think will be required. This ensures that you will have the log information when you need it.

FIGURE 15.1
You configure the logs in the Event Log settings dialog box.

You configure the logs in the Event Viewer under Log, Settings. A screen appears that looks similar to the one shown in Figure 15.1. The options are as follows:

◆ **Change Settings for.** This setting tells the system the log for which you are changing the settings.

◆ **Maximum Log Size.** This setting specifies the total size to which the log can grow. For most applications, the default setting of 512KB should be enough. If you will be auditing many events or have several pieces of software that will use the applications log, you might want to increase this number until the log holds the amount of traffic generated in about three days.

◆ **Event Log Wrapping.** This setting tells the system what to do if the log becomes full.

Using the Event Log

Perform advanced problem resolution, including using the event log service.

Even on a system that is completely functional, you should see some activity (see Figure 15.2). There are five basic events that you will see in the logs. The first is that of informational items that alert you that things are happening on the system. These are represented by blue circles with the letter *i* in them.

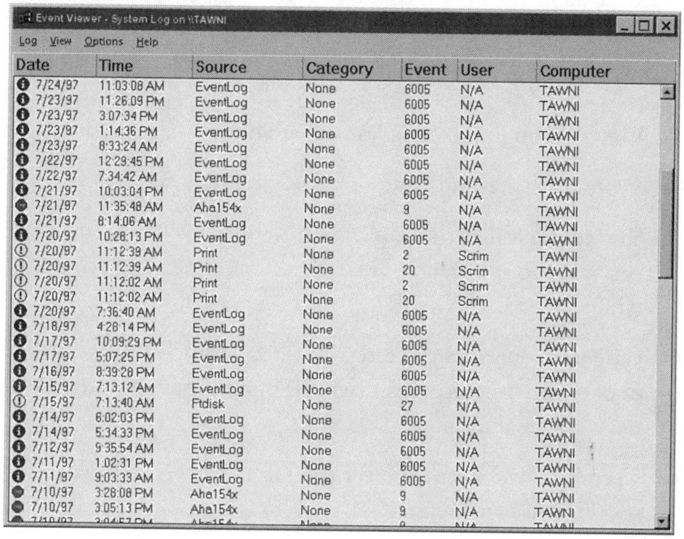

FIGURE 15.2
Here the Event Viewer shows the system log and the list of events.

Warning messages indicate there are more severe problems, but do not stop the system. These are yellow circles with an *!* in them. Warnings often lead to a stop error. Most stop errors indicate that some part of Windows NT is not functioning and are shown as red stop signs.

The other two errors are normally on the Security menu. Violations (failures) of security are shown as locks, and access events (successes) are shown as keys. To help you locate events in the Event Viewer, the following subsections discuss these topics:

◆ Filtering

◆ Searching for events

◆ Following the sequence of events

Filtering

The event logs can list thousands of events. To make the job of finding the problem easier, you can filter the log. To filter the log, choose View, Filter from the menu. You will see the Filter dialog box appear (see Figure 15.3).

In the Filter dialog box, you can view a subset of the many options that are available for filtering. The following list covers the different items that you can filter on.

◆ **View From.** Sets the earliest date that you want to see.

◆ **View Through.** Sets the last date that you want to see.

◆ **Types.** Specifies the types of events that you want to see.

◆ **Source.** Identifies the application, service, or driver for which you want to see events. The source could be something like FTDISK or BROWSER.

◆ **Category.** Specifies the category of the error. The system log does not usually use this category, but instead specifies the area that you are auditing.

◆ **User.** Tells the Event Viewer to look for errors that have the specified user name.

◆ **Computer.** Tells the Event Viewer to look for errors that have the computer name.

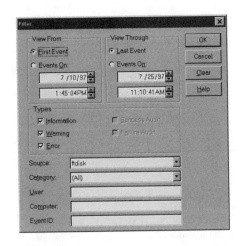

FIGURE 15.3
In the Filter dialog box, you can enable conditions on the events listed.

◆ **Event ID.** Tells the Event Viewer to list only the errors with the specified event ID.

When you want to go back to seeing all events, choose View, All Events.

Searching for Events

Searching for an event is similar to filtering, but in many cases it is more useful for troubleshooting because it enables you to see the events surrounding the one that you are looking for. You can find an event by choosing View, Find.

The Find dialog box (see Figure 15.4) enables you to enter the search criteria. The options are almost the same as those in the Filter Events dialog box. However, you will notice that dates are missing. You can now look for any piece of text in the details of the event and can choose to search up or down.

Following the Sequence of Events

In a perfect world, a computer would be able to tell you what is wrong and what needs to be fixed, and then fix it. We don't live in that world. When you go into the Event Viewer, you need to be able to follow the sequence of events to find the problem with the system.

You should first scan down the system log until you see the EventLog item as the source of an information message. Every time you start the system, the event log service is started; each time the service starts, it writes an entry in the log to mark this point.

This point is close to, but not necessarily, the first entry. There are several drivers that reside at a lower layer than the Event Viewer, and you should check the times of the next few errors in the list to see when they occurred. If they happened seconds before the EventLog entry, they are probably the cause of the problem.

After you find the first error that occurred in the system startup, double-click to see the event details (see Figure 15.5). Now use the Previous button to move up the list (although this is counterintuitive).

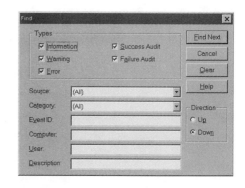

FIGURE 15.4
The Find dialog box from the Event Viewer enables you to search for certain events.

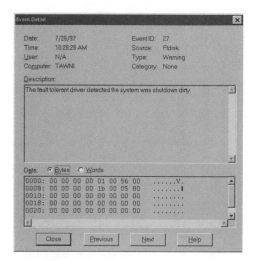

FIGURE 15.5
The Event Viewer can also show the details of an event.

As you move through the list, you will see the errors in the order of occurrence. Jumping into the log and double-clicking on the first error that occurred often leads you to an incorrect assumption about the cause of the problem. This error is the last one to occur and is normally caused by the other listed errors.

Finding More Information

If you have worked with the event logs in Windows NT, you know that the information that is displayed in the event details can sometimes be relatively cryptic. Therefore, you need to be able to find more information using the event ID or other clues that are in the information.

There are two very good sources for information about Windows NT errors. Microsoft TechNet is a solid and very current source of information that is available for a monthly subscription rate. The other source is the Internet. The Microsoft site has a full suite of information about things that have already happened to other users.

TechNet

TechNet is probably the best source for troubleshooting information for Windows NT and all the Microsoft products. Shipped to subscribers on a monthly basis, TechNet comes on at least two CDs.

The interface is simple to use, with the contents list in a folder with the structure on the left and the contents on the right (see Figure 15.6).

After you have TechNet up, you can search for information. In Figure 15.7, a simple search has been entered.

Figure 15.8 shows the results.

On the Internet

Another great source of information is the Internet. Many sites can provide you with information about Windows NT. When it comes to troubleshooting, the best place to start is the Microsoft support site at **www.microsoft.com/support**. One of the items on the support site is the troubleshooting wizards (see Figure 15.9). These wizards step you through the process of troubleshooting and provide you with solutions that come from the Microsoft technical staff.

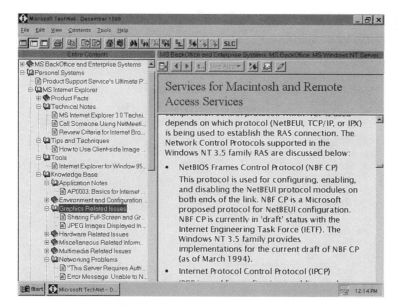

FIGURE 15.6
TechNet is your source for technical resources.

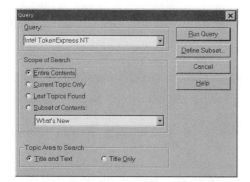

FIGURE 15.7
The TechNet search window with the system
set to search for Intel token express.

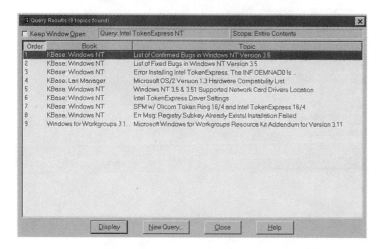

FIGURE 15.8
The results of the search in Figure 15.7 appear
in the TechNet archives.

FIGURE 15.9
You can find the NT troubleshooting wizard at the Microsoft support site; here is one of the initial screens you will see.

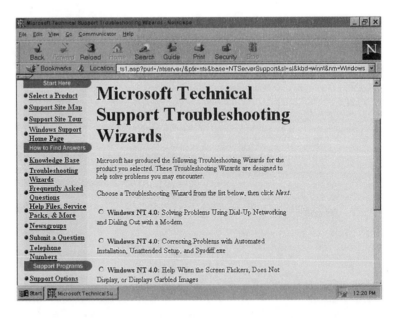

The other important area on the support page is the knowledge base, where report problems are listed and resolutions are published (see Figure 15.10).

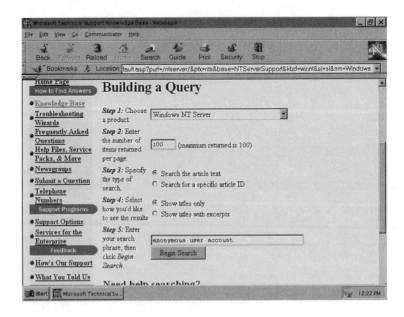

FIGURE 15.10
The knowledge base lists reported problems and publishes resolutions.

BLUE SCREEN ERRORS

Perform advanced problem resolution, including diagnosing and interpreting a blue screen.

Probably the most frustrating errors are blue screen errors. These are cases where the operating system fails to start or abruptly stops working, and you are left with hexadecimal information on the screen.

You can get several pieces of information from the blue screen. Usually these are enough to get by the critical problem. Most of the blue screen errors are caused by either device drivers or hardware. The following sections help you better understand blue screens:

◆ Interpreting blue screens

◆ Understanding information on the blue screen

◆ Debugging interactively

> **EXAM TIP**
>
> **Focus on the Big Picture** The Enterprise exam focuses more on the big picture of blue screen analysis than the procedure required. Ensure that you have an understanding of the tools available, and how you can connect to a machine to enable the debugging; it is on these areas that the exam will test you.

Interpreting Blue Screens

There are two ways to deal with a blue screen. Many troubleshooters simply reboot the system and if the problem continues, they reinstall the operating system. In many cases, you can avoid reinstallation by simply reading the information on the screen. You can also use some of the tools that are provided by Windows NT to diagnose and then fix the problem.

Understanding the Information on the Blue Screen

When a stop error occurs, the system displays the character mode stop screen, which includes five main sections:

◆ **Debug Port Status Indicators.** This describes the status of the serial port. If the port is in use, that information will be used for debugging.

◆ **BugCheck Information.** This displays the actual error code and any parameters that the developer included in the error-trapping routines. If this section displays only the top line, the error has also affected the areas that are used to display such information.

◆ **Driver Information.** This area lists the drivers that were loaded when the stop error occurred. There are three items of information given for each driver: the memory location into which the driver was loaded, the time the driver was created (this is the offset in seconds since 1970; use CVTIME.EXE to convert these to human dates), and the name of the driver. The BugCheck Information sometimes includes a pointer to the instruction that causes the ABEND (abnormal end) error. You can use this information to figure out which driver was involved.

◆ **Kernel Build Number and Stack Dump.** This area provides the information on the current build number and a dump of the last instructions that were executed.

◆ **Debug Port Information.** This area indicates the baud rate and other COM settings for the debug port that is in use.

The following is an example of what a stop screen might look like (this example is a simulation only):

```
DSR CTS SND
*** STOP:  0x0000000A (0x00000000,0x0000001A,0x00000000,0xFC873D6C)
IRQL_NOT_LESS_OR_EQUAL*** Address fc873d6c has base at fc870000—®i8042prt.SYS
CPUID:GenuineIntel 5.1.5 irql:1f    SYSVER 0Xf0000421
Dll Base   DateStmp—Name                Dll Base   DateStmp—Name
80100000   2fc653bc—ntoskrnl.exe        80400000   2fb24f4a—®hal.dll
80010000   2faae87f—ncrc810.sys         80013000   2faae8ca—®SCSIPORT.SYS
8001b000   2faae8c5—Scsidisk.sys        8029e000   2fc15d19—®Fastfat.sys
fc820000   2faae8af—Floppy.sys          fc830000   2fb16eef—®Scsicdrm.SYS
fc840000   2faae8ff—FS_Rec.SYSfc850000  2faae8b7—Null.SYS
fc860000   2faae8a1—Beep.SYS            fc870000   31167860—®i8042prt.SYS
fc880000   2faae8b5—Mouclass.SYS        fc890000   2faae8b4—®Kbdclass.SYS
fc8b0000   2faae88d—VIDEOPRT.SYS        fc8c0000   2fb67626—®ati.SYS
fc8a0000   2faae892—vga.sys             fc8e0000   2faae8fd—®Msfs.SYS
fc8f0000   2faae8ec—npfs.SYS            fc900000   2faae91a—®ndistapi.sys
fc910000   2fc4f4b2—ntfs.SYS            fc980000   2fc12af6—®NDIS.SYS
fc970000   2faaee1e—asyncmac.sys        fc9a0000   2dd47963—®epront.sys
fc9b0000   2fb52712—ndiswan.sys         fc9e0000   2faae945—®TDI.SYS
fc9c0000   2fae6a5f—nbf.sys             fc9f0000   2faec8b1—®afd.sys
fca00000   2faaee1f—rasarp.sys          fca10000   2fbf9993—®streams.sys
fca30000   2fc1557b—tcpip.sys           fca50000   2e6ce2d3—®ubnb.sys
fca60000   2e64646c—mcsxns.sys          fca70000   2fc0daf7—®netbt.sys
Address     dword dump    Build [1381]                        —®Name
8014004c fc873d6c fc873d6c ff05e051 00000000 ff05e04b 0000002f—®i8042prt.SYS
8014007c 801400c4 801400c4 00000000 00000023 00000023 00000037—®ntoskrnl.exe
80140098 fc87258e fc87258e 801400e8 00000030 ff0d141c ff0d1598—®i8042prt.SYS
8014009c 801400e8 801400e8 00000030 ff0d141c ff0d1598 00000002—®ntoskrnl.exe
801400b0 801400f8 801400f8 00000000 fc873d6c 00000008 00010202—®ntoskrnl.exe
801400b8 fc873d6c fc873d6c 00000008 00010202 ff0ced88 ff0d1598—®i8042prt.SYS
801400e0 801400c4 801400c4 fca460f4 ffffffff fc874f78 fc870418—®ntoskrnl.exe
```

```
801400e4 fca460f4 fca460f4 ffffffff fc874f78 fc870418 ffffffff—®tcpip.sys
801400ec fc874f78 fc874f78 fc870418 ffffffff 80140110 8013be2a—®i8042prt.SYS
801400f0 fc870418 fc870418 ffffffff 80140110 8013be2a ff0ced88—®i8042prt.SYS
801400f8 80140110 80140110 8013be2a ff0ced88 ff0d1350 80137502—®ntoskrnl.exe
801400fc 8013be2a 8013be2a ff0ced88 ff0d1350 80137052 00000031—®ntoskrnl.exe
Kernel Debugger Using: COM2 (Port 0x2f8, Baud Rate 19200)
Beginning dump of physical memory
Physical memory dump complete. Contact your system administrator or technical support group.
```

In many cases, if you look closely at the error, you will see where the error occurred. In this case, the I8042PRT.SYS is the likely cause, and you would probably be able to fix the problem with an emergency repair.

Debugging Interactively

In some cases, you need to go further than just looking at the screen. There are two ways that you can do so: You can set up the problematic computer to create a dump file and use utilities to verify it, or you can interactively debug the problematic computer using another computer, either with a null modem cable or remotely. In the \support\debug folder on the Windows NT distribution CD, a kernel debugger for each of the platforms can be used for installation. The kernel debuggers use basic serial communications and each needs some configuration. The tasks involved in preparing for a debugging session are outlined in Step by Step 15.1.

STEP BY STEP

15.1 Preparing for a Debugging Session

1. Set up the serial connection.

2. Configure the problematic computer.

3. Place the symbol tree on the diagnosing computer.

4. Set up the debugger on the problematic computer.

5. Start the debugger on the diagnosing computer.

   After you have completed the preparations for debugging a screen by following the preceding steps, you must then ensure that you have set all of the configuration options correctly. The upcoming sections discuss this configuration in more detail.

In using the kernel debugger, you must do some configuration. In the upcoming sections, you learn about the following:

◆ BOOT.INI switches

◆ Modem configuration

◆ The symbol tree

◆ The debugging command

You will look at the configuration requirements and the command used with the kernel debugger.

BOOT.INI Switches

For the system that you will debug to know where to send the information (to the serial port rather than the screen), you need to modify the BOOT.INI file. The following list provides you with the switches that you should add to the version of Windows NT you will boot:

◆ **/Debug.** This switch tells NT to load the kernel debugger during the boot and to keep the debugger in memory.

◆ **/Crashdebug.** This switch is similar to the /Debug option; however, with /Crashdebug, the debugging code will be available only if the system crashes. In most cases, this switch is a better option because the debugger code will not be in memory and therefore won't interfere with the problem.

◆ **/Debugport.** Use this switch to indicate the communications port that you will use.

◆ **/Baudrate.** Select the baud rate for the connection that you will use for debugging.

> N O T E
>
> **Change from Read-Only** Remember that the C:\BOOT.INI file is a read-only system file. To edit this file, you must remove these attributes. If you are unable to boot the system and the file is on an NTFS partition, you should try an emergency repair first. If that repair fails, you can install another copy of Windows NT to give you access to the original boot disk.

Modem Configuration

If you are going to use a local computer to perform the debugging, you only need to provide a null modem cable. If you need to connect remotely, you must configure a modem on the system.

You need to use an external modem to perform the debugging across a remote connection, and you must be able to configure the modem beforehand. If you cannot do this on the problematic system, you must do so on another system and move the modem to the problematic computer.

You need to configure the following settings for your modem.

Remember that if you move the modem after configuring it, you will either have to store the settings or maintain power to the modem.

◆ Auto answer mode: On

◆ Hardware compression: Disabled

◆ Error detection: Disabled

◆ Flow control: Disabled

◆ Baud rate: 9,600 bps for Intel computers, and 19,200 bps for RISC-based computers

The Symbol Tree

The symbol tree is used in debugging to provide the information about what the code does at various locations. This information is different for every version of Windows NT. The symbol library for a standard single processor version of Windows NT is in the \support\debug\symbol\platform folder on the CD-ROM.

If you have installed a service pack or you are working with a HAL other than the basic single-processor HAL, you will need to create a symbol set for the system. Step by Step 15.2 outlines how to do this.

> **NOTE**
>
> **Question on Debugger Remote Capabilities** The exam will have a question on the remote capabilities of the debugger. Ensure that you are aware that a machine can dial in through RAS and remotely debug a machine.

STEP BY STEP

15.2 Creating a Symbol Set for the System

1. Copy to your hard drive the correct folder structure from the Support folder on the CD.

2. Copy the symbols from the distribution media for the updates in the same order that you applied them.

3. For multiprocessor systems, you must rename some of the symbol files. The standard kernel debugger files are named NTOSKRNL.DBG for kernel and HAL.DBG for the HAL. On a multiprocessor computer, you need to rename NTKRNLMP.DBG as NTOSKRNL.DBG. These files are in the \Exe folder.

   The symbol library is a critical component to debugging the blue screens. Ensure that you are using a symbol library that is current with the version of NT with which you are working.

Next, you need to set up the host with a series of environment variables so that the debugger has the basic information it needs. You can do this using the SET command (for help on this, type **SET /?** at a command prompt).

♦ **_NT_DEBUG_PORT.** The COM port being used.

♦ **_NT_DEBUG_BAUD_RATE.** The baud rate for the port.

♦ **_NT_SYMBOL_PATH.** The folder where the symbols folder is located.

♦ **_NT_LOG_FILE_OPEN.** The name of a log file (this is optional).

Debugging Commands

After you have the system up and running, you can begin to debug the remote system. To do this, run the kernel debugger for the platform of the problematic machine. You need to be aware of some command-line switches:

♦ **–b.** Sends a debug breakpoint to the remote system that causes execution on the target computer to stop as soon as possible.

♦ **–c.** Requests a communications resynchronization when the systems connect.

♦ **–m.** Watches the modem control lines. This places the debugger in terminal mode if there is no CD (carrier detect).

♦ **–n.** Loads the symbols immediately (by default, they are loaded in a deferred mode).

♦ **–v.** Turns on verbose mode.

♦ **–x.** Forces the debugger to break in immediately when an exception occurs. By default, the application is left to deal with the error.

MEMORY DUMP FILES

Perform advanced problem resolution, including configuring a memory dump.

Sometimes you will be unable to resolve the problem using the kernel debugger. When this happens, you might want to have Windows NT create a dump file and then either try to analyze it yourself or send it to Microsoft for analysis.

This section discusses configuring Windows NT to create a dump file. It also discusses the utilities that you can use to check the dump file. The memory dump file contains the information needed by the DUMPEXAM utility to enable you to troubleshoot the kernel stop error.

Configuring NT to Create a DMP File

Configuring Windows NT to create a dump file is very easy. The tasks for setting this up are outlined in Step by Step 15.3. Remember that the dump file is in the Windows root folder and is the size of physical RAM. Therefore, if your server has 512MB of RAM, the file will be 512MB and this space must be available. In this case, choose another location for the dump file and ensure that there is enough disk space.

STEP BY STEP

15.3 Configuring NT to Create a DMP File

1. Right-click the My Computer Icon.

2. Choose the Startup/Shutdown tab (see Figure 15.11).

3. Under Recovery, click the "Write debugging information to" check box.

You can select to overwrite an existing dump file by checking "Overwrite any existing file."

You can enter another location for the dump file by entering the location (and name) into the text box.

4. Click OK.

After you have completed the preceding steps, if your system crashes and causes a blue screen, the contents of your physical memory are stored in a DMP file in the location specified in step 3.

FIGURE 15.11

Use the Startup/Shutdown configuration tab to configure the actions based on blue screen occurrences.

Using Dump File Utilities

Three utilities come with Windows NT that enable you to work with the memory dump files that are created. You can find each of these utilities on the Windows NT server CD-ROM. These utilities are the following:

◆ **DUMPCHK.** This utility checks that the dump file is in order by verifying all the addresses and listing the errors and system information.

◆ **DUMPEXAM.** This utility creates a text file that can provide the same information that was on the blue screen at the time the stop error occurred. You need the symbol files and the kernel debugger extensions as well as IMAGEHLP.DLL to run DUMPEXAM.

◆ **DUMPFLOP.** This utility backs up the dump file to a series of floppies so that you can send them to Microsoft.

CASE STUDY: TROUBLESHOOTING A BLUE SCREEN

ESSENCE OF THE CASE

Here are the essential elements in this case:

• The system appears to function normally until the performance monitor is used; then a stop error is created.

• You have created a memory dump with the relevant information for analysis by a Microsoft engineer.

• You have documented all error messages.

SCENARIO

You receive a call from a client at a provincial government department. The client is attempting to complete some optimization to its Windows NT server. Every time that the client launched the Performance Monitor, the system crashed and a blue screen error appeared. You attempt to analyze the blue screen message and document all listed error messages. You restart the system, and everything appears to function without a problem. You check the Event Viewer and it shows no error messages that would have caused the system to display a blue screen. You decide to re-create the error—however, you make sure to maintain a full memory dump file so that you can attempt to isolate the problem. You enable the option to write the debugging information to a memory dump file, and then continue to run the performance monitor with the same blue screen error occurring. Using the DUMPEXAM utility, you could not locate any possible problems. It is time to look elsewhere for assistance.

CASE STUDY: TROUBLESHOOTING A BLUE SCREEN

ANALYSIS

To help you solve the problem, you turn to various resources to search for the error messages that were displayed in your memory dump and blue screens. You run searches on the TechNet CD that you had handy, and located a possible answer to the problem. The client was running Windows NT server 4.0 without any of the service packs loaded; it appears that the client's copy of a DLL that came with the original version of NT 4.0 was known to conflict with certain network cards, and crashed when either the performance monitor or the network monitor was used to monitor network statistics. You load the Windows NT service packs, but cannot monitor this system without any additional errors. Many times the answers have already been released, however, without the error message, and your copy of TechNet you might have had a very difficult time in isolating the problem.

CHAPTER SUMMARY

The following list summarizes the key points to take away from this chapter:

◆ The Event Viewer is a very powerful troubleshooting tool. Through the Event Viewer, you can view three logs: the system log, the application log, and the security log.

◆ Cross-reference the events in the Event Viewer with knowledge base articles found on Microsoft TechNet for troubleshooting help.

◆ Interpreting blue screens can be very difficult; use memory dump files and the following utilites to view your memory dumps to help you isolate the problems:

  • DUMPCHK

  • DUMPEXAM

  • DUMPFLOP

◆ If the problem persists, you might have to use the kernel debugger that is included on the NT server CD-ROM in the \Support\debug folder.

◆ The kernel debugger can be used to monitor a remote machine through a null modem, or by using the RAS service into a machine that is connected to the problematic computer through a null modem.

KEY TERMS

- blue screen stop error
- Event Viewer
- system log
- security log
- application log
- TechNet
- kernel build number
- symbol tree
- HAL
- memory dump

This section enables you to assess how well you understood the material in the chapter. Review and exam questions test your knowledge of the tasks and concepts specified in the objectives. The exercises provide you with opportunities to engage in the sorts of tasks that comprise the skill sets the objectives reflect.

For more review and exam type questions, see the Top Score test engine on the CD-ROM that comes with this book.

Exercises

15.1 Looking at the Event Viewer

The Event Viewer is one of the first places that you need to look if your system is not working right. This exercise is meant to help you look at the Event Viewer and view the errors that occur. The first step is to create an error situation, the second to look at the results in the viewer.

Time Estimate: 20 minutes

Creating an Event Situation. In this part of the exercise, you create several entries in the event logs so that you will have something to look at in the following steps.

1. From the Start button, choose Settings, Control Panel.

2. Double-click the Services icon and locate the Server service.

3. Click Startup and choose Disabled.

4. Click OK and then Close to shut the Services dialog box.

5. Close the Control Panel and restart the computer.

6. You should receive an error stating that "At least one service or driver failed during system startup. Use Event Viewer to examine the event log for details." Click OK to accept the message—you will look at this shortly.

7. Create a printer by choosing Start, Settings, Printers, Add Printer.

8. The printer should be on My Computer. Use any port and printer driver you want. Use the default name and do not share the printer. Do not attempt to print a test page.

9. When prompted, enter the location of the NT source files.

10. Open the User Manager (for Domains) and choose Policy, Audit.

11. Turn on all auditing. (If you are currently auditing, ensure that you note what is on so you can reset the system later.)

12. Create a test user called Bill.

13. Close User Manager and open the Services icon in the Control Panel.

14. Change the startup for the Server service back to Automatic.

15. Shut down and restart the computer.

Looking at Events. You have now generated many events. In this section, you look at the information that was added to the Event Viewer.

APPLY YOUR LEARNING

1. Start the Event Viewer by choosing Start, Programs, Administrative Tools, Event Viewer.

2. You should see at least one error condition in the log. (Depending on the installed components, you might see several.)

3. Filter the events to see only events from the Service Control Manager. Choose View, Filter Events. In the Source drop-down list, choose Service Control Manager.

4. You will see at least one stop error. Double-click the first error to open the details.

5. Choose Next to step through the errors (when you reach the bottom, Event Viewer will ask you if you want to start at the top again). Choose No.

6. As you look through the events, you will notice that at least one error will be created because the Server service did not start. (Try disabling other services and restarting. This will give you other dependency errors that occur when a service required has not started.)

7. Choose View, Filter Events again, and this time choose Print as the source.

8. There should be at least two Warning events. Double-click the events to see the details and then move through them all. The Warnings indicate that files were added and that a printer was created.

9. Choose View, All Events to redisplay the full list.

10. To see the events in the Security log, choose Log, Security.

11. Scroll through the log looking for Account Manager entries.

12. Find Event ID 624 and double-click the entry. This should be the creation of the account for Bill.

13. Filter the events to see which are generated by the system. Choose View, Filter Events, then enter **SYSTEM** as the user.

14. Open the event details and scroll through the events.

15. Close the Event Viewer.

16. In the User Manager, turn off all auditing (if you had auditing on previously, then reset auditing to its previous setting).

Review Questions

1. Which tools can be used to view security audit logs?

2. What can you do when your system encounters a fatal stop error (blue screen)?

3. If a service does not start when you boot Windows NT, where should you look to see what caused the problem?

4. To enable debugging of your Windows NT system, what BOOT.INI switch must be used?

APPLY YOUR LEARNING

Exam Questions

1. Which of the following information is available within the Event Viewer?

    A. Error messages from services and devices

    B. Informational messages from applications

    C. Security messages from the operating system

    D. The date and time of system startup

    E. All of the above

2. Which of the following are utilities used to view the contents of a memory dump file?

    A. DUMPCHECK

    B. DUMPEXAM

    C. DUMPCHK

    D. DUMPVIEW

3. Which of the following logs are contained in the Event Viewer?

    A. Security

    B. Network

    C. System

    D. Application

Answers to Review Questions

1. The Event Viewer is a utility that can be used to view the security logs within Windows NT. See "Troubleshooting Tools" and "The Event Viewer."

2. There are three ways to deal with blue screen errors. You can read the screen for clues as to the problem, you can interactively debug the blue screen through a serial link, or you can create a dump file that you can analyze offline or send to Microsoft. See "Blue Screen Errors."

3. You should check the Event Viewer's system log. Locate the EventLog entry and work up through the series of events to see what failed first and what other errors were caused by this problem. See "Using the Event Log."

4. To enable debugging on your system, use the /DEBUG switch in BOOT.INI. See the section "BOOT.INI Switches."

Answers to Exam Questions

1. E. All of the listed information can be viewed in the Event Viewer. See the section "The Event Log."

2. B. C. DUMPEXAM and DUMPCHK are utilities used to view the contents of a memory dump. See the section "Dump File Utilities."

3. A. C. D. The Event Viewer contains the system log, security log, and the application log. See the section "Examining the Parts of the Event Log."

FINAL REVIEW

Fast Facts: Windows NT Server 4 Enterprise Exam

Fast Facts: Windows NT Server 4 Exam

Fast Facts: Windows NT Workstation 4 Exam

Fast Facts: Networking Essentials Exam

Study and Exam Prep Tips

Practice Exam

The fast facts listed in this section are designed as a refresher of key points and topics that are required to succeed on the Windows NT server 4.0 in the Enterprise exam. By using these summaries of key points, you can spend an hour prior to your exam to refresh key topics, and ensure that you have a solid understanding of the objectives and information required for you to succeed in each major area of the exam.

The following are the main categories Microsoft uses to arrange the objectives:

- ◆ Planning
- ◆ Installation and configuration
- ◆ Managing resources
- ◆ Connectivity
- ◆ Monitoring and optimization
- ◆ Troubleshooting

For each of these main sections, or categories, the assigned objectives are reviewed, and following each objective, review material is offered.

PLANNING

Plan the implementation of a directory services architecture. Considerations include the following:

- ◆ Selecting the appropriate domain model
- ◆ Supporting a single logon account
- ◆ Enabling users to access resources in different domains

Fast Facts: Windows NT Server 4 Enterprise Exam

The main goals of directory services are the following:

- One user, one account
- Universal resource access
- Centralized administration
- Directory synchronization

To ensure that you are selecting the best plan for your network, always address each of the goals of directory services.

The requirements for setting up a trust are as follows:

- The trust relationship can be established only between Windows NT Server domains.
- The domains must be able to make an RPC connection. To establish an RPC connection, you must ensure that a network connection exists between the domain controllers of all participating domains.

- The trust relationship must be set up by a user with administrator access.
- You should determine the number and type of trusts prior to the implementation.
- You must decide where to place the user accounts, as that is the trusted domain.

Trust relationships enable communication between domains. The trusts must be organized, however, to achieve the original goal of directory services. Windows NT domains can be organized into one of four different domain models:

- The single-domain model
- The single-master domain model
- The multiple-master domain model
- The complete-trust model

Table 1 summarizes the advantages and disadvantages of the domain models.

TABLE 1
PROFILING THE DOMAIN MODELS

Domain Model	Advantages	Disadvantages
Single-domain model	Centralized administration.	Limited to 40,000 user accounts. No trust relationships. No distribution of resources.
Single-master domain model	Centralized administration. Distributed resources.	Limited to 40,000 user accounts.
Multiple-master domain model	Unlimited number of user accounts; each master domain can host 40,000 user accounts. Distributed resources. Complex trust relationships.	No centralized administration of user accounts.
Complete-trust model	Unlimited number of user accounts; each domain can host 40,000 user accounts. Complex trust relationships.	No centralized administration of user accounts.

Plan the disk drive configuration for various requirements. Requirements include choosing a fault-tolerance method.

Windows NT Server 4 supports the following fault-tolerant solutions:

◆ RAID Level 0 (disk striping)

◆ RAID Level 1 (disk mirroring)

◆ RAID Level 5 (disk striping with parity)

A comparison of the three fault-tolerance options might help to summarize the information and to ensure that you have a strong understanding of the options available in Windows NT Server 4 (see Table 2).

Choose a protocol for various situations. The protocols include the following:

◆ TCP/IP

◆ TCP/IP with DHCP and WINS

◆ NWLink IPX/SPX Compatible Transport Protocol

◆ Data Link Control (DLC)

◆ AppleTalk

Windows NT Server 4 comes bundled with several protocols that can be used for interconnectivity with other systems and for use within a Windows NT environment. You examine the various protocols, then try to define when each protocol best fits your network needs. The protocols discussed to prepare you for the enterprise exam are the following:

◆ **NetBEUI.** The NetBEUI protocol is the easiest to implement and has wide support across platforms. The protocol uses NetBIOS broadcasts to locate other computers on the network. This process of locating other computers requires additional network traffic and can slow down your entire network. Because NetBEUI uses broadcasts to locate computers, it is not routable; in other words, you cannot access computers that are not on your physical network. Most Microsoft and IBM OS/2 clients support this protocol. NetBEUI is best suited to small networks with no

TABLE 2
SUMMARY OF FAULT-TOLERANCE OPTIONS IN WINDOWS NT SERVER 4

Disk Striping	*Disk Mirroring/ Disk Duplexing*	*Disk Striping with Parity*
No fault tolerance.	Complete disk duplication.	Data regeneration from stored parity information.
Minimum of two physical disks, maximum of 32 disks.	Two physical disks	Minimum of three physical disks, maximum of 32 disks.
100 percent available disk utilization.	50 percent available disk utilization.	Dedicates the equivalent of one disk's space in the set for parity information. The more disks, the higher the utilization.
Cannot include a system/boot partition.	Includes all partition types.	Cannot include a system/boot partition.
Excellent read/write performance.	Moderate read/write performance.	Excellent read and moderate write performance.

requirements for routing the information to remote networks or to the Internet.

◆ **TCP/IP.** Transmission Control Protocol/Internet Protocol, or TCP/IP, is the most common protocol—more specifically, it is the most common suite of protocols. TCP/IP is an industry-standard protocol that is supported by most network operating systems. Because of this acceptance throughout the industry, TCP/IP enables your Windows NT system to connect to other systems with a common communication protocol.

The following are advantages of using TCP/IP in a Windows NT environment:

- The capability to connect dissimilar systems

- The capability to use numerous standard connectivity utilities, including File Transfer Protocol (FTP), Telnet, and PING

- Access to the Internet

If your Windows NT system is using TCP/IP as a connection protocol, it can communicate with many non-Microsoft systems. Some of the systems it can communicate with are the following:

- Any Internet-connected system

- UNIX systems

- IBM mainframe systems

- DEC Pathworks

- TCP/IP-supported printers directly connected to the network

◆ **NWLink IPX/SPX Compatible.** The IPX protocol has been used within the NetWare environment for years. By developing an IPX-compatible protocol, Microsoft enables Windows NT systems to communicate with NetWare systems.

NWLink is best suited to networks requiring communication with existing NetWare servers and for existing NetWare clients.

Other utilities must be installed, however, to enable the Windows NT Server system to gain access into the NetWare security. Gateway Services for NetWare/Client Services for NetWare (GSNW/CSNW) must be installed on the Windows NT server to enable the computer to be logged on to a NetWare system. GSNW functions as a NetWare client, but it also can share the connection to the Novell box with users from the Windows NT system. This capability enables a controlled NetWare connection for file and print sharing on the NetWare box, without requiring the configuration of each NT client with a duplicate network redirector or client.

◆ **DataLink Control.** The DLC protocol was originally used for connectivity in an IBM mainframe environment, and maintains support for existing legacy systems and mainframes. The DLC protocol is also used for connections to some network printers.

◆ **AppleTalk.** Windows NT Server can configure the AppleTalk protocol to enable connectivity with Apple Macintosh systems. This protocol is installed with the Services for the Macintosh included with your Windows NT Server CD-ROM. The AppleTalk protocol enables Macintosh computers on your network to access files and printers set up on the Windows NT server. It also enables your Windows NT clients to print to Apple Macintosh printers.

The AppleTalk protocol is best suited to connectivity with the Apple Macintosh.

INSTALLATION AND CONFIGURATION

Install Windows NT Server to perform various server roles. Server roles include the following:

◆ Primary domain controller

◆ Backup domain controller

◆ Member server

The following are different server roles into which Windows NT Server can be installed:

◆ **Primary Domain Controller.** The Primary Domain Controller (PDC) is the first domain controller installed into a domain. As the first computer in the domain, the PDC creates the domain. This fact is important to understand because it establishes the rationale for needing a PDC in the environment. Each domain can contain only one PDC. All other domain controllers in the domain are installed as Backup Domain Controllers. The PDC handles user requests and logon validation, and it offers all the standard Windows NT Server functionality. The PDC contains the original copy of the Security Accounts Manager (SAM), which contains all user accounts and security permissions for your domain.

◆ **Backup Domain Controller.** The Backup Domain Controller (BDC) is an additional domain controller used to handle logon requests by users in the network. To handle the logon requests, the BDC must have a complete copy of the domain database, or SAM. The BDC also runs the Netlogon service; however, the Netlogon service in a BDC functions a little differently than in a PDC. In the PDC, the Netlogon

service handles synchronization of the SAM database to all the BDCs.

◆ **Member server.** In both of the domain controllers, PDC or BDC, the computer has an additional function: The domain controllers handle logon requests and ensure that the SAM is synchronized throughout the domain. These functions add overhead to the system. A computer that handles the server functionality you require without the overhead of handling logon validation is called a *member server*. A member server is a part of the domain, but it does not need a copy of the SAM database and does not handle logon requests. The main function of a member server is to share resources.

After you have installed your computer into a specific server role, you might decide to change the role of the server. This can be a relatively easy task if you are changing a PDC to a BDC or vice versa. If you want to change a domain controller to a member server or member server to a domain controller, however, you must reinstall into the required server role. A member server has a local database that does not participate in domain synchronization. In changing roles, a member server must be reinstalled to ensure that the account database and the appropriate services are installed.

Configure protocols and protocol bindings. Protocols include the following:

◆ TCP/IP

◆ TCP/IP with DHCP and WINS

◆ NWLink IPX/SPX Compatible Transport Protocol

◆ DLC

◆ AppleTalk

You install a new protocol in Windows NT Server through the Network Properties dialog box.

> **N O T E**
>
> **NetBEUI Not Discussed** This list does not include the NetBEUI protocol, as there are no configuration options available for this protocol.

Following are the protocols, and the configuration options available with each:

◆ **TCP/IP.** The following tabs are available for configuration in the Microsoft TCP/IP Properties dialog box:

- **IP Address.** The IP Address tab enables you to configure the IP address, the subnet mask, and the default gateway. You also can enable the system to allocate IP address information automatically through the use of the DHCP server.

  An IP address is a 32-bit address that is broken into four octets and used to identify your network adapter card as a TCP/IP host. Each IP address must be a unique address. If you have any IP address conflicts on your computer, you cannot use the TCP/IP protocol.

  Your IP address is then grouped into a subnet. The process you use to subnet your network is to assign a subnet mask. A *subnet mask* is used to identify the computers local to your network. Any address outside your subnet is accessed through the default gateway, also called the *router*. The default gateway is the address of the router that handles all routing of your TCP/IP information to computers, or hosts, outside your subnet.

- **DNS.** The DNS tab shows you the options available for configuring your TCP/IP protocol to use a DNS server. The Domain Name System (DNS) server translates TCP/IP host names of remote computers into IP addresses. Remember that an IP address is a unique address for each computer. The DNS server contains a database of all the computers you can access by host name. This database is used when you access a Web page on the Internet. Working with the naming scheme is easier than using the IP address of the computer.

- **WINS Address.** The WINS Address tab enables you to configure your primary and secondary Windows Internet Names Services (WINS) server addresses. WINS is used to reduce the number of NetBIOS broadcast messages sent across the network to locate a computer. By using a WINS server, you keep the names of computers on your network in a WINS database. The WINS database is dynamic.

  In configuring your WINS servers, you can enter your primary WINS server and a secondary WINS server. Your system searches the primary WINS server database first, then the secondary database if no match was found in the primary one.

- **DHCP Relay.** The DHCP relay agent is used to find your DHCP servers across routers. DHCP addresses are handed out by the DHCP servers. The client request, however, is made with a broadcast message. Broadcast messages do not cross routers; therefore, this protocol might place some restrictions on your systems. The solution is to use a DHCP relay agent to assist the clients in finding the DHCP server across a router.

In configuring your DHCP relay agent, you can specify the seconds threshold and the maximum number of hops to use in searching for the DHCP servers. At the bottom of the tab, you can enter the IP addresses of the DHCP servers you want to use.

- **Routing.** In an environment in which multiple subnets are used, you can configure your Windows NT Server as a multihomed system. In other words, you can install multiple network adapters, each connecting to a different subnet. If you enable the Enable IP Forwarding option, your computer acts as a router, forwarding the packets through the network cards in the multihomed system to the other subnet.

◆ **NWLINK IPX/SPX Compatible.** The configuration of the NWLink protocol is simple in comparison to the TCP/IP protocol. It is this simplicity that makes it a popular protocol to use.

The NWLink IPX/SPX Properties dialog box has two tabs:

- **General.** On the General tab, you have the option to assign an internal network number. This eight-digit hexadecimal number format is used by some programs with services that can be accessed by NetWare clients.

  You also have the option to select a frame type for your NWLink protocol. The frame type you select must match the frame type of the remote computer with which you need to communicate. By default, Windows NT Server uses the Auto Frame Type Detection setting, which scans the network and loads the first frame type it encounters.

- **Routing.** The Routing tab of the NWLink IPX/SPX Properties dialog box is used to

enable or disable the Routing Information Protocol (RIP). If you enable RIP routing over IPX, your Windows NT Server can act as an IPX router.

◆ **DLC.** The configuration of DLC is done through Registry parameters. The DLC protocol is configured based on three timers:

- **T1.** The response timer

- **T2.** The acknowledgment delay timer

- **Ti.** The inactivity timer

The Registry contains the entries that can be modified to configure DLC. You can find the entries at

HKEY_LOCAL_MACHINE\SYSTEM\Current ControlSet\Services\DLC\Parameters\ELNKIII *adapter name*

◆ **AppleTalk.** To install the AppleTalk protocol, you install Services for Macintosh.

Table 3 reviews the protocols that you can configure for your NT enterprise (including the subcomponents—tabs—of each protocol).

TABLE 3
PROTOCOLS TO CONFIGURE

Protocol	Subcomponent (Tab)
TCP/IP	IP Address
	DNS
	WINS Address
	DHCP Relay
	Routing
NWLink IPX/SPX Compatible	General
	Routing
AppleTalk	General
	Routing

The binding order is the sequence your computer uses to select which protocol to use for network communications. Each protocol is listed for each network-based service, protocol, and adapter available.

The Bindings tab contains an option, Show Bindings for, that can be used to select the service, adapter, or protocol you want to modify in the binding order. By clicking the appropriate button, you can enable or disable each binding, or move up or down in the binding order.

Configure Windows NT Server core services. Services include the following:

◆ Directory Replicator

◆ Computer Browser

In this objective, you look at configuring some of the core services in the Windows NT Server. These services are the following:

◆ **Server service.** The Server service answers network requests. By configuring Server service, you can change the way your server responds and, in a sense, the role it plays in your network environment. To configure Server service, you must open the Network dialog box. To do this, double-click the Network icon in the Control Panel. Select the Services tab. In the Server dialog box, you have four optimization settings. Each of these settings modifies memory management based on the role the server is playing. These options are the following:

• **Minimize Memory Used.** The Minimize Memory Used setting is used when your Windows NT Server system is accessed by less than 10 users.

This setting allocates memory so a maximum of 10 network connections can be properly maintained. By restricting the memory for

network connections, you make more memory available at the local or desktop level.

• **Balance.** The Balance setting can be used for a maximum of 64 network connections. This setting is the default when using NetBEUI software. Like the Minimize setting, Balance is best used for a relatively low number of users connecting to a server that also can be used as a desktop computer.

• **Maximize Throughput for File Sharing.** The Maximize Throughput for File Sharing setting allocates the maximum amount of memory available for network connections. This setting is excellent for large networks in which the server is being accessed for file and print sharing.

• **Maximize Throughput for Network Applications.** If you are running distributed applications, such as SQL Server or Exchange Server, the network applications do their own memory caching. Therefore, you want your system to enable the applications to manage the memory. You accomplish this by using the Maximize Throughput for Network Applications setting. This setting also is used for very large networks.

◆ **Computer Browser service.** The Computer Browser service is responsible for maintaining the list of computers on the network. The browse list contains all the computers located on the physical network. As a Windows NT Server, your system plays a big role in the browsing of a network. The Windows NT Server acts as a master browser or backup browser.

The selection of browsers is through an election. The election is called by any client computer or when a preferred master browser computer starts up. The election is based on broadcast messages.

Every computer has the opportunity to nominate itself, and the computer with the highest settings wins the election.

The election criteria are based on three things:

- The operating system (Windows NT Server, Windows NT Workstation, Windows 95, Windows for Workgroups)

- The version of the operating system (NT 4.0, NT 3.51, NT 3.5)

- The current role of the computer (master browser, backup browser, potential browser)

◆ **Directory Replicator service.** You can configure the Directory Replicator service to synchronize an entire directory structure across multiple servers.

In configuring the directory service, you must select the export server and all the import servers. The export server is the computer that holds the original copy of the directory structure and files. Each import server receives a complete copy of the export server's directory structure. The Directory Replicator service monitors the directory structure on the export server. If the contents of the directory change, the changes are copied to all the import servers. The file copying and directory monitoring is completed by a special service account you create. You must configure the Directory Replicator service to use this service account. The following access is required for your Directory Replicator service account:

- The account should be a member of the Backup Operators and Replicators groups.

- There should be no time or logon restrictions for the account.

- The Password Never Expires option should be selected.

- The User Must Change Password At Next Logon option should be turned off.

When configuring the export server, you have the option to specify the export directory. The default export directory is C:\WINNT\system32\repl\export\.

In the Import Directories section of the Directory Replication dialog box, you can select the import directory. The default import directory is C:\WINNT\system32\repl\import.

Remember that the default directory for executing logon scripts in a Windows NT system is C:\WINNT\system32\repl\import\scripts.

Configure hard disks to meet various requirements. Requirements include the following:

◆ Providing duplication

◆ Improving performance

All hard disk configuration can be done using the Disk Administrator tool. The different disk configurations you need to understand for the enterprise exam are the following:

◆ **Stripe set.** A stripe set gives you improved disk read and write performance; however, it supplies no fault tolerance. A minimum of two disks is required, and the configuration can stripe up to 32 physical disks. A stripe set cannot include the system partition.

◆ **Volume set.** A volume set enables you to extend partitions beyond one physical disk; however, it supplies no fault tolerance. To extend a volume set, you must use the NTFS file system.

◆ **Disk mirroring.** A mirror set uses two physical disks and provides full data duplication. Often referred to as RAID level 1, disk mirroring is a useful solution to assigning duplication to the system partition, as well as any other disks that might be in the system.

◆ **Stripe set with parity.** A stripe set with parity enables fault tolerance in your system. A minimum of three physical disks is required, and a maximum of 32 physical disks can be included in a stripe set with parity. A stripe set with parity cannot include the system partition of your Windows NT system.

The solution that supplies the best duplication and optimization mix is the stripe set with parity.

Configure printers. Tasks include the following:

◆ Adding and configuring a printer

◆ Implementing a printer pool

◆ Setting print priorities

The installation of a printer is a fairly simplistic procedure and is not tested heavily on the exam; however, the printer pool is a key point. The items to remember about printer pools are as follows:

◆ All printers in a printer pool must be able to function using the same printer driver.

◆ A printer pool can have a maximum of eight printers in the pool.

Configure a Windows NT Server computer for various types of client computers. Client computer types include the following:

◆ Windows NT Workstation

◆ Windows 95

◆ Macintosh

The Network Client Administrator is found in the Administrative Tools group. You can use the Network Client Administrator program to do the following:

◆ **Make a Network Installation Startup Disk.** This option creates an MS-DOS boot disk that contains commands required to connect to a network server and that automatically installs Windows NT Workstation, Windows 95, or the DOS network clients.

◆ **Make an Installation Disk Set.** This option enables the creation of installation disks for the DOS network client, LAN Manager 2.2c for DOS, or LAN Manager 2.2c for OS/2.

◆ **Copy Client-Based Network Administration Tools.** This option enables you to share the network administration tools with client computers. The client computers that can use the network administration tools are Windows NT Workstation and Windows 95 computers.

◆ **View Remoteboot Client Information.** This option enables you to view the remoteboot client information. To install remoteboot, go to the Services tab of the Network dialog box.

When installing a client computer, you must ensure that your Windows NT system is prepared for and configured for the client. The Windows clients can connect to the Windows NT server without any configuration required on the server; however, some configuration is required on the client computers. For the Apple Macintosh client, the NT server must install the services for the Macintosh, which includes the AppleTalk protocol. This protocol enables the seamless connection between the Windows NT system and the Apple clients.

Managing Resources

Manage user and group accounts. Considerations include the following:

- ◆ Managing Windows NT user accounts
- ◆ Managing Windows NT user rights
- ◆ Managing Windows NT groups
- ◆ Administering account policies
- ◆ Auditing changes to the user account database

AGLP stands for Accounts/Global Groups/Local Groups/Permissions. When you want to assign permissions to any resource, you should follow a few simple rules. All user accounts are placed into global groups, and global groups get assigned into local groups. The local groups have the resources and permissions assigned to them.

When you are working with groups across trust relationships, the following guidelines are useful:

- ◆ Always gather users into global groups. Remember that global groups can contain only user accounts from the same domain. You might have to create the same named global group in multiple domains.

- ◆ If you have multiple account domains, use the same name for a global group that has the same types of members. Remember that when multiple domains are involved, the group name is referred to as DOMAIN\GROUP.

- ◆ Before the global groups are created, determine whether an existing local group meets your needs. There is no sense in creating duplicate local groups.

- ◆ Remember that the local group must be created where the resource is located. If the resource is on a Domain Controller, create the local group in the Domain Account Database. If the resource is on a Windows NT Workstation or Windows NT Member Server, you must create the group in that system's local account database.

- ◆ Be sure to set the permissions for a resource before you make the global groups a member of the local group assigned to the resource. That way, you set the security for the resource.

Create and manage policies and profiles for various situations. Policies and profiles include the following:

- ◆ Local user profiles

- ◆ Roaming user profiles

- ◆ System policies

You can configure system policies to do the following:

- ◆ Implement defaults for hardware configuration— for all computers using the profile or for a specific machine.

- ◆ Restrict the changing of specific parameters that affect the hardware configuration of the participating system.

- ◆ Set defaults for all users in the areas of their personal settings that the users can configure.

- ◆ Restrict users from changing specific areas of their configuration to prevent tampering with the system. An example is disabling all Registry editing tools for a specific user.

- ◆ Apply all defaults and restrictions on a group level rather than just a user level.

Some common implementations of user profiles are the following:

◆ Locking down display properties to prevent users from changing the resolution of their monitor. Display properties can be locked down as a whole or on each individual property page of display properties. You adjust this setting by clicking the Control Panel, Display, Restrict Display option of the Default User Properties dialog box.

◆ Setting a default color scheme or wallpaper. You can do this by clicking the Desktop option of the Default User Properties dialog box.

◆ If you want to restrict access to portions of the Start menu or desktop, you can do this by clicking the Shell, Restrictions option of the Default User Properties dialog box.

◆ If you need to limit the applications that the user can run at a workstation, you can do so by clicking the System, Restrictions option of the Default User Properties dialog box. You can also use this option to prevent the user from modifying the Registry.

◆ You can prevent users from mapping or disconnecting network drives by clicking the Windows NT Shell, Restrictions option of the Default User Properties dialog box.

Profiles and policies can be very powerful tools to assist in the administrative tasks in your environment. The following list reviews each of the main topics covered in this objective:

◆ **Roaming profiles.** The user portion of the Registry is downloaded from a central location, allowing the user settings to follow the user anywhere within the network environment.

◆ **Local profiles.** The user settings are stored at each workstation and are not copied to other computers. Each workstation that you use will have different desktop and user settings.

◆ **System policies.** System policies enable the administrator to restrict user configuration changes on systems. This enables the administrator to maintain the settings of the desktop of systems without the fear that a user can modify them.

◆ **Computer policies.** Computer policies allow the lockdown of common machine settings that affect all users of that computer.

Administer remote servers from various types of client computers. Client computer types include the following:

◆ Windows 95

◆ Windows NT Workstation

This objective focuses on the remote administration tools available for your Windows NT Server. The following list summarizes the key tools:

◆ **Remote Administration Tools for Windows 95.** Allows User Manager, Server Manager, Event Viewer, and NTFS file permissions to be executed from the Windows 95 computer.

◆ **Remote Administration for Windows NT.** Allows User Manager, Server Manager, DHCP Manager, System Policy Editor, Remote Access Admin, Remote Boot Manager, WINS Manager, and NTFS file permissions to be executed from a Windows NT machine.

◆ **Web Based Administration.** Allows for common tasks to be completed through an Internet connection into the Windows NT Server.

Manage disk resources. Tasks include the following:

◆ Creating and sharing resources

◆ Implementing permissions and security

◆ Establishing file auditing

Windows NT has two levels of security for protecting your disk resources:

◆ Share permissions

◆ NTFS permissions

NTFS permissions enable you to assign more comprehensive security to your computer system. NTFS permissions can protect you at the file level. Share permissions, on the other hand, can be applied only to the folder level. NTFS permissions can affect users logged on locally or across the network to the system where the NTFS permissions are applied. Share permissions are in effect only when the user connects to the resource through the network.

The combination of Windows NT share permissions and NTFS permissions determines the ultimate access a user has to a resource on the server's disk. When share permissions and NTFS permissions are combined, no preference is given to one or the other. The key factor is which of the two effective permissions is the most restrictive.

For the exam, remember the following tips relating to managing resources:

◆ Users can be assigned only to global groups in the same domain.

◆ Only global groups from trusted domains can become members of local groups in trusting domains.

◆ NTFS permissions are assigned only to local groups in all correct test answers.

◆ Only NTFS permissions give you file-level security.

CONNECTIVITY

Configure Windows NT Server for interoperability with NetWare servers by using various tools. The tools include the following:

◆ Gateway Service for NetWare

◆ Migration Tool for NetWare

Gateway Service for NetWare (GSNW) performs the following functions:

◆ GSNW enables Windows NT Servers to access NetWare file and print resources.

◆ GSNW enables the Windows NT Servers to act as a gateway to the NetWare file and print resources. The Windows NT Server enables users to borrow the connection to the NetWare server by setting it up as a shared connection.

The Migration Tool for NetWare (NWCONV) transfers file and folder information and user and group account information from a NetWare server to a Windows NT domain controller. The Migration Tool can preserve the folder and file permissions if it is being transferred to an NTFS partition.

Connectivity between Windows NT and a NetWare server requires the use of GSNW. If the user and file information from NetWare is to be transferred to a Windows NT Server, the NetWare Conversion utility, NWCONV, is used for this task. The following list summarizes the main points in this section on NetWare connectivity:

◆ GSNW can be used as a gateway between Windows NT clients and a NetWare server.

◆ GSNW acts as a NetWare client to the Windows NT Server, allowing the NT server to have a connection to the NetWare server.

◆ GSNW is a service in Windows NT, and is installed using the Control Panel.

◆ For GSNW to be used as a gateway into a NetWare server, a gateway user account must be created and placed in a NetWare group called NTGATEWAY.

◆ In configuring the GSNW as a gateway, you can assign permissions to the gateway share by accessing the GSNW icon in the Control Panel.

◆ For GSNW to be functional, the NWLINK IPX/SPX protocol must be installed and configured.

◆ To convert user and file information from a NetWare server to a Windows NT server, you can use the NWCONV.EXE utility.

◆ NWCONV requires that GSNW be installed prior to any conversion being carried out.

◆ To maintain the NetWare folder- and file-level permissions in the NWCONV utility, you must convert to an NTFS partition on the Windows NT system.

Install and configure multiprotocol routing to serve various functions. Functions include the following:

◆ Internet router

◆ BOOTP/DHCP Relay Agent

◆ IPX router

Multiprotocol routing gives you flexibility in the connection method used by your clients, and in maintaining security. Check out the following:

◆ **Internet router.** Setting up Windows NT as an Internet router is as simple as installing two network adapters in the system, then enabling IP routing in the TCP/IP protocol configuration. This option enables Windows NT to act as a

static router. Note that Windows NT cannot exchange Routing Information Protocol (RIP) routing packets with other IP RIP routers unless the RIP routing software is installed.

◆ **IPX router.** You enable the IPX router by installing the IPX RIP router software by choosing Control Panel, Networks, Services.

After installing the IPX RIP router, Windows NT can route IPX packets over the network adapters installed. Windows NT uses the RIP to exchange its routing table information with other RIP routers.

The inclusion of the industry-standard protocols, and tools to simplify the configuration and extension of your NT network into other environments, makes this operating system a very powerful piece of your heterogenous environment. The following are the main factors to focus on for this objective:

◆ A strong understanding of the functionality of each of the Windows NT protocols—with a strong slant toward TCP/IP and the configuration options available. Understanding and configuration of the DHCP server are also tested on this exam.

◆ The services used to resolve the IP addresses and names of hosts in a TCP/IP environment. DNS service, WINS Service, the Hosts file, and the LMHosts files are among the services tested.

◆ The routing mechanisms available in Windows NT. These mechanisms are powerful, and largely unknown to the vast majority of NT administrators. Ensure that you review the configuration and functionality of Internet or IP routing, as well as the IPX routing tools available.

Install and configure Internet Information Server, and install and configure Internet services. Services include the following:

◆ The World Wide Web

◆ DNS

◆ Intranets

Internet Information Server (IIS) uses Hypertext Transfer Protocol (HTTP), File Transfer Protocol (FTP), and the Gopher service to provide Internet publishing services to your Windows NT Server computer.

IIS provides a graphical administration tool called the Internet Service Manager. With this tool, you can centrally manage, control, and monitor the Internet services in your Windows NT network. The Internet Service Manager uses the built-in Windows NT security model, so it offers a secure method of remotely administering your Web sites and other Internet services.

IIS is an integrated component in Windows NT Server 4.0. The IIS services are installed using the Control Panel, Networks icon or during the installation phase. The following list summarizes the key points in installing and configuring IIS:

◆ The three Internet services included in IIS are HTTP, FTP, and Gopher.

◆ HTTP is used to host Web pages from your Windows NT server system.

◆ FTP is a protocol used for transferring files across the Internet using the TCP/IP protocol.

◆ Gopher is used to create a set of hierarchical links to other computers or to annotate files or folders.

◆ The Internet Service Manager is the utility used to manage and configure your Internet services in IIS.

◆ The Internet Service Manager has three views that you can use to view your services. The three views are Report View, Servers View, and Services View.

Install and configure Remote Access Service (RAS). Configuration options include the following:

◆ Configuring RAS communications

◆ Configuring RAS protocols

◆ Configuring RAS security

RAS supports the Serial Line Internet Protocol (SLIP) and Point-to-Point Protocol (PPP) line protocols, and the NetBEUI, TCP/IP, and IPX network protocols.

RAS can connect to a remote computer using any of the following media:

◆ **Public Switched Telephone Network (PSTN).** (PSTN is also known simply as the phone company.) RAS can connect using a modem through an ordinary phone line.

◆ **X.25.** A packet-switched network. Computers access the network through a Packet Assembler Disassembler (PAD) device. X.25 supports dial-up or direct connections.

◆ **Null modem cable.** A cable that connects two computers directly. The computers then communicate using their modems (rather than network adapter cards).

◆ **ISDN.** A digital line that provides faster communication and more bandwidth than a normal phone line. (It also costs more, which is why not everybody has it.) A computer must have a special ISDN card to access an ISDN line.

RAS is designed for security. The following are some of RAS's security features:

◆ **Auditing.** RAS can leave an audit trail, enabling you to see who logged on when and what authentication they provided.

◆ **Callback security.** You can enable the RAS server to use callback (hang up all incoming calls and call the caller back), and you can limit callback numbers to prearranged sites that you know are safe.

◆ **Encryption.** RAS can encrypt logon information, or it can encrypt all data crossing the connection.

◆ **Security hosts.** In case Windows NT is not safe enough, you can add an extra dose of security by using a third-party intermediary security host—a computer that stands between the RAS client and the RAS server and requires an extra round of authentication.

◆ **PPTP filtering.** You can tell Windows NT to filter out all packets except ultra safe Point-to-Point Tunneling Protocol (PPTP) packets.

RAS can be a very powerful and useful tool in enabling you to extend the reaches of your network to remote and traveling users. The following list summarizes main points for RAS in preparation for the exam:

◆ RAS supports SLIP and PPP line protocols.

◆ With PPP, RAS can support NetBEUI, NWLINK, and TCP/IP across the communication line.

◆ RAS uses the following media to communicate with remote systems: PSTN, X.25, Null Modem cable, and ISDN.

◆ The RAS security features available are auditing, callback security, encryption, and PPTP filtering.

◆ To install RAS, click the Network icon in the Control Panel.

Monitoring and Optimization

Establish a baseline for measuring system performance. Tasks include creating a database of measurement data.

You can use numerous database utilities to analyze the data collected. The following are some of the databases that Microsoft provides:

◆ Performance Monitor

◆ Microsoft Excel

◆ Microsoft Access

◆ Microsoft FoxPro

◆ Microsoft SQL Server

The following list summarizes the key items to focus on when you are analyzing your computer and network:

◆ Establish a baseline measurement of your system when functioning at its normal level. Later, you can use the baseline in comparative analysis.

◆ Establish a database to maintain the baseline results and any subsequent analysis results on the system, to compare trends and identify potential pitfalls in your system.

◆ The main resources to monitor are memory, the processor, the disks, and the network.

The following list summarizes the tools used to monitor your NT server that are available and are built into Windows NT Server 4.0:

◆ Server Manager

◆ Windows NT Diagnostics

◆ Response Probe

- Performance Monitor
- Network Monitor

Monitor performance of various functions by using Performance Monitor. Functions include the following:

- Processor
- Memory
- Disk
- Network

To summarize the main views used within Performance Monitor, review the following list:

- **Chart view.** This view is very useful for viewing the objects and counters in a real-time mode. This mode enables you to view the data in a graphical format. You can also use the chart view to view the contents of a log file.

- **Log view.** This view enables you to set all the options required for creating a log of your system resources or objects. After this log is created, you can view it by using the chart view.

- **Alert view.** Use the alert view to configure warnings or alerts of your system resources or objects. In this view, you can configure threshold levels for counters and can then launch an action based on the threshold values being exceeded.

- **Report view.** The report view enables you to view the object and counters as an averaged value. This view is useful for comparing the values of multiple systems that are configured similarly.

When monitoring the disk, remember to activate the disk counters using the command diskperf –y. If you do not enter this command, you can select counter but will not see any activity displayed. In the case of a software RAID system, start diskperf with the -ye option.

When you want to monitor TCP/IP counters, make sure that SNMP is installed. Without the SNMP service installed, the TCP/IP counters are not available.

Performance Monitor is a graphical utility that you can use for monitoring and analyzing your system resources within Windows NT. You can enable objects and counters within Performance Monitor; it is these elements that enable the logging and viewing of system data.

In preparing you for this objective, this section introduces numerous objects and counters that you use with Performance Monitor. To prepare for the exam, you need to understand the following key topics:

- The four views available in Performance Monitor are the report view, the log view, the chart view, and the alert view.

- The main resources to monitor in any system are the disk, the memory, the network, and the processor.

- Each of the main resources is grouped as a separate object, and within each object are counters. A counter is the type of data available from a type of resource or object. Each counter might also have multiple instances. An instance is available if multiple components in a counter are listed.

- To enable the disk counters to be active, you must run the DISKPERF utility.

Monitor network traffic by using Network Monitor. Tasks include the following:

- Collecting data
- Presenting data
- Filtering data

Network Monitor is a network packet analyzer that comes with Windows NT Server 4. Actually, two versions of Network Monitor are available from Microsoft.

The first version comes with Windows NT Server 4 (simple version). This version can monitor the packets (frames) sent or received by a Windows NT Server 4 computer. The second version comes with Microsoft Systems Management Server (full version). This version can monitor all traffic on the network.

By fully understanding the various components found while analyzing traffic, you will be more successful in locating potential network bottlenecks and offering relevant optimization recommendations. The main components that need to be monitored with your network traffic analysis are the following:

- ◆ Locate and classify each service. Analyze the amount of traffic generated from each individual service, the frequency of the traffic, and the overall effect the traffic has on the network segment.

- ◆ Understand the three different types of frames: broadcast, multicast, and directed.

- ◆ Review the contents of a frame and ensure that you can find the destination address, source address, and data located in each frame.

The following points summarize the key items to understand in building a strong level of knowledge in using Network Monitor as a monitoring tool:

- ◆ Two versions of Network Monitor are available: the scaled-down version that is built into the Windows NT Server operating system, and the full version that is a component of Microsoft Systems Management Server.

- ◆ The Network Monitor windows consist of four sections: Graph, Session Statistics, Station Statistics, and Total Statistics.

- ◆ After Network Monitor captures some data, you use the display window of Network Monitor to view the frames. The three sections of the display window are the Summary pane, the Detail pane, and the Hexadecimal pane.

Identify performance bottlenecks and optimize performance for various results. Results include the following:

- ◆ Controlling network traffic

- ◆ Controlling the server load

To optimize the logon traffic in your Windows NT network, you should consider four main points:

- ◆ Determine the hardware required to increase performance.

- ◆ Configure the domain controllers to increase the number of logon validations.

- ◆ Determine the number of domain controllers needed.

- ◆ Determine the best location for each of the domain controllers.

The following are a few good points to follow in optimizing file-session traffic:

- ◆ Remove any excess protocols that are loaded.

- ◆ Reduce the number of wide area network (WAN) links required for file transfer.

The following are three points to consider when attempting to optimize server browser traffic:

- ◆ Reduce the number of protocols.

- ◆ Reduce the number of entries in the browse list.

- ◆ Increase the amount of time between browser updates.

Trust relationships generate a large amount of network traffic. In optimizing your system, attempt to keep the number of trusts very low.

TROUBLESHOOTING

Choose the appropriate course of action to take to resolve installation failures.

Troubleshooting a Windows NT system requires that you have a strong understanding of the processes and tools available to you. To be an effective troubleshooter, first and foremost you must have experience. The following is a list of some common installation problems:

◆ Hard disk problems

◆ Unsupported CD-ROMs

◆ Network adapter problems and conflicts

◆ Naming problems (each computer must be uniquely named, following the NetBIOS naming conventions)

Always use the hardware compatibility list to ensure that your components are supported by Windows NT.

Choose the appropriate course of action to take to resolve boot failures.

For startup errors, try the following:

◆ Check for missing files that are involved in the boot process, including NTLDR, NTDE-TECT.COM, BOOT.INI, NTOSKRNL.EXE, and OSLOADER (RISC).

◆ Modify BOOT.INI for options.

◆ Create an NT boot disk for bypassing the boot process from the hard disk.

◆ Use the Last Known Good option to roll back to the last working set of your Registry settings.

Choose the appropriate course of action to take to resolve configuration errors. Tasks include the following:

◆ Backing up and restoring the Registry

◆ Editing the Registry

You can resolve many problems that you encounter within Windows NT by configuring the Registry. However, before you make any Registry configurations, you must have a strong understanding of the keys within the Registry and always back up the Registry prior to making any modifications to ensure a smooth rollback if additional problems occur. The following are the main tools used to modify the Registry:

◆ REGEDT32

◆ REGEDIT

For configuration problems, remember the following:

◆ Using the Registry for configuration and troubleshooting can cause additional problems if you do not maintain a full understanding of the Registry.

◆ Always back up the Registry prior to editing the contents.

◆ You can back up and restore the local Registry by using REGEDT32.

Choose the appropriate course of action to take to resolve printer problems.

For troubleshooting printers, you should do the following:

◆ Understand and review the overview of the printing process.

◆ Understand the files involved in the printing process.

◆ As a first step in troubleshooting a printer, always verify that the printer is turned on and online.

◆ Note that the most common errors associated with a printer are an invalid printer driver or incorrect resource permissions set for a user.

Choose the appropriate course of action to take to resolve RAS problems.

The following is a list of some of the problems that you might encounter with RAS:

◆ You must ensure that the protocol you are requesting from the RAS client is available on the RAS server. There must be at least one common protocol or the connection will fail.

◆ If you are using NetBEUI, ensure that the name you are using on the RAS client is not in use on the network to which you are attempting to connect.

◆ If you are attempting to connect using TCP/IP, you must configure the RAS server to provide you with an address.

You can use the Remote Access Admin tool to monitor the ports as well as the active connections of your RAS server.

Numerous RAS settings can cause some problems with your RAS connections. Ensure that you understand the installation process, as well as any configuration settings required to enable your RAS server. You can avoid some of the common problems that can occur by doing the following:

◆ Ensuring that the modem and communication medium are configured and functional prior to installing RAS. It can be very difficult to modify settings after the installation, so it is recommended to have all hardware tested and working first.

◆ Verifying that dial-in permissions have been enabled for the required users. This small task is commonly forgotten in your RAS configuration.

Choose the appropriate course of action to take to resolve connectivity problems.

To test and verify your TCP/IP settings, you can use the following utilities:

◆ IPCONFIG

◆ PING

The most effective method for troubleshooting connectivity is to understand thoroughly the installation and configuration options of each of the network protocols. If you understand the options available, you can narrow down the possible problem areas very quickly. Also ensure that you use utilities such as IPCONFIG and PING to test your connections.

Choose the appropriate course of action to take to resolve resource access and permission problems.

You should keep in mind two main issues about permissions:

◆ The default permissions for both share and NTFS give the Windows NT group Everyone full control over the files and folders. Whenever you format a drive as NTFS or first share a folder, you should remove these permissions. The Everyone group contains everyone, including guests and any other user who, for one reason or another, can connect to your system.

◆ The NTFS folder permission delete takes precedence over any file permissions. In all other cases, the file permissions take precedence over the folder permissions.

Choose the appropriate course of action to take to resolve fault-tolerance failures. Fault-tolerance methods include the following:

◆ Tape backup

◆ Mirroring

◆ Stripe set with parity

In using the NTBACKUP tool, the primary thing that you need to do is to determine the frequency and type of backup that you will do. There are three main types of backups that you might want to perform:

◆ **Full.** This backs up all the files that you mark, and marks the files as having been backed up. This is the longest of the backups because it transfers the most data.

◆ **Differential.** This backs up all the files that have changed since the last backup. A differential backup does not mark the files as being backed up. As time passes since the last full backup, the differentials become increasingly larger. However, you need only reload the full backup and the differential to return to the position of the last backup.

◆ **Incremental.** This backs up any files that have changed since the last backup, and then marks them as having been backed up. If your system crashes, you need to start by loading a full backup and then each incremental backup since that full backup.

If you are mirroring the system partition, the disks and partitions should be absolutely identical. Otherwise, the MBR/DBR (master boot record/disk boot record) that contains the driver information will not be correct.

Although ARC naming looks complicated, it is really rather simple. The name is in four parts, of which you use three. The syntax is as follows:

```
multi/scsi(#)disk(#)rdisk(#)partition(#)
```

The following list outlines the parts of the name:

◆ **multi/scsi.** You use either multi or scsi, not both. Use multi in all cases except when using a scsi controller that cannot handle int13 (hard disk access) BIOS routines. Such cases are uncommon. The number is the logical number of the controller with the first controller being 0, the second being 1, and so forth.

◆ **disk.** When you use a scsi disk, you use the disk parameter to indicate which of the drives on the controller is the drive you are talking about. Again, the numbers start at 0 for the first drive and then increase for each subsequent drive.

◆ **rdisk.** Use this parameter for the other controllers in the same way as you use the disk parameter for scsi.

◆ **partition.** This is the partition on the disk that you are pointing at. The first partition is 1, the second is 2, and so forth. Remember that you can have up to four primary partitions, or three primary and one extended. The extended partition is always the last one, and the first logical drive in the partition will have the partition's number. Other drives in the extended partition each continue to add one.

Breaking a mirror set. The boot floppy will get the operating system up and running. You should immediately back up the mirrored copy of the mirror set. To back up the drive, you must break your mirror set. To do this, perform the tasks outlined in Step by Step FF.1.

STEP BY STEP

FF.1 Breaking the Mirror Set

1. Run the Disk Administrator.

2. From the Disk Administrator, click the remaining fragment of the mirrored set.

3. Choose Fault Tolerance, Break Mirror set from the menu.

    At the end of these three steps, you should notice that the mirror set has been broken, and you can now back up the drive.

Regenerating a stripe set with parity. Fixing a stripe set with parity is simple. Perform the tasks outlined in Step by Step FF.2 to regenerate your stripe set with parity.

STEP BY STEP

FF.2 Regenerating the Stripe Set

1. Physically replace the faulty disk drive.

2. Start the Disk Administrator.

3. Select the stripe set with parity that you need to repair and then Ctrl+click the free space of the drive you added to fix the stripe set.

4. Choose Fault Tolerant, Regenerate. Note that this process can take some time, although the process takes less time than restoring from tape.

   The drives regenerate all the required data from the parity bits and the data bits, and upon completion your stripe set with parity is completely functional.

◆ **Share permissions.** A common problem when troubleshooting share resources is in the share permissions. Ensure that the minimum functional permissions have been assigned. Always remove the Everyone group from having full control of a share.

◆ **Combining NTFS and share permissions.** When combining these permissions, remember that NT uses the most restrictive of the permissions when combining. As a rule, use the NTFS permissions as the highest level of permissions, and use the share permissions mainly for access to the folder or share.

◆ **Tape backups.** In any system that you are using, ensure that you have a good backup strategy. Any component in your system can be faulty, and it is your responsibility to have a recovery plan in case of emergencies.

◆ **Disk mirroring.** If you are implementing disk mirroring in your system, ensure that you have created a fault-tolerant boot disk that you can use in case of drive failure. By having this disk pre-configured and handy, you can break the mirror set and replace the drive with very little down-time for your server.

◆ **Stripe set with parity.** This system automatically regenerates data if a drive is faulty. Although your system performance will dramatically decline, it is still a functional box and you risk no possibility of losing any data. If you find that a drive in your stripe set is faulty, replace the drive and use the regenerate command from the Disk Administrator.

Perform advanced problem resolution. Tasks include the following:

◆ Diagnosing and interpreting a blue screen

◆ Configuring a memory dump

◆ Using the event log service

Three utilities come with Windows NT that enable you to work with the memory dump files that are created. You can find all of these utilities on the Windows NT Server CD-ROM. Each utility can be a very helpful tool. The following list briefly describes these utilities:

◆ **DUMPCHK.** This utility checks that the dump file is in order by verifying all the addresses and listing the errors and system information.

◆ **DUMPEXAM.** This creates a text file that can provide the same information that was on the blue screen at the time the stop error occurred.

You need the symbol files and the kernel debugger extensions as well as IMAGEHLP.DLL to run DUMPEXAM.

◆ **DUMPFLOP.** This utility backs up the dump file to a series of floppies so that you can send them to Microsoft.

The following list summarizes the key points required for this objective:

◆ The Event Viewer is a very powerful troubleshooting tool. The three logs that can be viewed through the Event Viewer are the system log, the application log, and the security log.

◆ Cross-reference the events in the Event Viewer with knowledge base articles found on Microsoft TechNet for troubleshooting help.

◆ Interpreting blue screens can be very difficult. Use memory dump files and the following utilities to view your memory dumps to help you isolate the problem:

- DUMPCHK

- DUMPEXAM

- DUMPFLOP

◆ If the problem persists, you might have to use the kernel debugger that is included on the NT Server CD-ROM in the \Support\debug folder.

◆ You can use the kernel debugger to monitor a remote machine through a null modem, or by using the RAS service into a machine that is connected to the problematic computer through a null modem.

Fast Facts

Now that you have thoroughly read through this book, worked through the exercises and got as much hands-on exposure to NT Server as you could, you've now booked your exam. This chapter is designed as a last-minute cram for you as you walk out the door on your way to the exam. You can't reread the whole book in an hour, but you will be able to read this chapter in that time.

This chapter is organized by objective category, giving you not just a summary, but a rehash of the most important point form facts that you need to know. Remember that this is meant to be a review of concepts and a trigger for you to remember wider definitions. In addition to what is in this chapter, make sure you know what is in the glossary because this chapter does not define terms. If you know what is in here and the concepts that stand behind it, chances are the exam will be a snap.

WINDOWS NT SERVER 4 EXAM

PLANNING

Remember: Here are the elements that Microsoft says they test on for the "Planning" section of the exam.

◆ Plan the disk drive configuration for various requirements. Requirements include: choosing a file system and fault tolerance method

◆ Choose a protocol for various situations. Protocols include: TCP/IP, NWLink IPX/SPX Compatible Transport, and NetBEUI

Minimum requirement for installing NT Server on an Intel machine is 468DX/33, 16MB of RAM, and 130MB of free disk space.

The login process on an NT Domain is as follows:

1. WinLogon sends the user name and password to the Local Security Authority (LSA).

2. The LSA passes the request to the local NetLogon service.

3. The local NetLogon service sends the logon information to the NetLogon service on the domain controller.

4. The NetLogon service on the domain controller passes the information to the domain controller's Security Accounts Manager (SAM).

5. The SAM asks the domain directory database for approval of the user name and password.

6. The SAM passes the result of the approval request to the domain controller's NetLogon service.

7. The domain controller's NetLogon service passes the result of the approval request to the client's NetLogon service.

8. The client's NetLogon service passes the result of the approval request to the LSA.

9. If the logon is approved, the LSA creates an access token and passes it to the WinLogon process.

10. WinLogon completes the logon, thus creating a new process for the user and attaching the access token to the new process.

The system partition is where your computer boots and it must be on an active partition.

The boot partition is where the WINNT folder is found and it contains the NT program files. It can be on any partition (not on a volume set, though).

NT supports two forms of software-based fault tolerance: Disk Mirroring (RAID 1) and Stripe Sets with Parity (RAID 5).

Disk Mirroring uses 2 hard drives and provides 50% disk space utilization.

Stripe sets with Parity use between 3 and 32 hard drives and provides an (n-1)/n*100% utilization (n = number of disks in the set).

Disk duplexing provides better tolerance than mirroring because it does mirroring with separate controllers on each disk.

NT Supports 3 file systems: NTFS, FAT, and CDFS (it no longer supports HPFS, the OS/2 file system nor does it support FAT32, a file system used by Windows 95).

The following table is a comparison of NTFS and FAT features.

Table 1.1 shows a quick summary of the differences between file systems:

SUMMARY TABLE 1
FAT VERSUS NTFS COMPARISON

Feature	FAT	NTFS
File name length	255	255
8.3 file name compatibility	Yes	Yes
File size	4 GB	16 EB
Partition size	4 GB	16 EB
Directory structure	Linked list	B-tree
Local security	No	Yes
Transaction tracking	No	Yes
Hot fixing	No	Yes
Overhead	1 MB	>4 MB
Required on system partition for RISC-based computers	Yes	No
Accessible from MS-DOS/ Windows 95	Yes	No
Accessible from OS/2	Yes	No
Case-sensitive	No	POSIX only
Case preserving	Yes	Yes

Feature	FAT	NTFS
Compression	No	Yes
Efficiency	200 MB	400 MB
Windows NT formattable	Yes	Yes
Fragmentation level	High	Low
Floppy disk formattable	Yes	No

The following is a table to summarize the protocols commonly used by NT for network communication:

SUMMARY TABLE 2
PRIMARY PROTOCOL USES

Protocol	Primary Use
TCP/IP	Internet and WAN connectivity
NWLink	Interoperability with NetWare
NetBEUI	Interoperability with old Lan Man networks

The main points regarding TCP/IP are as follows:

◆ Requires IP Address, and Subnet Mask to function (default Gateway if being routed)

◆ Can be configured manually or automatically using DHCP server running on NT

◆ Common address resolution methods are WINS and DNS

INSTALLATION AND CONFIGURATION

Remember: Here are the elements that Microsoft says they test on for the "Installation and Configuration" section of the exam.

◆ Install Windows NT Server on Intel-based platforms.

◆ Install Windows NT Server to perform various server roles. Server roles include: Primary domain controller, Backup domain controller, and Member server.

◆ Install Windows NT Server by using various methods. Installation methods include: CD-ROM, Over-the-network, Network Client Administrator, and Express versus custom.

◆ Configure protocols and protocol bindings. Protocols include: TCP/IP, NWLink IPX/SPX Compatible Transport, and NetBEUI.

◆ Configure network adapters. Considerations include: changing IRQ, IObase, and memory addresses and configuring multiple adapters.

◆ Configure Windows NT server core services. Services include: Directory Replicator, License Manager, and Other services.

◆ Configure peripherals and devices. Peripherals and devices include: communication devices, SCSI devices, tape devices drivers, UPS devices and UPS service, mouse drivers, display drivers, and keyboard drivers.

◆ Configure hard disks to meet various requirements. Requirements include: allocating disk space capacity, providing redundancy, improving security, and formatting.

◆ Configure printers. Tasks include: adding and configuring a printer, implementing a printer pool, and setting print priorities.

◆ Configure a Windows NT Server computer for various types of client computers. Client computer types include: Windows NT Workstation, Microsoft Windows 95, and Microsoft MS-DOS-based.

The Hardware Compatibility list is used to ensure that NT supports all computer components.

NT can be installed in 3 different configurations in a domain: Primary Domain Controller, Backup Domain Controller, and Member Server.

Two sources can be used for installation files: CD-ROM or network share (which is the hardware specific files from the CD copied onto a server and shared).

Three Setup diskettes are required for all installations when a CD-ROM is not supported by the operating system present on the computer at installation time (or if no operating system exists and the computer will not boot from the CD-ROM).

WINNT and WINNT32 are used for network installation; WINNT32 for installations when NT is currently present on the machine you are installing to and WINNT when it is not.

The following table is a summary of the WINNT and WINNT32 switches:

SUMMARY TABLE 3
WINNT AND WINNT32 SWITCH FUNCTIONS

Switch	Function
/B	Prevents creation of the three setup disks during the installation process
/S	Indicates the location of the source files for NT installation (e.g., /S:D:\NTFiles)
/U	Indicates the script file to use for an unattended installation (e.g., /U:C:\Answer.txt)
/UDF	Indicates the location of the uniqueness database file which defines unique configuration for each NT machine being installed (e.g., /UDF:D:\Answer.UDF)
/T	Indicates the place to put the temporary installation files
/OX	Initiates only the creation of the three setup disks

Switch	Function
/F	Indicates not to verify the files copied to the setup diskettes
/C	Indicates not to check for free space on the setup diskettes before creating them

To remove NT from a computer you must do the following:

1. Remove all the NTFS partitions from within Windows NT and reformat them with FAT (this ensures that these disk areas will be accessible by non-NT operating systems).

2. Boot to another operating system, such as Windows 95 or MS-DOS.

3. Delete the Windows NT installation directory tree (usually WINNT).

4. Delete pagefile.sys.

5. Turn off the hidden, system, and read-only attributes for NTBOOTDD.SYS, BOOT.INI, NTLDR, and NTDETECT.COM and then delete them. You might not have all of these on your computer, but if so, you can find them all in the root directory of your drive C.

6. Make the hard drive bootable by placing another operating system on it (or SYS it with DOS or Windows 95 to allow the operating system with does exist to boot).

The Client Administrator allows you to do the following:

◆ Make Network Installation Startup disk: shares files and creates bootable diskette for initiating client installation.

◆ Make Installation Disk Set: copies installation files to diskette for installing simple clients like MS-DOS network client 3.0.

◆ Copy Client-Based Network Administration Tools: creates a folder which can be attached to from Windows NT Workstation and Windows 95 clients to install tools for administering an NT Server from a workstation.

MANAGING RESOURCES

Remember: Here are the elements that Microsoft says they test on for the "Managing Resources" section of the exam.

◆ Manage user and group accounts. Considerations include: managing Windows NT groups, managing Windows NT user rights, administering account policies, and auditing changes to the user account database.

◆ Create and manage policies and profiles for various situations. Policies and profiles include: local user profiles, roaming user profiles, and system policies.

◆ Administer remote servers from various types of client computers. Client computer types include: Windows 95 and Windows NT Workstation.

◆ Manage disk resources. Tasks include: copying and moving files between file systems, creating and sharing resources, implementing permissions and security, and establishing file auditing.

Network properties dialog box lets you install and configure the following:

◆ Computer and Domain names

◆ Services

◆ Protocols

◆ Adapters

◆ Bindings

When configuring NWLink ensure that if more than one frame type exists on your network that you don't use AutoDetect or only the first frame type encountered will be detected from then on.

The following table shows you three TCP/IP command-line diagnostic tools and what they do:

SUMMARY TABLE 4
TCP/IP COMMAND LINE DIAGNOSTIC TOOLS

Tool	Function
IPConfig	Displays the basic TCP/IP configuration of each adapter card on a computer (with/all displays detailed configuration information)
Ping	Determines connectivity with another TCP/IP host by sending a message that is echoed by the recipient if received
Tracert	Traces each hop on the way to a TCP/IP host and indicates points of failure if they exist

Network adapter card configuration of IRQ and I/O port address may or may not be configurable from the Network Properties dialog box; it depends on the card.

To allow NT computers to participate in a domain, a computer account must be created for each one.

Windows 95 clients need special profiles and policies created on a Windows 95 machine and then copied onto an NT Server to participate in domain profile and policy configuration.

Windows 95 clients need printer drivers installed on an NT Server acting as a print controller to print to an NT controller printer.

Typical services tested for NT Server are listed and described in the following table:

SUMMARY TABLE 5
NT SERVER SERVICES AND THEIR FUNCTIONS

Service	Function
DNS	Provides TCP/IP address resolution using a static table and can be use for non-Microsoft hosts
WINS	Provides TP/IP address resolution using a dynamic table and can be used for Microsoft hosts
DHCP	Provides automatic configuration of TCP/IP clients for Microsoft clients
Browser	Provides a list of domain resources to Network Neighborhood and Server Manager
Replicator	Provides import and export services for automated file distribution between NT computers (Servers can be export and import, Workstations can only be import)

REGEDT32.EXE and REGEDIT are used to view and modify registry settings in NT.

The five registry subtrees are:

◆ **HKEY_LOCAL_MACHINE.** Stores all the computer-specific configuration data.

◆ **HKEY_USERS.** Stores all the user-specific configuration data.

◆ **HKEY_CURRENT_USER.** Stores all configuration data for the currently logged on user.

◆ **HKEY_CLASSES_ROOT.** Stores all OLE and file association information.

◆ **HKEY_CURRENT_CONFIG.** Stores information about the hardware profile specified at startup.

REGEDT32.EXE allows you to see and set security on the registry and allows you to open the registry in read-only mode, but does not allow you to search by key value.

NT checking for serial mice at boot may disable a UPS. To disable that check, place the /noserialmice in the boot line in the BOOT.INI file.

The SCSI adapters icon in the Control Panel lets you add and configure SCSI devices as well as CD-ROM drives.

Many changes made in the disk administrator require that you choose the menu Partition, Commit Changes for them to take effect.

Although you can set drive letters manually, the following is how NT assigns letters to partitions and volumes:

1. Beginning from the letter C:, assign consecutive letters to the first primary partition on each physical disk.

2. Assign consecutive letters to each logical drive, completing all on one physical disk before moving on to the next.

3. Assign consecutive letters to the additional primary partitions, completing all on one physical disk before moving on to the next.

Disk Administrator allows for the creation of two kinds of partitions (primary and extended) and four kinds of volumes (volume set, stripe set, mirror set, and stripe set with parity). The following table is a summary of their characteristics:

SUMMARY TABLE 6
PARTITION CHARACTERISTICS

Object	Characteristics
Primary partition	Non-divisible disk unit which can be marked active and can be made bootable.
	Can have up to four on a physical drive.
	NT system partition must be on a primary.
Extended partition	Divisible disk unit which must be divided into logical disks (or have free space used in a volume) in order to function as space storage tool.
	Can have only one on a physical drive.
	Logical drive within can be the NT boot partition.
Volume Set	Made up of 2-32 portions of free space which do not have to be the same size and which can be spread out over between 1 and 32 disks of many types (IDE, SCSI, etc.).
	Can be added to if formatted NTFS.
	Cannot contain NT boot or system partition.
	Removing one portion of the set destroys the volume and the data is lost.
	Is not fault tolerant.
Stripe Set	Made up of 2-32 portions of free space which have to be the same size and which can be spread out over between 2 and 32 disks of many types (IDE, SCSI, etc.).
	Cannot be added to and removing one portion of the set destroys the volume and the data is lost.
	Is not fault tolerant.
Mirror Set	Made up of 2 portions of free space which have to be the same size and which must be on 2 physical disks.
	Identical data is written to both mirror partitions and they are treated as one disk.
	If one disk stops functioning the other will continue to operate.
	The NT Boot and System partitions can be held on a mirror set.
	Has a 50% disk utilization rate.
	Is fault tolerant.
Stripe Set with Parity	Made up of 3-32 portions of free space which have to be the same size and must be spread out over the same number of physical disks.
	Maintains fault tolerance by creating parity information across a stripe.
	If one disk fails, the stripe set will continue to function, albeit with a loss of performance.
	The NT Boot and System partitions cannot be held on a Stripe Set with Parity.
	Is fault tolerant.

Disk Administrator can be used to format partitions and volumes either FAT or NTFS.

If you have any clients who access a shared printer that are not using NT or are not using the same hardware platform as your printer server then you must install those drivers when you share the printer.

By assigning different priorities for printers associated with the same print device you can create a hierarchy among users' print jobs, thus ensuring that the print jobs of some users print sooner than others.

By adjusting the printer schedule you can ensure that jobs sent to particular printers are only printed at certain hours of the day.

A printer has permissions assigned to it. The following is a list of the permissions for printers.

- **No Access.** Completely restricts access to the printer.

- **Print.** Allows a user or group to submit a print job, and to control the settings and print status for that job.

- **Manage Documents.** Allows a user or group to submit a print job, and to control the settings and print status for all print jobs.

- **Full Control.** Allows a user to submit a print job, and to control the settings and print status for all documents as well as for the printer itself. In addition, the user or group may share, stop sharing, change permissions for, and even delete the printer.

Printer pools consist of one or more print devices that can use the same print driver controlled by a single printer.

MS-DOS users must have print drivers installed locally on their computers.

The assignment of permissions to resources should use the following procedure:

1. Create user accounts.

2. Create global groups for the domain and populate the groups with user accounts.

3. Create local groups and assign them rights and permissions to resources and programs in the domain.

4. Place global groups into the local groups you have created, thereby giving the users who are members of the global groups access to the system and its resources.

The built-in local groups in a Windows NT Domain are as follows:

- Administrators

- Users

- Guests

- Backup Operators

- Replicator

- Print Operators

- Server Operators

- Account Operators

The built-in global groups in an NT Domain are as follows:

- Domain Admins

- Domain Users

- Domain Guests

The system groups on an NT server are as follows:

- Everyone

- Creator Owner

◆ Network

◆ Interactive

The built-in users on an NT server are as follows:

◆ Administrator

◆ Guest

The following table describes the buttons on the User Properties dialog box and their functions:

SUMMARY TABLE 7
BUTTONS ON THE USER PROPERTIES DIALOG BOX

Button	Function
Groups	Enables you to add and remove group memberships for the account. The easiest way to grant rights to a user account is to add it to a group that possesses those rights.
Profile	Enables you to add a user profile path, a logon script name, and a home directory path to the user's environment profile. You learn more about the Profile button in the following section.
Hours	Enables you to define specific times when the users can access the account. (The default is always.)
Logon To	Enables you to specify up to 8 workstations from which the user can log on. (The default is all workstations.)
Account	Enables you to provide an expiration date for the account. (The default is never.) You also can specify the account as global (for regular users in this domain) or domain local.

The following table is a summary of the account policy fields:

SUMMARY TABLE 8
ACCOUNT POLICY FIELDS

Button	Function
Maximum Password Age	The maximum number of days a password can be in effect until it must be changed.
Minimum Password Age	The minimum number of days a password must stay in effect before it can be changed.
Minimum Password Length	The minimum number of characters a password must include.
Password Uniqueness	The number of passwords that NT remembers for a user; these passwords cannot be reused until they are no longer remembered.
Account Lockout	The number of incorrect passwords that can be input by a user before the account becomes locked. Reset will automatically set the count back to 0 after a specified length of time. In addition the duration of lockout is either a number of minutes or forever (until an administrator unlocks it).
Forcibly disconnect remote users from server when logon hours expire	In conjunction with logon hours, this checkbox enables forcible disconnection of a user when authorized hours come to a close.
Users must log on in order to change password	Ensures that a user whose password has expired cannot change his or her password but has to have it reset by an administrator.

Account SIDs are unique; therefore, if an account is deleted, the permissions cannot be restored by re-creating an account with the same name.

Local profiles are only available from the machine on which they were created, whereas roaming profiles can be accessed from any machine on the network.

A mandatory profile is a roaming profile that users cannot change. They have the extension .MAN.

Hardware profiles can be used with machines that have more than one hardware configuration (such as laptops).

The System Policy editor (POLEDIT) has two modes, Policy File mode and Registry Mode.

The application of system policies is as follows:

1. When you log in, the NT Config.pol is checked. If there is an entry for the specific user, then any registry settings indicated will be merged with, and overwrite if necessary, the user's registry.

2. If there is no specific user entry, any settings for groups that the user is a member of will be applied to the user.

3. If the user is not present in any groups and not listed explicitly then the Default settings will be applied.

4. If the computer that the user is logging in on has an entry, then the computer settings are applied.

5. If there is not a computer entry for the user then the default computer policy is applied.

Windows 95 policies are not compatible with NT and therefore Windows 95 users must access a Windows 95 policy created on an Windows 95 machine and copied to an NT machine and named Config.Pol.

The Net Use command line can be used to map a drive letter to a network share; using the /persistent switch ensures that it is reconnected at next logon.

FAT long file names under NT have 8.3 aliases created to ensure backward compatibility. The following is an example of how aliases are generated from 5 files that all have the same initial characters:

Team meeting Report #3.doc	TEAMME~1.DOC
Team meeting Report #4.doc	TEAMME~2.DOC
Team meeting Report #5.doc	TEAMME~3.DOC
Team meeting Report #6.doc	TEAMME~4.DOC
Team meeting Report #7.doc	TE12B4~1.DOC

A long file name on a FAT partition uses one file name for the 8.3 alias and then one more FAT entry for every 13 characters in the name.

A FAT partition can be converted to NTFS without loss of data through the command line

CONVERT <drive>: /FS:NTFS

NTFS supports compression as a file attribute that can be set in the file properties.

Compression can be applied to a folder or a drive and the effect is that the files within are compressed and any file copied into it will also become compressed.

Compression can be applied through the use of the COMPACT.EXE program through the syntax

COMPACT <file or directory path> [/switch]

The available switches for COMPACT are as follows:

SUMMARY TABLE 9
COMPACT SWITCHES

Switch	Function
/C	Compress
/U	Uncompress
/S	Compress an entire directory tree
/A	Compress hidden and system files
/I	Ignore errors and continue compressing
/F	Force compression even if the objects are already compressed
/Q	Display only summary information

Share-level permissions apply only when users access a resource over the network, not locally. The share-level permissions are:

- **No Access**. Users with No Access to a share can still connect to the share, but nothing appears in File Manager except the message You do not have permission to access this directory.

- **Read.** Allows you to display folder and file names, display file content and attributes, run programs, open folders inside the shared folder.

- **Change.** Allows you to create folders and files, change file content, change file attributes, delete files and folders, do everything READ permission allows.

- **Full Control.** Allows you to change file permissions and do everything change allows for.

Share-level permissions apply to the folder that is shared and apply equally to all the contents of that share.

Share-level permissions apply to any shared folder, whether on FAT or NTFS.

NTFS permissions can only be applied to any file or folder on an NTFS partition.

The actions that can be performed against an NTFS object are as follows:

- ◆ Read (R)
- ◆ Write (W)
- ◆ Execute (X)
- ◆ Delete (D)
- ◆ Change Permissions (P)
- ◆ Take Ownership (O)

The NTFS permissions available for folders are summarized in the following table:

SUMMARY TABLE 10
NTFS FOLDER PERMISSIONS

Permission	Action permitted
No Access	none
List	RX
Read	RX
Add	WX
Add & Read	RXWD
Change	RXWD
Full Control	RXWDPO

The NTFS permissions available for files are summarized in the following table:

SUMMARY TABLE 11
NTFS FILE PERMISSIONS

Permission	Action permitted
No Access	none
Read	RX
Add & Read	RX
Change	RXWD
Full Control	RXWDPO

If a user is given permission to a resource and a group or groups that the user is a member is also given access then the effective permission the user has is the cumulation of all of the user permissions. This applies unless any of the permissions are set to No Access in which case the user has no access to the resource.

If a user is given permission to a shared resource and is also given permission to that resource through NTFS permissions then the effective permission is the most restrictive permission.

The File Child Delete scenario manifests itself when someone has full control to a folder but is granted a permission which does not enable deletion (Read or No Access, for example). The effect is that a user will be able to delete files inside the folder even though sufficient access does not appear to be present.

To close the File Child Delete loophole, do not grant a user Full Control access to a folder but instead, use special Directory permissions to assign RXWDPO access; this eliminates the File Child Delete permission.

Access Tokens do not refresh and a user needs to log off and log back on if changed permissions are to take effect.

MONITORING AND OPTIMIZATION

Remember: Here are the elements that Microsoft says they test on for the "Monitoring and Optimization" section of the exam.

◆ Monitor performance of various functions by using Performance Monitor. Functions include: processor, memory, disk, and network.

◆ Identify performance bottlenecks.

Performance monitor has 4 views: chart, alert, log, and report.

The subsystems that are routinely monitored are: Memory, Disk, Network, and Processor.

Disk counters can be enabled through the command line:

Diskperf –y

Or

Diskperf –ye (for RAID disks and volumes)

TROUBLESHOOTING

Remember: Here are the elements that Microsoft says they test on for the "Troubleshooting" section of the exam.

◆ Choose the appropriate course of action to take to resolve installation failures.

◆ Choose the appropriate course of action to take to resolve boot failures.

◆ Choose the appropriate course of action to take to resolve configuration errors.

◆ Choose the appropriate course of action to take to resolve printer problems.

◆ Choose the appropriate course of action to take to resolve RAS problems.

◆ Choose the appropriate course of action to take to resolve connectivity problems.

◆ Choose the appropriate course of action to take to resolve fault tolerance problems. Fault-tolerance methods include: tape backup, mirroring, stripe set with parity, and disk duplexing.

The acronym DETECT can be used to define the troubleshooting process and stands for:

◆ Discover the problem.

◆ Explore the boundaries.

◆ Track the possible approaches.

◆ Execute an Approach.

◆ Check for success.

◆ Tie up loose ends.

An NTHQ diskette can test a computer to ensure that NT will successfully install on it.

The following list identifies possible sources of installation problems:

◆ Media errors

◆ Insufficient disk space

◆ Non-supported SCSI adapter

◆ Failure of dependency service to start

◆ Inability to connect to the domain controller

◆ Error in assigning domain name

The files involved in the boot process are identified in the following table for both Intel and RISC machines:

SUMMARY TABLE 12
FILES INVOLVED IN THE BOOT PROCESS

Intel	*RISC*
NTLDR	OSLOADER.EXE
BOOT.INI	NTOSKRNL.EXE
NTDETECT.COM	
NTOSKRNL.EXE	

In the NT boot process (in BOOT.INI) ARC paths define the physical position of the NT operating system files and come in two forms:

Scsi(0)disk(0)rdisk(0)partition(1)\WINNT

Multi(0)disk(0)rdisk(0)partition(1)\WINNT

SCSI arc paths define hard drives which are SCSI and which have their bios disabled. The relevant parameters are:

◆ SCSI: the SCSI controller starting from 0

◆ DISK: the physical disk starting from 0

◆ PARTITION: the partition on the disk stating from 1

◆ \folder: the folder in which the NT files are located

MULTI arc paths define hard drives which are non-SCSI or SCSI with their bios enabled. The relevant parameters are:

◆ MULTI: the controller starting from 0

◆ RDISK: the physical disk starting from 0

◆ PARTITION: the partition on the disk stating from 1

◆ \folder: the folder in which the NT files are located

Partitions are numbered as follows:

1. The first primary partition on each disk gets the number 0.

2. Each additional primary partition then is given a number, incrementing up from 0.

3. Each logical drive is then given a number in the order they appear in the Disk Administrator.

Switches on boot lines in the boot.ini file define additional boot parameters. The following table lists the switches you need to know about and their function:

SUMMARY TABLE 13
BOOT.INI FILE SWITCHES

Switch	Function
/basevideo	Loads standard VGA video driver (640x480, 16 color)
/sos	Displays each driver as it is loaded
/noserialmice	Prevents autodetection of serial mice on COM ports which may disable a UPS connected to the port

A recovery disk can be used to bypass problems with system partition. Such a disk contains the following files (broken down by hardware platform):

SUMMARY TABLE 14
FILES ON A FAULT-TOLERANT BOOT DISKETTE

Intel	RISC
NTLDR	OSLOADER.EXE
NTDETECT.COM	HAL.DLL

Intel	RISC
BOOT.INI	*.PAL (for Alpha machines)
BOOTSECT.DOS (allows you to boot to DOS)	
NTBOOTDD.SYS (the SCSI driver for a hard drive with SCSI bios not enabled)	

An Emergency repair disk can be used to recover an NT system if the registry becomes corrupted and must be used in conjunction with the three setup diskettes used to install NT.

The RDISK programs allows you to update the \REPAIR folder which in turn is used to update your repair diskette.

The Event Viewer allows you to see three log files: System Log, Security Log, and Application Log.

The Windows NT Diagnostics program allows you to see (but not modify) configuration settings for much of your hardware and environment.

The course of action to take when a stop error occurs (blue screen) can be configured from the System Properties dialog box (in the Control Panel) on the Startup/Shutdown tab.

To move the spool file from one partition to another, use the Advanced Tab on the Server Properties dialog box; this can be located from the File, Server Properties menu in the Printers dialog box.

Common RAS problems include the following:

◆ User Permission: user not enabled to use RAS in User Manager for Domains.

◆ Authentication: often caused by incompatible encryption methods (client using different encryption than server is configured to receive).

◆ Callback with Multilink: Client configured for callback but is using multilink; server will only call back to a single number, thereby removing multilink functionality.

◆ Autodial at Logon: Shortcuts on desktop referencing server-based applications or files causes autodial to kick in when logon is complete.

User can't login may be caused by a number of factors including:

◆ Incorrect user name or password

◆ Incorrect domain name

◆ Incorrect user rights (inability to log on locally to an NT machine, for example)

◆ Netlogon service on server is stopped or paused

◆ Domain controllers are down

◆ User is restricted in system policies from logging on at a specific computer

The right to create backups and restore from backups using NT Backup is granted to the groups Administrators, Backup Operators, and Server Operators by default.

NT Backup will only backup files to tape, no other media is supported.

The following table summarizes the backup types available in NT backup:

SUMMARY TABLE 15
BACKUP TYPES AVAILABLE IN NTBACKUP

Type	Backs Up	Marks?
Normal	All selected files and folders	Yes
Copy	All selected files and folders	No
Incremental	Selected files and folders not marked as backed up	Yes
Differential	Selected files and folders not marked as backed up	No
Daily Copy	Selected files and folders changed that day	No

The local registry of a computer can be backed up by selecting the Backup Local Registry checkbox in the Backup Information dialog box.

Data from tape can be restored to the original location or to an alternate location and NTFS permissions can be restored or not, however, you cannot change the names of the objects being restored until the restore is complete.

Backup can be run from a command line using the NTBACKUP command in the syntax:

Ntbackup backup path [switches]

Some command line backup switches are shown in the following table:

SUMMARY TABLE 16
NTBACKUP COMMAND LINE SWITCHES

Switch	Function
/a	Append the current backup to the backup already on the tape
/v	Verify the backed up files when complete
/d "text"	Add an identifying description to the backup tape
/t option	Specify the backup type. Valid options are: normal, copy, incremental, differential, and daily

To recover from a failed mirror set you must do the following:

1. Shut down your NT server and physically replace the failed drive.

2. If required, boot NT using a recovery disk.

3. Start the Disk Administrator using the menu Start, Programs, Administrative Tools (Common), Disk Administrator.

4. Select the mirror set by clicking on it.

5. From the Fault Tolerance menu choose Break Mirror. This action exposes the remaining partition as a volume separate from the failed one.

6. Reestablish the mirror set if desired by selecting the partition you desire to mirror and a portion of free space equal in size and choosing the menu Fault Tolerance, Establish Mirror.

To regenerate a stripe set with parity, do the following:

1. Shut down your NT server and physically replace the failed drive.

2. Start the Disk Administrator using the menu Start, Programs, Administrative Tools (Common), Disk Administrator.

3. Select the stripe set with parity by clicking on it.

4. Select an area of free space as large or larger than the portion of the stripe set that was lost when the disk failed.

5. Choose Fault Tolerance, Regenerate.

Hopefully, this has been a helpful tool in your final review before the exam. You might find after reading this that there are some places in the book you need to revisit. Just remember to stay focused and answer all the questions. You can always go back and check the answers for the questions you are unsure of. Good luck!

Now that you have thoroughly read through this book, worked through the exercises, and picked up as much hands-on exposure to NT Workstation as possible, you're ready to take your exam. This chapter is designed to be a last-minute cram for you as you walk out the door on your way to the exam. You can't re-read the whole book in an hour, but you will be able to read this chapter in that time. This chapter is organized by objective category and summarizes the basic facts you need to know regarding each objective. If you know what is in here, chances are the exam will be a snap.

Fast Facts

WINDOWS NT WORKSTATION 4 EXAM

PLANNING

Remember: Here are the elements that Microsoft says they test on in the "Planning" section of the exam.

- ◆ Create unattended installation files.

- ◆ Plan strategies for sharing and securing resources.

- ◆ Choose the appropriate file system to use in a given situation. File systems and situations include: NTFS, FAT, HPFS, security, and dual-boot systems.

The files used for unattended installation are

- ◆ An unattended answer file (UNATTEND.TXT)

- ◆ A uniqueness database file (a .UDF file)

- ◆ SYSDIFF.EXE

- ◆ WINDIFF.EXE

Some switches available for WINNT32.EXE are useful for unattended installations:

- ◆ /u:*answerfile* (where *answerfile* might be UNATTEND.TXT, for example)

◆ /s:*sourcepath* (where *sourcepath* might be e:\i386, for example)

◆ /udf:*userid*,x:\udf.txt

The content of the OEM directory is copied to the destination machine before NT is installed to allow for additional file or application installation after NT has been installed.

SYSDIFF.EXE can be used to create a snapshot file, a difference file, and/or an .INF file.

.INF files are preferred over difference files because .INF files contain instructions on how to install the software, whereas the difference file contains the whole software package in one large file.

WINDIFF.EXE is used to compare one NT system to another.

The built-in groups in NT Workstation are

◆ Users

◆ Power Users

◆ Administrators

◆ Guests

◆ Backup Operators

◆ Replicator

Table 1 lists the default rights assigned to users or groups on an NT Workstation.

Table 2 lists the built-in capabilities of the built-in groups.

TABLE 1
ASSIGNMENT OF DEFAULT USER RIGHTS

Right	Administrators	Power Users	Users	Guests	Everyone	Backup Operators
Access This Computer from the Network	X	X				X
Back Up Files and Directories	X					X
Change the System Time	X	X				
Force Shutdown from a Remote System	X	X				
Load and Unload Device Drivers	X					
Log On Locally	X	X	X	X	X	X
Manage Auditing and Security Log	X					
Restore Files and Directories	X					X
Shut Down the System	X	X	X		X	X
Take Ownership of Files or Other Objects	X					

TABLE 2
BUILT-IN USER CAPABILITIES

Built-In Capability	Administrators	Power Users	Users	Guests	Everyone	Backup Operators
Create and Manage User Accounts	X	X				
Create and Manage Local Groups	X	X				
Lock the Workstation	X	X	X	X	X	X
Override the Lock of the Workstation	X					
Format the Hard Disk	X					
Create Common Groups	X	X				
Share and Stop Sharing Directories	X	X				
Share and Stop Sharing Printers	X	X				

The following special groups are maintained by NT:

◆ Network

◆ Interactive

◆ Everyone

◆ Creator Owner

Table 3 shows the advantages and disadvantages of storing home directories on a server and on a local computer.

Table 4 shows the advantages and disadvantages of running applications from a server and from a local machine.

TABLE 3
HOME DIRECTORIES ON THE SERVER VERSUS HOME DIRECTORIES ON THE LOCAL COMPUTER

Server-Based Home Directories	*Local Home Directories*
Centrally located so that users can access them from any location on the network.	Available only on the local machine. For roaming users (who log in from more than one computer on the network), the directory is not accessible from other systems.
During a regular backup of the server, information in users' home directories is also backed up.	Often users' local workstations are not backed up regularly as part of a scheduled backup process. If a user's machine fails, the user cannot recover the lost data.
Windows NT does not provide a way to limit the size of a user's directory. Thus, if a lot of information is being stored in home directories, the directories use up a lot of server disk space.	If a user stores a lot of information in his home directory, the space is taken up on his local hard drive instead of the server.
If the server is down, the user won't have access to her files.	The user has access to his files even when the network is down because the files are stored locally.
Some network bandwidth is consumed due to the over-the-network access of data or files.	No network traffic is generated by a user accessing his or her files.

TABLE 4
SHARED NETWORK APPLICATIONS VERSUS LOCALLY INSTALLED APPLICATIONS

Shared Network Applications	*Locally Installed Applications*
Take up less disk space on the local workstation.	Use more local disk space.
Easier to upgrade/control.	Upgrades must "touch" every machine locally.
Use network bandwidth.	Use no network bandwidth for running applications.
Slower response time because applications are accessed from the server.	Faster, more responsive.
If the server is down, users can't run applications.	Users can run applications regardless of server status.

NT Workstation supports the following file formats:

◆ FAT16 (a universal standard format)

◆ NTFS (an NT proprietary format)

◆ CDFS (CD-ROM format)

NT Workstation does not support these file formats:

◆ FAT32 (supported by Windows 95 OSR2 and Windows 98)

◆ HPFS (supported by OS/2)

Table 5 provides a comparison between FAT and NTFS.

TABLE 5

COMPARISON OF NTFS AND FAT FILE SYSTEMS USING WINDOWS NT WORKSTATION

Feature	FAT	NTFS
Support for long filenames (up to 255 characters)	Yes	Yes
Compression	No	Yes
Security	No	Yes
Dual-boot capabilities with non–Windows NT systems	Yes	No
Maximum file/partition size	4GB	16EB
Recommended partition size	0–400MB	400MB–16EB
Capability to format a floppy	Yes	No
Recoverability (transaction logging)	No	Yes

INSTALLATION AND CONFIGURATION

Remember: Here are the elements that Microsoft says they test on in the "Installation and Configuration" section of the exam.

- ◆ Install Windows NT Workstation on an Intel platform in a given situation.

- ◆ Set up a dual-boot system in a given situation.

- ◆ Remove Windows NT Workstation in a given situation.

- ◆ Install, configure, and remove hardware components for a given situation. Hardware components include: network adapter drivers, SCSI device drivers, tape device drivers, UPSs, multimedia devices, display drivers, keyboard drives, and mouse drivers.

- ◆ Use Control Panel applications to configure a Windows NT Workstation computer in a given situation.

- ◆ Upgrade to Windows NT Workstation 4.0 in a given situation.

- ◆ Configure server-based installation for wide-scale deployment in a given situation.

NTHQ.EXE (available on the Workstation CD-ROM) can be used to evaluate a computer for NT installation. It is used to verify hardware and produce a report indicating which components are and are not on the HCL.

Table 6 lists the minimum hardware requirements for NT Workstation installation.

NT Workstation supports four installation types. Table 7 lists the components installed with each of the four installation types.

TABLE 6

WINDOWS NT WORKSTATION 4.0 MINIMUM INSTALLATION REQUIREMENTS

Component	Minimum Requirement
CPU	32-bit Intel x86-based (80486/33 or higher) microprocessor or compatible (the 80386 microprocessor is no longer supported)
	Intel Pentium, Pentium Pro, or Pentium II microprocessor
	Digital Alpha AXP-based RISC microprocessor
	MIPS Rx400-based RISC microprocessor
	PowerPC-based RISC microprocessor
Memory	Intel x86-based computers: 12MB RAM
	RISC-based computers: 16MB RAM
Hard disk	Intel x86-based computers: 110MB
	RISC-based computers: 148MB
Display	VGA or better resolution
Other drives	Intel x86-based computers require a high-density 3 ½" floppy drive and a CD-ROM drive (unless you are planning to install Windows NT over a network)
Optional	Network adapter card
	Mouse or other pointing device, such as a trackball

TABLE 7

VARYING COMPONENTS IN FOUR SETUP OPTIONS

Component	Typical	Portable	Compact	Custom
Accessibility options	X	X	None	All options
Accessories	X	X	None	All options
Communications programs	X	X	None	All options
Games			None	All options
Windows Messaging			None	All options
Multimedia	X	X	None	All options

Windows NT Workstation can be installed using a variety of procedures given different circumstances:

- ◆ Locally, by using the three Setup floppy disks and a CD-ROM

- ◆ Locally, by using the CD-ROM and creating and using the three Setup floppy disks

- ◆ Locally, using the CD without Setup floppy disks, but by booting instead to an operating system that recognizes the CD-ROM

- ◆ Locally, by booting to the CD-ROM from a computer that recognizes the CD-ROM as a boot device

- ◆ Over the network, by creating and using the three Setup floppy disks

- ◆ Over the network, but without the Setup floppies

When you're installing NT on a computer with an existing operating system present, if the computer recognizes either the CD-ROM or a supported network adapter and connection to a network share on which the installation files are present, you can use one of two programs to install NT:

- ◆ **WINNT.EXE.** For installation from existing non-NT operating systems

- ◆ **WINNT32.EXE.** For installation or upgrade from existing NT installations

Table 8 describes the switches available for use with WINNT.EXE and WINNT32.EXE.

Dual booting is a method of installing two operating systems on a single machine and letting the user choose which will boot at startup time (only one can be booted at any time).

TABLE 8
SWITCHES FOR MODIFYING THE **WINNT.EXE** AND **WINNT32.EXE** INSTALLATION PROCESSES

Switch	Effect
/b	Prevents creation of the three Setup boot disks. Create a temporary folder named WIN_NT.˜BT and copy to it the boot files that would normally be copied to the three floppies. The contents of the temporary folder are used instead of the Setup boot disks to boot the machine when the user is prompted to restart.
/c	Skips the step of checking for available free space. (This switch cannot be used with WINNT32.EXE.)
/I:*inf_file*	Specifies the name of the Setup information file. The default filename is DOSNET.INF.
/f	Prevents verification of files as they are copied. (This switch cannot be used with WINNT32.EXE.)
/l	Creates a log file called $WINNT.LOG, which lists all errors that occur as files are being copied to the temporary directory. (This switch cannot be used with WINNT32.EXE.)
/ox	Creates the three Setup boot disks and then stops.
/s:*server_path*	Specifies the location of the installation source files.
/u	Allows all or part of an installation to proceed unattended (as detailed in Chapter 1, "Planning"). The /b option for floppyless installation is automatically invoked, and the /s option for location of the source files must be used. The /u option can be followed with the name of an answer file to fully automate installation.
/udf	During an unattended installation, specifies settings unique to a specific computer, which are contained in a uniqueness database file (see Chapter 1).
/w	This *undocumented* flag enables the WINNT.EXE program to execute in Windows (normally, it must be executed from an MS-DOS command prompt).
/x	Prevents creation of the three Setup boot disks. You must already have the three boot disks.

NT Workstation can dual boot with any of the following operating systems:

- MS-DOS

- Microsoft Windows (3.1, 3.11, 95, 98)

- OS/2

- Microsoft Windows NT (Server or Workstation, any version)

Dual booting with an operating system other than NT (Server or Workstation) requires that at least the primary partition be formatted FAT.

If you remove NT Workstation from a machine, you must SYS (for the OS that remains) on the primary partition to remove the following:

- All paging files (C:\PAGEFILE.SYS)

- C:\BOOT.INI, C:\BOOTSECT.DOS, C:\NTDETECT.COM, C:\NTLDR (these are hidden, system, read only files)

- *.PAL (on Alpha computers)

- NTBOOTDD.SYS (on computers with SCSI drives with the BIOS disabled)

- The *winnt_root* folder

- The C:\Program files\Windows Windows NT folder

Most device drivers not written for NT 4.0 will not work with NT 4.0 (that includes network adapter drivers for NT 3.51 and Windows 95).

All mass storage device installation and settings (including those for tape drives and IDE hard drives) are configured from the SCSI icon in the Control Panel.

During boot, NT's automatic hardware detection process can cause a UPS to shut off because of a pulse that's sent through the COM port to detect a serial mouse. This can be prevented by including the /noserialmice switch in the boot line of the BOOT.INI file.

MANAGING RESOURCES

Remember: Here are the elements that Microsoft says they test on in the "Managing Resources" section of the exam.

- Create and manage local user accounts and local group accounts to meet given requirements.

- Set up and modify user profiles.

- Set up shared folders and permissions.

- Set permissions on NTFS partitions, folders, and files.

- Install and configure printers in a given environment.

Using local groups to assign rights and permissions on an NT Workstation can reduce administrative overhead.

The following account policies can be set from the User Manager:

- **Maximum Password Age.** This option enables you to specify how long a user's password is valid. The default is that passwords expire in 42 days.

- **Minimum Password Age.** This specifies how long a user must keep a particular password before she can change it again. If you force a user to change her password, and you leave this set to Allow Changes Immediately, after the user has changed her password once, she can change it right back to the old one. If you are requiring password changes for security reasons, this breaks down your security. For that reason, you may want to set a minimum password age.

- **Minimum Password Length.** The default on Windows NT is to allow blank passwords. Once again, for security reasons, you may not want to allow this. You can set a minimum password length of up to 14 characters, which is the maximum password length allowed under Windows NT.

◆ **Password Uniqueness.** If you want to force users to use a different password each time they change their passwords, you can set a value for password uniqueness. If you set the password uniqueness value to remember two passwords, when a user is prompted to change her password, she cannot use the same password again until she changes her password for the third time. The maximum password uniqueness value is 24.

◆ **Lockout After Bad Logon Attempts.** Setting a value for this option prevents the account from being used after this number is reached, even if the right password is finally entered. If you set this value to five, which is the default when Account Lockout is enabled, on the sixth attempt, a person cannot log on to Windows NT—even if the user (or hacker) types in the correct username and password.

◆ **Reset Counter After.** This value specifies when to refresh the counter for bad logon attempts. The default value is 30 minutes. That means if Account Lockout is set to five and a user tries to log on unsuccessfully four times, he can stop, wait 45 minutes, and then try again. The counter will have been reset by then, and he can try to log on five more times before the account will be locked out.

◆ **Lockout Duration.** This value specifies how long the account should remain locked if the lockout counter is exceeded. It is generally more secure to set Lockout Duration to forever so that the administrator must unlock the account. That way, the administrator is warned of the activity on that account.

◆ **Users Must Log On to Change Password.** This setting requires a user to log on successfully

before changing his password. If a user's password expires, the user cannot log on until the administrator changes the password for the user.

Home directories can be created so that each user who logs on has a specific location on the local machine or the network where he or she can store personal information.

In order to use RAS, a user must be granted dial-in permission in the User Manager.

You create new accounts through User Manager. Two accounts are created automatically when NT is installed: Administrator and Guest.

The following password options can be configured for a user when the account is created:

◆ **User Must Change Password at Next Logon.** When this is selected (which is the default when creating new users), the user is prompted to change his password when he logs on to Windows NT. This setting is not compatible with the account policy that forces a user to log on to change his password. If both are selected, the user must contact the administrator to change the password.

◆ **User Cannot Change Password.** Setting this option prevents a user from changing her password. If both this setting and User Must Change Password are selected, you get an error message stating that you cannot check both options for the same user when you attempt to add the account.

◆ **Password Never Expires.** You can use this option to override the setting for password expiration in the Account Policy. This option tends to be used for accounts that will be assigned to services, but it can be granted to user accounts as well. If you have both this option and User Must Change Password at Next Logon selected, a warning tells you that the user will not be required to change her password.

◆ **Account Disabled.** Instead of deleting a user's account when he or she leaves the company, it is a good idea to disable the account. If the user will be replaced, it is likely that the new individual who's hired will need the same rights and permissions the previous user had. By disabling the account, you prevent the previous employee from accessing your Windows NT Workstation or domain. When the new individual is hired, however, you can rename the old account to the new name and have the user change the password.

◆ **Account Locked Out.** This option is visible only if you have Account Lockout enabled in the Account Policy. You, as an administrator, can never check this box; it will be grayed out. The only time this box is available is when a user's account has been locked out because it has exceeded the specified number of bad logon attempts. If the Lockout Duration is set to forever, the administrator must go into that user's account and uncheck the Account Locked Out check box.

Table 9 lists the buttons available from a user's Properties dialog box in User Manager.

TABLE 9
USER PROPERTY BUTTONS IN USER MANAGER

Button	Enables You to Modify...
Groups	The groups the user is a member of
Profile	The user's profile path, login script path, and home directory location
Account	The user's account expiration date and account type
Hours	The hours a user can log in to the computer
Dialin	Whether the user can dial in using RAS and what callback features (if any) are enabled

You can create account templates to reduce the amount of administration that's required to create groups of similar accounts. Accounts created from a template inherit the template's configuration for the following features:

◆ Account Description option

◆ User Must Change Password at Next Logon option

◆ User Cannot Change Password option

◆ Password Never Expires option

◆ Group memberships

◆ All user-environment profile properties

◆ All dial-in properties

In account configuration, the %UserName% variable can represent individual users' login names whenever they're needed to access or create a folder. (For example, you might use it when creating home folders called by the users' login names.)

When a user leaves the company, it is always better to disable his account than to delete it for the following reasons:

◆ A disabled account cannot be used to log in (rendering it unuseable).

◆ Deleting an account also deletes the SID associated with it, thus removing the permissions for that user from all locations on the network.

◆ A user whose account is deleted will have to have her permissions restored everywhere if she should return.

◆ Renaming an account grants the permissions of the former user to the new user.

Local groups can be created to grant access to Workstation resources and to assign users' rights on the system. The following local groups are created when NT Workstation is installed:

◆ **Administrators.** The Administrators group has full control over the Windows NT Workstation. This account has the most control on the computer. However, members of the Administrators group do not automatically have control over all files on the system. By using an NTFS partition, a user can configure a file's permissions to restrict access from the administrator. If the administrator needs to access the file, she can take ownership of the file and then access it. Administrative privilege is one of three levels of privilege you can assign to a user in Windows NT. It is the highest level of privilege that can be assigned.

◆ **Guests.** The Guests group is used to give someone limited access to the resources on the Windows NT Workstation. The Guest account is automatically added to this group. The Guests group is one of the three levels of privilege you can assign to a Windows NT user account.

◆ **Users.** The Users group provides a user with the necessary rights to use the computer. By default, all accounts created on Windows NT Workstation are put into the Users group, except for the built-in Administrator and Guest accounts. User privilege is one of the three levels of privilege you can assign in Windows NT.

◆ **Power Users.** The Power Users group gives members the ability to perform certain system tasks without giving them complete administrative control over the machine. One of the tasks a power user can perform is the sharing of directories. An ordinary user on Windows NT Workstation cannot share directories.

◆ **Backup Operators.** The Backup Operators group gives its members the ability to bypass the security placed on any file when using the NT Backup utility. This allows them complete resource access, but only for the specialized job of backing up files, not for general access.

◆ **Replicator.** The Replicator group is used only to enable directory replication. This process allows file transfer to take place between an export computer (which must be an NT Server) and an import computer (which can be NT Workstation or NT Server). You will not see questions regarding this group and its service on the NT Workstation exam; but if you want more information, you can consult the NT Server book in this MCSE series.

Group accounts cannot be renamed.

User profiles fall into two categories: local and roaming. In addition, roaming user profiles fall into two categories: mandatory and personal. A local profile is located on a specific machine and takes effect only when a user logs onto that machine. A roaming profile is available over the network and can be accessed from any machine that has network connectivity to the machine holding the profile. Mandatory profiles (which have the extension .MAN) are read only and, therefore, cannot be changed by a user.

Shared folders allow users to access Workstation resources from the network (by default, no resources are made generally accessible to users over the network).

The following permissions are available on shared folders:

◆ **No Access.** If a user or group is given the No Access permission to a shared folder, that user or group cannot open the shared folder even though he will see the shared folder on the network. The

No Access permission overrides all other permissions a user or group might have to the folder.

◆ **Read.** The Read permission allows a user or group to display files and subfolders within the shared folder. It also allows the user or group to execute programs that might be located within the shared folder.

◆ **Change.** The Change permission allows a user or group to add files or subfolders to the shared folder and to append or delete information from existing files and subfolders. The Change permission also encompasses everything included within the Read permission.

◆ **Full Control.** If a user or group is given the Full Control permission, that user or group has the ability to change the file permissions and to perform all tasks allowed by the Change permission.

In order to share a folder on an NT Workstation, you must have that right. It is given by default to the built-in Administrators and Power Users groups.

You can share a folder remotely by using the Server Manager. Shares can be created, modified, or removed from a folder through the folder share permissions (accessible by right-clicking the folder and choosing Sharing).

If a user is given individual permission to access a folder and is also a member of one or more groups which are given access, the user's effective permission is the combination of the permissions (the highest level). This is true unless one of the permissions is No Access, in which case the No Access permission prevails over all others.

The permission granted to a share is also the permission granted to the tree structure inside that share. Sharing one folder within another shared folder gives two points of access and, potentially, two levels of access to the same resource.

Shared permissions apply only to network access; NTFS permissions apply both over the network and locally.

Table 10 describes the access permissions available on NTFS.

TABLE 10
STANDARD NTFS PERMISSIONS

Permission	Folder	File
Read (R)	Enables the user to display the folder and subfolders, attributes, and permissions	Enables the user to display the file, its attributes, and its permissions
Write (W)	Enables the user to add files or folders, change attributes for the folder, and display permissions	Enables the user to change file attributes and add or append data to the file
Execute (X)	Enables the user to make changes to subfolders, display permissions, and display attributes	Enables the user to run a file if it is an executable and display attributes and permissions
Delete (D)	Enables the user to remove the folder	Enables the user to remove the file
Change Permission (P)	Enables the user to modify folder permissions	Enables the user to modify file permissions
Take Ownership (O)	Enables the user to take ownership of the folder	Enables the user to take ownership of a file

Table 11 lists the standard NTFS file permissions and the granular permissions that comprise them.

TABLE 11
STANDARD NTFS FILE PERMISSIONS

Standard File Permission	Individual NTFS Permissions
No Access	(None)
Read	(RX)
Change	(RWXD)
Full Control	(All Permissions)

Table 12 lists the standard NTFS folder permissions and the default file permissions for files within those folders.

You (or any user) can take ownership of an NTFS resource provided that you meet one or more of the following criteria:

◆ **You must be the owner of the file or folder.** You must be the user who created it.

◆ **You must have been granted Full Control.** This includes the ability to Change Permissions (P).

◆ **You must have been given special access to Change Permissions (P).** A user can be given just this one permission to a file or folder.

◆ **You must have been given special access to Take Ownership (O).** With the ability to Take Ownership, a user can give himself the right to Change Permissions (P).

◆ **You must be a member of the Administrators group.**

If a user is granted individual NTFS permissions to a resource and is also a member of one or more groups that have been granted access, the effective permission for the user is the cumulative permission from all the access levels. This is the case unless any level is No Access, in which case the No Access level prevails over all others.

When shared permissions are combined with NTFS permissions for accessing a resource over the network, the lowest permission (share or NTFS) prevails. If the user is accessing locally, however, only NTFS permission applies.

TABLE 12
STANDARD NTFS FOLDER PERMISSIONS

Standard Folder Permissions	Individual NTFS Folder Permissions	Individual NTFS File Permissions
No Access	(None)	(None)
Read	(RX)	(RX)
Change	(RWXD)	(RWXD)
Add	(WX)	(Not Applicable)
Add & Read	(RWX)	(RX)
List	(RX)	(Not Applicable)
Full Control	(All)	(All)

When you copy a file from one folder to another, the permissions of the destination folder are applied to the new copy of the file. When you move a file from one folder to another and the folders are on different partitions, the permissions on the destination folder apply to the moved file. When you move a file from one folder to another on the same partition, the file retains its original permissions.

It's important that you remember the definitions of the following printing terms:

- **Printer**. The software component for printing. Also referred to as a *logical printer*, it is the software interface between the application and the print device.

- **Print device.** The actual hardware the paper comes out of. This is what you would traditionally think of as a printer. In Windows NT terminology, however, it is called a print device.

- **Print job.** The information that is sent to the print device. It contains both the data and the commands for print processing.

- **Print spooler.** A collection of DLLs (Dynamic Link Libraries) that accept, process, schedule, and distribute print jobs.

- **Creating a printer.** The process of defining a printer from your Windows NT Workstation. When you create a printer, you specify that the machine on which you are creating it will be the print server for that print device. You must create a printer if no other Windows NT system has created it yet, or if the print device is on a non–Windows NT operating system such as Windows 95.

- **Connecting to a printer.** A process that is necessary when the print device has already been defined by another Windows NT system and a printer has been created on that Windows NT system. If that is the case, in order to use the printer, you just need to connect to the printer from your Windows NT Workstation.

- **Print server.** The computer that created the printer and on which the printer is defined. Typically this is a Windows NT Server. However, a Windows NT Workstation or even a Windows 95 system can act as a print server.

- **Print queue.** The list of print jobs on the print server that are waiting to print.

- **Printer driver.** The software that enables applications to communicate properly with the print device.

- **Spooling.** The process of storing documents on the hard disk and then sending them to the printer. After the document has been stored on the hard disk, the user regains control of the application.

You can configure a printer pool by assigning two or more printer ports to the same printer and enabling printer pooling.

To allow other users to access a printer over the network, you must share the printer. Printer permissions can be set to control access to a printer. Table 13 lists those permissions.

TABLE 13
CAPABILITIES GRANTED WITH PRINTER PERMISSIONS

Capability	Full Control	Manage Documents	Print	No Access
Print documents	X	X	X	
Pause, resume, restart, and cancel the user's own documents	X	X	X	
Connect to a printer	X	X	X	
Control job settings for all documents	X	X		
Pause, restart, and delete all documents	X	X		
Share a printer	X			
Change printer properties	X			
Delete a printer	X			
Change printer permissions		X		

In a printer's properties dialog box, you can set the availability of the printer to allow it to hold documents until a certain time of the day.

Spool settings include the following options:

- **Spool Print Documents So Program Finishes Printing Faster.** If you choose this option, the documents will spool. This option has two choices within it:

  - *Start Printing After Last Page Is Spooled.* This prevents documents from printing until they are completely spooled. The application that is printing is not available during the spooling. To use this option, you must have enough space on the partition of the spool directory to hold the entire print job.

  - *Start Printing Immediately.* This enables a document to start printing before it has spooled completely, which speeds up printing.

- **Print Directly to the Printer.** This prevents the document from spooling. Although it speeds up printing, this is not an option for a shared printer, which would must support multiple incoming documents simultaneously.

- **Hold Mismatched Documents.** This prevents incorrect documents from printing. Incorrect documents are those that do not match the configuration of the printer.

- **Print Spooled Documents First.** Spooled documents will print ahead of partially spooled documents, even if they have a lower priority. This speeds up printing.

- **Keep Documents After They Have Printed.** Documents remain in the spooler after they have been printed.

If the print queue becomes jammed, you can clear corrupted print items by stopping and restarting the Spooler service from the Services icon in the Control Panel. The spool directory is, by default, located in Systemroot\system32\spool\printers, but that location can be changed via the File menu in the printer properties dialog box.

CONNECTIVITY

Remember: Here are the elements that Microsoft says they test on in the "Connectivity" section of the exam.

- Add and configure the network components of Windows NT Workstation.

- Use various methods to access network resources.

- Implement Windows NT Workstation as a client in a NetWare environment.

- Use various configurations to install Windows NT Workstation as a TCP/IP client.

- Configure and install Dial-Up Networking in a given situation.

- Configure Microsoft Peer Web Services in a given situation.

NDIS 4.0 enables the following on an NT Workstation computer:

- An unlimited number of network adapter cards.

- An unlimited number of network protocols can be bound to a single network adapter card.

- Independence between protocols and adapter card drivers.

- Communication links between adapter cards and their drivers.

The major characteristics of TCP/IP include the following:

- Routing support

- Connectivity with the Internet

- Interoperability with most possible operating systems and computer types

- Support as a client for Dynamic Host Configuration Protocol (DHCP)

- Support as a client for Windows Internet Name Service (WINS)

- Support as a client for Domain Name System (DNS)

- Support for Simple Network Management Protocol (SNMP)

The following are the major characteristics of NWLink:

- Connectivity with NetWare resources

- Routing support

- Supported by a wide variety of other operating systems

- Large installation base

The main characteristics of NetBEUI include

- No routing support.

- Transmissions are broadcast-based and, therefore, generate a lot of traffic.

- Fast performance on small LANs.

- Small memory overhead.

- No tuning options.

DLC protocol is primarily used for connecting NT Workstations to printers directly attached to the network through network interface cards.

Two network programming interfaces are available to allow programmers to access the network:

◆ **NetBIOS (Network Basic Input/Output System).** The original network API supported by Microsoft. IBM originally developed NetBIOS.

◆ **Windows Sockets (also called WinSock).** A newer network API originally developed by the UNIX community. Now Microsoft also supports it.

Table 14 describes the IPC mechanisms available in NT Workstation.

The Network applet in the Control Panel allows you to change names, services, protocols, adapters, and bindings for network configuration.

In order to be part of an NT domain, an NT computer must have an account that was created by someone with the right to add computer accounts in the domain (by default, an administrator).

If NWLink is installed and NT is left to autoconfigure the frame type, NT will expect 802.2 frames unless others are detected, in which case it will configure to the frame type it sees first. To use multiple NWLink frame types, you must make a Registry setting change.

Client Services for NetWare gives an NT Workstation the capability to access files and printers from a NetWare server, provided that NWLink is also installed on the Workstation. When installed on an NT Workstation, NWLink allows the workstation to connect to an application running on a NetWare server.

TABLE 14
TYPES OF INTERPROCESS COMMUNICATIONS

IPC Mechanism	Typical Uses
Named pipes	Named pipes establish a guaranteed bidirectional communications channel between two computers. After the pipe is established, either computer can read data from or write data to the pipe.
Mailslots	Mailslots establish a unidirectional communications channel between two computers. Receipt of the message is not guaranteed, and no acknowledgment is sent if the data is received.
Windows Sockets (WinSock)	WinSock is an API that enables applications to access transport protocols such as TCP/IP and NWLink.
RPCs	RPCs enable the various components of distributed applications to communicate with one another via the network.
Network Dynamic Data Exchange (NetDDE)	NetDDE is an older version of an RPC that is based on NetBIOS.
Distributed ActiveX Component Object Model (DCOM)	DCOM is an RPC based on Microsoft technology; it enables the components of a distributed application to be located on multiple computers across a network simultaneously.

TCP/IP is the default protocol installed on NT Workstation and requires at least a TCP/IP address and subnet mask to function properly. You can configure an NT Workstation to automatically receive TCP/IP configuration information from a DHCP server by selecting the Obtain Address from DHCP Server option button in the TCP/IP Properties dialog box. Two tools, IPCONFIG and PING, can be used to test the configuration and function of TCP/IP on your NT Workstation.

NT Workstation can act as a RAS client or a RAS server with one concurrent incoming connection. As a client, it can connect to servers using the SLIP, PPP, and PPTP protocols; as a client, it supports incoming connections using PPP or PPTP. Whether acting as a RAS client or a RAS server, an NT Workstation must have the RAS service installed. Table 15 lists the features of the three line protocols mentioned here.

PPTP connections require a PPP or LAN connection to a server with a Virtual Private Network (VPN) configured on it and provide for secure and encrypted communication.

In order for a user to log on to an NT Workstation using RAS, the user account must be configured in User Manager to allow dialin.

Peer Web Services allows for FTP, WWW, and Gopher connections from Internet or intranet clients.

TABLE 15
RAS LINE PROTOCOLS AND FEATURES

Feature	SLIP	PPP	PPTP
Supports NT as server	No	Yes	Yes
Supports NT as client	Yes	Yes	Yes
Passes TCP/IP	Yes	Yes	Yes
Passes NetBEUI	No	Yes	Yes
Passes NWLink	No	Yes	Yes
Supports DHCP over RAS	No	Yes	No
Requires PPP or LAN connection	No	No	Yes
Supports VPNs	No	No	Yes
Supports password encryption	No	Yes	Yes
Supports transmission encryption	No	No	Yes

RUNNING APPLICATIONS

Remember: Here are the elements that Microsoft says they test on in the "Running Applications" section of the exam.

◆ Start applications on Intel and RISC platforms in various operating system environments.

◆ Start applications with various priorities.

NT Workstation supports (to a greater or lesser extent) applications written for the following operating systems:

◆ Windows NT and Windows 95

◆ MS-DOS

◆ Windows 3.x

◆ OS/2

◆ POSIX

MS-DOS applications invoke an NT Virtual DOS machine, which emulates a DOS environment. Windows 16-bit applications invoke an NT Virtual DOS machine (unless one is already running) and then run a Win16 emulator called WOW.EXE.

By default, Win16 applications all run in the same NTVDM. However, if desired, you can configure them to run in separate NTVDMs. The following list summarizes the advantages and disadvantages of running Win16 applications in separate NTVDMs.

Advantages:

◆ Win16 applications will now use preemptive multitasking. An ill-behaved Win16 application will no longer prevent other Win16 applications from executing normally because each Win16 application will have its own memory space and thread of execution.

◆ Win16 applications will now be more reliable because they will not be affected by the problems of other Win16 applications.

◆ Win16 applications can now take advantage of multiprocessor computers. When Win16 applications are run in a common NTVDM, they must share a single thread of execution. The generation of individual NTVDMs also creates individual threads of execution, and each thread can potentially be executed on a different processor. The operating system could now schedule each NTVDM's thread of execution to run on whichever processor is available. In a system with multiple processors, this can lead to multiprocessing. If the Win16 applications were running in a common NTVDM, their single thread of execution would be able to run only on a single processor, no matter how many processors existed on the computer.

◆ Windows NT will enable Win16 applications running in separate memory spaces to continue to participate in OLE and dynamic data exchange (DDE).

Disadvantages:

◆ There is additional overhead in running separate NTVDMs.

◆ Some older Win16 applications did not use the standards of OLE and DDE. These applications would not function properly if they were run in separate memory spaces. These applications must be run in a common memory space to function correctly. Lotus for Windows 1.0 is an example of this type of application.

NT offers four methods for running Win16 applications in separate NTVDMs:

◆ Anytime you start a Win16 application from the Start menu using the Run option, you can select the Run in Separate Memory Space option. This technique must be applied every time an application is run from the Run dialog box.

◆ At a command prompt, you can start a Win16 application using the command syntax start /separate *application*. For example, to start Word 6.0 you could type the following:

```
start /separate c:\office16\word\winword.exe
```

This technique must be applied every time the application is run from a command prompt.

◆ Shortcuts that point to Win16 applications can be configured to always run in a separate memory space. To do that, use the appropriate option on the Shortcut tab of the properties dialog box for the shortcut. Although this causes an application to run in a separate memory space every time the shortcut is used, it applies only to the particular shortcut that's modified, and not to any other shortcuts that have been created to that application.

◆ You can configure all files with a particular extension to always run in a separate memory space when the data document is double-clicked on in the Windows NT Explorer. To do this, you edit the File Types tab of the View, Options properties.

The OS/2 subsystem allows you to run OS/2 1.x character-based applications on Intel machines. On RISC machines, you must run OS/2 applications in NTVDMs by using the /FORCEDOS switch when running the applications from a command prompt or shortcut. You configure OS/2 applications by editing a CONFIG.SYS file using an OS/2 text editor. This creates a temporary file that is then converted to Registry settings (no CONFIG.SYS file is actually stored on the hard drive).

NT provides POSIX.1 support in its POSIX subsystem. This subsystem supports the following features for POSIX applications:

◆ **Case-sensitive file naming.** NTFS preserves case for both directory and filenames.

◆ **Hard links.** POSIX applications can store the same data in two differently named files.

◆ **An additional time stamp on files.** This tracks the last time the file was accessed. The default on FAT volumes is to track only the last time the file was modified.

Application support differs across different hardware platforms. Table 16 lists the kinds of support that applications have. *Binary* means that the same application will run across all hardware platforms; *source* means that a different compile is required for each hardware platform.

TABLE 16
APPLICATION COMPATIBILITY ACROSS WINDOWS NT PLATFORMS

Platform	MS-DOS	Win16	Win32	OS/2	POSIX
Intel	Binary	Binary	Source	Binary	Source
Alpha	Binary	Binary	Source*	Binary**	Source
Mips	Binary	Binary	Source	Binary**	Source
PowerPC	Binary	Binary	Source	Binary**	Source

* Third-party utilities such as Digital FX!32 enable Win32-based Intel programs to execute on Digital Alpha AXP microprocessors. Although these utilities are interpreting the code on-the-fly, they end up performing faster on the Alpha as a result of the increased processor speed.
** Only bound applications can be run on the three RISC hardware platforms. They will run in a Windows NTVDM because the OS/2 subsystem is not provided in RISC-based versions of Windows NT.

All applications run at a default priority set by the application itself (between 0 and 31). This priority determines its relative access to the CPU and, as a result, how quickly it responds to user interaction.

You can assign priority levels to applications through the use of command prompt switches. Table 17 lists the priority levels, their base priorities, and the commands you use to assign them.

NT boosts the priority of the application in the foreground by anywhere from 0 to 2 points (this ensures that foreground applications are more responsive than background applications). The "boost from" base is set on the Performance tab of the Control Panel's System application.

TABLE 17
BASE PRIORITY LEVELS UNDER WINDOWS NT

Priority Level	Base Priority	Command Line
Low	4	start /low executable.exe
Normal	8	start /normal executable.exe
High	13	start /high executable.exe
Realtime	24	start /realtime executable.exe

MONITORING AND OPTIMIZATION

Remember: Here are the elements that Microsoft says they test on in the "Monitoring and Optimization" section of the exam.

◆ Monitor system performance by using various tools.

◆ Identify and resolve a given performance problem.

◆ Optimize system performance in various areas.

Task Manager (accessible by right-clicking the taskbar and choosing Task Manager) allows you to see and end applications and processes on your system.

Performance Monitor allows you to monitor counters for specific computer and application objects and to tune the performance of your computer based on what you find.

In order to monitor disk counters, you must first enable them through the use of the command DISKPERF -y (or DISKPERF -YE for volume sets and RAID disks).

Table 18 describes the objects you will find in the Performance Monitor (others may be present depending on the services or applications you have installed).

Four views are available in the Performance Monitor:

◆ **Chart view.** Real-time line graphs of counters.

◆ **Log view.** Stored statistics useable by other views at a later time.

◆ **Alert view.** Monitored thresholds that generate events if the thresholds are crossed.

◆ **Report view.** Real-time text-displayed statistics on counters.

Performance Monitor can be used to monitor a local machine or an NT Server or Workstation to which the user has Administrative rights.

TABLE 18
COMMON OBJECTS ALWAYS AVAILABLE IN THE PERFORMANCE MONITOR

Object	Description
Cache	The file system cache is an area of physical memory that holds recently used data.
Logical Disk	Disk partitions and other logical views of disk space.
Memory	Random access memory used to store code and data.
Objects	Certain system software objects.
Paging File	File used to support virtual memory allocated by the system.
Physical Disk	Hardware disk unit.
Process	Software object that represents a running program.
Processor	Hardware unit that executes program instructions.
Redirector	File system that diverts file requests to network servers.
System	Counters that apply to all system hardware and software.
Thread	The part of a process that uses the processor.

The Server Manager allows you to see who is currently logged on to a computer and what resources they are using, to see available shares on your Workstation, to start or stop sharing resources, and to see what type of access is being made to all in-use resources.

WINMSD allows you to view configuration information about your computer.

You may want to monitor and tune the following components:

◆ Memory

◆ Processor

◆ Disks

◆ Network

The Event Viewer allows you to view information logged to any of three logs:

◆ **System log.** A log of events detected by NT that have to do with system functioning (the starting and stopping of services or their failure).

◆ **Security log.** A log of audited events that have to do with resource access (success or failure).

◆ **Application log.** A log of events recorded by applications running on NT that are configured to create such events.

You can archive any of these logs for viewing at a later time or for event archive.

An emergency repair disk enables you to recover Registry and system settings should they become corrupt. By performing the following two steps, you can be sure your ERD remains up-to-date:

1. Using the RDISK.EXE utility, update the Repair directory to save the repair information on your hard drive.

2. Using the RDISK.EXE utility, write the Repair information to a floppy disk.

You can perform a repair by booting to and using the three installation disks required to install NT from a CD-ROM and by specifying that you want to repair your system when asked.

The LastKnownGood configuration is a set of Registry settings that record the state of the NT configuration at the time of the last successful login. If you encounter problems with your system resulting from a change you've made in the current session, reboot and choose to restore LastKnownGood. Every time you log in, the LastKnownGood configuration is overwritten with the current configuration of your hardware (whether it functions properly or not).

TROUBLESHOOTING

Remember: Here are the elements that Microsoft says they test on in the "Troubleshooting" section of the exam.

◆ Choose the appropriate course of action to take when the boot process fails.

◆ Choose the appropriate course of action to take when a print job fails.

◆ Choose the appropriate course of action to take when the installation process fails.

◆ Choose the appropriate course of action to take when an application fails.

◆ Choose the appropriate course of action to take when a user cannot access a resource.

◆ Modify the Registry using the appropriate tool in a given situation.

◆ Implement advanced techniques to resolve various problems.

The acronym DETECT can be used to define the troubleshooting process:

D	Discover the problem
E	Explore the boundaries
T	Track the possible approaches
E	Execute an approach
C	Check for success
T	Tie up loose ends

Table 19 identifies the files involved in the boot process for both Intel and RISC machines.

TABLE 19
BOOT PROCESS FILES

Intel	RISC
NTLDR	OSLOADER.EXE
BOOT.INI	NTOSKRNL.EXE
NTDETECT.COM	
NTOSKRNL.EXE	
NTBOOTDD.SYS (for SCSI drives with BIOS disabled)	

In the NT boot process (in BOOT.INI), ARC paths define the physical position of the NT operating system files. ARC paths follow one of two formats:

scsi(0)disk(0)rdisk(0)partition(1)*folder*

multi(0)disk(0)rdisk(0)partition(1)*folder*

The first type, scsi ARC paths, define hard drives that are SCSI but have the BIOS disabled. The relevant parameters are

◆ **scsi.** The SCSI controller, starting from 0.

◆ **disk.** The physical disk, starting from 0.

◆ **partition.** The partition on the disk, starting from 1.

◆ ***folder*.** The folder in which the NT files are located.

The second type, multi ARC paths, define hard drives that are non-SCSI or are SCSI with the BIOS enabled. The relevant parameters are

◆ **multi.** The controller, starting from 0.

◆ **rdisk.** The physical disk, starting from 0.

◆ **partition.** The partition on the disk, starting from 1.

◆ ***folder*.** The folder in which the NT files are located.

Partitions are numbered according to the following pattern:

1. The first primary partition on each disk gets the number 1.

2. Each additional primary partition is then given a number, incrementing up from 1.

3. Each logical drive is then given a number in the order they appear in the Disk Administrator.

Switches on boot lines in the BOOT.INI file define additional boot parameters. Table 20 lists the switches you need to know and their functions.

TABLE 20
BOOT.INI SWITCHES

Switch	Function
/basevideo	Loads standard VGA video driver (640×480, 16-color)
/sos	Displays each driver as it is loaded
/noserialmice	Prevents autodetection of serial mice on COM ports, which can disable a UPS connected to the port

A recovery disk can be used to bypass problems with a system partition. This disk must be formatted in NT and will contain the files listed in Table 21 (broken down by hardware platform).

TABLE 21
FILES ON THE RECOVERY DISK

Intel	RISC
NTLDR	OSLOADER.EXE
NTDETECT.COM	HAL.DLL
BOOT.INI	*.PAL (for Alpha machines)
BOOTSECT.DOS (allows you to boot to DOS)	
NTBOOTDD.SYS (the SCSI driver for a hard drive with SCSI BIOS not enabled)	

An emergency repair disk can be used to repair an NT system if the Registry becomes corrupted. The repair disk must be used in conjunction with the three setup disks used to install NT.

The RDISK program allows you to update the \REPAIR folder, which in turn is used to update your repair disk.

The following list identifies possible sources of installation problems:

◆ Media errors

◆ Insufficient disk space

◆ Non-supported SCSI adapters

◆ Failure of dependency service to start

◆ Inability to connect to the domain controller

◆ Error in assigning domain names

Application failures generally result from incorrect application configuration, not from incorrect NT configuration.

If applications do not run, check the following:

◆ An MS-DOS application may be trying to access hardware directly.

◆ Two Win16 applications running in the same NTVDM may be conflicting.

◆ Win32 applications may be compiled for a different processor.

Services are interrelated: If one service fails, it may affect others as well. Therefore, you need to make sure that you get to the root of a service failure, and you're not just treating the symptoms.

Two programs are available for viewing and modifying the Registry:

◆ REGEDIT.EXE

◆ REGEDT32.EXE

The Network Monitor tool can be used to analyze network traffic in and out of the adapter on an NT Workstation computer.

Twelve chapters of this book have looked at objectives and components of the Microsoft Networking Essentials exam. After reading all of that, what is it that you must really know? What should you read as you sit and wait in the parking lot of the testing center—right up until the hour before going in to gamble your $100 and pride?

The following material covers the salient points of the 12 previous chapters and the points that make excellent test fodder. Although there is no substitute for real-world, hands-on experience, knowing what to expect on the exam can be equally meaningful. The information that follows is the networking equivalent of *Cliffs Notes*, providing the information you must know in each of the four sections to pass the exam. Don't just memorize the concepts given; attempt to understand the reason why they are so, and you will have no difficulties passing the exam.

NETWORKING ESSENTIALS EXAM

STANDARDS AND TERMINOLOGY

The Standards and Terminology section is designed to test your understanding and knowledge of terms used in networking, as well as some of the more common standards that have been implemented in the industry.

Define Common Networking Terms for LANs and WANs

The Networking Essentials exam does not really test on definitions of terms. You are asked questions though, and, based on these questions, you need to understand the definitions of the terms used in order to successfully answer the questions.

The best mechanism to study for this area would be to be able to review the key terms found in every chapter and provide the correct definition for each term. Below is a list of some of the more general networking terms you should be aware of.

- **peer-to-peer networking**. A networking model where both the services and the client are performed by the same computer.

- **client/server networking**. A networking model where a specific role of providing services or acting as a client (not both) is performed by a computer.

- **centralized computing**. A form of computing where all the processing is done by one central computer.

- **distributed computing**. A form of computing where all the processing is shared by many different computers.

- **file services**. Services allowing for the storage and access of files.

- **print services**. Services that allow the sharing of a printer.

- **file and print server**. A server that provides file and print services.

- **application server**. A server that provides some high-end application used by many different computers.

- **token-ring network**. A network that follows a logical topology of a ring, but a physical topology of a star. The computers are connected to a concentrator known as an MSAU or MAU. Computers rely on the possession of a token before the transmission of data on the network. This type of network is known as a deterministic network.

- **ethernet network**. This type of a network is run as a logical bus, but can take on the physical topology of a bus or a star. The concentrator used by these computers, when in a star topology, is called a hub. This type of network is known as a contention-based network because each device contends with every other device for network access.

- **LAN**. Also known as a Local Area Network. Often characterized by fast transmission speeds and short distances between devices, and by the fact that the company running the network has control over all devices and transmission media.

- **WAN**. Also known as a Wide Area Network. When compared to a LAN, a WAN is often characterized by lower data transmission rates and the coverage of long distances, and by the fact that a third party is involved with the supply and maintenance of the transmission media.

Compare a File and Print Server with an Application Server

A file server is a service that is involved with giving access to files and directories on the network. The purpose of the file server is to give large numbers of users access to a centrally stored set of files and directories.

A print server is a computer or device that gives large number of users access to a centrally maintained printing device. A computer that is a file server often acts as print server, too. These types of computers are known as file and print servers.

An application server is responsible for running applications such as Exchange Server or SQL Server on the network. Application servers perform services that often require a more advanced level of processing than a user's personal computer is able to provide.

Compare User-Level Security with Access Permission Assigned to a Shared Directory on a Server

User-level security is a security model in which access to resources is given on a user-by-user basis, a group-by-group basis, or both. This type of access restriction allows an administrator to grant access to resources and affords users seemless access to those resources. User-level security is offered by Windows NT in both the workgroup and domain models.

The permissions to a shared directory are:

◆ **Read**. The user is allowed to read files within a share. He can also see all files and subdirectories.

◆ **Change**. The user can modify existing files and directories and create new files and directories within the share.

◆ **Full Control**. The user can see, modify, delete, and take ownership of all files and directories within the share.

◆ **No Access**. The user cannot access any files or directories within the share.

Share-level permissions apply to anyone accessing the share over the network and do not apply to users who are interactive on the computer where the share resides. Share-level permissions can be set on both FAT and NTFS partitions.

Compare a Client/Server Network with a Peer-to-Peer Network

A client/server network is one in which a computer has a specific role. A server is a computer, often with more

RAM, more hard drive space, and a faster CPU than the other machines. A server services requests from clients. These requests could be for the use of files and printers, application services, communication services, and database services.

Clients are the computers on which users work. These computers typically are not as powerful as servers. Client computers are designed to submit requests to the server.

Peer-to-peer networks are made up of several computers that play the roles of both a client and a server; thus there is no dedicated computer running file and printer services, application services, communication services, or database services.

Compare the Implications of Using Connection-Oriented Communications with Connectionless Communications

In general, connection-oriented communication differs from connectionless communication as follows:

◆ **Connection-oriented mode**. Error correction and flow control are provided at internal nodes along the message path.

◆ **Connectionless mode**. Internal nodes along the message path do not participate in error correction and flow control.

In connection-oriented mode, the chain of links between the source and destination nodes forms a kind of logical pathway connection. The nodes forwarding the data packet can track which packet is part of which connection. This enables the internal nodes to provide flow control as the data moves along the path. For example, if an internal node determines that a link is malfunctioning, the node can send a notification message backward through the path to the source computer. Furthermore, because the internal node distinguishes among individual, concurrent connections in which it participates, this node can transmit (or forward) a "stop sending" message for one of its connections without stopping all communications through the node. Another feature of connection-oriented communication is that internal nodes provide error correction at each link in the chain. Therefore, if a node detects an error, it asks the preceding node to retransmit.

SPX and TCP are two major examples of connection-oriented protocols.

Connectionless mode does not provide these elaborate internal control mechanisms; instead, connectionless mode relegates all error-correcting and retransmitting processes to the source and destination nodes. The end nodes acknowledge the receipt of packets and retransmit if necessary, but internal nodes do not participate in flow control and error correction (other than simply forwarding messages between the end nodes).

IPX and UDP are two major examples of connection-oriented protocols.

The advantage of connectionless mode is that connectionless communications can be processed more quickly and more simply because the internal nodes only forward data and thus don't have to track connections or provide retransmission or flow control.

Distinguish Whether SLIP or PPP Is Used as the Communications Protocol for Various Situations

Two other standards vital to network communication are Serial Line Internet Protocol (SLIP) and Point-to-Point Protocol (PPP). SLIP and PPP were designed to

support dial-up access to networks based on the Internet transport protocols. SLIP is a simple protocol that functions at the Physical layer, whereas PPP is a considerably enhanced protocol that provides Physical layer and Data Link layer functionality.

Windows NT supports both SLIP and PPP from the client end using the Dial-Up Networking application. On the server end, Windows NT RAS (Remote Access Service) supports PPP but doesn't support SLIP. In other words, Windows NT can act as a PPP server but not as a SLIP server.

PPP

PPP was defined by the Internet Engineering Task Force (IETF) to improve on SLIP by providing the following features:

◆ Security using password logon

◆ Simultaneous support for multiple protocols on the same link

◆ Dynamic IP addressing

◆ Improved error control

Different PPP implementations might offer different levels of service and negotiate service levels when connections are made. Because of its versatility, interoperability, and additional features, PPP has surpassed SLIP as the most popular serial-line protocol.

SLIP

Developed to provide dial-up TCP/IP connections, SLIP is an extremely rudimentary protocol that suffers from a lack of rigid standardization in the industry, which sometimes hinders different vendor implementations of SLIP from operating with each other.

SLIP is most commonly used on older systems or for dial-up connections to the Internet via SLIP-server Internet hosts.

Certain dial-up configurations cannot use SLIP for the following reasons:

- SLIP supports the TCP/IP transport protocol only. PPP, however, supports TCP/IP, as well as a number of other transport protocols, such as NetBEUI, IPX, AppleTalk, and DECnet. In addition, PPP can support multiple protocols over the same link.

- SLIP requires static IP addresses. Because SLIP requires static, or preconfigured, IP addresses, SLIP servers do not support the Dynamic Host Configuration Protocol (DHCP), which assigns IP addresses dynamically or when requested. (DHCP enables clients to share IP addresses so that a relatively small number of IP addresses can serve a larger user base.) If the dial-up server uses DHCP to assign an IP address to the client, the dial-up connection won't use SLIP.

- SLIP does not support dynamic addressing through DHCP so SLIP connections cannot dynamically assign a WINS or DNS server.

Define the Communication Devices that Communicate at Each Level of the OSI Model

- **Repeater**. Operates at the Physical layer of the OSI model. The purpose of a repeater is to regenerate a signal, allowing a signal to travel beyond the maximum distance specified by the transmission media.

- **Hub**. Operates at the Physical layer. A hub is a concentrator that connects 10BASE-T cabling together on an Ethernet network. Some hubs also have the capability to act as a repeater.

- **MSAU**. Operates at the Physical layer. An MSAU performs the same purpose of a hub, but is used on token-ring networks.

- **Network Interface Card (NIC)**. Operates at the Data Link layer. A NIC is responsible for converting information in a computer to a signal that will be sent on the transmission media.

- **Bridge**. Operates at the Data Link layer of the OSI mode. A bridge is responsible for isolating network traffic on a cable segment. It performs this task by building address tables that contain the MAC address or hardware addresses of devices on ether side of it.

- **Router**. Operates at the Network layer of the OSI model. It is responsible for connecting different segments that have dissimilar logical network addresses.

- **Gateway**. Can appear at any level of the OSI model but is primarily seen at the Network layer and higher. The purpose of a gateway is to convert one network protocol to another.

Describe the Characteristics and Purpose of the Media Used in IEEE 802.3 and IEEE 802.5 Standards

The various media types used by the IEEE 802.3 and 802.5 are discussed below.

IEEE 802.3

This standard defines characteristics related to the MAC sublayer of the Data Link layer and the OSI Physical layer. Except for one minor distinction—frame type—IEEE 802.3 Ethernet functions identically to DIX Ethernet v.2.

The MAC sublayer uses a type of contention access called *Carrier Sense Multiple Access with Collision Detection (CSMA/CD)*. This technique reduces the incidence of collision by having each device listen to the network to determine whether it's quiet ("carrier sensing"); a device attempts to transmit only when the network is quiescent. This reduces but does not eliminate collisions because signals take some time to propagate through the network. As devices transmit, they continue to listen so they can detect a collision should it occur. When a collision occurs, all devices cease transmitting and send a "jamming" signal that notifies all stations of the collision. Each device then waits a random amount of time before attempting to transmit again. This combination of safeguards significantly reduces collisions on all but the busiest networks.

The IEEE 802.3 Physical layer definition describes signaling methods (both baseband and broadband), data rates, media, and topologies. Several Physical layer variants also have been defined. Each variant is named following a convention that states the signaling rate (1 or 10) in Mbps, baseband (BASE) or broadband (BROAD) mode, and a designation of the media characteristics.

The following list details the IEEE 802.3 variants of transmission media:

◆ **lBASE5**. This 1-Mbps network utilizes UTP cable with a signal range up to 500 meters (250 meters per segment). A star physical topology is used.

◆ **10BASE5**. Typically called Thick Ethernet, or Thicknet, this variant uses a large diameter (10 mm) "thick" coaxial cable with a 50-ohm impedance. A data rate of 10 Mbps is supported with a signaling range of 500 meters per cable segment on a physical bus topology.

◆ **10BASE2**. Similar to Thicknet, this variant uses a thinner coaxial cable that can support cable runs of 185 meters. (In this case, the "2" only indicates an approximate cable range.) The transmission rate remains at 10 Mbps, and the physical topology is a bus. This variant typically is called Thin Ethernet, or Thinnet.

◆ **10BASE-F**. This variant uses fiber-optic cables to support 10-Mbps signaling with a range of four kilometers. Three subcategories include *10BASE-FL* (fiber link), *10BASE-FB* (fiber backbone), and *10BASE-FP* (fiber passive).

◆ **10BROAD36**. This broadband standard supports channel signal rates of 10 Mbps. A 75-ohm coaxial cable supports cable runs of 1,800 meters (up to 3,600 meters in a dual-cable configuration) using a physical bus topology.

◆ **10BASE-T**. This variant uses UTP cable in a star physical topology. The signaling rate remains at 10 Mbps, and devices can be up to 100 meters from a wiring hub.

◆ **100BASE-X**. This proposed standard is similar to 10BASE-T but supports 100 Mbps data rates.

IEEE 802.5

The IEEE 802.5 standard was derived from IBM's Token Ring network, which employs a ring logical topology and token-based media-access control. Data rates of 1, 4, and 16 Mbps have been defined for this standard.

Explain the Purpose of NDIS and Novell ODI Network Standards

The *Network Driver Interface Specification (NDIS)*, a standard developed by Microsoft and the 3Com Corporation, describes the interface between the network transport protocol and the Data Link layer network adapter driver. The following list details the goals of NDIS:

◆ To provide a vendor-neutral boundary between the transport protocol and the network adapter card driver so that an NDIS-compliant protocol stack can operate with an NDIS-compliant adapter driver.

◆ To define a method for binding multiple protocols to a single driver so that the adapter can simultaneously support communications under multiple protocols. In addition, the method enables you to bind one protocol to more than one adapter.

The *Open Data-Link Interface (ODI)*, developed by Apple and Novell, serves the same function as NDIS. Originally, ODI was written for NetWare and Macintosh environments. Like NDIS, ODI provides rules that establish a vendor-neutral interface between the protocol stack and the adapter driver. This interface also enables one or more network drivers to support one or more protocol stacks.

PLANNING

The planning section on the exam tests your ability to apply networking components and standards when designing a network.

Select the Appropriate Media for Various Situations

Media choices include:

◆ Twisted-pair cable

◆ Coaxial cable

◆ Fiber-optic cable

◆ Wireless

Situational elements include:

◆ Cost

◆ Distance limitations

◆ Number of nodes

Summary Table 1 outlines the characteristics of the cable types discussed in this section.

Summary Table 2 compares the different types of wireless communication media in terms of cost, ease of installation, distance, and other issues.

SUMMARY TABLE 1
COMPARISON OF CABLE MEDIA

Cable Type	Cost	Installation	Capacity	Range	EMI
Coaxial Thinnet	Less than STP	Inexpensive/easy	10 Mbps typical	185 m	Less sensitive than UTP
Coaxial Thicknet	Greater than STP Less than Fiber	Easy	10 Mbps typical	500 m	Less sensitive than UTP
Shielded Twisted-Pair (STP)	Greater than UTP Less than Thicknet	Fairly easy	16 Mbps typical up to 500 Mbps	100 m typical	Less sensitive than UTP
Unshielded twisted-pair (UTP)	Lowest	Inexpensive/easy	10 Mbps typical up to 100 Mbps	100 m typical	Most sensitive
Fiber-optic	Highest	Expensive/ Difficult	100 Mbps typical	Tens of Kilometers	Insensitive

SUMMARY TABLE 2
COMPARISON OF WIRELESS MEDIA

Cable Type	Cost	Installation	Distance	Other Issues
Infrared	Cheapest of all the wireless	Fairly easy; may require line of sight	Under a kilometer	Can attenuate due to fog and rain
Laser	Similar to infrared	Requires line of site	Can span several kilometers	Can attenuate due to fog and rain
Narrow band radio	More expensive than infrared and laser; may need FCC license	Requires trained technicians and can involve tall radio towers	Can span hundreds of kilometers	Low power devices can attenuate; can be eavesdropped upon; can also attenuate due to fog, rain, and solar flares
Spread spectrum radio	More advanced technology than narrow band radio, thus more expensive	Requires trained technicians and can involve tall radio towers	Can span hundreds of kilometers	Low power devices can attenuate; can also attenuate due to fog, rain, and solar flares
Microwave	Very expensive as it requires link to satellites often	Requires trained technicians and can involve satellite dishes	Can span thousands of kilometers	Can be eavesdropped upon; can also attenuate due to fog, rain, and solar flares

Select the Appropriate Topology for Various Token-Ring and Ethernet Networks

The following four topologies are implemented by Ethernet and token-ring networks:

◆ **Ring**. Ring topologies are wired in a circle. Each node is connected to its neighbors on either side, and data passes around the ring in one direction only. Each device incorporates a receiver and a transmitter and serves as a repeater that passes the signal to the next device in the ring. Because the signal is regenerated at each device, signal degeneration is low. Most ring topologies are logical, and implemented as physical stars. Token-ring networks follow a ring topology.

◆ **Bus**. Star topologies require that all devices connect to a central hub. The hub receives signals from other network devices and routes the signals to the proper destinations. Star hubs can be interconnected to form tree or hierarchical network topologies. A star physical topology is often used to physically implement a bus or ring logical topology that is used by both Ethernet and token-ring networks.

◆ **Star**. Star topologies require that all devices connect to a central hub. The hub receives signals from other network devices and routes the signals to the proper destinations. Star hubs can be interconnected to form tree or hierarchical network topologies. A star physical topology is often used to physically implement a bus or ring logical topology that is used by both Ethernet and token-ring networks.

◆ **Mesh**. A mesh topology is really a hybrid model representing a physical topology because a mesh topology can incorporate all of the previous topologies. The difference is that in a mesh topology every device is connected to every other device on the network. When a new device is added, a connection to all existing devices must be made. Mesh topologies can be used by both Ethernet and token-ring networks.

Select the Appropriate Network and Transport Protocol or Protocols for Various Token-Ring and Ethernet Networks

Protocol choices include:

- ◆ DLC
- ◆ AppleTalk
- ◆ IPX
- ◆ TCP/IP
- ◆ NFS
- ◆ SMB

Data Link Control (DLC)

The Data Link Control (DLC) protocol does not provide a fully functioning protocol stack. In Windows NT systems, DLC is used primarily to access to Hewlett-Packard JetDirect network-interface printers. DLC also provides some connectivity with IBM mainframes. It is not a protocol that can be used to connect Windows NT or 95 computers together.

AppleTalk

AppleTalk is the computing architecture developed by Apple Computer for the Macintosh family of personal computers. Although AppleTalk originally supported only Apple's proprietary LocalTalk cabling system, the suite has been expanded to incorporate both Ethernet and token-ring Physical layers. Within Microsoft operating systems, AppleTalk is only supported by Windows NT Server. Windows NT Workstation and Windows 95 do not support AppleTalk. AppleTalk cannot be used for Microsoft to Microsoft operating system communication, only by NT servers supporting Apple clients.

The LocalTalk, EtherTalk, and TokenTalk Link Access Protocols (LLAP, ELAP, and TLAP) integrate AppleTalk upper-layer protocols with the LocalTalk, Ethernet, and token-ring environments.

Apple's *Datagram Deliver Protocol (DDP)* is a Network layer protocol that provides connectionless service between two sockets. The AppleTalk Transaction Protocol (ATP) is a connectionless Transport layer protocol. Reliable service is provided through a system of acknowledgments and retransmissions. The *AppleTalk File Protocol (AFP)* provides file services and is responsible for translating local file service requests into formats required for network file services. AFP directly translates command syntax and enables applications to perform file format translations. AFP is responsible for file system security and verifies and encrypts logon names and passwords during connection setup.

IPX

The *Internetwork Packet Exchange Protocol (IPX)* is a Network layer protocol that provides connectionless (datagram) service. (IPX was developed from the XNS protocol originated by Xerox.) As a Network layer protocol, IPX is responsible for internetwork routing and maintaining network logical addresses. Routing uses the RIP protocol (described later in this section) to make route selections. IPX provides similar functionality as UDP does in the TCP/IP protocol suite.

IPX relies on hardware physical addresses found at lower layers to provide network device addressing. IPX also uses sockets, or upper-layer service addresses, to deliver packets to their ultimate destinations. On the client, IPX support is provided as a component of the older DOS shell and the current DOS NetWare requester.

TCP/IP

TCP/IP is a broad protocol that covers many different areas. This summary presents some of the most important protocols within the TCP/IP protocol suite.

Internet Protocol (IP)

The *Internet Protocol (IP)* is a connectionless protocol that provides datagram service, and IP packets are most commonly referred to as IP datagrams. IP is a packet-switching protocol that performs the addressing and route selection.

IP performs packet disassembly and reassembly as required by packet size limitations defined for the Data Link and Physical layers being implemented. IP also performs error checking on the header data using a checksum, although data from upper layers is not error-checked.

Transmission Control Protocol (TCP)

The *Transmission Control Protocol (TCP)* is an internetwork connection-oriented protocol that corresponds to the OSI Transport layer. TCP provides full-duplex, end-to-end connections. When the overhead of end-to-end communication acknowledgment isn't required, the User Datagram Protocol (UDP) can be substituted for TCP at the Transport (host-to-host) level. TCP and UDP operate at the same layer.

TCP corresponds to SPX in the NetWare environment (see the NetWare IPX/SPX section). TCP maintains a logical connection between the sending and receiving computer systems. In this way, the integrity of the transmission is maintained. TCP detects any problems in the transmission quickly and takes action to correct them. The tradeoff is that TCP isn't as fast as UDP, due to the number of acknowledgments received by the sending host.

TCP also provides message fragmentation and reassembly and can accept messages of any length from upper-layer protocols. TCP fragments message streams into segments that can be handled by IP. When used with IP, TCP adds connection-oriented service and performs segment synchronization, adding sequence numbers at the byte level.

Windows Internet Naming Services (WINS)

Windows Internet Naming Service (WINS) provides a function similar to that of DNS, with the exception that it provides a NetBIOS name to IP address resolution. This is important because all of Microsoft's networking requires the capability to reference NetBIOS names. Normally NetBIOS names are obtained with the issuance of broadcasts, but because routers normally do not forward broadcasts, a WINS server is one alternative that can be used to issue IP addresses to NetBIOS name requests. WINS servers replace the need for LMHOSTS files on a computer.

Domain Name System (DNS)

The Domain Name System (DNS) protocol provides host name and IP address resolution as a service to client applications. DNS servers enable humans to use logical node names, utilizing a fully qualified domain name structure to access network resources. Host names can be up to 260 characters long. DNS servers replace the need for HOSTS files on a computer.

Network File System (NFS)

Network File System (NFS), developed by Sun Microsystems, is a family of file-access protocols that are a considerable advancement over FTP and Telnet. Since Sun made the NFS specifications available for public use, NFS has achieved a high level of popularity.

Server Messaging Blocks (SMB)

One protocol that is slightly independent is Microsoft's Server Messaging Blocks (SMB). SMBs are Microsoft's equivalent to NCP packets. Like NCP packets, SMBs operate at the Application layer of the OSI model.

SMBs allow machines on a Microsoft network to communicate with one another. Through the use of SMBs, file and print services can be shared. SMBs can use TCP/IP, NWLink (IPX/SPX), and NetBEUI because SMBs utilize a NetBIOS interface when communicating. For more information on NetBIOS names, see the following section.

Select the Appropriate Connectivity Devices for Various Token-Ring and Ethernet Networks

Connectivity devices include:

- ◆ **Repeaters**. Repeaters regenerate a signal and are used to expand LANs beyond cabling limits.
- ◆ **Bridges**. Bridges know the side of the bridge on which a node is located. A bridge passes only packets addressed to computers across the bridge, so a bridge can thus filter traffic, reducing the load on the transmission medium.
- ◆ **Routers**. Routers forward packets based on a logical (as opposed to a physical) address. Some

routers can determine the best path for a packet based on routing algorithms.

- ◆ **Brouters**. A brouter is a device that is a combination of a bridge and a router, providing both types of services.
- ◆ **Gateways**. Gateways function under a process similar to routers except that gateways can connect dissimilar network environments. A gateway replaces the necessary protocol layers of a packet so that the packet can circulate in the destination environment.

List the Characteristics, Requirements, and Appropriate Situations for WAN Connection Services

WAN connection services include:

- ◆ X.25
- ◆ ISDN
- ◆ Frame relay
- ◆ ATM

X.25

X.25 is a packet-switching network standard developed by the International Telegraph and Telephone Consultative Committee (CCITT), which has been renamed the International Telecommunications Union (ITU). The standard, referred to as *Recommendation X.25*, was introduced in 1974 and is now implemented most commonly in WANs.

At the time X.25 was developed, this flow control and error checking was essential because X.25 was developed around relatively unreliable telephone line communications. The drawback is that error checking and flow control slow down X.25. Generally, X.25 networks are implemented with line speeds up to 64 Kbps, although actual throughput seems slower due to the error correction controls in place. These speeds are suitable for the file transfer and terminal activity that comprised the bulk of network traffic when X.25 was defined, most of this traffic being terminal connections to mainframes. Such speeds, however, are inadequate to provide LAN-speed services, which typically require speeds of 1 Mbps or better. X.25 networks, therefore, are poor choices for providing LAN application services in a WAN environment. One advantage of X.25, however, is that it is an established standard that is used internationally. This, as well as lack of other services throughout the world, means that X.25 is more of a connection service to Africa, South America, and Asia, where a lack of other services prevails.

ISDN

The original idea behind ISDN was to enable existing phone lines to carry digital communications, and it was at one time touted as a replacement to traditional analog lines. Thus, ISDN is more like traditional telephone service than some of the other WAN services. ISDN is intended as a dial-up service and not as a permanent 24-hour connection.

ISDN separates the bandwidth into channels. Based upon how these channels are used, ISDN can be separated into two classes of service:

◆ **Basic Rate (BRI)**. Basic Rate ISDN uses three channels. Two channels (called B channels) carry the digital data at 64 Kbps. A third channel (called the D channel) provides link and signaling information at 16 Kbps. Basic Rate ISDN thus is referred to as 2B+D. A single PC transmitting

through ISDN can use both B channels simultaneously, providing a maximum data rate of 128 Kbps (or higher with compression).

◆ **Primary Rate (PRI)**. Primary Rate supports 23 64 Kbps B channels and one 64 Kbps D channel. The D channel is used for signaling and management, whereas the B channels provide the data throughput.

In a BRI line, if the line was currently being used for voice, this would only allow one of the B channels to be available for data. This effectively reduces the throughput of the BRI to 64 Kbps.

Frame Relay

Frame Relay was designed to support the *Broadband Integrated Services Digital Network (B-ISDN)*, which was discussed in the previous section. The specifications for Frame Relay address some of the limitations of X.25. As with X.25, Frame Relay is a packet-switching network service, but Frame Relay was designed around newer, faster fiber-optic networks.

Unlike X.25, Frame Relay assumes a more reliable network. This enables Frame Relay to eliminate much of the X.25 overhead required to provide reliable service on less reliable networks. Frame Relay relies on higher-level protocol layers to provide flow and error control.

Frame Relay typically is implemented as a public data network and, therefore, is regarded as a WAN protocol. The scope of Frame Relay, with respect to the OSI model, is limited to the Physical and Data Link layers.

Frame Relay provides permanent virtual circuits that supply permanent virtual pathways for WAN connections. Frame Relay services typically are implemented at line speeds from 56 Kbps up to 1.544 Mbps (T1).

Customers typically purchase access to a specific amount of bandwidth on a frame-relay service. This bandwidth is called the *committed information rate (CIR)*, a data rate for which the customer is guaranteed access. Customers might be permitted to access higher data rates on a pay-per-use temporary basis. This arrangement enables customers to tailor their network access costs based on their bandwidth requirements.

To use Frame Relay, you must have special Frame Relay-compatible connectivity devices (such as frame-relay-compatible routers and bridges).

Asynchronous Transfer Mode (ATM)

Asynchronous Transfer Mode (ATM) is a high-bandwidth switching technology developed by the ITU Telecommunications Standards Sector (ITU-TSS). An organization called the ATM Forum is responsible for defining ATM implementation characteristics. ATM can be layered on other Physical layer technologies, such as Fiber Distributed Data Interface (FDDI) and SONET.

Several characteristics distinguish ATM from other switching technologies. ATM is based on fixed-length 53-byte cells, whereas other technologies employ frames that vary in length to accommodate different amounts of data. Because ATM cells are uniform in length, switching mechanisms can operate with a high level of efficiency. This high efficiency results in high data transfer rates. Some ATM systems can operate at an incredible rate of 622 Mbps; a typical working speed for an ATM is around 155 Mbps.

The unit of transmission for ATM is called a cell. All cells are 53 bytes long and consist of a 5-byte header and 48 bytes of data. The 48-byte data size was selected by the standards committee as a compromise to suit both audio- and data-transmission needs. Audio information, for instance, must be delivered with little latency (delay) to maintain a smooth flow of sound. Audio engineers therefore preferred a small cell so that cells would be more readily available when needed. For data, however, large cells reduce the overhead required to deliver a byte of information.

Asynchronous delivery is another distinguishing feature of ATM. "Asynchronous" refers to the characteristic of ATM in which transmission time slots don't occur periodically but are granted at irregular intervals. ATM uses a technique called *label multiplexing*, which allocates time slots on demand. Traffic that is time-critical, such as voice or video, can be given priority over data traffic that can be delayed slightly with no ill effect. Channels are identified by cell labels, not by specific time slots. A high-priority transmission need not be held until its next time slot allocation. Instead, it might be required to wait only until the current 53-byte cell has been transmitted.

IMPLEMENTATION

The Implementation section of the exam tests your knowledge of how to implement, test, and manage an installed network.

Choosing an Administrative Plan to Meet Specified Needs, Including Performance Management, Account Management, and Security

Administrative plans can be broken down into three areas: performance management, account management, and security.

Performance Management

Performance management is best done through the establishment of a baseline of the network performance and a baseline of a computer's performance. Based upon the information in a baseline, the administrators of the network can establish when network or computer performance is abnormal.

Account Management

Account management within Windows NT is done through the use of groups. In a workgroup model, there exist local groups, or groups that are local to the computer. These groups are not seen on other machines in the network. Users are placed into these local groups and assigned permissions to resources, such as printers, shares, or files and directories.

Windows 95 computers do not have built-in groups. There also is no account database on a Windows 95 computer to provide user accounts.

Windows NT domain models do make use of user accounts and groups. Like the workgroup model, the domain model has user accounts and local groups. A domain model also has global groups. Global groups reside on a domain controller and can be referenced as a resource user by any Windows NT computer within the domain sharing resources.

Security

Windows 95 computers have the capability to provide share-level security, which involves password protecting resources.

Windows NT computers can provide user-level security, in which users are granted access to resources on a user or local group basis (workgroups and domains support this) and a global group basis (only domains support this).

Choosing a Disaster Recovery Plan for Various Situations

Disaster recovery applies to many different components on the network. The following sections describe the most common issues and solutions used in a disaster recovery program.

Uninterruptible Power Supply (UPS)

An uninterruptible power supply (UPS) is a special battery (or sometimes a generator) that supplies power to an electronic device in the event of a power failure. UPSs commonly are used with network servers to prevent a disorderly shutdown by warning users to log out. After a predetermined waiting period, the UPS software performs an orderly shutdown of the server. Many UPS units also regulate power distribution and serve as protection against power surges. Remember that in most cases, a UPS generally does not provide for continued network functionality for longer than a few minutes. A UPS is not intended to keep the server running through a long power outage, but rather to give the server time to do what it needs before shutting down. This can prevent the data loss and system corruption that sometimes result from sudden shutdown.

Tape Backup

Tape backups are done to store data offline in the event that the hard drive containing the data fails. There are three types of tape backups:

◆ **Full backup**. Backs up all specified files.

◆ **Incremental backup**. Backs up only those files that have changed since the last backup.

◆ **Differential backup**. Backs up the specified files if the files have changed since the last backup. This type doesn't mark the files as having been backed up, however. (A differential backup is somewhat like a copy command. Because the file is not marked as having been backed up, a later differential or incremental backup will back up the file again.)

RAID 1

In level 1, drives are paired or mirrored with each byte of information being written to each identical drive. You can duplex these devices by adding a separate drive controller for each drive. Disk mirroring is defined as two hard drives (one primary, one secondary) that use the same disk channel or controller cards and cable. Disk mirroring is most commonly configured by using disk drives contained in the server. Duplexing is a form of mirroring that involves the use of a second controller and that enables you to configure a more robust hardware environment.

RAID 5

RAID 5 uses striping with parity information written across multiple drives to enable fault-tolerance with a minimum of wasted disk space. This level also offers the advantage of enabling relatively efficient performance on writes to the drives, as well as excellent read performance.

Striping with parity is based on the principle that all data is written to the hard drive in binary code (ones and zeros). RAID 5 requires at least three drives because this version writes data across two of them and then creates the parity block on the third. If the first byte is 00111000 and the second is 10101001, the system computes the third by adding the digits together using this system:

1+1=0, 0+0=0, 0+1=1, 1+0=1

The sum of 00111000 and 10101001 is 10010001, which would be written to the third disk. If any of the

disks fail, the process can be reversed and any disk can be reconstructed from the data on the other two. Recovery includes replacing the bad disk and then regenerating its data through the Disk Administrator. A maximum of 32 disks can be connected in a RAID 5 array under Windows NT.

Given the Manufacturer's Documentation for the Network Adapter, Install, Configure, and Resolve Hardware Conflicts for Multiple Network Adapters in a Token-Ring or Ethernet Network

The following resources are configurable on network adapter cards:

- ◆ IRQ
- ◆ Base I/O port address
- ◆ Base memory address
- ◆ DMA channel
- ◆ Boot PROM
- ◆ MAC address
- ◆ Ring speed (token-ring cards)
- ◆ Connector type

Not all network adapter cards have all of these resources available for configuration. These resource settings on the network adapter card must be different than the settings found on other components used within the computer.

Some network adapter cards use jumper settings to configure these settings, others use software, and others can have this done through the operating system software, such as Windows 95 and Windows NT. The method of configuration is dependent upon the manufacturer.

Implementing a NetBIOS Naming Scheme for All Computers on a Given Network

NetBIOS is an interface that provides NetBIOS-based applications with access to network resources. Every computer on a Windows NT network must have a unique name for it to be accessible through the NetBIOS interface. This unique name is called a computer name or a NetBIOS name.

On a NetBIOS network, every computer must have a unique name. The computer name can be up to 15 characters long. A NetBIOS name can include alphanumeric characters and any of the following special characters:

! @ # $ % ^ & ( ) - _ ' { } . ~

Note that you cannot use a space or an asterisk in a NetBIOS name. Also, NetBIOS names are not case sensitive.

Selecting the Appropriate Hardware and Software Tools to Monitor Trends in the Network

The hardware and software tools described in the next five sections are used to monitor trends in a network.

Protocol Analyzer

This can be a hardware or software tool to analyze the traffic in a network. Protocol analyzers capture packets on a network and display their contents. The software version of this tool supplied by Microsoft is Network Monitor. Network Monitor ships with Windows NT as a scaled-down version that can only capture data between the host computer and those to which the host talks.

Event Viewer

This software tool is found on Windows NT. It reports one of three event types:

- ◆ **System Events**. Those generated by the operating system.

- ◆ **Application Events**. Those generated by any application that is programmed to make event calls to the Event Viewer.

- ◆ **Auditing**. Any auditing being performed on NTFS partitions or by users interacting with the network.

Performance Monitor

Windows NT's Performance Monitor tool lets you monitor important system parameters for the computers on your network in real time. Performance Monitor can keep an eye on a large number of system parameters, providing a graphical or tabular profile of system and network trends. Performance Monitor also can save performance data in a log for later reference. You can use Performance Monitor to track statistical measurements (called *counters*) for any of several hardware or software components (called *objects*).

System Monitor

Windows 95 includes a program called System Monitor that also allows information to be collected on the Windows 95 machine in real time. System Monitor collects information on different categories of items on the system. System Monitor is not as detailed as Windows NT's Performance Monitor.

Simple Network Management Protocol (SNMP)

SNMP is a TCP/IP protocol used to perform management operations on a TCP/IP network. SNMP-enabled devices allow for information to be sent to a management utility (this is called a *trap*). SNMP devices also allow for the setting and extraction of information (this is done by the issuance of a set or get command) found in their Management Information Base (MIB).

TROUBLESHOOTING

The Troubleshooting section of the exam covers many of the topics covered in previous sections. Emphasis of this section is to test your understanding of what can cause problems, and how to fix them.

Identifying Common Errors Associated with Components Required for Communications

The utilities described in the next four sections can be used to diagnose errors associated with components required for communications.

Protocol Analyzers

Protocol analyzers are either hardware or software products used to monitor network traffic, track network performance, and analyze packets. Protocol analyzers can identify bottlenecks, protocol problems, and malfunctioning network components.

Digital Volt Meter (DVM)

Digital volt meters are handheld electronic measuring tools that enable you to check the voltage of network cables. They also can be used to check the resistance of terminators. You can use a DVM to help you find a break or a short in a network cable.

DVMs are usually inexpensive battery-operated devices that have either a digital or needle readout and two metal prongs attached to the DVM by some wires a foot or more in length. By sending a small current through the wires and out through the metal prongs, resistance and voltages of terminators and wires can be measured.

Time-Domain Reflectometers (TDR)

Time-domain reflectometers send sound waves along a cable and look for imperfections that might be caused by a break or a short in the line. A good TDR can detect faults on a cable to within a few feet.

Oscilloscope

An oscilloscope measures fluctuations in signal voltage and can help find faulty or damaged cabling. Oscilloscopes are often more expensive electronic devices that show the signal fluctuations on a monitor.

Several diagnostic software tools provide information on virtually any type of network hardware, as well. A considerable number of diagnostic software packages are available for a variety of prices.

A common software tool distributed with most network cards is a Send/Receive package. This software tool allows two computers with network cards and cables to connect to each other. This tool does not rely on a networked operating system, nor can it be used to send data. It simply sends packets from one computer to the other, establishing that the network cards and underlying transmission media are connected and configured properly.

Diagnosing and Resolving Common Connectivity Problems with Cards, Cables, and Related Hardware

Most network problems occur on the transmission media or with the components that attach devices to the transmission media. All of these components operate at the Physical, DataLink, or Network levels of the OSI model. The components that connect PCs and enable them to communicate are susceptible to many kinds of problems.

Troubleshooting Cables and Connectors

Most network problems occur at the OSI Physical layer, and cabling is one of the most common causes. A cable might have a short or a break, or it might be attached to a faulty connector. Tools such as DVMs and TDRs help search out cabling problems.

Cabling problems can cause three major problems: An individual computer cannot access the network, a group of computers cannot access the network, or none of the computers can access the network.

On networks that are configured in a star topology, an individual cable break between the computer and hub or MSAU causes a failure in communication between

that individual computer and the rest of the network. This type of cable break does not cause problems between all of the other computers on the network.

A cable break in cables connecting multiple hubs causes a break in communications between the computers on one side of the cable break and the computers on the other side of the cable break. In most cases, the communications between computers within the broken segment can continue.

In the case of MSAU, the breakage of a cable connecting MSAUs often causes all computers on the ring to fail because the ring is not complete. A break in the cable on a bus topology also causes all computers on the network segment to be unable to communicate with any other computers on the network.

Try the following checks when troubleshooting network cabling problems:

◆ With 10BASE-T, make sure the cable used has the correct number of twists to meet the data-grade specifications.

◆ Look for electrical interference, which can be caused by tying the network cable together with monitor and power cords. Fluorescent lights, electric motors, and other electrical devices can cause interference if they are located too close to cables. These problems often can be alleviated by placing the cable away from devices that generate electromagnetic interference or by upgrading the cable to one that has better shielding.

◆ Make sure that connectors are pinned properly and crimped tightly.

◆ If excess shielding on coaxial cable is exposed, make sure it doesn't ground out the connector.

◆ Ensure that coaxial cables are not coiled tightly together. This can generate a magnetic field around the cable, causing electromagnetic interference.

◆ On coaxial Ethernet LANs, look for missing terminators or terminators with improper resistance ratings.

◆ Watch out for malfunctioning transceivers, concentrators, or T-connectors. All of these components can be checked by replacing the suspect devices.

◆ Test the continuity of the cable by using the various physical testing devices discussed in the previous section or by using a software-based cable testing utility.

◆ Make sure that all the component cables in a segment are connected. A user who moves his client and removes the T-connector incorrectly can cause a broken segment.

◆ Examine cable connectors for bent or broken pins.

◆ On token-ring networks, inspect the attachment of patch cables and adapter cables. Remember, patch cables connect MSAUs, and adapter cables connect the network adapter to the MSAU.

One advantage of a token-ring network is its built-in capability to monitor itself. token-ring networks provide electronic troubleshooting and, when possible, actually make repairs. When the token-ring network can't make its own repairs, a process called *beaconing* narrows down the portion of the ring in which the problem is most likely to exist.

Troubleshooting Network Adapter Cards

Network problems often result from malfunctioning network adapter cards. The process of troubleshooting the network adapter works like any other kind of troubleshooting process: Start with the simple. The following list details some aspects you can check if you think your network adapter card might be malfunctioning:

◆ Make sure the cable is properly connected to the card.

◆ Confirm that you have the correct network adapter card driver and that the driver is installed properly. Be sure the card is properly bound to the appropriate transport protocol.

◆ Make sure the network adapter card and the network adapter card driver are compatible with your operating system. If you use Windows NT, consult the Windows NT hardware compatibility list. If you use Windows 95 or another operating system, rely on the adapter card vendor specifications.

◆ Test for resource conflicts. Make sure another device isn't attempting to use the same resources. If you think a resource conflict might be the problem, but you can't pinpoint the conflict using Windows NT Diagnostics, Windows 95's Device Manager, or some other diagnostic program, try removing all the cards except the network adapter and then replacing the cards one by one. Check the network with each addition to determine which device is causing the conflict.

◆ Run the network adapter card's diagnostic software. This will often indicate which resource on the network card is failing.

◆ Examine the jumper and DIP switch settings on the card. Make sure the resource settings are consistent with the settings configured through the operating system.

◆ Make sure the card is inserted properly in the slot. Reseat if necessary.

◆ If necessary, remove the card and clean the connector fingers (don't use an eraser because it leaves grit on the card).

◆ Replace the card with one that you know works. If the connection works with a different card, you know the card is the problem.

Token-ring network adapters with failure rates that exceed a preset tolerance level might actually remove themselves from the network. Try replacing the card. Some token-ring networks also can experience problems if a token-ring card set at a ring speed of 16 Mbps is inserted into a ring using a 4 Mbps ring speed, and vice versa.

Troubleshooting Hubs and MSAUs

If you experience problems with a hub-based LAN, such as a 10BASE-T network, you often can isolate the problem by disconnecting the attached workstations one at a time. If removing one of the workstations eliminates the problem, the trouble may be caused by that workstation or its associated cable length. If removing each of the workstations doesn't solve the problem, the fault may lie with the hub. Check the easy components first, such as ports, switches, and connectors, and then use a different hub (if you have it) to see if the problem persists. If your hub doesn't work properly, call the manufacturer.

If you're troubleshooting a token-ring network, make sure the cables are connected properly to the MSAUs, with ring-out ports connecting to the ring-in ports throughout the ring. If you suspect the MSAU, isolate it by changing the ring-in and ring-out cables to bypass the MSAU. If the ring is now functional again, consider replacing the MSAU. In addition, you might find that if your network has MSAUs from more than one manufacturer, they are not wholly compatible. Impedance and other electrical characteristics can show slight differences between manufacturers, causing intermittent network problems. Some MSAUs (other than the 8228) are active and require a power supply. These MSAUs fail if they have a blown fuse or a bad power source. Your problem also might result from a misconfigured MSAU port. MSAU ports using the hermaphrodite connector need to be reinitialized with the setup tool. Removing drop cables and reinitializing each

MSAU port is a quick fix that is useful on relatively small token-ring networks.

Isolating problems with patch cables, adapter cables, and MSAUs is easier to do if you have a current log of your network's physical design. After you narrow down the problem, you can isolate potential problem areas from the rest of the network and then use a cable tester to find the actual problem.

Troubleshooting Modems

A modem presents all the potential problems you find with any other device. You must make sure that the modem is properly installed, that the driver is properly installed, and that the resource settings do not conflict with other devices. Modems also pose some unique problems because they must connect directly to the phone system, they operate using analog communications, and they must make a point-to-point connection with a remote machine.

The online help files for both Windows NT and Windows 95 include a topic called the Modem Troubleshooter. The Modem Troubleshooter leads you to possible solutions for a modem problem by asking questions about the symptoms. As you answer the questions (by clicking the gray box beside your answer), the Modem Troubleshooter zeroes in on more specific questions until (ideally) it leads you to a solution.

Some common modem problems are as follows:

◆ **Dialing problems**. The dialing feature is improperly configured. For instance, the modem isn't dialing 9 to bypass your office switchboard, or it is dialing 9 when you're away from your office. The computer also could be dialing an area code or an international code when it shouldn't. Check the dialing properties for the connection.

◆ **Connection problems**. You cannot connect to another modem. Your modem and the other modem might be operating at different speeds.

Verify that the maximum speed setting for your modem is the highest speed that both your modem and the other modem can use. Also make sure the Data Bits, Parity, and Stop Bits settings are consistent with the remote computer.

◆ **Digital phone systems**. You cannot plug a modem into a telephone line designed for use with digital phone systems. These digital phone systems are commonplace in most office environments.

◆ **Protocol problems**. The communicating devices are using incompatible line protocols. Verify that the devices are configured for the same or compatible protocols. If one computer initiates a connection using PPP, the other computer must be capable of using PPP.

Repeaters, Bridges, and Routers

Issues dealing with repeaters, bridges, and routers are often more technically advanced than those covered in a book such as Networking Essentials. Companies such as Cisco, Bay Networks, and 3Com have their own dedicated books and courses on dealing with the installation, configuration, and troubleshooting of repeaters, bridges, and routers. In general, there are some basic troubleshooting steps you can do when working with these three devices.

Repeaters are responsible for regenerating a signal sent down the transmission media. The typical problem with repeaters is that they do not work—that is, the signal is not being regenerated. If this is the case, the signal being sent to devices on the other side of the repeater from the sending device will not receive the signal.

Problems with bridges are almost identical to that of a repeater. The signal being sent to devices on the other side of the bridge from the sending device will be received. Other issues with bridges are that the table of which devices are on which interface of the bridge can

get corrupt. This can lead from one to all machines not receiving packets on the network. Diagnostic utilities provided by the bridge's manufacturer can resolve this type of problem.

Problems with routers can be complex, and troubleshooting them often involves a high level of understanding of the different protocols in use on the network, as well as the software and commands used to program a router. There are generally two types of router problems.

The first router problem that is commonly found is that packets are just not being passed through because the router is 'dead' or simply not functioning. The second common problem with routers is that the routing tables within the routers are corrupted or incorrectly programmed. This problem either leads to computers on different networks being unable to communicate with each other or to the fact that certain protocols simply do not work.

Resolve Broadcast Storms

A *broadcast storm* is a sudden flood of broadcast messages that clogs the transmission medium, approaching 100 percent of the bandwidth. Broadcast storms cause performance to decline and, in the worst case, computers cannot even access the network. The cause of a broadcast storm is often a malfunctioning network adapter, but a broadcast storm also can be caused when a device on the network attempts to contact another device that either doesn't exist or for some reason doesn't respond to the broadcast.

If the broadcast messages are viable, a network-monitoring or protocol-analysis tool often can determine the source of the storm. If the broadcast storm is caused by a malfunctioning adapter throwing illegible packets onto the line, and a protocol analyzer can't find the source, try to isolate the offending PC by removing computers from the network one at a time until the line returns to normal.

Identify and Resolve Network Performance Problems

If your network runs slower than it used to run (or slower than it ought to run), the problem might be that the present network traffic exceeds the level at which the network can operate efficiently. Some possible causes for increased traffic are new hardware (such as a new workstation) or new software (such as a network computer game or some other network application). A generator or another mechanical device operating near the network could cause a degradation of network performance. In addition, a malfunctioning network device could act as a bottleneck. Ask yourself what has changed since the last time the network operated efficiently, and begin there with your troubleshooting efforts.

A performance monitoring tool, such as Windows NT's Performance Monitor or Network Monitor, can help you look for bottlenecks that are adversely affecting your network. For instance, the increased traffic could be the result of increased usage. If usage exceeds the capacity of the network, you might want to consider expanding or redesigning your network. You also might want to divide the network into smaller segments by using a router or a bridge to reduce network traffic. A protocol analyzer can help you measure and monitor the traffic at various points on your network.

Study and Exam Prep Tips

This chapter provides you with some general guidelines for preparing for the exam. It is organized into three sections. The first section addresses your pre-exam preparation activities, covering general study tips. This is followed by an extended look at the Microsoft Certification exams, including a number of specific tips that apply to the Microsoft exam formats. Finally, it addresses changes in Microsoft's testing policies and how they might affect you.

To better understand the nature of preparation for the test, it is important to understand learning as a process. You probably are aware of how you best learn new material. Maybe outlining works best for you, or maybe you are a visual learner who needs to "see" things. Whatever your learning style, test preparation takes time. While it is obvious that you can't start studying for these exams the night before you take them, it is very important to understand that learning is a developmental process. Understanding the process helps you focus on what you know and what you have yet to learn.

Thinking about how you learn should help you recognize that learning takes place when we are able to match new information to old. You have some previous experience with computers and networking, and now you are preparing for this certification exam. Using this book, software, and supplementary materials will not just add incrementally to what you know. As you study, you actually change the organization of your knowledge to integrate this new information into your existing knowledge base. This will lead you to a more comprehensive understanding of the tasks and concepts outlined in the objectives and related to computing in general. Again, this happens as an iterative process rather than a singular event. Keep this model of

learning in mind as you prepare for the exam, and you will make better decisions on what to study and how much to study.

STUDY TIPS

There are many ways to approach studying, just as there are many different types of material to study. However, the tips that follow should work well for the type of material covered on the certification exams.

Study Strategies

Although individuals vary in the ways they learn information, some basic principles of learning apply to everyone. You should adopt some study strategies that take advantage of these principles. One of these principles is that learning can be broken into various depths. *Recognition* (of terms, for example) exemplifies a surface level of learning: You rely on a prompt of some sort to elicit recall. *Comprehension or understanding* (of the concepts behind the terms, for instance) represents a deeper level of learning. The ability to analyze a concept and apply your understanding of it in a new way or to address a unique setting represents further depth of learning.

Your learning strategy should enable you to know the material a level or two deeper than mere recognition. This will help you to do well on the exam(s). You will know the material so thoroughly that you can easily handle the recognition-level types of questions used in multiple-choice testing. You will also be able to apply your knowledge to solve novel problems.

Macro and Micro Study Strategies

One strategy that can lead to this deeper learning includes preparing an outline that covers all the objectives and subobjectives for the particular exam you are working on. You should then delve a bit further into the material and include a level or two of detail beyond the stated objectives and subobjectives for the exam. Finally, flesh out the outline by coming up with a statement of definition or a summary for each point in the outline.

This outline provides two approaches to studying. First, you can study the outline by focusing on the organization of the material. Work your way through the points and subpoints of your outline with the goal of learning how they relate to one another. For example, be sure you understand how each of the main objective areas is similar to and different from one another. Then do the same thing with the subobjectives. Also, be sure you know which subobjectives pertain to each objective area and how they relate to one another.

Next, you can work through the outline and focus on learning the details. Memorize and understand terms and their definitions, facts, rules and strategies, advantages and disadvantages, and so on. In this pass through the outline, attempt to learn detail as opposed to the big picture (the organizational information that you worked on in the first pass through the outline).

Research shows that attempting to assimilate both types of information at the same time seems to interfere with the overall learning process. Separate your studying into these two approaches, and you will perform better on the exam than if you attempt to study the material in a more conventional manner.

Active Study Strategies

In addition, the process of writing down and defining the objectives, subobjectives, terms, facts, and definitions promotes a more active learning strategy than merely reading the material does. In human information processing terms, writing forces you to engage in more active encoding of the information. Simply reading over it constitutes passive processing.

Next, determine whether you can apply the information you have learned by attempting to create examples and scenarios of your own. Think about how or where you could apply the concepts you are learning. Again, write down this information to process the facts and concepts in a more active fashion.

The hands-on nature of the Step by Step tutorials and the exercises at the end of the chapters provide further active learning opportunities that will reinforce concepts.

Common Sense Strategies

Finally, you should also follow common sense practices in studying: Study when you are alert, reduce or eliminate distractions, take breaks when you become fatigued, and so on.

Pre-Testing Yourself

Pre-testing allows you to assess how well you are learning. One of the most important aspects of learning is what has been called "meta-learning." Meta-learning has to do with realizing when you know something well or when you need to study some more. In other words, you recognize how well or how poorly you have learned the material you are studying. For most people, this can be difficult to assess objectively on their own. Therefore, practice tests are useful because they reveal more objectively what you have and have not learned. You should use this information to guide review and further studying. Developmental learning takes place as you cycle through studying, assessing how well you have learned, reviewing, and assessing again, until you feel you are ready to take the exam.

You may have noticed the practice exam included in this book. Use it as part of this process. In addition to the Practice Exam, the Top Score software on the CD-ROM also provides a variety of ways to test yourself before you take the actual exam. By using the Top Score Practice Exams, you can take an entire practice test. By using the Top Score Study Cards, you can take an entire practice exam or you can focus on a particular objective area, such as Planning, Troubleshooting, or Monitoring and Optimization. By using the Top Score Flash Cards, you can test your knowledge at a level beyond that of recognition; you must come up with the answers in your own words. The Flash Cards also enable you to test your knowledge of particular objective areas.

You should set a goal for your pre-testing. A reasonable goal would be to score consistently in the 90-percent range (or better). See Appendix D, "Using the Top Score Software," for more detailed explanation of the test engine.

Exam Prep Tips

Having mastered the subject matter, the final preparatory step is to understand how the exam will be presented. Make no mistake about it, a Microsoft Certified Professional (MCP) exam will challenge both your knowledge and your test-taking skills! This section starts with the basics of exam design, reviews a new type of exam format, and concludes with hints that are targeted to each of the exam formats.

The MCP Exam

Every MCP exam is released in one of two basic formats. What's being called *exam format* here is really little more than a combination of the overall exam structure and the presentation method for exam questions.

Each exam format utilizes the same types of questions. These types or styles of questions include multiple-rating (or scenario-based) questions, traditional multiple-choice questions, and simulation-based questions. It's important to understand the types of questions you will be asked and the actions required to properly answer them.

Understanding the exam formats is essential to good preparation because the format determines the number of questions presented, the difficulty of those questions, and the amount of time allowed to complete the exam.

Exam Format

There are two basic formats for the MCP exams: the traditional fixed-form exam and the adaptive form. As its name implies, the fixed-form exam presents a fixed set of questions during the exam session. The adaptive format, however, uses only a subset of questions drawn from a larger pool during any given exam session.

Fixed-Form

A fixed-form, computerized exam is based on a fixed set of exam questions. The individual questions are presented in random order during a test session. If you take the same exam more than once, you won't necessarily see the exact same questions. This is because two or three final forms are typically assembled for every fixed-form exam Microsoft releases. These are usually labeled Forms A, B, and C.

The final forms of a fixed-form exam are identical in terms of content coverage, number of questions, and allotted time, but the questions themselves are different. You may have noticed, however, that some of the same questions appear on, or rather are shared across, different final forms. When questions are shared across multiple final forms of an exam, the percentage of sharing is generally small. Many final forms share no questions, but some older exams may have ten to fifteen percent duplication of exam questions on the final exam forms.

Fixed-form exams also have a fixed time limit in which you must complete the exam. The Top Score software on the CD-ROM that accompanies this book provides fixed-form exams.

Finally, the score you achieve on a fixed-form exam (which is always reported for MCP exams on a scale of 0 to 1,000) is based on the number of questions you answer correctly. The exam passing score is the same for all final forms of a given fixed-form exam.

The typical format for the fixed-form exam is this:

◆ 50–60 questions

◆ 75–90 minute testing time

◆ Question review is allowed, including the opportunity to change your answers

Adaptive Form

An adaptive form exam has the same appearance as a fixed-form exam, but it differs in both how questions are selected for presentation and how many questions actually are presented. Although the statistics of adaptive testing are fairly complex, the process is concerned with determining your level of skill or ability with the exam subject matter. This ability assessment begins with the presentation of questions of varying levels of difficulty and ascertains at what difficulty level you can reliably answer them. Finally, the ability assessment determines if that ability level is above or below the level required to pass that exam.

Examinees at different levels of ability will then see quite different sets of questions. Examinees who demonstrate little expertise with the subject matter will demonstrate little expertise with the subject matter will

continue to be presented with relatively easy questions. Examinees who demonstrate a high level of expertise will be presented progressively more-difficult questions. Both individuals may answer the same number of questions correctly, but because the higher-expertise examinee can correctly answer more-difficult questions, he or she will receive a higher score and is more likely to pass the exam.

The typical design for the adaptive form exam is this:

◆ 20–25 questions

◆ 90 minute testing time (although this is likely to be reduced to 45–60 minutes in the near future)

◆ Question review is not allowed, providing no opportunity to change your answers

The Adaptive Exam Process

Your first adaptive exam will be unlike any other testing experience you have had. In fact, many examinees have difficulty accepting the adaptive testing process because they feel they were not provided the opportunity to adequately demonstrate their full expertise.

You can take consolation in the fact that adaptive exams are painstakingly put together after months of data gathering and analysis and are just as valid as a fixed-form exam. The rigor introduced through the adaptive testing methodology means that there is nothing arbitrary about what you'll see! It is also a more efficient means of testing that requires less time to conduct and complete.

As you can see from Figure 1, a number of statistical measures drive the adaptive examination process. The one that's most immediately relevant to you is the ability estimate. Accompanying this test statistic are the standard error of measurement, the item characteristic curve, and the test information curve.

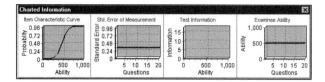

FIGURE 1
Microsoft's adaptive testing demonstration program.

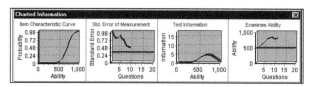

FIGURE 2
The changing statistics in an adaptive exam.

The standard error, which is the key factor in determining when an adaptive exam will terminate, reflects the degree of error in the exam ability estimate. The item characteristic curve reflects the probability of a correct response relative to examinee ability. Finally, the test information statistic provides a measure of the information contained in the set of questions the examinee has answered, again relative to the ability level of the individual examinee.

When you begin an adaptive exam, the standard error has already been assigned a target value below which it must drop for the exam to conclude. This target value reflects a particular level of statistical confidence in the process. The examinee ability is initially set to the mean possible exam score, which is 500 for MCP exams.

As the adaptive exam progresses, questions of varying difficulty are presented. Based on your pattern of responses to those questions, the ability estimate is recalculated. Simultaneously, the standard error estimate is refined from its first estimated value of one toward the target value. When the standard error reaches its target value, the exam terminates. Thus, the more consistently you answer questions of the same degree of difficulty, the more quickly the standard error estimate drops and the fewer questions you will end up seeing during the exam session. This situation is depicted in Figure 2.

As you might suspect, one good piece of advice for taking an adaptive exam is to treat every exam question as if it is the most important. The adaptive scoring algorithm is attempting to discover a pattern of responses

that reflects some level of proficiency with the subject matter. Incorrect responses almost guarantee that additional questions must be answered (unless, of course, you get every question wrong). This is because the scoring algorithm must adjust to information that is not consistent with the emerging pattern.

New Question Types

A variety of question types can appear on MCP exams. Examples of multiple-choice questions and scenario-based questions appear throughout this book and the Top Score software. Simulation-based questions are new to the MCP exam series.

Simulation Questions

Simulation-based questions reproduce the look and feel of key Microsoft product features for the purpose of testing. The simulation software used in MCP exams has been designed to look and act, as much as possible, just like the actual product. Consequently, answering simulation questions in an MCP exam entails completing one or more tasks just as if you were using the product itself.

The format of a typical Microsoft simulation question is straightforward. It presents a brief scenario or problem statement along with one or more tasks that must be completed to solve the problem. The next section provides an example of a simulation question for MCP exams.

A Typical Simulation Question

It sounds obvious, but the first step when you encounter a simulation is to carefully read the question (see Figure 3). Do not go straight to the simulation application! Assess the problem being presented and identify the conditions that make up the problem scenario. Note the tasks that must be performed or outcomes that must be achieved to answer the question, and then review any instructions on how to proceed.

The next step is to launch the simulator by using the button provided. After clicking the Show Simulation button, you will see a feature of the product, like the dialog box shown in Figure 4. The simulation application will partially cover the question text on many test center machines. Feel free to reposition the simulation or to move between the question text screen and the simulation using hot-keys and point-and-click navigation or even by clicking the simulation launch button again.

It is important to understand that your answer to the simulation question is not recorded until you move on to the next exam question. This gives you the added capability to close and reopen the simulation application (using the launch button) on the same question without losing any partial answer you may have made.

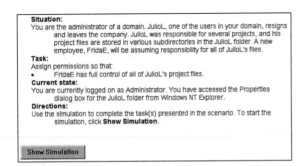

Situation:
You are the administrator of a domain. JulioL, one of the users in your domain, resigns and leaves the company. JulioL was responsible for several projects, and his project files are stored in various subdirectories in the JulioL folder. A new employee, FridaE, will be assuming responsibility for all of JulioL's files.
Task:
Assign permissions so that:
• FridaE has full control of all of JulioL's project files.
Current state:
You are currently logged on as Administrator. You have accessed the Properties dialog box for the JulioL folder from Windows NT Explorer.
Directions:
Use the simulation to complete the task(s) presented in the scenario. To start the simulation, click **Show Simulation**.

Show Simulation

FIGURE 3
Typical MCP exam simulation question with directions.

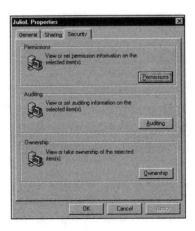

FIGURE 4
Launching the simulation application.

The third step is to use the simulator as you would the actual product to solve the problem or perform the defined tasks. Again, the simulation software is designed to function, within reason, just as the product does. But don't expect the simulation to reproduce product behavior perfectly. Most importantly, do not allow yourself to become flustered if the simulation does not look or act exactly like the product. Figure 5 shows the solution to the sample simulation problem.

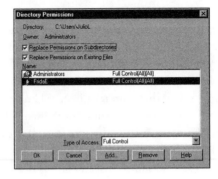

FIGURE 5
The solution to the simulation example.

There are two final points that will help you tackle simulation questions. First, respond only to what is being asked in the question. Do not solve problems that you are not asked to solve. Second, accept what is being asked of you. You may not entirely agree with conditions in the problem statement, the quality of the desired solution, or sufficiency of defined tasks to adequately solve the problem. Always remember that you are being tested on your ability to solve the problem as it has been presented.

The solution to the simulation problem shown in Figure 5 perfectly illustrates both of these points. As you'll recall from the question scenario (refer to Figure 3), you were asked to assign appropriate permissions to a new user called FridaE. You were not instructed to make any other changes in permissions. Thus, if you had modified or removed Administrator permissions, this item would have been scored wrong on an MCP exam.

Putting It All Together

Given all these different pieces of information, the task is now to assemble a set of tips that will help you successfully tackle the different types of MCP exams.

More Pre-Exam Preparation Tips

Generic exam preparation advice is always useful. Follow these general guidelines:

◆ Become familiar with the product. Hands-on experience is one of the keys to success on any MCP exam. Review the exercises and the Step by Step tutorials in the book.

◆ Review the current exam preparation guide on the Microsoft MCP Web site. The documentation Microsoft makes publicly available over the Web identifies the skills every exam is intended to test.

◆ Memorize foundational technical detail as appropriate. But remember, MCP exams are generally heavy on problem solving and application of knowledge more than they are on questions that require only rote memorization.

◆ Take any of the available practice tests. We recommend the one included in this book and those you can create using the Top Score software on the CD-ROM. While these are fixed-format exams, they provide preparation that is also valuable for taking an adaptive exam. Because of the nature of adaptive testing, it is not possible for these practice exams to be offered in the adaptive format. However, fixed-format exams provide the same types of questions as adaptive exams and are the most effective way to prepare for either type of exam. As a supplement to the material included with this book, try the free practice tests available on the Microsoft MCP Web site.

◆ Look on the Microsoft MCP Web site for samples and demonstration items. These tend to be particularly valuable for one significant reason: They allow you to become familiar with any new testing technologies before you encounter them on an MCP exam.

During the Exam Session

Similarly, the generic exam-taking advice you've heard for years applies when taking an MCP exam:

◆ Take a deep breath and try to relax when you first sit down for your exam. It is very important to control the pressure you may (naturally) feel when taking exams.

◆ You will be provided scratch paper. Take a moment to write down any factual information and technical detail that you committed to short-term memory.

◆ Carefully read all information and instruction screens. These displays have been put together to give you information relevant to the exam you are taking.

◆ Accept the Non-Disclosure Agreement and preliminary survey as part of the examination process. Complete them accurately and quickly move on.

◆ Read the exam questions carefully. Reread each question to identify all relevant detail.

◆ Tackle the questions in the order they are presented. Skipping around won't build your confidence; the clock is always counting down.

◆ Don't rush, but at the same time, don't linger on difficult questions. The questions vary in degree of difficulty. Don't let yourself be flustered by a particularly difficult or verbose question.

Fixed-Form Exams

Building from this basic preparation and test-taking advice, you also need to consider the challenges presented by the different exam designs. Because a fixed-form exam is composed of a fixed, finite set of questions, add these tips to your strategy for taking a fixed-form exam:

◆ Note the time allotted and the number of questions appearing on the exam you are taking. Make a rough calculation of how many minutes you can spend on each question, and use that number to pace yourself through the exam.

◆ Take advantage of the fact that you can return to and review skipped or previously answered questions. Mark the questions you can't answer confidently, noting the relative difficulty of each question on the scratch paper provided. When you reach the end of the exam, return to the more difficult questions.

◆ If there is session time remaining when you have completed all questions (and you aren't too fatigued!), review your answers. Pay particular attention to questions that seem to have a lot of detail or that required graphics.

◆ As for changing your answers, the rule of thumb here is *don't*! If you read the question carefully and completely and you felt like you knew the right answer, you probably did. Don't second-guess yourself. If, as you check your answers, one stands out as clearly incorrect, however, of course you should change it. But if you are at all unsure, go with your first impression.

Adaptive Exams

If you are planning to take an adaptive exam, keep these additional tips in mind:

◆ Read and answer every question with great care. When reading a question, identify every relevant detail, requirement, or task that must be performed and double-check your answer to be sure you have addressed every one of them.

◆ If you cannot answer a question, use the process of elimination to reduce the set of potential answers, and then take your best guess. Stupid mistakes invariably mean additional questions will be presented.

◆ Forget about reviewing questions and changing your answers. Once you leave a question, whether you've answered it or not, you cannot return to it. Do not skip any questions either. If you do, that question is counted as incorrect!

Simulation Questions

You may encounter simulation questions on either the fixed-form or adaptive form exam. If you do, keep these tips in mind:

◆ Avoid changing any simulation settings that don't pertain directly to the problem solution. Solve the problem you are being asked to solve and nothing more.

◆ Assume default settings when related information has not been provided. If something has not been mentioned or defined, it is a non-critical detail that does not factor in to the correct solution.

◆ Be sure your entries are syntactically correct, paying particular attention to your spelling. Enter relevant information just as the product would require it.

◆ Close all simulation application windows after you complete the simulation tasks. The testing system software is designed to trap errors that could result when using the simulation application, but trust yourself over the testing software.

◆ If simulations are part of a fixed-form exam, you can return to skipped or previously answered questions and change your answer. However, if you choose to change your answer to a simulation question, or if you even attempt to review the settings you've made in the simulation application, your previous response to that simulation question will be deleted. If simulations are part of an adaptive exam, you cannot return to previous questions.

Final Considerations

Finally, a number of changes in the MCP program will impact how frequently you can repeat an exam and what you will see when you do.

◆ Microsoft has instituted a new exam retake policy. This new rule is "two and two, then one and two." That is, you can attempt any exam twice with no restrictions on the time between attempts. But after the second attempt, you must wait two weeks before you can attempt that exam again. After that, you will be required to wait two weeks between subsequent attempts. Plan to pass the exam in two attempts; if that's not possible, increase your time horizon for receiving an MCP credential.

◆ New questions are being seeded into the MCP exams. After performance data has been gathered on new questions, they will replace older questions on all exam forms. This means that the questions appearing on exams will change regularly.

◆ Many of the current MCP exams will be republished in adaptive format in the coming months. Prepare yourself for this significant change in testing format, as it is entirely likely that this will become the new preferred MCP exam format.

These changes mean that the brute-force strategies for passing MCP exams may soon completely lose their viability. So if you don't pass an exam on the first or second attempt, it is entirely possible that the exam will change significantly in form. It could be updated from fixed-form to adaptive form, or it might have a different set of questions or question types.

The intention of Microsoft is clearly not to make the exams more difficult by introducing unwanted change. Their intent is to create and maintain valid measures of the technical skills and knowledge associated with the different MCP credentials. Preparing for an MCP exam has always involved not only studying the subject matter, but also planning for the testing experience itself. With these changes, this is now more true than ever.

Practice Exam

This appendix consists of 70 questions representative of what you should expect on the actual exam. The answers are at the end. It is strongly suggested that when you take this practice exam, you treat it just as you would the actual exam at the test center. Time yourself, read carefully, and answer all the questions to the best of your ability.

Some of the questions are vague and require deduction on your part to come up with the best answer from the possibilities given. Many of them are verbose, requiring you to read a lot before you come to an actual question. These are skills you should acquire before attempting the actual exam. Run through the test, and if you score less than 750 (missing more than 13), try re-reading the chapters containing information where you were weak (use the index to find keywords to point you to the appropriate locations).

EXAM QUESTIONS

1. ABC Company has 500 users located in a single location. The MIS Director wants to administer the accounts and resources for the network in one central place. Which domain model is best for this situation?

   A. Single domain model

   B. Single master domain model

   C. Multiple master domain model

   D. Complete trust model

2. Big Company has 20,000 users who each have a Windows NT Workstation. For their domain, the MIS Director wants the MIS department to maintain user accounts and to manage the resources on the network. Which domain model is best for this situation?

   A. Single domain model

   B. Single master domain model

   C. Multiple master domain model

   D. Complete trust model

3. XYZ, Inc. has 100 users scattered in three locations. The administrators at each location want to control their own resources. However, the administrators at headquarters insist on creating all the user accounts. Which domain model is best for this situation?

   A. Single domain model

   B. Single master domain model

   C. Multiple master domain model

   D. Complete trust model

4. Required Results: Headquarters manages all user accounts; manufacturing must access resources at Headquarters and R&D. Optional Results: R&D can access resources at Manufacturing; headquarters can access resources at R&D.

   Solution: Implement a single domain model. Add the Domain Users group to the local Users group on any server that needs to be accessed by users.

A. The proposed solution produces the required results and produces both optional results.

B. The proposed solution produces the required results and produces only one optional result.

C. The proposed solution produces the required results but does not produce any optional results.

D. The proposed solution does not produce the required results.

5. Required Result: Users at Manufacturing must access resources at Headquarters and R&D. Optional Results: Users at Headquarters can access resources at Manufacturing; users at R&D can access resources at Manufacturing.

Solution: Create a domain for each location. Create trust relationships in which Manufacturing trusts R&D, and Manufacturing and Headquarters trust each other with a two-way trust. Assign domain users from each domain to the local Users group where users need to access resources.

A. The proposed solution produces the required result and produces both optional results.

B. The proposed solution produces the required result and produces only one optional result.

C. The proposed solution produces the required result but does not produce any optional results.

D. The proposed solution does not produce the required result.

6. How are the trusts configured in a single master domain model?

A. The master domain trusts all the resource domains in a one-way trust.

B. The resource domains trust the master domain with a one-way trust and trusts the other resource domains with two-way trusts.

C. The master domain is trusted by all the resource domains.

D. All the domains trust each other with two-way trusts.

7. What can be added to a local group in a resource domain in a multiple master domain model?

A. Members of the resource domain

B. Members of the resource domain and any master domain

C. Members of resource domain and global groups from the resource domain

D. Members of the resource domain and any master domain and global groups from any of these domains

8. Which utility is used to create trust relationships?

A. Server Manager

B. User Manager for Domains

C. Trust Manager

D. DNS Manager

9. The Sales domain trusts the HR domain. The HR domain trusts the Accounting domain. How can users in the Accounting domain access resources in the Sales domain?

A. Add a global group from the Accounting domain to a local group in the Sales domain.

B. Add a global group from the Accounting domain to a global group in the HR domain, and then add the global group from the HR domain to a local group in the Sales domain.

C. Add a global group from the Sales domain to a local group in the Accounting domain.

D. Users in the Accounting domain cannot access resources in the Sales domain.

10. Required Result: Administrators for the Concord domain need to administer the Richmond and Martinez domains.

Optional Results: Administrators for the Concord domain need to administer the member servers of the Richmond and Martinez domains; administrators for the Concord domain need to administer the Windows NT workstations of the Richmond and Martinez domains.

Solution: The three domains are configured in a single master domain model with the Concord domain as the master domain. The Domain Admins group from the Concord domain is added to the Administrators group of the Martinez and Richmond domains.

A. The proposed solution produces the required result and produces both optional results.

B. The proposed solution produces the required result and produces only one optional result.

C. The proposed solution produces the required result but does not produce any optional results.

D. The proposed solution does not produce the required result.

11. You are planning a complete trust domain model with four domains. How many trust relationships are required for this model?

A. 4

B. 6

C. 10

D. 12

12. On which disk partitioning scheme can you place a system partition?

A. Volume set

B. Stripe set without parity

C. Stripe set with parity

D. Disk mirror

13. Which fault-tolerant disk scheme requires the least overhead in disk storage?

A. Striping with parity

B. Disk mirroring

C. Disk duplexing

D. Striping without parity

14. How many physical disks can be included in a RAID 5 array?

A. 2

B. 3

C. 4

D. 32

15. Which file system can be used for a stripe set with parity? Select all that apply.

A. HPFS

B. FAT

C. CDFS

D. NTFS

16. A Windows NT Server has four physical disks. The first disk, which contains the WINNT directory on a 400 MB FAT partition, has 200 MB of

free space. The second disk has a 400 MB NTFS partition and 100 MB of free space. The third and fourth disks are unformatted with 500 MB of free space on each disk. Which fault-tolerant scheme would allow a 300 MB application to be installed on the disks? Select all that apply.

A. Make a stripe set with parity using all the free space on disks 1, 3, and 4.

B. Make a volume set using the remaining disk space on disk 2.

C. Make a mirror using all the free space on disks 3 and 4.

D. Make a mirror with the boot partition using free space on disk 4. Make a stripe set with parity using the remaining disk space on all four disks.

17. Required Result: Protect the operating system and Web data from a single disk failure.

Optional Result: Provide faster read access for Web data; enable file level permissions for the Web data.

Solution: Install Windows NT Server on a machine with three physical disks. Mirror the boot partition to another disk. Use the remaining disk space on the system disk and the other disks to create a stripe set with parity. Format the partition as NTFS. Place the Web data on the stripe set.

A. The proposed solution produces the required results and produces both optional results.

B. The proposed solution produces the required results and produces only one optional result.

C. The proposed solution produces the required results but does not produce any optional results.

D. The proposed solution does not produce the required results.

18. Your network includes Windows NT Servers and NetWare Servers running the IPX/SPX protocol. Which of the following protocols must be installed on the Windows NT Servers so that NetWare clients can connect to these servers?

A. NetBEUI

B. NWLink

C. TCP/IP

D. AppleTalk

19. Required Result: Allow access to the application for both Microsoft and NetWare clients. Optional Results: Minimize broadcast traffic on the network; minimize the number of protocols used on the network.

Solution: Install TCP/IP and the client software on the NetWare and Microsoft clients. Install TCP/IP on the new servers. Install a WINS Server and configure the Microsoft clients as WINS clients. Install WINS proxy agents on the network segments where the NetWare clients reside.

A. The proposed solution produces the required results and produces both optional results.

B. The proposed solution produces the required results and produces only one optional result.

C. The proposed solution produces the required results but does not produce any optional results.

D. The proposed solution does not produce the required results.

20. You want a server to provide WINS and DHCP services on the network. You also want this server to be a Gopher Server. How many protocols must be installed to support these services?

A. 1

B. 2

C. 3

D. 4

21. If an NT Workstation machine needs to migrate to another domain, what needs to happen? Select all that apply.

A. From the Server Manager, use Add to Domain; then, from the workstation machine, change the workstation name from My Computer properties.

B. From the Server Manager, use Add to Domain; then, from the workstation machine, change the workstation name from Network Neighborhood properties.

C. Reinstall and create the computer account during the installation.

D. On the local computer, add the computer account from the network applet in Control Panel.

22. To optimize your binding order, the protocols should be placed in what order?

A. The protocols used most often should be at the top of the binding order.

B. The least used protocols should be at the top of the binding order.

C. Binding order will not affect speed.

D. Stagger the protocols to keep a balanced load.

23. Where must information be placed for replication to occur?

A. Folders are placed in Systemroot\system32\repl\import.

B. Folders are placed in Systemroot\system32\repl\import\scripts.

C. Folders are placed in Systemroot\system32\repl\export\scripts.

D. Folders are placed in Systemroot\system32\repl\export.

24. With what file systems can a volume set be formatted?

A. FAT, HPFS, NTFS

B. HPFS, NTFS

C. FAT, NTFS

D. FAT, HPFS

25. With what file system can a volume set be formatted to extend it?

A. FAT

B. NTFS

C. FAT or NTFS

D. HPFS

26. After sharing a network printer for Windows NT and 95 clients, what else needs to be done to allow NT Workstation clients to use the printer?

A. Users just connect to the printer.

B. Users must right-click the printer under network neighborhood and choose to configure it to the appropriate port.

C. Users must install a printer driver locally.

D. Nothing else needs to be done. The printer will automatically be available for use.

27. By default, who can take ownership of a printer?

A. Only the Administrator

B. Everyone

C. Administrators, Print Operators, and Server Operators

D. Creator Owner

28. What file formats are supported for Macintosh Accessible Volumes?

    A. FAT

    B. NTFS

    C. HPFS

    D. FAT and NTFS

29. To create a new account, the user running the utility must be a member of either of which two groups?

    A. Administrators

    B. Account Operators

    C. Domain Users

    D. Guest

30. The goal of enterprise networking is for each user in the enterprise to have how many user accounts?

    A. 1

    B. 2

    C. 14

    D. 256

31. Global groups, as a general rule, contain:

    A. Resources

    B. Users

    C. Domains

    D. Text files

32. Local groups, as a general rule, are related to:

    A. Resources

    B. Users

    C. Domains

    D. Text files

33. Which of the following stores the user portion of the Registry?

    A. System policies

    B. User profiles

    C. Regedt32

    D. Login scripts

34. Implementing roaming profiles in Windows 95 differs from Windows NT in which of the following ways? Select all correct answers.

    A. Separate user profiles are not implemented automatically in Windows 95 as they are in Windows NT.

    B. The user portion of the Registry is saved in the file USER.DAT in Windows 95, whereas it is stored in NTUSER.DAT in Windows NT.

    C. The user profile path setting in the user's properties has no effect on Windows 95 clients.

    D. Windows NT roaming profile information is stored in the Windows NT Home Directory.

35. Using the System Policy Editor, you can create policies for which of the following? Select all correct answers.

    A. Domain

    B. Computer

    C. User

    D. Group

36. When using the Windows 95 Remote Administration Tools, which of the following can you manage on a Windows NT Server Domain? Select all correct answers.

A. Auditing

B. Print permission management

C. NTFS permissions

D. Dial-up connections

37. The Windows NT Server Tools for Windows NT Workstation include which of the following utilities? Select all correct answers.

A. DHCP Manager

B. System Policy Editor

C. Remote Access Admin

D. User Manager

38. The Web Administration tools are implemented as:

A. A CMD script

B. An ActiveX plug-in

C. A DirectX extension

D. An Internet Information Server extension

39. Which of the following is used as the entry point into the system for Windows NT users?

A. Share-level security

B. User-level security

C. Resource security

D. Attributes

40. Users whom you assign varying levels of permissions through group memberships have effective shared permissions of:

A. The accumulation of their individual shared permissions.

B. The lowest possible permissions.

C. Those permissions assigned the highest priority.

D. The permissions assigned to the highest priority group of which they belong.

41. If an NTFS file is moved to a new directory on the same volume, what will become of the permissions?

A. The file will maintain its existing permissions.

B. The file will assume permissions from the source.

C. The file will assume permissions from the target.

D. The file will abandon permissions.

42. How many connections to the NetWare server does GSNW require?

A. 1

B. 2

C. 4

D. 8

43. For the Migration Tool for NetWare to maintain directory and file permissions, what type of partition must the target be?

A. FAT

B. VFAT

C. NTFS

D. CDFS

44. To set up Windows NT as an Internet router, what two steps should you follow?

A. Install two network adapters in the system.

B. Enable IP routing.

C. Start GSNW.

D. Enable the NetBEUI protocol.

45. An NT router cannot exchange Routing Information Protocol (RIP) routing packets with other IP RIP routers unless

    A. GSNW is running.

    B. The RIP routing software is installed.

    C. NetBEUI is enabled.

    D. The Default Gateway has been defined.

46. What three publishing services does Internet Information Server use?

    A. WWW

    B. HTTP

    C. HTML

    D. FTP

    E. Gopher

47. Internet Information Server provides a graphical administration tool called:

    A. Internet Tool

    B. Server Manager

    C. User Manager

    D. Internet Service Manager

48. Internet services can be broken into what three components?

    A. Reverse lookup

    B. WWW

    C. Gopher

    D. FTP

49. DNS is the abbreviation for:

    A. Domain Name System

    B. Domain Name Service

    C. Dynamic Name System

    D. Dynamic Name Service

50. A sure way to find problems with RAS is to check the PPP.LOG. Which of the following statements are true of PPP logging? Choose two.

    A. It is enabled by default.

    B. Information is written to the PPP.LOG.

    C. You must edit the Registry to turn it on.

    D. It also contains logging information on modems.

51. Which of the following protocols does PPP support?

    A. TCP/IP

    B. NetBEUI

    C. IPX

    D. Appleshare

52. Mike needs to compare disk transfer rates between two computers. What counter should he select in Performance Monitor? Choose the best answer.

    A. Bytes Transferred

    B. %Disk Time

    C. Bytes Transferred/sec

    D. Disk Time

53. Scenario: Alice has taken over as administrator of a small network. The network consists of 150 users with two domains that fully trust each other. Three file servers are in DomainA of which the Primary Domain Controller is one.

    In DomainB, the Primary Domain Controller is a print server, and an application server also exists. No baseline has been created for the domain controllers of either domain also exists.

Required Result: A baseline must be created for each of the domain controllers.

Optional Result 1: A baseline must be created for the application server.

Optional Result 2: A baseline must be created for the print server.

Proposed Solution: Alice uses Performance Monitor on each domain controller and file server each day, throughout the day, for two weeks. She uses the Log view so that a log file can be created and referenced at a later date. Ratings:

A. The required result is met, and both optional results are also met.

B. The required result and one optional result is met.

C. The required result is met, and neither optional result is met.

D. The required result is not met, and one optional result is met.

E. None of the results is met.

54. A file server is being used by 65 users for storing files, as well as for installation source files. The server has 64 MB of RAM, a 9.2 GB fast SCSI drive, a 16-bit network card, and enabled shadow RAM. The users complain that access to the server is slow at different times of the day.

Required Result: Determine whether memory is the bottleneck.

Optional Result 1: Determine whether the disk is the bottleneck.

Optional Result 2: Improve the performance of the server.

Proposed Solution: Run Performance Monitor at different times throughout the day for a number of days, watching the counters of %Processor

Time, Page Faults/sec, and Processor Queue Length. Ratings:

A. The required result is met, and both optional results are also met.

B. The required result and one optional result is met.

C. The required result is met, and neither optional result is met.

D. The required result is not met, and one optional result is met.

E. None of the results is met.

55. Nancy is trying to verify that logon requests are reaching the server with the correct user name because a number of users are not getting validated. How can she verify that particular user names are being forwarded to the logon server?

A. Have each user go to the server and logon locally.

B. Have Nancy watch them enter their name and password to ensure that they are not making typos.

C. Run Network Monitor on the logon server and check the Hexadecimal pane to see whether the names are getting to the server.

D. It's not possible to verify that the information is reaching the server.

56. Where is the best place to modify the virtual memory settings in Windows NT 4?

A. Through the Registry

B. Through Control Panel, Services, Virtual Memory

C. Through Control Panel, System, Virtual Memory

D. Through WinMSD

57. Scenario: The Orion Organization has hired a consultant to assist with the deployment of 1,000 new computer systems, all of which will all be running Windows NT 4 Workstation.

    Required Result: The IS Manager wants the installations to be completely automated and be consistent between computers.

    Optional Result 1: The workstations should be installed to different resource domains based on their geographic locations and should have the correct time zone settings.

    Optional Result 2: All applications used in the Orion Organization should be included in the deployment process.

    Proposed Solution: Create an unattended script file for the installation process. Install all necessary software onto the first system using the unattended script file. Run the SYSDIFF utility to take a snapshot of all the software installed. Perform all remaining installations using the unattended script file and the SYSDIFF snapshot.

    This solution:

    A. Meets the required result and both optional results

    B. Meets the required result and only one optional result

    C. Meets only the required result

    D. Does not satisfy any required or optional results

58. During the installation of Windows NT Workstation, the installation program does not recognize a SCSI adapter. How can the third-party driver be installed?

    A. Install with the default SCSI driver and apply the third-party driver after the installation is complete.

    B. Press S to specify the third-party driver when the SCSI device-selection screen is presented.

    C. If the SCSI adapter cannot be selected, it is not on the NT Hardware Compatibility List and cannot be used.

    D. Replace the SCSI adapter with an adapter on the HCL list.

59. How can you force a user to select an operating system from the Boot menu when starting Windows NT?

    A. Do not enable a default choice.

    B. Set the timeout value to 0 in BOOT.INI.

    C. Set the timeout value to −1 in BOOT.INI.

    D. In the System applet of the Control Panel, set the Show List option on the Startup/Shutdown tab to 999 seconds.

60. You have updated your tape backup device's driver, and when you reboot, Windows NT fails to start. What can you do to fix this problem? Select the best answer.

    A. Boot using the [VGA Mode] setting.

    B. Use the Last Known Good configuration.

    C. Perform an emergency repair procedure.

    D. Boot into DOS and rename the REG.BAK file REG.DAT.

61. How do you create a mandatory user profile?

    A. In the System applet of the Control Panel, change the user's profile type to Mandatory on the User Profile tab.

    B. Rename the NTUSER.DAT file to NTUSER.MAN in the %Systemroot%\profiles\%username% directory.

C. In the System Policy Editor, configure the user profile to be Mandatory.

D. In User Manager, configure the Profile path to a central network location.

62. What permissions are required to pause, delete, and reorder jobs in the print queue?

A. No Access

B. Print

C. Manage Documents

D. Full Control

63. Under what conditions can a dial-in Windows NT Workstation client access NetWare resources by dialing into a Windows NT Server? Select all that apply.

A. The client dials in via a SLIP connection to a RAS Server running Gateway Services for NetWare.

B. The client dials in via a PPP connection to a RAS Server running Gateway Services for NetWare.

C. The client dials in via a NWLink PPP connection and has Client Services for NetWare installed.

D. The client dials in via a NetBEUI PPP connection and has Client Services for NetWare installed.

64. What utilities can be used to assign dial-in permissions to user accounts? Select all that apply.

A. Remote Access Admin

B. Server Manager

C. User Manager for Domains

D. Registry Editor

65. You want to connect to a printer hosted by a NetWare server. What must be configured on your Windows NT Workstation to enable connectivity? Select all that apply.

A. NWLink protocol

B. RIP for IPX

C. Client Services for NetWare

D. SAP Agent

66. The ACME Corporation has offices in St. Louis, Vancouver, and New Orleans. Each office has been installed with its own Windows NT domain. The ACME Corporation wants all user accounts in the domain to be managed at the head office in St. Louis. Select the trust relationships that must be established. Select all that apply.

A. St. Louis must trust Vancouver.

B. Vancouver must trust St. Louis.

C. New Orleans must trust St. Louis.

D. St. Louis must trust New Orleans.

67. Greg's account on the Omaha National Network is located in DOMAIN1. If you were to grant Greg access to a printer located on BDC2, what permission assignments need to be performed?

A. Create a new global group in DOMAIN1 and make Greg's account a member of the group. Create a local group in DOMAIN2 and assign it Print permissions. Remove the Everyone group from the permissions for the printer. Finally, assign the global group from DOMAIN1 to the local group in DOMAIN2.

B. Create a new local group in DOMAIN1 and make Greg's account a member of the group. Create a local group in DOMAIN2 and assign it Print permissions. Remove the Everyone group from the permissions for the printer. Finally, assign the local group from DOMAIN1 to the local group in DOMAIN2.

C. Create a new local group in DOMAIN1 and make Greg's account a member of the group. Create a global group in DOMAIN2 and assign it Print permissions. Remove the Everyone group from the permissions for the printer. Finally, assign the local group from DOMAIN1 to the global group in DOMAIN2.

D. This cannot be done because the trust relationship has been established in the wrong direction.

68. Charlene and Ron have user accounts in DOMAIN2. Anthony and Bernice have accounts in DOMAIN1. You need to grant all these users access to the accounting system on the member server MS1 in DOMAIN1. What group assignments must be performed?

A. Create a global group in DOMAIN1 and make all four users members of the group. Create a local group on PDC1 and assign permissions to it on the MS1 computer. Make the global group a member of the local group.

B. Create a global group in DOMAIN1 and make all four users members of the group. Create a local group on MS1 and assign permissions to it on the MS1 computer. Make the global group a member of the local group.

C. Create a global group in DOMAIN1 and make Anthony and Bernice members. Create another global group in DOMAIN2 and make Charlene and Ron members. Create a

local group on PDC1 and assign permissions to it on the MS1 computer. Make the two global groups members of the local group.

D. Create a global group in DOMAIN1 and make Anthony and Bernice members. Create another global group in DOMAIN2 and make Charlene and Ron members. Create a local group on MS1 and assign permissions to it on the MS1 computer. Make the two global groups members of the local group.

69. What is the largest stripe set that can be created using any of the available disks?

A. 2200 MB

B. 2000 MB

C. 1600 MB

D. 1500 MB

70. What program writes the contents of memory to a disk file when a STOP error occurs?

A. CRASHDUMP

B. DUMPCHK.EXE

C. DUMPFLOP.EXE

D. DUMPEXAM.EXE

ANSWERS

1. **A.** With a small number of users in one location and centralized administration of both accounts and resources, the single domain is the only possible answer.

2. **B.** Centralized administration of accounts and decentralized control of resources implies the single master model. Checking the size of the SAM for 20,000 users and computers yields a total

SAM of 30 MB (20 MB for users and 10 MB for computers). This is small enough for a single master.

3. **B**. Although the number of users is small, with the requirement for decentralized resource administration, the single master is the best choice.

4. **A**. With the single domain model, administration is centralized. In a single domain, the location of users is not important, so if the Domain Users group is added to all the servers where access is needed, all users can access all required resources regardless of location.

5. **D**. The trust between R&D and Manufacturing is in the wrong direction for the required result to be met.

6. **C**. All the domains with resources trust the single domain with user accounts.

7. **D**. Individual users and global groups from the local domain as well as any trusted domain can be added to local groups.

8. **B**. The Policies menu within User Manager for Domains is used to create trusts.

9. **D**. No trust relationship exists between the Sales and Accounting domains. Users from one domain cannot access resources in another domain unless a trust relationship is explicitly created between them.

10. **C**. The trust is correct, but Domain Admins is added only to the administrators group in the domain, which allows domain administration but not administration of member servers or Windows NT workstations.

11. **D**. All four domains must trust the other three domains, 4×3=12.

12. **D**. Only a disk mirror allows a system partition.

13. **A**. Although striping without parity requires no overhead, it's not a fault-tolerant scheme.

14. **D**. Up to 32 disks can be part of a RAID 5 array.

15. **B**. **D**. Any supported file system can be used for any of the disk arrays. HPFS is not supported for Windows NT 4.0. CDFS is the file system used to read data from CD-ROMs.

16. **A**. **C**. **D**. The mirror would be 1 GB, with 500 MB of usable space. A stripe set on three disks would yield 600 MB total, with 400 MB of usable space. A stripe set on four disks would yield 400 MB total, with 300 MB of usable space.

17. **A**. Mirroring the boot partition protects the operating system. The stripe set with parity protects the Web data and provides faster read access. The NTFS file system allows file-level permissions.

18. **B**. NWLink is Microsoft's implementation of IPX/SPX.

19. **A**. NetWare clients can connect by using TCP/IP if they have the protocol installed. TCP/IP uses few broadcasts, and a single protocol can be used for these requirements.

20. **A**. TCP/IP is the only protocol needed to support these services. A Gopher Server is part of IIS.

21. **B**. **D**. Reinstalling is not necessary.

22. **A**. To optimize the protocols, place the most used at the top of the list.

23. **D**. Files must be placed in Folders under the export folder to replicate.

24. **C**. A volume can be created and formatted with FAT or NTFS.

25. **B**. Only NTFS can be used on an extended volume.

26. **A**. A user may connect to a printer to install the driver.

27. **C**. Anyone with Full Control can take ownership.

28. **B**. MAC-accessible volumes must be formatted using NTFS.

29. **A. B.** To create a new account, the user running User Manager for Domains must be a member of either the Administrators local group or the Account Operators local group.

30. **A**. The goal of enterprise networking is for each user in the enterprise to have only *one* user account.

31. **B**. As a general rule, global groups contain users and local groups contain resources. The local groups are then related to resources and assigned the appropriate permissions.

32. **A**. Local groups contain resources and global groups contain users. The local groups are then related to resources and assigned the appropriate permissions.

33. **B**. User Profiles store the user portion of the Registry.

34. **A. B. C.** Implementing roaming profiles in Windows 95 differs from Windows NT in the following ways: Separate User profiles are not implemented automatically in Windows 95 as they are in Windows NT; the user portion of the Registry is saved in the file USER.DAT in Windows 95, whereas it is stored in NTUSER.DAT in Windows NT; and the user profile path setting in the user's properties has no effect on Windows 95 clients.

35. **B. C. D**. To create Computer, User, and Group policies, you must use the System Policy Editor.

36. **A. B. C.** The Windows 95 Remote Administration Tools enable a client running Windows 95 to manage NTFS permissions, auditing, and print permissions through the Network Neighborhood.

37. **D**. The Windows NT Server Tools for Windows NT Workstation include User Manager for Domains and not User Manager (a Workstation utility).

38. **D**. The Web Administration tools are implemented as an Internet Information Server extension.

39. **A**. Shares have a level of security, and they are also used as the entry point into the system for Windows NT users.

40. **A**. When users, through group membership, have been assigned varying levels of share permissions, their effective shared permissions are the accumulation of their individual shared permissions.

41. **A**. If a file is moved from one directory to another directory on the same NTFS volume, it retains the same NTFS permissions it had.

42. **A**. GSNW enables multiple Windows NT clients to share a single connection.

43. **C**. The Migration Tool for NetWare can preserve the directory and file permissions if it is being transferred to an NTFS partition.

44. **A. B**. To set up Windows NT as an Internet router, install two network adapters in the system, and then enable IP routing.

45. **B**. An NT router cannot exchange Routing Information Protocol (RIP) routing packets with other IP RIP routers unless the RIP routing software is installed.

46. **B. D. E**. Internet Information Server uses Hypertext Transfer Protocol (HTTP), File Transfer Protocol (FTP), and the Gopher services

to provide Internet publishing services to your Windows NT Server computer.

47. **D.** Internet Information Server provides a graphical administration tool called the Internet Service Manager.

48. **B. C. D.** Internet services can be broke into three components: World Wide Web services, FTP services, and Gopher services.

49. **A.** DNS is the abbreviation for Domain Name System.

50. B. C. If you have problems with PPP, you can log PPP debugging information to a file called PPP.Log in the \<winnt_root>\System32\Ras directory. To log PPP debugging information to PPP.Log, change the Registry value for \HKEY_LOCAL_MACHINE\System\ CurrentControlSet\Services\Rasman\PPP\ Logging to 1.

51. **A. B. C.** PPP supports TCP/IP, NetBEUI, and IPX.

52. **C.** Bytes Transferred/sec is the best selection because it gives relative information. Mike can see how many bytes are transferred in one second. Bytes Transferred provides the number of bytes transferred but no indication of how long it took.

53. **B.** Both domain controllers and the print server had a baseline created. The application server did not get a baseline created.

54. **C.** Monitoring Page Faults/sec can help determine whether memory is a bottleneck.

55. **C.** Run Network Monitor at the logon server and view the Hexadecimal pane to see whether the names are getting to the server correctly.

56. **C.** The settings are in Control Panel, System, Performance tab.

57. **D.** Although this solution appears to answer the required result, a uniqueness database file is required to do 1,000 installs. The UDF provides the unique settings required by each computer. Without the UDF, the computers would have to be renamed manually after the install is completed. In addition, the SYSDIFF procedure is performed incorrectly. The initial snapshot must be performed before the software is installed to the master template system.

58. **B.** You can specify third-party SCSI drivers during the SCSI-detection routine of the Windows NT installation.

59. **C.** Setting the timeout value to –1 eliminates the countdown timer for selecting the default operating system.

60. **B.** If your computer fails to start due to a newly installed driver, you can use the Last Known Good configuration to revert to the previous setup. Remember, you must not log on to Windows NT if you plan to use the Last Known Good configuration.

61. **B.** You create a mandatory profile by renaming the user's NTUSER.DAT file as NTUSER.MAN. NTUSER.DAT is stored in the %SystemRoot%\Profiles\ %Username% directory. Remember that if the user has been configured with a roaming profile, you must rename the NTUSER.DAT file in the configured roaming profile directory.

62. **C.** The Manage Documents permission allows a user to pause, delete, and reorder print jobs.

63. **B. C.** A dial-in client can access a NetWare server if the dial-in server is running Gateway Services for NetWare or if the client is running Client Services for NetWare and using the NWLink protocol when dialing in to the network.

64. **A. C**. Dial-in permissions can be set in Remote Access Admin and User Manager for Domains.

65. **A. C**. To use file and print services on a NetWare server, a Windows NT Workstation computer requires both the NWLink protocol and Client Services for NetWare.

66. **B. C**. If St. Louis is going to act as the Master Domain, both Vancouver and New Orleans must trust St. Louis.

67. **D**. The trust relationship is pointing in the wrong direction. If you want Greg to access any resources in DOMAIN2, DOMAIN2 must trust DOMAIN1.

68. **D**. Because the resource is located on a Member Server in DOMAIN2, the local group must be created in the account database of the Member Server.

69. **C**. The largest stripe set that can be created using any of the available disks is 1600 MB, using 400 MB from disks 0, 1, 3, and 4.

70. **A**. Although not a true executable, the CRASH-DUMP routine writes the contents of memory to the page file with an indicator that a memory dump has been written to the page file. When the system is restarted, the contents of the page file are written to the file %SystemRoot%\Memory.dmp by default.

APPENDIXES

Glossary

The following are key terms from this book. Know them in preparation for running an enterprise system, and know them in preparation for the Microsoft exam:

A

access token   A Windows NT object describing a user account and group memberships. This object is provided by the Local Security Authority on successful logon and validation and is attached to all user processes.

account lockout   A Windows NT Server security feature that locks a user account if a number of failed logon attempts occur within a specified amount of time, based on account policy lockout settings. (Locked accounts cannot log on.) See also *password parameters.*

account policy   A setting that controls the way passwords must be used by all user accounts of a domain or of an individual computer. Specifics include minimum password length, how often a user must change his or her password, and how often users can reuse old passwords. Account policy can be set for all user accounts in a domain when administering a domain, and for all user accounts of a single workstation or member server when administering a computer.

active partition   The disk partition that has been designated as being bootable. Although an NT system can have up to four partitions that are capable of booting, only one can be active at any one time.

Address Resolution Protocol (ARP)   The protocol within TCP/IP that determines whether a packet's source and destination addresses are in the Data-Link Control (DLC) or Internet Protocol (IP) format. ARP is necessary for proper packet routing on a TCP/IP network.

administrative share   A network share that is created and maintained by the Windows NT operating systems. Administrative shares are hidden and accessible only by users in the local Administrators account. All disk partitions have Administrative shares associated with them. For example, C$ is the share for the C drive.

AGLP (Accounts/Global/Local/Permissions)   The "best practice" process for applying permissions to user accounts and groups in a Windows NT domain.

Alert view   A view in the Performance Monitor in which thresholds for counters are set and then actions are taken when those thresholds are crossed.

API (Application Programming Interface)   A standard used to communicate between software applications. API calls are used to transfer information between programs.

application log   A server log accessible from the Event Viewer. This log records messages, warnings, and errors generated by applications running on your NT Server or Workstation.

ARC-path (Advanced RISC Computing path)   An industry-standard method of identifying the physical location of a partition on a hard drive. ARC-paths are used in the BOOT.INI file to identify the location of NT boot files.

B

backup browser   A computer chosen by an election process to maintain a list of resources on a network. These computers have browse clients directed to them by a master browser when a request for resources is made on a network.

Backup Domain Controller (BDC)   In a Windows NT Server domain, a computer running Windows NT Server that receives a copy of the domain's directory database, which contains all account and security policy information for the domain. The copy is synchronized periodically and automatically with the master copy on the primary domain controller (PDC). BDCs also authenticate user logons and can be promoted to function as PDCs as needed. Multiple BDCs can exist on a domain. See also *member server; PDC.*

baseline   A collection of the measurements of resources on your system that have been taken at normal usage of the system. This measurement is then used to compare for any changes to the system.

binding   A process that establishes the communication channel between a protocol driver (such as TCP/IP) and a network card.

blue screen stop error   The resulting screen after a system crash. The blue screen is comprised of event error codes and hexadecimal data.

boot partition   The volume, formatted for either an NTFS or FAT file system, that has the Windows NT operating system and its support files. The boot partition can be (but does not have to be) the same as the system partition. See also *partition; FAT; NTFS.*

BOOT.INI   A file, located on the system partition of an NT Server or Workstation, responsible for pointing the boot process to the correct boot files for the operating system chosen in the boot menu.

BOOTSECT.DOS   A file, located on the system partition, containing information required to boot an NT System to MS-DOS if a user requests it.

bottleneck   A system resource that is the limiting factor in the speed of processing. All systems have a bottleneck of some sort; the question is whether the bottleneck is significant in the context in which a server finds itself.

broadcast frame   Transmission of a message intended for all network recipients.

browser   Called the Computer Browser service, the browser maintains an up-to-date list of computers, and provides the list to applications when requested. This list is kept up to date by consulting with a master or backup browser on the network. The browser provides the computer lists displayed in the Network Neighborhood, Select Computer, and Select Domain dialog boxes, and (for Windows NT Server only) in the Server Manager window.

C

CACLS (Change the Access Control Lists)   A command-line utility that can be used to modify the access control lists.

call back   A security feature, enabled in the configuration of a RAS server, that requires that a RAS server call a client at a specific phone number (system or user-configured) when a client has initiated a RAS connection to the server. This feature is used either to transfer the bulk of long-distance charges to the server rather than the user, or to ensure that a user is authentic by being at a specific location rather than a hacker trying to gain unauthorized access to a network through RAS.

Chart view   A view in the Performance Monitor in which a dynamically updated line graph or histogram is displayed for the counters selected in the view configuration.

client access license   A license, required by all users connecting to an NT server, which provides legal access to NT server resources.

Client Administration tools   A set of applications which allow for the administration of an NT Domain Controller from a Windows 95 or Windows NT Workstation, or Windows NT Server computer. The Client Administration Tools provide the most commonly used administration tools but do not provide complete administration functionality.

Client Services for NetWare (CSNW)   Services included with Windows NT Workstation, enabling workstations to make direct connections to file and printer resources at NetWare servers running NetWare 2.x or later.

COMPACT.EXE   A command-line utility used to compress files on NTFS volumes. To see command-line options, type **compact /?** at the command prompt. Right-clicking any file or folder on an NTFS volume in Windows NT Explorer and clicking Properties to compress or uncompress the files can also access this utility.

Control Panel   A folder containing a number of applets (applications) that help you configure and monitor your system running Windows NT. This includes configuring hardware, software, network configurations, service startup parameters, and system properties.

CONVERT.EXE   A command-line utility used to convert an NT volume from FAT to NTFS. The command syntax is CONVERT <drive letter>: /fs:NTFS; an example of a command is CONVERT C: /fs:NTFS.

counter   A specific component of a Performance Monitor object that has a displayable value. For example, for the object Memory, one counter is Available Bytes.

D

default gateway   In TCP/IP, the intermediate network device on the local network that has knowledge of the network IDs of the other networks in the Internet so that it can forward the packets to other gateways until the packet is eventually delivered to a gateway connected to the specified destination.

DETECT (Discover, Explore, Track, Execute, Check, Tie-Up)   A recommended troubleshooting method for approaching NT problems.

differential backup   A backup method that backs up all files which do not have their archive attribute set and which does not set the archive attribute of those files it backs up.

directory replication   The copying of a master set of directories from a server (called an export server) to specified servers or workstations (called import computers) in the same or other domains. Replication simplifies the task of maintaining identical sets of directories and files on multiple computers, because only a single master copy of the data must be maintained. Files are replicated when they are added to an exported directory and every time a change is saved to the file.

Directory Service Manager for NetWare (DSMN)   An NT add-on that provides directory synchronization between an NT network and a NetWare network.

Directory Services   The network and specifically the account and security database used to combine your network into an organized structure. There are numerous implementations of directory services, and in previous versions of Windows NT, Microsoft referred to them as simply the domain models.

directory synchronization   A process for automatically transferring the account database, containing all user and security information, from the Primary Domain Controllers to all Backup Domain Controllers in your Windows NT environment.

Disk Administrator An administration program that enables an NT administrator to create, format, and maintain hard drive partitions, volumes, and fault-tolerant mechanisms.

disk duplexing A mirror set created with two hard drives controlled by separate disk controller cards. Disk duplexing provides more fault tolerance than standard mirror sets as it ensures that a controller card failure will not bring down the mirror set.

disk mirroring A fault-tolerant mechanism that provides a fully redundant or shadow copy of data (mirror set). Mirror sets provide an identical twin for a selected disk; all data written to the primary disk is also written to the shadow or mirror disk. This enables you to have instant access to another disk with a redundant copy of the information on a failed disk.

disk striping with parity A method of data protection in which data is striped in large blocks across all the disks in an array. The parity information provides data redundancy.

DISKPERF A utility used to enable the hard disk counters in the Performance Monitor.

domain In Windows NT, a collection of computers defined by the administrator of a Windows NT Server network that share a common directory database. A domain provides access to the centralized user accounts and group accounts maintained by the domain administrator. Each domain has a unique name.

domain master browser A kind of network name server that keeps a browse list of all the servers and domains on the network. The domain master browser for a domain is always the Primary Domain Controller.

Domain Name Service (DNS) A static, hierarchical name service for TCP/IP hosts. The network administrator configures the DNS with a list of host names and IP addresses, allowing users of workstations configured to query the DNS to specify remote systems by host names rather than IP addresses. For example, a workstation configured to use DNS name resolution could use the command **ping remotehost** rather than **ping 1.2.3.4** if the mapping for the system named remotehost were contained in the DNS database.

Dynamic Host Configuration Protocol (DHCP) A protocol that offers dynamic configuration of IP addresses and related information through the DHCP server service running on an NT Server. DHCP provides safe, reliable, and simple TCP/IP network configuration, prevents address conflicts, and helps conserve the use of IP addresses through centralized management of address allocation.

E

Emergency Repair Disk A disk containing configuration information for a specific NT Server or Workstation. This disk is created and updated using the RDISK utility and can be used with the three NT setup disks to recover from many NT system failures resulting from file and/or Registry corruption.

Event Viewer An administrative utility used to look at event logs. Three logs are provided to the Event Viewer: system, security, and application.

export computer In directory replication, a server from which a master set of directories is exported to specified servers or workstations (called import computers) in the same or other domains.

extended partition Created from free space on a hard disk, an extended partition can be subpartitioned into zero or more logical drives. Only one of the four partitions allowed per physical disk can be an extended partition, and no primary partition needs to be present to create an extended partition.

F

FAT (File Allocation Table)   A table or list maintained by some operating systems to keep track of the status of various segments of disk space used for file storage. Also referred to as the FAT file system, this method is used to format hard drives in DOS, Windows 95, and OS/2, and can be used in Windows NT.

FAT32   A variation of FAT that provides for more efficient file storage. This FAT variation is available only on Windows 95 and Windows 98 and is not readable by Windows NT.

fault tolerance   Ensuring data integrity when hardware failures occur. In Windows NT, the FTDISK.SYS driver provides fault tolerance. In Disk Administrator, fault tolerance is provided using mirror sets, stripe sets with parity, and volume sets.

fault-tolerant boot disk   A disk that contains the files required by NT to begin the boot and to point to the boot partition. The files required for an Intel system are BOOT.INI, NTDETECT.COM, NTLDR, and NTBOOTDD.SYS (if the hard drive is SCSI with BIOS disabled).

File and Print Services for NetWare (FPNW)   A service installed on an NT server that enables NetWare clients to access an NT server for the purposes of reading files and printing to NT-controlled printers. For this service to work, the NT Server must have NWLink installed on it.

filename alias   An 8.3-compatible short name given to a long filename created on an NT computer to allow MS-DOS and Windows 3.x clients to read files.

frame   The addressing and protocol information, as well as the data sent from one computer or host (routers, bridges, and so on) to another. There are three types of frames: broadcast, multicast, and directed.

frame type   The type of network package generated on a network. In NT configuration, this term refers to the type of network packages sent by a NetWare server that an NT client is configured to accept.

FTP (File Transfer Protocol)   FTP is the TCP/IP protocol for file transfer.

G

Gateway Services for NetWare (GSNW)   Included with Windows NT Server, these services enable a computer running Windows NT Server to connect to NetWare servers. Creating a gateway enables computers running only Microsoft client software to access NetWare resources through the gateway.

global group   For Windows NT Server, a group that can be used in its own domain, member servers and workstations of the domain, and trusting domains. In all those places, the group can be granted rights and permissions and can become a member of local groups. However, the group can contain only user accounts from its own domain. Global groups provide a way to create handy sets of users from inside the domain, available for use both in and out of the domain.

Global groups cannot be created or maintained on computers running Windows NT Workstation. However, for Windows NT Workstation computers that participate in a domain, domain global groups can be granted rights and permissions at those workstations, and can become members of local groups at those workstations.

GOPHER   The Internet Gopher is a distributed document-delivery system.

group account   A collection of user accounts. Giving a user account membership in a group gives that user all the rights and permissions granted to the group.

H

Hardware Compatibility List (HCL)   The Windows NT Hardware Compatibility List lists the devices supported by Windows NT. The latest version of the HCL can be downloaded from the Microsoft Web Page (microsoft.com) on the Internet.

hidden share   A network share which is configured not to show up in browse lists but to which you can connect explicitly if you know the share name. You can create hidden shares by appending a dollar sign ($) to the end of a share name, as in SECRET$. All Administrative shares are hidden shares.

hive   A section of the Registry that appears as a file on your hard disk. The Registry subtree is divided into hives (named for their resemblance to the cellular structure of a beehive). A hive is a discrete body of keys, subkeys, and values that is rooted at the top of the Registry hierarchy. A hive is backed by a single file and a .log file that are in the %SystemRoot%\system32\config or the %SystemRoot%\profiles\username folders. By default, most hive files (Default, SAM, Security, and System) are stored in the %SystemRoot%\system32\config folder. The %SystemRoot%\ profiles folder contains the user profile for each user of the computer. Because a hive is a file, it can be moved from one system to another, but can be edited only using Registry Editor.

Hkey_Local_Machine   A Registry subtree that maintains all the configuration information for the local machine, including hardware settings and software installed.

host name   The name assigned to any computer or service that can be accessed through the TCP/IP protocol. *Host name* is a commonly used term in the Internet community.

HTTP (Hypertext Transfer Protocol)   A standard used for accessing Web pages.

I

ICMP (Internet Control Message Protocol)   The protocol used to handle errors and control messages at the IP layer. ICMP is actually part of the IP protocol.

IIS (Internet Information Server)   The Internet components that are integrated into Windows NT server 4.0. This service enables your Windows NT system to function as an Internet server using the HTTP, FTP, or Gopher services.

import computer   In directory replication, the server or workstation that receives copies of the master set of directories from an export server.

incremental backup   A backup method that backs up all files which do not have their archive attribute set and which sets the archive attribute of those files it backs up.

installation disk set   A set of disks that contain a minimal configuration of NT used to initiate NT installation and repair.

IP (Internet Protocol)   IP is part of the TCP/IP suite. It is a network-layer protocol that governs packet forwarding.

IP address   An address used to identify a node on a network and to specify routing information. Each node on the network must be assigned a unique IP address, which is made up of the network ID, plus a unique host ID assigned by the network administrator. This address is typically represented in dotted-decimal notation, with the decimal value of each octet separated by a period (for example, 138.57.7.27). In Windows NT, the IP address can be configured statically on the client or configured dynamically through DHCP.

IPC (Interprocess Communication)   The exchange of information between processes through a secured message channel.

IPConfig A command-line utility that is used to determine the current TCP/IP configuration of a local computer. It is also used to request a new TCP/IP address from a DHCP server through the use of the /RELEASE and /RENEW switches. The /ALL switch displays a complete list of TCP/IP configurations.

IPX/SPX Transport protocols used in Novell NetWare networks. Windows NT implements IPX through NWLink.

L

LastKnownGood A set of Registry settings that records the hardware configuration of an NT computer at last successful login. LastKnownGood can be used to recover from incorrect hardware setup as long as logon does not occur between when the configuration was changed and the LastKnownGood was invoked.

License Manager An administrative utility that enables you to track the purchase of Client Access Licenses for an NT Server and/or Domain.

licensing mode An indicator of what kind of licensing is being used on an NT Server. The choices are per-server and per-seat.

local group For Windows NT Workstation, a group that can be granted permissions and rights only for its own workstation. However, the group can contain user accounts from its own computer and (if the workstation participates in a domain) user accounts and global groups both from its own domain and from trusted domains.

For Windows NT Server, a group that can be granted permissions and rights only for the domain controllers of its own domain. However, the group can contain user accounts and global groups both from its own domain and from trusted domains.

Local groups provide a way to create handy sets of users from both inside and outside the domain, to be used only at domain controllers of the domain.

local profile A profile stored on a local machine that is accessible only to a user who logs on to an NT computer locally.

Local Security Authority (LSA) The NT process responsible for directing logon requests to the local Security Accounts Manager (SAM) or to the SAM of a domain controller through the NetLogon service. The LSA is responsible for generating an Access Token after a user logon has been validated.

Log view A view in the Performance Monitor in which the configuration of a log is determined. Logs have no dynamic information; however, the resulting file can be analyzed using any of the other Performance Monitor views.

logical drive A subpartition of an extended partition on a hard disk.

logon script These are files containing commands that are used to set up a user's environment when connecting to the network.

M

MAC (Media Access Control) address The hardware address of a device that is connected to a network. For example, the hardware address of an Ethernet card is referred to as the MAC address.

mandatory profile A profile that is downloaded to the user's desktop each time he or she logs on. A mandatory user profile is created by an administrator and assigned to one or more users to create consistent or job-specific user profiles. A profile cannot be changed by the user and remains the same from one logon session to the next.

Master Boot Record (MBR)   The place on the disk that the initial computer startup is directed to go to initiate operating system boot. The MBR is located on the primary partition.

master browser   A kind of network name server that keeps a browse list of all the servers and domains on the network. Also referred to as *browse master.*

member server   A computer that runs Windows NT Server but is not a Primary Domain Controller (PDC) or Backup Domain Controller (BDC) of a Windows NT domain. Member servers do not receive copies of the directory database.

Migration Tool for NetWare   A tool included with Windows NT that enables you to transfer user and group accounts, volumes, folders, and files easily from a NetWare server to a computer running Windows NT Server.

multi-boot   A computer that runs two or more operating systems. For example, Windows 95, MS-DOS, and Windows NT operating systems can be installed on the same computer. When the computer is started, any one of the operating systems can be selected. Also known as *dual-boot.*

multicast packet   A single packet that is copied to a specific subset of network addresses. In contrast, broadcast packets are sent to all stations in a network.

Multilink protocol   A protocol that combines multiple physical links into a logical bundle. This aggregate link increases your bandwidth.

multiprotocol routing   Enabling one computer system to route the packets from dissimilar networking protocols.

N

Net Logon   For Windows NT Server, a feature that performs authentication of domain logons, and keeps the domain's directory database synchronized between the Primary Domain Controller (PDC) and the other Backup Domain Controllers (BDCs) of the domain.

NetBEUI   A network protocol usually used in small, department-size local area networks (LANs) of 1 to 200 clients. It is nonroutable and therefore not a preferred wide area network (WAN) protocol.

NetBIOS (Network Basic Input/Output System)   A standard network interface for IBM PCs. NetBIOS is used for locating named resources on a network.

network adapter   An expansion card or other device used to connect a computer to a LAN. Also called a *network card; network adapter card; adapter card; network interface card (NIC).*

Network Monitor   An administrative utility installed on an NT computer when the Network Monitor Tools and Agent service is installed. The network monitor provided with NT enables you to capture and analyze network traffic coming into and going out of the local network card. The SMS version of Network Monitor runs in promiscuous mode that allows monitoring of traffic on the local network.

network protocols   Communication "languages" that enable networked computer and devices to communicate with each other. Common network protocols are TCP/IP, NetBEUI, NWLink, and DLC (used for communicating with networked printers such as HP DirectJet).

network services   A process that performs a specific network system function and often provides an application programming interface (API) for other processes to call. Windows NT services are RPC-enabled, meaning that their API routines can be called from remote computers.

non-browser   A computer that is configured never to participate in browser elections and therefore can never become a master or backup browser.

normal backup   A method that backs up all files and then sets the archive attribute of those files it backs up. Sometimes referred to as a *full backup.*

NTBOOTDD.SYS   The driver for a SCSI boot device that does not have its BIOS enabled. NTBOOTDD.SYS is found on an NT system partition and is also required to create a fault-tolerant boot disk.

NTCONFIG.POL   A file that defines an NT system policy.

NTDETECT.COM   The program in the NT boot process responsible for generating a list of hardware devices. This list is later used to populate part of the HKEY_LOCAL_MACHINE subtree in the Registry.

NTFS   An advanced file system designed for use specifically within the Windows NT operating system. It supports file system recovery, extremely large storage media, long file names, and various features for the POSIX subsystem. It also supports object-oriented applications by treating all files as objects with user-defined and system-defined attributes.

NTFS compression   A compression type supported only on an NTFS volume. This supports file-level compression and is dynamic.

NTFS permissions   Local permissions on NTFS volumes that allow for the restriction of both local and network access to files and folders.

NTHQ   A program that executes from a disk that enables you to have hardware on a computer automatically checked against the HCL for NT compatibility.

NTLDR   The program responsible for booting an NT system. It is invoked when an NT computer is started and is responsible for displaying the boot menu (from the BOOT.INI file) and for starting the NTDETECT.COM program.

NTOSKRNL.EXE   The program responsible for maintaining the core of the NT operating system. When NTLDR has completed the boot process, control of NT is handed over to the NTOSKRNL.

NWCONV   The utility used within Windows NT to convert NetWare user and group information and file information from a Novell server into a Windows NT domain.

NWLink   A standard network protocol that supports routing and can support NetWare client/server applications, where NetWare-aware Sockets-based applications communicate with IPX\SPX Sockets-based applications.

O

object   A specific system category for which counters can be observed in Performance Monitor. Objects whose counters are frequently monitored are Memory, Processor, Network, and PhysicalDisk.

octet   An octet is eight bits. In networking, the term *octet* is often used in place of *byte,* as TCP/IP uses multiple octets in the addressing.

OSLOADER.EXE   The program on a RISC-based machine responsible for the function of the NTLDR on an Intel-based machine.

P

partition   A portion of a physical disk that functions as though it were a physically separate unit.

per-client licensing mode   An NT licensing mode that allocates server access on a per-person basis, not on a per-connection basis. Using a per-client license, a user can connect to many NT servers simultaneously.

per-server licensing mode   An NT licensing mode that allocates server access on a per-connection basis. This licensing mode allocates a certain number of simultaneous connections to a server, and when that number of connections is reached, no more users are allowed to access the server.

Performance Monitor   An administrative application used to monitor object counters on an NT computer to determine bottlenecks in the system and to increase overall efficiency.

persistent connection   A network connection from a client to a server that is automatically reestablished when disconnected.

PING   A command used to verify connections to one or more remote hosts. The PING utility uses the ICMP echo request and echo reply packets to determine whether a particular IP system on a network is functional. The PING utility is useful for diagnosing IP network or router failures.

Point-to-Point Protocol (PPP)   A set of industry-standard framing and authentication protocols that is part of Windows NT RAS to ensure interoperability with third-party remote access software. PPP negotiates configuration parameters for multiple layers of the OSI model.

Point-to-Point Tunneling Protocol (PPTP)   A new networking technology that supports multiprotocol virtual private networks (VPNs), enabling remote users to access corporate networks securely across the Internet by dialing into an Internet service provider (ISP) or by connecting directly to the Internet.

potential browser   A computer that is not currenly functioning as a browser on a network but which could, if needed, become one.

Primary Domain Controller (PDC)   In a Windows NT Server domain, the computer running Windows NT Server that authenticates domain logons and maintains the directory database for a domain. The PDC tracks changes made to accounts of all computers on a domain. It is the only computer to receive these changes directly. A domain has only one PDC.

primary partition   A partition is a portion of a physical disk that can be marked for use by an operating system. There can be up to four primary partitions (or up to three, if there is an extended partition) per physical disk. A primary partition cannot be subpartitioned.

print device   The actual hardware device that produces printed output.

printer   The software interface between the operating system and the print device. The printer defines where the document will go before it reaches the print device (to a local port, to a file, or to a remote print share), when it will go, and various other aspects of the printing process.

printer driver   A program that converts graphics commands into a specific printer language, such as PostScript or PCL.

printer pool   Two or more identical print devices associated with one printer.

protocol   See *network protocols.*

PSTN   Public Switched Telephone Network.

R

RAID (Redundant Array of Inexpensive Disks) RAID is a standard used for allowing fault tolerance for your computer systems disk drives. Windows NT supports RAID 1 and RAID 5. RAID 1 is disk mirroring, in which all data is duplicated across two drives. In RAID 5, the controllers write data a segment at a time and interleave parity among the segments. (A segment is a selectable number of blocks.) RAID 5 does not use a dedicated parity disk.

RDISK.EXE   A program used to create and update Emergency Repair Disks and the /REPAIR folder on an NT system.

REGEDIT.EXE   One of two Registry editors available in NT. This one has the same interface as the Registry editor available in Windows 95 and provides key value searching.

REGEDT32.EXE   One of two Registry editors available in NT. This one has a cascaded subtree interface and enables you to set Registry security.

regenerate   To rebuild a replaced hard drive in a stripe set with parity after hard drive failure. This process can be initiated from the Disk Administrator.

Registry   Windows NT's database repository for information about a computer's configuration. It is organized in a hierarchical structure, and is comprised of subtrees and their keys, hives, and value entries.

Registry Key   A specific Registry entry that has a configurable value.

Registry tree   A collection of similar Registry keys. HKEY_LOCAL_MACHINE is an example of a Registry tree.

Remote Access Service (RAS)   A service that provides remote networking for telecommuters, mobile workers, and system administrators who monitor and manage servers at multiple branch offices. Users with RAS on a Windows NT computer can dial in to access their networks remotely for services such as file and printer sharing, electronic mail, scheduling, and SQL database access.

Remote Procedure Call (RPC)   A common communication standard that enables processes to interact and communicate through a secured channel.

Report view   A view in Performance Monitor that displays in a single-page format current counter values.

reporting interval   In Performance Monitor, the interval at which a new set of statistical information is processed and delivered to the view or views currently operating.

Response Probe   A utility used to apply a controlled stress on a system and monitor the response. This tool is useful for determining a resource's capacity before placing it in a "live" production environment.

roaming profile   A profile that is enabled when an administrator enters a user profile path into the user account. The first time the user logs off, the local user profile is copied to that location. Thereafter, the server copy of the user profile is downloaded each time the user logs on (if it is more current than the local copy) and is updated each time the user logs off.

S

SCSI (Small Computer System Interface)   A standard high-speed parallel interface defined by the American National Standards Institute (ANSI).

SCSI adapter   An adapter used for connecting microcomputers to peripheral devices such as hard disks and printers, and to other computers and local area networks.

Security Accounts Manager (SAM)   The NT process responsible for querying the directory database to locate a specific user name and password combination when a user attempts to log on.

security log   A log that records security events and can be viewed through the Event Viewer. This log helps track changes to the security system and identify any possible breaches of security. For example, depending on the Audit settings in User Manager or User Manager for Domains, the security log might record attempts to log on the local computer. The security log contains both valid and invalid logon attempts as well as events related to resource use (such as creating, opening, or deleting files).

Serial Line Interface Protocol (SLIP) An older industry standard that is part of Windows NT RAS to ensure interoperabability with third-party remote access software. Windows NT supports SLIP as a client but not as a server; that is, an NT machine can connect to a SLIP server but cannot itself be a SLIP server.

Server Message Block (SMB) A file-sharing protocol designed to enable systems to access transparently files that reside on remote systems.

service A process that performs a specific system function and often provides an application programming interface (API) for other processes to call. Windows NT services are RPC-enabled, meaning that their API routines can be called from remote computers.

share permissions A set of permissions controlling access to a network share when that access is attempted over the network. Share permissions do not apply to local users of a system and can be applied only at the folder level.

sharing The process of making a resource available on the network. This resource can be a drive, a folder, or a printer.

/SOS A BOOT.INI switch indicating that on NT Server or Workstation boot, the list of drivers loading should be displayed. This switch is used for troubleshooting and is normally configured as part of the [VGA] boot option.

spooler Software that accepts documents sent by a user to be printed, and then stores those documents and sends them, one by one, to available printer(s).

standalone server An NT server that participates as part of a workgroup and not as a part of a domain.

stripe set The saving of data across identical partitions on different drives. A stripe set does not provide fault tolerance.

subnet mask A 32-bit value that enables the recipient of IP packets to distinguish the network ID portion of the IP address from the host ID.

system groups One or more groups maintained by NT for special purposes. The Everyone group is an example of a system group; it cannot be changed, as its membership is defined and maintained by NT.

system log A log that contains events logged by the Windows NT components and that can be looked at through Event Viewer. For example, the failure of a driver or other system component to load during startup is recorded in the system log.

system partition The volume that has the hardware-specific files needed to load Windows NT.

system policy A policy created with the System Policy Editor to control user work environments and actions, and to enforce system configuration for Windows NT clients. System policy can be implemented for specific users, groups, or computers, or for all users. System policy for users overwrites settings in the current user area of the Registry, and system policy for computers overwrites the current local machine area of the Registry. If you have clients who are using Windows 95, separate system policies need to be created for them on a Windows 95 system, as NT system policies are not compatible with Windows 95.

T

Take Ownership The process by which the ownership of a resource is transferred from one user to another. By default, administrators can take ownership of any NT resource.

Task Manager A utility integrated within Windows NT that enables you to monitor processes and applications on your system. You can also use the task manager to view processor and memory statistics.

TCP (Transmission Control Protocol) A protocol that provides end-to-end, connection-oriented, reliable transport layer (layer 4) functions over IP-controlled networks. TCP performs the following functions: flow control between two systems, acknowledgments of packets received, and end-to-end sequencing of packets. The protocol uses IP for delivery. TCP was originally developed by the Department of Defense to support interworking of dissimilar computers across a network.

TCP/IP (Transmission Control Protocol/Internet Protocol) A set of networking protocols that provide communications across interconnected networks made up of computers with diverse hardware architectures and various operating systems. TCP/IP includes standards for how computers communicate and conventions for connecting networks and routing traffic.

Telephony API (TAPI) Used by programs to make data/fax/voice calls, including the Windows NT applets HyperTerminal, Dial-Up Networking, Phone Dialer, and other Win32 communications applications written for Windows NT.

thread The object of a process that is responsible for executing code segments.

Tracert A TCP/IP troubleshooting utility to trace the route from one host to another. You can use this utility to locate the source of a transmission breakdown between TCP/IP hosts.

trust relationship A secured communication channel between Windows NT server domains, allowing for the sharing of user account database information. A trust relationship is used to establish the connections between domains in the Windows NT domain models.

U

UDP (User Datagram Protocol) A protocol that is part of the TCP/IP protocol suite and that provides a means for applications to access the connectionless features of IP. UDP operates at layer 4 of the OSI reference model and provides for the exchange of datagrams without acknowledgments or guaranteed delivery.

UNC (Universal Naming Convention) name A full Windows NT name of a resource on a network. It conforms to the *servername**sharename* syntax, where *servername* is the server's name and *sharename* is the name of the shared resource. UNC names of directories or files can also include the directory path under the share name, with the following syntax:

*servername**sharename**directory**filename*

UPS (Uninterruptible Power Supply) A battery-operated power supply connected to a computer to keep the system running during a power failure.

user account An identifier that consists of all the information that defines a user to Windows NT. This includes such things as the user name and password required for the user to log on, the groups in which the user account has membership, and the rights and permissions the user has for using the system and accessing its resources. For Windows NT Workstation, user accounts are managed with User Manager. For Windows NT Server, user accounts are managed with User Manager for Domains.

User Manager for Domains A Windows NT Server tool used to manage security for a domain or an individual computer. The tool administers user accounts, groups, and security policies.

user profile Profiles that save configuration information that can be retained on a user-by-user basis. This information includes all the per-user settings of the Windows NT environment, such as the desktop arrangement, personal program groups and the program items in those groups, screen colors, screen savers, network connections, printer connections, mouse settings, window size and position, and more. When a user logs on, the user's profile is loaded and the user's Windows NT environment is configured according to that profile.

user rights   Access permissions that allow the users and/or groups to perform specific functions and tasks on the Windows NT system.

V

volume set   A combination of partitions on a physical disk that appears as one logical drive.

W

Windows Internet Name Service (WINS)   A name-resolution service that resolves Windows NT networking computer names to IP addresses in a routed environment. A WINS server handles name registrations, queries, and releases.

WinLogon   The NT process that initiates login by presenting the logon dialog box to a user.

WINNT.EXE   The program used to install Windows NT from a non-NT platform.

WINNT32.EXE   The program used to install or upgrade Windows NT from an NT platform

workgroup   For Windows NT, a collection of computers that are grouped for viewing purposes. Each workgroup is identified by a unique name.

Overview of the Certification Process

You must pass rigorous certification exams to become a Microsoft Certified Professional. These certification exams provide a valid and reliable measure of your technical proficiency and expertise. The closed-book exams are developed in consultation with computer industry professionals who have on-the-job experience with Microsoft products in the workplace. These exams are conducted by an independent organization—Sylvan Prometric—at more than 1,200 Authorized Prometric Testing Centers around the world.

Currently Microsoft offers six types of certification, based on specific areas of expertise:

◆ **Microsoft Certified Professional (MCP).** Persons who attain this certification are qualified to provide installation, configuration, and support for users of at least one Microsoft desktop operating system, such as Windows NT Workstation. In addition, candidates can take elective exams to develop areas of specialization. MCP is the initial or first level of expertise.

◆ **Microsoft Certified Professional + Internet (MCP+Internet).** Persons who attain this certification are qualified to plan security, install and configure server products, manage server resources, extend service to run CGI scripts or ISAPI scripts, monitor and analyze performance, and troubleshoot problems. The expertise required is similar to that of an MCP with a focus on the Internet.

◆ **Microsoft Certified Systems Engineer (MCSE).** Persons who attain this certification are qualified to effectively plan, implement, maintain, and support information systems with Microsoft Windows NT and other Microsoft advanced systems and workgroup products, such as Microsoft Office and Microsoft BackOffice. MCSE is a second level of expertise.

◆ **Microsoft Certified Systems Engineer + Internet (MCSE+Internet).** Persons who attain this certification are qualified in the core MCSE areas and are qualified to enhance, deploy, and manage sophisticated intranet and Internet solutions that include a browser, proxy server, host servers, database, and messaging and commerce components. In addition, an MCSE+Internet–certified professional will be able to manage and analyze Web sites.

◆ **Microsoft Certified Solution Developer (MCSD).** Persons who attain this certification are qualified to design and develop custom business solutions by using Microsoft development tools, technologies, and platforms, including Microsoft Office and Microsoft BackOffice. MCSD is a second level of expertise with a focus on software development.

◆ **Microsoft Certified Trainer (MCT).** Persons who attain this certification are instructionally and technically qualified by Microsoft to deliver

Microsoft Education Courses at Microsoft-authorized sites. An MCT must be employed by a Microsoft Solution Provider Authorized Technical Education Center or a Microsoft Authorized Academic Training site.

> **NOTE**
>
> **Stay in Touch** For up-to-date information about each type of certification, visit the Microsoft Training and Certification World Wide Web site at http://www.microsoft.com/train_cert. You must have an Internet account and a WWW browser to access this information. You also can call the following sources:
>
> - Microsoft Certified Professional Program:
>   800-636-7544
>
> - Sylvan Prometric Testing Centers:
>   800-755-EXAM
>
> - Microsoft Online Institute (MOLI):
>   800-449-9333

How to Become a Microsoft Certified Professional (MCP)

To become an MCP, you must pass one operating system exam. The following list contains the names and exam numbers of all the operating system exams that will qualify you for your MCP certification (a * denotes an exam that is scheduled to be retired):

- Implementing and Supporting Microsoft Windows 95, #70-064 (formerly #70-063)

- Implementing and Supporting Microsoft Windows NT Workstation 4.02, #70-073

- Implementing and Supporting Microsoft Windows NT Workstation 3.51, #70-042*

- Implementing and Supporting Microsoft Windows NT Server 4.0, #70-067

- Implementing and Supporting Microsoft Windows NT Server 3.51, #70-043*

- Microsoft Windows for Workgroups 3.11–Desktop, #70-048*

- Microsoft Windows 3.1, #70-030*

- Microsoft Windows Architecture I, #70-160

- Microsoft Windows Architecture II, #70-161

How to Become a Microsoft Certified Professional + Internet (MCP+Internet)

To become an MCP with a specialty in Internet technology, you must pass the following three exams:

- Internetworking Microsoft TCP/IP on Microsoft Windows NT 4.0, #70-059

- Implementing and Supporting Microsoft Windows NT Server 4.0, #70-067

- Implementing and Supporting Microsoft Internet Information Server 3.0 and Microsoft Index Server 1.1, #70-077

  OR Implementing and Supporting Microsoft Internet Information Server 4.0, #70-087

How to Become a Microsoft Certified Systems Engineer (MCSE)

MCSE candidates must pass four operating system exams and two elective exams. The MCSE certification path is divided into two tracks: the Windows NT 3.51 track and the Windows NT 4.0 track.

The following lists show the core requirements (four operating system exams) for the Windows NT 3.51 track, the core requirements for the Windows NT 4.0 track, and the elective courses (two exams) you can choose from for either track.

The four Windows NT 3.51 track core requirements for MCSE certification are:

◆ Implementing and Supporting Microsoft Windows NT Server 3.51, #70-043*

◆ Implementing and Supporting Microsoft Windows NT Workstation 3.51, #70-042*

◆ Microsoft Windows 3.1, #70-030*

   OR Microsoft Windows for Workgroups 3.11, #70-048*

   OR Implementing and Supporting Microsoft Windows 95, #70-064

   OR Implementing and Supporting Microsoft Windows 98, #70-098

◆ Networking Essentials, #70-058

The four Windows NT 4.0 track core requirements for MCSE certification are:

◆ Implementing and Supporting Microsoft Windows NT Server 4.0, #70-067

◆ Implementing and Supporting Microsoft Windows NT Server 4.0 in the Enterprise, #70-068

◆ Microsoft Windows 3.1, #70-030*

   OR Microsoft Windows for Workgroups 3.11, #70-048*

   OR Implementing and Supporting Microsoft Windows 95, #70-064

   OR Implementing and Supporting Microsoft Windows NT Workstation 4.0, #70-073

   OR Implementing and Supporting Microsoft Windows 98, #70-098

◆ Networking Essentials, #70-058

For both the Windows NT 3.51 and the Windows NT 4.0 track, you must pass two of the following elective exams for MCSE certification:

◆ Implementing and Supporting Microsoft SNA Server 3.0, #70-013

   OR Implementing and Supporting Microsoft SNA Server 4.0, #70-085

◆ Implementing and Supporting Microsoft Systems Management Server 1.0, #70-014*

   OR Implementing and Supporting Microsoft Systems Management Server 1.2, #70-018

   OR Implementing and Supporting Microsoft Systems Management Server 2.0, #70-086

◆ Microsoft SQL Server 4.2 Database Implementation, #70-021

   OR Implementing a Database Design on Microsoft SQL Server 6.5, #70-027

   OR Implementing a Database Design on Microsoft SQL Server 7.0, #70-029

◆ Microsoft SQL Server 4.2 Database Administration for Microsoft Windows NT, #70-022

OR System Administration for Microsoft SQL Server 6.5 (or 6.0), #70-026

OR System Administration for Microsoft SQL Server 7.0, #70-028

◆ Microsoft Mail for PC Networks 3.2-Enterprise, #70-037

◆ Internetworking with Microsoft TCP/IP on Microsoft Windows NT (3.5–3.51), #70-053

OR Internetworking with Microsoft TCP/IP on Microsoft Windows NT 4.0, #70-059

◆ Implementing and Supporting Microsoft Exchange Server 4.0, #70-075*

OR Implementing and Supporting Microsoft Exchange Server 5.0, #70-076

OR Implementing and Supporting Microsoft Exchange Server 5.5, #70-081

◆ Implementing and Supporting Microsoft Internet Information Server 3.0 and Microsoft Index Server 1.1, #70-077

OR Implementing and Supporting Microsoft Internet Information Server 4.0, #70-087

◆ Implementing and Supporting Microsoft Proxy Server 1.0, #70-078

OR Implementing and Supporting Microsoft Proxy Server 2.0, #70-088

◆ Implementing and Supporting Microsoft Internet Explorer 4.0 by Using the Internet Explorer Resource Kit, #70-079

How to Become a Microsoft Certified Systems Engineer + Internet (MCSE+Internet)

MCSE+Internet candidates must pass seven operating system exams and two elective exams. The following lists show the core requirements and the elective courses (of which you need to pass two exams).

The seven MCSE+Internet core exams required for certification are:

◆ Networking Essentials, #70-058

◆ Internetworking with Microsoft TCP/IP on Microsoft Windows NT 4.0, #70-059

◆ Implementing and Supporting Microsoft Windows 95, #70-064

OR Implementing and Supporting Microsoft Windows NT Workstation 4.0, #70-073

OR Implementing and Supporting Microsoft Windows 98, #70-098

◆ Implementing and Supporting Microsoft Windows NT Server 4.0, #70-067

◆ Implementing and Supporting Microsoft Windows NT Server 4.0 in the Enterprise, #70-068

◆ Implementing and Supporting Microsoft Internet Information Server 3.0 and Microsoft Index Server 1.1, #70-077

OR Implementing and Supporting Microsoft Internet Information Server 4.0, #70-087

◆ Implementing and Supporting Microsoft Internet Explorer 4.0 by Using the Internet Explorer Resource Kit, #70-079

You must also pass two of the following elective exams:

- System Administration for Microsoft SQL Server 6.5, #70-026

- Implementing a Database Design on Microsoft SQL Server 6.5, #70-027

- Implementing and Supporting Web Sites Using Microsoft Site Server 3.0, #70-056

- Implementing and Supporting Microsoft Exchange Server 5.0, #70-076

    OR Implementing and Supporting Microsoft Exchange Server 5.5, #70-081

- Implementing and Supporting Microsoft Proxy Server 1.0, #70-078

    OR Implementing and Supporting Microsoft Proxy Server 2.0, #70-088

- Implementing and Supporting Microsoft SNA Server 4.0, #70-085

How to Become a Microsoft Certified Solution Developer (MCSD)

MCSD candidates must pass two core technology exams and two elective exams. The following lists show the required technology exams, plus the elective exams that apply toward obtaining the MCSD.

You must pass the following two core technology exams to qualify for MCSD certification:

- Microsoft Windows Architecture I, #70-160

- Microsoft Windows Architecture II, #70-161

You must also pass two of the following elective exams to become an MSCD:

- Microsoft SQL Server 4.2 Database Implementation, #70-021

    OR Implementing a Database Design on Microsoft SQL Server 6.5, #70-027

    OR Implementing a Database Design on Microsoft SQL Server 7.0, #70-029

- Developing Applications with C++ Using the Microsoft Foundation Class Library, #70-024

- Implementing OLE in Microsoft Foundation Class Applications, #70-025

- Programming with Microsoft Visual Basic 4.0, #70-065

    OR Developing Applications with Microsoft Visual Basic 5.0, #70-165

- Microsoft Access 2.0 for Windows-Application Development, #70-051

    OR Microsoft Access for Windows 95 and the Microsoft Access Development Toolkit, #70-069

- Developing Applications with Microsoft Excel 5.0 Using Visual Basic for Applications, #70-052

- Programming in Microsoft Visual FoxPro 3.0 for Windows, #70-054

Becoming a Microsoft Certified Trainer (MCT)

To understand the requirements and process for becoming a Microsoft Certified Trainer (MCT), you need to obtain the Microsoft Certified Trainer Guide document from the following WWW site:

```
http://www.microsoft.com/train_cert/mct/
```

From this page, you can read the document as Web pages, or you can display or download it as a Word file.

The MCT Guide explains the four-step process of becoming an MCT. The general steps for the MCT certification are described here:

1. Complete and mail a Microsoft Certified Trainer application to Microsoft. You must include proof of your skills for presenting instructional material. The options for doing so are described in the MCT Guide.

2. Obtain and study the Microsoft Trainer Kit for the Microsoft Official Curricula (MOC) course(s) for which you want to be certified. You can order Microsoft Trainer Kits by calling 800-688-0496 in North America. Other regions should review the MCT Guide for information on how to order a Trainer Kit.

3. Pass the Microsoft certification exam for the product for which you want to be certified to teach.

4. Attend the Microsoft Official Curriculum (MOC) course for which you want to be certified. You do this so that you can understand how the course is structured, how labs are completed, and how the course flows.

> **WARNING**
>
> **Be Sure to Get the MCT Guide!**
> You should consider the preceding steps to be a general overview of the MCT certification process. The precise steps that you need to take are described in detail on the WWW site mentioned earlier. Do not mistakenly believe the preceding steps make up the actual process you need to take.

If you are interested in becoming an MCT, you can receive more information by visiting the Microsoft Certified Training (MCT) WWW site at `http://www.microsoft.com/train_cert/mct/` or call 800-688-0496.

What's on the CD-ROM

This appendix offers a brief rundown of what you'll find on the CD-ROM that comes with this book. For a more detailed description of the newly developed Top Score test engine, exclusive to Macmillan Computer Publishing, see Appendix D, "Using the Top Score Software."

TOP SCORE

Top Score is a test engine developed exclusively for Macmillan Computer Publishing. It is, we believe, the best test engine available because it closely emulates the format of the standard Microsoft exams. In addition to providing a means of evaluating your knowledge of the exam material, Top Score features several innovations that help you to improve your mastery of the subject matter. For example, the practice tests allow you to check your score by exam area or category, which helps you determine which topics you need to study further. Other modes allow you to obtain immediate feedback on your response to a question, explanation of the correct answer, and even hyperlinks to the chapter in an electronic version of the book where the topic of the question is covered. Again, for a complete description of the benefits of Top Score, see Appendix D.

Before you attempt to run the Top Score software, make sure that autorun is enabled. If you prefer not to use autorun, you can run the application from the CD by double-clicking the START.EXE file from within Explorer.

EXCLUSIVE ELECTRONIC VERSION OF TEXT

As alluded to above, the CD-ROM also contains the electronic version of this book in Portable Document Format (PDF). In addition to the links to the book that are built into the Top Score engine, you can use that version of the book to help you search for terms you need to study or other book elements. The electronic version comes complete with all figures as they appear in the book.

COPYRIGHT INFORMATION AND DISCLAIMER

Macmillan Computer Publishing's Top Score test engine: Copyright 1998 New Riders Publishing. All rights reserved. Made in U.S.A.

Using the Top Score Software

GETTING STARTED

The installation procedure is very simple and typical of Windows 95 or Window NT 4 installations.

1. Put the CD into the CD-ROM drive. The autorun function starts, and after a moment, you see a CD-ROM Setup dialog box asking you if you are ready to proceed.

2. Click OK, and you are prompted for the location of the directory in which the program can install a small log file. Choose the default (C:\Program Files\), or type the name of another drive and directory, or select the drive and directory where you want it placed. Then click OK.

3. The next prompt asks you to select a start menu name. If you like the default name, click OK. If not, enter the name you would like to use. The Setup process runs its course.

When setup is complete, icons are displayed in the MCSE Top Score Software Explorer window that is open. For an overview of the CD's contents, double-click the CD-ROM Contents icon.

If you reach this point, you have successfully installed the exam(s). If you have another CD, repeat this process to install additional exams.

INSTRUCTIONS ON USING THE TOP SCORE SOFTWARE

Top Score software consists of the following three applications:

◆ Practice Exams

◆ Study Cards

◆ Flash Cards

The Practice Exams application provides exams that simulate the Microsoft certification exams. The Study Cards serve as a study aid organized around specific exam objectives. Both are in multiple-choice format. Flash Cards are another study aid that require responses to open-ended questions, which test your knowledge of the material at a level deeper than that of recognition memory.

To start the Study Cards, Practice Exams, or Flash Cards applications, follow these steps:

1. Begin from the overview of the CD contents (double-click the CD-ROM Contents icon). The left window provides you with options for obtaining further information on any of the Top Score applications as well as a way to launch them.

2. Click a "book" icon, and a listing of related topics appears below it in Explorer fashion.

3. Click an application name. This displays more detailed information for that application in the right window.

4. To start an application, click its book icon. Then click on the Starting the Program option. Do this for Practice Exams, for example. Information appears in the right window. Click on the button for the exam, and the opening screens of the application appear.

Further details on using each of the applications follow.

Using Top Score Practice Exams

The Practice Exams interface is simple and straightforward. Its design simulates the look and feel of the Microsoft certification exams. To begin a practice exam, click the button for the exam name. After a moment, you see an opening screen similar to the one shown in Figure D.1.

Click on the Next button to see a disclaimer and copyright screen. Read the information, and then click Top Score's Start button. A notice appears, indicating that the program is randomly selecting questions for the practice exam from the exam database (see Figure D.2). Each practice exam contains the same number of items as the official Microsoft exam. The items are selected from a larger set of 150–900 questions. The random selection of questions from the database takes some time to retrieve. Don't reboot; your machine is not hung!

> N O T E
>
> **Some Exams Follow a New Format**
> The number of questions will be the same for traditional exams. However, this will not be the case for exams that incorporate the new "adaptive testing" format. In that format, there is no set number of questions. See the chapter entitled "Study and Exam Prep Tips" in the Final Review section of the book for more details on this new format.

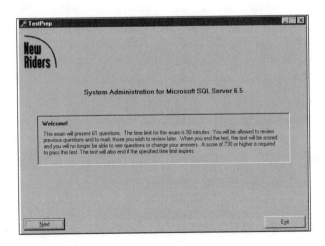

FIGURE D.1
Top Score Practice Exams opening screen.

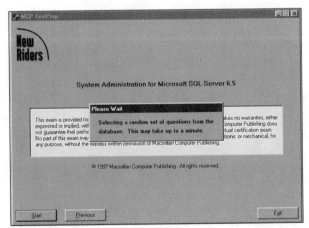

FIGURE D.2
Top Score's Please Wait notice.

After the questions have been selected, the first test item appears. See Figure D.3 for an example of a test item screen.

Notice several important features of this window. The question number and the total number of retrieved questions appears in the top-left corner of the window in the control bar. Immediately below that is a check box labeled Mark, which enables you to mark any exam item you would like to return to later. Across the screen from the Mark check box, you see the total time remaining for the exam.

The test question is located in a colored section (it's gray in the figure). Directly below the test question, in the white area, are response choices. Be sure to note that immediately below the responses are instructions about how to respond, including the number of responses required. You will notice that question items requiring a single response, such as that shown in Figure D.3, have radio buttons. Items requiring multiple responses have check boxes (see Figure D.4).

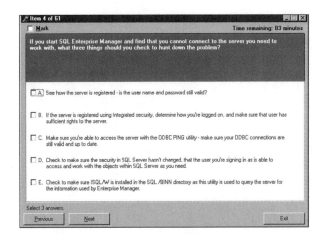

FIGURE D.4
A Top Score test item requiring multiple responses.

Some questions and some responses do not appear on the screen in their entirety. You will recognize such items because a scroll bar appears to the right of the question item or response. Use the scroll bar to reveal the rest of the question or response item.

The buttons at the bottom of the window enable you to move back to a previous test item, proceed to the next test item, or exit Top Score Practice Exams.

Some items require you to examine additional information referred to as *exhibits*. These screens typically include graphs, diagrams, or other types of visual information that you will need in order to respond to the test question. You can access Exhibits by clicking the Exhibit button, also located at the bottom of the window.

After you complete the practice test by moving through all of the test questions for your exam, you arrive at a summary screen titled Item Review (see Figure D.5).

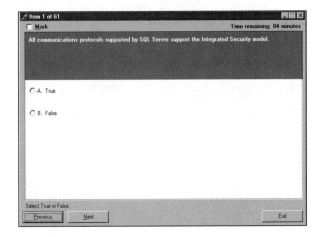

FIGURE D.3
A Top Score test item requiring a single response.

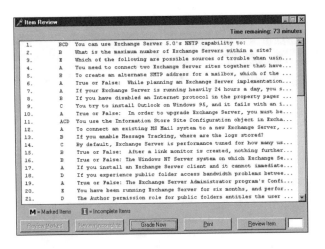

FIGURE D.5
The Top Score Item Review window.

This window enables you to see all the question numbers, your response(s) to each item, any questions you have marked, and any you've left incomplete. The buttons at the bottom of the screen enable you to review all the marked items and incomplete items in numeric order.

If you want to review a specific marked or incomplete item, simply type the desired item number in the box in the lower-right corner of the window and click the Review Item button. This takes you to that particular item. After you review the item, you can respond to the question. Notice that this window also offers the Next and Previous options. You can also select the Item Review button to return to the Item Review window.

> **NOTE**
>
> **Your Time Is Limited** If you exceed the time allotted for the test, you do not have the opportunity to review any marked or incomplete items. The program will move on to the next screen.

After you complete your review of the practice test questions, click the Grade Now button to find out how you did. An Examination Score Report is generated for your practice test (see Figure D.6). This report provides you with the required score for this particular certification exam, your score on the practice test, and a grade. The report also breaks down your performance on the practice test by the specific objectives for the exam. Click the Print button to print out the results of your performance.

You also have the option of reviewing those items that you answered incorrectly. Click the Show Me What I Missed button to view a summary of those items. You can print out that information if you need further practice or review; such printouts can be used to guide your use of Study Cards and Flash Cards.

Using Top Score Study Cards

To start the software, begin from the overview of the CD contents. Click the Study Cards icon to see a listing of topics. Clicking Study Cards brings up more detailed information for this application in the right window.

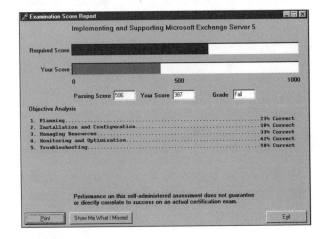

FIGURE D.6
The Top Score Examination Score Report window.

To launch Study Cards, click on Starting the Program. In the right window, click on the button for the exam in which you are interested. After a moment, an initial screen similar to that of the Practice Exams appears.

Click on the Next button to see the first Study Cards screen (see Figure D.7).

The interface for Study Cards is very similar to that of Practice Exams. However, several important options enable you to prepare for an exam. The Study Cards material is organized according to the specific objectives for each exam. You can opt to receive questions on all the objectives, or you can use the check boxes to request questions on a limited set of objectives. For example, if you have already completed a Practice Exam and your score report indicates that you need work on Planning, you can choose to cover only the Planning objectives for your Study Cards session.

You can also determine the number of questions presented by typing the number of questions you want into the option box at the right of the screen. You can control the amount of time you will be allowed for a review by typing the number of minutes into the Time Limit option box immediately below the one for the number of questions.

When you're ready, click the Start Test button, and Study Cards randomly selects the indicated number of questions from the question database. A dialog box appears, informing you that this process could take some time. After the questions are selected, the first item appears, in a format similar to that in Figure D.8.

Respond to the questions in the same manner you did for the Practice Exam questions. Radio buttons signify that a single answer is required, while check boxes indicate that multiple answers are expected.

Notice the menu options at the top of the window. You can pull down the File menu to exit from the program. The Edit menu contains commands for the copy function and even allows you to copy questions to the Windows clipboard.

Should you feel the urge to take some notes on a particular question, you can do so via the Options menu. When you pull it down, choose Open Notes, and Notepad opens. Type any notes you want to save for later reference. The Options menu also allows you to start over with another exam.

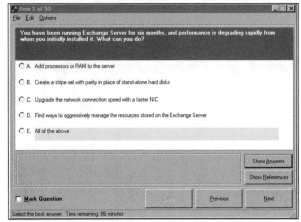

FIGURE D.8
A Study Cards item.

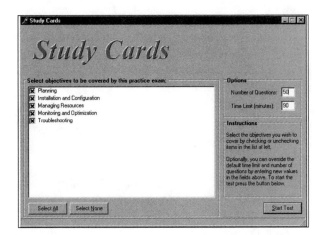

FIGURE D.7
The first Study Cards screen.

The Study Cards application provides you with immediate feedback of whether you answered the question correctly. Click the Show Answers button to see the correct answer, and it appears highlighted on the screen as shown in Figure D.9.

Study Cards also includes Item Review, Score Report, and Show Me What I Missed features that function the same as those in the Practice Exams application.

Using Top Score Flash Cards

Flash Cards offer a third way to use the exam question database. The Flash Cards items do not offer you multiple-choice answers to choose from; instead, they require you to respond in a short answer/essay format. Flash Cards are intended to help you learn the material well enough to respond with the correct answers in your own words, rather than just by recognizing the correct answer. If you have the depth of knowledge to answer questions without prompting, you will certainly be prepared to pass a multiple-choice exam.

You start the Flash Cards application in the same way you did Practice Exams and Study Cards. Click the Flash Cards icon, and then click Start the Program.

Click the button for the exam you are interested in, and the opening screen appears. It looks similar to the example shown in Figure D.10.

You can choose Flash Cards according to the various objectives, as you did Study Cards. Simply select the objectives you want to cover, enter the number of questions you want, and enter the amount of time you want to limit yourself to. Click the Start Test button to start the Flash Cards session, and you see a dialog box notifying you that questions are being selected.

The Flash Cards items appear in an interface similar to that of Practice Exams and Study Cards (see Figure D.11).

Notice, however, that although a question is presented, no possible answers appear. You type your answer in the white space below the question (see Figure D.12).

Compare your answer to the correct answer by clicking the Show Answers button (see Figure D.13).

You can also use the Show Reference button in the same manner as described earlier in the Study Cards sections.

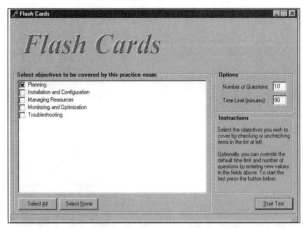

FIGURE D.10
The Flash Cards opening screen.

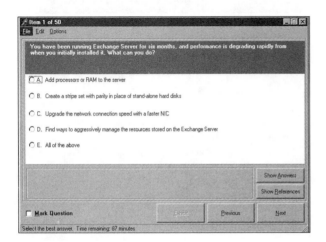

FIGURE D.9
The correct answer is highlighted.

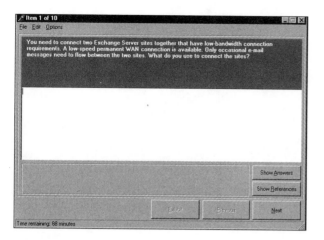

FIGURE D.11
A Flash Cards item.

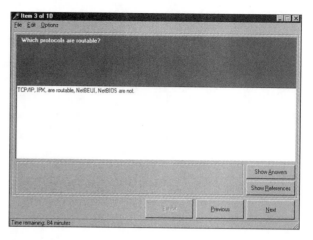

FIGURE D.12
A typed answer in Flash Cards.

The pull-down menus provide nearly the same functionality as those in Study Cards, with the exception of a Paste command on the Edit menu instead of the Copy Question command.

Flash Cards provide simple feedback; they do not include an Item Review or Score Report. They are intended to provide you with an alternative way of assessing your level of knowledge that will encourage you to learn the information more thoroughly than other methods do.

SUMMARY

The Top Score software's suite of applications provides you with several approaches to exam preparation. Use Practice Exams to do just that—practice taking exams, not only to assess your learning, but also to prepare yourself for the test-taking situation. Use Study Cards and Flash Cards as tools for more focused assessment and review and to reinforce the knowledge you are gaining. You will find that these three applications are the perfect way to finish off your exam preparation.

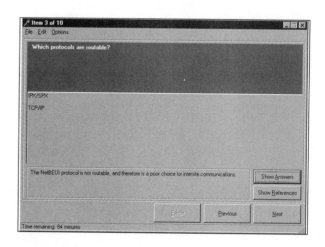

FIGURE D.13
The correct answer is shown.

Index

SYMBOLS

802.2 frame type, 86

A

absolute values, 341-342
Access Control Entries, *see* ACEs
Access Control Lists, *see* ACLs
Access Denied permission, 195
access tokens, 204-205
accessing
    network resources, 17
    restrictions, case studies, 172-173
    share levels, 199
    trust relationships, 20-24
Account Information dialog box, 26-27
Account Operators local group, auditing, 207
accounts
    centralized administration, 18
    complete trust model, 41
    disabling versus deleting, 640
    global, 26
    group management, 132
    local, 26-27
    multiple-master domain model, 35-39
        see also trusted domains
    one user, one account, 17
    permissions
        assigning, 28-29
        groups, 26-28
    policies, defining, 141-145

replication, configuring, 94
SAM (Security Accounts Manager), 15-16, 207
single-master domain model, 35
templates, 144-145
trust relationships, 25, 429
universal resource access, 17
user
    access tokens, 204-205
    adding with Web administration tools, 192-193
    audit selection, 209
    creating, 133-135
    domain controller distribution, requirements, 410-411
    intranet security, 422
    locking out, 135
    logon validation, 405-414
    logons, auditing, 211-212
    managing, 132
    memory requirements, 408-409
    Novell NetWare, migrating to NT, 271-274
    NTFS permissions, 196-199
    print auditing, 210-211
    properties, 133-135
    rights, auditing, 206
    share permissions, 194-196
    validation, 403
    Windows NT Workstation, creating, 109-110
ACEs (Access Control Entries), 204-205
ACK (Acknowledgments), 228
ACLs (Access Control Lists), 204-205
actions, auditing, 209-210

D

H

I-K

W-Z

FAST TRACK
SERIES

*The Accelerated Path to
Certification Success*

Fast Tracks provide an easy way to
review the key elements of each certification technology without being
bogged down with elementary-level
information.

These guides are perfect for when
you already have real-world, hands-
on experience. They're the ideal
enhancement to training courses,
test simulators, and comprehensive
training guides. *No fluff, simply what
you really need to pass the exam!*

LEARN IT FAST

Part I contains only the essential
information you need to pass the
test. With over 200 pages of information, it is a concise review for the
more experienced MCSE candidate.

REVIEW IT EVEN FASTER

Part II averages 50–75 pages, and
takes you through the test and into
the real-world use of the technology,
with chapters on:

1) Fast Facts Review Section
2) Hotlists of Exam-Critical Concepts
3) Sample Test Questions
4) The Insider's Spin (on taking the
exam)
5) Did You Know? (real-world
applications for the technology covered in the exam)

MCSE Fast Track:
Networking Essentials

1-56205-939-4,
$19.99, 9/98

MCSE Fast Track:
TCP/IP

1-56205-937-8,
$19.99, 9/98

MCSE Fast Track:
Windows 98

0-7357-0016-8,
$19.99, Q4/98

MCSE Fast Track:
Internet Information
Server 4

1-56205-936-X,
$19.99, 9/98

MCSE Fast Track:
Windows NT Server 4

1-56205-935-1,
$19.99, 9/98

MCSD Fast Track:
Solution Architectures

0-7357-0029-X,
$19.99, Q1/99

MCSE Fast Track:
Windows NT Server 4
Enterprise

1-56205-940-8,
$19.99, 9/98

MCSD Fast Track:
Visual Basic 6,
Exam 70-175

0-7357-0018-4,
$19.99, Q4/98

MCSE Fast Track:
Windows NT
Workstation 4

1-56205-938-6,
$19.99, 9/98

MCSD Fast Track:
Visual Basic 6,
Exam 70-176

0-7357-0019-2,
$19.99, Q4/98

TESTPREP SERIES

Practice and cram with the new, revised Second Edition TestPreps

Questions. Questions. And more questions. That's what you'll find in our New Riders *TestPreps*. They're great practice books when you reach the final stage of studying for the exam. We recommend them as supplements to our *Training Guides*.

What makes these study tools unique is that the questions are the primary focus of each book. All the text in these books support and explain the answers to the questions.

✓ **Scenario-based questions** challenge your experience.

✓ **Multiple-choice questions** prep you for the exam.

✓ **Fact-based questions** test your product knowledge.

✓ **Exam strategies** assist you in test preparation.

✓ **Complete yet concise explanations of answers** make for better retention.

✓ **Two practice exams** prepare you for the real thing.

✓ **Fast Facts** offer you everything you need to review in the testing center parking lot.

Practice, practice, practice, pass with New Riders TestPreps!

MCSE TestPrep: Networking Essentials, Second Edition

0-7357-0010-9, $19.99, 11/98

MCSE TestPrep: Windows 95, Second Edition

0-7357-0011-7, $19.99, 11/98

MCSE TestPrep: Windows NT Server 4, Second Edition

0-7357-0012-5, $19.99, 12/98

MCSE TestPrep: Windows NT Server 4 Enterprise, Second Edition

0-7357-0009-5, $19.99, 11/98

MCSE TestPrep: Windows NT Workstation 4, Second Edition

0-7357-0008-7, $19.99, 11/98

MCSE TestPrep: TCP/IP, Second Edition

0-7357-0025-7, $19.99, 12/98

MCSE TestPrep: Windows 98

1-56205-922-X, $19.99, Q4/98

FIRST EDITIONS

MCSE TestPrep: SQL Server 6.5 Administration, 0-7897-1597-X

MCSE TestPrep: SQL Server 6.5 Design and Implementation, 1-56205-915-7

MCSE TestPrep: Windows 95 70-64 Exam, 0-7897-1609-7

MCSE TestPrep: Internet Explorer 4, 0-7897-1654-2

MCSE TestPrep: Exchange Server 5.5, 0-7897-1611-9

MCSE TestPrep: IIS 4.0, 0-7897-1610-0

HOW TO CONTACT US

IF YOU NEED THE LATEST UPDATES ON A TITLE THAT YOU'VE PURCHASED:

1) Visit our Web site at www.newriders.com.

2) Click on the DOWNLOADS link, and enter your book's ISBN number, which is located on the back cover in the bottom right-hand corner.

3) In the DOWNLOADS section, you'll find available updates that are linked to the book page.

IF YOU ARE HAVING TECHNICAL PROBLEMS WITH THE BOOK OR THE CD THAT IS INCLUDED:

1) Check the book's information page on our Web site according to the instructions listed above, or

2) Email us at support@mcp.com, or

3) Fax us at (317) 817-7488 attn: Tech Support.

IF YOU HAVE COMMENTS ABOUT ANY OF OUR CERTIFICATION PRODUCTS THAT ARE NON-SUPPORT RELATED:

1) Email us at certification@mcp.com, or

2) Write to us at New Riders, 201 W. 103rd St., Indianapolis, IN 46290-1097, or

3) Fax us at (317) 581-4663.

IF YOU ARE OUTSIDE THE UNITED STATES AND NEED TO FIND A DISTRIBUTOR IN YOUR AREA:

Please contact our international department at international@mcp.com.

IF YOU WISH TO PREVIEW ANY OF OUR CERTIFICATION BOOKS FOR CLASSROOM USE:

Email us at pr@mcp.com. Your message should include your name, title, training company or school, department, address, phone number, office days/hours, text in use, and enrollment. Send these details along with your request for desk/examination copies and/or additional information.

WE WANT TO KNOW WHAT YOU THINK

To better serve you, we would like your opinion on the content and quality of this book. Please complete this card and mail it to us or fax it to 317-581-4663.

Name _____

Address _____

City _____ State _____ Zip _____

Phone_____ Email Address _____

Occupation _____

Which certification exams have you already passed? _____

_____

_____

_____

Which certification exams do you plan to take? _____

_____

_____

_____

What influenced your purchase of this book?
- ❑ Recommendation
- ❑ Table of Contents
- ❑ Magazine Review
- ❑ Reputation of New Riders
- ❑ Cover Design
- ❑ Index
- ❑ Advertisement
- ❑ Author Name

How would you rate the contents of this book?
- ❑ Excellent
- ❑ Good
- ❑ Below Average
- ❑ Very Good
- ❑ Fair
- ❑ Poor

What other types of certification products will you buy/have you bought to help you prepare for the exam?
- ❑ Quick reference books
- ❑ Study guides
- ❑ Testing software
- ❑ Other

What do you like most about this book? Check all that apply.
- ❑ Content
- ❑ Accuracy
- ❑ Listings
- ❑ Index
- ❑ Price
- ❑ Writing Style
- ❑ Examples
- ❑ Design
- ❑ Page Count
- ❑ Illustrations

What do you like least about this book? Check all that apply.
- ❑ Content
- ❑ Accuracy
- ❑ Listings
- ❑ Index
- ❑ Price
- ❑ Writing Style
- ❑ Examples
- ❑ Design
- ❑ Page Count
- ❑ Illustrations

What would be a useful follow-up book to this one for you?_____

Where did you purchase this book? _____

Can you name a similar book that you like better than this one, or one that is as good? Why?_____

_____

_____

How many New Riders books do you own? _____

What are your favorite certification or general computer book titles? _____

_____

What other titles would you like to see us develop?_____

_____

Any comments for us? _____

_____

_____

_____

Fold here and Scotch tape to mail

New Riders
201 W. 103rd St.
Indianapolis, IN 46290